PEARSON CUSTOM BUSINESS RESOURCES

EC 201
Principles of Microeconomics
Bobby L. Puryear
North Carolina State University

PEARSON

V092
ISBN 10: 1-269-68275-X
ISBN 13: 978-1-269-68275-6

PEARSON

Table of Contents

Economics:
Foundations and Models

Economics:
Foundations and Models

Chapter Outline and Learning Objectives

Is the Private Doctor's Office Going to Disappear?

Traditionally, most doctors in the United States have worked in private practices that they owned themselves or in partnership with other doctors. Like other businesspeople, a doctor hires workers—nurses, physician's assistants, and receptionists—and buys or rents machinery and equipment. A doctor's income represents the profits from his or her practice, or the difference between the revenue received from patients and their health insurance plans and the costs to the doctor of wages, rent, loans, and insurance.

Increasingly, rather than owning a private practice, many doctors have chosen to work as salaried employees of hospitals. Although in 2000 nearly 60 percent of doctors were in private practice, by 2013 fewer than 40 percent were. What explains the increasing number of doctors who are giving up their private practices to become salaried employees of hospitals? Some doctors choose private practice because they like being their own boss. Other doctors prefer the more regular hours of working for a hospital, where they are less likely to be woken up at 2 A.M. to treat a patient with a medical emergency. Economists believe, though, that the best explanation for doctors abandoning private practice is that the doctors are acting in response to changing *economic incentives*. In fact, one of the key ideas that we will explore in this text is that we can often predict behavior by assuming that people respond to economic incentives.

The economic incentives doctors face have changed in a number of ways. For example, soaring health care costs have led many private insurance companies, as well as the federal and state governments, to reduce the payments they make to doctors in return for treating patients. As a result, doctors in private practice have found their incomes fluctuating, which makes the steady income from a hospital salary more attractive. Congress passed President Barack Obama's package of health care changes in 2010. One rule requires most doctors and hospitals to convert to electronic medical record keeping. Although this change may improve the quality of health care, the computer systems required are expensive. Doctors can avoid this cost by leaving private practice for hospital employment. Other new rules have increased the amount of paperwork doctors must complete to be paid for treating patients.

AN INSIDE LOOK discusses how technological change is affecting medical care.

Sources: Robert Kocher and Nikhil R. Sahni, "Hospitals' Race to Employ Physicians," *New England Journal of Medicine*, Vol. 364, No. 19, May 12, 2011, pp. 1790–1793; Julie Creswell and Reed Abelson, "A Hospital War Reflects a Bind for Doctors in the U.S.," *New York Times*, November 30, 2012; and Scott Gottlieb, "The Doctor Won't See You Now: He's Clocked Out," *Wall Street Journal*, March 14, 2013.

Economics in Your Life

Will There Be Plenty of Jobs Available in the Health Care Industry?

The U.S. Health Resources and Services Administration (HRSA) forecasts that there will be 866,400 doctors in the United States in 2020. The HRSA also forecasts that 922,000 doctors will be needed in 2020. In other words, this federal government agency forecasts that there will be a shortage of about 56,000 doctors in 2020. The U.S. Bureau of Labor Statistics forecasts that 9 of the 20 fastest growing occupations over the next 10 years will be in the medical field. But the availability of these jobs depends on the reliability of the forecasts. What is the basis for the forecasts on the availability of jobs in health care, and how reliable are the forecasts? As you read this chapter, try to answer this question. You can check your answer against the one we provide at the end of this chapter.

Economists do not always agree on the answers to every question. In fact, as we will see, economists engage in lively debate on some issues. In addition, new problems and issues are constantly arising. So, economists are always at work developing new methods to analyze economic questions.

All the topics we discuss in this text illustrate a basic fact of life: To attain our goals, we must make choices. We must make choices because we live in a world of **scarcity**, which means that although our wants are *unlimited*, the resources available to fulfill those wants are *limited*. You might like to own a BMW and spend each summer vacationing at five-star European hotels, but unless Bill Gates is a close and generous relative, you probably lack the funds to fulfill these dreams. Every day, you make choices as you spend your limited income on the many goods and services available. The finite amount of time you have also limits your ability to attain your goals. If you spend an hour studying for your economics midterm, you have one hour less to study for your history midterm. Firms and the government are in the same situation as you: They must also attain their goals with limited resources. **Economics** is the study of the choices consumers, business managers, and government officials make to attain their goals, given their scarce resources.

We begin this chapter by discussing three important economic ideas: *People are rational, people respond to economic incentives*, and *optimal decisions are made at the margin*. Then, we consider the three fundamental questions that any economy must answer: *What* goods and services will be produced? *How* will the goods and services be produced? and *Who* will receive the goods and services produced? Next, we consider the role of *economic models* in analyzing economic issues. **Economic models** are simplified versions of reality used to analyze real-world economic situations. We will explore why economists use models and how they construct them. Finally, we will discuss the difference between microeconomics and macroeconomics, and we will preview some important economic terms.

Three Key Economic Ideas

As you try to achieve your goals, whether they involve buying a new computer or finding a part-time job, you will interact with other people in *markets*. A **market** is a group of buyers and sellers of a good or service and the institution or arrangement by which they come together to trade. Examples of markets are the markets for smartphones, houses, haircuts, stocks and bonds, and labor. Most of economics involves analyzing what happens in markets.

Scarcity A situation in which unlimited wants exceed the limited resources available to fulfill those wants.

Economics The study of the choices people make to attain their goals, given their scarce resources.

Economic model A simplified version of reality used to analyze real-world economic situations.

1 LEARNING OBJECTIVE

Explain these three key economic ideas: People are rational; people respond to economic incentives; and optimal decisions are made at the margin.

Market A group of buyers and sellers of a good or service and the institution or arrangement by which they come together to trade.

People Are Rational

Economists generally assume that people are rational. This assumption does *not* mean that economists believe everyone knows everything or always makes the "best" decision. It means that economists assume that consumers and firms use all available information as they act to achieve their goals. Rational individuals weigh the benefits and costs of each action, and they choose an action only if the benefits outweigh the costs. For example, if Apple charges a price of $299 for its latest iPhone, economists assume that the managers at Apple have estimated that this price will earn Apple the most profit. The managers may be wrong; perhaps a price of $325 would be more profitable, but economists assume that the managers at Apple have acted rationally, on the basis of the information available to them, in choosing the price. Of course, not everyone behaves rationally all the time. Still, the assumption of rational behavior is very useful in explaining most of the choices that people make.

People Respond to Economic Incentives

Human beings act from a variety of motives, including envy, compassion, and religious belief. While not ignoring other motives, economists emphasize that consumers and firms consistently respond to *economic incentives*. This point may seem obvious, but it is often overlooked. For example, according to an article in the *Wall Street Journal*, the FBI couldn't understand why banks were not taking steps to improve security in the face of an increase in robberies: "FBI officials suggest that banks place uniformed, armed guards outside their doors and install bullet-resistant plastic, known as a 'bandit barrier,' in front of teller windows." FBI officials were surprised that few banks took their advice. But the article also reported that installing bullet-resistant plastic costs $10,000 to $20,000, and a well-trained security guard receives $50,000 per year in salary and benefits. The average loss in a bank robbery is only about $1,200. The economic incentive to banks is clear: It is less costly to put up with bank robberies than to take additional security measures. FBI agents may be surprised by how banks respond to the threat of robberies—but economists are not.

The *Making the Connection* feature discusses a news story or another application related to the chapter material. Read this *Making the Connection* for a discussion of whether people respond to economic incentives even when deciding how much to eat and how much to exercise.

Making the Connection	**Does Health Insurance Give People an Incentive to Become Obese?**

Obesity is an increasing problem in the United States. The U.S. Centers for Disease Control and Prevention (CDC) defines obesity for an adult as having a body mass index (BMI) of 30 or greater. The BMI measures a person's weight relative to the person's height. (The exact formula is: BMI = (Weight in pounds/Height in inches^2 × 703.) A BMI of 30 is equivalent to a person 5'4" being 30 pounds overweight. Obesity is related to a variety of diseases, including heart disease, stroke, diabetes, and hypertension.

These two maps show the dramatic increase in obesity between 1994 and 2011. In 1994, in a majority of states between 10 percent and 14 percent of the adult population was obese, and in no state was more than 20 percent of the adult population obese. By 2011, in every state at least 20 percent of the adult population was obese, and in about three-quarters of the states, at least 25 percent of the adult population was obese.

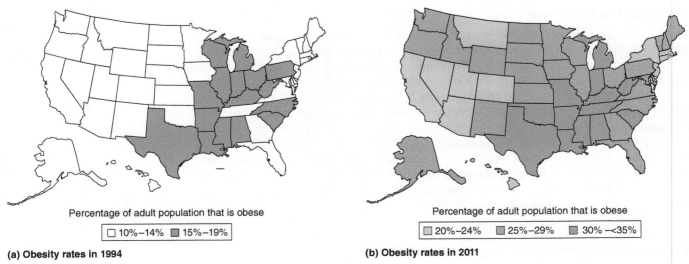

Percentage of adult population that is obese

| ☐ 10%–14% | ■ 15%–19% |

(a) Obesity rates in 1994

Percentage of adult population that is obese

| ☐ 20%–24% | ■ 25%–29% | ■ 30% –<35% |

(b) Obesity rates in 2011

Source: Centers for Disease Control and Prevention, "Prevalence of Self-Reported Obesity among U.S. Adults."

Many people who suffer from obesity have underlying medical conditions. For these people, obesity is an unfortunate medical problem that they cannot control. The fact that obesity is increasing, though, indicates that for some people obesity is the result of diet and lifestyle choices. Potential explanations for the increase in obesity include greater intake of high-calorie fast foods, insufficient exercise, and a decline in the physical activity associated with many jobs. The CDC recommends that teenagers get a minimum of 60 minutes of aerobic exercise per day, a standard that only 15 percent of high school students were meeting in 2013. In 1960, 50 percent of jobs in the United States required at least moderate physical activity. By 2013, only 20 percent of jobs did. As a result, a typical worker was burning off about 130 fewer calories per workday.

In addition to eating too much and not exercising enough, could health insurance be a cause of obesity? Obese people tend to suffer more medical problems and so incur higher medical costs. Obese people with health insurance that will reimburse them for only part of their medical bills or who have no health insurance must pay some or all of these higher medical bills themselves. People with health insurance that covers most of their medical bills will not suffer as large a monetary cost from being obese. In other words, by reducing some of the costs of obesity, health insurance may give people an economic incentive to gain weight.

At first glance, this argument may seem implausible. Some people suffer from medical conditions that can make physical activity difficult or that can cause weight gain even with moderate eating, so they may become obese whether they have health insurance or not. Some people are obese because of poor eating habits or lack of exercise, and they probably don't consider health insurance when deciding whether to have another slice of chocolate cake or to watch television instead of going to the gym. But if economists are correct about the importance of economic incentives, then we would expect that if we hold all other personal characteristics—such as age, gender, and income—constant, people with health insurance will be more likely to be overweight than people without health insurance.

Jay Bhattacharya and Kate Bundorf of Stanford University, Noemi Pace of the University of Venice, and Neeraj Sood of the University of Southern California, have analyzed the effects of health insurance on weight. Using a sample that followed nearly 80,000 people from 1989 to 2004, they found that after controlling for income, education, race, gender, age, and other factors, people with health insurance were significantly more likely to be overweight than people without health insurance. Having private health insurance increased BMI by 1.3 points, and having public health insurance, such as Medicaid, which is a program under which the government provides health care to low-income people, increased BMI by 2.3 points. These findings suggest that people respond to economic incentives even when making decisions about what they eat and how much they exercise.

Sources: Centers for Disease Control and Prevention, "Prevalence of Self-Reported Obesity among U.S. Adults," www.cdc .gov; Katherine M. Flegal, Margaret D. Caroll, Cynthia L. Ogden, and Lester R. Curtin, "Prevalence and Trends in Obesity among U.S. Adults, 1999–2008," *Journal of the American Medical Association*, Vol. 303, No. 3, January 20, 2010, pp. 235–241; Jay Bhattacharya, Kate Bundorf, Noemi Pace, and Neeraj Sood, "Does Health Insurance Make You Fat?" in Michael Grossman and Naci H. Mocan, eds., *Economic Aspects of Obesity*, Chicago: University of Chicago Press, 2011; and Tara Parker-Pope, "Less Active at Work, Americans Have Packed on Pounds," *New York Times*, May 25, 2011.

Your Turn: Test your understanding by doing related problems 1.6 and 1.7 at the end of this chapter.

Optimal Decisions Are Made at the Margin

Some decisions are "all or nothing." For instance, when an entrepreneur decides whether to open a new restaurant, she starts the new restaurant or she doesn't. When you decide whether to enter graduate school or to take a job, you enter graduate school or you don't. But rather than being all or nothing, most decisions in life involve doing a little more or a little less. If you are trying to decrease your spending and increase your saving, the decision is not really between saving all the money you earn or spending it all. Rather, many small choices are involved, such as whether to buy a caffè mocha at Starbucks every day or just three times per week.

Economists use the word *marginal* to mean "extra" or "additional." Should you watch another hour of television or spend that hour studying? The *marginal benefit* (*MB*) of watching more television is the additional enjoyment you receive. The *marginal cost* (*MC*) is the lower grade you receive from having studied a little less. Should Apple produce an additional 300,000 iPhones? Firms receive *revenue* from selling goods. Apple's marginal benefit is the additional revenue it receives from selling 300,000 more iPhones. Apple's marginal cost is the additional cost—for wages, parts, and so forth—of producing 300,000 more iPhones. *Economists reason that the optimal decision is to continue any activity up to the point where the marginal benefit equals the marginal cost—* MB = MC. Often we apply this rule without consciously thinking about it. Usually you will know whether the additional enjoyment from watching a television program is worth the additional cost involved in not spending that hour studying, without giving the decision a lot of thought. In business situations, however, firms often have to make careful calculations to determine, for example, whether the additional revenue received from increasing production is greater or less than the additional cost of the production. Economists refer to analysis that involves comparing marginal benefits and marginal costs as **marginal analysis**.

The special feature *Solved Problem* will increase your understanding of the material by leading you through the steps of solving an applied economic problem. After reading the problem, test your understanding by doing the related problems that appear at the end of the chapter. You can also complete Solved Problems on **www.myeconlab.com** and receive tutorial help.

Marginal analysis Analysis that involves comparing marginal benefits and marginal costs.

Solved Problem 1

A Doctor Makes a Decision at the Margin

A doctor receives complaints from patients that her office isn't open enough hours. So the doctor asks her office manager to analyze the effect of keeping her office open 9 hours per day rather than 8 hours. The doctor's office manager tells her: "Keeping the office open an extra hour is a good idea because the revenue from your practice will increase by $300,000 per year when the office is open 9 hours per day." Do you agree with the office manager's reasoning? What, if any, additional information do you need to decide whether the doctor should keep her office open an additional hour per day?

Solving the Problem

Step 1: **Review the chapter material.** This problem is about making decisions, so you may want to review the section "Optimal Decisions Are Made at the Margin."

Step 2: **Explain whether you agree with the office manager's reasoning.** We have seen that any activity should be continued to the point where the marginal benefit is equal to the marginal cost. In this case, the doctor should keep her office open up to the point where the additional revenue she receives from seeing more patients is equal to the marginal cost of keeping her office open an additional hour. The office manager has provided information on marginal revenue but not on marginal cost. So the office manager has not provided enough information to make a decision, and you should not agree with the office manager's reasoning.

Step 3: **Explain what additional information you need.** To make a correct decision, you would need information on the marginal cost of remaining open an extra hour per day. The marginal cost would include the additional salary to be paid to the office staff, any additional medical supplies that would be used, as well as any additional electricity or other utilities. The doctor would also need to take into account the nonmonetary cost of spending another hour working rather than spending time with her family and friends or in other leisure activities. The marginal revenue would depend on how many more patients the doctor can see in the extra hour. The doctor should keep her office open an additional hour if the marginal revenue of doing so is greater than the marginal cost. If the marginal cost is greater than the marginal revenue, then the doctor should continue to keep her office open for 8 hours.

Your Turn: For more practice, do related problems 1.8, 1.9, and 1.10 at the end of this chapter.

2 LEARNING OBJECTIVE

Discuss how an economy answers these questions: What goods and services will be produced? How will the goods and services be produced? Who will receive the goods and services produced?

Trade-off The idea that, because of scarcity, producing more of one good or service means producing less of another good or service.

Opportunity cost The highest-valued alternative that must be given up to engage in an activity.

The Economic Problem That Every Society Must Solve

Because we live in a world of scarcity, any society faces the *economic problem* that it has only a limited amount of economic resources—such as workers, machines, and raw materials—and so can produce only a limited amount of goods and services. Therefore, every society faces **trade-offs:** Producing more of one good or service means producing less of another good or service. In fact, the best measure of the cost of producing a good or service is the value of what has to be given up to produce it. The **opportunity cost** of any activity—such as producing a good or service—is the highest-valued alternative that must be given up to engage in that activity. The concept of opportunity cost is very important in economics and applies to individuals as much as it does to firms or society as a whole. Consider the example of a doctor who could receive a salary of $100,000 per year working as an employee of a hospital but decides to open his own private practice instead. In that case, the opportunity cost of the physician services he supplies to his own firm is the $100,000 he gives up by not working for the hospital, *even if he does not explicitly pay himself a salary.* As in this example, opportunity costs often do not involve actual payments of money.

Trade-offs force society to make choices when answering the following three fundamental questions:

1. *What* goods and services will be produced?
2. *How* will the goods and services be produced?
3. *Who* will receive the goods and services produced?

We will now briefly introduce each question.

What Goods and Services Will Be Produced?

How will society decide whether to produce more economics textbooks or more Blu-ray players? More daycare facilities or more football stadiums? Of course, "society" does not make decisions; only individuals make decisions. The answer to the question of what will be produced is determined by the choices that consumers, firms, and the government make. Every day, you help decide which goods and services firms will produce when you choose to buy an iPhone instead of a Samsung Galaxy or a caffè mocha rather than a chai tea. Similarly, Apple must choose whether to devote its scarce resources to making more iPhones or more iPads. The federal government must choose whether to spend more of its limited budget on breast cancer research or on repairing highways. In each case, consumers, firms, and the government face the problem of scarcity by trading off one good or service for another. And each choice made comes with an opportunity cost, measured by the value of the best alternative given up.

How Will the Goods and Services Be Produced?

Firms choose how to produce the goods and services they sell. In many cases, firms face a trade-off between using more workers or using more machines. For example, a local service station has to choose whether to provide car repair services using more diagnostic computers and fewer auto mechanics or fewer diagnostic computers and more auto mechanics. Similarly, movie studios have to choose whether to produce animated films using highly skilled animators to draw them by hand or fewer animators and more computers. In deciding whether to move production offshore to China, firms may need to choose between a production method in the United States that uses fewer workers and more machines and a production method in China that uses more workers and fewer machines.

Who Will Receive the Goods and Services Produced?

In the United States, who receives the goods and services produced depends largely on how income is distributed. The higher a person's income, the more goods and services he or she can buy. Often, people are willing to give up some of their income—and, therefore, some of their ability to purchase goods and services—by donating to charities to increase the incomes of poorer people. Each year, Americans donate about $300 billion to charity, or an average donation of $2,650 for each household in the country. An important policy question, however, is whether the government should intervene to make the distribution of income more equal. Such intervention already occurs in the United States, because people with higher incomes pay a larger fraction of their incomes in taxes and because the government makes payments to people with low incomes. There is disagreement over whether the current attempts to redistribute income are sufficient or whether there should be more or less redistribution.

Centrally Planned Economies versus Market Economies

To answer the three questions—what, how, and who—societies organize their economies in two main ways. A society can have a **centrally planned economy** in which the government decides how economic resources will be allocated. Or a society can have a **market economy** in which the decisions of households and firms interacting in markets allocate economic resources.

From 1917 to 1991, the most important centrally planned economy in the world was that of the Soviet Union, which was established when Vladimir Lenin and the Communist Party staged a revolution and took control of the Russian Empire. In the Soviet Union, the government decided what goods to produce, how the goods would be produced, and who would receive the goods. Government employees managed factories and stores. The objective of these managers was to follow the government's orders rather than to satisfy the wants of consumers. Centrally planned economies like that of the Soviet Union have not been successful in producing low-cost, high-quality goods and services. As a result, the standard of living of the average person in a centrally planned economy tends to be low. All centrally planned economies have also been political

Centrally planned economy An economy in which the government decides how economic resources will be allocated.

Market economy An economy in which the decisions of households and firms interacting in markets allocate economic resources.

dictatorships. Dissatisfaction with low living standards and political repression finally led to the collapse of the Soviet Union in 1991. Today, only North Korea still has a completely centrally planned economy.

All high-income democracies, including the United States, Canada, Japan, and the countries of Western Europe, have market economies. Market economies rely primarily on privately owned firms to produce goods and services and to decide how to produce them. Markets, rather than the government, determine who receives the goods and services produced. In a market economy, firms must produce goods and services that meet the wants of consumers, or the firms will go out of business. In that sense, it is ultimately consumers who decide what goods and services will be produced. Because firms in a market economy compete to offer the highest-quality products at the lowest price, they are under pressure to use the lowest-cost methods of production. For example, in the past 10 years, some U.S. firms have been under pressure to reduce their costs to meet competition from Chinese firms.

In a market economy, the income of an individual is determined by the payments he receives for what he has to sell. If he is a civil engineer, and firms are willing to pay a salary of $85,000 per year for engineers with his training and skills, he will have this amount of income to purchase goods and services. If the engineer also owns a house that he rents out, his income will be even higher. One of the attractive features of markets is that they reward hard work. Generally, the more extensive the training a person has received and the longer the hours the person works, the higher the person's income will be. Of course, luck—both good and bad—also plays a role here, as elsewhere in life. Someone might have a high income because she won the state lottery, while someone else might have a low income because he has severe medical problems. We can conclude that market economies respond to the question: "Who receives the goods and services produced?" with the answer: "Those who are most willing and able to buy them."

The Modern "Mixed" Economy

In the nineteenth and early twentieth centuries, the U.S. government engaged in relatively little regulation of markets for goods and services. Beginning in the middle of the twentieth century, government intervention in the economy dramatically increased in the United States and other market economies. This increase was primarily caused by the high rates of unemployment and business bankruptcies during the Great Depression of the 1930s. Some government intervention was also intended to raise the incomes of the elderly, the sick, and people with limited skills. For example, in the 1930s, the United States established the Social Security system, which provides government payments to retired and disabled workers, and minimum wage legislation, which sets a floor on the wages employers can pay workers in many occupations. In more recent years, government intervention in the economy has also expanded to meet goals such as the protection of the environment, the promotion of civil rights, and the provision of medical care to low-income people and the elderly.

Mixed economy An economy in which most economic decisions result from the interaction of buyers and sellers in markets but in which the government plays a significant role in the allocation of resources.

Some economists argue that the extent of government intervention makes it no longer accurate to refer to the U.S., Canadian, Japanese, and Western European economies as pure market economies. Instead, they should be referred to as *mixed economies*. A **mixed economy** is still primarily a market economy because most economic decisions result from the interaction of buyers and sellers in markets. However, the government plays a significant role in the allocation of resources.

One of the most important developments in the international economy in recent years has been the movement of China from being a centrally planned economy to being a more mixed economy. The Chinese economy suffered decades of economic stagnation following the takeover of the government in 1949 by Mao Zedong and the Communist Party. Although China remains a political dictatorship, the production of most goods and services is now determined in the market rather than by the government. The result has been rapid economic growth that in the future may lead to total production of goods and services in China surpassing total production in the United States.

Efficiency and Equity

Market economies tend to be more efficient than centrally planned economies. There are two types of efficiency. **Productive efficiency** occurs when a good or service is produced at the lowest possible cost. **Allocative efficiency** occurs when production is in accordance with consumer preferences. Markets tend to be efficient because they promote competition and facilitate voluntary exchange. With **voluntary exchange**, both the buyer and the seller of a product are made better off by the transaction. We know that they are both made better off because, otherwise, the buyer would not have agreed to buy the product or the seller would not have agreed to sell it. Productive efficiency is achieved when competition among firms forces them to produce goods and services at the lowest cost. Allocative efficiency is achieved when the combination of competition among firms and voluntary exchange between firms and consumers results in firms producing the mix of goods and services that consumers prefer the most. Competition will force firms to continue producing and selling goods and services as long as the additional benefit to consumers is greater than the additional cost of production. In this way, the mix of goods and services produced will match consumer preferences.

Although markets promote efficiency, they don't guarantee it. Inefficiency can arise from various sources. To begin with, it may take some time to achieve an efficient outcome. When Blu-ray players were introduced, for example, firms did not instantly achieve productive efficiency. It took several years for firms to discover the lowest-cost method of producing this good. Governments sometimes reduce efficiency by interfering with voluntary exchange in markets. For example, many governments limit the imports of some goods from foreign countries. This limitation reduces efficiency by keeping goods from being produced at the lowest cost. The production of some goods damages the environment. In this case, government intervention can increase efficiency because without such intervention, firms may ignore the costs of environmental damage and thereby fail to produce the goods at the lowest possible cost.

An economically efficient outcome is not necessarily desirable. Many people prefer economic outcomes that they consider fair or equitable, even if those outcomes are less efficient. **Equity** is harder to define than efficiency because there isn't an agreed upon definition of fairness. For some people, equity involves a more equal distribution of economic benefits than would result from an emphasis on efficiency alone. For example, some people support raising taxes on people with higher incomes to provide the funds for programs that aid the poor. Although governments may increase equity by reducing the incomes of high-income people and increasing the incomes of the poor, efficiency may be reduced. People have less incentive to open new businesses, supply labor, and save if the government takes a significant amount of the income they earn from working or saving. The result is that fewer goods and services are produced, and less saving takes place. As this example illustrates, *there is often a trade-off between efficiency and equity*. Government policymakers often confront this trade-off.

Productive efficiency A situation in which a good or service is produced at the lowest possible cost.

Allocative efficiency A state of the economy in which production is in accordance with consumer preferences; in particular, every good or service is produced up to the point where the last unit provides a marginal benefit to society equal to the marginal cost of producing it.

Voluntary exchange A situation that occurs in markets when both the buyer and the seller of a product are made better off by the transaction.

Equity The fair distribution of economic benefits.

Economic Models

3 LEARNING OBJECTIVE

Understand the role of models in economic analysis.

Economists rely on economic theories, or models (the words *theory* and *model* are used interchangeably), to analyze real-world issues, such as those involved with health care. As mentioned earlier, economic models are simplified versions of reality. Economists are certainly not alone in relying on models: An engineer may use a computer model of a bridge to help test whether it will withstand high winds, or a biologist may make a physical model of a nucleic acid to better understand its properties. One purpose of economic models is to make economic ideas sufficiently explicit and concrete so that individuals, firms, or the government can use them to make decisions. For example, the model of demand and supply is a simplified version of how the prices of products are determined by the interactions among buyers and sellers in markets.

Economists use economic models to answer questions. For example, will the United States have a sufficient number of doctors in 2020? For such a complicated question, economists often use several models to examine different aspects of the issue. For example, economists at the U.S. Bureau of Labor Statistics (BLS) build models that allow them to forecast future employment in different occupations. These models allow the BLS to forecast how many doctors there are likely to be at a future date. Economists also use models to forecast the demand for medical services. By separately forecasting the number of doctors and the demand for medical services, these models provide a forecast of whether there will be a sufficient number of doctors in 2020. As mentioned earlier, economists at the U.S. Health Resources and Services Administration (HRSA) have used models to forecast that there will be a shortage of about 56,000 doctors in 2020.

Sometimes economists use an existing model to analyze an issue, but in other cases, they have to develop a new model. To develop a model, economists generally follow these steps:

1. Decide on the assumptions to use in developing the model.
2. Formulate a testable hypothesis.
3. Use economic data to test the hypothesis.
4. Revise the model if it fails to explain the economic data well.
5. Retain the revised model to help answer similar economic questions in the future.

The Role of Assumptions in Economic Models

Any model is based on making assumptions because models have to be simplified to be useful. We cannot analyze an economic issue unless we reduce its complexity. For example, economic models make *behavioral assumptions* about the motives of consumers and firms. Economists assume that consumers will buy the goods and services that will maximize their well-being or their satisfaction. Similarly, economists assume that firms act to maximize their profits. These assumptions are simplifications because they do not describe the motives of every consumer and every firm. How can we know if the assumptions in a model are too simplified or too limiting? We can determine the usefulness of assumptions by forming hypotheses based on the assumptions and then testing the hypotheses using real-world information.

Forming and Testing Hypotheses in Economic Models

Economic variable Something measurable that can have different values, such as the incomes of doctors.

An **economic variable** is something measurable that can have different values, such as the incomes of doctors. In an economic model, a hypothesis is a statement that may be either correct or incorrect about an economic variable. An example of a hypothesis in an economic model is the statement that the falling incomes earned by primary care physicians—often referred to as *family doctors*—will result in a decline in the number of physicians choosing to enter primary care in the United States in 2020. An economic hypothesis is usually about a causal relationship; in this case, the hypothesis states that lower incomes cause, or lead to, fewer doctors entering primary care.

Before we can accept a hypothesis, we have to test it. To test a hypothesis, we analyze statistics on the relevant economic variables. In our example, we would gather statistics on the incomes of family doctors, the number of family doctors, and perhaps other variables as well. Testing a hypothesis can be tricky. For example, showing that the number of family doctors declined at a time when the average income of these doctors declined would not be enough to demonstrate that the decline in income *caused* the decline in the number of family doctors. Just because two things are correlated—that is, they happen at the same time—does not mean that one caused the other. For example, before entering practice, a doctor spends time in a teaching hospital as a resident in his or her field. Teaching hospitals determine how many residencies they will offer in a particular field. Suppose that teaching hospitals decreased the number of residencies in primary care at the same time that the incomes of family doctors were declining. In that case, the declining number of residencies, rather than the declining incomes, might have caused the decline in the number of family doctors. Over a period of time, many economic variables change, which complicates the testing of hypotheses. In fact, when economists disagree about a hypothesis, such as the effect of falling incomes on the number of family doctors, it is often because of disagreements over interpreting the statistical analysis used to test the hypothesis.

Note that hypotheses must be statements that could, in principle, turn out to be incorrect. Statements such as "Increasing the number of family doctors is good" or "Increasing the number of family doctors is bad" are value judgments rather than hypotheses because it is not possible to disprove them.

Economists accept and use an economic model if it leads to hypotheses that are confirmed by statistical analysis. In many cases, the acceptance is tentative, however, pending the gathering of new data or further statistical analysis. In fact, economists often refer to a hypothesis having been "not rejected," rather than having been "accepted," by statistical analysis. But what if statistical analysis clearly rejects a hypothesis? For example, what if a model leads to a hypothesis that declining incomes of family doctors will cause a decline in the number of these doctors, but the data reject this hypothesis? In this case, the model must be reconsidered. It may be that an assumption used in the model was too simplified or too limiting. For example, perhaps the model ignored the fact that family doctors were moving from owning their own practices to becoming salaried employees of hospitals, where they would be freed from the responsibilities involved in running their own businesses. This change in how primary care physicians are employed might explain why the data rejected the hypothesis.

The BLS has analyzed the accuracy of the projections it had made in 1996 of employment levels in 2006. Some projections were quite accurate, while others were less so. For instance, the BLS had projected that 677,917 physicians and surgeons would be employed in 2006, but actual employment was only 633,292, or about 7 percent less than projected. The error with respect to physician's assistants was much larger, with the projection being that 93,485 physician's assistants would be employed in 2006, but actual employment was only 65,628, or about 30 percent less than expected. Analyzing the errors in these projections helps the BLS to improve the models it uses to make projections of occupational employment.

The process of developing models, testing hypotheses, and revising models occurs not just in economics but also in disciplines such as physics, chemistry, and biology. This process is often referred to as the *scientific method*. Economics is a *social science* because it applies the scientific method to the study of the interactions among individuals.

Positive and Normative Analysis

As we build economic models and use them to answer questions, bear in mind the following important distinction: **Positive analysis** is concerned with *what is*, and **normative analysis** is concerned with *what ought to be*. Economics is about positive analysis, which measures the costs and benefits of different courses of action.

Positive analysis Analysis concerned with what is.

Normative analysis Analysis concerned with what ought to be.

We can use the federal government's minimum wage law to compare positive and normative analysis. In 2013, under this law, it was illegal for an employer to hire a worker at a wage less than $7.25 per hour. Without the minimum wage law, some firms and workers would voluntarily agree to a lower wage. Because of the minimum wage law, some workers have difficulty finding jobs, and some firms end up paying more for labor than they otherwise would have. A positive analysis of the federal minimum wage law uses an economic model to estimate how many workers have lost their jobs because of the law, its effect on the costs and profits of businesses, and the gains to workers receiving the minimum wage. After economists complete this positive analysis, the decision as to whether the minimum wage law is a good or a bad idea is a normative one and depends on how people evaluate the trade-off involved. Supporters of the law believe that the losses to employers and workers who are unemployed as a result of the law are more than offset by the gains to workers who receive higher wages than they would without the law. Opponents of the law believe the losses are greater than the gains. The assessment by any individual depends, in part, on that person's values and political views. The positive analysis an economist provides would play a role in the decision but can't by itself decide the issue one way or the other.

The *Don't Let This Happen to You* box alerts you to common pitfalls in thinking about economic ideas. After reading this box, test your understanding by working the related problem that appears at the end of the chapter.

Don't Let This Happen to You

Don't Confuse Positive Analysis with Normative Analysis

"Economic analysis has shown that the minimum wage law is a bad idea because it causes unemployment." Is this statement accurate? As of 2013, the federal minimum wage law prevents employers from hiring workers at a wage of less than $7.25 per hour. This wage is higher than some employers are willing to pay some workers. If there were no minimum wage law, some workers who currently cannot find any firm willing to hire them at $7.25 per hour would be able to find employment at a lower wage. Therefore, positive economic analysis indicates that the minimum wage law causes unemployment (although economists disagree about how much unemployment the minimum wage law causes). But, some workers who have jobs benefit from the minimum wage law because they are paid a higher wage than they otherwise would be. In other words, the minimum wage law creates both losers (the workers who become unemployed and the firms that have to pay higher wages) and winners (the workers who receive higher wages).

Should we value the gains to the winners more than we value the losses to the losers? The answer involves normative analysis. Positive economic analysis can show the consequences of a particular policy, but it cannot tell us whether the policy is "good" or "bad." So, the statement at the beginning of this box is inaccurate.

Your Turn: Test your understanding by doing related problem 3.9 at the end of this chapter.

Economics as a Social Science

Because economics studies the actions of individuals, it is a social science. Economics is therefore similar to other social science disciplines, such as psychology, political science, and sociology. As a social science, economics considers human behavior—particularly decision-making behavior—in every context, not just in the context of business. Economists have studied issues such as how families decide on the number of children to have, why people have difficulty losing weight or attaining other desirable goals, and why people often ignore relevant information when making decisions. Economics also has much to contribute to questions of government policy. Economists have played an important role in formulating government policies in areas such as the environment, health care, and poverty.

Making the Connection

Should Medical School Be Free?

The U.S. population continues to increase, which by itself would increase the demand for medical services. In addition, the average age of the population is rising, and older people need more medical care than do younger people. So, over time, the number of doctors needs to increase. As mentioned at the beginning of this chapter, the U.S. Health Resources and Services Administration (HRSA) estimates that the number of doctors needed to provide patient care will rise from about 805,000 in 2010 to 922,000 in 2020.

Can we be sure that these additional doctors will be available in 2020? The HRSA forecasts that, in fact, there will be a shortage of 56,000 doctors in 2020. The bulk of that shortage is likely to be in primary care physicians, or family doctors. Ordinarily, we expect that when consumers want more of a product, higher wages and salaries and more job openings will attract workers to that industry. For example, during the U.S. housing boom of the mid-2000s, the number of workers in the building trades—carpenters, plumbers, roofers, and others—increased rapidly. But producing more doctors is a long process. After completing his or her undergraduate education, a doctor spends four years in medical school and then three to five years at

Should these medical students have to pay tuition?

a teaching hospital, pursuing a residency in a particular field of medicine. Apparently convinced that hospitals will not train enough doctors unless they get help, Congress contributes $10 billion per year to teaching hospitals, based on the number of residents they train.

Peter Bach of the Sloan-Kettering Cancer Center and Robert Kocher of the Brookings Institution have proposed that medical schools should charge no tuition. They argue that nearly all students graduate from medical school owing money on student loans, with the average student owing more than $160,000. We might expect that these debts, although large, would not deter students from applying to medical school, because in 2013, the average income of physicians was more than $250,000 per year. Bach and Kocher argue, though, that the high cost of medical school has two bad outcomes: Some good students do not apply because they either do not want to be saddled with such large debts or are unable to borrow sufficient money, and many students avoid going into primary care—where average incomes are $190,000—in favor of specialties such as plastic surgery or anesthesiology—where average incomes are $325,000. Teaching hospitals pay doctors a salary of about $50,000 per year during their residencies. Bach and Kocher propose that hospitals continue to pay residents who pursue primary care but not pay residents who specialize. The money that hospitals would otherwise pay to these residents would be paid to medical schools instead to finance the free tuition. The plan would give residents an incentive to pursue primary care rather than to specialize. Critics of the Bach and Kocher proposal have questioned whether many students capable of being admitted to medical school actually are deterred by medical school tuition. They also question whether many residents who intend to specialize would choose primary care instead, even if specializing means they have to borrow to meet living expenses rather than paying for them with a hospital salary.

Like many other policy debates, the debate over whether changes should be made in how medical school is paid for has positive and normative elements. By gathering data and using economic models, we can assess some of the quantitative claims made by each side in the debate: What role does tuition play in a student's decision about whether to attend medical school? Have tuition increases had a large or a small effect on the number of applications to medical school? How do changes in expected future incomes affect the decisions of medical students about which specialty to choose? These are all positive questions, so it is possible to formulate quantitative answers. Ultimately, though, this debate also has a normative element. For instance, some doctors, economists, and policymakers argue that it is important that people living in low-income or rural areas have improved access to health care, so they are willing to support policies that would redirect medical students away from specialized fields and toward primary care. Other doctors, economists, and policymakers believe that medical students who enter specialized fields make a larger contribution to society than do students who enter primary care. A disagreement of this type is unlikely to be resolved by building models and analyzing data because the issue involved is essentially normative.

In 2010, President Obama and Congress enacted the Patient Protection and Affordable Care Act, which made major changes to the U.S. health care system. Most of the changes were in effect by 2014. Additional changes are likely as policymakers grapple with the rapidly escalating costs of health care. Whether Congress and the president will enact policies intended to increase the number of family doctors remains to be seen.

Sources: Uwe E. Reinhardt, "Producing More Primary-Care Doctors," *New York Times*, June 10, 2011; Uwe E. Reinhardt, "The Debt of Medical Students," *New York Times*, September 14, 2012; and Peter B. Bach and Robert Kocher, "Why Medical School Should Be Free," *New York Times*, May 28, 2011.

Your Turn: Test your understanding by doing related problem 3.6 at the end of this chapter.

Microeconomics and Macroeconomics

4 LEARNING OBJECTIVE

Distinguish between microeconomics and macroeconomics.

Economic models can be used to analyze decision making in many areas. We group some of these areas together as *microeconomics* and others as *macroeconomics*. **Microeconomics** is the study of how households and firms make choices, how they interact in markets, and how the government attempts to influence their choices. Microeconomic issues include explaining how consumers react to changes in product prices and how firms decide what prices to charge for the products they sell. Microeconomics also involves policy issues, such as analyzing the most efficient way to reduce teenage smoking, analyzing the costs and benefits of approving the sale of a new prescription drug, and analyzing the most efficient way to reduce air pollution.

Macroeconomics is the study of the economy as a whole, including topics such as inflation, unemployment, and economic growth. Macroeconomic issues include explaining why economies experience periods of recession and increasing unemployment and why, over the long run, some economies have grown much faster than others. Macroeconomics also involves policy issues, such as whether government intervention can reduce the severity of recessions.

The division between microeconomics and macroeconomics is not hard and fast. Many economic situations have *both* a microeconomic and a macroeconomic aspect. For example, the level of total investment by firms in new machinery and equipment helps to determine how rapidly the economy grows—which is a macroeconomic issue. But to understand how much new machinery and equipment firms decide to purchase, we have to analyze the incentives individual firms face—which is a microeconomic issue.

Microeconomics The study of how households and firms make choices, how they interact in markets, and how the government attempts to influence their choices.

Macroeconomics The study of the economy as a whole, including topics such as inflation, unemployment, and economic growth.

5 LEARNING OBJECTIVE

Define important economic terms.

A Preview of Important Economic Terms

Becoming familiar with certain important terms is a necessary step in learning economics. Here we provide a brief introduction to some of these terms.

- *Firm, company, or business.* A *firm* is an organization that produces a good or service. Most firms produce goods or services to earn profits, but there are also nonprofit firms, such as universities and some hospitals. Economists use the terms *firm, company,* and *business* interchangeably.

- *Entrepreneur.* An *entrepreneur* is someone who operates a business. In a market system, entrepreneurs decide what goods and services to produce and how to produce them. An entrepreneur starting a new business puts his or her own funds at risk. If an entrepreneur is wrong about what consumers want or about the best way to produce goods and services, his or her funds can be lost. Losing money in a failed business is not unusual: In the United States, about half of new businesses close within four years. Without entrepreneurs willing to assume the risk of starting and operating businesses, economic progress would be impossible in a market system.

- *Innovation.* There is a distinction between an *invention* and an *innovation.* An *invention* is a new good or a new process for making a good. An *innovation* is the practical application of an invention. (*Innovation* may also be used more broadly to refer to any significant improvement in a good or in the means of producing a good.) Much time often passes between the appearance of a new idea and its development for widespread use. For example, the Wright brothers first achieved self-propelled flight at Kitty Hawk, North Carolina, in 1903, but the Wright brothers' plane was very crude, and it wasn't until the introduction of the DC-3 by Douglas Aircraft in 1936 that regularly scheduled intercity airline flights became common in the United States. Similarly, the first digital electronic computer—the ENIAC—was developed in 1945, but the first IBM personal computer was not introduced until 1981, and widespread use of computers did not have a significant effect on the productivity of U.S. business until the 1990s.

- *Technology.* A firm's *technology* is the processes it uses to produce goods and services. In the economic sense, a firm's technology depends on many factors, such as the skill of its managers, the training of its workers, and the speed and efficiency of its machinery and equipment.

- *Goods.* *Goods* are tangible merchandise, such as books, computers, or Blu-ray players.

- *Services.* *Services* are activities done for others, such as providing haircuts or investment advice.

- *Revenue.* A firm's *revenue* is the total amount received for selling a good or service. We calculate it by multiplying the price per unit by the number of units sold.

- *Profit.* A firm's *profit* is the difference between its revenue and its costs. Economists distinguish between *accounting profit* and *economic profit*. In calculating accounting profit, we exclude the cost of some economic resources that the firm does not pay for explicitly. In calculating economic profit, we include the opportunity cost of all resources used by the firm. When we refer to *profit* in this text, we mean economic profit. It is important not to confuse *profit* with *revenue*.

- *Household.* A *household* consists of all persons occupying a home. Households are suppliers of factors of production—particularly labor—used by firms to make goods and services. Households also demand goods and services produced by firms and governments.

- *Factors of production, economic resources, or inputs.* Firms use *factors of production* to produce goods and services. The main factors of production are labor, capital, natural resources—including land—and entrepreneurial ability. Households earn income by supplying the factors of production to firms. Economists use the terms *factors of production, economic resources*, and *inputs* interchageably.

- *Capital.* In everyday speech, the word *capital* can refer to *financial capital* or to *physical capital*. Financial capital includes stocks and bonds issued by firms, bank accounts, and holdings of money. In economics, though, *capital* refers to physical capital, which includes manufactured goods that are used to produce other goods and services. Examples of physical capital are computers, factory buildings, machine tools, warehouses, and trucks. The total amount of physical capital available in a country is referred to as the country's *capital stock*.

- *Human capital.* *Human capital* refers to the accumulated training and skills that workers possess. For example, college-educated workers generally have more skills and are more productive than workers who have only high school degrees; therefore, college-educated workers have more human capital.

Continued

Economics in Your Life

Will There Be Plenty of Jobs Available in the Health Care Industry?

At the beginning of this chapter, we posed the question: "What is the basis for the forecasts on the availability of jobs in health care, and how reliable are the forecasts?" As the U.S. population increases and as the average age of the population rises, it seems likely that there will be an increase in the number of doctors, nurses, physician's assistants, and other health care workers. The U.S. Bureau of Labor Statistics (BLS) publishes the most widely used occupational forecasts. Economists at the BLS base these forecasts on economic models. The forecasts can be inaccurate, however. For example, in 1996, the BLS forecast that 93,485 physician's assistants would be employed in 2006, when in fact only 65,628 were. The BLS analyzes errors like these in attempting to improve its forecasts. So, it is likely that the BLS's forecasts will become more accurate over time, but it would be a mistake to expect the forecasts to be exact.

Conclusion

Economics is a group of useful ideas about how individuals make choices. Economists have put these ideas into practice by developing economic models. Consumers, business managers, and government policymakers use these models every day to help make choices. In this text, we explore many key economic models and give examples of how to apply them in the real world.

Reading newspapers and other periodicals is an important part of understanding the current business climate and learning how to apply economic concepts to a variety of real-world events. At the end of this chapter, you will see a two-page feature titled *An Inside Look*. This feature consists of an excerpt from an article that relates to the company or economic issue introduced at the start of the chapter and also to the concepts discussed in the chapter. A summary and an analysis with supporting graphs highlight the key economic points of the article. Read *An Inside Look* for a discussion of how technological changes, such as smartphones, affect how doctors provide health care. Test your understanding by answering the *Thinking Critically* questions.

FORBES

The Year 2020: The Doctor Will (NOT) See You Now!

It's the year 2020. 20/20, just like perfect vision.

And interestingly, it's also *your* vision. In today's world of health and wellness, computer-guided laser vision correction is so commonplace that eye glasses are hardly necessary and almost pure fashion. Except for the occasional "Google Glasses" that early innovators still wear as a badge of adoption.

The Exam Room of the Future

Today is the first time you've been to a doctor's office in two years. Yet, surprisingly, you're as compliant and up to date as can be. Over the past two years, you've had several interactions with your doctor including an ECG, simplified physical exam and evaluation of a sore throat. However, these evaluations were done from your home with one of the most essential components of care for both you and your physician–the smartphone. As you arrive, one of the first things you notice is that the waiting room is almost empty. Advances in digital appointments and off site care have changed the practice dynamics significantly. In fact, your family physician sees more patients virtually than in the real world. The digital receptionist acknowledges you by first name as you approach this holographic image. Face recognition has instantly identified you and a thermal scan has checked your body temperature to screen for the potential of any infectious conditions that would immediately shuttle you off to an isolation area.

You pick up an electronic tablet and have a seat in the specific color-coded, pod-like chair that the receptionist has indicated. There are some quick questions to answer on the tablet as electronic sensors built into the chair begin to analyze your weight, blood oxygen, and other key elements of your physiology. You're asked to do some basic tasks including standing, looking into a small scanner and to grasp two sensor handles. The analysis is compared directly with your electronic medical records and prompt questions about unusual changes or variations. Once the basic analysis has been completed, supplemental questions–culled from an extensive clinical database–are asked to preemptively identify health issues and problems that can be addressed much earlier.

You might be surprised to know that most of your "history and-physical" is now complete. An entire "healthprint" is on your physician's desktop. It contains a comprehensive physical exam that has been cross indexed against your past history and a large database of patients. Any outlying concerns can be addressed the good old-fashioned way. But leaving that up to the unpredictable and error-prone abilities of a nurse or doctor can be problematic!

"Looks like you're doing great!" Those are the first words you hear from an actual human–your doctor. And you're done…. But as you leave you can't stop and wonder if this "car-wash" type doctor visit is sub-optimal. What happened to the face time and human component of good old-fashioned medicine?

Examining the Exam

Let's take a closer look at what just happened in the future:

- It took 17 minutes–from start to finish. It's effective *and* efficient.
- The analytical and diagnostic acumen of the technology is, in many respects, superior to the physical skill set of your doctor.
- The data used for diagnosis and therapeutic recommendations are always current and reflect the best and brightest thinking in medicine.
- The depth and breadth of the database used for predictive information is massive. No individual physician can ever have the experience, intuition or processing power to come close.
- The human touch is still there–it's just reserved for more specific and valuable use.

Healthcare is in a great state of transition now. Financial concerns, reimbursement and coverage, and an aging population will be powerful drivers of change. Technology will be a beacon of innovation that will help address many of these concerns without the compromise of care. The innovation, and the rate of change, is simply amazing and the future is looking very healthy indeed.

Source: John Nosta, "The Year 2020: The Doctor Will (NOT) See You Now!" *Forbes*, August 15, 2012.

Key Points in the Article

Advances in technology may change the way patients interact with their doctors in 2020. Today, many people visit a doctor's office for routine physical exams or treatment of conditions such as the flu. This article predicts that by the end of this decade, many medical evaluations will be performed via smartphone from the convenience of the patient's home. There will still be occasions when an actual visit to the doctor's office is necessary, so the doctor's office will not disappear, but it will be drastically transformed as a result of technology. These changes, including electronic evaluations and diagnoses based on extensive, current databases, not only will reduce the amount of time required for a typical doctor's appointment but may also dramatically improve the quality of analysis and level of care that patients receive.

Analyzing the News

(a) Advances in technology continue to change many facets of the economy, and the doctor's office is no exception. Economic incentives are changing for both doctors and patients. Granted, the author of the article is speculating as to how basic medical care will be handled by the end of this decade, but based on ongoing improvements in technology, his ideas read more like fact than fiction. Smartphone technology has improved greatly over the past few years, so it is not hard to imagine these devices playing an ever-increasing role in our everyday lives. Being able to have routine medical tests and diagnoses performed electronically via smartphone will save time and money for doctors, laboratories, and patients, thereby increasing efficiency and potentially reducing costs.

(b) Imagine a routine trip to the doctor's office taking 17 minutes—from start to finish—and happening only once every two years. No more taking off an entire day from work or school every time a minor ailment arises. (You may not be interested in this improvement now, but your professors and your future employer will appreciate it.) Lost time from work or school can have a negative effect on productivity, decreasing economic efficiency. One key to the scenario presented in the article is that efficiency will be improved without sacrificing quality. The author also argues that the quality of medical care will be enhanced as well. Should this outcome occur, the additional benefits received from this way of delivering medical care would seem to outweigh the additional costs, including having less personal interaction with the doctor.

(c) The health care industry is changing and, with the passage of the Affordable Care Act in 2010, will continue to change. The chapter opener discusses the increasing number of doctors leaving private practice to become salaried employees of hospitals because of changes in health care laws and financial concerns. Other factors that will significantly affect health care in the coming years and that may also be a reason for doctors choosing hospital employment are the aging population and the increasing number of people covered by health insurance. The figure below shows recent data on the number of people aged 65 and older, the number of uninsured people, and projections for 2020. These numbers indicate a significant increase in demand for health care services in the coming years. Technological innovations such as those discussed in the article could prove invaluable in efficiently providing quality medical care to this growing number of patients.

Thinking Critically

1. One key economic idea is that people respond to economic incentives. Explain how the improvements in technology discussed in the article, along with the expected increase in the demand for health care, may affect the incentives for doctors leaving private practice for employment in hospitals.

2. The article speculates that improvements in technology will increase efficiency in the health care industry without compromising the quality of customer care. Suppose you want to develop an economic model to analyze the relationship between the increased efficiency resulting from the changes in technology used in a doctor's office and the corresponding level of care patients receive. Use information from the article to explain the steps you would take to develop this model.

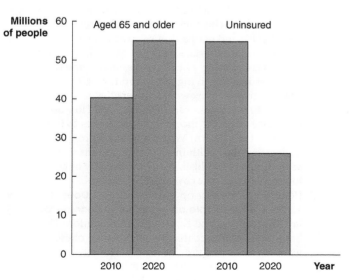

Technological innovations could help increase availability of health care to an aging population and the uninsured.

Data for people aged 65 and older and the uninsured are for 2010 and projected for 2020.

Source: U.S. Census Bureau and Congressional Budget Office.

Chapter Summary and Problems

Key Terms

Allocative efficiency	Economics	Market economy	Positive analysis
Centrally planned economy	Equity	Microeconomics	Productive efficiency
Economic model	Macroeconomics	Mixed economy	Scarcity
Economic variable	Marginal analysis	Normative analysis	Trade-off
	Market	Opportunity cost	Voluntary exchange

 Three Key Economic Ideas

LEARNING OBJECTIVE: Explain these three key economic ideas: People are rational; people respond to economic incentives; and optimal decisions are made at the margin.

Summary

Economics is the study of the choices consumers, business managers, and government officials make to attain their goals, given their scarce resources. We must make choices because of **scarcity**, which means that although our wants are unlimited, the resources available to fulfill those wants are limited. Economists assume that people are rational in the sense that consumers and firms use all available information as they take actions intended to achieve their goals. Rational individuals weigh the benefits and costs of each action and choose an action only if the benefits outweigh the costs. Although people act from a variety of motives, ample evidence indicates that they respond to economic incentives. Economists use the word **marginal** to mean extra or additional. The optimal decision is to continue any activity up to the point where the marginal benefit equals the marginal cost.

Visit **www.myeconlab.com** *to complete these exercises online and get instant feedback.*

Review Questions

1.1 Briefly discuss each of the following economic ideas: People are rational, people respond to economic incentives, and optimal decisions are made at the margin.

1.2 What is scarcity? Why is scarcity central to the study of economics?

Problems and Applications

1.3 Do you agree with the following statement: "The problem with economics is that it assumes that consumers and firms always make the correct decisions. But we know that everyone makes mistakes."

1.4 According to the FBI Bank Crime Statistics, there were more than 5,000 bank robberies in the United States in 2012. The FBI claims that banks have allowed themselves to become easy targets by refusing to install clear acrylic partitions, called *bandit barriers*, that separate bank tellers from the public. According to a special agent with the FBI, "Bandit barriers are a great deterrent. We've talked to guys who rob banks, and as soon as they see a bandit barrier, they go find another bank." Despite this finding, many banks have been reluctant to install these barriers. Wouldn't banks have a strong incentive to install bandit barriers to deter robberies? Why, then, do so many banks not do so?

Sources: "FBI Bank Crime Statistics 2012," www.fbi.gov; and Richard Cowen, "FBI: Banks Are to Blame for Rise in Robberies," NorthJersey .com, March 10, 2009.

1.5 The grading system plays an important role in student learning. In their book *Effective Grading: A Tool for Learning and Assessment in College*, Barbara Walvoord and Virginia Anderson state that "grading infuses everything that happens in the classroom." They also argue that grading "needs to be acknowledged and managed from the first moment that an instructor begins planning a class."
  a. How could the grading system a teacher uses affect the incentives of students to learn the course material?
  b. If teachers put too little weight in the grading scale on a certain part of the course, such as readings outside the textbook, how might students respond?
  c. Teachers often wish that students came to class prepared, having read the upcoming material. How could a teacher design the grading system to motivate students to come to class prepared?

Source: Barbara E. Walvoord and Virginia Johnson Anderson, *Effective Grading: A Tool for Learning and Assessment in College*, 2nd edition, San Francisco: Jossey-Bass, 2010, p. 1.

1.6 [Related to the Making the Connection: **Does Health Insurance Give People an Incentive to Become Obese?]** Many universities and corporations offer a health wellness program that helps their employees improve or maintain their health and get paid (a relatively small amount) for doing so. The programs vary but typically consist of employees completing a health assessment, receiving a program for healthy living, and monitoring their monthly health activities. Why would universities and corporations pay employees to take care of themselves? How does health insurance affect the incentive of employees to improve or maintain their health? Would a wellness program increase or decrease the health insurance premiums that an insurance company would charge the university or corporation to provide insurance coverage? Briefly explain.

1.7 [Related to the Making the Connection: **Does Health Insurance Give People an Incentive to Become Obese?]** Jay Bhattacharya and Kate Bundorf of Stanford University have found evidence that people who are obese and who work for firms that provide health insurance receive lower wages than workers at those firms who are not obese. At firms that do not provide health insurance, obese workers do not receive lower wages than workers who are not obese.

a. Why might firms that provide workers with health insurance pay a lower wage to obese workers than to workers who are not obese?

b. Is Bhattacharya and Bundorf's finding relevant to the question of whether health insurance provides people with an incentive to become obese? Briefly explain.

Source: Jay Bhattacharya and M. Kate Bundorf, "The Incidence of the Health Care Costs of Obesity," *Journal of Health Economics*, Vol. 28, No. 3, May 2009, pp. 649–658.

1.8 **[Related to** Solved Problem 1**]** In 2013, the president and chief executive officer of McDonald's, Don Thompson, said that McDonald's was considering serving breakfast all day, instead of stopping at 10:30 A.M. on weekdays and 11:00 A.M. on weekends. Several owners of McDonald's restaurants, however, point out that offering breakfast 24 hours a day presents two logistical problems: (1) Burgers and other meats need to be cooked at a higher temperature than eggs, so it would be difficult for employees to set the grill at the right temperature for both foods, and (2) scrambled eggs require employees to continually stir, while hamburgers don't require this attention. In addition, some customers might buy the cheaper breakfast rather than the more expensive lunch or dinner meals. If you were the president and chief executive officer of McDonald's, discuss how you would go about deciding whether to serve breakfast all day. Would your decision have to be all or nothing—either serve breakfast up to 10:30 A.M. or serve breakfast all day? Would you have to serve the entire breakfast menu all day?

Source: Susan Berfield and Leslie Patton, "What's So Hard About a 24/7 McMuffin?" *Bloomberg BusinessWeek*, May 6–12, 2013.

1.9 **[Related to** Solved Problem 1**]** Two students are discussing Solved Problem 1:

> **Joe:** I think the key additional information you need to know in deciding whether the doctor should keep the medical practice open 9 hours per day rather than 8 hours is the amount of profit she is currently making while being open 8 hours. Then, she can compare the profit earned from being open 9 hours with the profit earned from being open 8 hours. This information is more important than the additional revenue and additional cost of being open 1 more hour.
>
> **Jill:** Actually, Joe, knowing how much profits change when the medical practice stays open 1 more hour is exactly the same as knowing the additional revenue and the additional cost.

Briefly evaluate their discussion.

1.10 **[Related to** Solved Problem 1**]** Late in the semester, a friend tells you, "I was going to drop my psychology course so I could concentrate on my other courses, but I had already put so much time into the course that I decided not to drop it." What do you think of your friend's reasoning? Would it make a difference to your answer if your friend has to pass the psychology course at some point to graduate? Briefly explain.

1.11 In a paper written by Bentley College economists Patricia M. Flynn and Michael A. Quinn, the authors state:

> We find evidence that Economics is a good choice of major for those aspiring to become a CEO [chief executive officer]. When adjusting for size of the pool of graduates, those with undergraduate degrees in Economics are shown to have had a greater likelihood of becoming an S&P 500 CEO than any other major.

A list of famous economics majors published by Marietta College includes business leaders Warren Buffett, Donald Trump, Ted Turner, Diane von Furstenberg, Steve Ballmer, and Sam Walton, as well as former presidents George H.W. Bush, Gerald Ford, and Ronald Reagan. Why might studying economics be particularly good preparation for being the top manager of a corporation or a leader in government?

Sources: Patricia M. Flynn and Michael A. Quinn, "Economics: A Good Choice of Major for Future CEOs," *Social Science Research Network*, November 28, 2006; and *Famous Economics Majors*, Marietta College, Marietta, Ohio, May 15, 2012.

 2

The Economic Problem That Every Society Must Solve

LEARNING OBJECTIVE: Discuss how an economy answers these questions: What goods and services will be produced? How will the goods and services be produced? Who will receive the goods and services produced?

Summary

Society faces **trade-offs**: Producing more of one good or service means producing less of another good or service. The **opportunity cost** of any activity—such as producing a good or service—is the highest-valued alternative that must be given up to engage in that activity. The choices of consumers, firms, and governments determine what goods and services will be produced. Firms choose how to produce the goods and services they sell. In the United States, who receives the goods and services produced depends largely on how income is distributed in the marketplace. In a **centrally planned economy**, most economic decisions are made by the government. In a **market economy**, most economic decisions are made by consumers and firms. Most economies, including that of the United States, are **mixed economies** in which most economic decisions are made by consumers and firms but in which the government also plays a significant role. There are two types of efficiency: productive efficiency and allocative efficiency. **Productive efficiency** occurs when a good or service is produced at the lowest possible cost. **Allocative efficiency** occurs when production corresponds with consumer preferences. **Voluntary exchange** is a situation that occurs in markets when both the buyer and the seller of a product are made better off by the transaction. **Equity** is more difficult to define than efficiency, but it usually involves a fair distribution of economic benefits. Government policymakers often face a trade-off between equity and efficiency.

Visit **www.myeconlab.com** to complete these exercises online and get instant feedback.

Review Questions

2.1 Why does scarcity imply that every society and every individual face trade-offs?

2.2 What are the three economic questions that every society must answer? Briefly discuss the differences in how centrally planned, market, and mixed economies answer these questions?

2.3 What is the difference between productive efficiency and allocative efficiency?

2.4 What is the difference between efficiency and equity? Why do government policymakers often face a trade-off between efficiency and equity?

Problems and Applications

2.5 When the price of Microsoft stock increased more than 27 percent in the first part of 2013, Bill Gates, who owns 436 million shares of Microsoft stock, once again became the world's richest person. Does Bill Gates face scarcity? Does everyone? Are there any exceptions?

Source: "Bill Gates Surpasses Carlos Slim to Become Richest Man in the World," Huffingtonpost.com, May 16, 2013.

2.6 Consider an organization that exists to help the poor. The members of the organization are discussing alternative methods of aiding the poor, when a proponent of one particular method asserts that: "If even one poor person is helped with this method, then all our time and money would have been worth it." If you were a member of the organization, how would you reply to this assertion?

2.7 In a market economy, why does a firm have a strong incentive to be productively efficient and allocatively efficient? What does the firm earn if it is productively and allocatively efficient, and what happens if it is not?

2.8 Would you expect new and better machinery and equipment to be adopted more rapidly in a market economy or in a centrally planned economy? Briefly explain.

2.9 Centrally planned economies have been less efficient than market economies.
   a. Has this difference in efficiency happened by chance, or is there some underlying reason?
   b. If market economies are more economically efficient than centrally planned economies, would there ever be

a reason to prefer having a centrally planned economy rather than a market economy?

2.10 Would you expect a centrally planned economy to be better at productive efficiency or allocative efficiency? Briefly explain.

2.11 Leonard Fleck, a philosophy professor at Michigan State University, has written:

> When it comes to health care in America, we have limited resources for unlimited health care needs. We want everything contemporary medical technology can offer that will improve the length or quality of our lives as we age. But as presently healthy taxpayers, we want costs controlled.

Why is it necessary for all economic systems to limit services such as health care? How does a market system prevent people from getting as many goods and services as they want?

Source: Leonard Fleck, *Just Caring: Health Care Rationing and Democratic Deliberation*, New York: Oxford University Press, 2009.

2.12 Suppose that your local police department recovers 100 tickets to a big NASCAR race in a drug raid. Police decide to distribute the tickets to residents and announce that tickets will be given away at 10 A.M. Monday at City Hall.
   a. What groups of people will be most likely to try to get the tickets? Think of specific examples and then generalize.
   b. What is the opportunity cost of distributing the tickets this way?
   c. Productive efficiency occurs when a good or service (such as the distribution of tickets) is produced at the lowest possible cost. Is this an efficient way to distribute the tickets? If possible, think of a more efficient method of distributing the tickets.
   d. Is this an equitable way to distribute the tickets? Explain.

3	**Economic Models**

LEARNING OBJECTIVE: Understand the role of models in economic analysis.

Summary

An **economic variable** is something measurable that can have different values, such as the wages of software programmers. Economists rely on economic models when they apply economic ideas to real-world problems. **Economic models** are simplified versions of reality used to analyze real-world economic situations. Economists accept and use an economic model if it leads to hypotheses that are confirmed by statistical analysis. In many cases, the acceptance is tentative, however, pending the gathering of new data or further statistical analysis. Economics is a *social science* because it applies the scientific method to the study of the interactions among individuals. Economics is concerned with positive analysis rather than normative analysis. **Positive analysis** is concerned with what is. **Normative analysis** is concerned with what ought to be. As a social science, economics considers human behavior in every context of decision making, not just in business.

Visit **www.myeconlab.com** to complete these exercises online and get instant feedback.

Review Questions

3.1 Why do economists use models? How are economic data used to test models?

3.2 Describe the five steps by which economists arrive at a useful economic model.

3.3 What is the difference between normative analysis and positive analysis? Is economics concerned mainly with normative analysis or positive analysis? Briefly explain.

Problems and Applications

3.4 Suppose an economist develops an economic model and finds that "it works great in theory, but it fails in practice." What should the economist do next?

3.5 Dr. Strangelove's theory is that the price of mushrooms is determined by the activity of subatomic particles that exist in another universe parallel to ours. When the subatomic particles are emitted in profusion, the price of mushrooms is high. When subatomic particle emissions are low, the price of mushrooms is also low. How would you go about testing Dr. Strangelove's theory? Discuss whether this theory is useful.

3.6 **[Related to the** Making the Connection: **Should Medical School Be Free?]** This feature explains that there are both positive and normative elements to the debate over whether medical schools should charge tuition and whether hospitals should continue to pay residents who pursue primary care but not residents who specialize. What economic statistics would be most useful in evaluating the positive elements in this debate? Assuming that these statistics are available or could be gathered, are they likely to resolve the normative issues in this debate?

3.7 **[Related to the** Chapter Opener**]** In recent years, many doctors have decided to give up running their private practices as small businesses and have become salaried employees of hospitals.
 a. What important differences exist between doctors' private practices and other small businesses, such as restaurants and hardware stores?
 b. How have the economic incentives a doctor faces when considering whether to operate a private practice or become a salaried employee of a hospital changed over the years?

3.8 **[Related to the** Chapter Opener**]** According to an article in the *New York Times*, hospitals sometimes complain that doctors do not work as hard when they become hospital employees as they do when they operate a private practice. How do the economic incentives a doctor faces to work hard change when the doctor closes a private practice and becomes a salaried employee of a hospital?

Source: Julie Crewell and Reed Abelson, "A Hospital War Reflects a Bind for Doctors in the U.S.," *New York Times*, November 30, 2012.

3.9 **[Related to the** Don't Let This Happen to You**]** Explain which of the following statements represent positive analysis and which represent normative analysis.
 a. A 50-cent-per-pack tax on cigarettes will lead to a 12 percent reduction in smoking by teenagers.
 b. The federal government should spend more on AIDS research.
 c. Rising wheat prices will increase bread prices.
 d. The price of coffee at Starbucks is too high.

3.10 In the United States, to receive a medical license, a doctor must complete a residency program at a hospital. Hospitals are not free to expand their residency programs in a particular medical specialty without approval from a Residency Review Committee (RRC), which is made up of physicians in that specialty. A hospital that does not abide by the rulings of the RRC runs the risk of losing its accreditation from the Accreditation Council for Graduate Medical Education (ACGME). The ACGME and the RRCs argue that this system makes it possible to ensure that residency programs do not expand to the point where they are not providing residents with high-quality training.
 a. How does this system help protect consumers?
 b. How might this system protect the financial interests of doctors more than the well-being of consumers?
 c. Briefly discuss whether you consider this system to be a good one. Is your conclusion an example of normative economics or of positive economics? Briefly explain.

Sources: Brian Palmer, "We Need More Doctors, Stat!" *Slate*, June 27, 2011; and Sean Nicholson, "Barriers to Entering Medical Specialties," Wharton School, September 2003.

Microeconomics and Macroeconomics

LEARNING OBJECTIVE: Distinguish between microeconomics and macroeconomics.

Summary

Microeconomics is the study of how households and firms make choices, how they interact in markets, and how the government attempts to influence their choices. **Macroeconomics** is the study of the economy as a whole, including topics such as inflation, unemployment, and economic growth.

Visit **www.myeconlab.com** to complete these exercises online and get instant feedback.

Review Question

4.1 Briefly discuss the difference between microeconomics and macroeconomics.

4.2 Is every economic issue either strictly microeconomic or strictly macroeconomic? Briefly explain.

Problems and Applications

4.3 Briefly explain whether each of the following is primarily a microeconomic issue or a macroeconomic issue.
 a. The effect of higher cigarette taxes on the quantity of cigarettes sold.
 b. The effect of higher income taxes on the total amount of consumer spending.
 c. The reasons the economies of East Asian countries grow faster than the economies of sub-Saharan African countries.
 d. The reasons for low rates of profit in the airline industry.

4.4 Briefly explain whether you agree with the following assertion: "Microeconomics is concerned with things that happen in one particular place, such as the unemployment rate in one city. In contrast, macroeconomics is concerned with things that affect the country as a whole, such as how the rate of teenage smoking in the United States would be affected by an increase in the tax on cigarettes."

A Preview of Important Economic Terms

LEARNING OBJECTIVE: Define important economic terms.

Summary

Becoming familiar with important terms is a necessary step in learning economics. These important economic terms include *capital, entrepreneur, factors of production, firm, goods, household, human capital, innovation, profit, revenue, services,* and *technology.*

Appendix

LEARNING OBJECTIVE

Review the use of graphs and formulas.

Using Graphs and Formulas

Graphs are used to illustrate key economic ideas. Graphs appear not just in economics textbooks but also on Web sites and in newspaper and magazine articles that discuss events in business and economics. Why the heavy use of graphs? Because they serve two useful purposes: (1) They simplify economic ideas, and (2) they make the ideas more concrete so they can be applied to real-world problems. Economic and business issues can be complicated, but a graph can help cut through complications and highlight the key relationships needed to understand the issue. In that sense, a graph can be like a street map.

Suppose you take a bus to New York City to see the Empire State Building. After arriving at the Port Authority Bus Terminal, you will probably use a map similar to the one shown here to find your way to the Empire State Building.

Maps are very familiar to just about everyone, so we don't usually think of them as being simplified versions of reality, but they are. This map does not show much more than the streets in this part of New York City and some of the most important buildings. The names, addresses, and telephone numbers of the people who live and work in the area aren't given. Almost none of the stores and buildings those people work and live in are shown either. The map doesn't indicate which streets allow curbside parking and which don't. In fact, the map shows almost nothing about the messy reality of life in this section of New York City, except how the streets are laid out, which is the essential information you need to get from the Port Authority Bus Terminal to the Empire State Building.

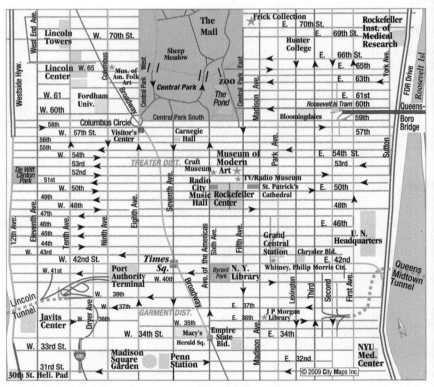

Street map of New York City. Copyright © 2011 City Maps Inc. Reprinted by permission.

Think about someone who says, "I know how to get around in the city, but I just can't figure out how to read a map." It certainly is possible to find your destination in a city without a map, but it's a lot easier with one. The same is true of using graphs in economics. It is possible to arrive at a solution to a real-world problem in economics and business without using graphs, but it is usually a lot easier if you use them.

Often, the difficulty students have with graphs and formulas is a lack of familiarity. With practice, all the graphs and formulas in this text will become familiar to you. Once you are familiar with them, you will be able to use them to analyze problems that would otherwise seem very difficult. What follows is a brief review of how graphs and formulas are used.

Graphs of One Variable

Figure A.1 displays values for *market shares* in the U.S. automobile market, using two common types of graphs. Market shares show the percentage of industry sales accounted for by different firms. In this case, the information is for groups of firms: the "Big Three"—Ford, General Motors, and Chrysler—as well as Japanese, European, and Korean firms. Panel (a) displays the information on market shares as a *bar graph*, where the market share of each group of firms is represented by the height of its bar. Panel (b) displays the same information as a *pie chart*, where the market share of each group of firms is represented by the size of its slice of the pie.

Information on economic variables is also often displayed in *time-series graphs*. Time-series graphs are displayed on a coordinate grid. In a coordinate grid, we can measure the value of one variable along the vertical axis (or *y*-axis) and the value of another variable along the horizontal axis (or *x*-axis). The point where the vertical axis intersects the horizontal axis is called the *origin*. At the origin, the value of both variables is zero. The points on a coordinate grid represent values of the two variables. In Figure A.2, we measure the number of automobiles and trucks sold worldwide by Ford Motor Company on the vertical axis, and we measure time on the horizontal axis. In time-series graphs, the height of the line at each date shows the value of the variable measured on the vertical axis. Both panels of Figure A.2 show Ford's worldwide sales during each year from 2001 to 2012. The difference between panel (a) and panel (b) illustrates the importance of the scale used in a time-series graph. In panel (a), the vertical axis starts at 0 and the distance between each value shown is the same. In this panel, the decline in

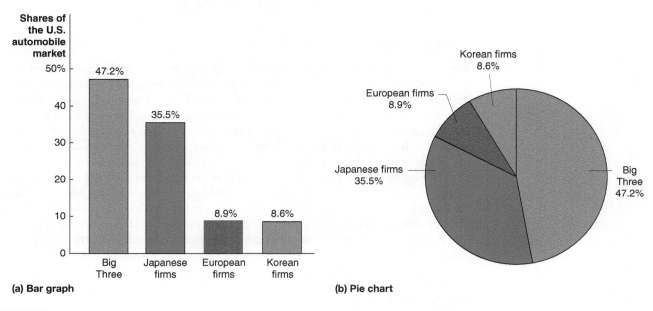

Figure A.1   Bar Graphs and Pie Charts

Values for an economic variable are often displayed as a bar graph or a pie chart. In this case, panel (a) shows market share data for the U.S. automobile industry as a bar graph, where the market share of each group of firms is represented by the height of its bar. Panel (b) displays the same information as a pie chart, where the market share of each group of firms is represented by the size of its slice of the pie. **Source:** "Auto Sales," *Wall Street Journal*, May 1, 2013.

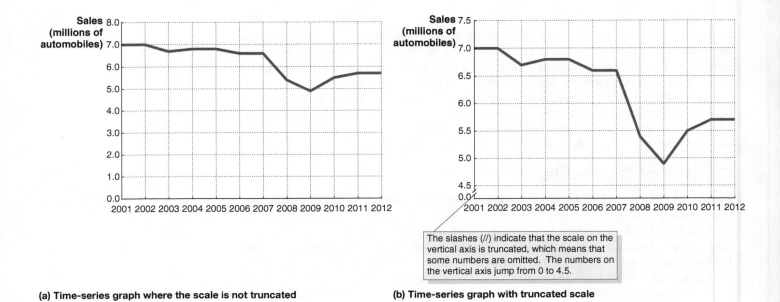

(a) Time-series graph where the scale is not truncated

(b) Time-series graph with truncated scale

The slashes (//) indicate that the scale on the vertical axis is truncated, which means that some numbers are omitted. The numbers on the vertical axis jump from 0 to 4.5.

Figure A.2 Time-Series Graphs

Both panels present time-series graphs of Ford Motor Company's worldwide sales during each year from 2001 to 2012. In panel (a), the vertical axis starts at 0 and the distance between each pair of values shown is the same. In panel (b), the scale on the vertical axis is truncated, which means that although it starts at zero, it then

jumps to 4.5 million. As a result, the fluctuations in Ford's sales appear smaller in panel (a) than in panel (b).
Source: Ford Motor Company, *Annual Report*, various years.

Ford's sales during 2008 and 2009 appears relatively small. In panel (b), the scale on the vertical axis is truncated, which means that although it starts at zero, it jumps to 4.5 million. As a result, the distance on the vertical axis from 0 to 4.5 million is much smaller than the distance from 4.5 million to 5.0 million. The slashes (//) near the bottom of the axis indicate that the scale is truncated. In panel (b), the decline in Ford's sales during 2008 and 2009 appears much larger than in panel (a). (Technically, the horizontal axis in both panels is also truncated because we start with 2001, not 0.)

Graphs of Two Variables

We often use graphs to show the relationship between two variables. Suppose you are interested in the relationship between the price of a pepperoni pizza and the quantity of pizzas sold per week in the small town of Bryan, Texas. A graph showing the relationship between the price of a good and the quantity of the good demanded at each price is called a *demand curve*. (As we will discuss later, in drawing a demand curve for a good, we have to hold constant any variables other than price that might affect the willingness of consumers to buy the good.) Figure A.3 shows the data collected on price and quantity. The figure shows a two-dimensional grid on which we measure the price of pizza along the *y*-axis and the quantity of pizza sold per week along the *x*-axis. Each point on the grid represents one of the price and quantity combinations listed in the table. We can connect the points to form the demand curve for pizza in Bryan, Texas. Notice that the scales on both axes in the graph are truncated. In this case, truncating the axes allows the graph to illustrate more clearly the relationship between price and quantity by excluding low prices and quantities.

Slopes of Lines

Once you have plotted the data in Figure A.3, you may be interested in how much the quantity of pizza sold increases as the price decreases. The *slope* of a line tells us how much the variable we are measuring on the *y*-axis changes as the variable we are measuring on the *x*-axis changes. We can use the Greek letter delta (Δ) to stand for the

Price (dollars per pizza)	Quantity (pizzas per week)	Points
$15	50	A
14	55	B
13	60	C
12	65	D
11	70	E

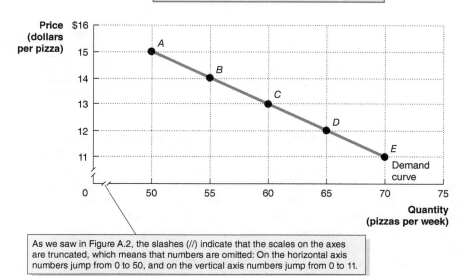

Figure A.3

Plotting Price and Quantity Points in a Graph

The figure shows a two-dimensional grid on which we measure the price of pizza along the vertical axis (or *y*-axis) and the quantity of pizza sold per week along the horizontal axis (or *x*-axis). Each point on the grid represents one of the price and quantity combinations listed in the table. By connecting the points with a line, we can better illustrate the relationship between the two variables.

As we saw in Figure A.2, the slashes (//) indicate that the scales on the axes are truncated, which means that numbers are omitted: On the horizontal axis numbers jump from 0 to 50, and on the vertical axis numbers jump from 0 to 11.

change in a variable. The slope is sometimes referred to as the rise over the run. So, we have several ways of expressing slope:

$$\text{Slope} = \frac{\text{Change in value on the vertical axis}}{\text{Change in value on the horizontal axis}} = \frac{\Delta y}{\Delta x} = \frac{\text{Rise}}{\text{Run}}.$$

Figure A.4 reproduces the graph from Figure A.3. Because the slope of a straight line is the same at any point, we can use any two points in the figure to calculate the slope of the line. For example, when the price of pizza decreases from $14 to $12, the quantity of pizza sold increases from 55 per week to 65 per week. Therefore, the slope is:

$$\text{Slope} = \frac{\Delta \text{Price of pizza}}{\Delta \text{Quantity of pizza}} = \frac{(\$12 - \$14)}{(65 - 55)} = \frac{-2}{10} = -0.2.$$

The slope of this line shows us how responsive consumers in Bryan, Texas, are to changes in the price of pizza. The larger the value of the slope (ignoring the negative sign), the steeper the line will be, which indicates that not many additional pizzas are sold when the price falls. The smaller the value of the slope, the flatter the line will be, which indicates a greater increase in pizzas sold when the price falls.

Taking into Account More Than Two Variables on a Graph

The demand curve graph in Figure A.4 shows the relationship between the price of pizza and the quantity of pizza demanded, but we know that the quantity of any good demanded depends on more than just the price of the good. For example, the quantity of pizza demanded in a given week in Bryan, Texas, can be affected by other variables—the price of hamburgers, whether an advertising campaign by local pizza parlors has begun that week, and so on. Allowing the values of any other variables to change will cause the position of the demand curve in the graph to change.

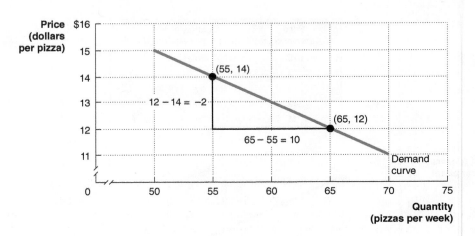

Figure A.4

Calculating the Slope of a Line

We can calculate the slope of a line as the change in the value of the variable on the *y*-axis divided by the change in the value of the variable on the *x*-axis. Because the slope of a straight line is constant, we can use any two points in the figure to calculate the slope of the line. For example, when the price of pizza decreases from \$14 to \$12, the quantity of pizza demanded increases from 55 per week to 65 per week. So, the slope of this line equals −2 divided by 10, or −0.2.

Suppose that the demand curve in Figure A.4 were drawn holding the price of hamburgers constant, at \$1.50. If the price of hamburgers rises to \$2.00, some consumers will switch from buying hamburgers to buying pizza, and more pizzas will be demanded at every price. The result on the graph will be to shift the line representing the demand curve to the right. Similarly, if the price of hamburgers falls from \$1.50 to \$1.00, some consumers will switch from buying pizza to buying hamburgers, and fewer pizzas will be demanded at every price. The result on the graph will be to shift the line representing the demand curve to the left.

The table in Figure A.5 shows the effect of a change in the price of hamburgers on the quantity of pizza demanded. On the graph, suppose that at first we are on the line labeled Demand curve$_1$. If the price of pizza is \$14 (point *A*), an increase in the price of

Figure A.5

Showing Three Variables on a Graph

The demand curve for pizza shows the relationship between the price of pizzas and the quantity of pizzas demanded, *holding constant other factors that might affect the willingness of consumers to buy pizza*. If the price of pizza is \$14 (point *A*), an increase in the price of hamburgers from \$1.50 to \$2.00 increases the quantity of pizzas demanded from 55 to 60 per week (point *B*) and shifts us to Demand curve$_2$. Or, if we start on Demand curve$_1$ and the price of pizza is \$12 (point *C*), a decrease in the price of hamburgers from \$1.50 to \$1.00 decreases the quantity of pizza demanded from 65 to 60 per week (point *D*) and shifts us to Demand curve$_3$.

Price (dollars per pizza)	Quantity (pizzas per week)		
	When the Price of Hamburgers = \$1.00	When the Price of Hamburgers = \$1.50	When the Price of Hamburgers = \$2.00
\$15	45	50	55
14	50	55	60
13	55	60	65
12	60	65	70
11	65	70	75

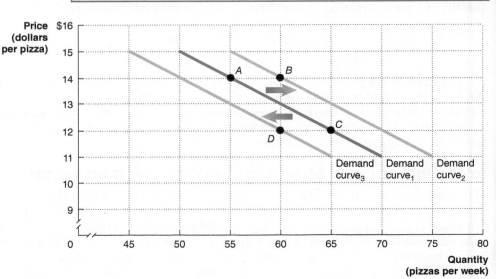

hamburgers from $1.50 to $2.00 increases the quantity of pizzas demanded from 55 to 60 per week (point B) and shifts us to Demand curve$_2$. Or, if we start on Demand curve$_1$ and the price of pizza is $12 (point C), a decrease in the price of hamburgers from $1.50 to $1.00 decreases the quantity of pizzas demanded from 65 to 60 per week (point D) and shifts us to Demand curve$_3$. By shifting the demand curve, we have taken into account the effect of changes in the value of a third variable—the price of hamburgers. We will use this technique of shifting curves to allow for the effects of additional variables many times in this text.

Positive and Negative Relationships

We can use graphs to show the relationships between any two variables. Sometimes the relationship between the variables is *negative*, meaning that as one variable increases in value, the other variable decreases in value. This was the case with the price of pizza and the quantity of pizzas demanded. The relationship between two variables can also be *positive*, meaning that the values of both variables increase or decrease together. For example, when the level of total income—or *disposable personal income*—received by households in the United States increases, the level of total *consumption spending*, which is spending by households on goods and services, also increases. The table in Figure A.6 shows the values (in billions of dollars) for income and consumption spending for 2009–2012. The graph plots the data from the table, with disposable personal income measured along the horizontal axis and consumption spending measured along the vertical axis. Notice that the points for 2010 and 2011 do not all fall exactly on the line. To examine the relationship between two variables, economists often use the straight line that best fits the data.

Determining Cause and Effect

When we graph the relationship between two variables, we usually want to draw conclusions about whether changes in one variable are causing changes in the other variable. Doing so can, however, lead to mistakes. Suppose you graph over the course of a year the number of homes in a neighborhood that have a fire burning in the fireplace and the number of leaves on trees in the neighborhood. You would get a relationship like

Year	Disposable Personal Income (billions of dollars)	Consumption Spending (billions of dollars)
2009	$10,722	$9,846
2010	11,127	10,216
2011	11,549	10,729
2012	11,931	11,120

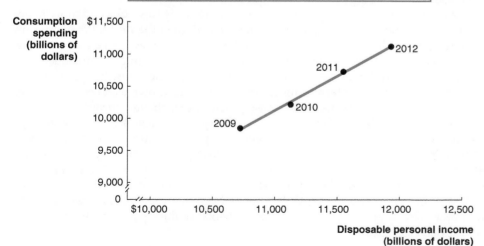

Figure A.6

Graphing the Positive Relationship between Income and Consumption

In a positive relationship between two economic variables, as one variable increases, the other variable also increases. This figure shows the positive relationship between disposable personal income and consumption spending. As disposable personal income in the United States has increased, so has consumption spending.
Source: U.S. Department of Commerce, Bureau of Economic Analysis.

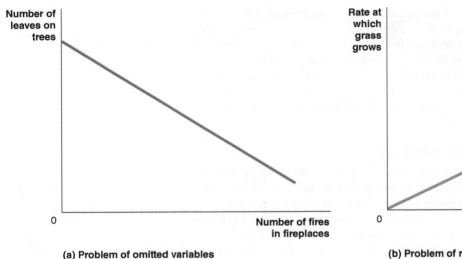

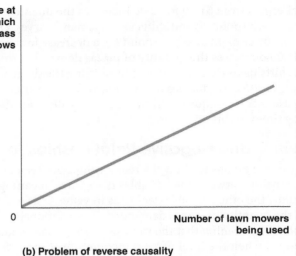

(a) Problem of omitted variables

(b) Problem of reverse causality

Figure A.7   Determining Cause and Effect

Using graphs to draw conclusions about cause and effect can be hazardous. In panel (a), we see that there are fewer leaves on the trees in a neighborhood when many homes have fires burning in their fireplaces. We cannot draw the conclusion that using fireplaces causes the leaves to fall because we have an *omitted*

variable—the season of the year. In panel (b), we see that more lawn mowers are used in a neighborhood during times when the grass grows rapidly and fewer lawn mowers are used when the grass grows slowly. Concluding that using lawn mowers *causes* the grass to grow faster would be making the error of *reverse causality*.

that shown in panel (a) of Figure A.7: The more fireplaces in use in the neighborhood, the fewer leaves the trees have. Can we draw the conclusion from this graph that using a fireplace causes trees to lose their leaves? We know, of course, that such a conclusion would be incorrect. In spring and summer, there are relatively few fireplaces being used, and the trees are full of leaves. In the fall, as trees begin to lose their leaves, fireplaces are used more frequently. And in winter, many fireplaces are being used and many trees have lost all their leaves. The reason that the graph in Figure A.7 is misleading about cause and effect is that there is obviously an *omitted variable* in the analysis—the season of the year. An omitted variable is one that affects other variables, and its omission can lead to false conclusions about cause and effect.

Although in our example the omitted variable is obvious, there are many debates about cause and effect where the existence of an omitted variable has not been clear. For instance, it has been known for many years that people who smoke cigarettes suffer from higher rates of lung cancer than do nonsmokers. For some time, tobacco companies and some scientists argued that there was an omitted variable—perhaps a failure to exercise or a poor diet—that made some people more likely to smoke and more likely to develop lung cancer. If this omitted variable existed, then the finding that smokers were more likely to develop lung cancer would not have been evidence that smoking *caused* lung cancer. In this case, however, nearly all scientists eventually concluded that the omitted variable did not exist and that, in fact, smoking does cause lung cancer.

A related problem in determining cause and effect is known as *reverse causality*. The error of reverse causality occurs when we conclude that changes in variable *X* cause changes in variable *Y* when, in fact, it is actually changes in variable *Y* that cause changes in variable *X*. For example, panel (b) of Figure A.7 plots the number of lawn mowers being used in a neighborhood against the rate at which grass on lawns in the neighborhood is growing. We could conclude from this graph that using lawn mowers *causes* the grass to grow faster. We know, however, that in reality, the causality is in the other direction. Rapidly growing grass during the spring and summer causes the increased use of lawn mowers. Slowly growing grass in the fall or winter or during periods of low rainfall causes the decreased use of lawn mowers.

Once again, in our example, the potential error of reverse causality is obvious. In many economic debates, however, cause and effect can be more difficult to determine.

For example, changes in the money supply, or the total amount of money in the economy, tend to occur at the same time as changes in the total amount of income people in the economy earn. A famous debate in economics was about whether the changes in the money supply caused the changes in total income or whether the changes in total income caused the changes in the money supply. Each side in the debate accused the other side of committing the error of reverse causality.

Are Graphs of Economic Relationships Always Straight Lines?

The graphs of relationships between two economic variables that we have drawn so far have been straight lines. The relationship between two variables is *linear* when it can be represented by a straight line. Few economic relationships are actually linear. For example, if we carefully plot data on the price of a product and the quantity demanded at each price, holding constant other variables that affect the quantity demanded, we will usually find a curved—or *nonlinear*—relationship rather than a linear relationship. In practice, however, it is often useful to approximate a nonlinear relationship with a linear relationship. If the relationship is reasonably close to being linear, the analysis is not significantly affected. In addition, it is easier to calculate the slope of a straight line, and it is also easier to calculate the area under a straight line. So, in this text, we often assume that the relationship between two economic variables is linear, even when we know that this assumption is not precisely correct.

Slopes of Nonlinear Curves

In some situations, we need to take into account the nonlinear nature of an economic relationship. For example, panel (a) of Figure A.8 shows the hypothetical relationship between Apple's total cost of producing iPhones and the quantity of iPhones produced. The relationship is curved rather than linear. In this case, the cost of production is increasing at an increasing rate, which often happens in manufacturing. In other words, as we move up the curve, its slope becomes larger. (Remember that with a straight line, the slope is always constant.) To see why, first remember that we calculate the slope of a curve by dividing the change in the variable on the y-axis by the change in the variable on the x-axis. As we move from point A to point B, the quantity produced increases by 1 million iPhones, while the total cost of production increases by $50 million. Farther up the curve, as we move from point C to point D, the change in quantity is the same—1 million iPhones—but the change in the total cost of production is now much larger—$250 million. Because the change in the y variable has increased, while the change in the x variable has remained the same, we know that the slope has increased.

To measure the slope of a nonlinear curve at a particular point, we measure the slope of the line that is tangent to that curve at that point. This tangent line will touch the curve only at that point. We can measure the slope of the tangent line just as we would measure the slope of any other straight line. In panel (b), the tangent line at point B has a slope equal to:

$$\frac{\Delta \text{Cost}}{\Delta \text{Quantity}} = \frac{75}{1} = 75.$$

The tangent line at point C has a slope equal to:

$$\frac{\Delta \text{Cost}}{\Delta \text{Quantity}} = \frac{150}{1} = 150.$$

Once again, we see that the slope of the curve is larger at point C than at point B.

Formulas

We have just seen that graphs are an important economic tool. In this section, we will review several useful formulas and show how to use them to summarize data and to calculate important relationships.

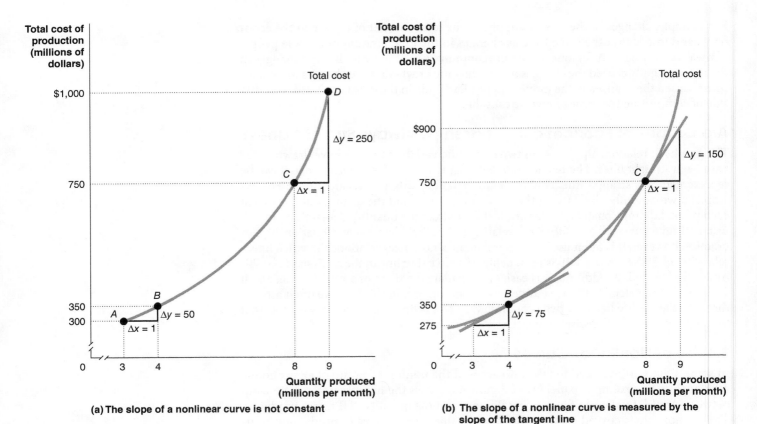

Figure A.8 **The Slope of a Nonlinear Curve**

The relationship between the quantity of iPhones produced and the total cost of production is curved rather than linear. In panel (a), when we move from point A to point B, the quantity produced increases by 1 million iPhones, while the total cost of production increases by $50 million. Farther up the curve, as we move from point C to point D, the change in quantity is the same—1 million iPhones—but the change in the total cost of production is now much larger—$250 million.

Because the change in the y variable has increased, while the change in the x variable has remained the same, we know that the slope has increased. In panel (b), we measure the slope of the curve at a particular point by calculating the slope of the tangent line at that point. The slope of the tangent line at point B is 75, and the slope of the tangent line at point C is 150.

Formula for a Percentage Change

One important formula is the percentage change. The *percentage change* is the change in some economic variable, usually from one period to the next, expressed as a percentage. A key macroeconomic measure is the real gross domestic product (GDP). GDP is the value of all the final goods and services produced in a country during a year. "Real" GDP is corrected for the effects of inflation. When economists say that the U.S. economy grew 2.8 percent during 2012, they mean that real GDP was 2.8 percent higher in 2012 than it was in 2011. The formula for making this calculation is:

$$\left(\frac{GDP_{2012} - GDP_{2011}}{GDP_{2011}} \right) \times 100,$$

or, more generally, for any two periods:

$$\text{Percentage change} = \left(\frac{\text{Value in the second period} - \text{Value in the first period}}{\text{Value in the first period}} \right) \times 100.$$

In this case, real GDP was $15,052 billion in 2011 and $15,471 billion in 2012. So, the growth rate of the U.S. economy during 2012 was:

$$\left(\frac{\$15,471 - \$15,052}{\$15,052}\right) \times 100 = 2.8\%.$$

Notice that it doesn't matter that in using the formula, we ignored the fact that GDP is measured in billions of dollars. In fact, when calculating percentage changes, *the units don't matter*. The percentage increase from $15,052 billion to $15,471 billion is exactly the same as the percentage increase from $15,052 to $15,471.

Formulas for the Areas of a Rectangle and a Triangle

Areas that form rectangles and triangles on graphs can have important economic meaning. For example, Figure A.9 shows the demand curve for Pepsi. Suppose that the price is currently $2.00 and that 125,000 bottles of Pepsi are sold at that price. A firm's *total revenue* is equal to the amount it receives from selling its product, or the quantity sold multiplied by the price. In this case, total revenue will equal 125,000 bottles times $2.00 per bottle, or $250,000.

The formula for the area of a rectangle is:

$$\text{Area of a rectangle} = \text{Base} \times \text{Height.}$$

In Figure A.9, the shaded rectangle also represents the firm's total revenue because its area is given by the base of 125,000 bottles multiplied by the price of $2.00 per bottle.

Areas that are triangles can also have economic significance. The formula for the area of a triangle is:

$$\text{Area of a triangle} = \frac{1}{2} \times \text{Base} \times \text{Height.}$$

The shaded area in Figure A.10 is a triangle. The base equals 150,000 − 125,000, or 25,000. Its height equals $2.00 − $1.50, or $0.50. Therefore, its area equals 1/2 × 25,000 × $0.50, or $6,250. Notice that the shaded area is a triangle only if the demand curve is a straight line, or linear. Not all demand curves are linear. However, the formula for the area of a triangle will usually still give a good approximation, even if the demand curve is not linear.

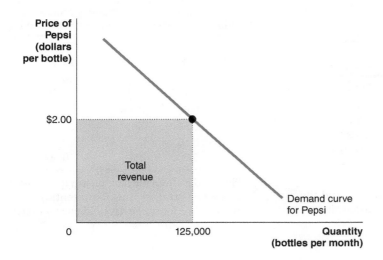

Figure A.9

Showing a Firm's Total Revenue on a Graph

The area of a rectangle is equal to its base multiplied by its height. Total revenue is equal to quantity multiplied by price. Here, total revenue is equal to the quantity of 125,000 bottles times the price of $2.00 per bottle, or $250,000. The area of the shaded rectangle shows the firm's total revenue.

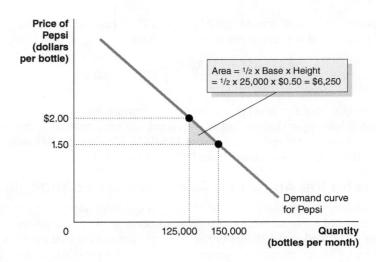

Figure A.10

The Area of a Triangle

The area of a triangle is equal to 1/2 multiplied by its base multiplied by its height. The area of the shaded triangle has a base equal to 150,000 − 125,000, or 25,000, and a height equal to $2.00 − $1.50, or $0.50. Therefore, its area is equal to 1/2 × 25,000 × $0.50, or $6,250.

Summary of Using Formulas

Whenever you use a formula, you should follow these steps:

1. Make sure you understand the economic concept the formula represents.
2. Make sure you are using the correct formula for the problem you are solving.
3. Make sure the number you calculate using the formula is economically reasonable. For example, if you are using a formula to calculate a firm's revenue and your answer is a negative number, you know you made a mistake somewhere.

 Using Graphs and Formulas

LEARNING OBJECTIVE: Review the use of graphs and formulas.

Visit **www.myeconlab.com** to complete these exercises online and get instant feedback.

Problems and Applications

A.1 The following table shows the relationship between the price of custard pies and the number of pies Jacob buys per week:

Price (dollars per pie)	Quantity of pies	Week
$3.00	6	July 2
2.00	7	July 9
5.00	4	July 16
6.00	3	July 23
1.00	8	July 30
4.00	5	August 6

a. Is the relationship between the price of pies and the number of pies Jacob buys a positive relationship or a negative relationship?

b. Plot the data from the table on a graph similar to Figure A.3. Draw a straight line that best fits the points.

c. Calculate the slope of the line.

A.2 The following table gives information on the quantity of glasses of lemonade demanded on sunny and overcast days:

Price (dollars per glass)	Quantity (glasses of lemonade per day)	Weather
$0.80	30	Sunny
0.80	10	Overcast
0.70	40	Sunny
0.70	20	Overcast
0.60	50	Sunny
0.60	30	Overcast
0.50	60	Sunny
0.50	40	Overcast

Plot the data from the table on a graph similar to Figure A.5. Draw two straight lines representing the two demand curves—one for sunny days and one for overcast days.

A.3 Using the information in Figure A.2, calculate the percentage change in Ford's auto sales from one year to the next. During which year did sales fall at the highest rate?

A.4 Real GDP in 2008 was $14,834 billion. Real GDP in 2009 was $14,418 billion. What was the percentage change in real GDP from 2008 to 2009. What do economists call the percentage change in real GDP from one year to the next?

A.5 Assume that the demand curve for Pepsi passes through the following two points:

Price per bottle of Pepsi (in dollars)	Number of bottles demanded
$2.50	100,000
1.25	200,000

a. Draw a graph with a linear demand curve that passes through these two points.

b. Show on the graph the areas representing total revenue at each price. Give the value for total revenue at each price.

A.6 What is the area of the triangle shown in the following figure?

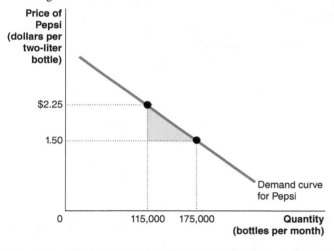

A.7 Calculate the slope of the total cost curve at point A and at point B in the following figure.

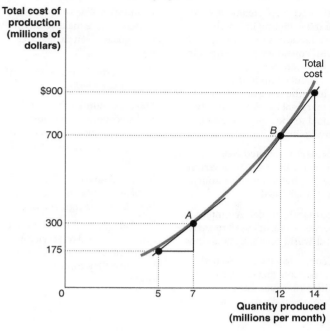

Glossary

Allocative efficiency A state of the economy in which production is in accordance with consumer preferences; in particular, every good or service is produced up to the point where the last unit provides a marginal benefit to society equal to the marginal cost of producing it.

Centrally planned economy An economy in which the government decides how economic resources will be allocated.

Economic model A simplified version of reality used to analyze real-world economic situations.

Economic variable Something measurable that can have different values, such as the incomes of doctors.

Economics The study of the choices people make to attain their goals, given their scarce resources.

Equity The fair distribution of economic benefits.

Macroeconomics The study of the economy as a whole, including topics such as inflation, unemployment, and economic growth.

Marginal analysis Analysis that involves comparing marginal benefits and marginal costs.

Market A group of buyers and sellers of a good or service and the institution or arrangement by which they come together to trade.

Market economy An economy in which the decisions of households and firms interacting in markets allocate economic resources.

Microeconomics The study of how households and firms make choices, how they interact in markets, and how the government attempts to influence their choices.

Mixed economy An economy in which most economic decisions result from the interaction of buyers and sellers in markets but in which the government plays a significant role in the allocation of resources.

Normative analysis Analysis concerned with what ought to be.

Opportunity cost The highest-valued alternative that must be given up to engage in an activity.

Positive analysis Analysis concerned with what is.

Productive efficiency A situation in which a good or service is produced at the lowest possible cost.

Scarcity A situation in which unlimited wants exceed the limited resources available to fulfill those wants.

Trade-off The idea that, because of scarcity, producing more of one good or service means producing less of another good or service.

Voluntary exchange A situation that occurs in markets when both the buyer and the seller of a product are made better off by the transaction.

Credits

Credits are listed in the order of appearance.

Photo

Véronique Burger/Science Source/Photo Researchers, Inc.; Burger/Phanie/SuperStock

Text

John Hechinger, "FBI Presses Banks to Boost Security as Robberies Rise," *Wall Street Journal*, October 8, 2002.

Trade-offs, Comparative Advantage, and the Market System

Trade-offs, Comparative Advantage, and the Market System

Chapter Outline and Learning Objectives

1 **Production Possibilities Frontiers and Opportunity Costs**
Use a production possibilities frontier to analyze opportunity costs and trade-offs.

2 **Comparative Advantage and Trade**
Describe comparative advantage and explain how it serves as the basis for trade.

3 **The Market System**
Explain the basic idea of how a market system works.

Managers at Tesla Motors Face Trade-Offs

Are all-electric cars the wave of the future? If you're like most drivers, you probably like the idea of skipping the gas station in favor of powering up your car by plugging it into an electric outlet. Yet, all-electric cars, such as the Chevrolet Volt and Nissan Leaf, have struggled to succeed in the marketplace for two key reasons: (1) The lithium batteries that power electric cars are costly, forcing up the prices of the cars, and (2) available batteries need to be recharged every 300 miles or so, making all-electric cars difficult to use on long trips.

Many people were therefore surprised when Tesla Motors announced in early 2013 that sales of its all-electric cars had been higher than expected and that it had made a profit for the first time. Tesla was founded in 2003 by billionaire Elon Musk, who also started the online payment system PayPal and the private space firm SpaceX. As many investors began to believe that Tesla was likely to become the first successful electric car company, the value of the firm soared to more than $200 billion.

Tesla manufactures its cars in Fremont, California. To compete in the automobile market, Tesla's managers must make many strategic decisions, such as whether to introduce new car models. In 2013, Tesla's only model, the Model S sedan, received the highest car rating ever from *Consumer Reports* and won the 2013 award for World Green Car of the Year. In 2014, Tesla introduced a second model, the Model X, a cross between a sport utility vehicle (SUV) and a minivan. The Model X was designed for families who would otherwise buy traditional gasoline-powered SUVs or minivans.

Tesla's managers must also decide how to sell and service its cars. Most cars are sold through dealerships, which also provide service for those cars. In 2013, however, Tesla had no dealerships. Instead, the company sold all of its cars online and relied on company-owned service centers to provide maintenance and repair services. Some economists have questioned whether Tesla will be able to meet its future sales goals without selling cars through dealerships.

Managers also make smaller-scale decisions. For instance, in scheduling production at its Fremont plant, Tesla's managers must decide each month the quantity of Model S sedans and Model X SUVs to manufacture. Like other decisions managers make, this one involves a trade-off: Producing more of one of these two models means producing fewer of the other.

AN INSIDE LOOK discusses how managers at Mercedes-Benz decide which models to manufacture and why the company chose to partner with Tesla Motors to develop electric-vehicle components.

Sources: Steven Russolillo, "Four Reasons Morgan Stanley Loves Tesla," *Wall Street Journal*, May 14, 2013; and Christopher F. Schuetze, "Will 2013 Be the Year of the Electric Car?" *New York Times*, January 7, 2013.

Economics in Your Life

The Trade-offs When You Buy a Car

When you buy a traditional gasoline-powered car, you probably consider factors such as safety and fuel efficiency. To increase fuel efficiency, automobile manufacturers make cars that are small and light. Large cars absorb more of the impact of an accident than do small cars. As a result, people are usually safer driving large cars than small cars. What can we conclude from these facts about the relationship between safety and fuel efficiency? Under what circumstances would it be possible for automobile manufacturers to make cars that are both safer and more fuel efficient? As you read the chapter, try to answer these questions. You can check your answers against those provided at the end of this chapter.

Scarcity A situation in which unlimited wants exceed the limited resources available to fulfill those wants.

In a market system, managers at most firms must make decisions like those made by Tesla's managers. These decisions reflect a key fact of economic life: *Scarcity requires trade-offs*. **Scarcity** exists because we have unlimited wants but only limited resources available to fulfill those wants. Goods and services are scarce. So, too, are the economic resources, or *factors of production*—workers, capital, natural resources, and entrepreneurial ability—used to make goods and services. Your time is scarce, which means you face trade-offs: If you spend an hour studying for an economics exam, you have one less hour to spend studying for a psychology exam or going to the movies. If your university decides to use some of its scarce budget to buy new computers for the computer labs, those funds will not be available to buy new books for the library or to resurface the student parking lot. If Tesla decides to devote some of the scarce workers and machinery in its Fremont assembly plant to producing more Model X SUVs, those resources will not be available to produce more Model S sedans.

Households and firms make many of their decisions in markets. Trade is a key activity that takes place in markets. Trade results from the decisions of millions of households and firms spread around the world. By engaging in trade, people can raise their incomes. In this chapter, we provide an overview of how the market system coordinates the independent decisions of these millions of households and firms. We begin our analysis of the economic consequences of scarcity and the working of the market system by introducing an important economic model: the *production possibilities frontier*.

1 LEARNING OBJECTIVE

Use a production possibilities frontier to analyze opportunity costs and trade-offs.

Production Possibilities Frontiers and Opportunity Costs

As we saw in the chapter opener, Tesla operates an automobile factory in Fremont, California, where it assembles two car models. Because the firm's resources—workers, machinery, materials, and entrepreneurial skills—are limited, Tesla faces a trade-off: Resources devoted to producing one model are not available for producing the other model. Economic models can be useful in analyzing many questions. We can use a simple model called the *production possibilities frontier* to analyze the trade-offs Tesla faces in its Fremont plant. A **production possibilities frontier (*PPF*)** is a curve showing the maximum attainable combinations of two products that may be produced with available resources and current technology. In Tesla's case, the company produces only Model S sedans and Model X SUVs at the Fremont plant, using workers, materials, robots, and other machinery.

Production possibilities frontier (*PPF*) A curve showing the maximum attainable combinations of two products that may be produced with available resources and current technology.

Graphing the Production Possibilities Frontier

Figure 1 uses a production possibilities frontier to illustrate the trade-offs that Tesla faces. The numbers from the table are plotted in the graph. The line in the graph represents Tesla's production possibilities frontier. If Tesla uses all its resources to produce Model S sedans, it can produce 80 per day—point *A* at one end of the production possibilities frontier. If Tesla uses all its resources to produce Model X SUVs, it can produce 80 per day—point *E* at the other end of the production possibilities frontier. If Tesla devotes resources to producing both vehicles, it could be at a point like *B*, where it produces 60 sedans and 20 SUVs.

All the combinations either on the frontier—like points *A*, *B*, *C*, *D*, and *E*—or inside the frontier—like point *F*—are *attainable* with the resources available. Combinations on the frontier are *efficient* because all available resources are being fully utilized,

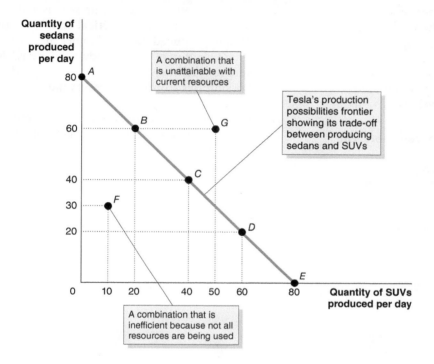

Tesla's Production Choices at Its Fremont Plant

Choice	Quantity of Sedans Produced	Quantity of SUVs Produced
A	80	0
B	60	20
C	40	40
D	20	60
E	0	80

Figure 1

Tesla's Production Possibilities Frontier

Tesla faces a trade-off: To build one more sedan, it must build one fewer SUV. The production possibilities frontier illustrates the trade-off Tesla faces. Combinations on the production possibilities frontier—like points *A*, *B*, *C*, *D*, and *E*—are *technically efficient* because the maximum output is being obtained from the available resources. Combinations inside the frontier—like point *F*—are *inefficient* because some resources are not being used. Combinations outside the frontier—like point *G*—are *unattainable* with current resources.

and the fewest possible resources are being used to produce a given amount of output. Combinations inside the frontier—like point *F*—are *inefficient* because maximum output is not being obtained from the available resources—perhaps because the assembly line is not operating at its capacity. Tesla might like to be beyond the frontier—at a point like *G*, where it would be producing 60 sedans and 50 SUVs per day—but points beyond the production possibilities frontier are *unattainable*, given the firm's current resources. To produce the combination at *G*, Tesla would need more machines and more workers.

Notice that if Tesla is producing efficiently and is on the production possibilities frontier, the only way to produce more of one vehicle is to produce fewer of the other vehicle. The **opportunity cost** of any activity is the highest-valued alternative that must be given up to engage in that activity. For Tesla, the opportunity cost of producing one more SUV is the number of sedans the company will not be able to produce because it has shifted those resources to producing the SUV. For example, in moving from point *B* to point *C*, the opportunity cost of producing 20 more SUVs per day is the 20 fewer sedans that Tesla can produce.

What point on the production possibilities frontier is best? We can't tell without further information. If consumer demand for SUVs is greater than the demand for sedans, the company is likely to choose a point closer to *E*. If demand for sedans is greater than the demand for SUVs, the company is likely to choose a point closer to *A*.

Opportunity cost The highest-valued alternative that must be given up to engage in an activity.

Solved Problem 1

Drawing a Production Possibilities Frontier for Tesla Motors

Suppose, for simplicity, that during any given week, the machinery and number of workers at Tesla Motors' Fremont plant cannot be increased. So the number of sedans or SUVs the company can produce during the week depends on how many hours are devoted to assembling each of the different models. Assume that SUVs are more difficult to assemble, so if Tesla devotes an hour to assembling sedans, it will produce 15 vehicles, but if Tesla devotes an hour to producing SUVs, it will produce only 10 vehicles. Assume that the plant can run for 8 hours per day.

a. Use the information given to complete the following table:

	Hours Spent Making		Quantity Produced per Day	
Choice	Sedans	SUVs	Sedans	SUVs
A	8	0	____	____
B	7	1	____	____
C	6	2	____	____
D	5	3	____	____
E	4	4	____	____
F	3	5	____	____
G	2	6	____	____
H	1	7	____	____
I	0	8	____	____

b. Use the data in the table to draw a production possibilities frontier graph illustrating Tesla's trade-off between assembling sedans and assembling SUVs. Label the vertical axis "Quantity of sedans produced per day." Label the horizontal axis "Quantity of SUVs produced per day." Make sure to label the values where Tesla's production possibilities frontier intersects the vertical and horizontal axes.

c. Label the points representing choice D and choice E. If Tesla is at choice D, what is its opportunity cost of making 10 more SUVs?

Solving the Problem

Step 1: **Review the chapter material.** This problem is about using production possibilities frontiers to analyze trade-offs, so you may want to review the section "Graphing the Production Possibilities Frontier."

Step 2: **Answer part (a) by filling in the table.** If Tesla can assemble 15 sedans in 1 hour, then with choice A, it can assemble 120 sedans and 0 SUVs. Because Tesla can assemble 10 SUVs in 1 hour, with choice B, it will produce 105 sedans and 10 SUVs. Using similar reasoning, you can fill in the remaining cells in the table as follows:

	Hours Spent Making		Quantity Produced per Day	
Choice	Sedans	SUVs	Sedans	SUVs
A	8	0	120	0
B	7	1	105	10
C	6	2	90	20
D	5	3	75	30
E	4	4	60	40
F	3	5	45	50
G	2	6	30	60
H	1	7	15	70
I	0	8	0	80

Step 3: **Answer part (b) by drawing the production possibilities frontier graph.**
Using the data in the table in Step 2, you should draw a graph that looks like this:

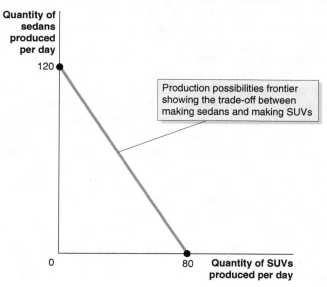

If Tesla devotes all 8 hours to assembling sedans, it will produce 120 sedans.
Therefore, Tesla's production possibilities frontier will intersect the vertical
axis at 120 sedans produced. If Tesla devotes all 8 hours to assembling SUVs,
it will produce 80 SUVs. Therefore, Tesla's production possibilities frontier
will intersect the horizontal axis at 80 SUVs produced.

Step 4: **Answer part (c) by labeling choices *D* and *E* on your graph.** The points for
choices *D* and *E* can be plotted using the information from the table:

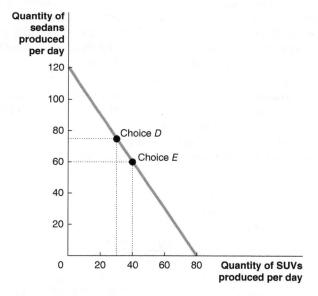

Moving from choice *D* to choice *E* increases Tesla's production of SUVs by 10
but lowers its production of sedans by 15. Therefore, Tesla's opportunity cost
of producing 10 more SUVs is making 15 fewer sedans.

Your Turn: For more practice, do related problem 1.10 at the end of this chapter.

Increasing Marginal Opportunity Costs

We can use the production possibilities frontier to explore issues concerning the economy as a whole. Suppose we divide all the goods and services produced in the economy into just two types: military goods and civilian goods. In Figure 2, we let tanks represent military goods and automobiles represent civilian goods. If all the country's resources are devoted to producing military goods, 400 tanks can be produced in one year. If all resources are devoted to producing civilian goods, 500 automobiles can be produced in one year. Devoting resources to producing both goods results in the economy being at other points along the production possibilities frontier.

Notice that this production possibilities frontier is bowed outward rather than being a straight line. Because the curve is bowed out, the opportunity cost of automobiles in terms of tanks depends on where the economy currently is on the production possibilities frontier. For example, to increase automobile production from 0 to 200—moving from point *A* to point *B*—the economy has to give up only 50 tanks. But to increase automobile production by another 200 vehicles—moving from point *B* to point *C*—the economy has to give up 150 tanks.

As the economy moves down the production possibilities frontier, it experiences *increasing marginal opportunity costs* because increasing automobile production by a given quantity requires larger and larger decreases in tank production. Increasing marginal opportunity costs occur because some workers, machines, and other resources are better suited to one use than to another. At point *A*, some resources that are well suited to producing automobiles are forced to produce tanks. Shifting these resources into producing automobiles by moving from point *A* to point *B* allows a substantial increase in automobile production, without much loss of tank production. But as the economy moves down the production possibilities frontier, more and more resources that are better suited to tank production are switched to automobile production. As a result, the increases in automobile production become increasingly smaller, while the decreases in tank production become increasingly larger. We would expect in most situations that production possibilities frontiers will be bowed outward rather than linear as in the Tesla example discussed earlier.

The idea of increasing marginal opportunity costs illustrates an important economic concept: *The more resources already devoted to an activity, the smaller the payoff to devoting additional resources to that activity.* For example, the more hours you have already spent studying economics, the smaller the increase in your test grade from each additional hour you spend—and the greater the opportunity cost of using the hour in that way. The more funds a firm has devoted to research and development during a given year, the smaller the amount of useful knowledge it receives from each additional dollar—and the greater the opportunity cost of using the funds in that way. The more funds the federal government spends cleaning up the environment during a given year, the smaller the reduction in pollution from each additional dollar—and, once again, the greater the opportunity cost of using the funds in that way.

Figure 2

Increasing Marginal Opportunity Costs

As the economy moves down the production possibilities frontier, it experiences *increasing marginal opportunity costs* because increasing automobile production by a given quantity requires larger and larger decreases in tank production. For example, to increase automobile production from 0 to 200—moving from point *A* to point *B*—the economy has to give up only 50 tanks. But to increase automobile production by another 200 vehicles—moving from point *B* to point *C*—the economy has to give up 150 tanks.

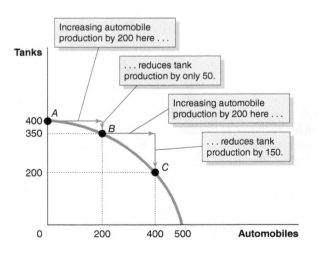

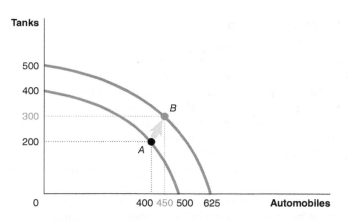

(a) Shifting out the production possibilities frontier

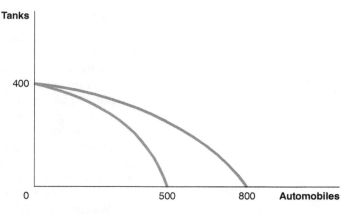

(b) Technological change in the automobile industry

Figure 3   Economic Growth

Panel (a) shows that as more economic resources become available and technological change occurs, the economy can move from point A to point B, producing more tanks and more automobiles. Panel (b) shows the results of technological change in the automobile industry that increases the quantity of vehicles workers can produce per year while leaving unchanged the maximum quantity of tanks they can produce. Outward shifts in the production possibilities frontier represent *economic growth*.

Economic Growth

At any given time, the total resources available to any economy are fixed. Therefore, if, for example, the United States produces more automobiles, it must produce less of something else—tanks in our example. Over time, though, the resources available to an economy may increase. For example, both the labor force and the capital stock—the amount of machinery and other physical capital available in the country—may increase. The increase in the available labor force and the capital stock shifts the production possibilities frontier outward for the U.S. economy and makes it possible to produce both more automobiles and more tanks. Panel (a) of Figure 3 shows that the economy can move from point A to point B, producing more tanks and more automobiles.

Similarly, technological change makes it possible to produce more goods with the same number of workers and the same amount of machinery, which also shifts the production possibilities frontier outward. Technological change need not affect all sectors equally. Panel (b) of Figure 3 shows the results of technological change in the automobile industry that increases the quantity of automobiles workers can produce per year while leaving unchanged the quantity of tanks they can produce.

Outward shifts in the production possibilities frontier represent **economic growth** because they allow the economy to increase the production of goods and services, which ultimately raises the standard of living. In the United States and other high-income countries, the market system has aided the process of economic growth, which over the past 200 years has greatly increased the well-being of the average person.

Economic growth The ability of the economy to increase the production of goods and services.

Comparative Advantage and Trade

We can use the concepts of the production possibilities frontier and opportunity costs to understand the basic economic activity of *trade*. Markets are fundamentally about **trade**, which is the act of buying and selling. Sometimes we trade directly, as when children trade one baseball card for another baseball card. But often we trade indirectly: We sell our labor services as, say, an accountant, a salesperson, or a nurse for money, and then we use the money to buy goods and services. Although in these cases trade takes place indirectly, ultimately the accountant, salesperson, or nurse is trading his or her services for food, clothing, and other goods and services. One of the great benefits of trade is that it makes it possible for people to become better off by increasing both their production and their consumption.

2 LEARNING OBJECTIVE

Describe comparative advantage and explain how it serves as the basis for trade.

Trade The act of buying and selling.

Specialization and Gains from Trade

Consider the following situation: You and your neighbor both have fruit trees on your properties. Initially, suppose you have only apple trees and your neighbor has only cherry trees. In this situation, if you both like apples and cherries, there is an obvious opportunity for both of you to gain from trade: You trade some of your apples for some of your neighbor's cherries, making you both better off. But what if there are apple and cherry trees growing on both of your properties? In that case, there can still be gains from trade. For example, your neighbor might be very good at picking apples, and you might be very good at picking cherries. It would make sense for your neighbor to concentrate on picking apples and for you to concentrate on picking cherries. You can then trade some of the cherries you pick for some of the apples your neighbor picks. But what if your neighbor is actually better at picking both apples and cherries than you are?

We can use production possibilities frontiers (*PPFs*) to show how your neighbor can benefit from trading with you *even though she is better than you are at picking both apples and cherries*. (For simplicity, and because it will not have any effect on the conclusions we draw, we will assume that the *PPFs* in this example are straight lines.) The table in Figure 4 shows how many apples and how many cherries you and your neighbor can pick in one week. The graph in the figure uses the data from the table to construct *PPFs*. Panel (a) shows your *PPF*. If you devote all your time to picking apples, you can pick 20 pounds of apples per week. If you devote all your time to picking cherries, you can pick 20 pounds per week. Panel (b) shows that if your neighbor devotes all her time to picking apples, she can pick 30 pounds. If she devotes all her time to picking cherries, she can pick 60 pounds.

The *PPFs* in Figure 4 show how many apples and cherries you and your neighbor can consume, *without trade*. Suppose that when you don't trade with your neighbor, you pick and consume 8 pounds of apples and 12 pounds of cherries per week. This

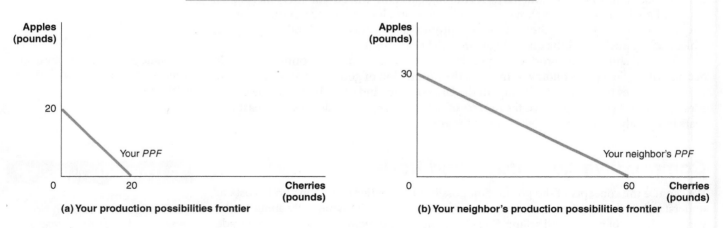

	You		Your Neighbor	
	Apples	Cherries	Apples	Cherries
Devote all time to picking apples	20 pounds	0 pounds	30 pounds	0 pounds
Devote all time to picking cherries	0 pounds	20 pounds	0 pounds	60 pounds

(a) Your production possibilities frontier

(b) Your neighbor's production possibilities frontier

Figure 4 **Production Possibilities for You and Your Neighbor, without Trade**

The table shows how many pounds of apples and how many pounds of cherries you and your neighbor can each pick in one week. The graphs use the data from the table to construct *PPFs* for you and your neighbor. Panel (a) shows your *PPF*. If you devote all your time to picking apples and none to picking cherries, you can pick 20 pounds. If you devote all your time to picking cherries, you can pick 20 pounds. Panel (b) shows that if your neighbor devotes all her time to picking apples, she can pick 30 pounds. If she devotes all her time to picking cherries, she can pick 60 pounds.

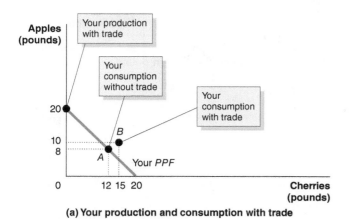

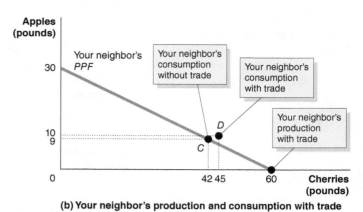

Figure 5 Gains from Trade

When you don't trade with your neighbor, you pick and consume 8 pounds of apples and 12 pounds of cherries per week—point *A* in panel (a). When your neighbor doesn't trade with you, she picks and consumes 9 pounds of apples and 42 pounds of cherries per week—point *C* in panel (b). If you specialize in picking apples, you can pick 20 pounds. If your neighbor specializes in picking cherries, she can pick 60 pounds. If you trade 10 pounds of your apples for 15 pounds of your neighbor's cherries, you will be able to consume 10 pounds of apples and 15 pounds of cherries—point *B* in panel (a). Your neighbor can now consume 10 pounds of apples and 45 pounds of cherries—point *D* in panel (b). You and your neighbor are both better off as a result of the trade.

combination of apples and cherries is represented by point *A* in panel (a) of Figure 5. When your neighbor doesn't trade with you, she picks and consumes 9 pounds of apples and 42 pounds of cherries per week. This combination of apples and cherries is represented by point *C* in panel (b).

After years of picking and consuming your own apples and cherries, suppose your neighbor comes to you one day with the following proposal: She offers to trade you 15 pounds of her cherries for 10 pounds of your apples the next week. Should you accept this offer? As we can show, you should accept because you will end up with more apples and more cherries to consume. To take advantage of her proposal, you should specialize in picking only apples rather than splitting your time between picking apples and picking cherries. We know specializing will allow you to pick 20 pounds of apples. You can trade 10 pounds of apples to your neighbor for 15 pounds of her cherries. The result is that you will be able to consume 10 pounds of apples and 15 pounds of cherries (point *B* in panel (a) of Figure 5). You are clearly better off as a result of trading with your neighbor: You can now consume 2 more pounds of apples and 3 more pounds of cherries than you were consuming without trading. You have moved beyond your *PPF*!

Your neighbor has also benefited from the trade. By specializing in picking only cherries, she can pick 60 pounds. She trades 15 pounds of cherries to you for 10 pounds of apples. She can then consume 10 pounds of apples and 45 pounds of cherries (point *D* in panel (b) of Figure 5). This combination is 1 more pound of apples and 3 more pounds of cherries than she was consuming before trading with you. She also has moved beyond her *PPF*. Table 1 summarizes the changes in production and consumption that result from your trade with your neighbor. (In this example, we chose one specific rate of trading cherries for apples—15 pounds of cherries for 10 pounds of apples. There are, however, many other rates of trading cherries for apples that would also make you and your neighbor better off.)

Absolute Advantage versus Comparative Advantage

Perhaps the most remarkable aspect of the preceding example is that your neighbor benefits from trading with you even though she is better than you at picking both apples and cherries. **Absolute advantage** is the ability of an individual, a firm, or a country to produce more of a good or service than competitors, using the same amount of resources. Your neighbor has an absolute advantage over you in picking both apples and

Absolute advantage The ability of an individual, a firm, or a country to produce more of a good or service than competitors, using the same amount of resources.

Table 1

A Summary of the Gains from Trade

	You		Your Neighbor	
	Apples (in pounds)	Cherries (in pounds)	Apples (in pounds)	Cherries (in pounds)
Production *and* consumption *without* trade	8	12	9	42
Production *with* trade	20	0	0	60
Consumption *with* trade	10	15	10	45
Gains from trade (increased consumption)	2	3	1	3

cherries because she can pick more of each fruit than you can in the same amount of time. Although it seems that your neighbor should pick her own apples *and* her own cherries, we have just seen that she is better off specializing in picking cherries and leaving picking apples to you.

We can consider further why both you and your neighbor benefit from specializing in picking only one fruit. First, think about the opportunity cost to each of you of picking the two fruits. We saw from the *PPF* in Figure 4 that if you devoted all your time to picking apples, you would be able to pick 20 pounds of apples per week. As you move down your *PPF* and shift time away from picking apples to picking cherries, you have to give up 1 pound of apples for each pound of cherries you pick (the slope of your *PPF* is −1.) Therefore, your opportunity cost of picking 1 pound of cherries is 1 pound of apples. By the same reasoning, your opportunity cost of picking 1 pound of apples is 1 pound of cherries. Your neighbor's *PPF* has a different slope, so she faces a different trade-off: As she shifts time from picking apples to picking cherries, she has to give up 0.5 pound of apples for every 1 pound of cherries she picks (the slope of your neighbor's *PPF* is −0.5). As she shifts time from picking cherries to picking apples, she gives up 2 pounds of cherries for every 1 pound of apples she picks. Therefore, her opportunity cost of picking 1 pound of apples is 2 pounds of cherries, and her opportunity cost of picking 1 pound of cherries is 0.5 pound of apples.

Table 2 summarizes the opportunity costs for you and your neighbor of picking apples and cherries. Note that even though your neighbor can pick more apples in a week than you can, the *opportunity cost* of picking apples is higher for her than for you because when she picks apples, she gives up more cherries than you do. So, even though she has an absolute advantage over you in picking apples, it is more costly for her to pick apples than it is for you. The table also shows that her opportunity cost of picking cherries is lower than yours. **Comparative advantage** is the ability of an individual, a firm, or a country to produce a good or service at a lower opportunity cost than competitors. In picking apples, your neighbor has an *absolute advantage* over you, while you have a *comparative advantage* over her. Your neighbor has both an absolute advantage and a comparative advantage over you in picking cherries. As we have seen, you are better off specializing in picking apples, and your neighbor is better off specializing in picking cherries.

Comparative advantage The ability of an individual, a firm, or a country to produce a good or service at a lower opportunity cost than competitors.

Comparative Advantage and the Gains from Trade

We have just arrived at an important economic principle: *The basis for trade is comparative advantage, not absolute advantage.* The fastest apple pickers do not necessarily do

Table 2

Opportunity Costs of Picking Apples and Cherries

	Opportunity Cost of Picking 1 Pound of Apples	Opportunity Cost of Picking 1 Pound of Cherries
You	1 pound of cherries	1 pound of apples
Your Neighbor	2 pounds of cherries	0.5 pound of apples

Don't Let This Happen to You

Don't Confuse Absolute Advantage and Comparative Advantage

First, make sure you know the definitions:

- **Absolute advantage.** The ability of an individual, a firm, or a country to produce more of a good or service than competitors, using the same amount of resources. In our example, your neighbor has an absolute advantage over you in both picking apples and picking cherries.
- **Comparative advantage.** The ability of an individual, a firm, or a country to produce a good or service at a lower opportunity cost than competitors. In our example, your neighbor has a comparative advantage in picking cherries, but you have a comparative advantage in picking apples.

Keep these two key points in mind:

1. It is possible to have an absolute advantage in producing a good or service without having a comparative advantage. This is the case with your neighbor picking apples.
2. It is possible to have a comparative advantage in producing a good or service without having an absolute advantage. This is the case with your picking apples.

Your Turn: Test your understanding by doing related problem 2.5 at the end of this chapter.

---

much apple picking. If the fastest apple pickers have a comparative advantage in some other activity—picking cherries, playing Major League Baseball, or being industrial engineers—they are better off specializing in that activity. Individuals, firms, and countries are better off if they specialize in producing goods and services for which they have a comparative advantage and obtain the other goods and services they need by trading.

Solved Problem 2

Comparative Advantage and the Gains from Trade

Suppose that Canada and the United States both produce maple syrup and honey, which are sold for the same price in both countries. These are the combinations of the two goods that each country can produce in one day using the same amounts of capital and labor:

Canada		United States	
Honey (in tons)	Maple Syrup (in tons)	Honey (in tons)	Maple Syrup (in tons)
0	60	0	50
10	45	10	40
20	30	20	30
30	15	30	20
40	0	40	10
		50	0

a. Which country has a comparative advantage in producing maple syrup? Which country has a comparative advantage in producing honey?
b. Suppose that Canada is currently producing 30 tons of honey and 15 tons of maple syrup, and the United States is currently producing 10 tons of honey and 40 tons of maple syrup. Demonstrate that Canada and the United States can both be better off if they specialize in producing only one good and trade for the other.
c. Illustrate your answer to question (b) by drawing a *PPF* for the United States and a *PPF* for Canada. Show on your *PPFs* the combinations of honey and maple syrup produced and consumed in each country before and after trade.

Solving the Problem

Step 1: **Review the chapter material.** This problem is about comparative advantage, so you may want to review the section "Absolute Advantage versus Comparative Advantage."

Step 2: Answer part (a) by calculating which country has a comparative advantage in each activity. Remember that a country has a comparative advantage in producing a good if it can produce the good at the lowest opportunity cost. When Canada produces 1 more ton of honey, it produces 1.5 tons less of maple syrup. When the United States produces 1 more ton of honey, it produces 1 ton less of maple syrup. Therefore, the United States' opportunity cost of producing honey—1 ton of maple syrup—is lower than Canada's—1.5 tons of maple syrup. When Canada produces 1 more ton of maple syrup, it produces 0.67 ton less of honey. When the United States produces 1 more ton of maple syrup, it produces 1 ton less of honey. Therefore, Canada's opportunity cost of producing maple syrup—0.67 ton of honey—is lower than that of the United States—1 ton of honey. We can conclude that the United States has a comparative advantage in the production of honey and Canada has a comparative advantage in the production of maple syrup.

Step 3: Answer part (b) by showing that specialization makes Canada and the United States better off. We know that Canada and the United States should each specialize where it has a comparative advantage. If both countries specialize, Canada will produce 60 tons of maple syrup and 0 tons of honey, and the United States will produce 0 tons of maple syrup and 50 tons of honey. After both countries specialize, the United States could then trade 30 tons of honey to Canada for 40 tons of maple syrup. (Other mutually beneficial trades are possible as well.) We can summarize the results in a table:

	Before Trade		After Trade	
	Honey (in tons)	Maple Syrup (in tons)	Honey (in tons)	Maple Syrup (in tons)
Canada	30	15	30	20
United States	10	40	20	40

The United States is better off after trade because it can consume the same amount of maple syrup and 10 more tons of honey. Canada is better off after trade because it can consume the same amount of honey and 5 more tons of maple syrup.

Step 4: Answer part (c) by drawing the *PPFs*.

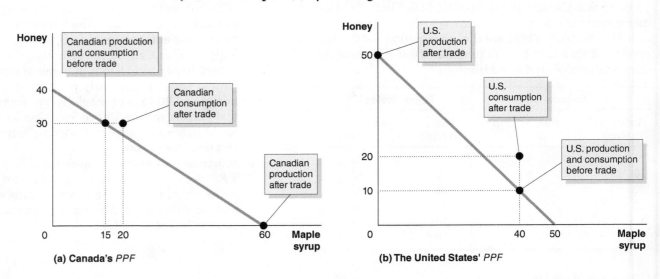

(a) Canada's *PPF*

(b) The United States' *PPF*

Your Turn: For more practice, do related problems 2.6 and 2.7 at the end of this chapter.

Making the Connection

Comparative Advantage, Opportunity Cost, and Housework

What's the most efficient way to divide up household chores?

Among roommates, married couples, and other people living together, dividing up the household chores can be a source of stress. Traditionally among married couples, women did most of the housework, such as preparing meals, cleaning, and doing the laundry. In 1965, married women with children averaged about 32 hours of housework per week, while married men averaged only 4 hours. Today, women average about 18 hours of housework, while men average about 10 hours.

Housework doesn't seem to be part of buying, selling, and the usual topics of business and economics. In fact, we can use basic economic concepts to analyze housework. Consider first the most efficient way to divide up household chores. Suppose Jack and Jill need to decide how they will get the cooking and laundry done. Assume Jack has an absolute advantage over Jill in both chores, but he has a big advantage over Jill in cooking—he takes much less time to prepare very tasty meals—but is only a little faster than Jill in doing the laundry. In other words, assuming they have the same amount of time available to do housework, Jack has a comparative advantage in cooking, while Jill has a comparative advantage in doing the laundry. So rather than Jack and Jill both doing some of the cooking and some of the laundry, they would be better off if Jack follows his comparative advantage and does all the cooking, while Jill follows her comparative advantage and does all the laundry.

Economics can also provide some insight into the decline in the number of hours spent on housework since the 1960s. Combined, men and women now spend more than 20 percent fewer hours on housework. This decline has been partly driven by technology, particularly improvements in household appliances, such as dishwashers and microwave ovens. The decline in the number of hours women devote to housework also reflects the greater job opportunities available to women today compared with the 1960s. The opportunity cost to a woman of spending time on housework and childcare is the wage she gives up by not spending that time in paid work. If a woman could work for an hour at a wage of $20 but spends that hour doing household chores, the opportunity cost of the time spent on chores is $20. As job opportunities for women and the wages those jobs pay have increased, so has the opportunity cost of doing housework. So in addition to taking advantage of improved appliances, many families have found that the cost of hiring specialists in household chores, such as cleaning services and lawn care services, is lower than the cost of the wife (or husband) performing those chores.

As women's wages have risen relative to men's wages, the opportunity cost to women of doing housework has increased more than has the opportunity cost to men. So we would expect that in addition to women devoting fewer hours to housework, the gap between the hours women and men devote would narrow. In fact, between 1965 and 2011, the average number of hours women devote to housework declined from 32 hours per week to 18 hours. The average number of hours women devote to paid work increased from 8 hours per week to 21 hours.

Of course, changes in social attitudes also help explain changes in how men and women allocate their time. But we have seen that the basic economic concepts of comparative advantage and opportunity cost provide important insights into the not-so-wonderful world of household chores.

Sources: Kim Parker and Wendy Wang, "Modern Parenthood: Roles of Moms and Dads Converge as They Balance Work and Family," pewsocialtrends.org, March 13, 2013; Emily Oster, "You're Dividing the Chores Wrong," *Slate*, November 21, 2012; and Ellen Byron, "A Truce in the Chore Wars," *New York Times*, December 4, 2012.

Your Turn: Test your understanding by doing related problems 2.14 and 2.15 at the end of this chapter.

The Market System

We have seen that households, firms, and the government face trade-offs and incur opportunity costs because resources are scarce. We have also seen that trade allows people to specialize according to their comparative advantage. By engaging in trade, people can raise their incomes and their standard of living. Of course, trade in the modern world is much more complex than the examples we have considered so far. Trade today involves the decisions of millions of people around the world. How are the decisions of these millions of people coordinated? In the United States and most other countries, trade is carried out in markets. Markets also determine the answers to the three fundamental questions: What goods and services will be produced? How will the goods and services be produced? and Who will receive the goods and services produced?

Market A group of buyers and sellers of a good or service and the institution or arrangement by which they come together to trade.

Market is a group of buyers and sellers of a good or service and the institution or arrangement by which they come together to trade. Markets take many forms: They can be physical places, such as a local pizza parlor or the New York Stock Exchange, or virtual places, such as eBay or iTunes. In a market, the buyers are demanders of goods or services, and the sellers are suppliers of goods or services. Households and firms interact in two types of markets: *product markets* and *factor markets*. **Product markets** are markets for goods—such as computers—and services—such as medical treatment. In product markets, households are demanders and firms are suppliers. **Factor markets** are markets for the *factors of production*. **Factors of production** are the inputs used to make goods and services. Factors of production are divided into four broad categories:

Product market A market for goods—such as computers—or services—such as medical treatment.

Factor market A market for the factors of production, such as labor, capital, natural resources, and entrepreneurial ability.

Factors of production The inputs used to make goods and services.

- *Labor* includes all types of work, from the part-time labor of teenagers working at McDonald's to the work of senior managers in large corporations.
- *Capital* refers to physical capital, such as computers and machine tools, that is used to produce other goods.
- *Natural resources* include land, water, oil, iron ore, and other raw materials (or "gifts of nature") that are used in producing goods.
- An *entrepreneur* is someone who operates a business. *Entrepreneurial ability* is the ability to bring together the other factors of production to successfully produce and sell goods and services.

The Circular Flow of Income

Two key groups participate in markets:

- A *household* consists of all the individuals in a home. Households are suppliers of factors of production—particularly labor—employed by firms to make goods and services. Households use the income they receive from selling the factors of production to purchase the goods and services supplied by firms. We are familiar with households as suppliers of labor because most people earn most of their income by going to work, meaning they are selling their labor services to firms in the labor market. But households own the other factors of production as well, either directly or indirectly, by owning the firms that own these resources. All firms are owned by households. Small firms, like a neighborhood restaurant, might be owned by one person. Large firms, like Apple, are owned by millions of households that own shares of stock in them. When firms pay profits to the people who own them, the firms are paying for using the capital and natural resources that are supplied to them by those owners. So, we can generalize by saying that in factor markets, households are suppliers and firms are demanders.
- *Firms* are suppliers of goods and services. Firms use the funds they receive from selling goods and services to buy or hire the factors of production needed to make the goods and services.

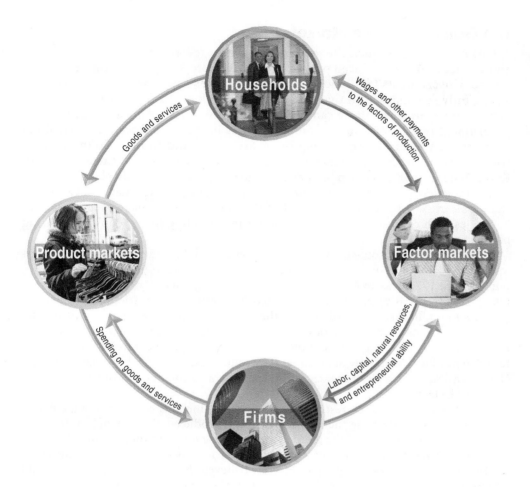

Figure 6

The Circular-Flow Diagram

Households and firms are linked together in a circular flow of production, income, and spending. The blue arrows show the flow of the factors of production. In factor markets, households supply labor, entrepreneurial ability, and other factors of production to firms. Firms use these factors of production to make goods and services that they supply to households in product markets. The red arrows show the flow of goods and services from firms to households. The green arrows show the flow of funds. In factor markets, households receive wages and other payments from firms in exchange for supplying the factors of production. Households use these wages and other payments to purchase goods and services from firms in product markets. Firms sell goods and services to households in product markets, and they use the funds to purchase the factors of production from households in factor markets.

We can use a simple economic model called the **circular-flow diagram** to see how participants in markets are linked. Figure 6 shows that in factor markets, households supply labor and other factors of production in exchange for wages and other payments from firms. In product markets, households use the payments they earn in factor markets to purchase the goods and services supplied by firms. Firms produce these goods and services using the factors of production supplied by households. In the figure, the blue arrows show the flow of factors of production from households through factor markets to firms. The red arrows show the flow of goods and services from firms through product markets to households. The green arrows show the flow of funds from firms through factor markets to households and the flow of spending from households through product markets to firms.

Like all economic models, the circular-flow diagram is a simplified version of reality. For example, Figure 6 leaves out the important role of government in buying goods from firms and in making payments, such as Social Security or unemployment insurance payments, to households. The figure also leaves out the roles played by banks, the stock and bond markets, and other parts of the *financial system* in aiding the flow of funds from lenders to borrowers. Finally, the figure does not show that some goods and services purchased by domestic households are produced in foreign countries and some goods and services produced by domestic firms are sold to foreign households. Despite these simplifications, the circular-flow diagram in Figure 6 is useful for seeing how product markets, factor markets, and their participants are linked together. One of the great wonders of the market system is that it manages to successfully coordinate the independent activities of so many households and firms.

Circular-flow diagram A model that illustrates how participants in markets are linked.

The Gains from Free Markets

Free market A market with few government restrictions on how a good or service can be produced or sold or on how a factor of production can be employed.

A **free market** exists when the government places few restrictions on how goods and services can be produced or sold or on how factors of production can be employed. Governments in all modern economies intervene more than is consistent with a fully free market. In that sense, we can think of the free market as being a benchmark against which we can judge actual economies. There are relatively few government restrictions on economic activities in the United States, Canada, the countries of Western Europe, Hong Kong, Singapore, and Estonia. So these countries come close to the free market benchmark. In countries such as Cuba and North Korea, the free market system has been rejected in favor of centrally planned economies with extensive government control over product and factor markets. Countries that come closest to the free market benchmark have been more successful than countries with centrally planned economies in providing their people with rising living standards.

The Scottish philosopher Adam Smith is considered the father of modern economics because his book *An Inquiry into the Nature and Causes of the Wealth of Nations*, published in 1776, was an early and very influential argument for the free market system. Smith was writing at a time when extensive government restrictions on markets were common. In many parts of Europe, the *guild system* prevailed. Under this system, governments would give guilds, or organizations of producers, the authority to control the production of a good. For example, the shoemakers' guild controlled who was allowed to produce shoes, how many shoes they could produce, and what price they could charge. In France, the cloth makers' guild even dictated the number of threads in the weave of the cloth.

Smith argued that such restrictions reduced the income, or wealth, of a country and its people by restricting the quantity of goods produced. Some people at the time supported the restrictions of the guild system because it was in their financial interest to do so. If you were a member of a guild, the restrictions served to reduce the competition you faced. But other people sincerely believed that the alternative to the guild system was economic chaos. Smith argued that these people were wrong and that a country could enjoy a smoothly functioning economic system if firms were freed from guild restrictions.

The Market Mechanism

In Smith's day, defenders of the guild system worried that if, for instance, the shoemakers' guild did not control shoe production, either too many or too few shoes would be produced. Smith argued that prices would do a better job of coordinating the activities of buyers and sellers than the guilds could. A key to understanding Smith's argument is the assumption that *individuals usually act in a rational, self-interested way*. In particular, individuals take those actions that are most likely to make themselves better off financially. This assumption of rational, self-interested behavior underlies nearly all economic analysis. In fact, economics can be distinguished from other disciplines that study human behavior—such as sociology and psychology—by its emphasis on the assumption of self-interested behavior. Adam Smith understood—as economists today understand—that people's motives can be complex. But when we analyze people in the act of buying and selling, the motivation of financial reward usually provides the best explanation for the actions people take.

For example, suppose that a significant number of consumers switch from buying regular gasoline-powered cars to buying gasoline/electric-powered hybrid cars, such as the Toyota Prius, or all-electric cars, such as the Tesla Model S. Firms will find that they can charge relatively higher prices for hybrid cars and electric cars than they can for regular cars. The self-interest of these firms will lead them to respond to consumers' wishes by producing more hybrid and electric cars and fewer regular cars. Or suppose that consumers decide that they want to eat less bread, pasta, and other foods that are high in carbohydrates. Then the prices firms can charge for bread and pasta will fall.

The self-interest of firms will lead them to produce less bread and pasta, which, in fact, is what has happened over the past 10 years.

Note that for the market mechanism to work in response to changes in consumers' wants, *prices must be flexible*. Changes in *relative prices*—the price of one good or service relative to the prices of other goods or services—provide information, or a signal, to both consumers and firms. For example, during 2010, consumers worldwide increased their demand for cattle and poultry. Because corn is fed to cattle and poultry, prices for corn soared relative to prices for other crops. Many farmers in the United States received this price signal and responded by increasing the amount of corn they planted and decreasing the amount of soybeans and wheat. One Kansas farmer was quoted as saying, "It seemed to me there was $100 to $150 per acre more money in the corn than there was in the beans. That's the kind of math that a lot of guys were using." By 2013, the United States was experiencing record corn crops. Similarly, falling prices for DVDs or music CDs in the 2000s were a signal to movie studios and record companies to devote fewer resources to these products and more resources to making movies and music available online.

In the United States today, governments at the federal, state, and local levels set or regulate the prices of only about 10 to 20 percent of goods and services. The prices of other goods and services are free to change as consumer wants change and as costs of production change.

In the case where consumers want more of a product, and in the case where they want less of a product, the market system responds without a guild or the government giving orders about how much to produce or what price to charge. In a famous phrase, Smith said that firms would be led by the "invisible hand" of the market to provide consumers with what they want. Firms respond *individually* to changes in prices by making decisions that *collectively* end up satisfying the wants of consumers.

| Making the Connection | ### A Story of the Market System in Action: How Do You Make an iPad? |

Apple produces the iPad. Because Apple's headquarters are in Cupertino, California, it seems reasonable to assume that iPads are also manufactured in that state. A poll by the *New York Times* showed that, in fact, a majority of people interviewed believed that iPads were manufactured in the United States, if not specifically in California. Although engineers at Apple designed the iPad, the company produces none of the components of the iPad, nor does it assemble the components into a finished product. Far from being produced entirely by one company in one country, the iPad requires the coordinated activities of thousands of workers and dozens of firms spread around the world.

Foxconn, which is based in Taiwan, assembles the iPad in factories in Shenzhen and Chengdu, China, and Jundiai, São Paulo, Brazil, and ships them to Apple for sale in the United States. Although Foxconn does final assembly, it doesn't make any of the components and, in fact, charges Apple less than $15 for assembling each iPad.

The following table lists some of the many suppliers of iPad components.

Each of these suppliers in turn relies on its own suppliers. For example, Broadcom designs the touchscreen controller for the iPad and supplies it to Apple, but it does not manufacture the components of the controller or assemble them. To manufacture the components, Broadcom relies on SilTerra, based in Malaysia; SMIC, based in mainland China; and Taiwan Semiconductor Manufacturing Corporation (TSMC) and UMC, based in Taiwan. TSMC's factories are for the most part not in Taiwan but in mainland China and Eastern Europe. To assemble the components, Broadcom uses several companies, including Amkor Technology, based in Chandler, Arizona, and STATS ChipPAC, based in Singapore.

The market coordinates the activities of the many people spread around the world who contribute to making an iPad.

Firm	Location of the Firm	iPad Component the Firm Supplies
AKM	Japan	Motion sensor
AU Optronics	Taiwan	Display
Broadcom	United States (California)	Touchscreen controller and wireless chip
Cirrus Logic	United States (Texas)	Audio chip
Corning	United States (New York)	Glass screen cover
Elpida	Japan	System memory
SK Hynix	South Korea	Flash memory
Infineon Technologies	Germany	Semiconductors
LG Electronics	South Korea	Display
Quicomm	United Kingdom	Wireless section
Samsung	South Korea	Display, flash memory, and applications processor
Sharp	Japan	Display
STMicroelectronics	France/Italy	Motion sensors
Texas Instruments	United States (Texas)	Touchscreen controller
Toshiba	Japan	Flash memory

All told, an iPad contains hundreds of parts that are designed, manufactured, and assembled by firms around the world. Many of these firms are not even aware of which other firms are also producing components for the iPad. Few of the managers of these firms have met managers of the other firms or shared knowledge of how their particular components are produced. In fact, no one person from Tim Cook, the chief executive officer of Apple, on down possesses the knowledge of how to produce all the components that are assembled into an iPad. Instead, the invisible hand of the market has led these firms to contribute their knowledge and resources to the process that ultimately results in an iPad available for sale in a store in the United States. Apple has so efficiently organized the process of producing the iPad that you can order a custom iPad with a personal engraving and have it delivered from an assembly plant in China or Brazil to your doorstep in the United States in as little as three days.

Sources: Marjorie Connelly, "Poll Finds Consumer Confusion on Where Apple Devices Are Made," *New York Times*, January 25, 2012; Andrew Rassweiler, "New iPad 32GB + 4G Carries $364.35 Bill of Materials," iSuppli.com, March 16, 2012; and Arik Hesseldahl, "Teardown Shows Apple iPad Mini Costs at Least $188 to Build," allthingsd.com, November 3, 2012.

Your Turn: Test your understanding by doing related problems 3.8 and 3.9 at the end of this chapter.

The Role of the Entrepreneur

Entrepreneur Someone who operates a business, bringing together the factors of production—labor, capital, and natural resources—to produce goods and services.

Entrepreneurs are central to the working of the market system. An **entrepreneur** is someone who operates a business. Entrepreneurs first determine what goods and services they believe consumers want and then decide how to produce those goods and services most profitably, using the available factors of production—labor, capital, and natural resources. Successful entrepreneurs are able to search out opportunities to provide new goods and services. Frequently these opportunities are created by new technology. Consumers and existing businesses often do not at first realize that the new technology makes new products feasible. For example, even after the development of the internal combustion engine had made automobiles practicable, Henry Ford remarked, "If I had asked my customers what they wanted, they would have said a faster horse." Because consumers often cannot evaluate a new product before it exists, some of the most successful entrepreneurs, such as the late Steve Jobs of Apple, rarely use *focus groups*, or meetings with consumers in which the consumers are asked what new products they would like to see. Instead, entrepreneurs think of products that consumers may not even realize they need, such as, in Jobs's case, an MP3 player—iPod—or a tablet computer—iPad. Entrepreneurs are important to the economy because they are often responsible for making new products widely available to consumers, as Henry Ford did with the automobile and Steve Jobs did with the iPod.

The firms entrepreneurs found are typically small at first, as Apple and Ford were. Table 3 lists some of the important products entrepreneurs at small firms introduced during the twentieth century.

Entrepreneurs put their own funds at risk when they start businesses. If they are wrong about what consumers want or about the best way to produce goods and services, they can lose those funds. In fact, it is not unusual for entrepreneurs who eventually achieve great success to fail at first. For instance, early in their careers, both Henry Ford and Sakichi Toyoda, who eventually founded the Toyota Motor Corporation, started companies that quickly failed. Research by Richard Freeman of Harvard University has shown that a typical entrepreneur earns less than an employee at a large firm who has the same education and other characteristics. Few entrepreneurs make the fortunes earned by Mark Zuckerberg, Steve Jobs, or Bill Gates.

Product	Inventor
Air conditioning	William Haviland Carrier
Airplane	Orville and Wilbur Wright
Automobile, mass produced	Henry Ford
Biomagnetic imaging	Raymond Damadian
Biosynthetic insulin	Herbert Boyer
DNA fingerprinting	Alec Jeffries
FM radio	Edwin Howard Armstrong
Helicopter	Igor Sikorsky
High-resolution CAT scanner	Robert Ledley
Hydraulic brake	Malcolm Lockheed
Integrated circuit	Jack Kilby
Microprocessor	Ted Hoff
Optical scanner	Everett Franklin Lindquist
Oral contraceptives	Carl Djerassi
Overnight delivery service	Fred Smith
Personal computer	Steve Jobs and Steve Wozniak
Quick-frozen foods	Clarence Birdseye
Safety razor	King Gillette
Soft contact lens	Kevin Tuohy
Solid fuel rocket engine	Robert Goddard
Supercomputer	Seymour Cray
Vacuum tube	Philo Farnsworth
Zipper	Gideon Sundback

Table 3

Important Products Introduced by Entrepreneurs at Small Firms

Source: William J. Baumol, *The Microtheory of Innovative Entrepreneurship*, Princeton, NJ: Princeton University Press, 2010, and various sources. Note that the person who first commercially developed a particular product is sometimes disputed by historians.

Entrepreneurs make a vital contribution to economic growth through their roles in responding to consumer demand and introducing new products. Government policies that encourage entrepreneurship are also likely to increase economic growth and raise the standard of living. In the next section, we consider the legal framework required for a successful market in which entrepreneurs can succeed.

The Legal Basis of a Successful Market System

In a free market, government does not restrict how firms produce and sell goods and services or how they employ factors of production. But the absence of government intervention is not enough for the market system to work well. Government has to take active steps to provide a *legal environment* that will allow markets to operate efficiently.

Protection of Private Property For the market system to work well, individuals must be willing to take risks. Someone with $250,000 can be cautious and keep it safely in a bank—or even in cash, if the person doesn't trust banks. But the market system won't work unless a significant number of people are willing to risk their funds by investing them in businesses. Investing in businesses is risky in any country. Many businesses fail every year in the United States and other high-income countries. But in high-income countries, someone who starts a new business or invests in an existing business doesn't have to worry that the government, the military, or criminal gangs might decide to seize the business or demand payments for not destroying the business. Unfortunately, in many poor countries, owners of businesses are not well protected from having their businesses seized by the government or from having their profits taken by criminals. Where these problems exist, opening a business can be extremely risky. Cash can be concealed easily, but a business is difficult to conceal or move.

Property rights The rights individuals or firms have to the exclusive use of their property, including the right to buy or sell it.

Property rights are the rights individuals or firms have to the exclusive use of their property, including the right to buy or sell it. Property can be tangible, physical property, such as a store or factory. Property can also be intangible, such as the right to an idea. Two amendments to the U.S. Constitution guarantee property rights: The Fifth Amendment states that the federal government shall not deprive any person "of life, liberty, or property, without due process of law." The Fourteenth Amendment extends this guarantee to the actions of state governments: "No state ... shall deprive any person of life, liberty, or property, without due process of law." Similar guarantees exist in every high-income country. Unfortunately, in many developing countries, such guarantees do not exist or are poorly enforced.

In any modern economy, *intellectual property rights* are very important. Intellectual property includes books, films, software, and ideas for new products or new ways of producing products. To protect intellectual property, the federal government grants a *patent* that gives an inventor—often a firm—the exclusive right to produce and sell a new product for a period of 20 years from the date the patent was filed. For instance, because Microsoft has a patent on the Windows operating system, other firms cannot sell their own versions of Windows. The government grants patents to encourage firms to spend money on the research and development necessary to create new products. If other companies could freely copy Windows, Microsoft would not have spent the funds necessary to develop it. Just as a new product or a new method of making a product receives patent protection, new books, films, and software receive *copyright* protection. Under U.S. law, the creator of a book, film, or piece of music has the exclusive right to use the creation during the creator's lifetime. The creator's heirs retain this exclusive right for 50 years after the death of the creator.

In providing copyright protection for only a limited time, Congress provides economic incentives to creators while eventually—after the period of copyright has ended—allowing the creators' works to be freely available. The longer the period of copyright, the more likely it is that some consumers will not gain access to the copyrighted work and the longer the wait before others can use the copyrighted work in their own work, for instance, by writing a sequel to a copyrighted book.

Making the Connection	### Who Owns *The Wizard of Oz*?

The U.S. Congress provides copyright protection to authors to give them an economic incentive to invest the time and effort required to write a book. While a book is under copyright, only the author—or whoever the author sells the copyright to—can legally publish a paper or digital copy of the book. Once the copyright expires, however, the book enters the *public domain* and anyone is free to publish the book. Copies of classic books, such as *Huckleberry Finn* or *Oliver Twist*, are usually available from many publishers.

L. Frank Baum wrote *The Wonderful Wizard of Oz* in 1900. The copyright on the book expired years ago and many publishers now sell their own versions of the book. While these publishers can't claim copyright of Baum's words, because those words are in the public domain, they can claim copyright on a new design of the book or on any new illustrations they create.

A similar situation exists with the famous 1939 MGM film *The Wizard of Oz*. Warner Brothers, which now owns the copyright to the film, does not have a legal right to any of the words or incidents in the film that were taken directly from Baum's book. However, Warner Brothers does have a copyright on any dialogue or incidents that were written specifically for the film as well as the design of the film sets and the actors' costumes. Warner Brothers was aggressive in defending its copyright when Walt Disney announced that it was making a film called *Oz The Great and Powerful*. As a copyright lawyer put it: "The MGM film presented the story in a certain way, and it's those things—the embellishments, the creative decisions—that Disney cannot use."

The Wonderful Wizard of Oz is a classic book from 1900 that became a classic film in 1939. A remake of the film in 2013 raised copyright issues.

Disney had to be careful even in minor details to avoid violating Warner Brothers' copyright. For example, it made the green makeup of the Wicked Witch of the West a different shade from that in the earlier film. Disney also changed the location of the Yellow Brick Road and the name of Munchkin Country to avoid infringing on Warner Brothers' copyright. Shortly before the film was released in early 2013, Disney's lawyers decided that the hairstyles of some of the Munchkins in the completed film had to be digitally altered because they appeared too close to the hairstyles in the earlier film.

Most economists believe that copyrights provide needed protection for authors and creators of movies or other artistic works. However, the roadblocks Warner Brothers placed in the way of Disney making a new *Oz* film show that copyrights may deter others from producing new work that might infringe on a copyrighted work.

Sources: Brooks Barnes, "We Aren't in the Old Kansas, Toto," *New York Times*, February 28, 2013; and Eriq Gardner, "Disney, Warner Bros. Fighting Over 'Wizard of Oz' Trademarks," *Hollywood Reporter*, February 12, 2012.

Your Turn: Test your understanding by doing related problem 3.17 at the end of this chapter.

Enforcement of Contracts and Property Rights Business activity often involves someone agreeing to carry out some action in the future. For example, you may borrow $20,000 to buy a car and promise the bank—by signing a loan contract—that you will pay back the money over the next five years. Or Facebook may sign a licensing agreement with a small technology company, agreeing to use that company's technology for a period of several years in return for a fee. Usually these agreements take the form of legal contracts. For the market system to work, businesses and individuals have to rely on these contracts being carried out. If one party to a legal contract does not fulfill its obligations—perhaps the small company had promised Facebook exclusive use of its technology but then began licensing it to other companies—the other party can go to court to have the agreement enforced. Similarly, if property owners in the United States believe that the federal or state government has violated their rights under the Fifth or Fourteenth Amendments, they can go to court to have their rights enforced.

But going to court to enforce a contract or private property rights will be successful only if the court system is independent and judges are able to make impartial decisions on the basis of the law. In the United States and other high-income countries, the court systems have enough independence from other parts of the government and enough protection from intimidation by outside forces—such as criminal gangs—that they are able to make their decisions based on the law. In many developing countries, the court systems lack this independence and will not provide a remedy if the government violates private property rights or if a person with powerful political connections decides to violate a business contract.

If property rights are not well enforced, fewer goods and services will be produced. This reduces economic efficiency, leaving the economy inside its production possibilities frontier.

Continued

Economics in Your Life

The Trade-offs When You Buy a Car

At the beginning of the chapter, we asked you to think about two questions: With respect to traditional gasoline-powered cars, what is the relationship between safety and fuel efficiency? and Under what circumstances would it be possible for automobile manufacturers to make cars safer and more fuel efficient? To answer the first question, you have to recognize that there is a trade-off between safety and fuel efficiency. With the technology available at any particular time, an automobile manufacturer can increase fuel efficiency by making a car smaller and lighter. But driving a lighter car increases your chances of being injured if you have an accident. The trade-off between safety and fuel efficiency would look much like the relationship in Figure 1. To get more of both safety and gas mileage, automobile makers would have to discover new technologies that allow them to make cars lighter and safer at the same time. Such new technologies would make points like G in Figure 1 attainable.

Conclusion

We have seen that by trading in markets, people are able to specialize and pursue their comparative advantage. Trading on the basis of comparative advantage makes all participants in trade better off. The key role of markets is to facilitate trade. In fact, the market system is a very effective means of coordinating the decisions of millions of consumers, workers, and firms. At the center of the market system is the consumer. To be successful, firms must respond to the desires of consumers. These desires are communicated to firms through prices. To explore how markets work, we must study the behavior of consumers and firms.

Read *An Inside Look* on the next page to explore the trade-offs managers face at luxury carmaker Mercedes-Benz and why the company chose to partner with Tesla Motors to develop electric-vehicle components.

CAR AND DRIVER

Mercedes-Benz Execs Talk 13 New Models, Electric Cars, and Hybrid AMGs

Mercedes-Benz has never had a stronger first quarter in the United States than it has had in 2013, but the German automaker isn't about to slow down. The company is taking strides to secure its position over the long term and to bolster its global sales with 13 all-new new models by 2020. These vehicles aren't just refreshes and redesigns; the Stuttgart-based marque will introduce 13 new nameplates—vehicles without a predecessor. We know there will be the front-drive-based GLA-class crossover and the S-class will add coupe and convertible variants, but the bulk of the plan remains a mystery. Hoping to fill in some of the unknowns, we sat down with four of the most influential executives at Mercedes-Benz: Thomas Weber, head of R&D; Dieter Zetsche, Daimler chairman and head of Mercedes-Benz cars; Jörg Prigl, vice president of small-car development; and Ola Källenius, chairman of Mercedes-Benz AMG. Here's what they had to say about the future of Mercedes:

Car and Driver [C/D]: We're struggling to find 13 obvious holes in the Mercedes-Benz lineup. What kinds of vehicles are coming? Should we expect Mercedes versions of BMW's Gran Turismos?

Thomas Weber: To build such a vehicle is easy. To be successful is the name of the game. You also must be careful not to say a current trend is a trend forever. We will certainly add long-wheelbase models targeting the Asian markets. As we look at these new models, we need to beat our competitors in three areas: design, powertrains, and environmental and safety technologies.

C/D: Is there any concern that the $30,825 CLA250 might dilute the brand image in the U.S. or cannibalize C-class sales?

Dieter Zetsche: Our more-mature, more-affluent customers are very good to us. At the same time, the A-class has an average age drop of 10 years [in Europe]. It's all about striking the right balance. The new S-class will move into Rolls-Royce Ghost territory. Just as we introduce small cars, we keep the light shining on the brand.

Jörg Prigl: If we saw that as a risk, we shouldn't have done the CLA. We are not fighting for the loyal customers we have.

C/D: Electric vehicles have failed to take off in the U.S. Why bring the electric B-class to market?

Prigl: Technology leadership in a potential future drivetrain is a must for us. The partnership with Tesla will help us speed up and beat the competition. If you believe you can do this alone as an automaker, you will fail. The battery cell should not be done by the OEM [Auto Parts]. There should be huge competition among suppliers to get the cell right. The specific know-how for the automaker is in the packaging and the battery management. Tesla provides the complete powertrain for the B-class Electric Drive, but the calibration is split between Tesla and Mercedes-Benz.

C/D: The Geneva auto show was dominated by a pair of hybrid supercars, the McLaren P1 and the Ferrari LaFerrari. At what point will tightening environmental regulations force AMG to adopt hybrid powertrains?

Ola Källenius: The SLS AMG Electric Drive is a glimpse of the future, but we took two steps forward to take one step back. Hybrids are the next logical step, likely in five to seven years. For now, with conventional gas measures we can reduce emissions another 20 percent. The immediate future is relatively clear. Downsize and direct injection is where combustion is headed, but it is inevitable that we will have to electrify these cars.

C/D: Why isn't Mercedes making a big investment in carbon fiber like BMW and the Volkswagen Group have?

Källenius: Carbon fiber is for a hypercar. Taking out weight is a decathlon. You need to work with all the materials. Right now, the industry is at a peak; every new car going forward will shave off weight ....

Source: Eric Tingwall, "Mercedes-Benz Execs Talk 13 New Models, Electric Cars, and Hybrid AMGs," *Car and Driver*, April 10, 2013.

Key Points in the Article

Mercedes is planning 13 new models by 2020, including a new crossover vehicle; new variations of its S-class automobile; redeveloped entry-level vehicles; and the introduction of an electric car. With these new models, the managers at Mercedes are making choices about how to use new designs, upgraded powertrains, and advances in technology to deal with environmental and safety concerns. In addition, these managers have also chosen to partner with Tesla Motors to develop electric-vehicle components. Making the optimal choices will be important for Mercedes to remain one of the most competitive and successful high-end automobile manufacturers in the world.

Analyzing the News

(a) Automobile manufacturers must decide what type of cars to bring to market. Mercedes has two challenges in introducing a new entry-level car in the United States. First, for a high-end manufacturer like Mercedes, image is very important, and even the perception that the company is catering to a lower-income consumer can be damaging. Second, Mercedes does not want to sacrifice sales of its more profitable C-class models for these new lower-price A-class models. Suppose Mercedes produced only A-class and C-class vehicles and in 2013 had the capability of producing a total of 30,000 vehicles. This capacity is represented by PPF_{2013} in the figure below. This curve shows that Mercedes would have to sacrifice production (and therefore sales) of one type of vehicle to produce more of the other. The executives at Mercedes expect their market to continue to grow, and they do not believe that introducing the new A-class model will take sales away from the C-class. Mercedes will therefore have to produce a larger number of automobiles, which is represented by PPF_{2020} in the figure.

(b) Despite disappointing sales figures for electric vehicles, Mercedes has decided to introduce its electric B-class model in the U.S. market. Mercedes believes that the market for electric vehicles will grow, and it needs to be at the forefront of development in order to beat the competition. Mercedes faced a trade-off when deciding on the development of its electric vehicle. Rather than build this vehicle completely in-house, Mercedes chose to partner with Tesla, believing that Tesla's experience in producing electric vehicles would be advantageous for both companies and make the B-class a success. In choosing to take advantage of Tesla's expertise and technology, Mercedes gave up some level of control, but it chose this path believing it would increase the potential for building a vehicle that would have strong sales.

(c) As emissions standards continue to tighten and gas-mileage requirements continue to grow, lighter-weight cars will become a bigger part of our future. One decision Mercedes has made is to *not* invest heavily in lightweight carbon fiber for use in production, but rather to reduce the weight of all materials over the next several years. Here again, Mercedes faced a trade-off between investing in one specific technology and waiting to see what the future holds in terms of other lighter-weight production options that it can use in its manufacturing.

Thinking Critically

1. Suppose that from 2013 to 2020, the resources Mercedes-Benz uses to produce its automobiles remain constant, while improvements in technology in 2020 allow Mercedes to produce the additional quantity of A-class models shown in the figure below, but no additional C-class models. Draw a graph that illustrates this technology change. Be sure to show both the 2013 and new 2020 *PPF*s. What is the opportunity cost to Mercedes-Benz of producing one C-class model in 2013? In 2020?

2. Assume that the figure below accurately represents Mercedes-Benz's *PPF*s for 2013 and 2020, and that in 2020 it has customer orders for 35,000 A-class models and 20,000 C-class models. Explain whether Mercedes can fill all of these orders.

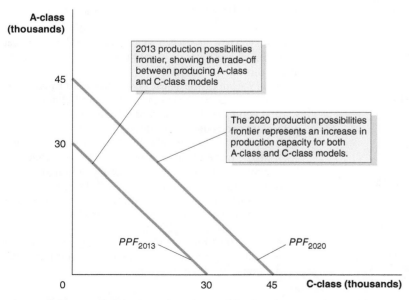

Choosing between producing a Mercedes A-class model and producing a C-class model.

Chapter Summary and Problems

Key Terms

Absolute advantage	Entrepreneur	Market	Property rights
Circular-flow diagram	Factor market	Opportunity cost	Scarcity
Comparative advantage	Factors of production	Product market	Trade
Economic growth	Free market	Production possibilities frontier (*PPF*)	

1 Production Possibilities Frontiers and Opportunity Costs

LEARNING OBJECTIVE: Use a production possibilities frontier to analyze opportunity costs and trade-offs.

Summary

The **production possibilities frontier (*PPF*)** is a curve that shows the maximum attainable combinations of two products that may be produced with available resources. The *PPF* is used to illustrate the trade-offs that arise from **scarcity**. Points on the frontier are technically efficient. Points inside the frontier are inefficient, and points outside the frontier are unattainable. The **opportunity cost** of any activity is the highest-valued alternative that must be given up to engage in that activity. Because of increasing marginal opportunity costs, production possibilities frontiers are usually bowed out rather than straight lines. This illustrates the important economic concept that the more resources that are already devoted to any activity, the smaller the payoff from devoting additional resources to that activity is likely to be. **Economic growth** is illustrated by shifting a production possibilities frontier outward.

Visit **www.myeconlab.com** to complete these exercises online and get instant feedback.

Review Questions

1.1 What do economists mean by *scarcity*? Can you think of anything that is not scarce according to the economic definition?

1.2 What is a production possibilities frontier? How can we show efficiency on a production possibilities frontier? How can we show inefficiency? What causes a production possibilities frontier to shift outward?

1.3 What does increasing marginal opportunity costs mean? What are the implications of this idea for the shape of the production possibilities frontier?

Problems and Applications

1.4 Draw a production possibilities frontier that shows the trade-off between the production of cotton and the production of soybeans.
  a. Show the effect that a prolonged drought would have on the initial production possibilities frontier.
  b. Suppose genetic modification makes soybeans resistant to insects, allowing yields to double. Show the effect of this technological change on the initial production possibilities frontier.

1.5 **[Related to the** Chapter Opener**]** One of the trade-offs Tesla faces is between safety and the maximum range someone can drive an all-electric car before having to recharge it. For example, adding steel to a car makes it safer but also heavier, which results in fewer miles between recharges. Draw a hypothetical production possibilities frontier that Tesla engineers face that shows this trade-off.

1.6 **[Related to** Chapter Opener**]** According to an article on *CNNMoney*, in May 2013 CEO Elon Musk of Tesla Motors announced plans for a large expansion of Tesla's network of supercharger stations by the end of the year. The network of supercharger stations will stretch from Los Angeles to New York and cover most metropolitan areas in the United States and Supercharger stations allow the all-electric cars to be recharged in about an hour. Musk stated that: "It is very important to address this issue of long-distance travel."
  a. Why is it important for Tesla Motors to address the issue of long-distance travel?
  b. Tesla Motors, like other firms, faces many strategic decisions and trade-offs. What would be the opportunity cost to Tesla Motors to expanding the supercharger networks?

Source: Chris Isidore, "Tesla Tripling Supercharger Network for LA to NY Trip," *CNNMoney*, May 31, 2013.

1.7 Suppose you win free tickets to a movie plus all you can eat at the snack bar for free. Would there be a cost to you to attend this movie? Explain.

1.8 Suppose we can divide all the goods produced by an economy into two types: consumption goods and capital goods. Capital goods, such as machinery, equipment, and computers, are goods used to produce other goods.
  a. Use a production possibilities frontier graph to illustrate the trade-off to an economy between producing consumption goods and producing capital goods. Is it likely that the production possibilities frontier in this situation will be a straight line (as in Figure 1) or bowed out (as in Figure 2)? Briefly explain.
  b. Suppose a technological change occurs that has a favorable effect on the production of capital goods but not consumption goods. Show the effect on the production possibilities frontier.

c. Suppose that Lichtenstein and Luxembourg currently have identical production possibilities frontiers but that Lichtenstein devotes only 5 percent of its resources to producing capital goods over each of the next 10 years, while Luxembourg devotes 30 percent. Which country is likely to experience more rapid economic growth in the future? Illustrate using a production possibilities frontier graph. Your graph should include production possibilities frontiers for Lichtenstein and Luxembourg today and in 10 years.

1.9 Use the following production possibilities frontier for a country to answer the questions.

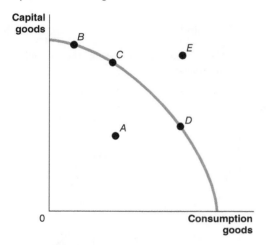

a. Which point or points are unattainable? Briefly explain why.
b. Which point or points are efficient? Briefly explain why.
c. Which point or points are inefficient? Briefly explain why.
d. At which point is the country's future growth rate likely to be the highest? Briefly explain why.

1.10 **[Related to** Solved Problem 1**]** You have exams in economics and chemistry coming up, and you have 5 hours available for studying. The following table shows the trade-offs you face in allocating the time you will spend in studying each subject:

	Hours Spent Studying		Midterm Score	
Choice	Economics	Chemistry	Economics	Chemistry
A	5	0	95	70
B	4	1	93	78
C	3	2	90	84
D	2	3	86	88
E	1	4	81	90
F	0	5	75	91

a. Use the data in the table to draw a production possibilities frontier graph. Label the vertical axis "Score on economics exam," and label the horizontal axis "Score on chemistry exam." Make sure to label the values where your production possibilities frontier intersects the vertical and horizontal axes.

b. Label the points representing choice C and choice D. If you are at choice C, what is your opportunity cost of increasing your chemistry score by 4 points?
c. Under what circumstances would choice A be a sensible choice?

1.11 Suppose the U.S. president is attempting to decide whether the federal government should spend more on research to find a cure for heart disease. He asks you, one of his economic advisors, to prepare a report discussing the relevant factors he should consider. Use the concepts of opportunity cost and trade-offs to discuss some of the main issues you would deal with in your report.

1.12 Suppose that the federal government is deciding which of two cancer treatment therapies it will allow Medicare to pay for (assuming that only one treatment therapy will be funded): Therapy A, which will prolong the average life span of patients receiving the treatment by 24 months and will cost $750,000 per patient treated, or therapy B, which will prolong the average life span of patients receiving the treatment by 20 months and will cost $25,000 per patient treated. What factors should the federal government take into consideration in making its decision?

1.13 Lawrence Summers served as secretary of the Treasury in the Clinton administration from 1999 to 2001 and as director of the National Economic Council in the Obama administration from 2009 to 2010. He has been quoted as giving the following defense of the economic approach:

> There is nothing morally unattractive about saying: We need to analyze which way of spending money on health care will produce more benefit and which less, and using our money as efficiently as we can. I don't think there is anything immoral about seeking to achieve environmental benefits at the lowest possible costs.

Would it be more ethical to reduce pollution without worrying about the cost, or by taking the cost into account? Briefly explain.

Source: David Wessel, "Precepts from Professor Summers," *Wall Street Journal*, October 17, 2002.

1.14 In *The Wonderful Wizard of Oz* and his other books about the Land of Oz, L. Frank Baum observed that if people's wants were limited enough, most goods would not be scarce. According to Baum, this was the case in Oz:

> There were no poor people in the Land of Oz, because there was no such thing as money.... Each person was given freely by his neighbors whatever he required for his use, which is as much as anyone may reasonably desire. Some tilled the lands and raised great crops of grain, which was divided equally among the whole population, so that all had enough. There were many tailors and dressmakers and shoemakers and the like, who made things that any who desired them might wear. Likewise there were jewelers who made ornaments for the person, which pleased and beautified the people, and these ornaments also were free to those who asked for them. Each man and woman, no

matter what he or she produced for the good of the community, was supplied by the neighbors with food and clothing and a house and furniture and ornaments and games. If by chance the supply ever ran short, more was taken from the great storehouses of the Ruler, which were afterward filled up again when there was more of any article than people needed... .

You will know, by what I have told you here, that the Land of Oz was a remarkable country. I do not suppose such an arrangement would be practical with us.

Do you agree with Baum that the economic system in Oz wouldn't work in the contemporary United States? Briefly explain why or why not.

Source: L. Frank Baum, *The Emerald City of Oz*, 1910, pp. 30–31.

2 Comparative Advantage and Trade

LEARNING OBJECTIVE: Describe comparative advantage and explain how it serves as the basis for trade.

Summary

Fundamentally, markets are about **trade**, which is the act of buying or selling. People trade on the basis of comparative advantage. An individual, a firm, or a country has a **comparative advantage** in producing a good or service if it can produce the good or service at the lowest opportunity cost. People are usually better off specializing in the activity for which they have a comparative advantage and trading for the other goods and services they need. It is important not to confuse comparative advantage with absolute advantage. An individual, a firm, or a country has an **absolute advantage** in producing a good or service if it can produce more of that good or service using the same amount of resources. It is possible to have an absolute advantage in producing a good or service without having a comparative advantage.

Visit **www.myeconlab.com** to complete these exercises online and get instant feedback.

Review Questions

2.1 What is absolute advantage? What is comparative advantage? Is it possible for a country to have a comparative advantage in producing a good without also having an absolute advantage? Briefly explain.

2.2 What is the basis for trade: absolute advantage or comparative advantage? How can an individual or a country gain from specialization and trade?

Problems and Applications

2.3 Look again at the information in Figure 4. Choose a rate of trading cherries for apples different from the rate used in the text (15 pounds of cherries for 10 pounds of apples) that will allow you and your neighbor to benefit from trading. Prepare a table like Table 1 to illustrate your answer.

2.4 Using the same amount of resources, the United States and Canada can both produce lumberjack shirts and

lumberjack boots, as shown in the following production possibilities frontiers:

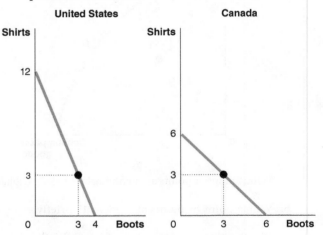

a. Who has a comparative advantage in producing lumberjack boots? Who has a comparative advantage in producing lumberjack shirts? Explain your reasoning.

b. Does either country have an absolute advantage in producing both goods? Explain.

c. Suppose that both countries are currently producing three pairs of boots and three shirts. Show that both can be better off if they each specialize in producing one good and then trade for the other.

2.5 **[Related to** Don't Let This Happen to You**]** In the 1950s, the economist Bela Balassa compared 28 manufacturing industries in the United States and Britain. In every one of the 28 industries, Balassa found that the United States had an absolute advantage. In these circumstances, would there have been any gain to the United States from importing any of these products from Britain? Explain.

2.6 **[Related to** Solved Problem 2**]** Suppose Iran and Iraq both produce oil and olive oil, which are sold for the same prices in both countries. The following table shows the combinations of both goods that each country can produce in a day, measured in thousands of barrels, using the same amounts of capital and labor:

Iraq		Iran	
Oil	Olive Oil	Oil	Olive Oil
0	8	0	4
2	6	1	3
4	4	2	2
6	2	3	1
8	0	4	0

a. Who has the comparative advantage in producing oil? Explain.

b. Can these two countries gain from trading oil and olive oil? Explain.

2.7 **[Related to** Solved Problem 2**]** Suppose that France and Germany both produce schnitzel and wine. The following table shows combinations of the goods that each country can produce in a day:

France		Germany	
Wine (bottles)	Schnitzel (pounds)	Wine (bottles)	Schnitzel (pounds)
0	8	0	15
1	6	1	12
2	4	2	9
3	2	3	6
4	0	4	3
		5	0

a. Who has a comparative advantage in producing wine? Who has a comparative advantage in producing schnitzel?

b. Suppose that France is currently producing 1 bottle of wine and 6 pounds of schnitzel, and Germany is currently producing 3 bottles of wine and 6 pounds of schnitzel. Demonstrate that France and Germany can both be better off if they specialize in producing only one good and then trade for the other.

2.8 Can an individual or a country produce beyond its production possibilities frontier? Can an individual or a country consume beyond its production possibilities frontier? Explain.

2.9 If Nicaragua can produce with the same amount of resources twice as much coffee as Columbia, explain how Columbia could have a comparative advantage in producing coffee.

2.10 Imagine that the next time the Indianapolis Colts play the New England Patriots at Lucas Oil Stadium in Indianapolis, Colts star quarterback Andrew Luck has a temporary lack of judgment and plans to sell Colts memorabilia during the game because he realizes that he can sell five times more Colts products than any other player. Likewise, imagine that you are a creative and effective manager at work and that you tell your employees that during the next six months, you plan to clean the offices because you can clean five times better than the cleaning staff. What error in judgment are both Andrew and you making? Why shouldn't Andrew and you do what you are better than anyone else at doing?

2.11 Is specialization and trade between individuals and countries more about having a job or about obtaining a higher standard of living? Individually, if you go from a situation of not trading with others (you produce everything yourself) to a situation of trading with others, do you still have a job? Does your standard of living increase? Likewise, if a country goes from not trading with other countries to trading with other countries, does it still have jobs? Does its standard of living increase?

2.12 In colonial America, the population was spread thinly over a large area, and transportation costs were very high because it was difficult to ship products by road for more than short distances. As a result, most of the free population lived on small farms, where they not only grew their own food but also usually made their own clothes and very rarely bought or sold anything for money. Explain why the incomes of these farmers were likely to rise as transportation costs fell. Use the concept of comparative advantage in your answer.

2.13 During the 1928 presidential election campaign, Herbert Hoover, the Republican candidate, argued that the United States should import only products that could not be produced here. Do you believe that this would be a good policy? Explain.

2.14 **[Related to the** Making the Connection: **Comparative Advantage, Opportunity Cost, and Housework]** In discussing dividing up household chores, Emily Oster, an economist at the University of Chicago, advises that: "No, you shouldn't always unload the dishwasher because you're better at it." If you are better at unloading the dishwasher, why shouldn't you be the one to unload it?

Source: Emily Oster, "Your're Dividing the Chores Wrong," *Slate*, November 21, 2012.

2.15 **[Related to the** Making the Connection: **Comparative Advantage, Opportunity Cost, and Housework]**According to the U.S. Bureau of Labor Statistics, the amount of time men devote to housework has been increasing, while the amount of time women devote to housework has been decreasing. Briefly explain whether there is an economic explanation for these trends.

Source: U.S. Bureau of Labor Statistics, *American Time Use Survey*.

3 The Market System

LEARNING OBJECTIVE: Explain the basic idea of how a market system works.

Summary

A **market** is a group of buyers and sellers of a good or service and the institution or arrangement by which they come together to trade. **Product markets** are markets for goods and services, such as computers and medical treatment. **Factor markets** are markets for the **factors of production**, such as labor, capital, natural resources, and entrepreneurial ability. A **circular-flow diagram** shows how participants in product markets and factor markets are linked. Adam Smith argued in his 1776 book *The Wealth of Nations* that in a **free market**, where the government does not control the production of goods and services, changes in prices lead firms to produce the goods and services most desired by consumers. If consumers demand more of a good, its price will rise. Firms respond to rising prices by increasing production. If consumers demand less of a good, its price will fall. Firms respond to falling prices by producing less of a good. An **entrepreneur** is someone who operates a business. In the market system, entrepreneurs are responsible for organizing the production of goods and services. The market system will work well only if there is protection for **property rights**, which are the rights of individuals and firms to use their property.

Visit **www.myeconlab.com** to complete these exercises online and get instant feedback.

Review Questions

3.1 What is a circular-flow diagram, and what does it demonstrate?

3.2 What are the two main categories of participants in markets? Which participants are of greatest importance in determining what goods and services are produced?

3.3 What is a free market? In what ways does a free market economy differ from a centrally planned economy?

3.4 What is an entrepreneur? Why do entrepreneurs play a key role in a market system?

3.5 Under what circumstances are firms likely to produce more of a good or service? Under what circumstances are firms likely to produce less of a good or service?

3.6 What are private property rights? What role do they play in the working of a market system? Why are independent courts important for a well-functioning economy?

Problems and Applications

3.7 Identify whether each of the following transactions will take place in the factor market or in the product market and whether households or firms are supplying the good or service or demanding the good or service:
   a. George buys a Tesla Model S.
   b. Tesla increases employment at its Fremont plant.
   c. George works 20 hours per week at McDonald's.
   d. George sells the land he owns to McDonald's so that it can build a new restaurant.

3.8 [Related to the Making the Connection: **A Story of the Market System in Action: How Do You Make an iPad?**] In *The Wealth of Nations*, Adam Smith wrote the following (Book I, Chapter II): "It is not from the benevolence

of the butcher, the brewer, or the baker, that we expect our dinner, but from their regard to their own interest." Briefly discuss what he meant by this.

3.9 [Related to the Making the Connection: **A Story of the Market System in Action: How Do You Make an iPad?**] According to an article in the *Wall Street Journal*, the parts contained in the BlackBerry Torch smartphone include a power management chip made by Texas Instruments (United States); a memory chip made by Samsung (South Korea); a GPS receiver made by CSR (United Kingdom); a radio frequency (RF) transceiver made by Dialog Semiconductor (Germany); an RF transceiver made by Renesas (Japan); an application and communications processor made by Marvell (United States); a video image processor made by STMicroelectronics (Switzerland); and plastic and stamped metal parts made by several firms in China. A firm in Mexico carries out final assembly of the Torch before it is shipped to BlackBerry for sale in the United States and other countries. Is it necessary for the managers in all these firms to know how the components of the Torch are manufactured and how the components are assembled into a smartphone? Is it necessary for the chief executive officer (CEO) of BlackBerry to know this information? Briefly explain.

Source: Jennifer Valentino-DeVries and Phred Dvorak, "Piece by Piece: The Suppliers Behind the New BlackBerry Torch Smartphone," *Wall Street Journal*, August 16, 2010.

3.10 In many parts of Europe during the mid-1770s, governments gave guilds, or organizations of producers, the authority to control who was allowed to produce a good, the amount of the good produced, and the price charged for the good. Would you expect more competition among producers in a *guild system* or in a market system? Was the consumer or the producer at the center of the guild system, and which is at the center of the market system? How would the two systems compare over time in terms of innovation of new products and technologies?

3.11 In a speech at the New York University Law School, Federal Reserve Chairman Ben Bernanke stated:

> Writing in the eighteenth century, Adam Smith conceived of the free-market system as an "invisible hand" that harnesses the pursuit of private interest to promote the public good. Smith's conception remains relevant today, notwithstanding the enormous increase in economic complexity since the Industrial Revolution.

Briefly explain the idea of the invisible hand. What is so important about the idea of the invisible hand?

Source: Ben S. Bernanke, "Financial Regulation and the Invisible Hand," speech made at the New York University Law School, New York, New York, April 11, 2007.

3.12 Evaluate the following argument: "Adam Smith's analysis is based on a fundamental flaw: He assumes that people are motivated by self-interest. But this isn't true. I'm not selfish, and most people I know aren't selfish."

3.13 Writing in the *New York Times*, Michael Lewis argued that "a market economy is premised on a system of incentives designed to encourage an ignoble human trait: self-interest." Do you agree that self-interest is an "ignoble human trait"? What incentives does a market system provide to encourage self-interest?

Source: Michael Lewis, "In Defense of the Boom," *New York Times*, October 27, 2002.

3.14 Some economists have been puzzled that although entrepreneurs take on the risk of losing money by starting new businesses, on average their incomes are lower than those of people with similar characteristics who go to work at large firms. Economist William Baumol believes part of the explanation for this puzzle may be that entrepreneurs are like people who buy lottery tickets. On average, people who don't buy lottery tickets are left with more money than people who buy tickets because lotteries take in more money than they give out. Baumol argues that "the masses of purchasers who grab up the [lottery] tickets are not irrational if they receive an adequate payment in another currency: psychic rewards."

a. What are "psychic rewards"?

b. What psychic rewards might an entrepreneur receive?

c. Do you agree with Baumol that an entrepreneur is like someone buying a lottery ticket? Briefly explain.

Source: William J. Baumol, *The Microtheory of Innovative Entrepreneurship*, Princeton, NJ: Princeton University Press, 2010.

3.15 The 2009 International Property Rights Index study states:

> [T]hose developing countries that respect property rights grow on average faster than those that fail to provide sound legal and political environments and protection for physical property rights.

Why would the protection of property rights be likely to increase economic growth in a developing, or low-income, country?

Source: Gaurav Tiwari, "Report: Property Rights Linked to Economic Security," *International Property Rights Index 2012 Report*.

3.16 According to an article on Phillyburbs.com, some farmers in rural Pennsylvania are causing a "stink" by using pig manure for fertilizer. The farmers purchase the pig manure, which is an organic fertilizer, from a nearby pork processing plant and spread it across the fields where they grow corn and soybeans. The article asserts that the farmers switched to pig manure because of the skyrocketing price of chemical fertilizers. Some of the residents of Milford, however, have complained about the smell, but the "farmers are likely protected under Pennsylvania's Right to Farm Act, which allows farmers to engage in practices that are common to agriculture."

a. What price signal did the farmers respond to in their switch to the organic pig manure fertilizer?

b. According to the Pennsylvania Right to Farm Act, do the farmers or the townspeople have the property right to the smell of the air around the farms? (Some of the residents did ask the township to urge the farmers to plow under the manure to reduce its stench.)

Source: Amanda Cregan, "Milford Farmers Switch to Pig Manure Causing a Stink for Neighbors," Phillyburbs.com, March 6, 2013.

3.17 **[Related to the** Making the Connection: **Who Owns *The Wizard of Oz*?]** The British historian Thomas Macaulay once remarked that copyrights are "a tax on readers." In what sense are copyrights a tax on readers? If copyrights are a tax on readers, why do governments enact them?

Glossary

Absolute advantage The ability of an individual, a firm, or a country to produce more of a good or service than competitors, using the same amount of resources.

Circular-flow diagram A model that illustrates how participants in markets are linked.

Comparative advantage The ability of an individual, a firm, or a country to produce a good or service at a lower opportunity cost than competitors.

Economic growth The ability of an economy to produce increasing quantities of goods and services.

Entrepreneur Someone who operates a business, bringing together the factors of production—labor, capital, and natural resources—to produce goods and services.

Factor market A market for the factors of production, such as labor, capital, natural resources, and entrepreneurial ability.

Factors of production Labor, capital, natural resources, and other inputs used to produce goods and services.

Free market A market with few government restrictions on how a good or service can be produced

or sold or on how a factor of production can be employed.

Market A group of buyers and sellers of a good or service and the institution or arrangement by which they come together to trade.

Opportunity cost The highest-valued alternative that must be given up to engage in an activity.

Product market A market for goods—such as computers—or services—such as medical treatment.

Production possibilities frontier (*PPF*) A curve showing the maximum attainable

combinations of two products that may be produced with available resources and current technology.

Property rights The rights individuals or firms have to the exclusive use of their property, including the right to buy or sell it.

Scarcity A situation in which unlimited wants exceed the limited resources available to fulfill those wants.

Trade The act of buying and selling.

Credits

Where Prices Come From:
The Interaction of Demand and Supply

From Chapter 3 of *Economics*, Fifth Edition. R. Glenn Hubbard and Anthony Patrick O'Brien. Copyright © 2015 by Pearson Education, Inc. All rights reserved.

Where Prices Come From: The Interaction of Demand and Supply

Chapter Outline and Learning Objectives

1 **The Demand Side of the Market**
  Discuss the variables that influence demand.

2 **The Supply Side of the Market**
  Discuss the variables that influence supply.

3 **Market Equilibrium: Putting Demand and Supply Together**
  Use a graph to illustrate market equilibrium.

4 **The Effect of Demand and Supply Shifts on Equilibrium**
  Use demand and supply graphs to predict changes in prices and quantities.

Smartphones: The Indispensible Product?

If you're like most students, professors, and businesspeople, you carry your cellphone or smartphone everywhere you go. With a cellphone, you can make and receive phone calls and text messages. With a smartphone, you can do much more: send and receive e-mails, check Facebook and other social media sites, share photos, and stream videos. By 2013, more than two million smartphones were being sold *per day* worldwide.

Ten years ago, the BlackBerry, sold by the Canadian-based firm Research in Motion, was the only widely used smartphone. The BlackBerry was expensive, though, and most buyers were businesspeople who wanted to send and answer e-mails while away from the office. When Apple introduced the iPhone in 2007, smartphones started to become popular with a wider market of consumers, including students. With the release of the iPhone 3G in 2008, Apple announced that a section of its immensely popular iTunes music and video store would be devoted to applications (or "apps") for the iPhone. Major software companies, as well as individuals writing their first software programs, have posted games, calendars, dictionaries, and many other types of apps to the iTunes store. Apple sold more than 3 million iPhones within a month of launching the iPhone 3G.

Although initially Apple had a commanding share of the smartphone market, competitors soon appeared. Companies such as Samsung, Nokia, HTC, LG, Huawei, Microsoft, Sony, ZTE, and Panasonic introduced smartphones. Most of these manufacturers followed Apple in developing apps or providing users access to online app stores.

The intense competition among firms selling smartphones is a striking example of how the market responds to changes in consumer tastes. As many consumers indicated that they would pay more for a smartphone than a regular cellphone, firms scrambled to meet the demand for smartphones. Although intense competition is not always good news for firms trying to sell products, it is great news for consumers because it increases the available choice of products and lowers the prices consumers pay for those products.

AN INSIDE LOOK discusses how Google faced the problem of not having enough of its Nexus 4 smartphones to meet customer demand, while Apple worried about overproduction of its iPhone 5.

Sources: Brian X. Chen, "Smartphones Finally Surpass the Feature Phone," *New York Times*, April 26, 2013; Eric Pfanner, "Competition Designed to Spread Basic Technologies," *New York Times*, April 18, 2013; and Brad Reed, "A Brief History of Smartphones," pcworld.com, June 18, 2010.

Economics in Your Life

Will You Buy an Apple iPhone or a Samsung Galaxy?

Suppose you want to buy a smartphone and are choosing between an Apple iPhone and a Samsung Galaxy S. If you buy an iPhone, you will have access to more applications—or "apps"—that can increase the enjoyment and performance of your smartphone. In addition, the iPhone is thin, lightweight, and sleek looking. One strategy Samsung can use to overcome these advantages is to compete based on price and value. Would you choose to buy a Galaxy S if it had a lower price than a comparable iPhone? If your income increased, would it affect your decision about which smartphone to buy? As you read this chapter, try to answer these questions. You can check your answers against those we provide at the end of this chapter.

In this chapter, we explore the model of demand and supply, which is the most powerful tool in economics.

Because economic models rely on assumptions, the models are simplifications of reality. In some cases, the assumptions of a model may not seem to describe exactly the economic situation being analyzed. For example, the model of demand and supply assumes that we are analyzing a **perfectly competitive market**, which is a market where there are many buyers and sellers, all the products sold are identical, and there are no barriers to new firms entering the market. These assumptions are very restrictive and apply exactly to only a few markets, such as the markets for wheat and other agricultural products. Experience has shown, however, that the model of demand and supply can be very useful in analyzing markets where competition among sellers is intense, even if there are relatively few sellers and the products being sold are not identical. In fact, in recent studies, the model of demand and supply has been successful in analyzing markets with as few as four buyers and four sellers. In the end, the usefulness of a model depends on how well it can predict outcomes in a market. As we will see in this chapter, this model is often successful in predicting changes in quantities and prices in many markets.

We begin studying the model of demand and supply by discussing consumers and the demand side of the market, before turning to firms and the supply side. Throughout this text, we will apply this model to understand business, the economy, and economic policy.

Perfectly competitive market A market that meets the conditions of (1) many buyers and sellers, (2) all firms selling identical products, and (3) no barriers to new firms entering the market.

The Demand Side of the Market

1 LEARNING OBJECTIVE

Discuss the variables that influence demand.

In a market system consumers ultimately determine which goods and services will be produced. The most successful businesses are the ones that respond best to consumer demand. But what determines consumer demand for a product? Certainly, many factors influence the willingness of consumers to buy a particular product. For example, consumers who are considering buying a smartphone, such as an Apple iPhone or a Samsung Galaxy S, will make their decisions based on, among other factors, the income they have available to spend and the effectiveness of the advertising campaigns of the companies that sell smartphones. The main factor in most consumer decisions, though, is the price of the product. So, it makes sense to begin with price when analyzing how consumers decide to buy a product. It is important to note that when we discuss demand, we are considering not what a consumer *wants* to buy but what the consumer is both willing and *able* to buy.

Demand Schedules and Demand Curves

Tables that show the relationship between the price of a product and the quantity of the product demanded are called **demand schedules**. The table in Figure 1 shows the number of smartphones consumers would be willing to buy over the course of a week at five different prices. The amount of a good or service that a consumer is willing and able to purchase at a given price is called the **quantity demanded**. The graph in Figure 1 plots the numbers from the table as a **demand curve**, which shows the relationship between the price of a product and the quantity of the product demanded. (Note that, for convenience, we made the demand curve in Figure 1 a straight line, or linear. There is no reason that all demand curves need to be straight lines.) The demand curve in Figure 1 shows the **market demand**, which is the demand by all the consumers of a given good or service. The market for a product, such as restaurant meals, that is sold locally would include all the consumers in a city or a relatively small area. The market for a product, such as smartphones, that is sold internationally would include all the consumers in the world.

Demand schedule A table that shows the relationship between the price of a product and the quantity of the product demanded.

Quantity demanded The amount of a good or service that a consumer is willing and able to purchase at a given price.

Demand curve A curve that shows the relationship between the price of a product and the quantity of the product demanded.

Market demand The demand by all the consumers of a given good or service.

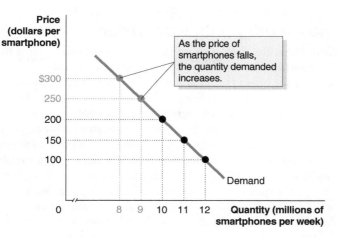

As the price of smartphones falls, the quantity demanded increases.

Figure 1

A Demand Schedule and Demand Curve

As the price changes, consumers change the quantity of smartphones they are willing to buy. We can show this as a *demand schedule* in a table or as a *demand curve* on a graph. The table and graph both show that as the price of smartphones falls, the quantity demanded increases. When the price of smartphones is $300, consumers buy 8 million smartphones per week. When the price falls to $250, consumers buy 9 million. Therefore, the demand curve for smartphones is downward sloping.

The demand curve in Figure 1 slopes downward because consumers will buy more smartphones as the price falls. When the price of smartphones is $300, consumers buy 8 million smartphones per week. When the price falls to $250, consumers buy 9 million. Buyers demand a larger quantity of a product as the price falls because the product becomes less expensive relative to other products and because they can afford to buy more at a lower price.

The Law of Demand

The inverse relationship between the price of a product and the quantity of the product demanded is called the **law of demand**: Holding everything else constant, when the price of a product falls, the quantity demanded of the product will increase, and when the price of a product rises, the quantity demanded of the product will decrease. The law of demand holds for any market demand curve. Economists have found only a very few exceptions to this law.

Law of demand The rule that, holding everything else constant, when the price of a product falls, the quantity demanded of the product will increase, and when the price of a product rises, the quantity demanded of the product will decrease.

What Explains the Law of Demand?

It makes sense that consumers will buy more of a good when its price falls and less of a good when its price rises, but let's look more closely at why this result holds. When the price of a product falls, consumers buy a larger quantity because of the *substitution effect* and the *income effect*.

Substitution Effect The **substitution effect** refers to the change in the quantity demanded of a good that results from a change in price making the good more or less expensive *relative* to other goods that are *substitutes*. When the price of smartphones falls, people will substitute buying smartphones for other goods, such as regular cellphones or even tablet computers, such as the iPad.

Substitution effect The change in the quantity demanded of a good that results from a change in price making the good more or less expensive relative to other goods that are substitutes.

Income Effect The **income effect** of a price change refers to the change in the quantity demanded of a good that results from the effect of a change in the good's price on consumers' *purchasing power*. Purchasing power is the quantity of goods a consumer can buy with a fixed amount of income. When the price of a good falls, the increased purchasing power of consumers' incomes will usually lead them to purchase a larger quantity of the good. When the price of a good rises, the decreased purchasing power of consumers' incomes will usually lead them to purchase a smaller quantity of the good.

Income effect The change in the quantity demanded of a good that results from the effect of a change in the good's price on consumers' purchasing power.

Note that although we can analyze them separately, the substitution effect and the income effect occur simultaneously whenever a price changes. So, a fall in the price of smartphones leads consumers to buy more smartphones both because the smartphones are now less expensive relative to substitute products and because the purchasing power of consumers' incomes has increased.

Holding Everything Else Constant: The *Ceteris paribus* Condition

Ceteris paribus ("all else equal") condition The requirement that when analyzing the relationship between two variables—such as price and quantity demanded—other variables must be held constant.

Notice that the definition of the law of demand contains the phrase *holding everything else constant*. In constructing the market demand curve for smartphones, we focused only on the effect that changes in the price of smartphones would have on the quantity consumers would be willing and able to buy. We were holding constant other variables that might affect the willingness of consumers to buy smartphones. Economists refer to the necessity of holding all variables other than price constant in constructing a demand curve as the **_ceteris paribus_ condition**. *Ceteris paribus* means "all else equal" in Latin.

What would happen if we allowed a change in a variable—other than price—that might affect the willingness of consumers to buy smartphones? Consumers would then change the quantity they demanded at each price. We can illustrate this effect by shifting the market demand curve. A shift of a demand curve is *an increase or a decrease in demand*. A movement along a demand curve is *an increase or a decrease in the quantity demanded*. As Figure 2 shows, we shift the demand curve to the right if consumers decide to buy more smartphones at each price, and we shift the demand curve to the left if consumers decide to buy less at each price.

Variables That Shift Market Demand

Many variables other than price can influence market demand. These five are the most important:

- Income
- Prices of related goods
- Tastes
- Population and demographics
- Expected future prices

We next discuss how changes in each of these variables affect the market demand curve.

Normal good A good for which the demand increases as income rises and decreases as income falls.

Income The income that consumers have available to spend affects their willingness and ability to buy a good. Suppose that the market demand curve in Figure 1 represents the willingness of consumers to buy smartphones when average household income is $50,000. If average household income rises to $52,000, the demand for smartphones will increase, which we show by shifting the demand curve to the right. A good is a **normal good** when the demand for the good increases following a rise in

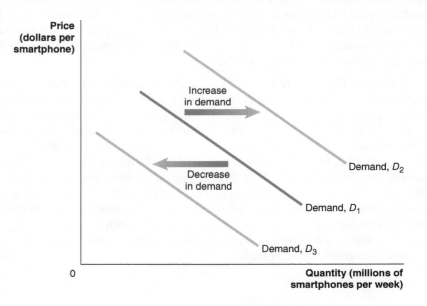

Figure 2

Shifting the Demand Curve

When consumers increase the quantity of a product they want to buy at a given price, the demand curve shifts to the right, from D_1 to D_2. When consumers decrease the quantity of a product they want to buy at a given price, the demand curve shifts to the left, from D_1 to D_3.

income and decreases following a fall in income. Most goods are normal goods, but the demand for some goods falls when income rises and rises when income falls. For instance, as your income rises, you might buy less canned tuna or fewer instant noodles and buy more shrimp or whole grain pasta. A good is an **inferior good** when the demand for the good decreases following a rise in income and increases following a fall in income. So, for you, canned tuna and instant noodles would be examples of inferior goods—not because they are of low quality but because you buy less of them as your income increases.

Inferior good A good for which the demand increases as income falls and decreases as income rises.

Prices of Related Goods The prices of other goods can also affect consumers' demand for a product. Consumers who would use a smartphone primarily for making phone calls could use a regular cellphone instead. Consumers who would use a smartphone to answer e-mails or surf the Web could use a tablet computer instead. Goods and services that can be used for the same purpose are called **substitutes**. When two goods are substitutes, the more you buy of one, the less you will buy of the other. A decrease in the price of a substitute causes the demand curve for a good to shift to the left. An increase in the price of a substitute causes the demand curve for a good to shift to the right.

Substitutes Goods and services that can be used for the same purpose.

Suppose that the market demand curve in Figure 1 represents the willingness and ability of consumers to buy smartphones during a week when the average price of tablet computers is $700. If the average price of tablets falls to $600, how will the market demand for smartphones change? Consumers will demand fewer smartphones at every price. We show this change by shifting the demand curve for smartphones to the left.

Making the Connection	Are Tablet Computers Substitutes for E-Readers?

Two products are rarely perfect substitutes for each other in the sense that consumers use them for exactly the same purpose. For example, if you want to read e-books, you would buy an e-reader, such as Barnes & Noble's Nook, Amazon's Kindle, or Kobo's Aura HD. If you want to send and receive e-mails, check your Facebook page, or watch a video, you would probably buy a tablet computer, such as Apple's iPad or Samsung's Galaxy Tab. Although you could use tablet computers to read e-books, tablets have higher prices and are often heavier than e-readers, which makes them less comfortable to hold for an extended period of reading. In addition, tablets typically don't display text as sharply as e-readers.

So e-readers and tablets are substitutes—but they aren't perfect substitutes. To correctly forecast sales and produce the correct quantity of e-readers, firms that produce them need to evaluate how close a substitute consumers consider e-readers and tablets to be. If people who read a lot of e-books strongly prefer e-readers to tablets, then e-reader sales are likely to be higher than if those people consider e-readers and tablets close substitutes.

By 2013, it had become clear that consumers considered the two products close substitutes. E-reader sales were falling much faster than many industry analysts had been expecting. Although 23 million e-readers were sold worldwide in 2011, only 16 million were sold in 2012, and as few as 5.8 million were expected to be sold in 2013. In July 2013, Barnes & Noble's CEO William Lynch resigned after losses from selling the Nook e-reader more than offset the company's profits from its retail stores. As one analyst explained: "It's looking like e-readers were a device for a particular moment in time that, more rapidly than we or anyone else thought, has been replaced by a new technology." Unfortunately for firms selling e-readers, consumers decided that tablets were a close substitute.

By 2013, many consumers saw the tablet computer as a close substitute for the e-reader.

Sources: Jeffrey A. Trachtenberg, "Barnes & Noble Pulls Back After Losses In Tablet Wars," *Wall Street Journal*, June 25, 2013; Brian X. Chen, "E-Reader Market Shrinks Faster Than Many Predicted," *New York Times*, December 20, 2012; Tom Gara, "The Future of the Nook," *Wall Street Journal*, May 9, 2013; Erik Sofge, "The Best E-Reader: Kobo's Aura HD," *Wall Street Journal*, May 3, 2013; and Tom Gara, "One More Casualty Of Barnes & Noble's Nook Problems: Its CEO," *Wall Street Journal*, July 8, 2013.

Your Turn: Test your understanding by doing related problem 1.12 at the end of this chapter.

Complements Goods and services that are used together.

Goods and services that are used together—such as hot dogs and hot dog buns—are called **complements**. When two goods are complements, the more consumers buy of one, the more they will buy of the other. A decrease in the price of a complement causes the demand curve for a good to shift to the right. An increase in the price of a complement causes the demand curve for a good to shift to the left.

Many people use applications, or "apps," on their smartphones. So, smartphones and apps are complements. Suppose the market demand curve in Figure 1 represents the willingness of consumers to buy smartphones at a time when the average price of an app is $2.99. If the average price of apps falls to $0.99, consumers will buy more apps *and* more smartphones, and the demand curve for smartphones will shift to the right.

Tastes Consumers can be influenced by an advertising campaign for a product. If Apple, Samsung, LG, and other firms making smartphones begin to advertise heavily, consumers are more likely to buy smartphones at every price, and the demand curve will shift to the right. An economist would say that the advertising campaign has affected consumers' *taste* for smartphones. Taste is a catchall category that refers to the many subjective elements that can enter into a consumer's decision to buy a product. A consumer's taste for a product can change for many reasons. Sometimes trends play a substantial role. For example, the popularity of low-carbohydrate diets caused a decline in demand for some goods, such as bread and donuts, and an increase in demand for beef. In general, when consumers' taste for a product increases, the demand curve will shift to the right, and when consumers' taste decreases, the demand curve will shift to the left.

Demographics The characteristics of a population with respect to age, race, and gender.

Population and Demographics As the population of a country increases, the number of consumers and the demand for most products will increase. The **demographics** of a population refers to its characteristics, with respect to age, race, and gender. As the demographics of a country or region change, the demand for particular goods will increase or decrease because different categories of people tend to have different preferences for those goods. For instance, Hispanics are expected to increase from 17 percent of the U.S. population in 2012 to 29 percent in 2050. This increase will expand demand for Spanish-language books and cable television channels, among other goods and services.

Making the Connection | **Coke and Pepsi Are Hit by U.S. Demographics**

Traditionally, consumption of soft drinks, such as Coca-Cola and Pepsi-Cola, has been much higher among people aged 30 and below than among older consumers. For many years, the demographics of soft drink consumption did not pose a problem for U.S. soft drink companies. As one generation aged and moved on to drinking coffee, tea, and other beverages, another generation of soft drink buyers took its place. In recent years, though, soft drink companies have begun to experience gradually decreasing sales in the United States.

One reason for declining soft drink sales is that the average age of the U.S. population is increasing. Following the end of World War II in 1945, the United States experienced a "baby boom," as birthrates rose and remained high through the early 1960s. Falling birthrates after 1965 mean that the baby boom generation is larger than the generations before and after it. As the baby boomers have aged and reduced their soft drink consumption, the generations that have followed have been smaller.

Even worse news for the soft drink companies is that younger consumers are not buying as much Coke, Pepsi, and other soft drinks as their parents and grandparents did. Younger consumers are more likely to buy energy drinks, water, juice, coffee, or tea than past generations. Part of the move away from soda is due to increased publicity about the potential health problems resulting from drinking soda. Some public health advocates argue that the amount of added sugars in many soft drinks make them unsafe and have called on the federal government to regulate the ingredients in soft

Younger consumers are buying more water and juice and less Coke and Pepsi than previous generations.

drinks. Many schools have reduced the availability of sodas in cafeterias and vending machines. As a result, consumption per person of carbonated soft drinks declined by more than 15 percent in the United States between 2005 and 2013. In early 2013, Pepsi announced that in just the past year, its soda sales in North America had declined by about 5 percent. The double problem of an aging population and a younger population not as inclined to drink soda led an article in the *Wall Street Journal* to ask: "Is This the End of the Soft-Drink Era?"

There were, however, some rays of sunshine for U.S. soft drink companies. Although demographics were hurting the demand for soft drinks in the United States, a growing population of young people worldwide meant that the global demand for soft drinks, particularly in developing countries, was increasing. U.S. soft drink companies responded to this opportunity. Coca-Cola announced a multiyear plan to increase sales in foreign markets, including investments of $5 billion in new bottling plants in India and $4 billion in China. As Indra K. Nooyi, PepsiCo's chairman and chief executive officer, put it in the company's *Annual Report*: "Looking back to 2006, emerging and developing markets accounted for 24 percent of our net revenue; in 2012, they represented 35 percent of our net revenue. And over the long term, we are looking to grow our business in these markets at high single digits to low double digits."

Clearly, soft drink companies needed to be aware of the effects of changing demographics on the demand for their products.

Sources: Mike Esterl, "Is This the End of the Soft-Drink Era?" *Wall Street Journal*, January 18, 2013; "PepsiCo Beats Expectations Despite Soda Struggles," Associated Press, April 13, 2013; PepsiCo, *2012 Annual Report*, www.pepsico.com /annual12/; and Stephanie Strom, "Health Officials Urge F.D.A. to Limit Sweeteners in Sodas," *New York Times*, February 13, 2013.

Your Turn: Test your understanding by doing related problem 1.13 at the end of this chapter.

Expected Future Prices Consumers choose not only which products to buy but also when to buy them. For instance, if enough consumers become convinced that houses will be selling for lower prices in three months, the demand for houses will decrease now, as some consumers postpone their purchases to wait for the expected price decrease. Alternatively, if enough consumers become convinced that the price of houses will be higher in three months, the demand for houses will increase now, as some consumers try to beat the expected price increase.

Table 1 summarizes the most important variables that cause market demand curves to shift. Note that the table shows the shift in the demand curve that results from an *increase* in each of the variables. A *decrease* in these variables would cause the demand curve to shift in the opposite direction.

A Change in Demand versus a Change in Quantity Demanded

It is important to understand the difference between a *change in demand* and a *change in quantity demanded*. A change in demand refers to a shift of the demand curve. A shift occurs if there is a change in one of the variables—*other than the price of the product*—that affects the willingness of consumers to buy the product. A change in quantity demanded refers to a movement along the demand curve as a result of a change in the product's price. Figure 3 illustrates this important distinction. If the price of smartphones falls from $300 to $250, the result will be a movement along the demand curve from point *A* to point *B*—an increase in quantity demanded from 8 million to 9 million. If consumers' incomes increase, or if another factor changes that makes consumers want more of the product at every price, the demand curve will shift to the right—an increase in demand. In this case, the increase in demand from D_1 to D_2 causes the quantity of smartphones demanded at a price of $300 to increase from 8 million at point *A* to 10 million at point *C*.

Table 1

Variables That Shift Market Demand Curves

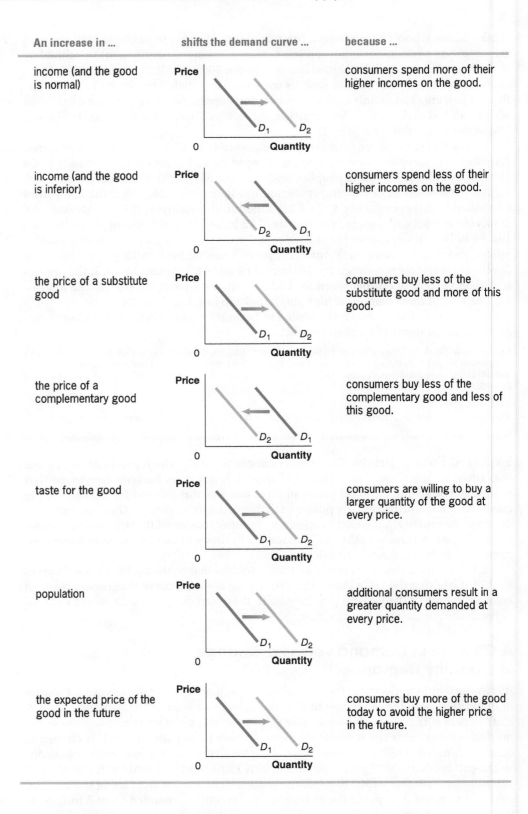

An increase in ...	shifts the demand curve ...	because ...
income (and the good is normal)	D_1 D_2	consumers spend more of their higher incomes on the good.
income (and the good is inferior)	D_2 D_1	consumers spend less of their higher incomes on the good.
the price of a substitute good	D_1 D_2	consumers buy less of the substitute good and more of this good.
the price of a complementary good	D_2 D_1	consumers buy less of the complementary good and less of this good.
taste for the good	D_1 D_2	consumers are willing to buy a larger quantity of the good at every price.
population	D_1 D_2	additional consumers result in a greater quantity demanded at every price.
the expected price of the good in the future	D_1 D_2	consumers buy more of the good today to avoid the higher price in the future.

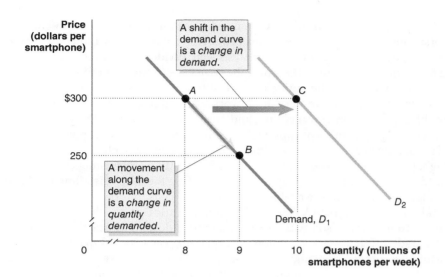

A shift in the demand curve is a *change in demand*.

A movement along the demand curve is a *change in quantity demanded*.

Demand, D_1

D_2

Figure 3

A Change in Demand versus a Change in Quantity Demanded

If the price of smartphones falls from $300 to $250, the result will be a movement along the demand curve from point A to point B—an increase in quantity demanded from 8 million to 9 million. If consumers' incomes increase, or if another factor changes that makes consumers want more of the product at every price, the demand curve will shift to the right—an increase in demand. In this case, the increase in demand from D_1 to D_2 causes the quantity of smartphones demanded at a price of $300 to increase from 8 million at point A to 10 million at point C.

Making the Connection

Forecasting the Demand for iPhones

One of the most important decisions that managers of any large firm face is which new products to develop. A firm must devote people, time, and money to design a new product, negotiate with suppliers, formulate a marketing campaign, and perform many other tasks. But any firm has only limited resources and so faces a trade-off: Resources used to develop one product will not be available to develop another product. Ultimately, the products a firm chooses to develop will be those that it believes will be the most profitable. So, to decide which products to develop, firms need to forecast the demand for those products.

David Sobotta, who worked at Apple for 20 years and eventually became its national sales manager, has described discussions at Apple during 2002 about whether to develop a tablet computer. According to Sobotta, representatives of the U.S. National Institutes of

Will demand for iPhones continue to grow despite increasing competition?

Health urged Apple to develop a tablet computer, arguing that it would be particularly useful to doctors, nurses, and hospitals. In 2001, Bill Gates, chairman of Microsoft, had predicted that "within five years ... [tablet PCs] will be the most popular form of PC sold in America." Apple's managers decided not to develop a tablet computer, however, because they believed the technology available at that time was too complex for an average computer user, and they also believed that the demand from doctors and nurses would be small. Apple's forecast was correct. Despite Bill Gates's prediction, in 2006 tablet computers made up only 1 percent of the computer market. According to Sobotta, "Apple executives had a theory that the route to success will not be through selling thousands of relatively expensive things, but millions of very inexpensive things like iPods."

Apple continued to work on smartphones, developing the technology to eliminate keyboards in favor of touchscreen displays. Rather than proceeding immediately to build a tablet computer, Steve Jobs, then Apple's CEO, realized he could use this technology in a different way: "I thought 'My God we can build a phone out of this.' " From its introduction in 2007, the iPhone was an immediate success. By mid-2013, Apple had sold more than 350 million iPhones worldwide.

As Apple attempts to forecast demand for its iPhone, it needs to consider two factors: competition from other firms producing smartphones and competition from substitute goods. By 2013, industry analysts were divided as to whether Apple would be able to maintain its share of the smartphone market in the face of increasing competition from other firms. The outlook for substitute goods was also mixed. Smartphones were an increasing share of the overall worldwide cellphone market. Many consumers were shifting from regular cellphones and music players, such as iPods, to smartphones. The increasing availability of apps, including new mobile payment apps that can be used in place of credit cards, was increasing the usefulness of smartphones. Some consumers, though, preferred the use of tablets, such as Apple's iPad or Samsung's Galaxy Tab, with their larger screens, for checking e-mails or surfing the Web. Installing the Skype app even made it possible to use a tablet to make phone calls.

Taking these factors together, Apple was optimistic that its iPhone sales would double by 2016 in comparison with 2012. As any firm does in forecasting demand, Apple faced a trade-off: If it was too cautious in expanding capacity or buying components for smartphones, other firms might seize a large share of the market. But, if Apple was too optimistic, it ran the risk of spending on capacity to produce more units than it could actually sell—an outcome that might turn potential profits into losses. Apple spent several billion dollars to buy large quantities of motion sensors, screens, and other components from suppliers. That will be money well spent … if the forecast of demand turns out to be accurate. Time will tell whether the future demand for smartphones will be as large as Apple and other firms were forecasting.

Source: "Apple Reports Second Quarter Results: 37.4 Million iPhones Sold; 19.5 Million iPads Sold," www.apple.com, April 23, 2013; Jérémie Bouchaud, "Apple and Samsung Are Top Buyers of MEMS Motion Sensors in Handsets and Tablets," www.isuppli.com, April 1, 2013; Jay Yarow, "CITI: Apple Is Pretty Much Doomed," www.businessinsider.com, March 6, 2013; David Sobotta, "What Jobs Told Me on the iPhone," *Guardian* (London), January 3, 2007; "Jobs Says iPad Idea Came Before iPhone," Associated Press, January 2, 2010; and "More Smartphones Were Shipped in Q1 2013 Than Feature Phones, an Industry First According to IDC," www.idc.com, April 25, 2013.

Your Turn: Test your understanding by doing related problem 1.17 at the end of this chapter.

2 LEARNING OBJECTIVE

Discuss the variables that influence supply.

Quantity supplied The amount of a good or service that a firm is willing and able to supply at a given price.

Supply schedule A table that shows the relationship between the price of a product and the quantity of the product supplied.

Supply curve A curve that shows the relationship between the price of a product and the quantity of the product supplied.

The Supply Side of the Market

Just as many variables influence the willingness and ability of consumers to buy a particular good or service, many variables influence the willingness and ability of firms to sell a good or service. The most important of these variables is price. The amount of a good or service that a firm is willing and able to supply at a given price is the **quantity supplied**. Holding other variables constant, when the price of a good rises, producing the good is more profitable, and the quantity supplied will increase. When the price of a good falls, selling the good is less profitable, and the quantity supplied will decrease. In addition, devoting more and more resources to the production of a good results in increasing marginal costs. If, for example, Apple, Samsung, LG, and other firms increase production of smartphones during a given time period, they are likely to find that the cost of producing additional smartphones increases as their suppliers run existing factories for longer hours and pay higher prices for components and higher wages for workers. With higher marginal costs, firms will supply a larger quantity only if the price is higher.

Supply Schedules and Supply Curves

A **supply schedule** is a table that shows the relationship between the price of a product and the quantity of the product supplied. The table in Figure 4 is a supply schedule showing the quantity of smartphones that firms would be willing to supply per month at different prices. The graph in Figure 4 plots the numbers from the table as a **supply curve**, which shows the relationship between the price of a product and the quantity of

Supply Schedule	
Price (dollars per smartphone)	Quantity (millions of smartphones per week)
$300	12
250	11
200	10
150	9
100	8

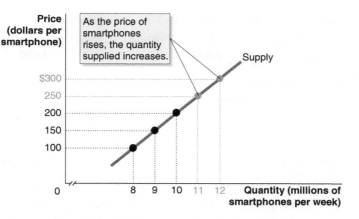

As the price of smartphones rises, the quantity supplied increases.

Figure 4

A Supply Schedule and Supply Curve

As the price changes, Apple, Samsung, LG, and other firms producing smartphones change the quantity they are willing to supply. We can show this as a *supply schedule* in a table or as a *supply curve* on a graph. The supply schedule and supply curve both show that as the price of smartphones rises, firms will increase the quantity they supply. At a price of $250 per smartphone, firms will supply 11 million smartphones per week. At a price of $300, firms will supply 12 million.

the product supplied. The supply schedule and supply curve both show that as the price of smartphones rises, firms will increase the quantity they supply. At a price of $250 per smartphone, firms will supply 11 million smartphones per week. At a higher price of $300, firms will supply 12 million. (Once again, we are assuming for convenience that the supply curve is a straight line, even though not all supply curves are actually straight lines.)

The Law of Supply

The *market supply curve* in Figure 4 is upward sloping. We expect most supply curves to be upward sloping, according to the **law of supply**, which states that, holding everything else constant, increases in price cause increases in the quantity supplied, and decreases in price cause decreases in the quantity supplied. Notice that the definition of the law of supply—like the definition of the law of demand—contains the phrase *holding everything else constant*. If only the price of the product changes, there is a movement along the supply curve, which is *an increase or a decrease in the quantity supplied*. As Figure 5 shows, if any other variable that affects the willingness of firms to supply a good changes, the supply curve will shift, which is *an increase or a decrease in supply*. When firms increase the quantity of a product they want to sell at a given price, the supply curve shifts to the right. The shift from S_1 to S_3 represents *an increase in supply*. When firms decrease the quantity of a product they want to sell at a given price, the supply curve shifts to the left. The shift from S_1 to S_2 represents *a decrease in supply*.

Law of supply The rule that, holding everything else constant, increases in price cause increases in the quantity supplied, and decreases in price cause decreases in the quantity supplied.

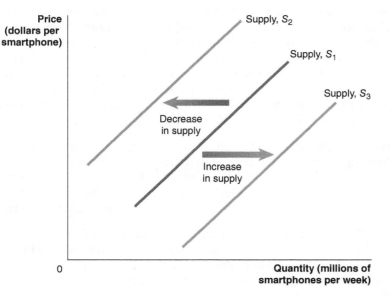

Figure 5

Shifting the Supply Curve

When firms increase the quantity of a product they want to sell at a given price, the supply curve shifts to the right. The shift from S_1 to S_3 represents an *increase in supply*. When firms decrease the quantity of a product they want to sell at a given price, the supply curve shifts to the left. The shift from S_1 to S_2 represents a *decrease in supply*.

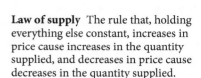

Variables That Shift Market Supply

The following are the most important variables that shift market supply:

- Prices of inputs
- Technological change
- Prices of substitutes in production
- Number of firms in the market
- Expected future prices

We next discuss how changes in each of these variables affect the market supply curve.

Prices of Inputs The factor most likely to cause the supply curve for a product to shift is a change in the price of an *input*. An input is anything used in the production of a good or service. For instance, if the price of a component of smartphones, such as memory chips, rises, the cost of producing smartphones will increase, and smartphones will be less profitable at every price. The supply of smartphones will decline, and the market supply curve for smartphones will shift to the left. Similarly, if the price of an input declines, the supply of smartphones will increase, and the market supply curve will shift to the right.

Technological change A positive or negative change in the ability of a firm to produce a given level of output with a given quantity of inputs.

Technological Change A second factor that causes a change in supply is **technological change**, which is a positive or negative change in the ability of a firm to produce a given level of output with a given quantity of inputs. Positive technological change occurs whenever a firm is able to produce more output using the same amount of inputs. In other words, the *productivity* of the firm's workers or machines has increased. If a firm can produce more output with the same amount of inputs, its costs will be lower, and the good will be more profitable to produce at any given price. As a result, when positive technological change occurs, the firm will increase the quantity supplied at every price, and its supply curve will shift to the right.

Negative technological change is relatively rare, although it could result from an earthquake or another natural disaster or from a war that reduces the ability of firms to supply as much output with a given amount of inputs. Negative technological change will raise firms' costs, and firms will earn lower profits from producing the good. Therefore, negative technological change will cause the market supply curve to shift to the left.

Prices of Substitutes in Production Firms often choose which good or service they will produce. Alternative products that a firm could produce are called *substitutes in production*. Many of the firms that produce smartphones also produce other consumer electronics. For example, Apple produces the iPad and Samsung produces the Galaxy Tab. These products typically use similar components and are often assembled in the same factories. If the price of smartphones increases relative to the price of tablet computers, smartphones will become more profitable, and Apple, Samsung, and other firms making smartphones will shift some of their productive capacity from tablets toward smartphones. The firms will offer more smartphones for sale at every price, so the supply curve for smartphones will shift to the right.

Number of Firms in the Market A change in the number of firms in the market will change supply. When new firms *enter* a market, the supply curve shifts to the right, and when existing firms leave, or *exit*, a market, the supply curve shifts to the left. In 2013, for instance, Amazon was widely expected to enter the market for smartphones. Amazon's entry will shift the market supply curve for smartphones to the right.

Expected Future Prices If a firm expects that the price of its product will be higher in the future, it has an incentive to decrease supply now and increase it in the future. For instance, if Apple believes that prices for smartphones are temporarily low—perhaps because of a recession—it may store some of its production today to sell later on, when it expects prices to be higher.

Table 2

Variables That Shift Market Supply Curves

An increase in ...	shifts the supply curve ...	because ...
the price of an input		the costs of producing the good rise.
productivity		the costs of producing the good fall.
the price of a substitute in production		more of the substitute is produced and less of the good is produced.
the number of firms in the market		additional firms result in a greater quantity supplied at every price.
the expected future price of the product		less of the good will be offered for sale today to take advantage of the higher price in the future.

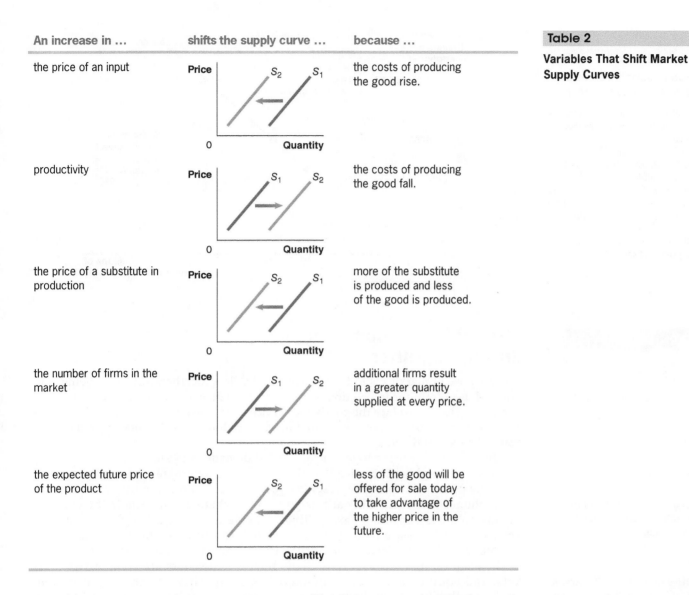

Table 2 summarizes the most important variables that cause market supply curves to shift. Note that the table shows the shift in the supply curve that results from an *increase* in each of the variables. A *decrease* in these variables would cause the supply curve to shift in the opposite direction.

A Change in Supply versus a Change in Quantity Supplied

We noted earlier the important difference between a change in demand and a change in quantity demanded. There is a similar difference between a *change in supply* and a *change in quantity supplied*. A change in supply refers to a shift of the supply curve. The supply curve will shift when there is a change in one of the variables—*other than the price of the product*—that affects the willingness of suppliers to sell the product. A change in quantity supplied refers to a movement along the supply curve as a result of a change in the product's price. Figure 6 illustrates this important distinction. If the price of smartphones rises from $200 to $250, the result will be a movement up the supply curve from point A to point B—an increase in quantity supplied from 10 million to 11 million. If the price of an input decreases, or if another factor changes that causes sellers to supply more of a product at every price, the supply curve will shift to the right—an increase in supply. In this case, the increase in supply from S_1 to S_2 causes the quantity of smartphones supplied at a price of $250 to increase from 11 million at point B to 13 million at point C.

Figure 6

A Change in Supply versus a Change in Quantity Supplied

If the price of smartphones rises from $200 to $250, the result will be a movement up the supply curve from point *A* to point *B*—an increase in quantity supplied by Apple, Samsung, Nokia, and other firms from 10 million to 11 million. If the price of an input decreases, or if another factor changes that causes sellers to supply more of the product at every price, the supply curve will shift to the right—an increase in supply. In this case, the increase in supply from S_1 to S_2 causes the quantity of smartphones supplied at a price of $250 to increase from 11 million at point *B* to 13 million at point *C*.

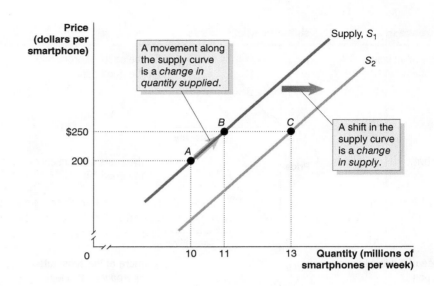

Use a graph to illustrate market equilibrium.

Market equilibrium A situation in which quantity demanded equals quantity supplied.

Competitive market equilibrium A market equilibrium with many buyers and sellers.

Market Equilibrium: Putting Demand and Supply Together

The purpose of markets is to bring buyers and sellers together. Instead of being chaotic and disorderly, the interaction of buyers and sellers in markets ultimately results in firms being led to produce the goods and services that consumers want most. To understand how this process happens, we first need to see how markets work to reconcile the plans of buyers and sellers.

In Figure 7, we bring together the market demand curve and the market supply curve for smartphones. Notice that the demand curve crosses the supply curve at only one point. This point represents a price of $200 and a quantity of 10 million smartphones per week. Only at this point of **market equilibrium** is the quantity of smartphones consumers are willing and able to buy equal to the quantity of smartphones firms are willing and able to sell. In this case, the *equilibrium price* is $200, and the *equilibrium quantity* is 10 million. As we noted at the beginning of the chapter, markets that have many buyers and sellers are competitive markets, and equilibrium in these markets is a **competitive market equilibrium**. In the market for smartphones, there are many buyers but only about 20 firms. Whether 20 firms are enough for our model of demand and supply to apply to this

Figure 7

Market Equilibrium

Where the demand curve crosses the supply curve determines market equilibrium. In this case, the demand curve for smartphones crosses the supply curve at a price of $200 and a quantity of 10 million smartphones. Only at this point is the quantity of smartphones consumers are willing to buy equal to the quantity that Apple, Samsung, LG, and other firms are willing to sell: The quantity demanded is equal to the quantity supplied.

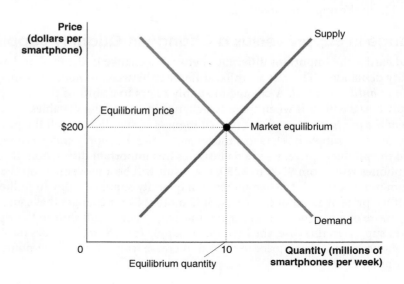

market is a matter of judgment. In this chapter, we are assuming that the market for smartphones has enough sellers to be competitive.

How Markets Eliminate Surpluses and Shortages

A market that is not in equilibrium moves toward equilibrium. Once a market is in equilibrium, it remains in equilibrium. To see why, consider what happens if a market is not in equilibrium. Suppose that the price in the market for smartphones was $250 rather than the equilibrium price of $200. As Figure 8 shows, at a price of $250, the quantity of smartphones supplied would be 11 million, and the quantity of smartphones demanded would be 9 million. When the quantity supplied is greater than the quantity demanded, there is a **surplus** in the market. In this case, the surplus is equal to 2 million smartphones (11 million − 9 million = 2 million). When there is a surplus, firms will have unsold goods piling up, which gives them an incentive to increase their sales by cutting the price. Cutting the price will simultaneously increase the quantity demanded and decrease the quantity supplied. This adjustment will reduce the surplus, but as long as the price is above $200, there will be a surplus, and downward pressure on the price will continue. Only when the price falls to $200 will the market be in equilibrium.

Surplus A situation in which the quantity supplied is greater than the quantity demanded.

If, however, the price were $100, the quantity demanded would be 12 million, and the quantity supplied would be 8 million, as shown in Figure 8. When the quantity demanded is greater than the quantity supplied, there is a **shortage** in the market. In this case, the shortage is equal to 4 million smartphones (12 million − 8 million = 4 million). When a shortage occurs, some consumers will be unable to buy smartphones at the current price. In this situation, firms will realize that they can raise the price without losing sales. A higher price will simultaneously increase the quantity supplied and decrease the quantity demanded. This adjustment will reduce the shortage, but as long as the price is below $200, there will be a shortage, and upward pressure on the price will continue. Only when the price rises to $200 will the market be in equilibrium.

Shortage A situation in which the quantity demanded is greater than the quantity supplied.

At a competitive market equilibrium, all consumers willing to pay the market price will be able to buy as much of the product as they want, and all firms willing to accept the market price will be able to sell as much of the product as they want. As a result, there will be no reason for the price to change unless either the demand curve or the supply curve shifts.

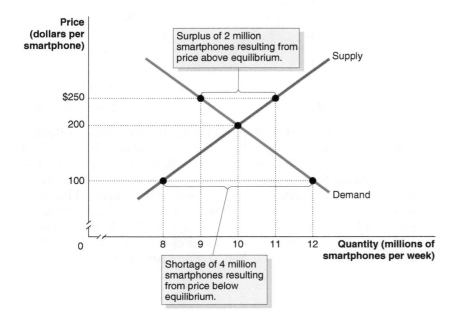

Figure 8

The Effect of Surpluses and Shortages on the Market Price

When the market price is above equilibrium, there will be a *surplus*. A price of $250 for smartphones results in 11 million smartphones being supplied but only 9 million being demanded, or a surplus of 2 million. As Apple, Nokia, LG, and other firms cut the price to dispose of the surplus, the price will fall to the equilibrium of $200. When the market price is below equilibrium, there will be a *shortage*. A price of $100 results in 12 million smartphones being demanded but only 8 million being supplied, or a shortage of 4 million. As firms find that consumers who are unable to find smartphones available for sale are willing to pay higher prices to get them, the price will rise to the equilibrium of $200.

Demand and Supply Both Count

Keep in mind that the interaction of demand and supply determines the equilibrium price. Neither consumers nor firms can dictate what the equilibrium price will be. No firm can sell anything at any price unless it can find a willing buyer, and no consumer can buy anything at any price without finding a willing seller.

Solved Problem 3

Demand and Supply Both Count: A Tale of Two Letters

Which letter is likely to be worth more: one written by Abraham Lincoln or one written by his assassin, John Wilkes Booth? Lincoln is one of the greatest presidents, and many people collect anything he wrote. The demand for letters written by Lincoln surely would seem to be much greater than the demand for letters written by Booth. Yet, when R.M. Smythe and Co. auctioned off on the same day a letter written by Lincoln and a letter written by Booth, the Booth letter sold for $31,050, and the Lincoln letter sold for only $21,850. Use a demand and supply graph to explain how the Booth letter has a higher market price than the Lincoln letter, even though the demand for letters written by Lincoln is greater than the demand for letters written by Booth.

Solving the Problem

Step 1: **Review the chapter material.** This problem is about prices being determined at market equilibrium, so you may want to review the section "Market Equilibrium: Putting Demand and Supply Together."

Step 2: **Draw demand curves that illustrate the greater demand for Lincoln's letters.** Begin by drawing two demand curves. Label one "Demand for Lincoln's letters" and the other "Demand for Booth's letters." Make sure that the Lincoln demand curve is much farther to the right than the Booth demand curve.

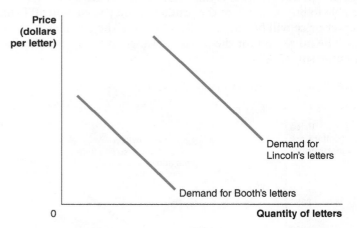

Step 3: **Draw supply curves that illustrate the equilibrium price of Booth's letters being higher than the equilibrium price of Lincoln's letters.** Based on the demand curves you have just drawn, think about how it might be possible for the market price of Lincoln's letters to be lower than the market price of Booth's letters. This outcome can occur only if the supply of Lincoln's letters is much greater than the supply of Booth's letters. Draw on your graph a supply curve for Lincoln's letters and a supply curve for Booth's letters that will result in an equilibrium price of Booth's letters of $31,050 and an equilibrium price of Lincoln's letters of $21,850. You have now solved the problem.

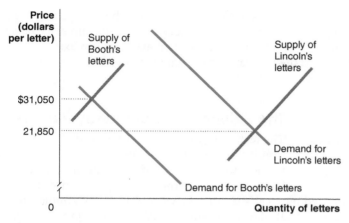

Extra Credit: The explanation for this puzzle is that both demand and supply count when determining market price. The demand for Lincoln's letters is much greater than the demand for Booth's letters, but the supply of Booth's letters is very small. Historians believe that only eight letters written by Booth exist today. (Note that the supply curves for letters written by Booth and by Lincoln are upward sloping, even though only a fixed number of each of these letters is available and, obviously, no more can be produced. The upward slope of the supply curves occurs because the higher the price, the larger the quantity of letters that will be offered for sale by people who currently own them.)

Your Turn: For more practice, do related problems 3.5, 3.6, and 3.7 at the end of this chapter.

The Effect of Demand and Supply Shifts on Equilibrium

4 LEARNING OBJECTIVE

Use demand and supply graphs to predict changes in prices and quantities.

We have seen that the interaction of demand and supply in markets determines the quantity of a good that is produced and the price at which it is sold. We have also seen that several variables cause demand curves to shift and other variables cause supply curves to shift. As a result, demand and supply curves in most markets are constantly shifting, and the prices and quantities that represent equilibrium are constantly changing. In this section, we look at how shifts in demand and supply curves affect equilibrium price and quantity.

The Effect of Shifts in Supply on Equilibrium

If Amazon enters the market for smartphones, the market supply curve for smartphones will shift to the right. Figure 9 shows the supply curve shifting from S_1 to S_2.

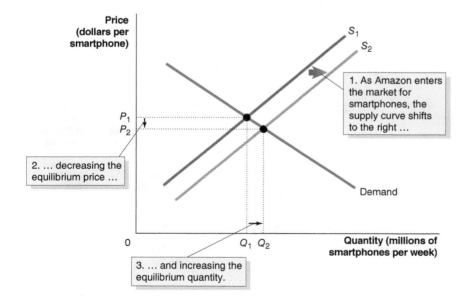

Figure 9

The Effect of an Increase in Supply on Equilibrium

If a firm enters a market, as Amazon is expected to enter the market for smartphones, the equilibrium price will fall, and the equilibrium quantity will rise:

1. As Amazon enters the market for smartphones, a larger quantity of smartphones will be supplied at every price, so the market supply curve shifts to the right, from S_1 to S_2, which causes a surplus of smartphones at the original price, P_1.

2. The equilibrium price falls from P_1 to P_2.

3. The equilibrium quantity rises from Q_1 to Q_2.

When the supply curve shifts to the right, there will be a surplus at the original equilibrium price, P_1. The surplus is eliminated as the equilibrium price falls to P_2, and the equilibrium quantity rises from Q_1 to Q_2. If an existing firm exits the market, the supply curve will shift to the left, causing the equilibrium price to rise and the equilibrium quantity to fall.

<table>
<tr><td>Making
the
Connection</td><td>

The Falling Price of Blu-ray Players

The technology for playing prerecorded movies has progressed rapidly during the past 30 years. Video cassette recorders (VCRs) were introduced in Japan in 1976 and in the United States in 1977. As the first way of recording TV programs or</td></tr>
</table>

playing prerecorded movies, VHS players were immensely popular. In 1997, though, digital video disc (DVD) players became available in the United States. DVDs could store more information than could the VHS tapes played on VCRs and could produce a crisper picture. Within a few years, sales of DVD players were greater than sales of VCRs, and by 2006 the movie studios had stopped releasing films on VHS tapes. In 2006, Blu-ray players were introduced. Because Blu-ray discs can store up to 50 gigabytes of data, compared with fewer than 5 gigabytes on a typical DVD, Blu-ray players can reproduce high-definition images that DVD players cannot.

When firms began selling VCRs, DVD players, and Blu-ray players, they initially charged high prices that declined rapidly within a few years. As this figure shows, the average price of a Blu-ray player was about $800 in May 2006, but it had declined to about $95 in 2013. Sales of Blu-ray players rose from about 425,000 in 2006 to 13.3 million in 2013. The figure shows that the decline in price and increase in quantity resulted from a large shift to the right of the supply curve. The supply curve in 2013 was much farther to the right than the supply curve in 2006 for two reasons: First, after Samsung introduced the first Blu-ray player—at a price of $999—other firms entered the industry, increasing the quantity supplied at every price. Second, the prices of the parts used in manufacturing Blu-ray players, particularly the laser components, declined sharply. As the cost of manufacturing the players declined, the quantity supplied at every price increased.

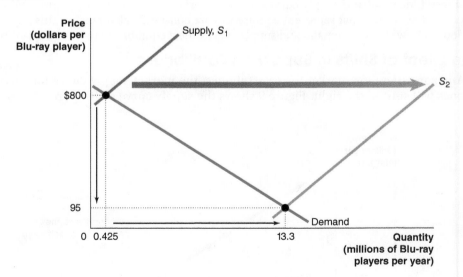

Source: Sarah McBride, "New DVD Players Resolve Battle of Formats," *Wall Street Journal*, January 4, 2007; Yukari Iwatani Kane and Miguel Bustillo, "Dreaming of a Blu Christmas," *Wall Street Journal*, December 23, 2009; and "DEG 2012 Year-End Home Entertainment Report," www.degonline.org.

Your Turn: Test your understanding by doing related problem 4.5 at the end of this chapter.

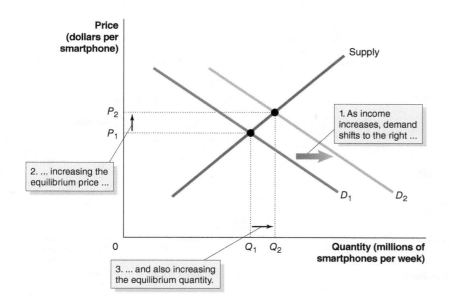

Figure 10

The Effect of an Increase in Demand on Equilibrium

Increases in income will cause the equilibrium price and quantity to rise:
1. Because smartphones are a normal good, as income increases, the quantity demanded increases at every price, and the market demand curve shifts to the right, from D_1 to D_2, which causes a shortage of smartphones at the original price, P_1.
2. The equilibrium price rises from P_1 to P_2.
3. The equilibrium quantity rises from Q_1 to Q_2.

The Effect of Shifts in Demand on Equilibrium

Because smartphones are a normal good, when incomes increase, the market demand curve shifts to the right. Figure 10 shows the effect of a demand curve shifting to the right, from D_1 to D_2. This shift causes a shortage at the original equilibrium price, P_1. To eliminate the shortage, the equilibrium price rises to P_2, and the equilibrium quantity rises from Q_1 to Q_2. In contrast, if the price of a substitute good, such as tablet computers, were to fall, the demand for smartphones would decrease, shifting the demand curve to the left. When the demand curve shifts to the left, both the equilibrium price and quantity will decrease.

The Effect of Shifts in Demand and Supply over Time

Whenever only demand or only supply shifts, we can easily predict the effect on equilibrium price and quantity. But, what happens if *both* curves shift? For instance, in many markets, the demand curve shifts to the right over time as population and income increase. The supply curve also often shifts to the right as new firms enter the market and positive technological change occurs. Whether the equilibrium price in a market rises or falls over time depends on whether demand shifts to the right more than does supply. Panel (a) of Figure 11 shows that when demand shifts to the right more than supply, the equilibrium price rises, while panel (b) shows that when supply shifts to the right more than demand, the equilibrium price falls.

Table 3 summarizes all possible combinations of shifts in demand and supply over time and the effects of the shifts on equilibrium price (*P*) and quantity (*Q*). For example, the entry in red in the table shows that if the demand curve shifts to the right and the supply curve also shifts to the right, the equilibrium quantity will increase, while the equilibrium price may increase, decrease, or remain unchanged. To make sure you understand each entry in the table, draw demand and supply graphs to check whether you can reproduce the predicted changes in equilibrium price and quantity. If the entry in the table says the predicted change in equilibrium price or quantity can be either an increase or a decrease, draw two graphs similar to panels (a) and (b) of Figure 11, one showing the equilibrium price or quantity increasing and the other showing it decreasing. Note also that in the ambiguous cases where either price or quantity might increase or decrease, it is also possible that price or quantity might remain unchanged. Be sure you understand why this is true.

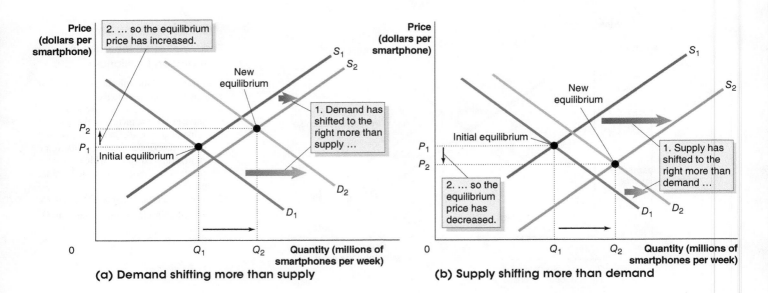

Figure 11 Shifts in Demand and Supply over Time

Whether the price of a product rises or falls over time depends on whether demand shifts to the right more than supply.

In panel (a), demand shifts to the right more than supply, and the equilibrium price rises:

1. Demand shifts to the right more than supply.
2. The equilibrium price rises from P_1 to P_2.

In panel (b), supply shifts to the right more than demand, and the equilibrium price falls:

1. Supply shifts to the right more than demand.
2. The equilibrium price falls from P_1 to P_2.

Table 3

How Shifts in Demand and Supply Affect Equilibrium Price (P) and Quantity (Q)

	Supply Curve Unchanged	Supply Curve Shifts to the Right	Supply Curve Shifts to the Left
Demand Curve Unchanged	Q unchanged P unchanged	Q increases P decreases	Q decreases P increases
Demand Curve Shifts to the Right	Q increases P increases	Q increases P increases or decreases	Q increases or decreases P increases
Demand Curve Shifts to the Left	Q decreases P decreases	Q increases or decreases P decreases	Q decreases P increases or decreases

Solved Problem 4

What Has Caused the Decline in Beef Consumption?

Whether you like to eat hamburger or roast beef, the source of the meat is a farmer who raises cattle. An article in the *New York Times* discussed how the cost to farmers of raising cattle for beef had been increasing. At the same time, consumer tastes had been changing, leading to a decline in the demand for beef. Use demand and supply graphs to illustrate your answers to the following questions:

a. Can we use this information to be certain whether the equilibrium quantity of beef will increase or decrease?

b. Can we use this information to be certain whether the equilibrium price of beef will increase or decrease?

Solving the Problem

Step 1: **Review the chapter material.** This problem is about how shifts in demand and supply curves affect the equilibrium price, so you may want to review the section "The Effect of Shifts in Demand and Supply over Time."

Step 2: **Answer part (a) using demand and supply analysis.** You are given the information that consumer tastes have changed, leading to a decline in demand for beef. So, the demand curve for beef has shifted to the left. You are also given the information that the cost of raising beef has increased. So, the supply curve for beef has also shifted to the left. The following graph shows both these shifts:

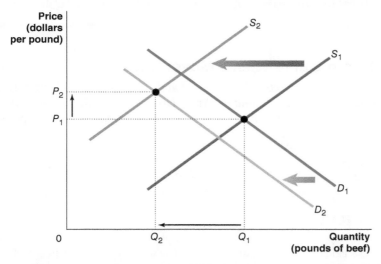

As Table 3 summarizes, if the demand curve and the supply curve both shift to the left, the equilibrium quantity must decrease. Therefore, we can answer part (a) by stating that we are certain that the equilibrium quantity of beef will decrease.

Step 3: **Answer part (b) using demand and supply analysis.** The graph we drew in Step 2 showed the equilibrium price of beef increasing. But given the information provided, the following graph would also be correct:

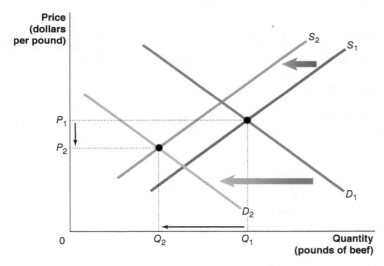

Unlike the graph in Step 2, which showed the equilibrium price increasing, this graph shows the equilibrium price decreasing. The uncertainty about whether the equilibrium price will increase or decrease is consistent with what we saw in Table 3 when the demand curve and the supply curve both shift to the left. Therefore, we can answer part (b) by stating that we cannot be certain whether the equilibrium price of beef will increase or decrease.

Extra Credit: During 2012 and 2013, the equilibrium quantity of beef decreased while the equilibrium price of beef increased. We can conclude that *both* the decrease in demand for beef and the decrease in the supply of beef contributed to the decline in beef consumption. That the price of beef rose indicates that the decrease in supply had a larger effect on equilibrium in the beef market than did the decrease in demand.

Sources: Theopolis Waters, "US Beef Prices Set New High as Spring Barbecue Season Heats Up," www.reuters.com, May 3, 2013; and Mark Bittman, "We're Eating Less Meat. Why?" *New York Times*, January 10, 2012.

Your Turn: For more practice, do related problems 4.6, 4.7, and 4.8 at the end of this chapter.

Shifts in a Curve versus Movements along a Curve

When analyzing markets using demand and supply curves, it is important to remember that *when a shift in a demand or supply curve causes a change in equilibrium price, the change in price does not cause a further shift in demand or supply.* Suppose an increase in

Don't Let This Happen to You

Remember: A Change in a Good's Price Does *Not* Cause the Demand or Supply Curve to Shift

Suppose a student is asked to draw a demand and supply graph to illustrate how an increase in the price of oranges would affect the market for apples, with other variables being constant. He draws the graph on the left and explains it as follows: "Because apples and oranges are substitutes, an increase in the price of oranges will cause an initial shift to the right in the demand curve for apples, from D_1 to D_2. However, because this initial shift in the demand curve for apples results in a higher price for apples, P_2, consumers will find apples less desirable, and the demand curve will shift to the left, from D_2 to D_3, resulting in a final equilibrium price of P_3." Do you agree or disagree with the student's analysis?

You should disagree. The student has correctly understood that an increase in the price of oranges will cause the demand curve for apples to shift to the right. But, the second demand curve shift the student describes, from D_2

to D_3, will not take place. Changes in the price of a product do not result in shifts in the product's demand curve. Changes in the price of a product result only in movements along a demand curve.

The graph on the right shows the correct analysis. The increase in the price of oranges causes the demand curve for apples to increase from D_1 to D_2. At the original price, P_1, the increase in demand initially results in a shortage of apples equal to $Q_3 - Q_1$. But, as we have seen, a shortage causes the price to increase until the shortage is eliminated. In this case, the price will rise to P_2, where both the quantity demanded and the quantity supplied are equal to Q_2. Notice that the increase in price causes a decrease in the *quantity demanded*, from Q_3 to Q_2, but does *not* cause a decrease in demand.

Your Turn: Test your understanding by doing related problems 4.13 and 4.14 at the end of this chapter.

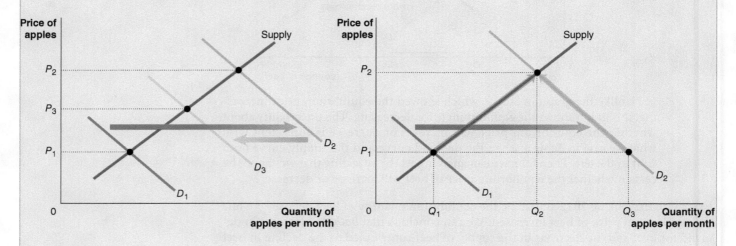

supply causes the price of a good to fall, while everything else that affects the willingness of consumers to buy the good is constant. The result will be an increase in the quantity demanded but not an increase in demand. For demand to increase, the whole curve must shift. The point is the same for supply: If the price of the good falls but everything else that affects the willingness of sellers to supply the good is constant, the quantity supplied decreases, but the supply does not. For supply to decrease, the whole curve must shift.

Continued

Economics in Your Life

Will You Buy an Apple iPhone or a Samsung Galaxy?

At the beginning of this chapter, we asked you to consider two questions: Would you choose to buy a Samsung Galaxy S if it had a lower price than a comparable Apple iPhone? and Would your decision be affected if your income increased? To determine the answer to the first question, you have to recognize that the iPhone and the Galaxy S are substitutes. If you consider the two smartphones to be close substitutes, then you are likely to buy the one with the lower price. In the market, if consumers generally believe that the iPhone and the Galaxy S are close substitutes, a fall in the price of the iPhone will increase the quantity of iPhones demanded and decrease the demand for Galaxy Ss. Suppose that you are currently leaning toward buying the Galaxy S because its price is lower than the price of the iPhone. If an increase in your income would cause you to change your decision and buy the iPhone, then the Galaxy S is an inferior good for you.

Conclusion

The interaction of demand and supply determines market equilibrium. The model of demand and supply is a powerful tool for predicting how changes in the actions of consumers and firms will cause changes in equilibrium prices and quantities. As we have seen in this chapter, we can use the model to analyze markets that do not meet all the requirements for being perfectly competitive. As long as there is intense competition among sellers, the model of demand and supply can often successfully predict changes in prices and quantities.

Read *An Inside Look* on the next page for a discussion of how Google dealt with the problem of not having enough of its Nexus 4 smartphones to meet customer demand, and how Apple dealt with overproduction of its iPhone 5.

Google and Apple Face Supply and Demand Concerns in the Smartphone Market

MOTLEY FOOL

Google's Smartphone Production Problems

Predicting mobile computing sales is a tough one, especially when rolling out a relatively new product. Unless the production numbers match sales expectations perfectly, investors are going to be disappointed. Just ask **Apple** (NASDAQ: AAPL).

On Monday [January 14, 2013], Apple cut orders from its iPhone 5 manufacturers by as much as half due to lack of demand. Forget that production changes often occur after the busy holiday shopping season, or that Apple could have previously placed massive orders to adjust supply chain problems with its new iPhone, or any other fair reason. Investors weren't interested. Apple stock proceeded to drop over 3%, and remains below $500 a share.

Google (NASDAQ: GOOG) and its Nexus 4 smartphone partner LG have found themselves in a similar situation as Apple, though on the opposite end of the spectrum. The problem for Google is too much demand internationally for its low-cost smartphone. It took all of 20 minutes for Google's Play store to sell out of what was then its new Nexus 4 for the international market, and the backlog of orders isn't improving.

He said, she said

In response to concerns about production keeping up with Nexus 4

demand, a director in Google's U.K. offices said, "Supplies with the manufacturer [LG] are erratic," not exactly a glowing recommendation for LG. One estimate put the number of Google Nexus 4 sales since its release a couple of months ago at 370,000; not bad, but paltry compared to Apple and Samsung numbers. So, when in doubt, apparently you blame the supplier.

However, LG isn't taking Google's insinuations about production problems lying down. In a recent interview, an LG executive pulled no punches when asked what the problems were in keeping Nexus 4 phones in stock. According to the LG exec, Google underestimated demand, particularly in the U.K. and Germany, by as much as 10 times the number of Nexus 4's needed to fill orders.

The price for being wrong

The impact of its Nexus 4 supply issues on Google's bottom line will be negligible when it announces earnings Jan. 22. The Nexus is, after all, relatively new to market and Google certainly has other sources of revenue. But Google's inability to meet demand will hurt its share price in the near term, but will be little more than a hiccup in the overall scheme of things.

The flip side of Google's production issue is Apple. According to estimates, Apple sold around 50 million smartphones in the recently completed Q4 of 2012. But because of declining sales expectations this quarter,

Apple cut component deliveries and its share price got beaten down. Can you imagine if Apple planned for 40 million units, and were then forced to announce a ramp-up in production to meet demand for 10 more million iPhones? You can bet share prices would have soared.

Is it any wonder **Microsoft** (NASDAQ: MSFT) hasn't released sales data for its Surface tablet, or why it was initially rolled out on such a minimal basis, with temporary retail outlets? If Microsoft CEO Steve Ballmer had shot for the moon relative to Surface sales, and didn't meet those lofty expectations, he'd feel the wrath of shareholders all the way up in Redmond, Wa. Of course, if Ballmer undershot expectations, and then was having production difficulty filling orders, shareholders would again be on the warpath.

When it's said and done, supply and demand forecasting isn't an exact science. Sure, there's information that can be gleaned from changes in orders and amounts, but let's keep it in perspective. Do Google's issues with LG threaten to derail the online leader? Of course not. Take the 4% drop in Google's share price the past week for what it is: an opportunity.

Source: Tim Brugger, "Google's Smartphone Production Problems," *Motley Fool*, January 18, 2013.

Key Points in the Article

The demand for Google's Nexus 4 smartphone and the production problems prevented the company from supplying enough of the product to fill its orders. Google blamed the shortage on the phone's manufacturer, LG, while LG executives claimed that Google severely underestimated demand for the smartphone, especially in some European markets. Although Google was dealing with the problem of underproduction, Apple was worried about overproduction of its iPhone 5. In January 2013, Apple cut orders from its iPhone 5 manufacturers by as much as half due to falling demand. For both Google and Apple, the production issues resulted in declines in the companies' stock prices.

Analyzing the News

(a) At the beginning of 2013, Apple and Google found themselves dealing with significant, but different, demand and supply issues. Apple reduced its orders of iPhone 5s from its manufacturers by as much as 50 percent due to insufficient demand, while Google sought ways to increase production of its Nexus 4 due to high demand. Both companies misjudged the demand for their smartphones. Figure 1 below shows a decrease in demand as a shift to the left of the demand curve from D_1 to D_3, which illustrates the situation Apple faced for its iPhone 5. All else equal, a decrease in demand would decrease equilibrium price from P_1 to P_3 and decrease equilibrium quantity from Q_1 to Q_3. Google faced an increase in demand for the Nexus 4, which is represented in Figure 1 by a shift to the right of the demand curve from D_1 to D_2. All else equal, an increase in demand would increase equilibrium price from P_1 to P_2 and increase equilibrium quantity from Q_1 to Q_2.

(b) On the supply side, Google blamed the Nexus 4 manufacturer, LG, for not being able to supply enough product, and LG blamed Google for underestimating Nexus 4 sales. Regardless of which company was ultimately at fault, Google needed to increase the supply of its smartphones to meet the growing demand. By blaming Google for the supply problem, the executives at LG implied that their company had the capability of producing enough smartphones to cover the backlog of orders, so increasing the supply of Nexus 4 phones would apparently not be an issue on the manufacturing end. An increase in supply, which Google needed, is represented in Figure 2 by a shift from S_1 to S_2. All else equal, an increase in supply would decrease the equilibrium price from P_1 to P_3 and increase the equilibrium quantity from Q_1 to Q_2.

(c) Apple expected sales of its iPhone 5 to decline in the first quarter of 2013 and chose to cut production of its smartphone in light of this expectation. A decrease in supply, such as Apple's reduction in production, is represented in Figure 2 by a shift from S_1 to S_3. All else equal, a decrease in supply would increase the equilibrium price from P_1 to P_2 and decrease the equilibrium quantity from Q_1 to Q_3.

Thinking Critically

1. Draw a demand and supply graph for the smartphone market. Show the change in the equilibrium price and quantity after Amazon enters the market by selling a smartphone.

2. Suppose that the federal government starts a new program that offers to reimburse low-income people for half the price of a new smartphone. Use a demand and supply graph of the smartphone market to show the effect on equilibrium price and quantity as a result of Amazon entering the market and the government beginning this program. Can we be sure whether the equilibrium quantity of smartphones will increase? Can we be sure whether the equilibrium price of smartphones will increase? Briefly explain.

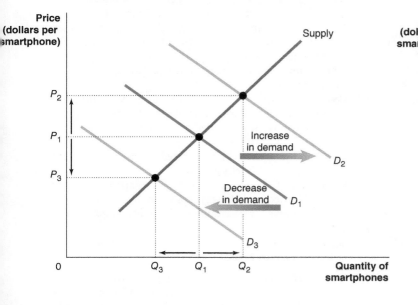

Figure 1

An increase in demand for smartphones shifts the demand curve to the right. All else equal, equilibrium price and equilibrium quantity both increase. A decrease in demand would have the opposite effect.

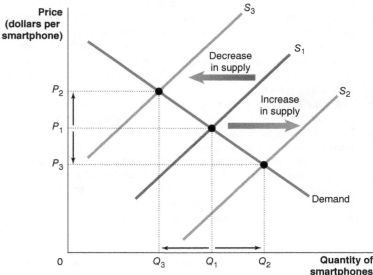

Figure 2

An increase in supply of smartphones shifts the supply curve to the right. All else equal, equilibrium price decreases and equilibrium quantity increases. A decrease in supply would have the opposite effect.

Chapter Summary and Problems

Key Terms

Ceteris paribus ("all else equal") condition

Competitive market equilibrium

Complements

Demand curve

Demand schedule

Demographics

Income effect

Inferior good

Law of demand

Law of supply

Market demand

Market equilibrium

Normal good

Perfectly competitive market

Quantity demanded

Quantity supplied

Shortage

Substitutes

Substitution effect

Supply curve

Supply schedule

Surplus

Technological change

 ## The Demand Side of the Market

LEARNING OBJECTIVE: Discuss the variables that influence demand.

Summary

The model of demand and supply is the most powerful tool in economics. The model applies exactly only to **perfectly competitive markets**, where there are many buyers and sellers, all the products sold are identical, and there are no barriers to new sellers entering the market. But, the model can also be useful in analyzing markets that don't meet all these requirements. The **quantity demanded** is the amount of a good or service that a consumer is willing and able to purchase at a given price. A **demand schedule** is a table that shows the relationship between the price of a product and the quantity of the product demanded. A **demand curve** is a graph that shows the relationship between the price of a product and the quantity of the product demanded. **Market demand** is the demand by all consumers of a given good or service. The **law of demand** states that *ceteris paribus*—holding everything else constant—the quantity of a product demanded increases when the price falls and decreases when the price rises. Demand curves slope downward because of the **substitution effect**, which is the change in quantity demanded that results from a price change making one good more or less expensive relative to another good, and the income effect, which is the change in quantity demanded of a good that results from the effect of a change in the good's price on consumer purchasing power. Changes in income, the prices of related goods, tastes, population and demographics, and expected future prices all cause the demand curve to shift. **Substitutes** are goods that can be used for the same purpose. **Complements** are goods that are used together. A **normal good** is a good for which demand increases as income increases. An **inferior good** is a good for which demand decreases as income increases. **Demographics** refers to the characteristics of a population with respect to age, race, and gender. A change in demand refers to a shift of the demand curve. A change in quantity demanded refers to a movement along the demand curve as a result of a change in the product's price.

Visit www.myeconlab.com to complete these exercises online and get instant feedback.

Review Questions

1.1 What is a demand schedule? What is a demand curve?

1.2 What do economists mean when they use the Latin expression *ceteris paribus*?

1.3 What is the difference between a change in demand and a change in quantity demanded?

1.4 What is the law of demand? Use the substitution effect and the income effect to explain why an increase in the price of a product causes a decrease in the quantity demanded.

1.5 What are the main variables that will cause the demand curve to shift? Give an example of each.

Problems and Applications

1.6 For each of the following pairs of products, state which are complements, which are substitutes, and which are unrelated.
  a. New cars and used cars
  b. Houses and washing machines
  c. UGG boots and Kindle e-readers
  d. iPads and Kindle e-readers

1.7 **[Related to the** Chapter Opener**]** When smartphones based on the Android operating system were first introduced, there were relatively few applications, or "apps," available for them. Now, there are many more apps available for Android-based smartphones. Are these apps substitutes or complements for smartphones? How has the increase in the availability of apps for these smartphones affected the demand for Apple iPhones? Briefly explain.

1.8 **[Related to the** Chapter Opener**]** Smart TVs, unlike traditional TVs, can connect directly to the Internet. Smart TVs made up 27 percent of all televisions sold worldwide in 2012.
  a. Should smart TVs be considered a substitute good for smartphones? Briefly explain.
  b. If smart TVs are a substitute for smartphones, how would a decline in the price of smart TVs affect the demand curve for smartphones? Include a graph in your answer.

  Source: Greg Tarr, "Smart TVs Rise to 27% of TV Shipments," www.twice.com, February 21, 2013.

1.9 State whether each of the following events will result in a movement along the demand curve for McDonald's Big Mac hamburgers or whether it will cause the curve to shift. If the demand curve shifts, indicate whether it will shift to the left or to the right and draw a graph to illustrate the shift.
  a. The price of Burger King's Whopper hamburger declines.
  b. McDonald's distributes coupons for $1.00 off the purchase of a Big Mac.

c. Because of a shortage of potatoes, the price of French fries increases.

d. Fast-food restaurants post nutrition warning labels.

e. The U.S. economy enters a period of rapid growth in incomes.

1.10 Suppose that the following table shows the quantity demanded of UGG boots at five different prices in 2014 and 2015:

Price	Quantity Demanded (thousands of pairs of boots)	
	2014	2015
$160	5,000	4,000
170	4,500	3,500
180	4,000	3,000
190	3,500	2,500
200	3,000	2,000

Name two different variables that could cause the quantity demanded of UGG boots to change from 2014 to 2015 as indicated in the table.

1.11 Suppose that the curves in the following graph represent two demand curves for traditional wings (basket of six) at Buffalo Wild Wings. What would cause a movement from point A to point B on D_1? Name two variables that would cause a movement from point A to point C.

1.12 [Related to the Making the Connection: **Are Tablet Computers Substitutes for E-Readers?**] Are smartphones a closer substitute for tablet computers, such as the iPad, or for e-readers, such as the Kindle? Briefly explain.

1.13 [Related to the Making the Connection: **Coke and Pepsi Are Hit by U.S. Demographics**] Since 1979, China has had a policy that allows couples to have only one child. This policy has caused a change in the demographics of China. Between 1980 and 2011, the share of the population under age 14 decreased from 36 percent to 19 percent. And, as parents attempt to ensure that the lone child is a son, the number of newborn males relative to females has increased. Choose three goods and explain how the demand for them has been affected by China's one-child policy.

Sources: World Bank, *World Development Indicators*, May 2013; and "China's Family Planning: Illegal Children Will Be Confiscated" and "China's Population: Only and Lonely," *Economist*, July 21, 2011.

1.14 Suppose the following table shows the price of a base model Toyota Prius hybrid and the quantity of Priuses sold for three years. Do these data indicate that the demand curve for Priuses is upward sloping? Explain.

Year	Price	Quantity
2012	$31,880	35,265
2013	30,550	33,250
2014	33,250	36,466

1.15 The following statement appeared in an article in the *New York Times* on the effects of changes in college tuition: "Some private colleges said that applications actually increased when they bolstered prices, apparently because families equated higher prices with quality." If applications increased when these colleges raised the tuition price they charged, did these colleges face upward sloping demand curves? Briefly explain.

Source: Andrew Martin, "Colleges Expect Lower Enrollment," *New York Times*, January 10, 2013.

1.16 Richard Posner is a federal court judge who also writes on economic topics. A newspaper reporter summarized Posner's views on the effect of online bookstores and e-books on the demand for books:

> Posner's [argument] is that the disappearance of bookstores is to be celebrated and not mourned, partly because e-books and online stores will reduce the cost of books and thus drive up demand for them.

Do you agree with Posner's statement, as given by the reporter? Briefly explain.

Source: Christopher Shea, "Judge Posner Hails the Demise of Bookstores," *Wall Street Journal*, January 13, 2011.

1.17 [Related to the Making the Connection: **Forecasting the Demand for iPhones**] An article in the *Wall Street Journal* in 2013 was titled "In India, iPhone Lags Far Behind." According to the article, the difficulty Apple was having selling iPhones in India was "no small matter as Apple's growth slows in the U.S. and other mature markets."

a. What does the article mean by "mature markets"?

b. Why would sales of iPhones be likely to be slower in mature markets than in countries such as India?

c. Would forecasting sales in mature markets be easier or harder than forecasting sales in countries such as India? Briefly explain.

Source: Dhanya Ann Thoppil, Amol Sharma, and Jessica E. Lessin, "In India, iPhone Lags Far Behind," *Wall Street Journal*, February 26, 2013.

---

2 | The Supply Side of the Market

LEARNING OBJECTIVE: Discuss the variables that influence supply.

Summary

The **quantity supplied** is the amount of a good that a firm is willing and able to supply at a given price. A **supply schedule** is a table that shows the relationship between the price of a product and the quantity of the product supplied. A **supply curve** is a curve that shows the relationship between the price of a product and the quantity of the product supplied. When the price of a product rises, producing the product is more profitable, and a greater amount will be supplied. The **law of supply** states that, holding everything else constant, the quantity of a product supplied increases when the price rises and decreases when the price falls. Changes in the prices of inputs, technology, the prices of substitutes in production, expected future prices, and the number of firms in a market all cause the supply curve to shift. **Technological change** is a positive or negative change in the ability of a firm to produce a given level of output with a given quantity of inputs. A change in supply refers to a shift of the supply curve. A change in quantity supplied refers to a movement along the supply curve as a result of a change in the product's price.

Visit **www.myeconlab.com** to complete these exercises online and get instant feedback.

Review Questions

2.1 What is a supply schedule? What is a supply curve?

2.2 What is the difference between a change in supply and a change in the quantity supplied?

2.3 What is the law of supply? What are the main variables that will cause a supply curve to shift? Give an example of each.

Problems and Applications

2.4 Briefly explain whether each of the following statements describes a change in supply or a change in the quantity supplied:

  a. To take advantage of high prices for snow shovels during a snowy winter, Alexander Shovels, Inc., decides to increase output.

  b. The success of the Apple iPhone leads more firms to begin producing smartphones.

  c. In the six months following the Japanese earthquake and tsunami in 2011, production of automobiles in Japan declined by 20 percent.

2.5 Suppose that the curves in the following graph represent two supply curves for traditional wings (basket of six) at Buffalo Wild Wings. What would cause a movement from point *A* to point *B* on S_1? Name two variables that would cause a movement from point *A* to point *C*.

2.6 Suppose that the following table shows the quantity supplied of UGG boots at five different prices in 2014 and 2015:

Price	Quantity Supplied (thousands of pairs of boots)	
	2014	2015
$160	3,000	2,000
170	3,500	2,500
180	4,000	3,000
190	4,500	3,500
200	5,000	4,000

Name two different variables that would cause the quantity supplied of UGG boots to change from 2014 to 2015 as indicated in the table.

2.7 Will each firm in the smartphone industry always supply the same quantity as every other firm at each price? What factors might cause the quantity of smartphones supplied by different firms to be different at a particular price?

2.8 If the price of a good increases, is the increase in the quantity of the good supplied likely to be smaller or larger, the longer the time period being considered? Briefly explain.

---

3 **Market Equilibrium: Putting Demand and Supply Together**

LEARNING OBJECTIVE: Use a graph to illustrate market equilibrium.

Summary

Market equilibrium occurs where the demand curve intersects the supply curve. A **competitive market equilibrium** has a market equilibrium with many buyers and sellers. Only at this point is the quantity demanded equal to the quantity supplied. Prices above equilibrium result in **surpluses**, with the quantity supplied being greater than the quantity demanded. Surpluses cause the market price to fall. Prices below equilibrium result in **shortages**, with the quantity demanded being greater than the quantity supplied. Shortages cause the market price to rise.

Visit **www.myeconlab.com** to complete these exercises online and get instant feedback.

Review Questions

3.1 What do economists mean by *market equilibrium*?

3.2 What do economists mean by a *shortage*? By a *surplus*?

3.3 What happens in a market if the current price is above the equilibrium price? What happens if the current price is below the equilibrium price?

Problems and Applications

3.4 Briefly explain whether you agree with the following statement: "When there is a shortage of a good, consumers eventually give up trying to buy it, so the demand for the good declines, and the price falls until the market is finally in equilibrium."

3.5 **[Related to** Solved Problem 3**]** In *The Wealth of Nations*, Adam Smith discussed what has come to be known as the "diamond and water paradox":

  Nothing is more useful than water: but it will purchase scarce anything; scarce anything can be had in exchange for it. A diamond, on the contrary, has scarce any value in use; but a very great quantity of other goods may frequently be had in exchange for it.

Graph the market for diamonds and the market for water. Show how it is possible for the price of water to be much lower than the price of diamonds, even though the demand for water is much greater than the demand for diamonds.

Source: Adam Smith, *An Inquiry into the Nature and Causes of the Wealth of Nations*, Vol. I, Oxford, UK: Oxford University Press, 1976; original edition, 1776.

3.6 **[Related to** Solved Problem 3**]** An article discusses the market for autographs by Mickey Mantle, the superstar centerfielder for the New York Yankees during the 1950s and 1960s: "At card shows, golf outings, charity dinners, Mr. Mantle signed his name over and over." One expert on sport autographs is quoted as saying, "He was a real good signer.... He is not rare." Yet the article quotes another expert as saying, "Mr. Mantle's autograph ranks No. 3 of most-popular autographs, behind Babe Ruth and Muhammad Ali." A baseball signed by Mantle is likely to sell for the relatively high price of $250 to $400. By contrast, baseballs signed by Whitey Ford, a teammate of Mantle's on the Yankees, typically sell for less than $150. Use one graph to show both the demand and supply for autographs by Whitey Ford and the demand and supply for autographs by Mickey Mantle. Show how it is possible for the price of Mantle's autographs to be higher than the price of Ford's autographs, even though the supply of Mantle autographs is larger than the supply of Ford autographs.

Source: Beth DeCarbo, "Mantle Autographs Not Rare, but Collectors Don't Care," *Wall Street Journal*, August 4, 2008.

3.7 **[Related to** Solved Problem 3**]** Comic book fans eagerly compete to buy copies of *Amazing Fantasy* No. 15, which contains the first appearance of the superhero Spider-Man. At the same time the publisher printed copies of the comic for the U.S. market, with the price printed on the cover in cents, it printed copies for the U.K. market, with the price printed on the cover in British pence. About 10 times as many U.S. copies of *Amazing Fantasy* No. 15 have survived as U.K. copies. Yet in auctions that occurred at about the same time in 2013, a U.S. copy sold for $29,000, while a U.K. copy in the same condition sold for only $10,755. Use a demand and supply graph to explain how the U.S. version of the comic has a higher price than the U.K. version, even though the supply of the U.S. version is so much greater than the supply of the U.K. version.

Source: Auction price data from: *GPA Analysis for CGC Comics*, www.comics.gpanalysis.com.

3.8 If a market is in equilibrium, is it necessarily true that all buyers and sellers are satisfied with the market price? Briefly explain.

3.9 During 2013, an article in the *Wall Street Journal* stated: "Steel prices have slumped this month, setting off a scramble among steelmakers to maintain prices ... despite a nationwide glut."
   a. What does the article mean by a "glut"? What does a glut imply about the quantity demanded of steel relative to the quantity supplied?
   b. Why would steel prices slump if there is a glut in the steel market?
   c. Is it likely that steel companies would succeed in maintaining steel prices in the face of a glut in the market? Briefly explain.

Source: John W. Miller, "Steelmakers Pinched by Price Plunge," *Wall Street Journal*, April 26, 2013.

The Effect of Demand and Supply Shifts on Equilibrium

LEARNING OBJECTIVE: Use demand and supply graphs to predict changes in prices and quantities.

Summary

In most markets, demand and supply curves shift frequently, causing changes in equilibrium prices and quantities. Over time, if demand increases more than supply, equilibrium price will rise. If supply increases more than demand, equilibrium price will fall.

Visit **www.myeconlab.com** to complete these exercises online and get instant feedback.

Review Questions

4.1 Draw a demand and supply graph to show the effect on the equilibrium price in a market in the following situations:
   a. The demand curve shifts to the right.
   b. The supply curve shifts to the left.

4.2 If, over time, the demand curve for a product shifts to the right more than the supply curve does, what will happen to the equilibrium price? What will happen to the equilibrium price if the supply curve shifts to the right more than the demand curve? For each case, draw a demand and supply graph to illustrate your answer.

Problems and Applications

4.3 According to an article in the *Wall Street Journal*, one of the effects of an increase in the demand for corn was a decline in the number of U.S. farmers growing rice: "The number of acres dedicated to rice likely will decline 3% this spring compared with last year, to 2.61 million acres." Use a demand and supply graph to analyze the effect on the equilibrium price of rice resulting from the increase in the demand for corn.

Source: Owen Fletcher, "Farmers Lose Their Taste for Rice," *Wall Street Journal*, April 1, 2013.

4.4 According to an article on the wine market in the *Wall Street Journal*, "many farmers in recent years stopped planting new [grape] vines, and some even switched to nuts, vegetables and other fruit." But at the same time, "Americans kept drinking more wine." Use demand and supply graphs to illustrate your answers to the following questions:
   a. Can we use this information to be certain whether the equilibrium quantity of wine will increase or decrease?
   b. Can we use this information to be certain whether the equilibrium price of wine will increase or decrease?

Source: Mike Esterl, "Fewer Grapes, More Drinkers," *Wall Street Journal*, June 8, 2012.

4.5 **[Related to the** Making the Connection**]** More than half of homes in the United States are heated by burning natural gas. According to an article in the *Wall Street Journal*, demand for natural gas decreased during the winter of 2012 because of unusually warm weather. At the same time, "robust production [of natural gas] from U.S. shale fields has created record supplies." Use demand and supply graphs to illustrate your answers to the following questions:

a. Can we use this information to be certain whether the equilibrium quantity of natural gas increased or decreased?

b. Can we use this information to be certain whether the equilibrium price of natural gas increased or decreased?

Source: Christian Berthelsen, "Natural-Gas Futures Slide," *Wall Street Journal*, January 11, 2012.

4.6 [Related to Solved Problem 4**]** The demand for watermelons is highest during summer and lowest during winter. Yet, watermelon prices are normally lower in summer than in winter. Use a demand and supply graph to demonstrate how this is possible. Be sure to carefully label the curves in your graph and to clearly indicate the equilibrium summer price and the equilibrium winter price.

4.7 [Related to Solved Problem 4**]** According to one observer of the lobster market: "After Labor Day, when the vacationers have gone home, the lobstermen usually have a month or more of good fishing conditions, except for the occasional hurricane." Use a demand and supply graph to explain whether lobster prices are likely to be higher or lower during the fall than during the summer.

Source: Jay Harlow, "Lobster: An Affordable Luxury," www.Sallybernstein.com.

4.8 [Related to Solved Problem 4**]** An article in the *Wall Street Journal* discussed the market for gasoline in the United States during the summer of 2013. Compared with the previous summer, the article stated that there will be "lower demand, as cars become more efficient" and "growth in oil production from hydraulic fracturing of shale deposits in the U.S."

a. Draw a demand and supply graph of the market for gasoline to analyze the situation described in this article. Be sure to indicate the equilibrium price and quantity of gasoline in the summer of 2012, the equilibrium price and quantity of gasoline in the summer of 2013, and any shifts in the demand curve and supply curve for gasoline.

b. Can you be certain from your analysis whether the equilibrium price of gasoline would increase or decrease? Can you be certain whether the equilibrium quantity of gasoline would increase or decrease? Briefly explain.

Source: Ángel González, "Drivers Can Expect a Break On Summer Gas Prices," *Wall Street Journal*, April 14, 2013.

4.9 Years ago, an apple producer argued that the United States should enact a tariff, or a tax, on imports of bananas. His reasoning was that "the enormous imports of cheap bananas into the United States tend to curtail the domestic consumption of fresh fruits produced in the United States."

a. Was the apple producer assuming that apples and bananas are substitutes or complements? Briefly explain.

b. If a tariff on bananas acts as an increase in the cost of supplying bananas in the United States, use two demand and supply graphs to show the effects of the apple producer's proposal. One graph should show the effect on the banana market in the United States, and the other graph should show the effect on the apple market in the United States. Be sure to label the change in equilibrium price and quantity in each market and any shifts in the demand and supply curves.

Source: Douglas A. Irwin, *Peddling Protectionism: Smoot-Hawley and the Great Depression*, Princeton, NJ: Princeton University Press, 2011, p. 22.

4.10 An article in the *Wall Street Journal* noted that the demand for video Internet advertising was increasing at the same time that the number of Internet sites accepting advertising was also increasing. After reading the article, a student argues: "From this information, we know that the price of Internet ads should rise, but we don't know whether the total quantity of Internet ads will increase or decrease." Is the student's analysis correct? Illustrate your answer with a demand and supply graph.

Source: Suzanne Vranica, "Web Video: Bigger and Less Profitable," *Wall Street Journal*, March 14, 2013.

4.11 Historically, the production of many perishable foods, such as dairy products, was highly seasonal. As the supply of those products fluctuated, prices tended to fluctuate tremendously—typically by 25 to 50 percent or more—over the course of the year. One effect of mechanical refrigeration, which was commercialized on a large scale in the last decade of the nineteenth century, was that suppliers could store perishables from one season to the next. Economists have estimated that as a result of refrigerated storage, wholesale prices rose by roughly 10 percent during peak supply periods, while they fell by almost the same amount during the off season. Use a demand and supply graph for each season to illustrate how refrigeration affected the market for perishable food.

Source: Lee A. Craig, Barry Goodwin, and Thomas Grennes, "The Effect of Mechanical Refrigeration on Nutrition in the U.S.," *Social Science History*, Vol. 28, No. 2, Summer 2004, pp. 327–328.

4.12 If the equilibrium price and quantity of a product were $100 and 1,000 units per month in 2013 and are $150 and 800 units per month in 2014, did this product experience a larger shift in its demand curve or supply curve from 2013 to 2014? Briefly explain.

4.13 [Related to the Don't Let This Happen to You**]** A student writes the following: "Increased production leads to a lower price, which in turn increases demand." Do you agree with his reasoning? Briefly explain.

4.14 [Related to the Don't Let This Happen to You**]** A student was asked to draw a demand and supply graph to illustrate the effect on the market for smartphones of a fall in the price of displays used in smartphones, holding everything else constant. She drew the following graph and explained it as follows:

Displays are an input to smartphones, so a fall in the price of displays will cause the supply curve for smartphones to shift to the right (from S_1 to S_2). Because this shift in the supply curve results in a lower price (P_2), consumers will want to buy more smartphones, and the demand curve will shift to the right (from D_1 to D_2). We know that

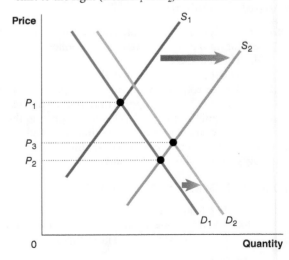

more smartphones will be sold, but we can't be sure whether the price of smartphones will rise or fall. That depends on whether the supply curve or the demand curve has shifted farther to the right. I assume that the effect on supply is greater than the effect on demand, so I show the final equilibrium price (P_3) as being lower than the initial equilibrium price (P_1).

Explain whether you agree or disagree with the student's analysis. Be careful to explain exactly what—if anything—you find wrong with her analysis.

4.15 Following are four graphs and four market scenarios, each of which would cause either a movement along the supply curve for Pepsi or a shift of the supply curve. Match each scenario with the appropriate graph.
  a. A decrease in the supply of Coke
  b. A drop in the average household income in the United States from $52,000 to $50,000
  c. An improvement in soft drink bottling technology
  d. An increase in the prices of sugar and high-fructose corn syrup

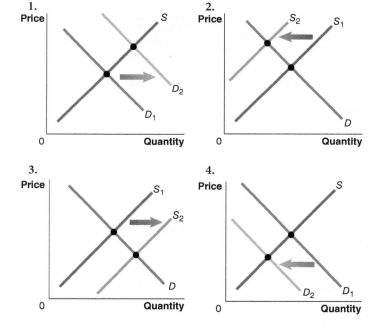

4.16 Proposals have been made to increase government regulation of firms providing childcare services by, for instance, setting education requirements for childcare workers. Suppose that these regulations increase the quality of childcare and cause the demand for childcare services to increase. At the same time, assume that complying with the new government regulations increases the costs of firms providing childcare services. Draw a demand and supply graph to illustrate the effects of these changes in the market for childcare services. Briefly explain whether the total quantity of childcare services purchased will increase or decrease as a result of regulation.

4.17 Which of the following graphs best represents what happens in the market for hotel rooms at a ski resort during the winter? Briefly explain. From the graph that you picked, what would be the result during the winter if hotel rates stayed at their summer level?

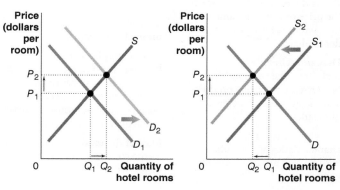

4.18 The following graphs show the supply and demand curves for two markets. One of the markets is for Tesla automobiles, and the other is for a cancer-fighting drug, without which lung cancer patients will die. Briefly explain which graph most likely represents which market.

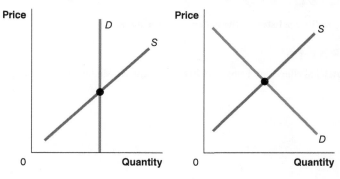

Glossary

***Ceteris paribus* ("all else equal") condition** The requirement that when analyzing the relationship between two variables—such as price and quantity demanded—other variables must be held constant.

Competitive market equilibrium A market equilibrium with many buyers and sellers.

Complements Goods and services that are used together.

Demand curve A curve that shows the relationship between the price of a product and the quantity of the product demanded.

Demand schedule A table that shows the relationship between the price of a product and the quantity of the product demanded.

Demographics The characteristics of a population with respect to age, race, and gender.

Income effect The change in the quantity demanded of a good that results from the effect of a change in the good's price on consumers' purchasing power, holding all other factors constant.

Inferior good A good for which the demand increases as income falls and decreases as income rises.

Law of demand The rule that, holding everything else constant, when the price of a product falls, the quantity demanded of the product will increase, and when the price of a product rises, the quantity demanded of the product will decrease.

Law of supply The rule that, holding everything else constant, increases in price cause increases in the quantity supplied, and decreases in price cause decreases in the quantity supplied.

Market demand The demand by all the consumers of a given good or service.

Market equilibrium A situation in which quantity demanded equals quantity supplied.

Normal good A good for which the demand increases as income rises and decreases as income falls.

Perfectly competitive market A market that meets the conditions of (1) many buyers and sellers, (2) all firms selling identical products, and (3) no barriers to new firms entering the market.

Quantity demanded The amount of a good or service that a consumer is willing and able to purchase at a given price.

Quantity supplied The amount of a good or service that a firm is willing and able to supply at a given price.

Shortage A situation in which the quantity demanded is greater than the quantity supplied.

Substitutes Goods and services that can be used for the same purpose.

Substitution effect The change in the quantity demanded of a good that results from a change in price making the good more or less expensive relative to other goods that are substitutes.

Supply curve A curve that shows the relationship between the price of a product and the quantity of the product supplied.

Supply schedule A table that shows the relationship between the price of a product and the quantity of the product supplied.

Surplus A situation in which the quantity supplied is greater than the quantity demanded.

Technological change A change in the ability of a firm to produce a given level of output with a given quantity of inputs.

Credits

Credits are listed in the order of appearance.

Photo

Ariel Skelley/Blend Images/Corbis; Wavebreak Media/Thinkstock; Eric Audras/Alamy; Susanna Bates/EPA/Landov

Economic Efficiency, Government Price Setting, and Taxes

From Chapter 4 of *Economics*, Fifth Edition. R. Glenn Hubbard and Anthony Patrick O'Brien. Copyright © 2015 by Pearson Education, Inc. All rights reserved.

Economic Efficiency, Government Price Setting, and Taxes

Chapter Outline and Learning Objectives

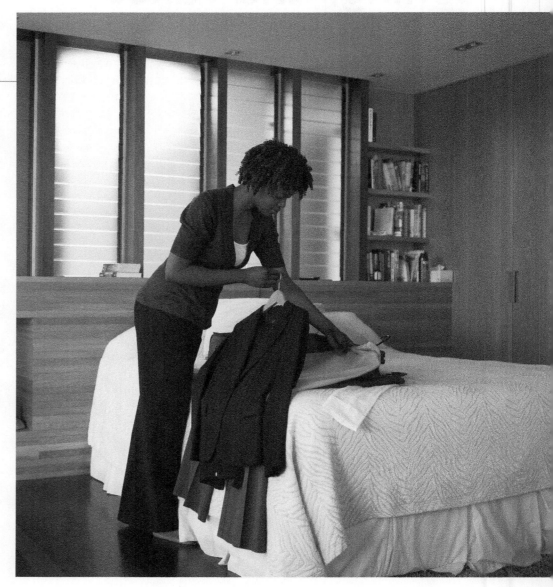

The Sharing Economy, Phone Apps, and Rent Control

The role of markets is to bring together buyers and sellers. Recently, Internet start-up companies have created rental markets for short-term use of apartments, cars, boats, bicycles, and other goods. For example, people who download the Airbnb app can search for short-term room rentals in 30,000 cities in 192 countries. The suppliers in this market typically want to earn extra money by renting their house, apartment, or sometimes just a single room, for a few days. Airbnb, Roomorama, Getaround, RelayRides, and SnapGoods, among other sites, facilitate peer-to-peer rentals. The *Economist* magazine has referred to the rapid increase in the number of people using these sites as the rise of the "sharing economy."

Airbnb was founded in 2008 and is based in San Francisco. More than 2.5 million people rented rooms using the site in 2012. Despite this success, Airbnb has run into problems, particularly in cities that have rent control regulations. In New York, San Francisco, Los Angeles, and nearly 200 smaller cities in the United States, apartments are subject to rent control by the local government. Rent control puts a legal limit on the rent that landlords can charge for an apartment. Supporters of rent control argue it is necessary to preserve affordable apartments in cities where equilibrium market rents would be above what middle- and lower-income people are willing and able to pay. But, as we will see in this chapter, rent controls cause a shortage of apartments and give people an incentive to list their apartments on Airbnb or other sites at rents far above the controlled rents. In San Francisco, a number of landlords complain that some high-income renters have moved out of the city but have kept their rent-controlled apartments in order to rent them using the apartment-sharing sites.

Some observers argue that the difficulty governments face regulating peer-to-peer rental sites will make it impossible to enforce rent control rules. Rent control supporters argue that city governments should do a better job of enforcing regulations that they believe some users of Airbnb and other sites are violating. As the head of the San Francisco Tenants Union noted: "All you have to do is sit in front of the computer for a few hours, and you can identify a lot of the lawbreakers. But there's no enforcement by the city."

AN INSIDE LOOK AT POLICY explains how the sharing economy is benefiting consumers by giving them access to previously unavailable products and services, including rooms to rent from homeowners.

Sources: "The Rise of the Sharing Economy" and "All Eyes on the Sharing Economy," *Economist*, March 9, 2013; "NYC Judge: Renting Apartments Using Airbnb Illegal," Associated Press, May 22, 2013; Steven T. Jones, "Airbnb's Tax and Tenant Law Violations Headed for Hearings," sfbg.com, March 28, 2013; and C.W. Nevius, "Rent Control Sometimes Benefitting the Rich," *San Francisco Chronicle*, June 16, 2012.

Economics in Your Life

Does Rent Control Make It Easier for You to Find an Affordable Apartment?

Suppose you have job offers in two cities. One factor in deciding which job to accept is whether you can find an affordable apartment. If one city has rent control, are you more likely to find an affordable apartment in that city, or would you be better off looking for an apartment in a city without rent control? As you read the chapter, try to answer this question. You can check your answer against the one we provide at the end of this chapter.

W̲e have seen that in a competitive market the price adjusts to ensure that the quantity demanded equals the quantity supplied. Stated another way, in equilibrium, every consumer willing to pay the market price is able to buy as much of the product as the consumer wants, and every firm willing to accept the market price can sell as much as it wants. Even so, consumers would naturally prefer to pay a lower price, and sellers would prefer to receive a higher price. Normally, consumers and firms have no choice but to accept the equilibrium price if they wish to participate in the market. Occasionally, however, consumers succeed in having the government impose a **price ceiling**, which is a legally determined maximum price that sellers may charge. Rent control is an example of a price ceiling. Firms also sometimes succeed in having the government impose a **price floor**, which is a legally determined minimum price that sellers may receive. In markets for farm products such as milk, the government has been setting price floors that are above the equilibrium market price since the 1930s.

Another way the government intervenes in markets is by imposing taxes. The government relies on the revenue raised from taxes to finance its operations. Unfortunately, whenever the government imposes a price ceiling, a price floor, or a tax, there are predictable negative economic consequences. It is important for government policymakers and voters to understand the negative consequences when evaluating these policies. Economists have developed the concepts of *consumer surplus*, *producer surplus*, and *deadweight loss* to analyze the economic effects of price ceilings, price floors, and taxes.

Price ceiling A legally determined maximum price that sellers may charge.

Price floor A legally determined minimum price that sellers may receive.

Distinguish between the concepts of consumer surplus and producer surplus.

Consumer Surplus and Producer Surplus

Consumer surplus measures the dollar benefit consumers receive from buying goods or services in a particular market. Producer surplus measures the dollar benefit firms receive from selling goods or services in a particular market. Economic surplus in a market is the sum of consumer surplus and producer surplus. As we will see, *when the government imposes a price ceiling or a price floor, the amount of economic surplus in a market is reduced*; in other words, price ceilings and price floors reduce the total benefit to consumers and firms from buying and selling in a market. To understand why this is true, we need to understand how consumer surplus and producer surplus are determined.

Consumer Surplus

Consumer surplus is the difference between the highest price a consumer is willing to pay for a good or service and the actual price the consumer pays. Suppose you are in Wal-Mart, and you see a DVD of *World War Z* on the shelf. The DVD doesn't have a price sticker, so you take it to the register to check the price. As you walk to the register, you think to yourself that $18 is the highest price you would be willing to pay. At the register, you find out that the price is actually $12, so you buy the DVD. Your consumer surplus in this example is $6: the difference between the $18 you were willing to pay and the $12 you actually paid.

We can use the demand curve to measure the total consumer surplus in a market. Demand curves show the willingness of consumers to purchase a product at different prices. Consumers are willing to purchase a product up to the point where the marginal benefit of consuming a product is equal to its price. The **marginal benefit** is the additional benefit to a consumer from consuming one more unit of a good or service. As a simple example, suppose there are only four consumers in the market for chai tea: Theresa, Tom, Terri, and Tim. Because these four consumers have different tastes for tea and different incomes, the marginal benefit each of them receives from consuming a cup of tea will be different. Therefore, the highest price each is willing to pay for a cup of tea is also different. In Figure 1, the information from the table is used to construct a demand curve for chai tea. For prices above $6 per cup, no tea is sold because $6 is the highest price any of the consumers is willing to pay. At a price of $5, both Theresa and

Consumer surplus The difference between the highest price a consumer is willing to pay for a good or service and the actual price the consumer pays.

Marginal benefit The additional benefit to a consumer from consuming one more unit of a good or service.

Consumer	Highest Price Willing to Pay
Theresa	$6
Tom	5
Terri	4
Tim	3

Figure 1

Deriving the Demand Curve for Chai Tea

With four consumers in the market for chai tea, the demand curve is determined by the highest price each consumer is willing to pay. For prices above $6, no tea is sold because $6 is the highest price any consumer is willing to pay. For prices of $3 and below, each of the four consumers is willing to buy a cup of tea.

Tom are willing to buy tea, so two cups are sold. At prices of $3 and below, all four consumers are willing to buy tea, and four cups are sold.

Suppose the market price of tea is $3.50 per cup. As Figure 2 shows, the demand curve allows us to calculate the total consumer surplus in this market. Panel (a) shows that the highest price Theresa is willing to pay is $6, but because she pays only $3.50, her consumer surplus is $2.50 (shown by the area of rectangle A). Similarly, Tom's consumer surplus is $1.50 (rectangle B), and Terri's consumer surplus is $0.50 (rectangle C). Tim is

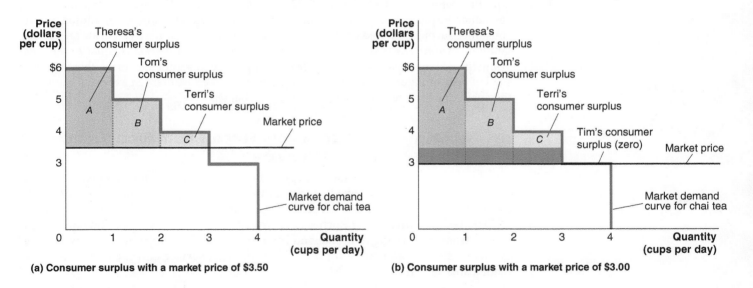

(a) Consumer surplus with a market price of $3.50

(b) Consumer surplus with a market price of $3.00

Figure 2 Measuring Consumer Surplus

Panel (a) shows the consumer surplus for Theresa, Tom, and Terri when the price of tea is $3.50 per cup. Theresa's consumer surplus is equal to the area of rectangle A and is the difference between the highest price she would pay—which is $6—and the market price of $3.50. Tom's consumer surplus is equal to the area of rectangle B, and

Terri's consumer surplus is equal to the area of rectangle C. Total consumer surplus in this market is equal to the sum of the areas of rectangles A, B, and C, or the total area below the demand curve and above the market price. In panel (b), consumer surplus increases by the dark blue area as the market price declines from $3.50 to $3.00.

Figure 3

Total Consumer Surplus in the Market for Chai Tea

The demand curve shows that most buyers of chai tea would have been willing to pay more than the market price of $2.00. For each buyer, consumer surplus is equal to the difference between the highest price he or she is willing to pay and the market price actually paid. Therefore, the total amount of consumer surplus in the market for chai tea is equal to the area below the demand curve and above the market price. Consumer surplus represents the benefit to consumers in excess of the price they paid to purchase a product.

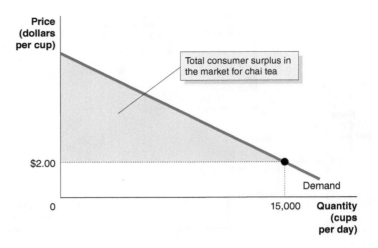

unwilling to buy a cup of tea at a price of $3.50, so he doesn't participate in this market and receives no consumer surplus. In this simple example, the total consumer surplus is equal to $2.50 + $1.50 + $0.50 = $4.50 (or the sum of the areas of rectangles A, B, and C). Panel (b) shows that a lower price will increase consumer surplus. If the price of tea falls from $3.50 per cup to $3.00, Theresa, Tom, and Terri each receive $0.50 more in consumer surplus (shown by the dark blue areas), so the total consumer surplus in the market rises to $6.00. Tim now buys a cup of tea but doesn't receive any consumer surplus because the price is equal to the highest price he is willing to pay. In fact, Tim is indifferent between buying the cup or not—his well-being is the same either way.

The market demand curves shown in Figures 1 and 2 do not look like the typical smooth demand curve because in this case we have only a small number of consumers, each consuming a single cup of tea. With many consumers, the market demand curve for chai tea will have the normal smooth shape shown in Figure 3. In this figure, the quantity demanded at a price of $2.00 is 15,000 cups per day. We can calculate total consumer surplus in Figure 3 the same way we did in Figures 1 and 2—by adding up the consumer surplus received on each unit purchased. Once again, we can draw an important conclusion: *The total amount of consumer surplus in a market is equal to the area below the demand curve and above the market price.* Consumer surplus is shown as the shaded area in Figure 3 and represents the benefit to consumers in excess of the price they paid to purchase a product—in this case, chai tea.

Making the Connection

The Consumer Surplus from Broadband Internet Service

Consumer surplus allows us to measure the benefit consumers receive in excess of the price they paid to purchase a product. Shane Greenstein of Northwestern University and Ryan McDevitt of the University of Rochester estimated the consumer surplus that households receive from subscribing to broadband Internet service. To carry out the analysis, they estimated the demand curve for broadband Internet service and then computed the shaded area shown in the following graph.

In the year they analyzed, 47 million consumers paid an average price of $36 per month to subscribe to a broadband Internet service. The demand curve shows the marginal benefit consumers receive from subscribing to a broadband Internet service rather than using dialup or doing without access to the Internet. The area below the demand curve and above the $36 price line represents the difference between the price consumers would have paid rather than do without broadband service and the $36 they did pay. The shaded area on the graph represents the total consumer surplus in the market for broadband Internet service. Greenstein and McDevitt estimate that the value of this

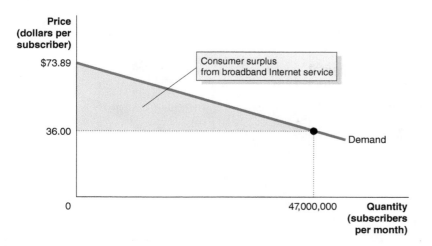

area is $890.4 million. This value is one month's benefit to the consumers who subscribe to a broadband Internet service.

Source: Shane Greenstein and Ryan C. McDevitt, "The Broadband Bonus: Estimating Broadband Internet's Economic Value," *Telecommunications Policy*, Vol. 35, No. 7, August 2011, pp. 617–632.

Your Turn: For more practice do related problem 1.11 at the end of this chapter.

Producer Surplus

Just as demand curves show the willingness of consumers to buy a product at different prices, supply curves show the willingness of firms to supply a product at different prices. The willingness to supply a product depends on the cost of producing it. Firms will supply an additional unit of a product only if they receive a price equal to the additional cost of producing that unit. **Marginal cost** is the additional cost to a firm of producing one more unit of a good or service. Consider the marginal cost to the firm Heavenly Tea of producing one more cup of tea: In this case, the marginal cost includes the ingredients to make the tea and the wages paid to the worker preparing the tea. Often, the marginal cost of producing a good increases as more of the good is produced during a given period of time. Increasing marginal cost is the key reason that supply curves are upward sloping.

Panel (a) of Figure 4 shows Heavenly Tea's producer surplus. For simplicity, we show Heavenly producing only a small quantity of tea. The figure shows that Heavenly's marginal cost of producing the first cup of tea is $1.25, its marginal cost of producing the second cup is $1.50, and so on. The marginal cost of each cup of tea is the lowest price Heavenly is willing to accept to supply that cup. The supply curve, then, is also a marginal cost curve. Suppose the market price of tea is $2.00 per cup. On the first cup of tea, the price is $0.75 higher than the lowest price that Heavenly is willing to accept. **Producer surplus** is the difference between the lowest price a firm would be willing to accept for a good or service and the price it actually receives. Therefore, Heavenly's producer surplus on the first cup is $0.75 (shown by the area of rectangle *A*), its producer surplus on the second cup is $0.50 (rectangle *B*), and its producer surplus on the third cup is $0.25 (rectangle *C*). Heavenly will not be willing to supply the fourth cup because the marginal cost of producing it is greater than the market price. Heavenly Tea's total producer surplus is equal to $0.75 + $0.50 + $0.25 = $1.50 (or the sum of the areas of rectangles *A*, *B*, and *C*). A higher price will increase producer surplus. For example, if the market price of chai tea rises from $2.00 to $2.25, Heavenly Tea's producer surplus will increase from $1.50 to $2.25. (Make sure you understand how the new level of producer surplus was calculated.)

The supply curve shown in panel (a) of Figure 4 does not look like the typical smooth curve because we are looking at a single firm producing only a small quantity of tea. With

Marginal cost The additional cost to a firm of producing one more unit of a good or service.

Producer surplus The difference between the lowest price a firm would be willing to accept for a good or service and the price it actually receives.

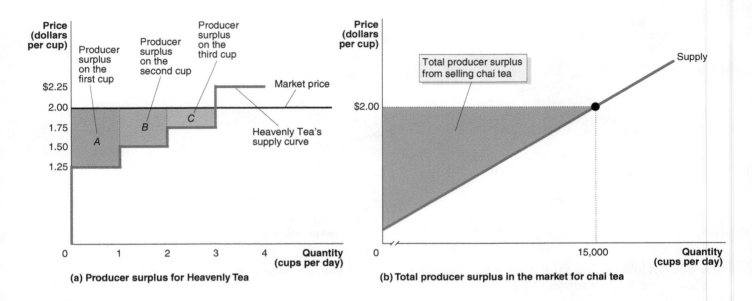

Figure 4 Measuring Producer Surplus

Panel (a) shows Heavenly Tea's producer surplus. The lowest price Heavenly Tea is willing to accept to supply a cup of tea is equal to its marginal cost of producing that cup. When the market price of tea is $2.00, Heavenly receives producer surplus of $0.75 on the first cup (the area of rectangle *A*), $0.50 on the second cup (rectangle *B*), and $0.25 on the third cup (rectangle *C*).

In panel (b), the total amount of producer surplus tea sellers receive from selling chai tea can be calculated by adding up for the entire market the producer surplus received on each cup sold. In the figure, total producer surplus is equal to the shaded area above the supply curve and below the market price.

many firms, the market supply curve for chai tea will have the normal smooth shape shown in panel (b) of Figure 4. In panel (b), the quantity supplied at a price of $2.00 is 15,000 cups per day. We can calculate total producer surplus in panel (b) the same way we did in panel (a): by adding up the producer surplus received on each cup sold. Therefore, *the total amount of producer surplus in a market is equal to the area above the market supply curve and below the market price*. The total producer surplus tea sellers receive from selling chai tea is shown as the shaded area in panel (b) of Figure 4.

What Consumer Surplus and Producer Surplus Measure

We have seen that consumer surplus measures the benefit to consumers from participating in a market, and producer surplus measures the benefit to producers from participating in a market. It is important to be clear about what these concepts are measuring. In a sense, consumer surplus measures the *net* benefit to consumers from participating in a market rather than the *total* benefit. That is, if the price of a product were zero, the consumer surplus in a market would be all of the area under the demand curve. When the price is not zero, consumer surplus is the area below the demand curve and above the market price. So, consumer surplus in a market is equal to the total benefit consumers receive minus the total amount they must pay to buy the good or service.

Similarly, producer surplus measures the *net* benefit received by producers from participating in a market. If producers could supply a good or service at zero cost, the producer surplus in a market would be all of the area below the market price. When cost is not zero, producer surplus is the area below the market price and above the supply curve. So, producer surplus in a market is equal to the total amount firms receive from consumers minus the cost of producing the good or service.

2 LEARNING OBJECTIVE

Understand the concept of economic efficiency.

The Efficiency of Competitive Markets

A *competitive market* is a market with many buyers and many sellers. An important advantage of the market system is that it results in efficient economic outcomes. But what does *economic efficiency* mean? The concepts we have developed so far in this chapter give us two ways to think about the economic efficiency of competitive markets. We can think in terms of marginal benefit and marginal cost. We can also think in terms of consumer surplus and producer surplus. As we will see, these two approaches lead to the same outcome, but using both can increase our understanding of economic efficiency.

Marginal Benefit Equals Marginal Cost in Competitive Equilibrium

Figure 5 again shows the market for chai tea. Recall from our discussion that the demand curve shows the marginal benefit received by consumers, and the supply curve shows the marginal cost of production. For this market to achieve economic efficiency, the marginal benefit from the last unit sold should equal the marginal cost of production. The figure shows that this equality occurs at competitive equilibrium where 15,000 cups per day are produced and marginal benefit and marginal cost are both equal to $2.00. Why is this outcome economically efficient? Because every cup of chai tea has been produced where the marginal benefit to buyers is greater than or equal to the marginal cost to producers.

Another way to see why the level of output at competitive equilibrium is efficient is to consider what the situation would be if output were at a different level. Suppose that output of chai tea was 14,000 cups per day. Figure 5 shows that at this level of output, the marginal benefit from the last cup sold is $2.20, while the marginal cost is only $1.80. This level of output is not efficient because 1,000 more cups could be produced for which the additional benefit to consumers would be greater than the additional cost of production. Consumers would willingly purchase those cups, and tea sellers would willingly supply them, making both consumers and sellers better off. Similarly, if the output of chai tea were 16,000 cups per day, the marginal cost of the 16,000th cup is $2.20, while the marginal benefit is only $1.80. Tea sellers would only be willing to supply this cup at a price of $2.20, which is $0.40 higher than consumers would be willing to pay. In fact, consumers would not be willing to pay the price tea sellers would need to receive for any cup beyond the 15,000th.

To summarize, we can say this: *Equilibrium in a competitive market results in the economically efficient level of output, at which marginal benefit equals marginal cost.*

Economic Surplus

Economic surplus in a market is the sum of consumer surplus and producer surplus. In a competitive market, with many buyers and sellers and no government restrictions, economic surplus is at a maximum when the market is in equilibrium. To see this point, let's look one

Economic surplus The sum of consumer surplus and producer surplus.

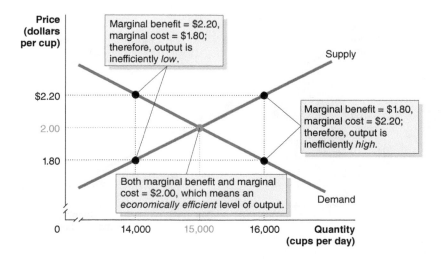

Figure 5

Marginal Benefit Equals Marginal Cost Only at Competitive Equilibrium

In a competitive market, equilibrium occurs at a quantity of 15,000 cups and a price of $2.00 per cup, where marginal benefit equals marginal cost. This level of output is economically efficient because every cup has been produced for which the marginal benefit to buyers is greater than or equal to the marginal cost to producers.

Figure 6

Economic Surplus Equals the Sum of Consumer Surplus and Producer Surplus

The economic surplus in a market is the sum of the blue area, representing consumer surplus, and the red area, representing producer surplus.

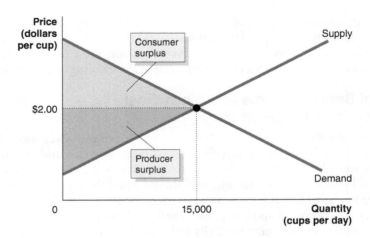

more time at the market for chai tea shown in Figure 6. The consumer surplus in this market is the blue area below the demand curve and above the line indicating the equilibrium price of $2.00. The producer surplus is the red area above the supply curve and below the price line.

Deadweight Loss

To show that economic surplus is maximized at equilibrium, consider a situation in which the price of chai tea is *above* the equilibrium price, as shown in Figure 7. At a price of $2.20 per cup, the number of cups consumers are willing to buy per day falls from 15,000 to 14,000. At competitive equilibrium, consumer surplus is equal to the sum of areas A, B, and C. At a price of $2.20, fewer cups are sold at a higher price, so consumer surplus declines to just the area of A. At competitive equilibrium, producer surplus is equal to the sum of areas D and E. At the higher price of $2.20, producer surplus changes to be equal to the sum of areas B and D. The sum of consumer and producer surplus—economic surplus—has been reduced to the sum of areas A, B, and D.

Figure 7

When a Market Is Not in Equilibrium, There Is a Deadweight Loss

Economic surplus is maximized when a market is in competitive equilibrium. When a market is not in equilibrium, there is a deadweight loss. For example, when the price of chai tea is $2.20 instead of $2.00, consumer surplus declines from an amount equal to the sum of areas A, B, and C to just area A. Producer surplus increases from the sum of areas D and E to the sum of areas B and D. At competitive equilibrium, there is no deadweight loss. At a price of $2.20, there is a deadweight loss equal to the sum of triangles C and E.

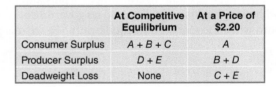

	At Competitive Equilibrium	At a Price of $2.20
Consumer Surplus	A + B + C	A
Producer Surplus	D + E	B + D
Deadweight Loss	None	C + E

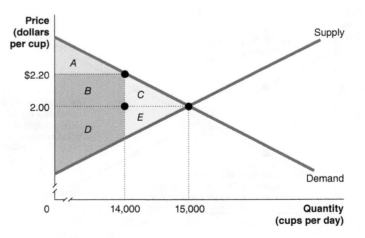

Notice that this sum is less than the original economic surplus by an amount equal to the sum of triangles *C* and *E*. Economic surplus has declined because at a price of $2.20, all the cups between the 14,000th and the 15,000th, which would have been produced in competitive equilibrium, are not being produced. These "missing" cups are not providing any consumer or producer surplus, so economic surplus has declined. The reduction in economic surplus resulting from a market not being in competitive equilibrium is called the **deadweight loss**. In the figure, deadweight loss is equal to the sum of the triangles *C* and *E*.

Deadweight loss The reduction in economic surplus resulting from a market not being in competitive equilibrium.

Economic Surplus and Economic Efficiency

Consumer surplus measures the benefit to consumers from buying a particular product, such as chai tea. Producer surplus measures the benefit to firms from selling a particular product. Therefore, economic surplus—which is the sum of the benefit to firms plus the benefit to consumers—is the best measure we have of the benefit to society from the production of a particular good or service. This gives us a second way of characterizing the economic efficiency of a competitive market: *Equilibrium in a competitive market results in the greatest amount of economic surplus, or total net benefit to society, from the production of a good or service.* Anything that causes the market for a good or service not to be in competitive equilibrium reduces the total benefit to society from the production of that good or service.

Now we can give a more general definition of *economic efficiency* in terms of our two approaches: **Economic efficiency** is a market outcome in which the marginal benefit to consumers of the last unit produced is equal to its marginal cost of production and in which the sum of consumer surplus and producer surplus is at a maximum.

Economic efficiency A market outcome in which the marginal benefit to consumers of the last unit produced is equal to its marginal cost of production and in which the sum of consumer surplus and producer surplus is at a maximum.

Government Intervention in the Market: Price Floors and Price Ceilings

3 LEARNING OBJECTIVE

Explain the economic effect of government-imposed price floors and price ceilings.

Notice that we have *not* concluded that every *individual* is better off if a market is at competitive equilibrium. We have concluded only that economic surplus, or the *total* net benefit to society, is greatest at competitive equilibrium. Any individual producer would rather receive a higher price, and any individual consumer would rather pay a lower price, but usually producers can sell and consumers can buy only at the competitive equilibrium price.

Producers or consumers who are dissatisfied with the competitive equilibrium price can lobby the government to legally require that a different price be charged. In the United States, the government only occasionally overrides the market outcome by setting prices. When the government does intervene, it can attempt to aid either sellers by requiring that a price be above equilibrium—a price floor—or buyers by requiring that a price be below equilibrium—a price ceiling. To affect the market outcome, the government must set a price floor that is above the equilibrium price or set a price ceiling that is below the equilibrium price. Otherwise, the price ceiling or price floor will not be *binding* on buyers and sellers. The preceding section demonstrates that moving away from competitive equilibrium will reduce economic efficiency. We can use the concepts of consumer surplus, producer surplus, and deadweight loss to understand more clearly the economic inefficiency of price floors and price ceilings.

Price Floors: Government Policy in Agricultural Markets

The Great Depression of the 1930s was the worst economic disaster in U.S. history, affecting every sector of the economy. Many farmers could sell their products only at very low prices. Farmers were able to convince the federal government to set price floors for many agricultural products. Government intervention in agriculture—often referred to as the *farm program*—has continued ever since. To understand how a price floor in

Figure 8

The Economic Effect of a Price Floor in the Wheat Market

If wheat farmers convince the government to impose a price floor of $8.00 per bushel, the amount of wheat sold will fall from 2.0 billion bushels per year to 1.8 billion. If we assume that farmers produce 1.8 billion bushels, producer surplus then increases by rectangle *A*—which is transferred from consumer surplus—and falls by triangle *C*. Consumer surplus declines by rectangle *A* plus triangle *B*. There is a deadweight loss equal to triangles *B* and *C*, representing the decline in economic efficiency due to the price floor. In reality, a price floor of $8.00 per bushel will cause farmers to expand their production from 2.0 billion to 2.2 billion bushels, resulting in a surplus of wheat.

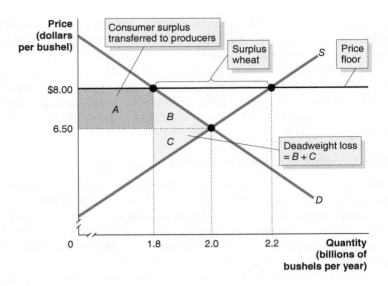

an agricultural market works, suppose that the equilibrium price in the wheat market is $6.50 per bushel, but the government decides to set a price floor of $8.00 per bushel. As Figure 8 shows, the price of wheat rises from $6.50 to $8.00, and the quantity of wheat sold falls from 2.0 billion bushels per year to 1.8 billion. Initially, suppose that production of wheat also falls to 1.8 billion bushels.

The producer surplus received by wheat farmers increases by an amount equal to the area of rectangle *A* and decreases by an amount equal to the area of triangle *C*. (This is the same result we saw in the market for chai tea in Figure 7) The area of rectangle *A* represents a transfer from consumer surplus to producer surplus. The total fall in consumer surplus is equal to the sum of the areas of rectangle *A* and triangle *B*. Wheat farmers benefit from this program, but consumers lose. There is also a deadweight loss equal to the areas of triangles *B* and *C* because economic efficiency declines as the price floor reduces the amount of economic surplus in the market for wheat. In other words, the price floor has caused the marginal benefit of the last bushel of wheat to be greater than the marginal cost of producing it. We can conclude that a price floor reduces economic efficiency.

We assumed initially that farmers reduce their production of wheat to the amount consumers are willing to buy. In fact, as Figure 8 shows, a price floor will cause the quantity of wheat that farmers want to supply to increase from 2.0 billion to 2.2 billion bushels. Because the higher price also reduces the amount of wheat consumers want to buy, the result is a surplus of 0.4 billion bushels of wheat (the 2.2 billion bushels supplied minus the 1.8 billion demanded).

The federal government's farm programs have often resulted in large surpluses of wheat and other agricultural products. In response, the government has usually either bought the surplus food or paid farmers to restrict supply by taking some land out of cultivation. Because both of these options are expensive, Congress passed the Freedom to Farm Act of 1996. The intent of the act was to phase out price floors and government purchases of surpluses and return to a free market in agriculture. To allow farmers time to adjust, the federal government began paying farmers *subsidies*, or cash payments based on the number of acres planted. Although the subsidies were originally scheduled to be phased out, Congress has passed additional farm bills that have resulted in the continuation of subsidies involving substantial federal government spending. In 2013, the Congressional Budget Office estimated that the farm bill then under consideration by Congress would result in federal spending of more than $960 billion over the following 10 years.

Making the Connection

Price Floors in Labor Markets: The Debate over Minimum Wage Policy

The minimum wage may be the most controversial "price floor." Supporters see the minimum wage as a way of raising the incomes of low-skilled workers. Opponents argue that it results in fewer jobs and imposes large costs on small businesses.

Since 2009, the national minimum wage as set by Congress has been $7.25 per hour for most occupations. It is illegal for an employer to pay less than this wage in these occupations. For most workers, the minimum wage is irrelevant because it is well below the wage employers are voluntarily willing to pay them. In 2013, only about 3 percent of workers in the United States earned the minimum wage or less. But for some low-skilled workers—such as workers in fast-food restaurants—the minimum wage is above the wage they would otherwise receive. The following figure shows the effect of the minimum wage on employment in the market for low-skilled labor.

Without a minimum wage, the equilibrium wage would be W_1 and the number of workers hired would be L_1. With a minimum wage set above the equilibrium wage, the number of workers employers demand declines from L_1 to L_2, and the quantity of labor supplied increases to L_3, leading to a surplus of workers unable to find jobs equal to $L_3 - L_2$. The quantity of labor supplied increases because the higher wage attracts more people to work. For instance, some teenagers may decide that working after school is worthwhile at the minimum wage of $7.25 per hour but would not be worthwhile at a lower wage.

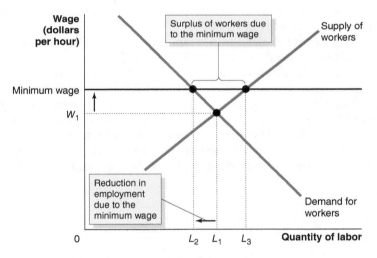

This analysis is very similar to our analysis of the wheat market in Figure 8. Just as a price floor in the wheat market leads to less wheat being consumed, a price floor in the labor market should lead to fewer workers being hired. Views differ sharply among economists, however, concerning how large a reduction in employment the minimum wage causes. For instance, David Card of the University of California, Berkeley, and Alan Krueger of Princeton University, conducted a study of fast-food restaurants in New Jersey and Pennsylvania. Their study indicated that the effect of minimum wage increases on employment is very small. This study has been controversial, however. Other economists have examined similar data and have come to the different conclusion that the minimum wage leads to a significant decrease in employment.

Whatever the extent of employment losses from the minimum wage, because it is a price floor, it will cause a deadweight loss, just as a price floor in the wheat market does. Therefore, many economists favor alternative policies for attaining the goal of raising the incomes of low-skilled workers. One policy many economists support is the *earned income tax credit*. The earned income tax credit reduces the amount of tax that low-income wage earners would otherwise pay to the federal government. Workers with very low incomes who do not owe any tax receive a payment from the government. Compared with the minimum wage, the earned income tax credit can increase the incomes of low-skilled workers without reducing employment. The earned income tax credit also places a lesser burden on the small businesses that employ many low-skilled workers and may cause a smaller loss of economic efficiency.

Sources: David Card and Alan B. Krueger, *Myth and Measurement: The New Economics of the Minimum Wage*, Princeton, J: Princeton University Press, 1995; David Neumark and William Wascher, "Minimum Wages and Employment: A Case Study of the Fast-Food Industry in New Jersey and Pennsylvania: Comment," *American Economic Review*, Vol. 90, No. 5, December 2000, pp. 1362–1396; and David Card and Alan B. Krueger, "Minimum Wages and Employment: A Case Study of the Fast-Food Industry in New Jersey and Pennsylvania: Reply," *American Economic Review*, Vol. 90, No. 5, December 2000, pp. 1397–1420.

Your Turn: Test your understanding by doing related problem 3.10 at the end of this chapter.

Price Ceilings: Government Rent Control Policy in Housing Markets

Support for governments setting price floors typically comes from sellers, and support for governments setting price ceilings typically comes from consumers. For example, when there is a sharp increase in gasoline prices, proposals are often made for the government to impose a price ceiling on the market for gasoline. As we saw in the chapter opener, a number of cities impose rent control, which puts a ceiling on the maximum rent that landlords can charge for an apartment. Figure 9 shows the market for apartments in a city that has rent control.

Without rent control, the equilibrium rent would be $2,500 per month, and 2,000,000 apartments would be rented. With a maximum legal rent of $1,500 per month, landlords reduce the quantity of apartments supplied to 1,900,000. The fall in the quantity of apartments supplied can be the result of landlords converting some apartments into offices, selling some off as condominiums, or converting some small apartment buildings into single-family homes. Over time, landlords may even abandon some apartment buildings. At one time in New York City, rent control resulted in landlords abandoning whole city blocks because they were unable to cover their costs with the rents the government allowed them to charge. In London, when rent controls were

Figure 9

The Economic Effect of a Rent Ceiling

Without rent control, the equilibrium rent is $2,500 per month. At that price, 2,000,000 apartments would be rented. If the government imposes a rent ceiling of $1,500 per month, the quantity of apartments supplied decreases to 1,900,000, and the quantity of apartments demanded increases to 2,100,000, resulting in a shortage of 200,000 apartments. Producer surplus equal to the area of rectangle *A* is transferred from landlords to renters, and there is a deadweight loss equal to the areas of triangles *B* and *C*.

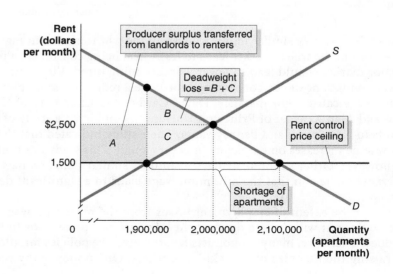

Don't Let This Happen to You

Don't Confuse "Scarcity" with "Shortage"

At first glance, the following statement seems correct: "There is a shortage of every good that is scarce." In everyday conversation, we describe a good as "scarce" if we have trouble finding it. For instance, if you are looking for a gift for a child, you might call the latest hot toy "scarce" if you are willing to buy it at its listed price but can't find it online or in any store. But economists have a broader definition of *scarce*. In the economic sense, almost everything—except undesirable things like garbage—is scarce.

A shortage of a good occurs only if the quantity demanded is greater than the quantity supplied at the current price. Therefore, the preceding statement—"There is a shortage of every good that is scarce"—is incorrect. In fact, there is no shortage of most scarce goods.

Your Turn: Test your understanding by doing related problem 3.14 at the end of this chapter.

---

applied to rooms and apartments located in a landlord's own home, the quantity of these apartments supplied decreased by 75 percent.

In Figure 9, with the rent ceiling of $1,500 per month, the quantity of apartments demanded rises to 2,100,000, resulting in a shortage of 200,000 apartments. Consumer surplus increases by rectangle *A* and falls by triangle *B*. Rectangle *A* would have been part of producer surplus if rent control were not in place. With rent control, it is part of consumer surplus. Rent control causes the producer surplus landlords receive to fall by rectangle *A* plus triangle *C*. Triangles *B* and *C* represent the deadweight loss, which results from rent control reducing the amount of economic surplus in the market for apartments. Rent control has caused the marginal benefit of the last apartment rented to be greater than the marginal cost of supplying it. We can conclude that a price ceiling, such as rent control, reduces economic efficiency. The appendix to this chapter shows how we can make quantitative estimates of the deadweight loss and provides an example of the changes in consumer surplus and producer surplus that can result from rent control.

Renters as a group benefit from rent controls—total consumer surplus is larger—but landlords lose. Because of the deadweight loss, the total loss to landlords is greater than the gain to renters. Notice also that although renters as a group benefit, the number of renters is reduced, so some renters are made worse off by rent controls because they are unable to find an apartment at the legal rent.

Black Markets and Peer-to-Peer Sites

To this point, our analysis of rent controls is incomplete. In practice, renters may be worse off and landlords may be better off than Figure 9 makes it seem. We have assumed that renters and landlords actually abide by the price ceiling, but sometimes they don't. Because rent control leads to a shortage of apartments, renters who would otherwise not be able to find apartments have an incentive to offer landlords rents above the legal maximum. When governments try to control prices by setting price ceilings or price floors, buyers and sellers often find a way around the controls. The result is a **black market** in which buying and selling take place at prices that violate government price regulations.

Airbnb and other peer-to-peer rental sites have provided landlords and tenants another way to avoid rent controls. Landlords can use these sites to convert a regular yearly rental into a series of short-term rentals for which they can charge above the legal maximum rent. Tenants can also use the sites to make a profit from rent controls. As we saw in the chapter opener, in San Francisco some tenants moved out of the city while keeping their rent-controlled apartments. They then rented out their apartments using

Black market A market in which buying and selling take place at prices that violate government price regulations.

peer-to-peer rental sites. Both San Francisco and New York have taken actions against peer-to-peer rental sites because some government officials believe the sites undermine rent control. Both cities have laws that prohibit landlords for renting apartments for less than 30 days. San Francisco also announced that anyone renting rooms through Airbnb and similar sites must pay the city's 14 percent hotel tax.

Some government officials in both cities, however, were reluctant to take actions that might limit the growth of the sharing economy of peer-to-peer rental sites. The sharing economy has the potential to improve economic efficiency and make available to consumers goods, such as cars, bikes, boats, and apartments, at lower prices. When cities have rent control laws, though, peer-to-peer sites perform a somewhat different function by making apartments available at rents higher than the legal price ceiling—apartments that renters might otherwise have difficulty finding because of the shortage caused by rent control. It remains to be seen whether local policymakers can resolve the conflict between putting legal ceilings on rents and encouraging peer-to-peer sites to operate in their cities.

Solved Problem 3

What's the Economic Effect of a Black Market in Renting Apartments?

In many cities that have rent controls, such as New York and San Francisco, the actual rents paid can be much higher than the legal maximum. Because rent controls cause a shortage of apartments, desperate tenants are often willing to pay landlords rents that are higher than the law allows, perhaps by writing a check for the legally allowed rent and paying an additional amount in cash. Look again at Figure 9.

Suppose that competition among tenants results in the black market rent rising to $3,500 per month. At this rent, tenants demand 1,900,000 apartments. Draw a graph showing the market for apartments and compare this situation with the one shown in Figure 9. Be sure to note any differences in consumer surplus, producer surplus, and deadweight loss.

Solving the Problem

Step 1: **Review the chapter material.** This problem is about price controls in the market for apartments, so you may want to review the section "Price Ceilings: Government Rent Control Policy in Housing Markets."

Step 2: **Draw a graph similar to Figure 9, with the addition of the black market price.**

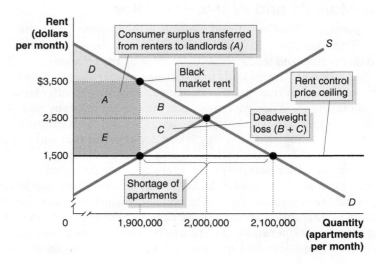

Step 3: Analyze the changes from Figure 9. The black market rent is now $3,500 per month—even higher than the original competitive equilibrium rent shown in Figure 9. So, consumer surplus declines by an amount equal to the sum of the areas of rectangle *A* and rectangle *E*. The remaining consumer surplus is triangle *D*. Note that rectangle *A*, which would have been part of consumer surplus without rent control, represents a transfer from renters to landlords. Compared with the situation shown in Figure 9, producer surplus has increased by an amount equal to the sum of the areas of rectangles *A* and *E*, and consumer surplus has declined by the same amount. Deadweight loss is equal to the sum of the areas of triangles *B* and *C*, the same as in Figure 9.

Extra Credit: This analysis leads to a surprising result: With an active black market in apartments, rent control may leave renters as a group worse off—with less consumer surplus—than if there were no rent control. There is one more possibility to consider, however. If enough landlords become convinced that they can get away with charging rents above the legal ceiling, the quantity of apartments supplied will increase. Eventually, the market could even end up at the competitive equilibrium, with an equilibrium rent of $2,500 and equilibrium quantity of 2,000,000 apartments. In that case, the rent control price ceiling becomes nonbinding, not because it was set below the equilibrium price but because it was not legally enforced.

Your Turn: For more practice, do related problem 3.15 at the end of this chapter.

Rent controls can also lead to an increase in racial and other types of discrimination. With rent controls, more renters are looking for apartments than there are apartments to rent. Landlords can afford to indulge their prejudices by refusing to rent to people they don't like. In cities without rent controls, landlords face more competition, which makes it more difficult to turn down tenants on the basis of irrelevant characteristics, such as race.

The Results of Government Price Controls: Winners, Losers, and Inefficiency

When the government imposes price floors or price ceilings, three important results occur:

- Some people win.
- Some people lose.
- There is a loss of economic efficiency.

The winners with rent control are the people who are paying less for rent because they live in rent-controlled apartments. Landlords may also gain if they break the law by charging rents above the legal maximum for their rent-controlled apartments, provided that those illegal rents are higher than the competitive equilibrium rents would be. The losers from rent control are the landlords of rent-controlled apartments who abide by the law and renters who are unable to find apartments to rent at the controlled price. Rent control reduces economic efficiency because fewer apartments are rented than would be rented in a competitive market (refer again to Figure 9). The resulting deadweight loss measures the decrease in economic efficiency.

Positive and Normative Analysis of Price Ceilings and Price Floors

Are rent controls, government farm programs, and other price ceilings and price floors bad? Questions of this type have no right or wrong answers. Economists are generally skeptical of government attempts to interfere with competitive market equilibrium. Economists know the role competitive markets have played in raising the average person's standard of living. They also know that too much government intervention has the potential to reduce the ability of the market system to produce similar increases in living standards in the future.

But the difference between positive and normative analysis is positive analysis is concerned with *what is*, and normative analysis is concerned with *what should be*. Our analysis of rent control and the federal farm programs in this chapter is positive analysis. We discussed the economic results of these programs. Whether these programs are desirable or undesirable is a normative question. Whether the gains to the winners more than make up for the losses to the losers and for the decline in economic efficiency is a matter of judgment and not strictly an economic question. Price ceilings and price floors continue to exist partly because people who understand their downside still believe they are good policies and therefore support them. The policies also persist because many people who support them do not understand the economic analysis in this chapter and so do not understand the drawbacks to these policies.

4 LEARNING OBJECTIVE

Analyze the economic impact of taxes.

The Economic Impact of Taxes

Supreme Court Justice Oliver Wendell Holmes once remarked: "Taxes are what we pay for a civilized society." When the government taxes a good or service, however, it affects the market equilibrium for that good or service. Just as with a price ceiling or price floor, one result of a tax is a decline in economic efficiency. Analyzing taxes is an important part of the field of economics known as *public finance*. In this section, we will use the model of demand and supply and the concepts of consumer surplus, producer surplus, and deadweight loss to analyze the economic impact of taxes.

The Effect of Taxes on Economic Efficiency

Whenever a government taxes a good or service, less of that good or service will be produced and consumed. For example, a tax on cigarettes will raise the cost of smoking and reduce the amount of smoking that takes place. We can use a demand and supply graph to illustrate this point. Figure 10 shows the market for cigarettes.

Without the tax, the equilibrium price of cigarettes would be $5.00 per pack, and 4 billion packs of cigarettes would be sold per year (point *A*). If the federal government requires sellers of cigarettes to pay a $1.00-per-pack tax, then their cost of selling cigarettes will increase by $1.00 per pack. This increase in costs causes the supply curve for cigarettes to shift up by $1.00 because sellers will now require a price that is $1.00 greater to supply the same quantity of cigarettes. In Figure 10, the supply curve shifts up by $1.00 to show the effect of the tax, and there is a new equilibrium price of $5.90 and a new equilibrium quantity of 3.7 billion packs (point *B*).

The federal government will collect tax revenue equal to the tax per pack multiplied by the number of packs sold, or $3.7 billion. The area shaded in green in Figure 10 represents the government's tax revenue. Consumers will pay a higher price of $5.90 per pack. Although sellers appear to be receiving a higher price per pack, once they have paid the tax, the price they receive falls from $5.00 per pack to $4.90 per pack. There is a loss of consumer surplus because consumers are paying a higher price. The price producers receive falls, so there is also a loss of producer surplus. Therefore, the tax on cigarettes has reduced *both* consumer surplus and producer surplus. Some of the reduction in consumer and producer surplus becomes tax revenue for the government. The rest of the reduction in consumer and producer surplus is equal to the deadweight loss from the tax, shown by the yellow-shaded triangle in the figure.

We can conclude that the true burden of a tax is not just the amount consumers and producers pay the government but also includes the deadweight loss. The deadweight loss from a tax is referred to as the *excess burden* of the tax. *A tax is efficient if it imposes a small excess burden relative to the tax revenue it raises.* One contribution economists make to government tax policy is to advise policymakers on which taxes are most efficient.

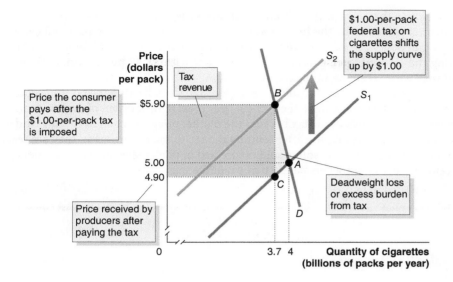

Figure 10

The Effect of a Tax on the Market for Cigarettes

Without the tax, market equilibrium occurs at point *A*. The equilibrium price of cigarettes is $5.00 per pack, and 4 billion packs of cigarettes are sold per year. A $1.00-per-pack tax on cigarettes will cause the supply curve for cigarettes to shift up by $1.00, from S_1 to S_2. The new equilibrium occurs at point *B*. The price of cigarettes will increase by $0.90, to $5.90 per pack, and the quantity sold will fall to 3.7 billion packs. The tax on cigarettes has increased the price paid by consumers from $5.00 to $5.90 per pack. Producers receive a price of $5.90 per pack (point *B*), but after paying the $1.00 tax, they are left with $4.90 (point *C*). The government will receive tax revenue equal to the green-shaded box. Some consumer surplus and some producer surplus will become tax revenue for the government, and some will become deadweight loss, shown by the yellow-shaded area.

Tax Incidence: Who Actually Pays a Tax?

The answer to the question "Who pays a tax?" seems obvious: Whoever is legally required to send a tax payment to the government pays the tax. But there can be an important difference between who is legally required to pay the tax and who actually *bears the burden* of the tax. The actual division of the burden of a tax between buyers and sellers is referred to as **tax incidence**. For example, the federal government currently levies an excise tax of 18.4 cents per gallon of gasoline sold. Gas station owners collect this tax and forward it to the federal government, but who actually bears the burden of the tax?

Tax incidence The actual division of the burden of a tax between buyers and sellers in a market.

Determining Tax Incidence on a Demand and Supply Graph Suppose that currently the federal government does not impose a tax on gasoline. In Figure 11, equilibrium in the retail market for gasoline occurs at the intersection of the demand curve and supply curve, S_1. The equilibrium price is $3.50 per gallon, and the equilibrium quantity is 144 billion gallons per year. Now suppose that the federal government imposes a 10-cents-per-gallon tax. As a result of the tax, the supply curve for gasoline will shift up by 10 cents per gallon. At the new equilibrium, where the demand curve intersects the supply curve, S_2, the price has risen by 8 cents per gallon, from $3.50 to

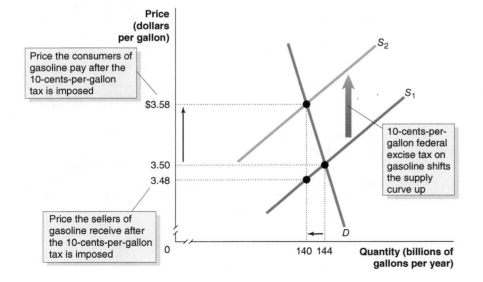

Figure 11

The Incidence of a Tax on Gasoline

With no tax on gasoline, the price would be $3.50 per gallon, and 144 billion gallons of gasoline would be sold each year. A 10-cents-per-gallon excise tax shifts up the supply curve from S_1 to S_2, raises the price consumers pay from $3.50 to $3.58, and lowers the price sellers receive from $3.50 to $3.48. Therefore, consumers pay 8 cents of the 10-cents-per-gallon tax on gasoline, and sellers pay 2 cents.

$3.58. Notice that only in the extremely unlikely case that demand is a vertical line will the market price rise by the full amount of the tax. Consumers are paying 8 cents more per gallon. Sellers of gasoline receive a new higher price of $3.58 per gallon, but after paying the 10-cents-per-gallon tax, they are left with $3.48 per gallon, or 2 cents less than they were receiving in the old equilibrium.

Although the sellers of gasoline are responsible for collecting the tax and sending the tax receipts to the government, they do not bear most of the burden of the tax. In this case, consumers pay 8 cents of the tax because the market price has risen by 8 cents, and sellers pay 2 cents of the tax because after sending the tax to the government, they are receiving 2 cents less per gallon of gasoline sold. Expressed in percentage terms, consumers pay 80 percent of the tax, and sellers pay 20 percent of the tax.

Solved Problem 4

When Do Consumers Pay All of a Sales Tax Increase?

A student makes the following statement: "If the federal government raises the sales tax on gasoline by $0.25, then the price of gasoline will rise by $0.25. Consumers can't get by without gasoline, so they have to pay the whole amount of any increase in the sales tax." Under what circumstances will the student's statement be true? Illustrate your answer with a graph of the market for gasoline.

Solving the Problem

Step 1: **Review the chapter material.** This problem is about tax incidence, so you may want to review the section "Tax Incidence: Who Actually Pays a Tax?"

Step 2: **Draw a graph like Figure 11 to illustrate the circumstances when consumers will pay all of an increase in a sales tax.**

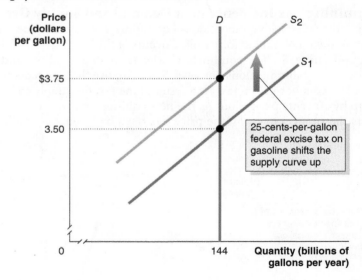

Step 3: **Use the graph to evaluate the statement.** The graph shows that consumers will pay all of an increase in a sales tax only if the demand curve is a vertical line. It is very unlikely that the demand for gasoline would look like this because we expect that for every good, an increase in price will cause a decrease in the quantity demanded. Because the demand curve for gasoline is not a vertical line, the statement is incorrect.

Your Turn: For more practice, do related problem 4.7 at the end of the chapter.

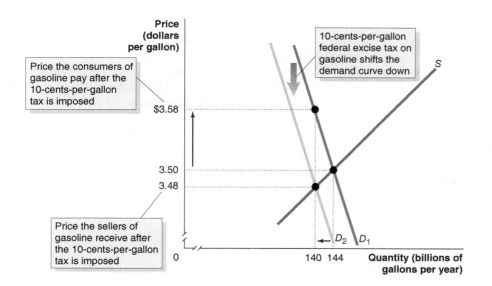

Price the consumers of gasoline pay after the 10-cents-per-gallon tax is imposed

Price the sellers of gasoline receive after the 10-cents-per-gallon tax is imposed

10-cents-per-gallon federal excise tax on gasoline shifts the demand curve down

Figure 12

The Incidence of a Tax on Gasoline Paid by Buyers

With no tax on gasoline, the demand curve is D_1. If a 10-cents-per-gallon tax is imposed that consumers are responsible for paying, the demand curve shifts down by the amount of the tax, from D_1 to D_2. In the new equilibrium, consumers pay a price of $3.58 per gallon, including the tax. Producers receive $3.48 per gallon. The result is the same as when producers were responsible for paying the tax.

Does It Make a Difference Whether the Government Collects a Tax from Buyers or Sellers?

We have already seen the important distinction between who is legally required to pay a tax and who actually *bears the burden* of a tax. We can reinforce this point by noting explicitly that the incidence of a tax does *not* depend on whether the government collects a tax from the buyers of a good or from the sellers. Figure 12 illustrates this point by showing the effect on equilibrium in the market for gasoline if a 10-cents-per-gallon tax is imposed on buyers rather than on sellers. That is, we are now assuming that instead of sellers having to collect the 10-cents-per-gallon tax at the pump, buyers are responsible for keeping track of how many gallons of gasoline they purchase and sending the tax to the government. (Of course, it would be very difficult for buyers to keep track of their purchases or for the government to check whether they were paying all of the taxes they owe. That is why the government collects the tax on gasoline from sellers.)

Figure 12 is similar to Figure 11 except that it shows the gasoline tax being imposed on buyers rather than on sellers. In Figure 12, the supply curve does not shift because nothing has happened to change the quantity of gasoline sellers are willing to supply at any given price. The demand curve has shifted, however, because consumers now have to pay a 10-cent tax on every gallon of gasoline they buy. Therefore, at every quantity, they are willing to pay a price 10 cents less than they would have without the tax. In the figure, we indicate the effect of the tax by shifting the demand curve down by 10 cents, from D_1 to D_2. Once the tax has been imposed and the demand curve has shifted down, the new equilibrium quantity of gasoline is 140 billion gallons, which is exactly the same as in Figure 11.

The new equilibrium price after the tax is imposed appears to be different in Figure 12 than in Figure 11, but if we include the tax, buyers will pay the same price and sellers will receive the same price in both figures. To see this point, notice that in Figure 11, buyers pay sellers a price of $3.58 per gallon. In Figure 12, they pay sellers only $3.48, but they must also pay the government a tax of 10 cents per gallon. So, the total price buyers pay remains $3.58 per gallon. In Figure 11, sellers receive $3.58 per gallon from buyers, but after they pay the tax of 10 cents per gallon, they are left with $3.48, which is the same amount they receive in Figure 12.

| Making the Connection | **Is the Burden of the Social Security Tax Really Shared Equally between Workers and Firms?** |

Most people who receive paychecks have several different taxes withheld by their employers, who forward these taxes directly to the government. In fact, after getting their first job, many people are shocked when they discover the gap between their gross pay and their net pay after taxes have been deducted. The largest tax many people of low or moderate income pay is FICA, which stands for the Federal Insurance Contributions Act. FICA funds the Social Security and Medicare programs, which provide income and health care to the elderly and disabled. FICA is sometimes referred to as the *payroll tax*. When Congress passed the act, it wanted employers and workers to equally share the burden of the tax. Currently, FICA is 15.3 percent of wages, with workers paying 7.65 percent, which is withheld from their paychecks, and employers paying the other 7.65 percent.

But does requiring workers and employers to each pay half the tax mean that the burden of the tax is also shared equally? Our discussion in this chapter shows that the answer is "no." In the labor market, employers are buyers, and workers are sellers. As we saw in the example of the federal tax on gasoline, whether the tax is collected from buyers or from sellers does not affect the incidence of the tax. Most economists believe, in fact, that the burden of FICA falls almost entirely on workers. The following figure, which shows the market for labor, illustrates why.

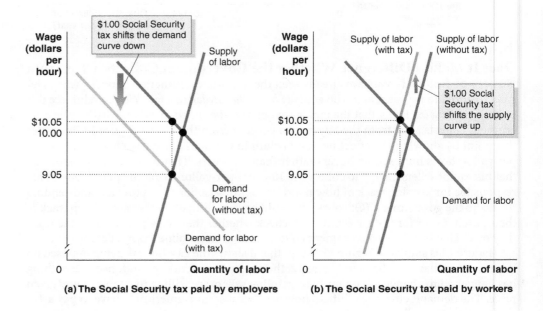

(a) The Social Security tax paid by employers   (b) The Social Security tax paid by workers

In the market for labor, the demand curve represents the quantity of labor demanded by employers at various wages, and the supply curve represents the quantity of labor supplied by workers at various wages. The intersection of the demand curve and the supply curve determines the equilibrium wage. In both panels, the equilibrium wage without a Social Security payroll tax is $10 per hour. For simplicity, let's assume that the payroll tax equals $1 per hour of work. In panel (a), we assume that employers must pay the tax. The tax causes the demand for labor curve to shift down by $1 at every quantity of labor because firms must now pay a $1 tax for every hour of labor they hire. We have drawn the supply curve for labor as being very steep because most economists believe the quantity of labor supplied by workers does not change much as the wage rate changes. In panel (a), after the tax is imposed, the equilibrium wage declines from $10 per hour to $9.05 per hour. Firms are now paying a total of $10.05 for every hour of work they hire: $9.05 in wages to workers and $1 in tax to the government. In other words, workers have paid $0.95 of the $1 tax, and firms have paid only $0.05.

Panel (b) shows that this result is exactly the same when the tax is imposed on workers rather than on firms. In this case, the tax causes the supply curve for labor to shift up by $1 at every quantity of labor because workers must now pay a tax of $1 for every hour they work. After the tax is imposed, the equilibrium wage increases to $10.05 per hour. But workers receive only $9.05 after they have paid the $1.00 tax. Once again, workers have paid $0.95 of the $1 tax, and firms have paid only $0.05.

Although the figure presents a simplified analysis, it reflects the conclusion of most economists who have studied the incidence of FICA: Even though Congress requires employers to pay half the tax and workers to pay the other half, in fact, the burden of the tax falls almost entirely on workers. This conclusion would not be changed even if Congress revised the law to require either employers or workers to pay all of the tax. The forces of demand and supply working in the labor market, and not Congress, determine the incidence of the tax.

Your Turn: Test your understanding by doing related problems 4.8 and 4.9 at the end of this chapter.

Continued

Economics in Your Life

Does Rent Control Make It Easier for You to Find an Affordable Apartment?

At the beginning of the chapter, we posed the following question: If you have job offers in two different cities, one with rent control and one without, will you be more likely to find an affordable apartment in the city with rent control? In answering the question, this chapter has shown that although rent control can keep rents lower than they might otherwise be, it can also lead to a permanent shortage of apartments. You may have to search for a long time to find a suitable apartment, and landlords may even ask you to give them payments "under the table," which would make your actual rent higher than the controlled rent. Finding an apartment in a city without rent control should be much easier, although the rent may be higher.

Conclusion

Our discussion of the model of demand and supply shows that markets free from government intervention eliminate surpluses and shortages and do a good job of responding to the wants of consumers. As we have seen in this chapter, both consumers and firms sometimes try to use the government to change market outcomes in their favor. The concepts of consumer surplus, producer surplus, and deadweight loss allow us to measure the benefits consumers and producers receive from competitive market equilibrium. These concepts also allow us to measure the effects of government price floors and price ceilings and the economic impact of taxes.

Read *An Inside Look at Policy* on the next page for an example of regulatory and legal challenges facing companies like Airbnb and Uber that promote the sharing economy.

WASHINGTON POST

The Sharing Economy: How Do You Stop Something You Can't Keep Up With?

At one time, the sharing economy looked unstoppable.

In the aftermath of the 2008 recession, everybody was looking for ways to save and generally be smarter about using the diminishing amount of what they had. By some accounts the total value of everything people are sharing today—from apartments to cars to used clothing to unused parking spaces—is close to $26 billion. Yet, even the icons of the sharing economy—companies such as Airbnb and Uber—continue to face a host of regulatory and legal challenges that could impede, if not completely foil, their plans for future growth faster than they can disrupt the markets of the incumbents.

The more recent signs that the sharing economy may not be unstoppable are the new legal troubles swirling around Airbnb, the international couchsurfing community that already has a Tumblr- and Instagram-like valuation of $1 billion. In New York City, where apartment vacancy rates remain around 2 percent—regulators and lawmakers are concerned that Airbnb might be violating New York City's "illegal hotel" laws that prohibit apartment owners from renting out rooms for less than 29 days at a time. The laws, which were originally intended to dissuade greedy landlords from drying up the housing supply even more by transforming residential buildings into pricey boutique hotels—now seem to apply equally as well to the cash-strapped condo owner with an extra room to let out for a few days.

With regard to its regulatory headaches, Airbnb is not alone. Think of mobile car-hailing business Uber, which has been involved in legal battles with regulators since Day 1. Even after Uber cleared initial regulatory hurdles in Washington, it still didn't make it any easier for a ride-sharing company like Sidecar to enter the market in its wake. If a company with access to a fleet of cars scared regulators, imagine what they felt when they learned that anyone could start picking up total strangers in their personal cars ....

You can see where this is going—whether it's apartments, condos, cars or bikes—market incumbents are making no secret of the fact that they don't like the sharing economy. Fundamentally, "sharing" means that they will sell less of whatever they offer to consumers. Therefore, incumbents have an incentive to convince regulators and lawmakers that sharing economy start-ups are somehow "illegal." In the name of protecting the interests of the consumer, they trot out all the regulations, codes and laws that are potentially being violated. In the case of Airbnb, it's easy to see how lawmakers and regulators might be convinced to shut down certain economic activity if there's the implied specter of transients coming and going from seedy apartments all over the city at all hours of the day and night.

But all of that assumes these sharing economy companies are something fundamentally new, a radical change to how the economy operates. That's not quite true. What's actually happening is that these sharing economy companies are going places where Adam Smith's "invisible hand" cannot. They are re-calibrating supply and demand, giving consumers access to otherwise unused capacity or idle assets. Instead of representing an entirely new underground economy, the companies of the sharing economy represent more of a supplement, adding capacity while driving down prices in ways that help consumers.

So, no, don't worry, the sharing economy is not illegal. Until the pace of regulatory change catches up to the pace of technological change, though, we can expect more of these legal and regulatory challenges to the likes of Airbnb and Uber. Until regulators understand how a route calculated via GPS might differ from the mileage calculated by a car's odometer or a taxi's taximeter, how could it be otherwise? The good news is that, as long as the entrenched market incumbents continue to argue that they're only acting to protect the interests of consumers, you can rest assured that the sharing economy is not going away anytime soon.

Source: Dominic Basulto, "The Sharing Economy: How Do You Stop Something You Can't Keep Up with?" *Washington Post*, May 24, 2013.

Key Points in the Article

Recent regulatory and legal challenges threaten the existence of Airbnb and Uber, two relatively new companies that are a part of the sharing economy. New York City lawmakers are exploring the possibility that Airbnb, a company that facilitates short-term room rentals in private residences, may be violating the city's hotel laws, which prohibit homeowners from renting rooms for less than 29 consecutive days. Uber, an on-demand car service company, is also involved in legal battles in several cities for potentially violating taxicab regulations. Established businesses in these industries argue that these new companies are not being subjected to the same level of regulatory laws, thereby gaining an unfair advantage.

Analyzing the News

Airbnb's primary business is matching homeowners who want to rent out rooms for a short period with travelers looking for short-term rentals. In New York City, hotel laws prohibit the renting of private rooms for less than 29 consecutive days, so some hotel and government regulators have accused Airbnb and the homeowners of violating these laws. In New York City, hotel rooms are subject to a 15 percent tax. Customers renting rooms through Airbnb are not subject to these taxes, and this loss of tax revenue may be a concern for lawmakers. The figure below shows a hypothetical example of a tax on the market for these private rooms. Without the tax, the equilibrium price is $100 per night, with a quantity of 5,000 rooms being rented each week. With a 15 percent tax ($15), the supply curve shifts up by $15, increasing the price the consumer pays to $107.50, decreasing the price the homeowner receives to $92.50, and decreasing the quantity of rooms rented to 4,200. The tax revenue is equal to $63,000 ($15 per room × 4,200 rooms).

Airbnb is competing with the established hotel industry, which is concerned that this new sharing economy will hurt their business. Customers using companies like Airbnb to rent rooms will cause a decrease in the demand for hotel rooms, which, all else equal, will decrease the equilibrium price and equilibrium quantity of hotel rooms. This loss of business and drop in revenue are certainly factors in the decision of the hotel industry to push lawmakers to apply regulations to companies conducting business in the sharing economy.

Businesses in the sharing economy are benefiting consumers by giving them access to previously unavailable products and services. With Airbnb, consumers are able to choose from a wider variety of options when it comes to renting a room, which could lower the equilibrium price of rooms. This access has the potential to increase efficiency in the market by increasing consumer surplus.

Thinking Critically About Policy

1. The figure below shows the market for private rooms before and after the imposition of a 15 percent tax. What can you tell about the burden of the tax from the figure? What effect does the tax have on economic efficiency? Use the figure to show any change in efficiency resulting from the imposition of the tax.

2. Suppose that you are a legislator in New York considering whether to exempt people using Airbnb from the rule that rooms in private homes have to be rented for at least 29 consecutive days. What considerations would you take into account in making a decision? Briefly explain whether your analysis of this issue is entirely positive, entirely normative, or a mixture of the two.

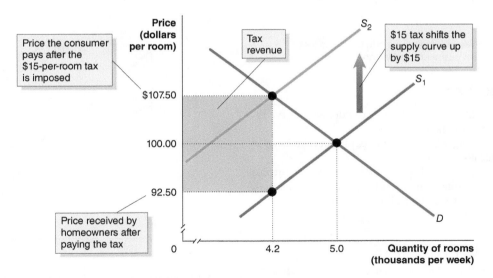

The market for private rooms before and after the imposition of a 15 percent hotel tax.

Chapter Summary and Problems

Key Terms

Black market

Consumer surplus

Deadweight loss

Economic efficiency

Economic surplus

Marginal benefit

Marginal cost

Price ceiling

Price floor

Producer surplus

Tax incidence

 Consumer Surplus and Producer Surplus

LEARNING OBJECTIVE: Distinguish between the concepts of consumer surplus and producer surplus.

Summary

Although most prices are determined by demand and supply in markets, the government sometimes imposes *price ceilings* and *price floors*. A **price ceiling** is a legally determined maximum price that sellers may charge. A **price floor** is a legally determined minimum price that sellers may receive. Economists analyze the effects of price ceilings and price floors using *consumer surplus, producer surplus,* and *deadweight loss.* **Marginal benefit** is the additional benefit to a consumer from consuming one more unit of a good or service. The demand curve is also a marginal benefit curve. **Consumer surplus** is the difference between the highest price a consumer is willing to pay for a good or service and the actual price the consumer pays. The total amount of consumer surplus in a market is equal to the area below the demand curve and above the market price. **Marginal cost** is the additional cost to a firm of producing one more unit of a good or service. The supply curve is also a marginal cost curve. **Producer surplus** is the difference between the lowest price a firm is willing to accept for a good or service and the price it actually receives. The total amount of producer surplus in a market is equal to the area above the supply curve and below the market price.

Visit **www.myeconlab.com** to complete these exercises online and get instant feedback.

Review Questions

1.1 What is marginal benefit? Why is the demand curve referred to as a marginal benefit curve?

1.2 What is marginal cost? Why is the supply curve referred to as a marginal cost curve?

1.3 What is consumer surplus? How does consumer surplus change as the equilibrium price of a good rises or falls?

1.4 What is producer surplus? How does producer surplus change as the equilibrium price of a good rises or falls?

Problems and Applications

1.5 Suppose your friend tells you that he recently purchased a particular product for $1,000 but that the product was "priceless." Although your friend is probably exaggerating, what would the consumer surplus equal for his "priceless" product?

1.6 Suppose that a frost in Florida reduces the size of the orange crop, which causes the supply curve for oranges to

shift to the left. Briefly explain whether consumer surplus will increase or decrease and whether producer surplus will increase or decrease. Use a demand and supply graph to illustrate your answers.

1.7 A student makes the following argument: "When a market is in equilibrium, there is no consumer surplus. We know this because in equilibrium, the market price is equal to the price consumers are willing to pay for the good." Briefly explain whether you agree with the student's argument.

1.8 How does consumer surplus differ from the total benefit consumers receive from purchasing products? Similarly, how does producer surplus differ from the total revenue that firms receive from selling products? Under what special case will consumer surplus equal the total benefit consumers receive from consuming a product? Under what special case will producer surplus equal the total revenue firms receive from selling a product?

1.9 In the graph below, is the consumer surplus larger with demand curve D_1 or demand curve D_2? Briefly explain. Compare the producer surplus with demand curve D_1 and with demand curve D_2.

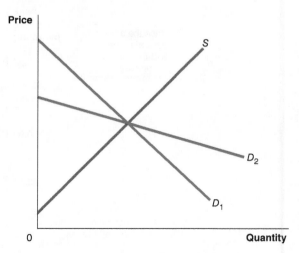

1.10 Assume that the following graph illustrates the market for a breast cancer–fighting drug, without which breast cancer patients cannot survive. What is the consumer surplus in this market? How does it differ from the consumer surplus in the markets you have studied up to this point?

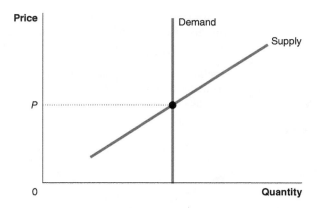

1.11 [**Related to the** Making the Connection: **The Consumer Surplus from Broadband Internet Service**] The *Making the Connection* states that the value of the area representing consumer surplus from broadband Internet service is $890.4 million. Use the information from the graph in the *Making the Connection* to show how this value was calculated.

1.12 The following graph shows the market for tickets to a concert that will be held in a local arena that seats 15,000 people. What is the producer surplus in this market? How does it differ from the producer surplus in the markets you have studied up to this point?

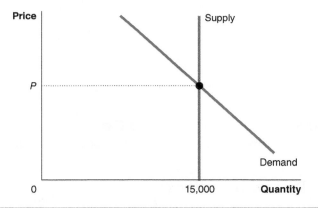

1.13 A study estimates that the total consumer surplus gained by people participating in auctions on eBay in a recent year was $7 billion. Is it likely that the total consumer surplus for the items bought in these auctions was higher or lower than it would have been if consumers had purchased these items for fixed prices in retail stores?

Source: Ravi Bapna, Wolfgang Jank, and Galit Shmueli, "Consumer Surplus in Online Auctions," *Information Systems Research*, Vol. 19, No. 4, December 2008, pp. 400–416.

1.14 Movies, songs, and books are covered by copyrights, which allow the creators of these works to keep other people from reproducing them without permission. Many people, though, violate copyright laws by using file-sharing services that allow them to download copies of songs and movies at a zero price.
  a. Does file sharing increase the consumer surplus from consuming existing songs and movies? Draw a demand curve to illustrate your answer. The demand curve should indicate the price when file sharing is not possible, the zero price with file sharing, and the amount of consumer surplus with and without file sharing.
  b. What are the likely effects of file sharing in the long run? Is file sharing likely to increase the total consumer surplus from consuming songs and movies in the long run? Briefly explain.

Source: Joel Waldfogel, "Bye, Bye, Miss American Pie? The Supply of New Recorded Music Since Napster," National Bureau of Economic Research Working Paper 16882, March 2011.

---

2 | The Efficiency of Competitive Markets

LEARNING OBJECTIVE: Understand the concept of economic efficiency.

Summary

Equilibrium in a competitive market is **economically efficient**. **Economic surplus** is the sum of consumer surplus and producer surplus. Economic efficiency is a market outcome in which the marginal benefit to consumers from the last unit produced is equal to the marginal cost of production and in which the sum of consumer surplus and producer surplus is at a maximum. When the market price is above or below the equilibrium price, there is a reduction in economic surplus. The reduction in economic surplus resulting from a market not being in competitive equilibrium is called the **deadweight loss**.

 Visit **www.myeconlab.com** to complete these exercises online and get instant feedback.

Review Questions

2.1 Define *economic surplus* and *deadweight loss*.
2.2 What is economic efficiency? Why do economists define *efficiency* in this way?

Problems and Applications

2.3 Briefly explain whether you agree with the following statement: "A lower price in a market always increases economic efficiency in that market."
2.4 Briefly explain whether you agree with the following statement: "If at the current quantity, marginal benefit is greater than marginal cost, there will be a deadweight loss in the market. However, there is no deadweight loss when marginal cost is greater than marginal benefit."

2.5 Using a demand and supply graph, illustrate and briefly explain the effect on consumer surplus and producer surplus of the price in a market being below the equilibrium price. Show any deadweight loss on your graph.

2.6 Briefly explain whether you agree with the following statement: "If consumer surplus in a market increases, producer surplus must decrease."

2.7 Does an increase in economic surplus in a market always mean that economic efficiency in the market has increased? Briefly explain.

2.8 Using the following graph, show the effects on consumer surplus and producer surplus of an increase in supply from S_1 to S_2. By how much does economic surplus increase?

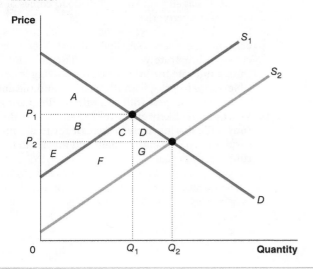

2.9 A student argues: "Economic surplus is greatest at the level of output where the difference between marginal benefit and marginal cost is largest." Do you agree? Briefly explain.

2.10 Using the following graph, explain why economic surplus would be smaller if Q_1 or Q_3 were the quantity produced than if Q_2 is the quantity produced.

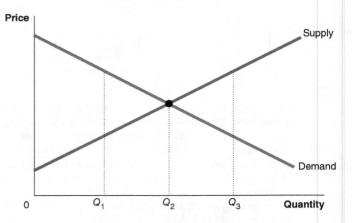

<table>
<tr><td>**3**</td><td>

Government Intervention in the Market: Price Floors and Price Ceilings
LEARNING OBJECTIVE: Explain the economic effect of government-imposed price floors and price ceilings.
</td></tr>
</table>

Summary

Producers or consumers who are dissatisfied with the equilibrium in a market can attempt to convince the government to impose a price floor or a price ceiling. Price floors usually increase producer surplus, decrease consumer surplus, and cause a deadweight loss. Price ceilings usually increase consumer surplus, reduce producer surplus, and cause a deadweight loss. The results of the government imposing price ceilings and price floors are that some people win, some people lose, and a loss of economic efficiency occurs. Price ceilings and price floors can lead to a **black market**, in which buying and selling take place at prices that violate government price regulations. Positive analysis is concerned with *what is*, and normative analysis is concerned with *what should be*. Positive analysis shows that price ceilings and price floors cause deadweight losses. Whether these policies are desirable or undesirable, though, is a normative question.

Visit **www.myeconlab.com** to complete these exercises online and get instant feedback.

Review Questions

3.1 Why do some consumers tend to favor price controls while others tend to oppose them?

3.2 Do producers tend to favor price floors or price ceilings? Briefly explain.

3.3 What is a black market? Under what circumstances do black markets arise?

3.4 Can economic analysis provide a final answer to the question of whether the government should intervene in markets by imposing price ceilings and price floors? Briefly explain.

Problems and Applications

3.5 The following graph shows the market for apples. Assume that the government has imposed a price floor of $10 per crate.

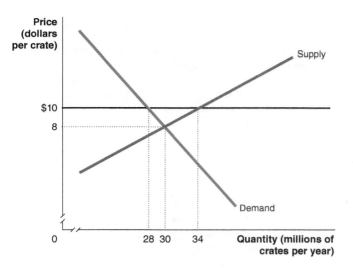

a. How many crates of apples will be sold to consumers after the price floor has been imposed?

b. Will there be a shortage or a surplus? If there is a shortage or a surplus, how large will it be?

c. Will apple producers benefit from the price floor? If so, explain how they will benefit.

3.6 Use the information on the kumquat market in the table to answer the following questions:

Price (per Crate)	Quantity Demanded (Millions of Crates per Year)	Quantity Supplied (Millions of Crates per Year)
$10	120	20
15	110	60
20	100	100
25	90	140
30	80	180
35	70	220

a. What are the equilibrium price and quantity? How much revenue do kumquat producers receive when the market is in equilibrium? Draw a graph showing the market equilibrium and the area representing the revenue kumquat producers receive.

b. Suppose the federal government decides to impose a price floor of $30 per crate. Now how many crates of kumquats will consumers purchase? How much revenue will kumquat producers receive? Assume that the government does not purchase any surplus kumquats. On your graph from question (a), show the price floor, the change in the quantity of kumquats purchased, and the revenue kumquat producers receive after the price floor is imposed.

c. Suppose the government imposes a price floor of $30 per crate and purchases any surplus kumquats from producers. Now how much revenue will kumquat producers receive? How much will the government spend on purchasing surplus kumquats? On your graph from question (a), show the area representing the amount the government spends to purchase the surplus kumquats.

3.7 Suppose that the government sets a price floor for milk that is above the competitive equilibrium price and that the government does not purchase any surplus milk.

a. Draw a graph showing this situation. Be sure your graph shows the competitive equilibrium price, the price floor, the quantity that would be sold in competitive equilibrium, and the quantity that would be sold with the price floor.

b. Compare the economic surplus in this market when there is a price floor and when there is not.

3.8 A newspaper headline reads: "State Officials Take on Pricing Regulations to Try to Provide Better, Dependable Income to Dairy Farmers." Is providing dependable income to dairy farmers a good policy goal for government officials? How are government officials likely to try to achieve this goal using pricing regulations? Should government officials use regulations to try to provide dependable incomes to every business in the country?

Source: Tim Darragh, "Thirsty for More Milk," *Morning Call*, (Allentown, PA) July 12, 2010.

3.9 According to an article in the *New York Times*, the Venezuelan government "imposes strict price controls that are intended to make a range of foods and other goods more affordable for the poor. They are often the very products that are the hardest to find."

a. Why would imposing price controls on goods make them hard to find?

b. One of the goods subject to price controls was toothpaste. Draw a graph to illustrate this situation. On your graph, be sure to indicate the areas representing consumer surplus, producer surplus, and deadweight loss.

Source: William Neuman, "With Venezuelan Cupboards Bare, Some Blame Price Controls," *New York Times*, April 20, 2012.

3.10 **[Related to the** Making the Connection: **Price Floors in Labor Markets: The Debate over Minimum Wage Policy]** Some economists studying the effects of the minimum wage law have found that it tends to reduce the employment of black teenagers relative to white teenagers. Does the graph in the *Making the Connection* help you understand why black teenagers may have been disproportionately affected by the minimum wage law? Briefly explain.

3.11 **[Related to the** Chapter Opener**]** The cities of Peabody and Woburn are five miles apart. Woburn enacts a rent control law that puts a ceiling on rents well below their competitive market value. Predict the effect of this law on the competitive equilibrium rent in Peabody, which does not have a rent control law. Illustrate your answer with a demand and supply graph.

3.12 **[Related to the** Chapter Opener**]** If San Francisco were to repeal its rent control law, would the prices for short-term rentals in the city listed on Airbnb and other peer-to-peer sites be likely to rise or fall? Briefly explain.

3.13 **[Related to the** Chapter Opener**]** The competitive equilibrium rent in the city of Lowell is currently $1,000 per month. The government decides to enact rent control and establish a price ceiling of $750 per month for apartments. Briefly explain whether rent control is likely to make each of the following people better or worse off:

a. Someone currently renting an apartment in Lowell
b. Someone who will be moving to Lowell next year and who intends to rent an apartment
c. A landlord who intends to abide by the rent control law
d. A landlord who intends to ignore the law and illegally charge the highest rent possible for his apartments

3.14 **[Related to the** Don't Let This Happen to You**]** Briefly explain whether you agree with the following statement: "If there is a shortage of a good, it must be scarce, but there is not a shortage of every scarce good."

3.15 **[Related to** Solved Problem 3**]** Use the information on the market for apartments in Bay City in the table to answer the following questions:

Rent	Quantity Demanded	Quantity Supplied
$500	375,000	225,000
600	350,000	250,000
700	325,000	275,000
800	300,000	300,000
900	275,000	325,000
1,000	250,000	350,000

a. In the absence of rent control, what is the equilibrium rent and what is the equilibrium quantity of apartments rented? Draw a demand and supply graph of the market for apartments to illustrate your answer. In equilibrium, will there be any renters who are unable to find an apartment to rent or any landlords who are unable to find a renter for an apartment?
b. Suppose the government sets a ceiling of $600 per month on rents. What is the quantity of apartments demanded, and what is the quantity of apartments supplied?
c. Assume that all landlords abide by the law. Use a demand and supply graph to illustrate the effect of this price ceiling on the market for apartments. Be sure to indicate on your graph each of the following: (i) the area representing consumer surplus after the price ceiling has been imposed, (ii) the area representing producer surplus after the price ceiling has been imposed, and (iii) the area representing the deadweight loss after the price ceiling has been imposed.
d. Assume that the quantity of apartments supplied is the same as you determined in (b). But now assume that landlords ignore the law and rent this quantity of apartments for the highest rent they can get. Briefly explain what this rent will be.

3.16 A student makes the following argument:

A price floor reduces the amount of a product that consumers buy because it keeps the price above the competitive market equilibrium. A price ceiling, though, increases the amount of a product that consumers buy because it keeps the price below the competitive market equilibrium.

Do you agree with the student's reasoning? Use a demand and supply graph to illustrate your answer.

3.17 University towns with major football programs experience an increase in demand for hotel rooms during home football weekends. Hotels respond to the increase in demand by increasing the prices they charge for rooms. Periodically, there is an outcry against the higher prices and accusations of "price gouging."

a. Draw a demand and supply graph of the market for hotel rooms in Boostertown for weekends with home football games and another graph for weekends without home football games. If the Boostertown city council passes a law stating that prices for rooms are not allowed to rise, what would happen to the market for hotel rooms during home football game weekends? Show your answer on your graph.
b. If the prices of hotel rooms are not allowed to increase, what will be the effect on out-of-town football fans?
c. How might the city council's law affect the supply of hotel rooms over time? Briefly explain.
d. University towns are not the only places that face peak and nonpeak "seasons." Can you think of other locations that face a large increase in demand for hotel rooms during particular times of the year? Why do we typically not see laws limiting the prices hotels can charge during peak seasons?

3.18 Suppose that initially the gasoline market is in equilibrium, at a price of $3.50 per gallon and a quantity of 45 million gallons per month. Then a war in the Middle East disrupts imports of oil into the United States, shifting the supply curve for gasoline from S_1 to S_2. The price of gasoline begins to rise, and consumers protest. The federal government responds by setting a price ceiling of $3.50 per gallon. Use the graph to answer the following questions:

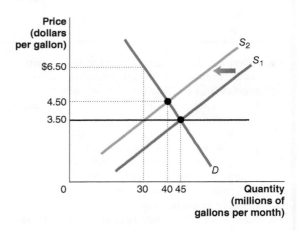

a. If there were no price ceiling, what would be the equilibrium price of gasoline, the quantity of gasoline demanded, and the quantity of gasoline supplied? Now assume that the price ceiling is imposed and that there is no black market in gasoline. What are the price of gasoline, the quantity of gasoline demanded, and the quantity of gasoline supplied? How large is the shortage of gasoline?

b. Assume that the price ceiling is imposed, and there is no black market in gasoline. Show on the graph the areas representing consumer surplus, producer surplus, and deadweight loss.

c. Now assume that there is a black market, and the price of gasoline rises to the maximum that consumers are willing to pay for the amount supplied by producers, at $3.50 per gallon. Show on the graph the areas representing producer surplus, consumer surplus, and deadweight loss.

d. Are consumers made better off with the price ceiling than without it? Briefly explain.

3.19 An editorial in the *Economist* magazine discusses the fact that in most countries—including the United States—it is illegal for individuals to buy or sell body parts, such as kidneys.

a. Draw a demand and supply graph for the market for kidneys. Show on your graph the legal maximum price of zero and indicate the quantity of kidneys supplied at this price. (*Hint:* Because we know that some kidneys are donated, the quantity supplied will not be zero.)

b. The editorial argues that buying and selling kidneys should be legalized:

> With proper regulation, a kidney market would be a big improvement over the current sorry state of affairs. Sellers could be checked for disease and drug use, and cared for after operations.... Buyers would get better kidneys, faster. Both sellers and buyers would do better than in the illegal market, where much of the money goes to middlemen.

Do you agree with this argument? Should the government treat kidneys like other goods and allow the market to determine the price?

Source: "Psst, Wanna Buy a Kidney?" *Economist*, November 18, 2006, p. 15.

The Economic Impact of Taxes

LEARNING OBJECTIVE: Analyze the economic impact of taxes.

Summary

Most taxes result in a loss of consumer surplus, a loss of producer surplus, and a deadweight loss. The true burden of a tax is not just the amount consumers and producers pay to the government but also includes the deadweight loss. The deadweight loss from a tax is called the excess burden of the tax. **Tax incidence** is the actual division of the burden of a tax. In most cases, consumers and firms share the burden of a tax levied on a good or service.

Visit **www.myeconlab.com** to complete these exercises online and get instant feedback.

Review Questions

4.1 What is meant by *tax incidence*?

4.2 What do economists mean by an *efficient tax*?

4.3 Does who is legally responsible for paying a tax—buyers or sellers—make a difference in the amount of tax each pays? Briefly explain.

Problems and Applications

4.4 As explained in the chapter, economic efficiency is a market outcome in which the marginal benefit to consumers of the last unit produced is equal to its marginal cost of production. Using this explanation of economic efficiency, explain why a tax creates a deadweight loss.

4.5 Suppose the current equilibrium price of a quarter-pound hamburger is $5, and 10 million quarter-pound hamburgers are sold per month. After the federal government imposes a tax of $0.50 per hamburger, the equilibrium

price of hamburgers rises to $5.20, and the equilibrium quantity falls to 9 million. Illustrate this situation with a demand and supply graph. Be sure your graph shows the equilibrium price before and after the tax; the equilibrium quantity before and after the tax; and the areas representing consumer surplus after the tax, producer surplus after the tax, tax revenue collected by the government, and deadweight loss.

4.6 Use the following graph of the market for cigarettes to answer the questions:

a. According to the graph, how much is the government tax on cigarettes?

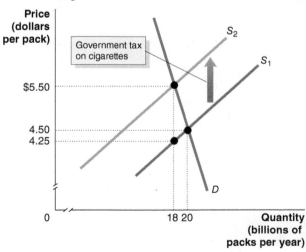

b. What price do producers receive after paying the tax?

c. How much tax revenue does the government collect?

d. How would the graph be different if the tax were collected from the buyers of cigarettes?

e. If the tax were collected from buyers, what would be the new equilibrium price that buyers pay producers of cigarettes?

f. Including the tax, what would be the total amount that cigarette buyers pay per pack?

4.7 **[Related to** Solved Problem 4**]** Suppose the federal government decides to levy a sales tax of $1.00 per pie on pizza. Briefly explain whether you agree with the following statement, made by a representative of the pizza industry:

> The pizza industry is very competitive. As a result, pizza sellers will have to pay the whole tax because they are unable to pass any of it on to consumers in the form of higher prices. Therefore, a sales tax of $1.00 per pie will result in pizza sellers receiving $1.00 less on each pie sold, after paying the tax.

Illustrate your answer with a graph.

4.8 **[Related to the** Making the Connection: **Is the Burden of the Social Security Tax Really Shared Equally Between Workers and Firms?]** If the price consumers pay and the price sellers receive are not affected by whether consumers or sellers collect a tax on a good or service, why does the government usually collect a tax from sellers rather than from consumers?

4.9 **[Related to the** Making the Connection: **Is the Burden of the Social Security Tax Really Shared Equally Between Workers and Firms?]** Suppose the government imposes a payroll tax of $1 per hour of work and collects the tax from employers. Use a graph for the market for labor to show the effect of the payroll tax, assuming the special case of a vertical supply curve of labor. By how much does the new equilibrium wage that employers pay workers fall?

4.10 The following graph shows the effect of a tax imposed on soft drinks. Use this graph to answer the questions:

a. Which areas in the graph represent the excess burden (deadweight loss) of the tax?

b. Which areas represent the revenues collected by the government from the tax?

c. Would this tax on soft drinks be considered efficient? Briefly explain.

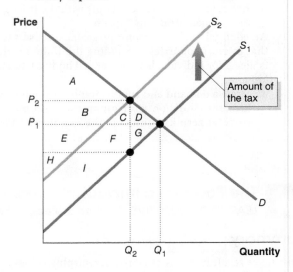

Appendix

Quantitative Demand and Supply Analysis

LEARNING OBJECTIVE

Use quantitative demand and supply analysis.

Graphs help us understand economic change *qualitatively*. For instance, a demand and supply graph can tell us that if household incomes rise, the demand curve for a normal good will shift to the right, and the price of the good will rise. Often, though, economists, business managers, and policymakers want to know more than the qualitative direction of change; they want a *quantitative estimate* of the size of the change.

In this chapter, we carried out a qualitative analysis of rent controls. We saw that imposing rent controls involves a trade-off: Renters as a group gain, but landlords lose, and the market for apartments becomes less efficient, as shown by the deadweight loss. To better evaluate rent controls, we need to know more than just that these gains and losses exist; we need to know how large they are. A quantitative analysis of rent controls will tell us how large the gains and losses are.

Demand and Supply Equations

The first step in a quantitative analysis is to supplement our use of demand and supply curves with demand and supply *equations*. Economists use data on prices, quantities, and other economic variables to statistically estimate equations for demand and supply curves. For example, suppose that economists have estimated that the demand for apartments in New York City is:

$$Q^D = 4,750,000 - 1,000P,$$

and the supply of apartments is:

$$Q^S = -1,000,000 + 1,300P.$$

We have used Q^D for the quantity of apartments demanded per month, Q^S for the quantity of apartments supplied per month, and P for the apartment rent, in dollars per month. In reality, both the quantity of apartments demanded and the quantity of apartments supplied will depend on more than just the rental price of apartments in New York City. The demand for apartments in New York City will also depend, for instance, on the average incomes of families in the New York area and on the rents of apartments in the surrounding cities. For simplicity, we will ignore these other factors.

With no government intervention, we know that at competitive market equilibrium, the quantity demanded must equal the quantity supplied, or:

$$Q^D = Q^S.$$

We can use this equation, which is called an *equilibrium condition*, to solve for the equilibrium monthly apartment rent by setting the quantity demanded from the demand equation equal to the quantity supplied from the supply equation:

$$4,750,000 - 1,000P = -1,000,000 + 1,300P$$
$$5,750,000 = 2,300P$$
$$P = \frac{5,750,000}{2,300} = \$2,500.$$

Figure A.1

Graphing Supply and Demand Equations

After statistically estimating supply and demand equations, we can use the equations to draw supply and demand curves. In this case, the equilibrium rent for apartments is $2,500 per month, and the equilibrium quantity of apartments rented is 2,250,000. The supply equation tells us that at a rent of $769, the quantity of apartments supplied will be zero. The demand equation tells us that at a rent of $4,750, the quantity of apartments demanded will be zero. The areas representing consumer surplus and producer surplus are also indicated on the graph.

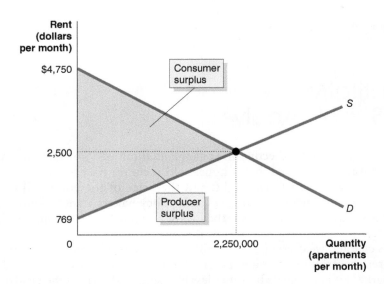

We can then substitute this price back into either the supply equation or the demand equation to find the equilibrium quantity of apartments rented:

$$Q^D = 4{,}750{,}000 - 1{,}000P = 4{,}750{,}000 - 1{,}000\,(2{,}500) = 2{,}250{,}000,$$

or

$$Q^S = -1{,}000{,}000 + 1{,}300P = -1{,}000{,}000 + 1{,}300\,(2{,}500) = 2{,}250{,}000.$$

Figure A.1 illustrates the information from these equations in a graph. The figure shows the values for rent when both the quantity supplied and the quantity demanded are zero. These values can be calculated from the demand and supply equations by setting Q^D and Q^S equal to zero and solving for price:

$$Q^D = 0 = 4{,}750{,}000 - 1{,}000P$$

$$P = \frac{4{,}750{,}000}{1{,}000} = \$4{,}750$$

and:

$$Q^S = 0 = -1{,}000{,}000 + 1{,}300P$$

$$P = \frac{-1{,}000{,}000}{-1{,}300} = \$769.23.$$

Calculating Consumer Surplus and Producer Surplus

Figure A.1 shows consumer surplus and producer surplus in this market. Recall that the sum of consumer surplus and producer surplus equals the net benefit that renters and landlords receive from participating in the market for apartments. We can use the values from the demand and supply equations to calculate the value of consumer surplus and producer surplus. Remember that consumer surplus is the area below the demand curve and above the line representing market price. Notice that this area forms a right triangle because the demand curve is a straight line—it is *linear*. The area of a triangle is equal to ½ × Base × Height. In this case, the area is:

$$^1\!/_2 \times (2{,}250{,}000) \times (4{,}750 - 2{,}500) = \$2{,}531{,}250{,}000.$$

So, this calculation tells us that the consumer surplus in the market for rental apartments in New York City is about $2.5 billion per month.

We can calculate producer surplus in a similar way. Remember that producer surplus is the area above the supply curve and below the line representing market price.

Because the supply curve is also a straight line, producer surplus in the figure is equal to the area of the right triangle:

$$\frac{1}{2} \times 2{,}250{,}000 \times (2{,}500 - 769) = \$1{,}947{,}375{,}000.$$

This calculation tells us that the producer surplus in the market for rental apartments in New York City is about $1.9 billion per month.

We can use the same type of analysis to measure the effect of rent control on consumer surplus, producer surplus, and economic efficiency. For instance, suppose the city imposes a rent ceiling of $1,500 per month. Figure A.2 can help guide us as we measure the effect.

First, we can calculate the quantity of apartments that will actually be rented by substituting the rent ceiling of $1,500 into the supply equation:

$$Q^S = -1{,}000{,}000 + (1{,}300 \times 1{,}500) = 950{,}000.$$

We also need to know the price on the demand curve when the quantity of apartments is 950,000. We can do this by substituting 950,000 for quantity in the demand equation and solving for price:

$$950{,}000 = 4{,}750{,}000 - 1{,}000P$$

$$P = \frac{-3{,}800{,}000}{-1{,}000} = \$3{,}800.$$

Compared with its value in competitive equilibrium, consumer surplus has been reduced by a value equal to the area of triangle B but increased by a value equal to the area of rectangle A. The area of triangle B is:

$$\frac{1}{2} \times (2{,}250{,}000 - 950{,}000) \times (3{,}800 - 2{,}500) = \$845{,}000{,}000,$$

and the area of rectangle A is Base $\times$ Height, or:

$$(\$2{,}500 - \$1{,}500) \times (950{,}000) = \$950{,}000{,}000.$$

The value of consumer surplus in competitive equilibrium was $2,531,250,000. As a result of the rent ceiling, it will be increased to:

$$(\$2{,}531{,}250{,}000 + 950{,}000{,}000) - \$845{,}000{,}000 = \$2{,}636{,}250{,}000.$$

Compared with its value in competitive equilibrium, producer surplus has been reduced by a value equal to the sum of the areas of triangle C and rectangle A. The area of triangle C is:

$$\frac{1}{2} \times (2{,}250{,}000 - 950{,}000) \times (2{,}500 - 1{,}500) = \$650{,}000{,}000.$$

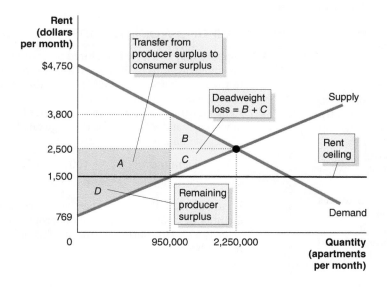

Figure A.2

Calculating the Economic Effect of Rent Controls

Once we have estimated equations for the demand and supply of rental housing, a diagram can guide our numerical estimates of the economic effects of rent control. Consumer surplus falls by an amount equal to the area of triangle B and increases by an amount equal to the area of rectangle A. Producer surplus falls by an amount equal to the sum of the areas of rectangle A and triangle C. The remaining producer surplus is equal to the area of triangle D. Deadweight loss is equal to the sum of the areas of triangles B and C.

We have already calculated the area of rectangle *A* as $950,000,000. The value of producer surplus in competitive equilibrium was $1,947,375,000. As a result of the rent ceiling, it will be reduced to:

$$\$1,947,375,000 - \$650,000,000 - \$950,000,000 = \$347,375,000.$$

The loss of economic efficiency, as measured by the deadweight loss, is equal to the value represented by the areas of triangles *B* and *C*, or:

$$\$845,000,000 + \$650,000,000 = \$1,495,000,000$$

The following table summarizes the results of the analysis (the values are in millions of dollars):

Consumer Surplus		Producer Surplus		Deadweight Loss	
Competitive Equilibrium	Rent Control	Competitive Equilibrium	Rent Control	Competitive Equilibrium	Rent Control
$2,531	$2,636	$1,947	$347	$0	$1,495

Qualitatively, we know that imposing rent control will make consumers better off, make landlords worse off, and decrease economic efficiency. The advantage of the analysis we have just gone through is that it puts dollar values on the qualitative results. We can now see how much consumers have gained, how much landlords have lost, and how great the decline in economic efficiency has been. Sometimes the quantitative results can be surprising. Notice, for instance, that after the imposition of rent control, the deadweight loss is actually much greater than the remaining producer surplus. Of course, these results are dependent on the numbers we chose for the demand and supply curve equations. Choosing different numbers would have changed the results.

Economists often study issues where the qualitative results of actions are apparent, even to non-economists. You don't have to be an economist to understand who wins and who loses from rent control or that if a company cuts the price of its product, its sales will increase. Business managers, policymakers, and the general public do, however, need economists to measure quantitatively the effects of different actions—including policies such as rent control—so that they can better assess the results of these actions.

Quantitative Demand and Supply Analysis

LEARNING OBJECTIVE: Use quantitative demand and supply analysis.

Visit www.myeconlab.com to complete these exercises online and get instant feedback.

Review Questions

A.1 In a linear demand equation, what economic information is conveyed by the intercept on the price axis? Similarly, what economic information is conveyed by the intercept on the price axis in a linear supply equation?

A.2 Suppose you were assigned the task of choosing a price that maximizes economic surplus in a market. What price would you choose? Why?

A.3 Consumer surplus is used as a measure of a consumer's net benefit from purchasing a good or service. Explain why consumer surplus is a measure of net benefit.

A.4 Why would economists use the term *deadweight loss* to describe the impact on consumer surplus and producer surplus from a price control?

Problems and Applications

A.5 Suppose that you have been hired to analyze the impact on employment from the imposition of a minimum wage in the labor market. Further suppose that you estimate the demand and supply functions for labor, where *L* stands for the quantity of labor (measured in thousands of workers) and *W* stands for the wage rate (measured in dollars per hour):

Demand: $L^D = 100 - 4W$

Supply: $L^S = 6W$

First, calculate the free market equilibrium wage and quantity of labor. Now suppose the proposed minimum wage is $12. How large will the surplus of labor in this market be?

A.6 The following graphs illustrate the markets for two different types of labor. Suppose an identical minimum wage is imposed in both markets. In which market will the minimum wage have the largest impact on employment? Why?

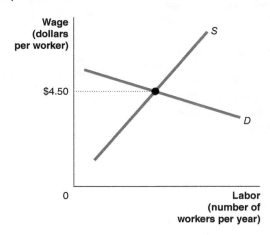

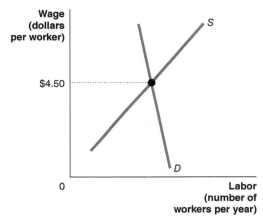

A.7 Suppose that you are the vice president of operations of a manufacturing firm that sells an industrial lubricant in a competitive market. Further suppose that your economist gives you the following demand and supply functions:

Demand: $Q^D = 45 - 2P$

Supply: $Q^S = -15 + P$

What is the consumer surplus in this market? What is the producer surplus?

A.8 The following graph shows a market in which a price floor of $3.00 per unit has been imposed. Calculate the values of each of the following:

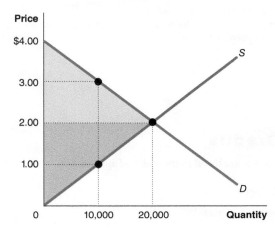

a. The deadweight loss
b. The transfer of producer surplus to consumers or the transfer of consumer surplus to producers
c. Producer surplus after the price floor is imposed
d. Consumer surplus after the price floor is imposed

A.9 Construct a table like the one in this appendix, but assume that the rent ceiling is $2,000 rather than $1,500.

Glossary

Black market A market in which buying and selling take place at prices that violate government price regulations.

Consumer surplus The difference between the highest price a consumer is willing to pay for a good or service and the actual price the consumer pays.

Deadweight loss The reduction in economic surplus resulting from a market not being in competitive equilibrium.

Economic efficiency A market outcome in which the marginal benefit to consumers of the last unit produced is equal to its marginal cost of production and in which the sum of consumer surplus and producer surplus is at a maximum.

Economic surplus The sum of consumer surplus and producer surplus.

Marginal benefit The additional benefit to a consumer from consuming one more unit of a good or service.

Marginal cost The additional cost to a firm of producing one more unit of a good or service.

Price ceiling A legally determined maximum price that sellers may charge.

Price floor A legally determined minimum price that sellers may receive.

Producer surplus The difference between the lowest price a firm would be willing to accept for a good or service and the price it actually receives.

Tax incidence The actual division of the burden of a tax between buyers and sellers in a market.

Credits

Credits are listed in the order of appearance.

Photo

Elasticity:
The Responsiveness of Demand and Supply

From Chapter 6 of *Economics*, Fifth Edition. R. Glenn Hubbard and Anthony Patrick O'Brien. Copyright © 2015 by Pearson Education, Inc.

Elasticity:
The Responsiveness of Demand and Supply

Chapter Outline and **Learning Objectives**

1 **The Price Elasticity of Demand and Its Measurement**
Define price elasticity of demand and understand how to measure it.

2 **The Determinants of the Price Elasticity of Demand**
Understand the determinants of the price elasticity of demand.

3 **The Relationship between Price Elasticity of Demand and Total Revenue**
Understand the relationship between the price elasticity of demand and total revenue.

4 **Other Demand Elasticities**
Define cross-price elasticity of demand and income elasticity of demand and understand their determinants and how they are measured.

5 **Using Elasticity to Analyze the Disappearing Family Farm**
Use price elasticity and income elasticity to analyze economic issues.

6 **The Price Elasticity of Supply and Its Measurement**
Define price elasticity of supply and understand its main determinants and how it is measured.

Do People Respond to Changes in the Price of Gasoline?

"Get ready for a roller coaster." This advice came from Steve Mosby, a partner with Admo Energy, a supplier of gasoline to retailers. Mr. Mosby was referring to swings in gasoline prices that were predicted for the summer of 2013. The fluctuations in gasoline prices over the previous few years had been much larger than normal.

But do fluctuations in gas prices have much effect on sales of gasoline? Some people would say that they don't. These people argue that consumers don't vary the quantity of gas they buy as the price fluctuates because the number of miles they need to drive to get to work or school or to run errands is roughly constant. Actual consumer behavior contradicts this argument. For example, in September 2012, when the average price of gasoline was $3.91 per gallon, U.S. consumers bought about 5 percent less gasoline than they had during September 2011, when the average price of gasoline was $3.66 per gallon.

When gasoline prices have reached $4 per gallon on several occasions in recent years, consumers found many ways to cut back on the quantity they purchased. As Dennis Jacobe, chief economist of Gallup, a public opinion poll firm, put it: "At $4 a gallon, you get people who might have money to spend, but with the amount gasoline costs, they start to cut back in response to the price. At $4 a gallon ... they make fewer trips." In California, rising gas prices have resulted in a decline in the number of cars crossing the Golden Gate Bridge, as commuters switch to using buses and ferries. Car dealers report that sales of smaller, more fuel-efficient cars are increasing compared with sales of SUVs and other less fuel-efficient vehicles.

All businesses have a strong interest in knowing how much their sales will decrease as prices rise. Governments are also interested in knowing how consumers will react if the price of a product such as gasoline rises following a tax increase. In this chapter, we will explore what determines the responsiveness of the quantity demanded and the quantity supplied to changes in the market price.

Sources: Steve Everly, "'Get Ready for a Roller Coaster' as Gas Prices Swing Wildly," *Kansas City Star*, April 21, 2013; Meg Handley, "Memorial Day 2013: Higher Gas Prices, Fewer Travelers," *U.S. News & World Report*, May 23, 2013; and data on gasoline prices and consumption from the U.S. Energy Information Administration.

Economics in Your Life

How Much Do Gas Prices Matter to You?

What factors would make you more or less responsive to price when purchasing gasoline? Have you responded differently to price changes during different periods of your life? Why do consumers seem to respond more to changes in gas prices at a particular service station but seem less sensitive when gas prices rise or fall at all service stations? As you read this chapter, try to answer these questions. You can check your answers against those we provide at the end of this chapter.

W hether you are managing a service station, a pizza parlor, or a coffee shop, you need to know how an increase or a decrease in the price of your products will affect the quantity consumers are willing to buy. We know that cutting the price of a good increases the quantity demanded and that raising the price reduces the quantity demanded. But the critical question is: *How much* will the quantity demanded change as a result of a price increase or decrease? Economists use the concept of **elasticity** to measure how one economic variable—such as the quantity demanded—responds to changes in another economic variable—such as the price. For example, the responsiveness of the quantity demanded of a good to changes in its price is called the *price elasticity of demand*. Knowing the price elasticity of demand allows you to compute the effect of a price change on the quantity demanded.

We also know that the quantity of a good that consumers demand depends not just on the price of the good but also on consumer income and on the prices of related goods. As a manager, you would also be interested in measuring the responsiveness of demand to these other factors. As we will see, we can use the concept of elasticity here as well. We are also interested in the responsiveness of the quantity supplied of a good to changes in its price, which is called the *price elasticity of supply*.

Elasticity is an important concept not just for business managers but for policymakers as well. If the government wants to discourage teenage smoking, it can raise the price of cigarettes by increasing the tax on them. If we know the price elasticity of demand for cigarettes, we can calculate how many fewer packs of cigarettes will be demanded at a higher price. In this chapter, we will also see how policymakers use the concept of elasticity.

Elasticity A measure of how much one economic variable responds to changes in another economic variable.

Define price elasticity of demand and understand how to measure it.

Price elasticity of demand The responsiveness of the quantity demanded to a change in price, measured by dividing the percentage change in the quantity demanded of a product by the percentage change in the product's price.

The Price Elasticity of Demand and Its Measurement

The law of demand states that when the price of a product falls, the quantity demanded of the product increases. But the law of demand tells firms only that the demand curves for their products slope downward. More useful is a measure of the responsiveness of the quantity demanded to a change in price. This measure is called the **price elasticity of demand**.

Measuring the Price Elasticity of Demand

We might measure the price elasticity of demand by using the slope of the demand curve because the slope of the demand curve tells us how much quantity changes as price changes. Using the slope of the demand curve to measure price elasticity has a drawback, however: The measurement of slope is sensitive to the units chosen for quantity and price. For example, suppose a $1 per gallon decrease in the price of gasoline leads to an increase in the quantity demanded from 10.1 million gallons to 10.2 million gallons per day. The change in quantity is 0.1 million gallons, and the change in price is −$1, so the slope is $0.1/-1 = -0.1$. But if we measure price in cents, rather than in dollars, the slope is $0.1/-100 = -0.001$. If we measure price in dollars and gallons in thousands, instead of millions, the slope is $100/-1 = -100$. Clearly, the value we compute for the slope can change dramatically, depending on the units we use for quantity and price.

To avoid this confusion over units, economists use *percentage changes* when measuring the price elasticity of demand. Percentage changes are not dependent on units of measurement. No matter what units we use to measure the quantity of gasoline, 10 percent more gasoline is 10 percent more gasoline. Therefore, the price elasticity of demand is measured by dividing the percentage change in the quantity demanded by the percentage change in the product's price. Or:

$$\text{Price elasticity of demand} = \frac{\text{Percentage change in quantity demanded}}{\text{Percentage change in price}}.$$

It's important to remember that *the price elasticity of demand is not the same as the slope of the demand curve.*

If we calculate the price elasticity of demand for a price cut, the percentage change in price will be negative, and the percentage change in quantity demanded will be positive. Similarly, if we calculate the price elasticity of demand for a price increase, the percentage change in price will be positive, and the percentage change in quantity demanded will be negative. Therefore, the price elasticity of demand is always negative. In comparing elasticities, though, we are usually interested in their relative size. So, we often drop the minus sign and compare their *absolute values*. For example, although −3 is actually a smaller number than −2, we say that a price elasticity of −3 is larger than a price elasticity of −2.

Elastic Demand and Inelastic Demand

If the quantity demanded is very responsive to changes in price, the percentage change in quantity demanded will be *greater* than the percentage change in price, and the price elasticity of demand will be greater than 1 in absolute value. In this case, demand is **elastic**. For example, if a 10 percent decrease in the price of bagels results in a 20 percent increase in the quantity of bagels demanded, then:

$$\text{Price elasticity of demand} = \frac{20\%}{-10\%} = -2,$$

and we can conclude that the demand for bagels is elastic.

> **Elastic demand** Demand is elastic when the percentage change in the quantity demanded is *greater* than the percentage change in price, so the price elasticity is *greater* than 1 in absolute value.

When the quantity demanded is not very responsive to price, however, the percentage change in quantity demanded will be *less* than the percentage change in price, and the price elasticity of demand will be less than 1 in absolute value. In this case, demand is **inelastic**. For example, if a 10 percent decrease in the price of wheat results in a 5 percent increase in the quantity of wheat demanded, then:

$$\text{Price elasticity of demand} = \frac{5\%}{-10\%} = -0.5,$$

and we can conclude that the demand for wheat is inelastic.

> **Inelastic demand** Demand is inelastic when the percentage change in quantity demanded is *less* than the percentage change in price, so the price elasticity is *less* than 1 in absolute value.

In the special case where the percentage change in quantity demanded is equal to the percentage change in price, the price elasticity of demand equals −1 (or 1 in absolute value). In this case, demand is **unit elastic**.

An Example of Computing Price Elasticities

Suppose you own a service station, and you are trying to decide whether to cut the price you are charging for a gallon of gas. You are currently at point A in Figure 1, selling 1,000 gallons per day at a price of $4.00 per gallon. How many more gallons you will sell by cutting the price to $3.70 depends on the price elasticity of demand for gasoline at your service station. Let's consider two possibilities: If D_1 is the demand curve for gasoline at your station, your sales will increase to 1,200 gallons per day, point B. But if D_2 is your demand curve, your sales will increase only to 1,050 gallons per day, point C. We might expect—correctly, as we will see—that between these points, demand curve D_1 is *elastic*, and demand curve D_2 is *inelastic*.

> **Unit-elastic demand** Demand is unit elastic when the percentage change in quantity demanded is *equal to* the percentage change in price, so the price elasticity is equal to 1 in absolute value.

To confirm that D_1 is elastic between these points and that D_2 is inelastic, we need to calculate the price elasticity of demand for each curve. In calculating price elasticity between two points on a demand curve, though, we face a problem because we get a different value for price increases than for price decreases. Suppose we calculate the price elasticity for D_1 as the price is cut from $4.00 to $3.70. This 7.5 percent price cut increases the quantity demanded from 1,000 gallons to 1,200 gallons, or by 20 percent. Therefore, the price elasticity of demand between points A and B is 20/−7.5 = −2.7. Now let's calculate the price elasticity for D_1 as the price is *increased* from $3.70 to $4.00. This 8.1 percent price increase causes a decrease in the quantity demanded from 1,200 gallons to 1,000 gallons, or by 16.7 percent. So, now our measure of the price elasticity of demand between points A and B is −16.7/8.1 = −2.1. It can be confusing to have different

Figure 1

Elastic and Inelastic Demand

Along D_1, cutting the price from \$4.00 to \$3.70 increases the number of gallons demanded from 1,000 to 1,200 per day. Because the percentage change in quantity demanded is greater than the percentage change in price (in absolute value), demand is elastic between point A and point B. Along D_2, cutting the price from \$4.00 to \$3.70 increases the number of gallons demanded only from 1,000 to 1,050 per day. Because the percentage change in quantity demanded is smaller than the percentage change in price (in absolute value), demand is inelastic between point A and point C.

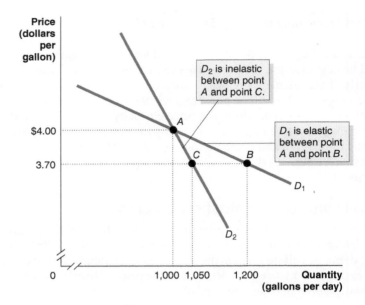

values for the price elasticity of demand between the same two points on the same demand curve. As we will see in the next section, economists use a formula that allows them to avoid this confusion when calculating elasticities.

The Midpoint Formula

We can use the *midpoint formula* to ensure that we have only one value of the price elasticity of demand between the same two points on a demand curve. The midpoint formula uses the *average* of the initial and final quantities and the initial and final prices. If Q_1 and P_1 are the initial quantity and price, and Q_2 and P_2 are the final quantity and price, the midpoint formula is:

$$\text{Price elasticity of demand} = \frac{(Q_2 - Q_1)}{\left(\dfrac{Q_1 + Q_2}{2}\right)} \div \frac{(P_2 - P_1)}{\left(\dfrac{P_1 + P_2}{2}\right)}.$$

The midpoint formula may seem challenging at first, but the numerator is just the change in quantity divided by the average of the initial and final quantities, and the denominator is just the change in price divided by the average of the initial and final prices.

Let's apply the formula to calculating the price elasticity of D_1 in Figure 1. Between point A and point B on D_1, the change in quantity is 200, and the average of the two quantities is 1,100. Therefore, there is an 18.2 percent change in quantity demanded. The change in price is −\$0.30, and the average of the two prices is \$3.85. Therefore, there is a −7.8 percent change in price. So, the price elasticity of demand is 18.2/−7.8 = −2.3. Notice these three results from calculating the price elasticity of demand using the midpoint formula:

1. As we suspected from examining Figure 1, demand curve D_1 is elastic between points A and B.
2. The value for the price elasticity calculated using the midpoint formula is between the two values we calculated earlier.
3. The midpoint formula will give us the same value whether we are moving from the higher price to the lower price or from the lower price to the higher price.

We can also use the midpoint formula to calculate the elasticity of demand between point A and point C on D_2. In this case, there is a 4.9 percent change in quantity and a −7.8 percent change in price. So, the elasticity of demand is 4.9/−7.8 = −0.6. Once again, as we suspected, demand curve D_2 is price inelastic between points A and C.

Solved Problem 1

Calculating the Price Elasticity of Demand

Suppose you own a service station, and you are currently selling gasoline for $3.50 per gallon. At this price, you can sell 2,000 gallons per day. You are considering cutting the price to $3.30 to attract drivers who have been buying their gas at competing stations. The following graph shows two possible increases in the quantity of gasoline sold as a result of your price cut. Use the information in the graph to calculate the price elasticity between these two prices on each of the demand curves. Use the midpoint formula in your calculations. State whether each demand curve is elastic or inelastic between these two prices.

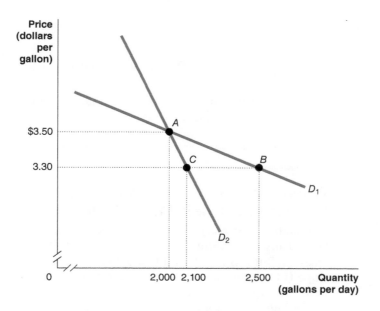

Solving the Problem

Step 1: **Review the chapter material.** This problem requires calculating the price elasticity of demand, so you may want to review the material in the section "The Midpoint Formula."

Step 2: **To begin using the midpoint formula, calculate the average quantity and the average price for demand curve D_1.**

$$\text{Average quantity} = \frac{2,000 + 2,500}{2} = 2,250$$

$$\text{Average price} = \frac{\$3.50 + \$3.30}{2} = \$3.40$$

Step 3: **Now calculate the percentage change in the quantity demanded and the percentage change in price for demand curve D_1.**

$$\text{Percentage change in quantity demanded} = \frac{2,500 - 2,000}{2,250} \times 100 = 22.2\%$$

$$\text{Percentage change in price} = \frac{\$3.30 - \$3.50}{\$3.40} \times 100 = -5.9\%$$

Step 4: **Divide the percentage change in the quantity demanded by the percentage change in price to arrive at the price elasticity for demand curve D_1.**

$$\text{Price elasticity of demand} = \frac{22.2\%}{-5.9\%} = -3.8$$

Because the elasticity is greater than 1 in absolute value, D_1 is price *elastic* between these two prices.

Step 5: **Calculate the price elasticity of demand curve D_2 between these two prices.**

$$\text{Percentage change in quantity demanded} = \frac{2,100 - 2,000}{2,050} \times 100 = 4.9\%$$

$$\text{Percentage change in price} = \frac{\$3.30 - \$3.50}{\$3.40} \times 100 = -5.9\%$$

$$\text{Price elasticity of demand} = \frac{4.9\%}{-5.9\%} = -0.8$$

Because the elasticity is less than 1 in absolute value, D_2 is price *inelastic* between these two prices.

Your Turn: For more practice, do related problem 1.7 at the end of this chapter.

When Demand Curves Intersect, the Flatter Curve Is More Elastic

Remember that elasticity is not the same thing as slope. While slope is calculated using changes in quantity and price, elasticity is calculated using percentage changes. But it *is* true that if two demand curves intersect, the one with the smaller slope (in absolute value)—the flatter demand curve—is more elastic, and the one with the larger slope (in absolute value)—the steeper demand curve—is less elastic. In Figure 1, for a given change in price, demand curve D_1 is more elastic than demand curve D_2.

Polar Cases of Perfectly Elastic and Perfectly Inelastic Demand

Perfectly inelastic demand The case where the quantity demanded is completely unresponsive to price and the price elasticity of demand equals zero.

Perfectly elastic demand The case where the quantity demanded is infinitely responsive to price and the price elasticity of demand equals infinity.

Although they do not occur frequently, you should be aware of the extreme, or polar, cases of price elasticity. If a demand curve is a vertical line, it is **perfectly inelastic**. In this case, the quantity demanded is completely unresponsive to price, and the price elasticity of demand equals zero. No matter how much price may increase or decrease, the quantity remains the same. For only a very few products will the quantity demanded be completely unresponsive to the price, making the demand curve a vertical line. The drug insulin is an example. Some diabetics must take a certain amount of insulin each day. If the price of insulin declines, it will not affect the required dose and therefore will not increase the quantity demanded. Similarly, a price increase will not affect the required dose or decrease the quantity demanded. (Of course, some diabetics may not be able to afford insulin at a higher price. If so, even in this case the demand curve may not be completely vertical and, therefore, not perfectly inelastic.)

If a demand curve is a horizontal line, it is **perfectly elastic**. In this case, the quantity demanded is infinitely responsive to price, and the price elasticity of demand equals infinity. If a demand curve is perfectly elastic, an increase in price causes the quantity demanded to fall to zero. Once again, perfectly elastic demand curves are rare, and it is important not to confuse *elastic* with *perfectly elastic*. Table 1 summarizes the different price elasticities of demand.

Table 1

Summary of the Price Elasticity of Demand

if demand is ...	then the absolute value of price elasticity is ...
elastic	greater than 1
inelastic	less than 1
unit elastic	equal to 1
perfectly elastic	equal to infinity
perfectly inelastic	equal to 0

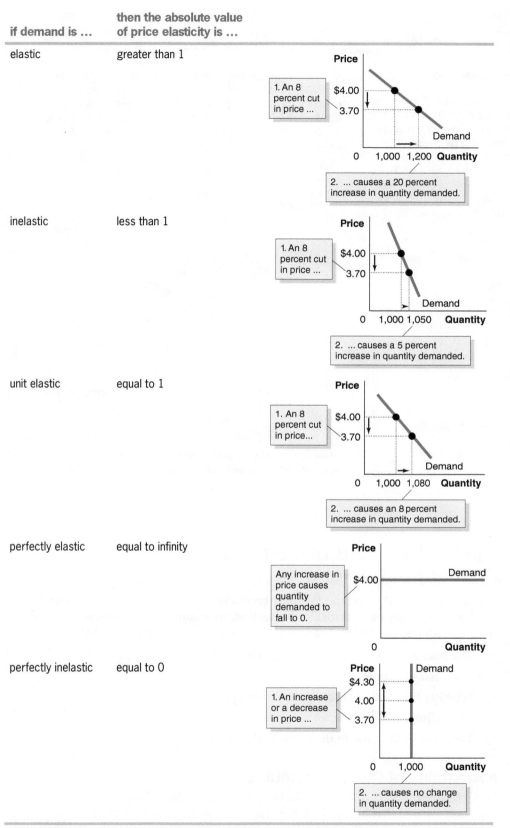

Note: The percentage changes shown in the boxes in the graphs were calculated using the midpoint formula and are rounded to the nearest whole number.

Don't Let This Happen to You

Don't Confuse Inelastic with Perfectly Inelastic

You may be tempted to simplify the concept of elasticity by assuming that any demand curve described as being inelastic is *perfectly* inelastic. You should never make this assumption because perfectly inelastic demand curves are rare. For example, consider the following problem: "Use a demand and supply graph to show how a decrease in supply affects the equilibrium quantity of gasoline. Assume that the demand for gasoline is inelastic." The following graph would be an *incorrect* answer to this problem.

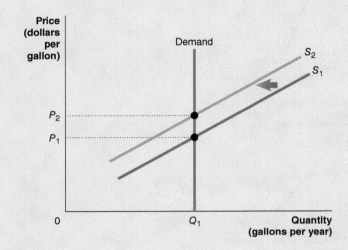

The demand for gasoline is inelastic, but it is not *perfectly* inelastic. When the price of gasoline rises, the quantity demanded falls. So, the correct answer to this problem would use a graph showing a typical downward-sloping demand curve rather than a vertical demand curve.

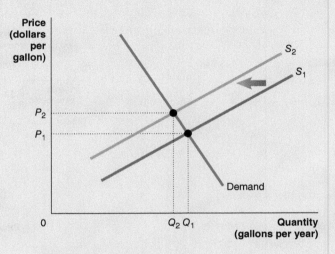

Your Turn: Test your understanding by doing related problem 1.10 at the end of this chapter.

---

2 LEARNING OBJECTIVE

Understand the determinants of the price elasticity of demand.

The Determinants of the Price Elasticity of Demand

We have seen that the demand for some products may be elastic, while the demand for other products may be inelastic. In this section, we examine why price elasticities differ among products. The key determinants of the price elasticity of demand are:

- The availability of close substitutes to the good
- The passage of time
- Whether the good is a luxury or a necessity
- The definition of the market
- The share of the good in the consumer's budget

Availability of Close Substitutes

How consumers react to a change in the price of a product depends on what alternatives they have to that product. So the availability of substitutes is the most important determinant of price elasticity of demand. For example, when the price of gasoline rises, consumers have few alternatives, so the quantity demanded falls only a little. But if the price of pizza rises, consumers have many alternative foods they can eat, so the quantity demanded is likely to fall substantially. In fact, a key constraint on a firm's pricing policies is how many close substitutes exist for its product. In general, *if a product has more substitutes available, it will have more elastic demand. If a product has fewer substitutes available, it will have less elastic demand.*

Passage of Time

It usually takes consumers some time to adjust their buying habits when prices change. If the price of chicken falls, for example, it takes a while before consumers decide to change from eating chicken for dinner once a week to eating it twice a week. If the price of gasoline increases, it also takes a while for consumers to decide to begin taking public transportation, to buy more fuel-efficient cars, or to find new jobs closer to where they live. *The more time that passes, the more elastic the demand for a product becomes.*

Luxuries versus Necessities

Goods that are luxuries usually have more elastic demand curves than goods that are necessities. For example, the demand for bread is inelastic because bread is a necessity, and the quantity that people buy is not very dependent on its price. Tickets to a concert are a luxury, so the demand for concert tickets is much more elastic than the demand for bread. *The demand curve for a luxury is more elastic than the demand curve for a necessity.*

Definition of the Market

In a narrowly defined market, consumers have more substitutes available. For example, if you own a service station and raise the price you charge for gasoline, many of your customers will switch to buying from a competitor. So, the demand for gasoline at one particular station is likely to be elastic. The demand for gasoline as a product, on the other hand, is inelastic because consumers have few alternatives (in the short run) to buying it. *The more narrowly we define a market, the more elastic demand will be.*

Share of a Good in a Consumer's Budget

Goods that take only a small fraction of a consumer's budget tend to have less elastic demand than goods that take a large fraction. For example, most people buy table salt infrequently and in relatively small quantities. The share of an average consumer's budget that is spent on salt is very low. As a result, even a doubling of the price of salt is likely to result in only a small decline in the quantity of salt demanded. "Big-ticket items," such as houses, cars, and furniture, take up a larger share in the average consumer's budget. Increases in the prices of these goods are likely to result in significant declines in the quantity demanded. In general, *the demand for a good will be more elastic the larger the share of the good in the average consumer's budget.*

Some Estimated Price Elasticities of Demand

Table 2 shows some estimated short-run price elasticities of demand. It's important to remember that estimates of the price elasticities of different goods can vary, depending on the data used and the time period over which the estimates were made. The results given in the table are consistent with our discussion of the determinants of price elasticity. Goods for which there are few substitutes, such as cigarettes, gasoline, and health insurance, are price inelastic, as are broadly defined goods, such as bread or beer. Particular brands of products such as Coca-Cola, Tide, or Post Raisin Bran

Table 2

Estimated Real-World Price Elasticities of Demand

Product	Estimated Elasticity	Product	Estimated Elasticity
Books (Barnes & Noble)	−4.00	Bread	−0.40
Books (Amazon)	−0.60	Water (residential use)	−0.38
DVDs (Amazon)	−3.10	Chicken	−0.37
Post Raisin Bran	−2.50	Cocaine	−0.28
Automobiles	−1.95	Cigarettes	−0.25
Tide (liquid detergent)	−3.92	Beer	−0.29
Coca-Cola	−1.22	Catholic school attendance	−0.19
Grapes	−1.18	Residential natural gas	−0.09
Restaurant meals	−0.67	Gasoline	−0.06
Health insurance (low-income households)	−0.65	Milk	−0.04
		Sugar	−0.04

See Text Credits at the end of this chapter for complete source list.

are price elastic. (This point is discussed further in the *Making the Connection* on the price elasticity of breakfast cereal.)

The table shows that the demand for books or DVDs bought from a particular retailer is typically price elastic. Note, though, that the demand for books from Amazon is inelastic, which indicates that consumers do not consider ordering from other online sites to be good substitutes for ordering from Amazon.

An increase in the price of grapes will lead some consumers to substitute other fruits, so demand for grapes is price elastic. Similarly, an increase in the price of new automobiles will lead some consumers to buy used automobiles or to continue driving their current cars, so demand for automobiles is also price elastic. The demand for necessities, such as natural gas and water, is price inelastic.

Making the Connection

The Price Elasticity of Demand for Breakfast Cereal

MIT economist Jerry Hausman has estimated the price elasticity of demand for breakfast cereal. He divided breakfast cereals into three categories: children's cereals, such as Trix and Froot Loops; adult cereals, such as Special K and Grape-Nuts; and family cereals, such as Corn Flakes and Raisin Bran. Some of the results of his estimates are given in the following table:

Cereal	Price Elasticity of Demand
Post Raisin Bran	−2.5
All family breakfast cereals	−1.8
All types of breakfast cereals	−0.9

Just as we would expect, the price elasticity for a particular brand of raisin bran was larger in absolute value than the elasticity for all family cereals, and the elasticity for all family cereals was larger than the elasticity for all types of breakfast cereals. If Post increases the price of its raisin bran by 10 percent, sales will decline by 25 percent, as many consumers switch to another brand of raisin bran. If the prices of all family breakfast cereals rise by 10 percent, sales will decline by 18 percent, as consumers switch to child or adult cereals. In both of these cases, demand is elastic.

But if the prices of all types of breakfast cereals rise by 10 percent, sales will decline by only 9 percent. Demand for all breakfast cereals is inelastic.

Source: Jerry A. Hausman, "Valuation of New Goods under Perfect and Imperfect Competition," in Timothy F. Bresnahan and Robert J. Gordon, eds., *The Economics of New Goods*, Chicago: University of Chicago Press, 1997.

Your Turn: Test your understanding by doing related problem 2.4 at the end of this chapter.

The Relationship between Price Elasticity of Demand and Total Revenue

3 LEARNING OBJECTIVE

Understand the relationship between the price elasticity of demand and total revenue.

Knowing the price elasticity of demand allows a firm to calculate how changes in price will affect its **total revenue**, which is the total amount of funds it receives from selling a good or service. Total revenue is calculated by multiplying price per unit by the number of units sold. When demand is inelastic, price and total revenue move in the same direction: An increase in price raises total revenue, and a decrease in price reduces total revenue. When demand is elastic, price and total revenue move inversely: An increase in price reduces total revenue, and a decrease in price raises total revenue.

Total revenue The total amount of funds a seller receives from selling a good or service, calculated by multiplying price per unit by the number of units sold.

To understand the relationship between price elasticity and total revenue, consider Figure 2. Panel (a) shows a demand curve for gasoline that is inelastic between point *A* and point *B*. (It was demand curve D_2 in Figure 1.) The total revenue received by the service station owner at point *A* equals the price of $4.00 multiplied by the 1,000 gallons sold, or $4,000. This amount equals the areas of rectangles *C* and *D* in the figure because together the rectangles have a height of $4.00 and a base of 1,000 gallons. Because this demand curve is inelastic between point *A* and point *B*, cutting

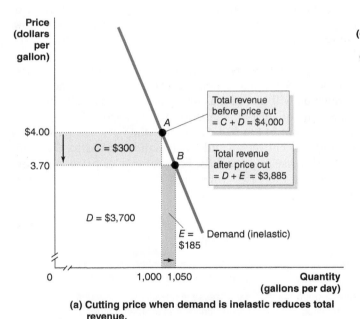

(a) Cutting price when demand is inelastic reduces total revenue.

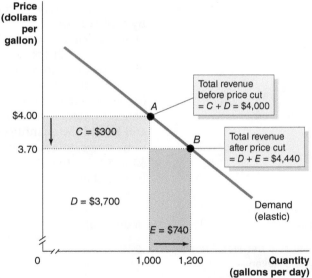

(b) Cutting price when demand is elastic increases total revenue.

Figure 2 **The Relationship between Price Elasticity and Total Revenue**

When demand is inelastic, a cut in price will decrease total revenue. In panel (a), at point *A*, the price is $4.00, 1,000 gallons are sold, and total revenue received by the service station equals $4.00 × 1,000 gallons, or $4,000. At point *B*, cutting the price to $3.70 increases the quantity demanded to 1,050 gallons, but the fall in price more than offsets the increase in quantity. As a result, revenue falls to

$3.70 × 1,050 gallons, or $3,885. When demand is elastic, a cut in the price will increase total revenue. In panel (b), at point *A*, the areas of rectangles *C* and *D* are still equal to $4,000. But at point *B*, the areas of rectangles *D* and *E* are equal to $3.70 × 1,200 gallons, or $4,440. In this case, the increase in the quantity demanded is large enough to offset the fall in price, so total revenue increases.

the price to $3.70 (point *B*) reduces total revenue. The new total revenue is shown by the areas of rectangles *D* and *E* and is equal to $3.70 multiplied by 1,050 gallons, or $3,885. Total revenue falls because the increase in the quantity demanded is not large enough to make up for the decrease in price. As a result, the $185 increase in revenue gained as a result of the price cut—rectangle *E*—is less than the $300 in revenue lost—rectangle *C*.

Panel (b) of Figure 2 shows a demand curve that is elastic between point *A* and point *B*. (It was demand curve D_1 in Figure 1.) With this demand curve, cutting the price increases total revenue. At point *A*, the areas of rectangles *C* and *D* are still equal to $4,000, but at point *B*, the areas of rectangles *D* and *E* are equal to $3.70 multiplied by 1,200 gallons, or $4,440. Here, total revenue rises because the increase in the quantity demanded is large enough to offset the lower price. As a result, the $740 increase in revenue gained as a result of the price cut—rectangle *E*—is greater than the $300 in revenue lost—rectangle *C*.

The third, less common possibility is that demand is unit elastic. In that case, a small change in price is exactly offset by a proportional change in the quantity demanded, leaving revenue unaffected. Therefore, when demand is unit elastic, neither a decrease nor an increase in price affects revenue. Table 3 summarizes the relationship between price elasticity and revenue.

Elasticity and Revenue with a Linear Demand Curve

Along most demand curves, elasticity is not constant at every point. For example, a straight-line, or linear, demand curve for gasoline is shown in panel (a) of Figure 3. (For simplicity, small quantities are used.) The numbers from the table are plotted in the graphs. The demand curve shows that when the price drops by $1 per gallon, consumers always respond by buying 2 more gallons per day. When the price is high and the quantity demanded is low, demand is elastic. Demand is elastic because a $1 drop in price is a smaller percentage change when the price is high, and an increase of 2 gallons is a larger percentage change when the quantity of gasoline purchased is low. By similar reasoning, we can see why demand is inelastic when the price is low and the quantity demanded is high.

Panel (a) in Figure 3 shows that when price is between $8 and $4 and quantity demanded is between 0 gallons and 8 gallons, demand is elastic. Panel (b) shows that over this same range, total revenue will increase as price falls. For example, in panel (a), as price falls from $7 to $6, the quantity demanded increases from 2 to 4, and in panel (b), total revenue increases from $14 to $24. Similarly, when price is between $4 and $0 and the quantity demanded is between 8 and 16, demand is inelastic. Over this same range, total revenue will decrease as price falls. For example, as price falls from $3 to $2 and the quantity demanded increases from 10 to 12, total revenue decreases from $30 to $24.

Table 3	If demand is …	then …	because …
The Relationship between Price Elasticity and Revenue	elastic	an increase in price reduces revenue	the decrease in quantity demanded is proportionally *greater* than the increase in price.
	elastic	a decrease in price increases revenue	the increase in quantity demanded is proportionally *greater* than the decrease in price.
	inelastic	an increase in price increases revenue	the decrease in quantity demanded is proportionally *smaller* than the increase in price.
	inelastic	a decrease in price reduces revenue	the increase in quantity demanded is proportionally *smaller* than the decrease in price.
	unit elastic	an increase in price does not affect revenue	the decrease in quantity demanded is proportionally *the same as* the increase in price.
	unit elastic	a decrease in price does not affect revenue	the increase in quantity demanded is proportionally *the same as* the decrease in price.

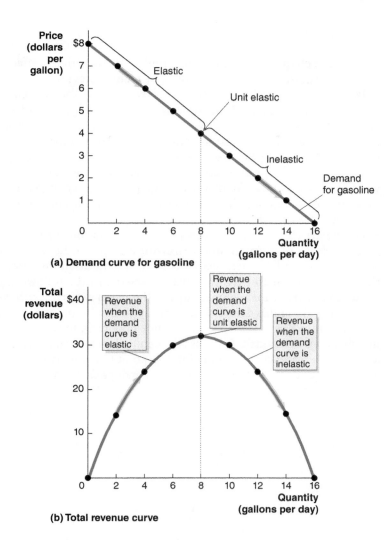

(a) Demand curve for gasoline

(b) Total revenue curve

Price	Quantity Demanded	Total Revenue
$8	0	$0
7	2	14
6	4	24
5	6	30
4	8	32
3	10	30
2	12	24
1	14	14
0	16	0

Figure 3   Elasticity Is Not Constant along a Linear Demand Curve

The data from the table are plotted in the graphs. Panel (a) shows that as we move down the demand curve for gasoline, the price elasticity of demand declines. In other words, at higher prices, demand is elastic, and at lower prices, demand is inelastic. Panel (b) shows that as the quantity of gasoline purchased increases from 0, revenue will increase until it reaches a maximum of $32 when 8 gallons are purchased. As purchases increase beyond 8 gallons, revenue falls because demand is inelastic on this portion of the demand curve.

Solved Problem 3

Price and Revenue Don't Always Move in the Same Direction

New York City officials believed they needed more revenue to maintain 35 city-owned recreation centers. To raise the additional revenue, the city's parks department increased the annual membership fee to use the centers from $75 to $150. According to an article in the *New York Times*, "the department had hoped to realize $4 million in new revenue, but in fact, it lost about $200,000." The article also explains that the parks department had expected a 5 percent decline in memberships due to the price increase.

a. What did the parks department believe about the price elasticity of demand for memberships in its recreation centers?

b. Is demand for memberships actually elastic or inelastic? Briefly explain. Illustrate your answer with a graph showing the demand curve for memberships as the parks department believed it to be and as it actually is.

Solving the Problem

Step 1: Review the chapter material. This problem deals with the effect of a price change on a firm's revenue, so you may want to review the section "The Relationship between Price Elasticity of Demand and Total Revenue."

Step 2: Answer part (a) by explaining how the parks department viewed the demand for memberships. Looking at Table 3, we can conclude that managers at the parks department must have thought the demand for memberships was inelastic because they believed that revenue would increase if they raised the price. The managers estimated that the quantity of memberships demanded would fall by 5 percent following the 100 percent price increase. Therefore, they must have believed that the price elasticity of demand for memberships was $-5\% / 100\% = -0.05$.

Step 3: Answer part (b) by explaining whether the demand for memberships is actually elastic or inelastic and by drawing a graph to illustrate your answer. Because revenue fell when the parks department raised the price, we know that demand for memberships must be elastic. In the following graph, D_1 shows the demand for memberships as the parks department believed it to be. Moving along this demand curve from point A to point B, an increase in the price from $75 to $150 causes a decline of only Q_1 to Q_2 in the quantity of memberships demanded. D_2 shows the demand curve as it actually is. Moving along this demand curve from point A to point C, the increase in price causes a much larger decline of Q_1 to Q_3 in memberships demanded.

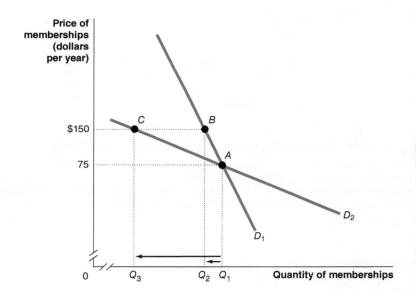

Your Turn: For more practice, do related problems 3.8 and 3.9 at the end of this chapter.

Estimating Price Elasticity of Demand

To estimate the price elasticity of demand, a firm needs to know the demand curve for its product. For a well-established product, economists can use historical data to statistically estimate the demand curve. To calculate the price elasticity of demand for a new product, firms often rely on market experiments, trying different prices and observing the change in quantity demanded that results.

For example, Apple introduced the first-generation iPhone in June 2007, at a price of $599. But demand for the iPhone was more elastic than Apple had expected, and when sales failed to reach Apple's projections, the company cut the price to $399 just two months later. Similarly, when 3D televisions were introduced into the U.S. market in early 2010, Sony and other manufacturers believed that sales would be strong despite prices being several hundred dollars higher than those for other high-end ultra-thin televisions. Once again, though, demand turned out to be more elastic than expected, and by December firms were cutting prices 40 percent or more in an effort to increase revenue.

Other Demand Elasticities

Elasticity is an important concept in economics because it allows us to quantify the responsiveness of one economic variable to changes in another economic variable. In addition to price elasticity, two other demand elasticities are important: *cross-price elasticity of demand* and *income elasticity of demand*.

Cross-Price Elasticity of Demand

Suppose you work at Apple, and you need to predict the effect of an increase in the price of Samsung's Galaxy Tab on the quantity of iPads demanded, holding other factors constant. You can do this by calculating the **cross-price elasticity of demand**, which is the percentage change in the quantity of iPads demanded divided by the percentage change in the price of Galaxy Tabs—or, in general:

Cross-price elasticity of demand
The percentage change in the quantity demanded of one good divided by the percentage change in the price of another good.

$$\text{Cross-price elasticity of demand} = \frac{\text{Percentage change in quantity demanded of one good}}{\text{Percentage change in price of another good}}.$$

The cross-price elasticity of demand is positive or negative, depending on whether the two products are substitutes or complements. Substitutes are products that can be used for the same purpose, such as two brands of tablet computers. Complements are products that are used together, such as tablet computers and applications that can be downloaded from online stores. An increase in the price of a substitute will lead to an increase in the quantity demanded, so the cross-price elasticity of demand will be positive. An increase in the price of a complement will lead to a decrease in the quantity demanded, so the cross-price elasticity of demand will be negative. Of course, if the two products are unrelated—such as tablet computers and peanut butter—the cross-price elasticity of demand will be zero. Table 4 summarizes the key points concerning the cross-price elasticity of demand.

Cross-price elasticity of demand is important to firm managers because it allows them to measure whether products sold by other firms are close substitutes for their products. For example, Pepsi-Cola and Coca-Cola spend heavily on advertising with the hope of convincing consumers that each cola tastes better than its rival. How can these firms tell whether their advertising campaigns have been effective? One way is by seeing whether the cross-price elasticity of demand has changed. If, for instance, Coca-Cola has a successful advertising campaign, when it increases the price of Coke, the percentage increase in sales of Pepsi should be smaller. In other words, the value of the cross-price elasticity of demand should have declined.

Table 4

Summary of Cross-Price Elasticity of Demand

If the products are …	then the cross-price elasticity of demand will be …	Example
substitutes	positive.	Two brands of tablet computers
complements	negative.	Tablet computers and applications downloaded from online stores
unrelated	zero.	Tablet computers and peanut butter

Table 5

Summary of Income Elasticity of Demand

If the income elasticity of demand is …	then the good is …	Example
positive but less than 1	normal and a necessity.	Bread
positive and greater than 1	normal and a luxury.	Caviar
negative	inferior.	High-fat meat

Income Elasticity of Demand

Income elasticity of demand A measure of the responsiveness of the quantity demanded to changes in income, measured by the percentage change in the quantity demanded divided by the percentage change in income.

The **income elasticity of demand** measures the responsiveness of the quantity demanded to changes in income. It is calculated as follows:

$$\text{Income elasticity of demand} = \frac{\text{Percentage change in quantity demanded}}{\text{Percentage change in income}}.$$

We know that if the quantity demanded of a good increases as income increases, then the good is a *normal good*. Normal goods are often further subdivided into *luxuries* and *necessities*. A good is a luxury if the quantity demanded is very responsive to changes in income, so that a 10 percent increase in income results in more than a 10 percent increase in the quantity demanded. Expensive jewelry and vacation homes are examples of luxuries. A good is a necessity if the quantity demanded is not very responsive to changes in income, so that a 10 percent increase in income results in less than a 10 percent increase in the quantity demanded. Food and clothing are examples of necessities. A good is *inferior* if the quantity demanded falls when income increases. Ground beef with a high fat content is an example of an inferior good. We should note that *normal good*, *inferior good*, *necessity*, and *luxury* are just labels economists use for goods with different income elasticities; the labels are not intended to be value judgments about the worth of these goods.

Because most goods are normal goods, during periods of economic expansion when consumer income is rising, most firms can expect—holding other factors constant—that the quantity demanded of their products will increase. Sellers of luxuries can expect particularly large increases. During recessions, falling consumer income can cause firms to experience increases in demand for inferior goods. For example, the demand for bus trips increases as consumers cut back on air travel, and supermarkets find that the demand for canned tuna increases relative to the demand for fresh salmon. Table 5 summarizes the key points about the income elasticity of demand.

Making the Connection	**Price Elasticity, Cross-Price Elasticity, and Income Elasticity in the Market for Alcoholic Beverages**

Many public policy issues are related to the consumption of alcoholic beverages. These issues include underage drinking, drunk driving, and the possible beneficial effects of red wine in lowering the risk of heart disease. Knowing how responsive the demand for alcohol is to changes in price provides insight into these policy issues. Christopher Ruhm of the University of Virginia and colleagues have estimated statistically the following elasticities. (*Spirits* refers to all beverages that contain alcohol, other than beer and wine.)

Price elasticity of demand for beer	−0.30
Cross-price elasticity of demand between beer and wine	−0.83
Cross-price elasticity of demand between beer and spirits	−0.50
Income elasticity of demand for beer	0.09

These results indicate that the demand for beer is inelastic. A 10 percent increase in the price of beer will result in a 3 percent decline in the quantity of beer demanded.

Somewhat surprisingly, both wine and spirits are complements for beer rather than substitutes. A 10 percent increase in the price of wine will result in an 8.3 percent *decrease* in the quantity of beer demanded. Previous studies of the price elasticity of beer had found that beer was a substitute for other alcoholic drinks. Ruhm and his colleagues argue that their results are more reliable because they use Uniform Product Code (UPC) scanner data on prices and quantities sold in grocery stores. They argue that these price data are more accurate than the data used in many previous studies that included the prices of only one brand each of beer, wine, and whiskey.

The results in the table also show that a 10 percent increase in income will result in a 0.9 percent *increase* in the quantity of beer demanded. So, beer is a normal good. According to the definitions given earlier, beer would be classified as a necessity because it has an income elasticity that is positive but less than 1.

Source: Christopher J. Ruhm, et al., "What U.S. Data Should Be Used to Measure the Price Elasticity of Demand for Alcohol," *Journal of Health Economics*, Vol. 31, No. 16, December 2012.

Your Turn: Test your understanding by doing related problem 4.8 at the end of this chapter.

Using Elasticity to Analyze the Disappearing Family Farm

5 LEARNING OBJECTIVE

Use price elasticity and income elasticity to analyze economic issues.

The concepts of price elasticity and income elasticity can help us understand many economic issues. For example, some people are concerned that the family farm is becoming an endangered species in the United States. Although food production continues to grow rapidly, the number of farms and farmers continue to dwindle. In 1950, the United States was home to more than 5 million farms, and more than 23 million people lived on farms. By 2013, only about 2 million farms remained, and fewer than 3 million people lived on them. The federal government has several programs that are intended to aid farmers. Many of these programs have been aimed at helping small, family-operated farms, but rapid growth in farm production, combined with low price and income elasticities for most food products, have made family farming difficult in the United States.

Productivity measures the ability of firms to produce goods and services with a given amount of economic inputs, such as workers, machines, and land. Productivity has grown very rapidly in U.S. agriculture. In 1950, the average U.S. wheat farmer harvested about 17 bushels from each acre of wheat planted. By 2013, because of the development of superior strains of wheat and improvements in farming techniques, the average American wheat farmer harvested 46 bushels per acre. So, even though the total number of acres devoted to growing wheat declined from about 62 million to about 56 million, total wheat production rose from about 1.0 billion bushels to about 2.3 billion.

Unfortunately for U.S. farmers, this increase in wheat production resulted in a substantial decline in wheat prices. Two key factors explain this decline: (1) The demand for wheat is inelastic, and (2) the income elasticity of demand for wheat is low. Even though the U.S. population has increased greatly since 1950 and the income of the average American is much higher than it was in 1950, the demand for wheat has increased only moderately. For all of the additional wheat to be sold, the price has had to decline. Because the demand for wheat is inelastic, the price decline has been substantial. Figure 4 illustrates these points.

A large shift in supply, a small shift in demand, and an inelastic demand curve combined to drive down the price of wheat from $19.29 per bushel in 1950 to $7.80 in 2013. (We measure the price in 1950 in terms of prices in 2013, to adjust for the general increase in prices since 1950.) With low prices, only the most efficiently run farms have been able to remain profitable. Small family–run farms have found it difficult to survive, and many of these farms have disappeared. The markets for most other food products are similar to the market for wheat. They are characterized by rapid output growth and low income and price elasticities. The result is the paradox of American farming: ever more abundant and cheaper food, supplied by fewer and fewer farms. American consumers have benefited, but most family farmers have not.

Figure 4

Elasticity and the Disappearing Family Farm

In 1950, U.S. farmers produced 1.0 billion bushels of wheat at a price of $19.29 per bushel. Over the next 60 years, rapid increases in farm productivity caused a large shift to the right in the supply curve for wheat. The income elasticity of demand for wheat is low, so the demand for wheat increased relatively little over this period. Because the demand for wheat is also inelastic, the large shift in the supply curve and the small shift in the demand curve resulted in a sharp decline in the price of wheat, from $19.29 per bushel in 1950 to $7.80 in 2013.
Source: U.S. Department of Agriculture, *Wheat Yearbook Tables*, May 21, 2013.

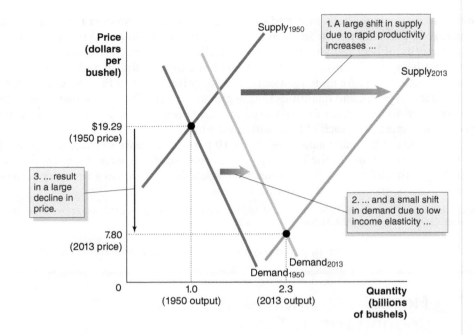

Solved Problem 5

Using Price Elasticity to Analyze a Policy of Taxing Gasoline

If the consumption of a product results in a negative externality, taxing the product may improve economic efficiency. Some economists and policymakers argue that driving cars and trucks involves a negative externality because burning gasoline increases emissions of greenhouse gases and contributes to the congestion that clogs many highways in and around big cities and to the accidents that take more than 30,000 lives per year. Some economists have suggested substantially increasing the federal excise tax on gasoline, which in 2013 was 18.4 cents per gallon. How much the tax would cause consumption to fall and how much revenue the tax would raise depend on the price elasticity of demand. Suppose that the price of gasoline is currently $4.00 per gallon, the quantity of gasoline demanded is

140 billion gallons per year, the price elasticity of demand for gasoline is −0.06, and the federal government decides to increase the excise tax on gasoline by $1.00 per gallon. The price of a product will not rise by the full amount of a tax increase unless the demand for the product is perfectly inelastic. In this case, suppose that the price of gasoline increases by $0.80 per gallon after the $1.00 excise tax is imposed.

a. What is the new quantity of gasoline demanded after the tax is imposed? How effective would a gas tax be in reducing consumption of gasoline in the short run?
b. How much revenue does the federal government receive from the tax?

Solving the Problem

Step 1: Review the chapter material. This problem deals with applications of the price elasticity of demand formula, so you may want to review the section "Measuring the Price Elasticity of Demand."

Step 2: Answer the first question in part (a) using the formula for the price elasticity of demand to calculate the new quantity demanded.

$$\text{Price elasticity of demand} = \frac{\text{Percentage change in quantity demanded}}{\text{Percentage change in price}}.$$

We can plug into the midpoint formula the values given for the price elasticity, the original price of $4.00, and the new price of $4.80 (= $4.00 + $0.80).

$$-0.06 = \frac{\text{Percentage change in quantity demanded}}{\frac{(\$4.80 - \$4.00)}{\left(\frac{\$4.00 + \$4.80}{2}\right)}}.$$

Or, rearranging and writing out the expression for the percentage change in the quantity demanded:

$$-0.011 = \frac{(Q_2 - 140\text{ billion})}{\left(\dfrac{140\text{ billion } + Q_2}{2}\right)}.$$

Solving for Q_2, the new quantity demanded is:

$$Q_2 = 138.5\text{ billion gallons.}$$

Step 3: **Answer the second question in part (a).** Because the price elasticity of demand for gasoline is so low, -0.06, even a substantial increase in the gasoline tax of $1.00 per gallon would reduce gasoline consumption by only a small amount: from 140 billion gallons of gasoline per year to 138.5 billion gallons. Note, though, that price elasticities typically increase over time. Economists estimate that the long-run price elasticity of gasoline is in the range of -0.40 to -0.60, so in the long run, the decline in the consumption of gasoline would be larger.

Step 4: **Calculate the revenue earned by the federal government to answer part (b).** The federal government would collect an amount equal to the tax per gallon multiplied by the number of gallons sold: $1 per gallon × 138.5 billion gallons = $138.5 billion.

Extra Credit: The tax of $138.5 billion calculated in Step 4 is substantial: about 12 percent of all the revenue the federal government raised from the personal income tax in 2012. It is also much larger than the roughly $25 billion the federal government receives each year from the existing 18.4-cents-per-gallon gasoline tax. We can conclude that raising the federal excise tax on gasoline would be a good way to raise revenue for the federal government, but, at least in the short run, increasing the tax would not greatly reduce the quantity of gasoline consumed. Notice that if the demand for gasoline were elastic, this result would be reversed: The quantity of gasoline consumed would decline much more, but so would the revenue that the federal government would receive from the tax increase.

Your Turn: For more practice, do related problems 5.2 and 5.3 at the end of this chapter.

The Price Elasticity of Supply and Its Measurement

Define price elasticity of supply and understand its main determinants and how it is measured.

We can use the concept of elasticity to measure the responsiveness of firms to a change in price, just as we used it to measure the responsiveness of consumers. We know from the law of supply that when the price of a product increases, the quantity supplied increases. To measure how much the quantity supplied increases when price increases, we use the *price elasticity of supply*.

Measuring the Price Elasticity of Supply

Just as with the price elasticity of demand, we calculate the **price elasticity of supply** by using percentage changes:

$$\text{Price elasticity of supply} = \frac{\text{Percentage change in quantity supplied}}{\text{Percentage change in price}}.$$

Price elasticity of supply The responsiveness of the quantity supplied to a change in price, measured by dividing the percentage change in the quantity supplied of a product by the percentage change in the product's price.

Notice that because supply curves are upward sloping, the price elasticity of supply will be a positive number. We categorize the price elasticity of supply the same way we categorized the price elasticity of demand: If the price elasticity of supply is less than 1, then supply is *inelastic*. For example, the price elasticity of supply of gasoline from U.S. oil refineries is about 0.20, and so it is inelastic; a 10 percent increase in the price of gasoline will result in only a 2 percent increase in the quantity supplied. If the price elasticity of supply is greater than 1, then supply is *elastic*. If the price elasticity of supply is equal to 1, the supply is *unit elastic*. As with other elasticity calculations, when we calculate the price elasticity of supply, we hold constant the values of other factors.

Determinants of the Price Elasticity of Supply

Whether supply is elastic or inelastic depends on the ability and willingness of firms to alter the quantity they produce as price increases. Often, firms have difficulty increasing the quantity of the product they supply during any short period of time. For example, a pizza parlor cannot produce more pizzas on any one night than is possible using the ingredients on hand. Within a day or two, it can buy more ingredients, and within a few months, it can hire more cooks and install additional ovens. As a result, the supply curve for pizza and most other products will be inelastic if we measure it over a short period of time, but the supply curve will be increasingly elastic the longer the period of time over which we measure it. Products that require resources that are themselves in fixed supply are an exception to this rule. For example, a French winery may rely on a particular variety of grape. If all the land on which that grape can be grown is already planted in vineyards, then the supply of that wine will be inelastic even over a long period.

Making the Connection	## Why Are Oil Prices So Unstable?

Bringing oil to market is a long process. Oil companies hire geologists to locate fields for exploratory oil well drilling. If significant amounts of oil are present, the company begins full-scale development of the field. The process from exploration to pumping significant amounts of oil can take years. This long process is the reason for the very low short-run price elasticity of supply for oil.

During the period from 2003 to mid-2008, the worldwide demand for oil increased rapidly as India, China, and some other developing countries increased both their manufacturing production and their use of automobiles. As the following graph shows, when supply is inelastic, an increase in demand can cause a large increase in price. The shift in the demand curve from D_1 to D_2 causes the equilibrium quantity of oil to increase only by 5 percent, from 80 million barrels per day to 84 million, but the equilibrium price rises by 75 percent, from $80 to $140 per barrel.

The world oil market is heavily influenced by the Organization of the Petroleum Exporting Countries (OPEC). OPEC has 11 members, including Saudi Arabia, Kuwait, Iran, Venezuela, and Nigeria. Together OPEC members own 75 percent of the world's proven oil reserves. Periodically, OPEC has attempted to force up the price of oil by reducing the quantity of oil its members supply. Since the 1970s, OPEC's attempts to reduce the quantity of oil in world markets have been successful only sporadically. As a result, the supply curve for oil shifts fairly frequently. Combined with the low price elasticities of oil supply and demand, these shifts in supply have caused the price of oil to fluctuate significantly over the past 40 years, from as low as $10 per barrel to more than $140.

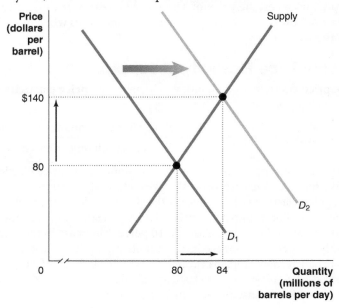

By mid-2008, the financial crisis that began in the United States had spread to other countries, resulting in a severe recession. As production and incomes fell during the recession, the worldwide demand for oil declined sharply. Over the space of a few months, the equilibrium price of oil fell from $140 per barrel to $40. As the following graph shows, once again, the extent of the price change reflected not only the size of the decline in demand but also the low short-run price elasticity of supply for oil.

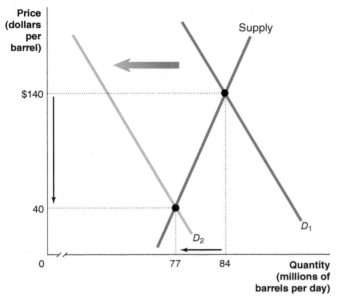

Over the long run, the elasticity of supply for oil is much higher than in the short run. High oil prices give oil companies an incentive to devise ways to extract oil from shale formations. Increases in the quantity of shale oil being pumped have led to forecasts that the United States could become the world's largest oil producer by 2020.

Your Turn: Test your understanding by doing related problem 6.3 at the end of this chapter.

Polar Cases of Perfectly Elastic and Perfectly Inelastic Supply

Although it occurs infrequently, it is possible for supply to fall into one of the polar cases of price elasticity. If a supply curve is a vertical line, it is *perfectly inelastic*. In this case, the quantity supplied is completely unresponsive to price, and the price elasticity of supply equals zero. Regardless of how much price may increase or decrease, the quantity remains the same. Over a brief period of time, the supply of some goods and services may be perfectly inelastic. For example, a parking lot may have only a fixed number of parking spaces. If demand increases, the price to park in the lot may rise, but no more spaces will become available. Of course, if demand increases permanently, over a longer period of time, the owner of the lot may buy more land and add additional spaces.

If a supply curve is a horizontal line, it is *perfectly elastic*. In this case, the quantity supplied is infinitely responsive to price, and the price elasticity of supply equals infinity. If a supply curve is perfectly elastic, a very small increase in price causes a very large increase in the quantity supplied. Just as with demand curves, it is important not to confuse a supply curve being elastic with its being perfectly elastic and not to confuse a supply curve being inelastic with its being perfectly inelastic. Table 6 summarizes the different price elasticities of supply.

Table 6

Summary of the Price Elasticity of Supply

If supply is...	then the value of price elasticity is ...	
elastic	greater than 1	
inelastic	less than 1	
unit elastic	equal to 1	
perfectly elastic	equal to infinity	
perfectly inelastic	equal to 0	

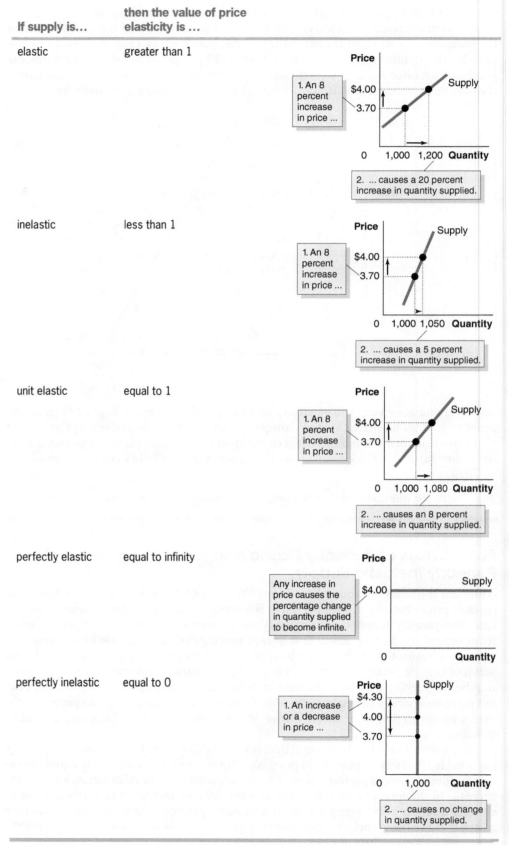

Note: The percentage increases shown in the boxes in the graphs were calculated using the midpoint formula.

Using Price Elasticity of Supply to Predict Changes in Price

Figure 5 illustrates the important point that, when demand increases, the amount by which price increases depends on the price elasticity of supply. The figure shows the demand and supply for parking spaces at a beach resort. In panel (a), on a typical summer weekend, equilibrium occurs at point A, where Demand$_{Typical}$ intersects a supply curve that is inelastic. The increase in demand for parking spaces on July 4th shifts the demand curve to the right, moving the equilibrium to point B. Because the supply curve is inelastic, the increase in demand results in a large increase in price—from $2.00 per hour to $4.00—but only a small increase in the quantity of spaces supplied—from 1,200 to 1,400.

In panel (b), supply is elastic, perhaps because the resort has vacant land that can be used for parking during periods of high demand. As a result, the change in equilibrium from point A to point B results in a smaller increase in price and a larger increase in the quantity supplied. An increase in price from $2.00 per hour to $2.50 is sufficient to increase the quantity of parking spaces supplied from 1,200 to 2,100. Knowing the price elasticity of supply makes it possible to predict more accurately how much price will change following an increase or a decrease in demand.

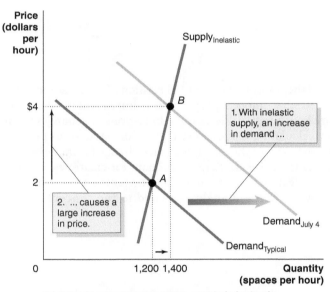

(a) Price increases more when supply is inelastic.

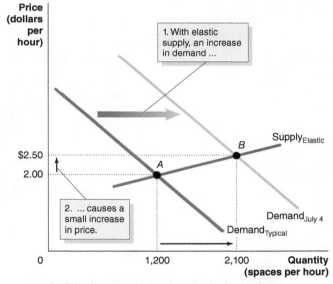

(b) Price increases less when supply is elastic.

Figure 5   Changes in Price Depend on the Price Elasticity of Supply

In panel (a), Demand$_{Typical}$ represents the typical demand for parking spaces on a summer weekend at a beach resort. Demand$_{July\,4}$ represents demand on July 4th. Because supply is inelastic, the shift in equilibrium from point A to point B results in a large increase in price—from $2.00 per hour to $4.00—but only a small increase in the quantity of spaces supplied—from 1,200 to 1,400.

In panel (b), supply is elastic. As a result, the change in equilibrium from point A to point B results in a smaller increase in price and a larger increase in the quantity supplied. An increase in price from $2.00 per hour to $2.50 is sufficient to increase the quantity of parking supplied from 1,200 to 2,100.

Continued

Economics in Your Life

How Much Do Gas Prices Matter to You?

At the beginning of the chapter, we asked you to think about three questions: What factors would make you more or less sensitive to price when purchasing gasoline? Have you responded differently to price changes during different periods of your life? and Why do consumers seem to respond more to changes in gas prices at a particular service station but seem less sensitive when gas prices rise or fall at all service stations? A number of factors are likely to affect your sensitivity to changes in gas prices, including how high your income is (and, therefore, how large a share of your budget is taken up by gasoline purchases), whether you live in an area with good public transportation (which can be a substitute for having to use your own car), and whether you live within walking distance of your school or job. Each of these factors may change over the course of your life, making you more or less sensitive to changes in gas prices. Finally, consumers respond to changes in the price of gas at a particular service station because gas at other service stations is a good substitute. But there are presently few good substitutes for gasoline as a product, so consumers respond much less to changes in prices at all service stations.

Conclusion

In this chapter, we have explored the important concept of elasticity. Table 7 summarizes the various elasticities we discussed. Computing elasticities is important in economics because it allows us to measure how one variable changes in response to changes in another variable. For example, by calculating the price elasticity of demand for its product, a firm can make a quantitative estimate of the effect of a price change on the revenue it receives. Similarly, by calculating the price elasticity of demand for cigarettes, the government can better estimate the effect of an increase in cigarette taxes on smoking.

Visit MyEconLab for a news article and analysis related to the concepts in this chapter.

Price Elasticity of Demand

Table 7

Summary of Elasticities

Formula: $\dfrac{\text{Percentage change in quantity demanded}}{\text{Percentage change in price}}$

Midpoint formula: $\dfrac{(Q_2 - Q_1)}{\left(\dfrac{Q_1 + Q_2}{2}\right)} \div \dfrac{(P_2 - P_1)}{\left(\dfrac{P_1 + P_2}{2}\right)}$

	Absolute Value of Price Elasticity	Effect on Total Revenue of an Increase in Price
Elastic	Greater than 1	Total revenue falls
Inelastic	Less than 1	Total revenue rises
Unit elastic	Equal to 1	Total revenue unchanged

Cross-Price Elasticity of Demand

Formula: $\dfrac{\text{Percentage change in quantity demanded of one good}}{\text{Percentage change in price of another good}}$

Types of Products	Value of Cross-Price Elasticity
Substitutes	Positive
Complements	Negative
Unrelated	Zero

Income Elasticity of Demand

Formula: $\dfrac{\text{Percentage change in quantity demanded}}{\text{Percentage change in income}}$

Types of Products	Value of Income Elasticity
Normal and a necessity	Positive but less than 1
Normal and a luxury	Positive and greater than 1
Inferior	Negative

Price Elasticity of Supply

Formula: $\dfrac{\text{Percentage change in quantity supplied}}{\text{Percentage change in price}}$

	Value of Price Elasticity
Elastic	Greater than 1
Inelastic	Less than 1
Unit elastic	Equal to 1

Chapter Summary and Problems

Key Terms

Cross-price elasticity of demand

Elastic demand

Elasticity

Income elasticity of demand

Inelastic demand

Perfectly elastic demand

Perfectly inelastic demand

Price elasticity of demand

Price elasticity of supply

Total revenue

Unit-elastic demand

 The Price Elasticity of Demand and Its Measurement

LEARNING OBJECTIVE: Define *price elasticity of demand* and understand how to measure it.

Summary

Elasticity measures how much one economic variable responds to changes in another economic variable. The **price elasticity of demand** measures how responsive the quantity demanded is to changes in price. The price elasticity of demand is equal to the percentage change in the quantity demanded divided by the percentage change in price. If the quantity demanded changes more than proportionally when price changes, the price elasticity of demand is greater than 1 in absolute value, and demand is **elastic**. If the quantity demanded changes less than proportionally when price changes, the price elasticity of demand is less than 1 in absolute value, and demand is **inelastic**. If the quantity demanded changes proportionally when price changes, the price elasticity of demand is equal to 1 in absolute value, and demand is **unit elastic**. **Perfectly inelastic demand** curves are vertical lines, and **perfectly elastic demand** curves are horizontal lines. Relatively few products have perfectly elastic or perfectly inelastic demand curves.

Visit **www.myeconlab.com** to complete these exercises online and get instant feedback.

Review Questions

1.1 Write the formula for the price elasticity of demand. Why isn't elasticity just measured by the slope of the demand curve?

1.2 If a 10 percent increase in the price of Cheerios causes a 25 percent reduction in the number of boxes of Cheerios demanded, what is the price elasticity of demand for Cheerios? Is the demand for Cheerios elastic or inelastic?

1.3 What is the midpoint formula for calculating price elasticity of demand? How else can you calculate the price elasticity of demand? What is the advantage of using the midpoint formula?

1.4 Draw a graph of a perfectly inelastic demand curve. Think of a product that would have a perfectly inelastic demand curve. Explain why demand for this product would be perfectly inelastic.

Problems and Applications

1.5 In the 2010 holiday season, Steve Richardson decided to cut the prices of his handcrafted wooden puzzles to increase sales. According to a newspaper account, "the number of orders at Stave Puzzles Inc., his Norwich, Vermont, business, hasn't been enough to offset the price cuts." Is the demand for these puzzles elastic or inelastic? Briefly explain.

Source: Emily Maltby, "In Season of Big Discounts, Small Shops Suffer," *Wall Street Journal*, November 24, 2010.

1.6 Suppose that the following table gives data on the price of rye and the number of bushels of rye sold in 2013 and 2014:

Year	Price (dollars per bushel)	Quantity (bushels)
2013	$3.00	8 million
2014	2.00	12 million

a. Calculate the change in the quantity of rye demanded divided by the change in the price of rye. Measure the quantity of rye in bushels.

b. Calculate the change in the quantity of rye demanded divided by the change in the price of rye, but this time measure the quantity of rye in millions of bushels. Compare your answer to the one you computed in (a).

c. Assuming that the demand curve for rye did not shift between 2013 and 2014, use the information in the table to calculate the price elasticity of demand for rye. Use the midpoint formula in your calculation. Compare the value for the price elasticity of demand to the values you calculated in (a) and (b).

1.7 **[Related to** Solved Problem 1**]** You own a hot dog stand that you set up outside the student union every day at lunchtime. Currently, you are selling hot dogs for a price of $3 each, and you sell 30 hot dogs a day. You are considering cutting the price to $2. The following graph shows two possible increases in the quantity sold as a result of your price cut. Use the information in the graph to calculate the price elasticity between these two prices on each of the demand curves. Use the midpoint formula to calculate the price elasticities.

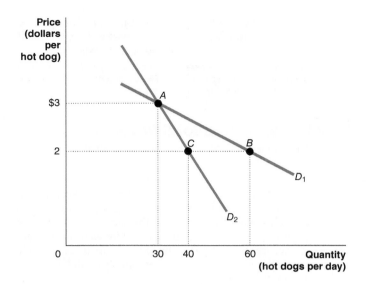

1.8 In the fall of 2006, Pace University in New York raised its annual tuition from $24,751 to $29,454. Freshman enrollment declined from 1,469 in the fall of 2005 to 1,131 in the fall of 2006. Assuming that the demand curve for places in the freshman class at Pace did not shift between 2005 and 2006, calculate the price elasticity of demand. Use the midpoint formula in your calculation. Is the demand for places in Pace's freshman class elastic or inelastic? Did the total amount of tuition Pace received from its freshman class rise or fall in 2006 compared with 2005?

Source: Karen W. Arenson, "At Universities, Plum Post at Top Is Now Shaky," *New York Times*, January 9, 2007.

1.9 In 1916, the Ford Motor Company sold 500,000 Model T Fords at a price of $440 each. Henry Ford believed that he could increase sales of the Model T by 1,000 cars for every dollar he cut the price. Use this information to calculate the price elasticity of demand for Model T Fords. Use the midpoint formula in your calculation.

1.10 [Related to the Don't Let This Happen to You**]** The publisher of a magazine gives his staff the following information:

Current price	$2.00 per issue
Current sales	150,000 copies per month
Current total costs	$450,000 per month

He tells the staff, "Our costs are currently $150,000 more than our revenues each month. I propose to eliminate this problem by raising the price of the magazine to $3.00 per issue. This will result in our revenue being exactly equal to our cost." Do you agree with the publisher's analysis? Explain. (*Hint:* Remember that a firm's revenue is calculated by multiplying the price of the product by the quantity sold.)

---

2 | Determinants of the Price Elasticity of Demand
LEARNING OBJECTIVE: Understand the determinants of the price elasticity of demand.

Summary

The main determinants of the price elasticity of demand for a good are the availability of close substitutes, the passage of time, whether the good is a necessity or a luxury, how narrowly the market for the good is defined, and the share of the good in the consumer's budget.

Visit **www.myeconlab.com** to complete these exercises online and get instant feedback.

Review Questions

2.1 Is the demand for most agricultural products elastic or inelastic? Briefly explain.

2.2 What are the key determinants of the price elasticity of demand for a product? Which determinant is the most important?

Problems and Applications

2.3 Briefly explain whether the demand for each of the following products is likely to be elastic or inelastic:
a. Milk
b. Frozen cheese pizza
c. Cola
d. Prescription medicine

2.4 [Related to the Making the Connection: The Price Elasticity of Demand for Breakfast Cereal**]** One study found that the price elasticity of demand for soda is −0.78, while the price elasticity of demand for Coca-Cola is −1.22. Coca-Cola is a type of soda, so why isn't its price elasticity the same as the price elasticity for soda as a product?

Source: Kelly D. Brownell and Thomas R. Frieden, "Ounces of Prevention—The Public Policy Case for Taxes on Sugared Beverages," *New England Journal of Medicine*, April 30, 2009, pp. 1805–1808.

2.5 The price elasticity of demand for crude oil in the United States has been estimated to be −0.06 in the short run and −0.45 in the long run. Why would the demand for crude oil be more price elastic in the long run than in the short run?

Source: John C. B. Cooper, "Price Elasticity of Demand for Crude Oil: Estimate for 23 Countries," *OPEC Review*, March 2003, pp. 1–8.

2.6 [Related to the Chapter Opener**]** An article in the *Dallas Morning News* discussed the market for green cars—hybrid gasoline and electric cars, electric cars, and diesel cars. One factor the article mentioned as affecting the market for green cars was the increasing gas mileage of conventional gasoline-powered cars. How would this factor be likely to affect the price elasticity of demand for green cars?

Source: Terry Box and Troy Oxford, "Green Cars Still a Small Part of New-Car Sales," *Dallas Morning News*, May 26, 2013.

2.7 The entrance fee into Yellowstone National Park in northwestern Wyoming is "$25 for a private, noncommercial vehicle; $20 for each snowmobile or motorcycle; or $12 for each visitor 16 and older entering by foot, bike, ski, etc." The fee provides the visitor with a seven-day entrance permit into Yellowstone and nearby Grand Teton National Park.

a. Would you expect the demand for entry into Yellowstone National Park for visitors in private, noncommercial vehicles to be elastic or inelastic? Briefly explain.

b. There are three general ways to enter the park: in a private, noncommercial vehicle; on a snowmobile or motorcycle; and by foot, bike, or ski. Which way would you expect to have the largest price elasticity of demand, and which would you expect to have the smallest price elasticity of demand? Briefly explain.

Source: National Park Service, Yellowstone National Park, "Fees, Reservations, and Permits," http://www.nps.gov/yell/planyourvisit /feesandreservations.htm, June 12, 2013.

---

3 The Relationship between Price Elasticity of Demand and Total Revenue

LEARNING OBJECTIVE: Understand the relationship between the price elasticity of demand and total revenue.

Summary

Total revenue is the total amount of funds received by a seller of a good or service. When demand is inelastic, a decrease in price reduces total revenue, and an increase in price raises total revenue. When demand is elastic, a decrease in price increases total revenue, and an increase in price decreases total revenue. When demand is unit elastic, an increase or a decrease in price leaves total revenue unchanged.

Visit **www.myeconlab.com** to complete these exercises online and get instant feedback.

Review Questions

3.1 If the demand for orange juice is inelastic, will an increase in the price of orange juice increase or decrease the revenue orange juice sellers receive?

3.2 The price of organic apples falls, and apple growers find that their revenue increases. Is the demand for organic apples elastic or inelastic?

Problems and Applications

3.3 **[Related to the** Chapter Opener**]** The Energy Information Administration estimated that in 2012 American consumers spent 4 percent of their incomes on gasoline. Would the elasticity of demand likely be greater or less if consumers had spent 8 percent of their incomes on gasoline? Briefly explain.

Source: Steve Everly, "'Get Ready for a Roller Coaster' as Gas Prices Swing Wildly," *Kansas City Star*, April 21, 2013.

3.4 Economists' estimates of price elasticities can differ somewhat, depending on the time period and on the markets in which the price and quantity data used in the estimates were gathered. An article in the *New York Times* contained the following statement from the Centers for Disease Control and Prevention: "A 10 percent increase in the price of cigarettes reduces consumption by 3 percent to 5 percent." Given this information, compute the range of the price elasticity of demand for cigarettes. Explain whether the demand for cigarettes is elastic, inelastic, or unit elastic. If cigarette manufacturers raise prices, will their revenue increase or decrease? Briefly explain.

Source: Shaila Dewan, "States Look at Tobacco to Balance the Budget," *New York Times*, March 20, 2009.

3.5 According to an article in the *New York Times*, in 2011 the Port Authority of New York and New Jersey was planning to increase the tolls on the bridges and tunnels crossing the Hudson River by as much as 50 percent. According to the article, "Revenue from the ... higher tolls would raise an additional $720 million for the agency ...." Is the Port Authority assuming that the demand for using bridges and tunnels crossing the Hudson is elastic or inelastic? Why might the Port Authority be reasonably confident in this assumption?

Source: Michael M. Grynbaum, "Port Authority Seeks Big Toll Increase," *New York Times*, August 5, 2011.

3.6 Use the following graph for Yolanda's Frozen Yogurt Stand to answer the questions.

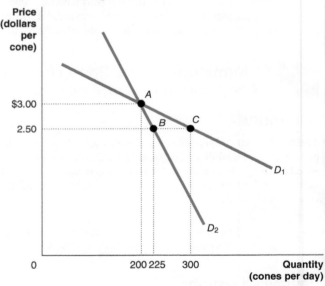

a. Use the midpoint formula to calculate the price elasticity of demand for D_1 between point A and point C and the price elasticity of demand for D_2 between point A and point B. Which demand curve is more elastic, D_1 or D_2? Briefly explain.

b. Suppose Yolanda is initially selling 200 cones per day at a price of $3.00 per cone. If she cuts her price to $2.50 per cone and her demand curve is D_1, what will be the change in her revenue? What will be the change in her revenue if her demand curve is D_2?

3.7 A sportswriter writing about the Cleveland Indians baseball team made the following observation: "If the Indians suddenly slashed all tickets to $10, would their attendance actually increase? Not all that much and revenue would drop dramatically." What is the sportswriter assuming about the price elasticity of demand for Indians' tickets?

Source: David Schoenfiel, "Chat with David Schoenfield," espn.com, November 27, 2012.

3.8 **[Related to** Solved Problem 3**]** Briefly explain whether you agree with Manager 2's reasoning:

Manager 1: "The only way we can increase the revenue we receive from selling our frozen pizzas is by cutting the price."

Manager 2: "Cutting the price of a product never increases the amount of revenue you receive. If we want to increase revenue, we have to increase price."

3.9 **[Related to** Solved Problem 3**]** If a firm increases the price of its product and its total revenue increases, will further increases in its price necessarily lead to further increases in its total revenue? Briefly explain.

3.10 According to an article in the *Wall Street Journal*, some small publishers have argued that Amazon has been increasing the prices it sells their books for on its Web site. Amazon was increasing the prices by reducing the discount it offered consumers on the retail prices of the books. One small nonfiction publisher said that Amazon had reduced the discount on its books from about 30 percent to about 16 percent. According to the author of the article: "For this publisher, that means less revenue and less profit as some buyers reject the more expensive books."

    a. Does the fact that some buyers will no longer buy the publisher's books at a higher price necessarily mean the publisher will earn less revenue? Briefly explain.

    b. What must be true about the price elasticity of demand for the publisher's books for the author's statement to be correct?

Source: David Streitfeld, "As Competition Wanes, Amazon Cuts Back Its Discounts," *Wall Street Journal*, July 4, 2013.

3.11 After parking rates were increased substantially from $10 to $16 per day at the "Big Blue Deck" at Detroit's Metro Airport, parking revenue increased from the previous December. Use the information in the following table to calculate the price elasticity of demand for parking spaces at the Big Blue Deck, using the midpoint formula. Assume that nothing happened between December 2007 and December 2008 to shift the demand curve for parking spaces. Be sure to state whether demand is elastic or inelastic.

Month	Rate	Revenue
December 2007	$10	$1,387,000
December 2008	16	1,448,000

Sources: Mary Francis Masson, "Metro Airport Parking Rate Hikes Worry Employees," *Detroit Free Press*, February 14, 2009; and Tanveer Ali, "Parking Dips; Revenue Soars," *Detroit News*, February 13, 2009.

3.12 The Delaware River Joint Toll Bridge Commission increased the toll from $0.50 to $1.00 on the bridges on Route 22 and Interstate 78 from New Jersey to Pennsylvania. Use the information in the following table to answer the questions. (Assume that besides the toll change, nothing occurred during the months that would affect consumer demand.)

		Number of Vehicles Crossing the Bridge	
Month	Toll	Route 22 Bridge	Interstate 78 Bridge
November	$0.50	519,337	728,022
December	1.00	433,691	656,257

    a. Calculate the price elasticity of demand for each bridge, using the midpoint formula.

    b. How much total revenue did the commission collect from these bridges in November? How much did it collect in December? Relate your answer to your answer in (a).

Source: Garrett Therolf, "Frugal Drivers Flood Free Bridge," *The Morning Call*, January 20, 2003.

 Other Demand Elasticities

LEARNING OBJECTIVE: Define *cross-price elasticity of demand* and *income elasticity of demand* and understand their determinants and how they are measured.

Summary

In addition to the elasticities already discussed, other important demand elasticities are the **cross-price elasticity of demand**, which is equal to the percentage change in the quantity demanded of one good divided by the percentage change in the price of another good, and the **income elasticity of demand**, which is equal to the percentage change in the quantity demanded divided by the percentage change in income.

Visit **www.myeconlab.com** to complete these exercises online and get instant feedback.

Review Questions

4.1 Define the *cross-price elasticity of demand*. What does it mean if the cross-price elasticity of demand is negative? What does it mean if the cross-price elasticity of demand is positive?

4.2 Define the *income elasticity of demand*. Use income elasticity to distinguish a normal good from an inferior good.

Is it possible to tell from the income elasticity of demand whether a product is a luxury good or a necessity good?

Problems and Applications

4.3 When lettuce prices doubled, from about $1.50 per head to about $3.00, the reaction of one consumer was quoted in a newspaper article: "I will not buy [lettuce] when it's $3 a head," she said, adding that other green vegetables can fill in for lettuce. "If bread were $5 a loaf we'd still have to buy it. But lettuce is not that important in our family."

    a. For this consumer's household, which product has the higher price elasticity of demand: bread or lettuce? Briefly explain.

    b. Is the cross-price elasticity of demand between lettuce and other green vegetables positive or negative for this consumer? Briefly explain.

Source: Justin Bachman, "Sorry, Romaine Only," *Associated Press*, March 29, 2002.

4.4 In the following graph, the demand for hot dog buns has shifted to the right because the price of hot dogs has fallen from $2.20 to $1.80 per package. Calculate the cross-price elasticity of demand between hot dogs and hot dog buns.

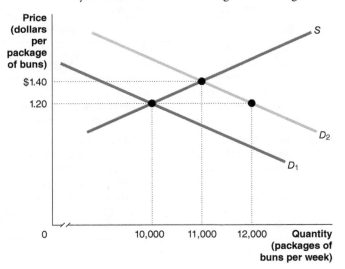

4.5 Are the cross-price elasticities of demand between the following pairs of products likely to be positive or negative? Briefly explain.
  a. Iced coffee and iced tea
  b. French fries and ketchup
  c. Steak and chicken
  d. Blu-ray players and Blu-ray discs

4.6 **[Related to the** Chapter Opener**]** During the spring of 2008, gasoline prices increased sharply in the United States. According to a newspaper article, rising gas prices had the following effect on the car market:

> Sales of Toyota's subcompact Yaris increased 46 percent, and Honda's tiny Fit had a record month. Ford's compact Focus model jumped 32 percent in April from a year earlier. All those models are rated at more than 30 miles per gallon for highway driving....

Sales of traditional SUVs are down more than 25 percent this year. In April, for example, sales of GM's Chevrolet Tahoe fell 35 percent. Full-size pickup sales have fallen more than 15 percent this year, with Ford's industry-leading F-Series pickup dropping 27 percent in April alone.

  a. Is the cross-price elasticity of demand between gasoline and high-mileage subcompact cars positive or negative? Is the cross-price elasticity of demand between gasoline and low-mileage SUVs and full-size pickups positive or negative? Briefly explain.
  b. How can we best think of the relationships among gasoline, subcompact cars, and SUVs? Briefly discuss which can be thought of as substitutes and which can be thought of as complements.

Source: Bill Vlasic, "As Gas Costs Soar, Buyers Flock to Small Cars," *New York Times*, May 2, 2008.

4.7 Rank the following four goods from lowest income elasticity of demand to highest income elasticity of demand. Briefly explain your ranking.
  a. Bread
  b. Pepsi
  c. Mercedes-Benz automobiles
  d. Laptop computers

4.8 **[Related to the** Making the Connection: Price Elasticity, Cross-Price Elasticity, and Income Elasticity in the Market for Alcoholic Beverages**]** The elasticities reported in this *Making the Connection* were calculated using price data for many brands of beer. Why might price elasticity estimates for a product be less reliable if they use data for only one brand of that product?

4.9 Consider firms selling three goods—one firm sells a good with an income elasticity of demand less than zero, one firm sells a good with an income elasticity of demand greater than zero but less than one, and one firm sells a good with an income elasticity of demand greater than one. In a recession, which firm is likely to see its sales decline the most? Which firm is likely to see its sales increase the most? Briefly explain.

5	**Using Elasticity to Analyze the Disappearing Family Farm**

LEARNING OBJECTIVE: Use price elasticity and income elasticity to analyze economic issues.

Summary

Price elasticity and income elasticity can be used to analyze many economic issues. One example is the disappearance of the family farm in the United States. Because the income elasticity of demand for food is low, the demand for food has not increased proportionally as incomes in the United States have grown. As farmers have become more productive, they have increased the supply of most foods. Because the price elasticity of demand for food is low, increasing supply has resulted in continually falling food prices.

Visit **www.myeconlab.com** to complete these exercises online and get instant feedback.

Review Questions

5.1 The demand for agricultural products is inelastic, and the income elasticity of demand for agricultural products is low. How do these facts help explain the decline of the family farm in the United States?

Problems and Applications

5.2 **[Related to** Solved Problem 5**]** According to a study by the U.S. Centers for Disease Control and Prevention, the price elasticity of demand for cigarettes is −0.25. Americans purchase about 360 billion cigarettes each year.
  a. If the federal tax on cigarettes were increased enough to cause a 50 percent increase in the price of cigarettes, what would be the effect on the quantity of cigarettes demanded?

b. Is raising the tax on cigarettes a more effective way to reduce smoking if the demand for cigarettes is elastic or if it is inelastic? Briefly explain.

Source: "Response to Increases in Cigarette Prices by Race/Ethnicity, Income, and Age Groups—United States, 1976–1993," *Morbidity and Mortality Weekly Report*, July 31, 1998.

5.3 **[Related to** Solved Problem 5**]** Suppose that the long-run price elasticity of demand for gasoline is −0.55. Assume that the price of gasoline is currently $4.00 per gallon, the quantity of gasoline is 140 billion gallons per year, and the federal government decides to increase the excise tax on gasoline by $1.00 per gallon. Suppose that in the long run the price of gasoline increases by $0.70 per gallon after the $1.00 excise tax is imposed.

a. What is the new quantity of gasoline demanded after the tax is imposed? How effective would a gas tax be in reducing consumption of gasoline in the long run?

b. How much does the federal government receive from the tax?

c. Compare your answers to those in *Solved Problem 5*.

5.4 Corruption has been a significant problem in Iraq. Opening and running a business in Iraq usually requires paying multiple bribes to government officials. We can think of there being a demand and supply for bribes, with the curves having the usual shapes: The demand for bribes will be downward sloping because the smaller the bribe, the more business owners will be willing to pay it. The supply of bribes will be upward sloping because the larger the bribe, the more government officials will be willing to run the risk of breaking the law by accepting the bribe. Suppose that the Iraqi government introduces a new policy to reduce corruption that raises the cost to officials of accepting bribes—perhaps by increasing the jail term for accepting a bribe. As a result, the supply curve for bribes will shift to the left. If we measure the burden on the economy from corruption by the total value of the bribes paid, what must be true of the demand for bribes if the government policy is to be effective? Illustrate your answer with a demand and supply graph. Be sure to show on your graph the areas representing the burden of corruption before and after the government policy is enacted.

Source: Frank R. Gunter, *The Political Economy of Iraq: Restoring Balance in a Post-Conflict Society*, Cheltenham, UK: Edward Elgar, 2013, Chapter 4.

5.5 The head of the United Kumquat Growers Association makes the following statement:

> The federal government is considering implementing a price floor in the market for kumquats. The government will not be able to buy any surplus kumquats produced at the price floor or to pay us any other subsidy. Because the demand for kumquats is elastic, I believe this program will make us worse off, and I say we should oppose it.

Explain whether you agree or disagree with this reasoning.

5.6 Will there be a greater loss of economic efficiency from a price ceiling when demand is elastic or inelastic? Illustrate your answer with a demand and supply graph.

The Price Elasticity of Supply and Its Measurement

LEARNING OBJECTIVE: Define *price elasticity of supply* and understand its main determinants and how it is measured.

Summary

The **price elasticity of supply** is equal to the percentage change in quantity supplied divided by the percentage change in price. The supply curves for most goods are inelastic over a short period of time, but they become increasingly elastic over longer periods of time. Perfectly inelastic supply curves are vertical lines, and perfectly elastic supply curves are horizontal lines. Relatively few products have perfectly elastic or perfectly inelastic supply curves.

Visit www.myeconlab.com to complete these exercises online and get instant feedback.

Review Questions

6.1 Write the formula for the price elasticity of supply. If an increase of 10 percent in the price of frozen pizzas results in a 9 percent increase in the quantity of frozen pizzas supplied, what is the price elasticity of supply for frozen pizzas? Is the supply of pizzas elastic or inelastic?

6.2 What is the main determinant of the price elasticity of supply?

Problems and Applications

6.3 **[Related to the** Making the Connection: Why Are Oil Prices So Unstable?**]** Refer again to the first graph in the *Making the Connection*. Suppose that demand had stayed at the level indicated in the graph, with the equilibrium price of oil remaining at $140 per barrel. Over long periods of time, high oil prices lead to greater increases in the quantity of oil supplied. In other words, the price elasticity of supply for oil increases. This happens because higher prices provide an economic incentive to recover oil from more costly sources, such as under the oceans, from tar sands, or from shale formations. If the supply of oil becomes more elastic, explain how the increase in demand shown in the figure will result in a lower equilibrium price than $140 per barrel and a higher equilibrium quantity than 84 million barrels per day. Illustrate your answer with a demand and supply graph.

6.4 Use the midpoint formula for calculating elasticity to calculate the price elasticity of supply between point *A* and point *B* for each panel of Figure 5.

6.5 Briefly explain whether you agree with the following statement: "The longer the period of time following an increase in the demand for apples, the greater the increase in the equilibrium quantity of apples and the smaller the increase in the equilibrium price."

6.6 Consider an increase in the demand for petroleum engineers in the United States. How would the supply of these engineers respond in the short run and in the long run? Conversely, consider a decrease in demand for lawyers. How would the supply of lawyers respond in the short run and in the long run?

6.7 On most days, the price of a rose is $1, and 8,000 roses are purchased. On Valentine's Day, the price of a rose jumps to $2, and 30,000 roses are purchased.

    a. Draw a demand and supply graph that shows why the price jumps.

    b. Based on this information, what do we know about the price elasticity of demand for roses? What do we know about the price elasticity of supply for roses? Calculate values for the price elasticity of demand and the price elasticity of supply or explain why you can't calculate these values.

6.8 Use the following graph of the market for basketball tickets at State University to answer these questions:

    a. What is the price elasticity of supply?

    b. Suppose the basketball team at State University goes undefeated in the first half of the season, and the demand for basketball tickets increases. Show the effects of this increase in demand on the graph. What happens to the equilibrium price and quantity of tickets? Briefly explain.

c. If the State University basketball team continues to do very well in future years, what is likely to happen to the price elasticity of supply of tickets to its games? Briefly explain.

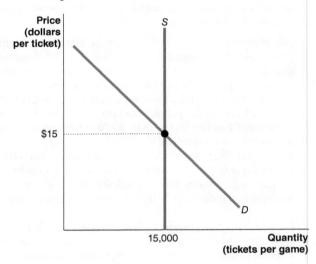

Glossary

Cross-price elasticity of demand The percentage change in the quantity demanded of one good divided by the percentage change in the price of another good.

Elastic demand Demand is elastic when the percentage change in the quantity demanded is *greater* than the percentage change in price, so the price elasticity is *greater* than 1 in absolute value.

Elasticity A measure of how much one economic variable responds to changes in another economic variable.

Income elasticity of demand A measure of the responsiveness of the quantity demanded to changes in income, measured by the percentage change in the quantity demanded divided by the percentage change in income.

Inelastic demand Demand is inelastic when the percentage change in quantity demanded is *less* than the percentage change in price, so the price elasticity is *less* than 1 in absolute value.

Perfectly elastic demand The case where the quantity demanded is infinitely responsive to price and the price elasticity of demand equals infinity.

Perfectly inelastic demand The case where the quantity demanded is completely unresponsive to price and the price elasticity of demand equals zero.

Price elasticity of demand The responsiveness of the quantity demanded to a change in price, measured by dividing the percentage change in the quantity demanded of a product by the percentage change in the product's price.

Price elasticity of supply The responsiveness of the quantity supplied to a change in price, measured by dividing the percentage change in the quantity supplied of a product by the percentage change in the product's price.

Total revenue The total amount of funds a seller receives from selling a good or service, calculated by multiplying price per unit by the number of units sold.

Unit-elastic demand Demand is unit elastic when the percentage change in quantity demanded is *equal to* the percentage change in price, so the price elasticity is equal to 1 in absolute value.

Credits

Credits are listed in the order of appearance.

Photo

Bill Aron/Science Source/Photo Researchers, Inc.

Text

Table 2, Estimated Real-World Price Elasticities of Demand, Kelly D. Brownell and Thomas R. Frieden, "Ounces of Prevention—The Public Policy Case for Taxes on Sugared Beverages," *New England Journal of Medicine*, April 30, 2009; Sheila M. Olmstead and Robert N. Stavins, "Comparing Price and Non-Price Approaches to Urban Water Conservation," Resources for the Future, Discussion paper 08-22, June 2008; Jonathan E. Hughes, Christopher R. Knittel, and Daniel Sperling, "Evidence of a Shift in the Short-Run Price Elasticity of Gasoline Demand," *Energy Journal*, Vol. 29, No. 1, January 2008; Robert P. Trost, Frederick Joutz, David Shin, and Bruce McDonwell, "Using Shrinkage Estimators to Obtain Regional Short-Run and Long-Run Price Elasticities of Residential Natural Gas Demand in the U.S.," George Washington University Working Paper, March 13, 2009; Lesley Chiou, "Empirical Analysis of Competition between Wal-Mart and Other Retail Channels," *Journal of Economics and Management Strategy*, Vol. 18, No. 2, Summer 2009; Judith Chevalier and Austan Goolsbee, "Price Competition Online: Amazon versus Barnes and Noble," *Quantitative Marketing and Economics*, Vol. 1, No. 2, June 2003; Henry Saffer and Frank Chaloupka, "The Demand for Illicit Drugs," *Economic Inquiry*, Vol. 37, No. 3, July 1999; "Response to Increases in Cigarette Prices by Race/Ethnicity, Income, and Age Groups—United States, 1976–1993," *Morbidity and Mortality Weekly Report*, July 31, 1998; James Wetzel and George Hoffer, "Consumer Demand for Automobiles: A Disaggregated Market Approach," *Journal of Consumer Research*, Vol. 9, No. 2, September 1982; Jerry A. Hausman, "The Price Elasticity of Demand for Breakfast Cereal," in Timothy F. Bresnahan and Robert J. Gordon, eds., *The Economics of New Goods*, Chicago: University of Chicago Press, 1997; Christopher J. Ruhm, et al., "What U.S. Data Should Be Used to Measure the Price Elasticity of Demand for Alcohol," *Journal of Health Economics*, Vol. 31, No. 16, December 2012; Susan Dynarski, Jonathan Gruber, and Danielle Li, "Cheaper By the Dozen: Using Sibling Discounts at Catholic Schools to Estimate the Price Elasticity of Private School Attendance," NBER Working Paper 15461, October 2009; and U.S. Department of Agriculture, Economic Research Service.

Comparative Advantage and the Gains from International Trade

From Chapter 9 of *Economics*, Fifth Edition. R. Glenn Hubbard and Anthony Patrick O'Brien. Copyright © 2015 by Pearson Education, Inc.
All rights reserved.

Comparative Advantage and the Gains from International Trade

Chapter Outline and Learning Objectives

Saving Jobs in the U.S. Tire Industry?

Between 2004 and 2008, Chinese tire companies tripled their exports to the United States. In response, in fall 2009, President Barack Obama announced that importers of Chinese tires used on cars and light trucks would have to pay the U.S. government a tariff equal to 35 percent of the tires' value. The purpose of the tariff was to protect jobs in the U.S. tire industry. In fall 2012, in a debate during his reelection campaign, President Obama argued that the tariff had served its purpose:

> We had a tire case in which … [China was] flooding us with cheap … tires …. And we put a stop to it and as a consequence saved jobs throughout America. … [Opponents] criticized me for being too tough in that tire case; said this wouldn't be good for American workers and that it would be protectionist. But I tell you, those workers don't feel that way.

Economists Gary Clyde Hufbauer and Sean Lowry of the Peterson Institute for International Economics believe the tire tariffs may have saved as many as 1,200 jobs in U.S. tire factories. But was the overall effect of the tariff on Chinese tires favorable to the U.S. economy? At the time it went into effect, owners of U.S. firms that sell Chinese tires claimed that the tariff would cause them losses. Bill Trimarco, the CEO of Hercules Tire & Rubber, located in Findlay, Ohio, argued: "This is an anti–small business policy.

A company like Goodyear won't get hit, but a lot of small businesses will be hard hit." Similarly, John Everett, owner of Cybert Tire & Car Care in New York City, noted: "This is a China tire, it costs me $69 today. Before it cost $39. It all gets passed to the customer."

Other businesspeople worried that the Chinese government might retaliate by raising tariffs on some imports from the United States. In fact, China did raise tariffs on some U.S. goods, including broiler chickens, causing lost sales and profits to those U.S. firms. Consumer groups also protested that consumers would suffer because the tariff raised the prices they paid for tires.

The tariff was enacted for a period of three years. When the three years had passed, the Obama administration allowed the tariff to expire without attempting to extend it. By 2013, imports of Chinese tires were rising rapidly to their pre-tariff levels.

Are tariffs and other attempts to protect U.S. firms from foreign competition good ideas? In this chapter, we will analyze this and other important questions related to international trade.

Sources: "Transcript of Final 2012 Presidential Debate, Part 2," cbsnews.com, October 22, 2012; Gary Clyde Hufbauer and Sean Lowry, "US Tire Tariffs: Saving Few Jobs at High Cost," Peterson Institute for International Economics, Policy Brief Number PB12-9, April 2012; Diana Ransom, "Burnt Rubber: Tire Firms Decry New Tariff," *Wall Street Journal*, September 30, 2009; and John Bussey, "Get-Tough Policy on Chinese Tires Falls Flat," *Wall Street Journal*, January 20, 2012.

Economics in Your Life

Have You Heard of the Tariff on Chinese Tires?

Politicians often support restrictions on trade because they want to convince people to vote for them. The workers in the industries these restrictions protect are likely to vote for the politicians because they believe that the restrictions will save their jobs. But most people do *not* work in industries that are protected from foreign competition by trade restrictions. Many people also have to pay higher prices for products, such as tires, that have tariffs imposed on them. How, then, did workers in the tire industry convince the federal government to impose a tariff on imports of Chinese tires, and why have so few people heard of this tariff? As you read this chapter, try to answer these questions. You can check your answers against those we provide at the end of this chapter.

Trade is simply the act of buying or selling. Is there a difference between trade that takes place within a country and international trade? Within the United States, domestic trade makes it possible for consumers in Ohio to eat salmon caught in Alaska and for consumers in Montana to drive cars built in Michigan or Kentucky. Similarly, international trade makes it possible for consumers in the United States to drink wine from France and use Blu-ray players from Japan. One significant difference between domestic trade and international trade is that international trade is more controversial. At one time, nearly all the televisions, shoes, clothing, and toys bought in the United States were also produced there. Today, firms in other countries produce most of these goods. This shift has benefited U.S. consumers because foreign-made goods have lower prices or higher quality than the U.S.-made goods they have replaced. At the same time, though, many U.S. firms that produced these goods have gone out of business, and their workers have had to find other jobs. Not surprisingly, opinion polls show that many Americans favor reducing international trade because they believe doing so will preserve jobs in the United States. But is this belief accurate?

We can use the tools of demand and supply to analyze markets for internationally traded goods and services. Trade in general—whether within a country or between countries—is based on the principle of comparative advantage. In this chapter, we look more closely at the role of comparative advantage in international trade. We also use the concepts of consumer surplus, producer surplus, and deadweight loss to analyze government policies that interfere with trade. With this background, we can return to the political debate over whether the United States benefits from international trade. We begin by looking at how large a role international trade plays in the U.S. economy.

The United States in the International Economy

International trade has grown tremendously over the past 50 years. The increase in trade is the result of the decreasing costs of shipping products around the world, the spread of inexpensive and reliable communications, and changes in government policies. Firms can use large container ships to send their products across oceans at low cost. Businesspeople today can travel to Europe or Asia, using fast, inexpensive, and reliable air transportation. The Internet, cellphones, and text messaging allow managers to communicate instantaneously and at a very low cost with customers and suppliers around the world. These and other improvements in transportation and communication have created an integrated global marketplace that earlier generations of businesspeople could only dream of.

Tariff A tax imposed by a government on imports.

Imports Goods and services bought domestically but produced in other countries.

Exports Goods and services produced domestically but sold in other countries.

Over the past 50 years, many governments have changed policies to facilitate international trade. For example, tariff rates have fallen. A **tariff** is a tax imposed by a government on *imports* into a country. **Imports** are goods and services bought domestically but produced in other countries. In the 1930s, the United States charged an average tariff rate above 50 percent. Today, the rate is less than 1.5 percent. In North America, most tariffs between Canada, Mexico, and the United States were eliminated following the passage of the North American Free Trade Agreement (NAFTA) in 1994. Twenty-eight countries in Europe have formed the European Union, which has eliminated all tariffs among member countries, greatly increasing both imports and **exports**, which are goods and services produced domestically but sold in other countries.

The Importance of Trade to the U.S. Economy

U.S. consumers buy increasing quantities of goods and services produced in other countries. At the same time, U.S. businesses sell increasing quantities of goods and services to consumers in other countries. Figure 1 shows that since 1970, both exports and imports have been steadily increasing as a fraction of U.S. gross domestic product (GDP). GDP is the value of all the final goods and services produced in a country

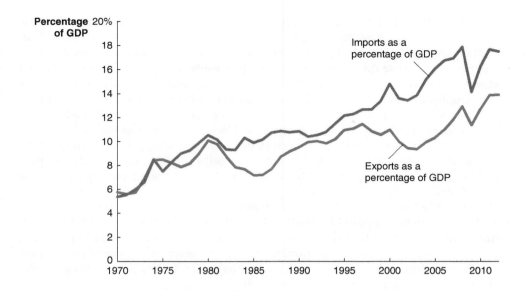

Figure 1

International Trade Is of Increasing Importance to the United States

Exports and imports of goods and services as a percentage of total production—measured by GDP—show the importance of international trade to an economy. Since 1970, both imports and exports have been steadily rising as a fraction of U.S. GDP.
Source: U.S. Department of Commerce, Bureau of Economic Analysis.

during a year. In 1970, exports and imports were both less than 6 percent of U.S. GDP. In 2012, exports were about 14 percent of GDP, and imports were about 18 percent.

Not all sectors of the U.S. economy are affected equally by international trade. For example, although it's difficult to import or export some services, such as haircuts and appendectomies, a large percentage of U.S. agricultural production is exported. Each year, the United States exports about 50 percent of its wheat and rice crops and 20 percent of its corn crop.

Many U.S. manufacturing industries also depend on trade. About 20 percent of U.S. manufacturing jobs depend directly or indirectly on exports. In some industries, such as pharmaceutical drugs, the products are directly exported. In other industries, such as steel, the products are used to make other products, such as bulldozers or machine tools, that are then exported. In all, about two-thirds of U.S. manufacturing industries depend on exports for at least 10 percent of jobs.

Making the Connection | **Goodyear and the Tire Tariff**

Goodyear Tire & Rubber Company, headquartered in Akron, Ohio, has been a leading U.S. manufacturing firm for more than a century. If you watch football or other events, you have probably seen the Goodyear blimp hovering in the sky. Although often thought of as a symbol of U.S. industry, Goodyear is in fact a global company with 52 manufacturing plants in 22 countries. As the following figure shows, today fewer than 40 percent of its tire sales occur in the United States and Canada, although more than half did as recently as 2000.

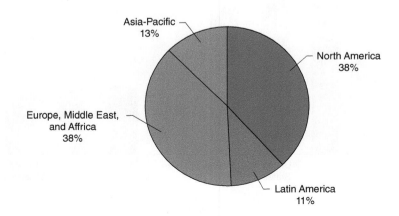

183

So when President Obama announced a 35 percent tariff on imports of Chinese tires in 2009, it was not necessarily good news for Goodyear for two key reasons. First, like many markets, tires are *differentiated*, meaning that many different types of tires are produced. Chinese firms concentrate primarily on producing inexpensive tires that consumers buy as replacement tires. Goodyear's North American production, sold under its Goodyear and Dunlop brands, sells more expensive tires that car manufacturers like General Motors and Ford buy to install on new cars. After the tariff had been in place for more than two years, a spokesman for Goodyear said: "The tariffs didn't have any material impact on our North American business. The stuff coming in from China is primarily low end. We got out of that market years ago." Second, Goodyear operates factories in China and some of the tires they produced there were exported to the United States and were subject to the tariff.

The Tire Industry Association, which represents both tire manufacturers and retailers who sell tires, had opposed the tariff. A spokesman for this association said the tariff "really hurt a lot of people in the industry—smaller businesses that geared up to bring these tires in from China." In addition, some manufacturers moved production from China to other low-wage countries, such as Mexico and Indonesia, whose exports to the United States were not subject to the tariff.

At the beginning of 2013, with the tire tariff having expired, Goodyear's profits rose more than 50 percent compared with the previous year, despite increases in imports of Chinese tires. Later in this chapter, we will consider further the effects of the tire tariff on the U.S. economy.

Sources: Jeff Bennett, "Goodyear Posts First-Quarter Profit," *Wall Street Journal,* April 26, 2013; John Bussey, "Get-Tough Policy on Chinese Tires Falls Flat," *Wall Street Journal*, January 20, 2012; Edmund L. Andrews, "U.S. Adds Tariffs on Chinese Tires," *New York Times*, September 12, 2009; and Goodyear Tire & Rubber Company, *Annual Report, 2012*.

Your Turn: Test your understanding by doing related problem 1.7 at the end of this chapter.

U.S. International Trade in a World Context

The United States is the second largest exporter in the world, just behind China, as Figure 2 illustrates. Six of the other seven leading exporting countries are also high-income countries. Although China is still a relatively low-income country, the rapid growth of the Chinese economy over the past 35 years has resulted in its becoming the largest exporter. Three of the top exporting countries are in East Asia, four are in Western Europe, and one is in North America.

Figure 2

The Eight Leading Exporting Countries, 2012

China is the leading exporting country, accounting for 9.3 percent of total world exports. The United States is second, with a 9.2 percent share. The values are the shares of total world exports of merchandise and commercial services.
Source: World Trade Organization, *International Trade Statistics*, 2012.

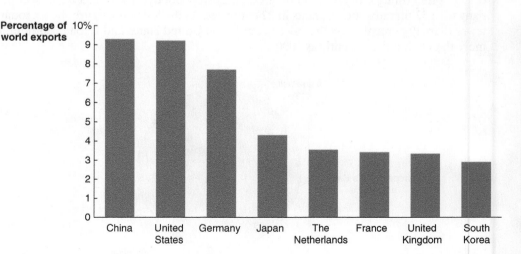

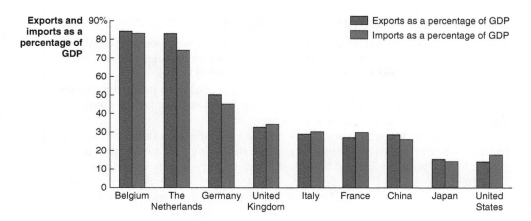

Figure 3

International Trade As a Percentage of GDP

International trade is still less important to the United States than it is to most other countries.
Source: Organization for Economic Cooperation and Development, *Country Statistical Profiles*.

Figure 3 shows that international trade is less important to the United States than it is to many other countries, with imports and exports being lower percentages of GDP. In some smaller countries, such as Belgium and the Netherlands, imports and exports make up more than half of GDP. In the larger European economies, imports and exports make up one-quarter to one-half of GDP.

Comparative Advantage in International Trade

2 LEARNING OBJECTIVE

Understand the difference between comparative advantage and absolute advantage in international trade.

Why have businesses around the world increasingly looked for markets in other countries? Why have consumers increasingly purchased goods and services made in other countries? People trade for one reason: Trade makes them better off. Whenever a buyer and seller agree to a sale, they must both believe they are better off; otherwise, there would be no sale. This outcome must hold whether the buyer and seller live in the same city or in different countries. As we will see, governments are more likely to interfere with international trade than they are with domestic trade, but the reasons for the interference are more political than economic.

A Brief Review of Comparative Advantage

Comparative advantage is the ability of an individual, a firm, or a country to produce a good or service at a lower opportunity cost than competitors. **Opportunity cost** is the highest-valued alternative that must be given up to engage in an activity. People, firms, and countries specialize in economic activities in which they have a comparative advantage. In trading, we benefit from the comparative advantage of other people (or firms or countries), and they benefit from our comparative advantage.

A good way to understand comparative advantage is to consider an example of you and your neighbor picking fruit. Your neighbor is better at picking both apples and cherries than you are. Your neighbor is a particularly skilled cherry picker, and every hour spent picking apples is an hour taken away from picking cherries. If your neighbor pick both types of fruit, the opportunity cost to your neighbor of picking her own apples is very high. You can pick apples at a much lower opportunity cost than your neighbor, so you have a comparative advantage in picking apples. Your neighbor can pick cherries at a much lower opportunity cost than you can, so she has a comparative advantage in picking cherries. Your neighbor is better off specializing in picking cherries, and you are better off specializing in picking apples. You can then trade some of your apples for some of your neighbor's cherries, and both of you will end up with more of each fruit.

Comparative advantage The ability of an individual, a firm, or a country to produce a good or service at a lower opportunity cost than competitors.

Opportunity cost The highest-valued alternative that must be given up to engage in an activity.

Comparative Advantage and Absolute Advantage

The principle of comparative advantage can explain why people pursue different occupations. It can also explain why countries produce different goods and services. International trade involves many countries importing and exporting many different goods and services. Countries are better off if they specialize in producing the goods for which they have a comparative advantage. They can then trade for the goods for which other countries have a comparative advantage.

We can illustrate why specializing on the basis of comparative advantage makes countries better off with a simple example involving just two countries and two products. Suppose the United States and Japan produce only cellphones and tablet computers, like Apple's iPad or Sony's Xperia. Assume that each country uses only labor to produce each good and that Japanese and U.S. cellphones and tablets are exactly the same. Table 1 shows how much each country can produce of each good with one hour of labor.

Notice that Japanese workers are more productive than U.S. workers in making both goods. In one hour, Japanese workers can make six times as many cellphones and one and one-half times as many tablets as U.S. workers. Japan has an *absolute advantage* over the United States in producing both goods. **Absolute advantage** is the ability to produce more of a good or service than competitors when using the same amount of resources. In this case, Japan can produce more of both goods using the same amount of labor as the United States.

It might seem at first that Japan has nothing to gain from trading with the United States because it has an absolute advantage in producing both goods. However, Japan should specialize and produce only cellphones and obtain the tablets it needs by exporting cellphones to the United States in exchange for tablets. The reason Japan benefits from trade is that although it has an *absolute advantage* in the production of both goods, it has a *comparative advantage* only in the production of cellphones. The United States has a comparative advantage in the production of tablets.

If it seems contrary to common sense that Japan should import tablets from the United States even though Japan can produce more of them per hour of labor, think about the opportunity cost to each country of producing each good. If Japan wants to produce more tablets, it has to switch labor away from cellphone production. Every hour of labor switched from producing cellphones to producing tablets increases tablet production by 6 and reduces cellphone production by 12. Japan has to give up 12 cellphones for every 6 tablets it produces. Therefore, the opportunity cost to Japan of producing one more tablet is 12/6, or 2 cellphones.

If the United States switches one hour of labor from cellphones to tablets, production of cellphones falls by 2 and production of tablets rises by 4. Therefore, the opportunity cost to the United States of producing one more tablet is 2/4, or 0.5 cellphone. The United States has a lower opportunity cost of producing tablets and, therefore, has a comparative advantage in making this product. By similar reasoning, we can see that Japan has a comparative advantage in producing cellphones. Table 2 summarizes the opportunity cost each country faces in producing these goods.

Absolute advantage The ability to produce more of a good or service than competitors when using the same amount of resources.

Table 1	Output per Hour of Work	
An Example of Japanese Workers Being More Productive Than American Workers	Cellphones	Tablets
Japan	12	6
United States	2	4

	Opportunity Costs	
	Cellphones	Tablets
Japan	0.5 tablet	2 cellphones
United States	2 tablets	0.5 cellphone

Table 2

The Opportunity Costs of Producing Cellphones and Tablets
The table shows the opportunity cost each country faces in producing cellphones and tablets. For example, the entry in the first row and second column shows that Japan must give up 2 cellphones for every tablet it produces.

How Countries Gain from International Trade

Can Japan really gain from producing only cellphones and trading with the United States for tablets? To see that it can, assume at first that Japan and the United States do not trade with each other. A situation in which a country does not trade with other countries is called **autarky**. Assume that in autarky, each country has 1,000 hours of labor available to produce the two goods, and each country produces the quantities of the two goods shown in Table 3. Because there is no trade, these quantities also represent consumption of the two goods in each country.

Increasing Consumption through Trade

Suppose now that Japan and the United States begin to trade with each other. The **terms of trade** is the ratio at which a country can trade its exports for imports from other countries. For simplicity, let's assume that the terms of trade end up with Japan and the United States being willing to trade one cellphone for one tablet.

Once trade has begun, the United States and Japan can exchange tablets for cellphones or cellphones for tablets. For example, if Japan specializes by using all 1,000 available hours of labor to produce cellphones, it will be able to produce 12,000 cellphones. It then could export 1,500 cellphones to the United States in exchange for 1,500 tablets. (Remember that we are assuming that the terms of trade are one cellphone for one tablet.) Japan ends up with 10,500 cellphones and 1,500 tablets. Compared with the situation before trade, Japan has the same number of tablets but 1,500 more cellphones. If the United States specializes in producing tablets, it will be able to produce 4,000 tablets. It could then export 1,500 tablets to Japan in exchange for 1,500 cellphones. The United States ends up with 2,500 tablets and 1,500 cellphones. Compared with the situation before trade, the United States has the same number of cellphones but 1,500 more tablets. Trade has allowed both countries to increase the quantities of goods consumed. Table 4 summarizes the gains from trade for the United States and Japan.

By trading, Japan and the United States are able to consume more than they could without trade. This outcome is possible because world production of both goods increases after trade. (In this example, our "world" consists of just the United States and Japan.)

Why does total production of cellphones and tablets increase when the United States specializes in producing tablets and Japan specializes in producing cellphones? A domestic analogy helps to answer this question: If a company shifts production from an old factory to a more efficient modern factory, its output will increase. The same thing happens in our example. Producing tablets in Japan and cellphones in the United States is inefficient. Shifting production to the more efficient country—the one with the comparative advantage—increases total production. The key point is: *Countries gain from specializing in producing goods in which they have a comparative advantage and trading for goods in which other countries have a comparative advantage.*

3 LEARNING OBJECTIVE

Explain how countries gain from international trade.

Autarky A situation in which a country does not trade with other countries.

Terms of trade The ratio at which a country can trade its exports for imports from other countries.

	Production and Consumption	
	Cellphones	Tablets
Japan	9,000	1,500
United States	1,500	1,000

Table 3

Production without Trade

Table 4

Gains from Trade for Japan and the United States

Without Trade		
Production and Consumption		
	Cellphones	Tablets
Japan	9,000	1,500
United States	1,500	1,000

With Trade						
	Production with Trade		**Trade**		**Consumption with Trade**	
	Cellphones	Tablets	Cellphones	Tablets	Cellphones	Tablets
Japan	12,000	0	Export 1,500	Import 1,500	10,500	1,500
United States	0	4,000	Import 1,500	Export 1,500	1,500	2,500

With trade, the United States and Japan specialize in the good they have a comparative advantage in producing . . .

. . . and export some of that good in exchange for the good the other country has a comparative advantage in producing.

Gains from Trade	
Increased Consumption	
Japan	1,500 Cellphones
United States	1,500 Tablets

The increased consumption made possible by trade represents the gains from trade.

Solved Problem 3

The Gains from Trade

The first discussion of comparative advantage appears in *On the Principles of Political Economy and Taxation*, a book written by the British economist David Ricardo in 1817. Ricardo provided a famous example of the gains from trade, using wine and cloth production in Portugal and England. The following table is adapted from Ricardo's example, with cloth measured in sheets and wine measured in kegs:

	Output per Year of Labor	
	Cloth	Wine
Portugal	100	150
England	90	60

a. Explain which country has an absolute advantage in the production of each good.

b. Explain which country has a comparative advantage in the production of each good.
c. Suppose that Portugal and England currently do not trade with each other. Each country has 1,000 workers, so each has 1,000 years of labor time to use in producing cloth and wine, and the countries are currently producing the amounts of each good shown in the following table:

	Cloth	Wine
Portugal	18,000	123,000
England	63,000	18,000

Show that Portugal and England can both gain from trade. Assume that the terms of trade are that one sheet of cloth can be traded for one keg of wine.

Solving the Problem

Step 1: **Review the chapter material.** This problem is about absolute and comparative advantage and the gains from trade, so you may want to review the sections "Comparative Advantage in International Trade," and "How Countries Gain from International Trade."

Step 2: **Answer part (a) by determining which country has an absolute advantage.** Remember that a country has an absolute advantage over another country when it can produce more of a good using the same resources. The first table in the problem shows that Portugal can produce more cloth *and* more wine with one year's worth of labor than can England. Therefore, Portugal has an absolute advantage in the production of both goods, and England does not have an absolute advantage in the production of either good.

Step 3: **Answer part (b) by determining which country has a comparative advantage.** A country has a comparative advantage when it can produce a good at a lower opportunity cost. To produce 100 sheets of cloth, Portugal must give up producing 150 kegs of wine. Therefore, Portugal's opportunity cost of producing 1 sheet of cloth is 150/100, or 1.5 kegs of wine. England has to give up producing 60 kegs of wine to produce 90 sheets of cloth, so its opportunity cost of producing 1 sheet of cloth is 60/90, or 0.67 keg of wine. The opportunity costs of producing wine can be calculated in the same way. The following table shows the opportunity cost to Portugal and England of producing each good.

	Opportunity Costs	
	Cloth	Wine
Portugal	1.5 kegs of wine	0.67 sheet of cloth
England	0.67 keg of wine	1.5 sheets of cloth

Portugal has a comparative advantage in wine because its opportunity cost is lower. England has a comparative advantage in cloth because its opportunity cost is lower.

Step 4: **Answer part (c) by showing that both countries can benefit from trade.** By now it should be clear that both countries will be better off if they specialize in producing the good for which they have a comparative advantage and trade for the other good. The following table is very similar to Table 4 and shows one example of trade making both countries better off. (To test your understanding, construct another example.)

Without Trade

	Production and Consumption	
	Cloth	Wine
Portugal	18,000	123,000
England	63,000	18,000

With Trade

	Production with Trade		Trade		Consumption with Trade	
	Cloth	Wine	Cloth	Wine	Cloth	Wine
Portugal	0	150,000	Import 18,000	Export 18,000	18,000	132,000
England	90,000	0	Export 18,000	Import 18,000	72,000	18,000

Gains from Trade

	Increased Consumption
Portugal	9,000 wine
England	9,000 cloth

Your Turn: For more practice, do related problems 3.5 and 3.6 at the end of this chapter.

Why Don't We See Complete Specialization?

In our example of two countries producing only two products, each country specializes in producing one of the goods. In the real world, many goods and services are produced in more than one country. For example, the United States, Japan, Germany, Canada, Mexico, India, China, and other countries produce automobiles. We do not see complete specialization in the real world for three main reasons:

- *Not all goods and services are traded internationally.* Even if, for example, Japan had a comparative advantage in the production of medical services, it would be difficult for Japan to specialize in producing medical services and then export them. There is no easy way for U.S. patients who need appendectomies to receive them from surgeons in Japan.

- *Production of most goods involves increasing opportunity costs.* Production of most goods involves increasing opportunity costs. In our example, if the United States devotes more workers to producing tablets, the opportunity cost of producing more tablets will increase. At some point, the opportunity cost of producing tablets in the United States may rise to the level of the opportunity cost of producing tablets in Japan. When that happens, international trade will no longer push the United States further toward specialization. The same will be true of Japan: The increasing opportunity cost of producing cellphones will cause Japan to stop short of complete specialization.

- *Tastes for products differ.* Most products are *differentiated*. Cellphones, tablets, cars, and televisions—to name just a few products—come with a wide variety of features. When buying automobiles, some people look for reliability and fuel efficiency, others look for room to carry seven passengers, and still others want styling and high performance. So, some car buyers prefer Toyota Prius hybrids, some prefer Chevy Suburbans, and others prefer BMWs. As a result, Japan, the United States, and Germany may each have a comparative advantage in producing different types of automobiles.

Does Anyone Lose as a Result of International Trade?

In our cellphone and tablet example, consumption increases in both the United States and Japan as a result of trade. Everyone gains, and no one loses. Or do they? In our

Don't Let This Happen to You

Remember That Trade Creates Both Winners and Losers

The following statement is from a Federal Reserve publication: "Trade is a win–win situation for all countries that participate." People sometimes interpret statements like this to mean that there are no losers from international trade. But notice that the statement refers to *countries*, not individuals. When countries participate in trade, they make their consumers better off by increasing the quantity of goods and services available to them. As we have seen, however, expanding trade eliminates the jobs of workers employed at companies that are less efficient than foreign companies. Trade also creates new jobs at companies that export products to foreign markets. It may be difficult, though, for workers who lose their jobs because of trade to easily find others. That is why in the United States the

federal government uses the Trade Adjustment Assistance program to provide funds for workers who have lost their jobs due to international trade. Qualified unemployed workers can use these funds to pay for retraining, searching for new jobs, or relocating to areas where new jobs are available. This program—and similar programs in other countries—recognizes that there are losers from international trade as well as winners.

Source: Federal Reserve Bank of Dallas, "International Trade and the Economy," www.dallasfed.org/educate/everyday/ev7.html.

Your Turn: Test your understanding by doing related problem 3.12 at the end of this chapter.

example, we referred repeatedly to "Japan" or the "United States" producing cellphones or tablets. But countries do not produce goods—firms do. In a world without trade, there would be cellphone and tablet firms in both Japan and the United States. In a world with trade, there would be only Japanese cellphone firms and U.S. tablet firms. Japanese tablet firms and U.S. cellphone firms would close. Overall, total employment would not change, and production would increase as a result of trade. Nevertheless, the owners of Japanese tablet firms, the owners of U.S. cellphone firms, and the people who work for them are worse off as a result of trade. The losers from trade are likely to do their best to convince the Japanese and U.S. governments to interfere with trade by barring imports of the competing products from the other country or by imposing high tariffs on them.

Where Does Comparative Advantage Come From?

Among the main sources of comparative advantage are the following:

- *Climate and natural resources.* This source of comparative advantage is the most obvious. Because of geology, Saudi Arabia has a comparative advantage in the production of oil. Because of climate and soil conditions, Costa Rica has a comparative advantage in the production of bananas, and the United States has a comparative advantage in the production of wheat.

- *Relative abundance of labor and capital.* Some countries, such as the United States, have many highly skilled workers and a great deal of machinery. Other countries, such as China, have many unskilled workers and relatively little machinery. As a result, the United States has a comparative advantage in the production of goods that require highly skilled workers or sophisticated machinery to make, such as aircraft and computer software. China has a comparative advantage in the production of goods, such as tools, clothing, and children's toys, that require unskilled workers and small amounts of simple machinery.

- *Technology.* Broadly defined, *technology* is the process firms use to turn inputs into goods and services. At any given time, firms in different countries do not all have access to the same technologies. In part, this difference is the result of past investments countries have made in supporting higher education or in providing support for research and development. Some countries are strong in *product technologies*, which involve the ability to develop new products. For example, firms in the United States have pioneered the development of such products as radios, televisions, digital computers, airliners, medical equipment, and many prescription drugs. Other countries are strong in *process technologies*, which involve the ability to improve the processes used to make existing products. For example, Japanese-based firms, such as Toyota and Honda, have succeeded by greatly improving the processes for designing and manufacturing automobiles.

- *External economies.* It is difficult to explain the location of some industries on the basis of climate, natural resources, the relative abundance of labor and capital, or technology. For example, why does southern California have a comparative advantage in making movies or Switzerland in making watches or New York in providing financial services? The answer is that once an industry becomes established in an area, firms located in that area gain advantages over firms located elsewhere. The advantages include the availability of skilled workers, the opportunity to interact with other firms in the same industry, and proximity to suppliers. These advantages result in lower costs to firms located in the area. Because these lower costs result from increases in the size of the industry in an area, economists refer to them as **external economies**.

External economies Reductions in a firm's costs that result from an increase in the size of an industry.

Leaving New York City Is Risky for Financial Firms

The name "Wall Street" is shorthand for the whole U.S. financial system of banks, brokerage houses, and other financial firms. Wall Street is also, of course, an actual street in the New York City borough of Manhattan. The New York Stock Exchange is located on Wall Street, and many financial firms have their headquarters in Manhattan. There are also a lot of financial firms located outside Manhattan, but many of the largest firms believe that there are advantages to being located close to Wall Street. For instance, in 1997, UBS, a large Swiss bank, moved its North American headquarters from Manhattan to Stamford, Connecticut, where it built the largest facility for trading financial securities in the world. By 2011, UBS had begun moving many of its bankers back to Manhattan and was expected to occupy more than 1 million square feet of the 3 World Trade Center building once construction was complete.

Financial firms benefit from the external economies of being located in New York City.

Other financial firms have also moved some operations out of Manhattan only to move them back. As one manager of a new hedge fund put it: "There were enough roadblocks to establishing a new fund that I didn't want to create another" by not being in Manhattan. He was hardly alone: In recent years more than 90 percent of new hedge funds have been located in Manhattan.

The original concentration of financial firms in Manhattan was something of a historical accident. In colonial times and up through the early nineteenth century, Philadelphia and Boston were at least close rivals to New York City as business and financial centers. In fact, Philadelphia had a larger population than New York City and was the headquarters of the federal government's first two central banks. New York City received a boost in its rivalry with other cities when the Erie Canal was completed in upstate New York in 1825. The canal resulted in crops and other raw materials being shipped to New York City rather than to other ports. This inflow led to the development of banking, insurance, and other financial firms. Coupled with the gradual increase in trading on the New York Stock Exchange, the increase in business resulting from the completion of the canal established New York City as the leading financial center in the country.

But the Erie Canal has long since ceased to operate, and most stock trading takes place electronically rather than on the floor of the New York Stock Exchange. So, why has New York continued to see a high concentration of financial firms, with some firms that temporarily left deciding to return? The answer is that financial firms benefit from the external economies of being located in New York City. Even in the Internet age, many financial deals are still conducted face-to-face, so not having a physical presence in Manhattan puts a firm at a disadvantage. Many people pursuing careers in finance also want to be physically located in Manhattan because that is where most of the highest-paying financial jobs are. Firms that have moved out of Manhattan have had more difficulty attracting and retaining the most productive workers. In addition, Manhattan also has a large concentration of firms that provide support services, such as software programming for running financial firms' computer systems.

Large financial firms located outside Manhattan, particularly those that heavily trade securities or attempt to make deals that involve mergers between firms, may have higher costs than firms located in Manhattan. Having many financial firms originally located in Manhattan was a historical accident, but external economies gave the area a comparative advantage in providing financial services once the industry began to grow there.

Sources: Juliet Chung, "Hedge Funds' Manhattan Migration," *Wall Street Journal*, January 14, 2012; Brett Philbin, "UBS Shifts Staff to New York," *Wall Street Journal*, July 13, 2011; and Charles V. Bagli, "Regretting Move, Bank May Return to Manhattan," *New York Times*, June 8, 2011.

Your Turn: Test your understanding by doing related problem 3.13 at the end of this chapter.

Comparative Advantage over Time: The Rise and Fall—and Rise—of the U.S. Consumer Electronics Industry

A country may develop a comparative advantage in the production of a good, and then, as time passes and circumstances change, the country may lose its comparative advantage in producing that good and develop a comparative advantage in producing other goods. For several decades, the United States had a comparative advantage in the production of consumer electronic goods, such as televisions, radios, and stereos. The comparative advantage of the United States in these products was based on having developed most of the underlying technology, having the most modern factories, and having a skilled and experienced workforce. Gradually, however, other countries, particularly Japan, gained access to the technology, built modern factories, and developed skilled workforces. As mentioned earlier, Japanese firms have excelled in process technologies, which involve the ability to improve the processes used to make existing products. By the 1970s and 1980s, Japanese firms were able to produce many consumer electronic goods more cheaply and with higher quality than could U.S. firms. Japanese firms Sony, Panasonic, and Pioneer replaced U.S. firms Magnavox, Zenith, and RCA as world leaders in consumer electronics.

By the mid-2000s, however, as the technology underlying consumer electronics had evolved, comparative advantage had shifted again, and several U.S. firms had surged ahead of their Japanese competitors. For example, Apple had developed the iPod, iPhone, and iPad; Linksys, a division of Cisco Systems, took the lead in home wireless networking technology; and TiVo pioneered the digital video recorder (DVR). As pictures and music converted to digital data, process technologies became less important than the ability to design and develop new products. These new consumer electronic products required skills similar to those in computer design and software writing, where the United States had long maintained a comparative advantage. Although for the most part these firms did not manufacture within the United States the products they designed and marketed, even that appeared to be changing as Apple announced in 2013 that its redesigned Mac Pro computer would be assembled in the United States.

Once a country has lost its comparative advantage in producing a good, its income will be higher and its economy will be more efficient if it switches from producing the good to importing it, as the United States did when it switched from producing televisions to importing them. As we will see in the next section, however, there is often political pressure on governments to attempt to preserve industries that have lost their comparative advantage.

Government Policies That Restrict International Trade

4 LEARNING OBJECTIVE

Analyze the economic effects of government policies that restrict international trade.

Free trade, or trade between countries that is without government restrictions, makes consumers better off. We can expand on this idea by using the concepts of consumer surplus and producer surplus. Figure 4 shows the market in the United States for the biofuel ethanol, which can be used as a substitute for gasoline. The figure shows the situation of autarky, where the United States does not trade with other countries. The equilibrium price of ethanol is $2.00 per gallon, and the equilibrium quantity is 6.0 billion gallons per year. The blue area represents consumer surplus, and the red area represents producer surplus.

Free trade Trade between countries that is without government restrictions.

Now suppose that the United States begins importing ethanol from Brazil and other countries that produce ethanol for $1.00 per gallon. Because the world market for ethanol is large, we will assume that the United States can buy as much ethanol as it wants without causing the *world price* of $1.00 per gallon to rise. Therefore, once imports of ethanol are permitted into the United States, U.S. firms will not be able to sell ethanol at prices higher than the world price of $1.00, and the U.S. price will become equal to the world price.

Figure 4

The U.S. Market for Ethanol under Autarky

This figure shows the market for ethanol in the United States, assuming autarky, where the United States does not trade with other countries. The equilibrium price of ethanol is $2.00 per gallon, and the equilibrium quantity is 6.0 billion gallons per year. The blue area represents consumer surplus, and the red area represents producer surplus.

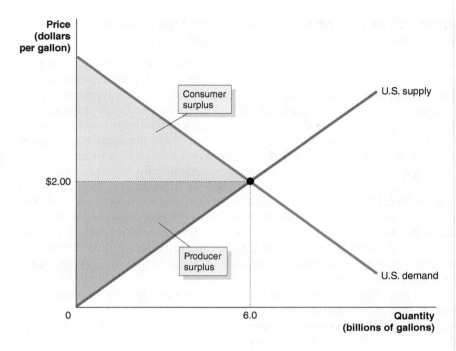

Figure 5 shows the result of allowing imports of ethanol into the United States. With the price lowered from $2.00 to $1.00, U.S. consumers increase their purchases from 6.0 billion gallons to 9.0 billion gallons. Equilibrium moves from point F to point G. In the new equilibrium, U.S. producers have reduced the quantity of ethanol they supply from 6.0 billion gallons to 3.0 billion gallons. Imports will equal 6.0 billion gallons, which is the difference between U.S. consumption and U.S. production.

Under autarky, consumer surplus would be area A in Figure 5. With imports, the reduction in price increases consumer surplus, so it is now equal to the sum of areas A,

Figure 5

The Effect of Imports on the U.S. Ethanol Market

When imports are allowed into the United States, the price of ethanol falls from $2.00 to $1.00. U.S. consumers increase their purchases from 6.0 billion gallons to 9.0 billion gallons. Equilibrium moves from point F to point G. U.S. producers reduce the quantity of ethanol they supply from 6.0 billion gallons to 3.0 billion gallons. Imports equal 6.0 billion gallons, which is the difference between U.S. consumption and U.S. production. Consumer surplus equals the sum of areas A, B, C, and D. Producer surplus equals the area E.

	Under Autarky	With Imports
Consumer Surplus	A	$A + B + C + D$
Producer Surplus	$B + E$	E
Economic Surplus	$A + B + E$	$A + B + C + D + E$

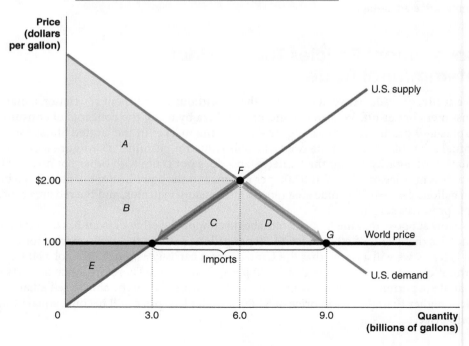

B, *C*, and *D*. Although the lower price increases consumer surplus, it reduces producer surplus. Under autarky, producer surplus was equal to the sum of areas *B* and *E*. With imports, it is equal to only area *E*. Economic surplus equals the sum of consumer surplus and producer surplus. Moving from autarky to allowing imports increases economic surplus in the United States by an amount equal to the sum of areas *C* and *D*.

We can conclude that international trade helps consumers but hurts firms that are less efficient than foreign competitors. As a result, these firms and their workers are often strong supporters of government policies that restrict trade. These policies usually take one of two forms: *tariffs* or *quotas* and *voluntary export restraints*.

Tariffs

The most common interferences with trade are *tariffs*, which are taxes imposed by a government on goods imported into the country. Like any other tax, a tariff increases the cost of selling a good. Figure 6 shows the effect of a tariff of $0.50 per gallon on ethanol imports into the United States. The $0.50 tariff raises the price of ethanol in the United States from the world price of $1.00 per gallon to $1.50 per gallon. At this higher price, U.S. ethanol producers increase the quantity they supply from 3.0 billion gallons to 4.5 billion gallons. U.S. consumers, though, cut back their purchases of ethanol from 9.0 billion gallons to 7.5 billion gallons. Imports decline from 6.0 billion gallons (9.0 billion − 3.0 billion) to 3.0 billion gallons (7.5 billion − 4.5 billion). Equilibrium moves from point *G* to point *H*.

By raising the price of ethanol from $1.00 to $1.50, the tariff reduces consumer surplus by the sum of areas *A*, *T*, *C*, and *D*. Area *A* is the increase in producer surplus from the higher price. The government collects tariff revenue equal to the tariff of $0.50 per gallon multiplied by the 3.0 billion gallons imported. Area *T* represents the government's tariff revenue. Areas *C* and *D* represent losses to U.S. consumers that are not captured by anyone. These areas are deadweight loss and represent the decline in economic efficiency resulting from the ethanol tariff. Area *C* shows the effect of U.S. consumers being forced to buy from U.S. producers who are less efficient than foreign producers, and area *D* shows the effect of U.S. consumers buying less ethanol than they would have at the world price. As a result of the tariff, economic surplus has been reduced by the sum of areas *C* and *D*.

We can conclude that the tariff succeeds in helping U.S. ethanol producers but hurts U.S. consumers and the efficiency of the U.S. economy.

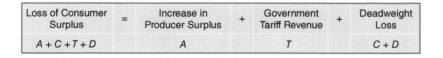

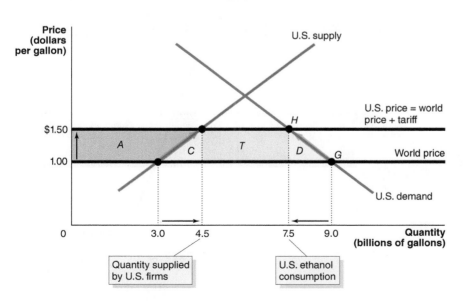

Figure 6

The Effects of a Tariff on Ethanol

Without a tariff on ethanol, U.S. producers will sell 3.0 billion gallons of ethanol, U.S. consumers will purchase 9.0 billion gallons, and imports will be 6.0 billion gallons. The U.S. price will equal the world price of $1.00 per gallon. The $0.50-per-gallon tariff raises the price of ethanol in the United States to $1.50 per gallon, and U.S. producers increase the quantity they supply to 4.5 billion gallons. U.S. consumers reduce their purchases to 7.5 billion gallons. Equilibrium moves from point *G* to point *H*. The ethanol tariff causes a loss of consumer surplus equal to the area *A* + *C* + *T* + *D*. The area *A* is the increase in producer surplus due to the higher price. The area *T* is the government's tariff revenue. The areas *C* and *D* represent deadweight loss.

Quotas and Voluntary Export Restraints

Quota A numerical limit a government imposes on the quantity of a good that can be imported into the country.

Voluntary export restraint (VER) An agreement negotiated between two countries that places a numerical limit on the quantity of a good that can be imported by one country from the other country.

A **quota** is a numerical limit on the quantity of a good that can be imported, and it has an effect similar to that of a tariff. A quota is imposed by the government of the importing country. A **voluntary export restraint (VER)** is an agreement negotiated between two countries that places a numerical limit on the quantity of a good that can be imported by one country from the other country. In the early 1980s, the United States and Japan negotiated a VER that limited the quantity of automobiles the United States would import from Japan. The Japanese government agreed to the VER primarily because it was afraid that if it did not, the United States would impose a tariff or quota on imports of Japanese automobiles. Quotas and VERs have similar economic effects.

The main purpose of most tariffs and quotas is to reduce the foreign competition that domestic firms face. For many years, Congress has imposed a quota on sugar imports to protect U.S. sugar producers. Figure 7 shows the actual statistics for the U.S. sugar market in 2012. The effect of a quota is very similar to the effect of a tariff. By limiting imports, a quota forces the domestic price of a good above the world price. In this case, the sugar quota limits sugar imports to 5.8 billion pounds per year (shown by the bracket in Figure 7), forcing the U.S. price of sugar up to $0.43 per pound, or $0.16 higher than the world price of $0.27 per pound. The U.S. price is above the world price because the quota keeps foreign sugar producers from selling the additional sugar in the United States that would drive the U.S. price down to the world price. At a price of $0.43 per pound, U.S. producers increase the quantity of sugar they supply from the 7.6 billion pounds they would supply at the world price to 17.3 billion pounds, and U.S. consumers cut back their purchases of sugar from the 25.7 billion pounds they would purchase at the world price to the 23.1 billion pounds they are willing to purchase at the higher U.S. price. If there were no import quota, equilibrium would be at the world price (point E), but with the quota equilibrium is at the U.S. price (point F).

Measuring the Economic Effect of the Sugar Quota

We can use the concepts of consumer surplus, producer surplus, and deadweight loss to measure the economic impact of the sugar quota. Without a sugar quota, the world price of $0.27 per pound would also be the U.S. price. In Figure 7, without a sugar quota, consumer surplus would equal the area above the $0.27 price line and below the demand curve. The sugar quota causes the U.S. price to rise to $0.43 and reduces

Figure 7

The Economic Effect of the U.S. Sugar Quota

Without a sugar quota, U.S. sugar producers would have sold 7.6 billion pounds of sugar, U.S. consumers would have purchased 25.7 billion pounds of sugar, and imports would have been 18.1 billion pounds. The U.S. price would have equaled the world price of $0.27 per pound. Because the sugar quota limits imports to 5.8 billion pounds (the bracket in the graph), the price of sugar in the United States rises to $0.43 per pound, and U.S. producers supply 17.3 billion pounds. U.S. consumers purchase 23.1 billion pounds rather than the 25.7 billion pounds they would purchase at the world price. Without the import quota, equilibrium would be at point E; with the quota, equilibrium is at point F. The sugar quota causes a loss of consumer surplus equal to the area $A + B + C + D$. The area A is the gain to U.S. sugar producers. The area B is the gain to foreign sugar producers. The areas C and D represent deadweight loss. The total loss to U.S. consumers in 2012 was $3.9 billion.

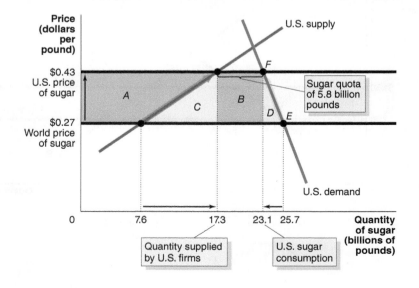

Loss of Consumer Surplus	=	Gain to U.S. Sugar Producers	+	Gain to Foreign Sugar Producers	+	Deadweight Loss
$A + C + B + D$		A		B		$C + D$
$3.90 billion	=	$1.99 billion	+	$0.93 billion	+	$0.98 billion

consumer surplus by the area $A + B + C + D$. Without a sugar quota, producer surplus received by U.S. sugar producers would be equal to the area below the $0.27 price line and above the supply curve. The higher U.S. price resulting from the sugar quota increases the producer surplus of U.S. sugar producers by an amount equal to area A.

A foreign producer must have a license from the U.S. government to import sugar under the quota system. Therefore, a foreign sugar producer that is lucky enough to have an import license also benefits from the quota because it is able to sell sugar in the U.S. market at $0.43 per pound instead of $0.27 per pound. Area B is the gain to foreign sugar producers. Areas A and B represent transfers from U.S. consumers of sugar to U.S. and foreign producers of sugar. Areas C and D represent losses to U.S. consumers that are not captured by anyone. These areas are deadweight loss and represent the decline in economic efficiency resulting from the sugar quota. Area C shows the effect of U.S. consumers being forced to buy from U.S. producers that are less efficient than foreign producers, and area D shows the effect of U.S. consumers buying less sugar than they would have at the world price.

Figure 7 provides enough information to calculate the dollar value of each of the four areas. The table in the figure shows the results of these calculations. The total loss to consumers from the sugar quota was $3.90 billion in 2012. About 51 percent of the loss to consumers, or $1.99 billion, was gained by U.S. sugar producers as increased producer surplus. About 24 percent, or $0.93 billion, was gained by foreign sugar producers as increased producer surplus, and about 25 percent, or $0.98 billion, was a deadweight loss to the U.S. economy. The U.S. International Trade Commission estimates that eliminating the sugar quota would result in the loss of about 3,000 jobs in the U.S. sugar industry. The cost to U.S. consumers of saving these jobs is equal to $3.9 billion/3,000, or about $1.3 million per job each year. In fact, this cost is an underestimate because eliminating the sugar quota would result in new jobs being created, particularly in the candy industry. Over the years, several U.S. candy companies—including the makers of Life Savers and Star Brite mints—have moved factories to other countries to escape the effects of the sugar quota. Partly as a result of the sugar quota, total employment in U.S. food and beverage firms that use sugar as an input declined from 717,192 in 1997 to 590,669 in 2011.

Solved Problem 4

Measuring the Economic Effect of a Quota

Suppose that the United States currently both produces and imports apples. The U.S. government then decides to restrict international trade in apples by imposing a quota that allows imports of only 4 million boxes of apples into the United States each year. The figure shows the results of imposing the quota.

Fill in the following table, using the prices, quantities, and letters in the figure:

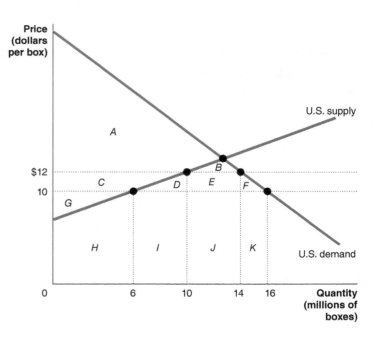

	Without Quota	With Quota
World price of apples		
U.S. price of apples		
Quantity supplied by U.S. firms		
Quantity demanded by U.S. consumers		
Quantity imported		
Area of consumer surplus		
Area of domestic producer surplus		
Area of deadweight loss		

Solving the Problem

Step 1: **Review the chapter material.** This problem is about measuring the economic effects of a quota, so you may want to review the sections "Quotas and Voluntary Export Restraints," and "Measuring the Economic Effect of the Sugar Quota."

Step 2: **Fill in the table.** After studying Figure 7, you should be able to fill in the table. Remember that consumer surplus is the area below the demand curve and above the market price.

	Without Quota	With Quota
World price of apples	$10	$10
U.S. price of apples	$10	$12
Quantity supplied by U.S. firms	6 million boxes	10 million boxes
Quantity demanded by U.S. consumers	16 million boxes	14 million boxes
Quantity imported	10 million boxes	4 million boxes
Area of consumer surplus	$A + B + C + D + E + F$	$A + B$
Area of domestic producer surplus	G	$G + C$
Area of deadweight loss	No deadweight loss	$D + F$

Your Turn: For more practice, do related problem 4.12 at the end of this chapter.

The High Cost of Preserving Jobs with Tariffs and Quotas

The sugar quota is not alone in imposing a high cost on U.S. consumers to save jobs at U.S. firms. Table 5 shows, for several industries, the costs tariffs and quotas impose on U.S. consumers per year for each job saved.

Many countries besides the United States also use tariffs and quotas to try to protect jobs. Table 6 shows the cost to Japanese consumers per year for each job saved as a result of tariffs and quotas in the listed industries. Note the staggering cost of $51 million for each job saved that is imposed on Japanese consumers by their government's restrictions on imports of rice.

Table 5

Preserving U.S. Jobs with Tariffs and Quotas Is Expensive

Product	Number of Jobs Saved	Cost to Consumers per Year for Each Job Saved
Benzenoid chemicals	216	$1,376,435
Luggage	226	1,285,078
Softwood lumber	605	1,044,271
Dairy products	2,378	685,323
Frozen orange juice	609	635,103
Ball bearings	146	603,368
Machine tools	1,556	479,452
Women's handbags	773	263,535
Canned tuna	390	257,640

Source: Federal Reserve Bank of Dallas, 2002 *Annual Report*, Exhibit 11.

Product	Cost to Consumers per Year for Each Job Saved
Rice	$51,233,000
Natural gas	27,987,000
Gasoline	6,329,000
Paper	3,813,000
Beef, pork, and poultry	1,933,000
Cosmetics	1,778,000
Radio and TV sets	915,000

Table 6

Preserving Japanese Jobs with Tariffs and Quotas Is Also Expensive

"Preserving Japanese Jobs with Tariffs and Quotas Is Also Expensive" by Yoko Sazabami, Shujiro Urata, and Hiroki Kawai from *Measuring the Cost of Protection in Japan*. Copyright © 1995 by the Institute for International Economics. Reprinted by permission.

Just as the sugar quota costs jobs in the candy industry, other tariffs and quotas cost jobs outside the industries immediately affected. For example, in 1991, the United States imposed tariffs on flat-panel displays used in laptop computers. The tariff was good news for U.S. producers of these displays but bad news for companies producing laptop computers. Toshiba, Sharp, and Apple all closed their U.S. laptop production facilities and moved production overseas. In fact, whenever one industry receives tariff or quota protection, other domestic industries lose jobs.

Making the Connection

The Effect on the U.S. Economy of the Tariff on Chinese Tires

We saw in the chapter opener that in 2009 the federal government imposed a tariff on imports of tires from China. The United Steelworkers Union, which represents workers in some U.S. tire factories, pushed for the tariff in order to save jobs. As with supporters of other tariffs and quotas who argue that these interferences with trade save jobs, the Steelworkers Union was focusing only on the jobs in tire manufacturing. We have seen that a tariff or quota makes it easier for domestic firms to compete against foreign firms that may have lower costs. More production by domestic firms means more employment at those firms, thereby saving jobs in that industry. But as we have also seen, other industries can see their costs rise as a result of the tariff or quota, causing firms in these industries to raise prices. In fact, the Tire Industry Association, which represents both tire manufacturers and tire retailers, opposed the tariff because it believed higher prices for Chinese tires might cause problems for the U.S. retailers who sold them. In addition, if consumers spend more on a good protected by a tariff, they have less to spend on other goods, thereby potentially reducing production and employment in other industries.

A tariff on tires increased the price of tires U.S. consumers purchased.

Economists Gary Clyde Hufbauer and Sean Lowry of the Petersen Institute for International Economics have estimated the effect of the tire tariff on the U.S. economy. The tariff succeeded in reducing imports of Chinese tires by raising their prices. Some consumers switched from Chinese tires to tires imported from other countries, whose prices were higher than the Chinese tires had been before the tariff. Hufbauer and

Lowry calculate that consumers spent about $800 million more on imported tires as a result of the tariff. In addition, U.S. manufacturers also increased prices as a result of the tariff, causing U.S. consumers to spend nearly $300 million more on U.S.-produced tires. Looking at the trends in employment among U.S. tire manufacturers, Hufbauer and Lowry conclude that the tariff saved at most 1,200 jobs. If the additional $1.1 billion consumers spent on tires as a result of the tariff is divided by the 1,200 jobs saved, the resulting value indicates that it cost U.S. consumers more than $900,000 per year for each job saved in the tire industry.

Because consumers spent more on tires as a result of the tariff, they had less to spend on other goods. Drawing on studies of the relationship between consumer spending and jobs in retailing, Hufbauer and Lowry estimate that the tariff resulted in a decline of 3,731 jobs in retailing. So, the short-run effect of the tariff during the years it was in effect would have been a net *decline* of 2,500 jobs.

This economic analysis indicates that the tire tariff was an expensive and ineffective way to preserve jobs.

Sources: Gary Clyde Hufbauer and Sean Lowry, "US Tire Tariffs: Saving Few Jobs at High Cost," Peterson Institute for International Economics, Policy Brief Number PB12-9, April 2012; Dylan Matthews, "How Obama's Tire Tariffs Have Hurt Consumers," *Washington Post*, October 23, 2013; and John Bussey, "Get-Tough Policy on Chinese Tires Falls Flat," *Wall Street Journal*, January 20, 2012.

Your Turn: Test your understanding by doing related problems 4.14 and 4.15 at the end of this chapter.

Gains from Unilateral Elimination of Tariffs and Quotas

Some politicians argue that eliminating U.S. tariffs and quotas would help the U.S. economy only if other countries eliminated their tariffs and quotas in exchange. It is easier to gain political support for reducing or eliminating tariffs or quotas if it is done as part of an agreement with other countries that involves their eliminating some of their tariffs or quotas. But as the example of the sugar quota shows, *the U.S. economy would experience a gain in economic surplus from the elimination of tariffs and quotas even if other countries did not reduce their tariffs and quotas.*

Other Barriers to Trade

In addition to tariffs and quotas, governments sometimes erect other barriers to trade. For example, all governments require that imports meet certain health and safety requirements. Sometimes, however, governments use these requirements to shield domestic firms from foreign competition. For example, a government may impose stricter health and safety requirements on imported goods than on goods produced by domestic firms.

Many governments also restrict imports of certain products on national security grounds. The argument is that in time of war, a country should not be dependent on imports of critical war materials. Once again, these restrictions are sometimes used more to protect domestic companies from competition than to protect national security. For example, for years, the U.S. government would buy military uniforms only from U.S. manufacturers, even though uniforms are not a critical war material.

5 LEARNING OBJECTIVE

Evaluate the arguments over trade policies and globalization.

The Arguments over Trade Policies and Globalization

The argument over whether the U.S. government should regulate international trade has continued since the early days of the country. One particularly controversial attempt to restrict trade took place during the Great Depression of the 1930s. At that time, the United States and other countries attempted to help domestic firms by raising tariffs on foreign imports. The United States started the process by passing the Smoot-Hawley Tariff in 1930, which raised average tariff rates to more than 50 percent. As other countries retaliated by raising their tariffs, international trade collapsed.

By the end of World War II in 1945, government officials in the United States and Europe were looking for a way to reduce tariffs and revive international trade. To help achieve this goal, they set up the General Agreement on Tariffs and Trade (GATT) in 1948. Countries that joined GATT agreed not to impose new tariffs or import quotas. In addition, a series of *multilateral negotiations*, called *trade rounds*, took place, in which countries agreed to reduce tariffs from the very high levels of the 1930s.

In the 1940s, most international trade was in goods, and the GATT agreement covered only goods. In the following decades, trade in services and products incorporating *intellectual property*, such as software programs and movies, grew in importance. Many GATT members pressed for a new agreement that would cover services and intellectual property, as well as goods. A new agreement was negotiated, and in January 1995, the GATT was replaced by the **World Trade Organization (WTO)**, headquartered in Geneva, Switzerland. More than 150 countries are currently members of the WTO.

World Trade Organization (WTO) An international organization that oversees international trade agreements.

Why Do Some People Oppose the World Trade Organization?

During the years immediately after World War II, many low-income, or developing, countries enacted high tariffs and restricted investment by foreign companies. When these policies failed to produce much economic growth, many of these countries decided during the 1980s to become more open to foreign trade and investment. This process became known as **globalization**. Most developing countries joined the WTO and began to follow its policies.

Globalization The process of countries becoming more open to foreign trade and investment.

During the 1990s, opposition to globalization began to increase. Over the years, protests, which have sometimes turned violent, have occurred in cities hosting WTO meetings. Why would attempts to reduce trade barriers with the objective of increasing income around the world cause such a furious reaction? The opposition to the WTO comes from three sources. First, some opponents are specifically against the globalization process that began in the 1980s and became widespread in the 1990s. Second, other opponents have the same motivation as the supporters of tariffs in the 1930s—to erect trade barriers to protect domestic firms from foreign competition. Third, some critics of the WTO support globalization in principle but believe that the WTO favors the interests of the high-income countries at the expense of the low-income countries. Let's look more closely at the sources of opposition to the WTO.

Anti-Globalization Many of those who protest at WTO meetings distrust globalization. Some believe that free trade and foreign investment destroy the distinctive cultures of many countries. As developing countries began to open their economies to imports from the United States and other high-income countries, the imports of food, clothing, movies, and other goods began to replace the equivalent local products. So, a teenager in Thailand might be sitting in a McDonald's restaurant, wearing Levi's jeans and a Ralph Lauren shirt, listening to a song by Lady Gaga on his iPhone, before downloading *World War Z* to his iPad. Globalization has increased the variety of products available to consumers in developing countries, but some people argue that this is too high a price to pay for what they see as damage to local cultures.

Globalization has also allowed multinational corporations to relocate factories from high-income countries to low-income countries. These new factories in Indonesia, Malaysia, Pakistan, and other countries pay much lower wages than are paid in the United States, Europe, and Japan and often do not meet the environmental or safety regulations that are imposed in high-income countries. Some factories use child labor, which is illegal in high-income countries. Some people have argued that firms with factories in developing countries should pay workers wages as high as those paid in high-income countries. They also believe these firms should abide by the health, safety, and environmental regulations that exist in the high-income countries.

The governments of most developing countries have resisted these proposals. They argue that when the currently rich countries were poor, they also lacked environmental or safety standards, and their workers were paid low wages. They argue that it is easier for rich countries to afford high wages and environmental and safety regulations than it is for poor countries. They also point out that many jobs that seem to have very low wages based on the standards of high-income countries are often better than the alternatives available to workers in low-income countries.

| Making the Connection | **The Unintended Consequences of Banning Goods Made with Child Labor** |

In many developing countries, such as Indonesia, Thailand, and Peru, children as young as seven or eight years old work ten or more hours a day. Reports of very young workers laboring long hours to produce goods for export have upset many people in high-income countries. In the United States, boycotts have been organized against stores that stock goods made in developing countries with child labor. Many people assume that if child workers in developing countries weren't working in factories making clothing, toys, and other products, they would be in school, as are children in high-income countries.

Would eliminating child labor, such as stitching soccer balls, improve the quality of children's lives?

In fact, children in developing countries usually have few good alternatives to work. Schooling is frequently available for only a few months each year, and even children who attend school rarely do so for more than a few years. Poor families are often unable to afford even the small costs of sending their children to school. Families may rely on the earnings of very young children to survive, as poor families once did in the United States, Europe, and Japan. There is substantial evidence that as incomes begin to rise in poor countries, families rely less on child labor. The United States eventually outlawed child labor, but not until 1938. In developing countries where child labor is common today, jobs producing export goods are usually better paying and less hazardous than the alternatives.

As preparations began in France for the 1998 World Cup, there were protests that Baden Sports—the main supplier of soccer balls—was purchasing the balls from suppliers in Pakistan that used child workers. France decided to ban all use of soccer balls made by child workers. Bowing to this pressure, Baden Sports moved production from Pakistan, where the balls were hand-stitched by child workers, to China, where the balls were machine-stitched by adult workers in factories. There was some criticism of the boycott of hand-stitched soccer balls at the time. In a broad study of child labor, three economists argued:

> Of the array of possible employment in which impoverished children might engage, soccer ball stitching is probably one of the most benign.... [In Pakistan] children generally work alongside other family members in the home or in small workshops.... Nor are the children exposed to toxic chemicals, hazardous tools or brutal working conditions. Rather, the only serious criticism concerns the length of the typical child stitcher's work-day and the impact on formal education.

In fact, the alternatives to soccer ball stitching for child workers in Pakistan turned out to be extremely grim. According to Keith Maskus, an economist at the University of Colorado and the World Bank, a "large proportion" of the children who lost their jobs stitching soccer balls ended up begging or in prostitution.

Sources: Tom Wright, "Pakistan Defends Its Soccer Industry," *Wall Street Journal*, April 26, 2010; Drusilla K. Brown, Alan V. Deardorff, and Robert M. Stern, "U.S. Trade and Other Policy Options to Deter Foreign Exploitation of Child Labor," in Magnus Blomstrom and Linda S. Goldberg, eds., *Topics in Empirical International Economics: A Festschrift in Honor of Bob Lispey*, Chicago: University of Chicago Press, 2001; Tomas Larsson, *The Race to the Top: The Real Story of Globalization,*

Washington, DC: Cato Institute, 2001, p. 48; and Eric V. Edmonds and Nina Pavcnik, "Child Labor in the Global Economy," *Journal of Economic Perspectives*, Vol. 19, No. 1, Winter 2005, pp. 199–220.

Your Turn: Test your understanding by doing related problem 5.5 at the end of this chapter.

"Old-Fashioned" Protectionism The anti-globalization argument against free trade and the WTO is relatively new. Another argument against free trade, called *protectionism*, has been around for centuries. **Protectionism** is the use of trade barriers to shield domestic firms from foreign competition. For as long as international trade has existed, governments have attempted to restrict it to protect domestic firms. As we saw with the analysis of the sugar quota, protectionism causes losses to consumers and eliminates jobs in the domestic industries that buy the protected product. In addition, by reducing the ability of countries to produce according to comparative advantage, protectionism reduces incomes.

Why, then, does protectionism attract support? Protectionism is usually justified on the basis of one of the following arguments:

- *Saving jobs.* Supporters of protectionism argue that free trade reduces employment by driving domestic firms out of business. It is true that when more-efficient foreign firms drive less-efficient domestic firms out of business, jobs are lost, but jobs are also lost when more-efficient domestic firms drive less-efficient domestic firms out of business. These job losses are rarely permanent. In the U.S. economy, jobs are lost and new jobs are created continually. No economic study has ever found a long-term connection between the total number of jobs available and the level of tariff protection for domestic industries. In addition, trade restrictions destroy jobs in some industries at the same time that they preserve jobs in others. The U.S. sugar quota may have saved jobs in the U.S. sugar industry, but it has also destroyed jobs in the U.S. candy industry.

- *Protecting high wages.* Some people worry that firms in high-income countries will have to start paying much lower wages to compete with firms in developing countries. This fear is misplaced, however, because free trade actually raises living standards by increasing economic efficiency. When a country practices protectionism and produces goods and services it could obtain more inexpensively from other countries, it reduces its standard of living. The United States could ban imports of coffee and begin growing it domestically. But doing so would entail a very high opportunity cost because coffee could only be grown in the continental United States in greenhouses and would require large amounts of labor and equipment. The coffee would have to sell for a very high price to cover these costs. Suppose the United States did ban coffee imports: Eliminating the ban at some future time would eliminate the jobs of U.S. coffee workers, but the standard of living in the United States would rise as coffee prices declined and labor, machinery, and other resources were moved out of coffee production and into production of goods and services for which the United States has a comparative advantage.

- *Protecting infant industries.* It is possible that firms in a country may have a comparative advantage in producing a good, but because the country begins production of the good later than other countries, its firms initially have higher costs. In producing some goods and services, substantial "learning by doing" occurs. As workers and firms produce more of the good or service, they gain experience and become more productive. Over time, these firms will have lower costs and can charge lower prices. As the firms in the "infant industry" gain experience, they will be able to compete successfully with foreign producers. Under free trade, however, they may not get a chance. The established foreign producers can sell the product at a lower price and drive domestic producers out of business before they gain enough experience to compete. To economists, the infant industry argument is the most persuasive of the protectionist arguments. It has a significant drawback,

Protectionism The use of trade barriers to shield domestic firms from foreign competition.

however. Tariffs used to protect an infant industry eliminate the need for the firms in the industry to become productive enough to compete with foreign firms. After World War II, the governments of many developing countries used the infant industry argument to justify high tariff rates. Unfortunately, most of their infant industries never grew up, and they continued for years as inefficient drains on their economies.

- *Protecting national security.* As already discussed, a country should not rely on other countries for goods that are critical to its military defense. For example, the United States would probably not want to import all its jet fighter engines from China. The definition of which goods are critical to military defense is a slippery one, however. In fact, it is rare for an industry to ask for protection without raising the issue of national security, even if its products have mainly nonmilitary uses.

Dumping

Dumping Selling a product for a price below its cost of production.

In recent years, the United States has extended protection to some domestic industries by using a provision in the WTO agreement that allows governments to impose tariffs in the case of *dumping*. **Dumping** is selling a product for a price below its cost of production. Using tariffs to offset the effects of dumping is controversial despite being allowed under the WTO agreement.

In practice, it is difficult to determine whether foreign companies are dumping goods because the true production costs of a good are not easy for governments to calculate. As a result, the WTO allows countries to determine that dumping has occurred if a product is exported for a lower price than it sells for on the home market. There is a problem with this approach, however. Often there are good business reasons for a firm to sell a product for different prices to different consumers. For example, the airlines charge business travelers higher ticket prices than leisure travelers. Firms also use "loss leaders"—products that are sold below cost, or even given away free—when introducing a new product or, in the case of retailing, to attract customers who will also buy full-price products. For example, during the holiday season, Wal-Mart sometimes offers toys at prices below what it pays to buy them from manufacturers. It's unclear why these normal business practices should be unacceptable when used in international trade.

Positive versus Normative Analysis

Economists emphasize the burden on the economy imposed by tariffs, quotas, and other government restrictions on free trade. Does it follow that these interferences are bad? The distinction between *positive analysis* and *normative analysis* is that positive analysis concerns what *is*. Normative analysis concerns what *ought to be*. Measuring the effect of the sugar quota on the U.S. economy is an example of positive analysis. Asserting that the sugar quota is bad public policy and should be eliminated is normative analysis. The sugar quota—like all other interferences with trade—makes some people better off and some people worse off, and it reduces total income and consumption. Whether increasing the profits of U.S. sugar companies and the number of workers they employ justifies the costs imposed on consumers and the reduction in economic efficiency is a normative question.

Most economists do not support interferences with trade, such as the sugar quota. Few people become economists if they don't believe that markets should usually be as free as possible. But the opposite view is certainly intellectually respectable. It is possible for someone to understand the costs of tariffs and quotas but still believe that tariffs and quotas are a good idea, perhaps because he or she believes unrestricted free trade would cause too much disruption to the economy.

The success of industries in getting the government to erect barriers to foreign competition depends partly on some members of the public knowing the costs of trade barriers but supporting them anyway. However, two other factors are also at work:

1. The costs tariffs and quotas impose on consumers are large in total but relatively small per person. For example, the sugar quota imposes a total burden of $3.90 billion per year on consumers. Spread across 314 million Americans, the burden is less than $12.50 per person: too little for most people to worry about, even if they know the burden exists.
2. The jobs lost to foreign competition are easy to identify, but the jobs created by foreign trade are less easy to identify.

In other words, the industries that benefit from tariffs and quotas benefit a lot—for example, the sugar quota increases the profits of U.S. sugar producers by almost $2 billion—whereas each consumer loses relatively little. This concentration of benefits and widely spread burdens makes it easy to understand why members of Congress receive strong pressure from some industries to enact tariffs and quotas and relatively little pressure from the general public to reduce them.

Continued

Economics in Your Life

Have You Heard of the Tariff on Chinese Tires?

At the beginning of the chapter, we asked you to consider how U.S. tire workers convinced the federal government to impose a tariff on Chinese tires and why relatively few people have heard of this tariff. In the chapter, we saw that trade restrictions tend to preserve relatively few jobs in the protected industries, while leading to job losses in other industries and costing consumers billions of dollars per year in higher prices. We have also seen, though, that *per person*, the burden of specific trade restrictions can be small. The sugar quota, for instance, imposes a per-person cost on consumers of only about $12.50 per year. Few people will take the trouble of writing a letter to their member of Congress or otherwise express their views to try to save $12.50 per year. In fact, few people will even spend the time to become aware that a specific trade restriction exists. So, if before you read this chapter you had never heard of the tire tariff, you are certainly not alone.

Conclusion

There are few issues economists agree upon more than the economic benefits of free trade. However, there are few political issues as controversial as government policy toward trade. Many people who would be reluctant to see the government interfere with domestic trade are quite willing to see it interfere with international trade. The damage high tariffs inflicted on the world economy during the 1930s shows what can happen when governments around the world abandon free trade. Whether future episodes of that type can be avoided is by no means certain.

Visit MyEconLab for a news article and analysis related to the concepts in this chapter.

Chapter Summary and Problems

Key Terms

Absolute advantage	External economies	Protectionism	Voluntary export restraint (VER)
Autarky	Free trade	Quota	
Comparative advantage	Globalization	Tariff	World Trade Organization (WTO)
Dumping	Imports	Terms of trade	
Exports	Opportunity cost		

 1 ## The United States in the International Economy

LEARNING OBJECTIVE: Discuss the role of international trade in the U.S. economy.

Summary

International trade has been increasing in recent decades, in part because of reductions in *tariffs* and other barriers to trade. A **tariff** is a tax imposed by a government on imports. The quantity of goods and services the United States imports and exports has been continually increasing. **Imports** are goods and services bought domestically but produced in other countries. **Exports** are goods and services produced domestically and sold to other countries. Today, the United States is the second leading exporting country in the world behind China, and about 20 percent of U.S. manufacturing jobs depend on exports.

Visit **www.myeconlab.com** to complete these exercises online and get instant feedback.

Review Questions

1.1 Briefly explain whether the value of U.S. exports is typically larger or smaller than the value of U.S. imports.

1.2 Are imports and exports now a smaller or larger fraction of GDP than they were 40 years ago?

1.3 Briefly explain whether you agree with the following statement: "International trade is more important to the U.S. economy than it is to most other economies."

Problems and Applications

1.4 If the United States were to stop trading goods and services with other countries, which U.S. industries would be likely to see their sales decline the most? Briefly explain.

1.5 Briefly explain whether you agree with the following statement: "Japan has always been much more heavily involved in international trade than are most other nations. In fact, today Japan exports a larger fraction of its GDP than Germany, Great Britain, or the United States."

1.6 Why might a smaller country, such as the Netherlands, be more likely to import and export larger fractions of its GDP than would a larger country, such as China or the United States?

1.7 **[Related to the** Chapter Opener **and the** Making the Connection: **Goodyear and the Tire Tariff]** Goodyear manufactures tires in the United States, so you might expect that the firm would benefit from a tariff on imports of Chinese tires. Yet Goodyear actually opposed the Obama administration's decision to impose the tariff. Briefly explain why Goodyear was not in favor of the tire tariff.

 2 ## Comparative Advantage in International Trade

LEARNING OBJECTIVE: Understand the difference between comparative advantage and absolute advantage in international trade.

Summary

Comparative advantage is the ability of an individual, a firm, or a country to produce a good or service at the lowest **opportunity cost**. **Absolute advantage** is the ability to produce more of a good or service than competitors when using the same amount of resources. Countries trade on the basis of comparative advantage, not on the basis of absolute advantage.

Visit **www.myeconlab.com** to complete these exercises online and get instant feedback.

Review Questions

2.1 What is the difference between absolute advantage and comparative advantage? Will a country always be an exporter of a good in the production of which it has an absolute advantage? Briefly explain.

2.2 A World Trade Organization (WTO) publication calls comparative advantage "arguably the single most powerful insight in economics." What is comparative advantage? What makes it such a powerful insight?

Source: World Trade Organization, "Understanding the WTO," www .wto.org/english/thewto_e/whatis_e/tif_e/fact3_e.htm.

Problems and Applications

2.3 Why do the goods that countries import and export change over time? Use the concept of comparative advantage in your answer.

2.4 In a newspaper column, Frank Wolak, a professor of economics at Stanford, referred to "the economic forces that lead to most children's toys being developed in the United States and mass-produced in China and other developing countries." What economic forces is he referring to? If a U.S. company develops a toy, why is a Chinese company likely to end up manufacturing the toy?

Source: Frank A. Wolak, "Our Comparative Advantage," *New York Times*, January 19, 2011.

2.5 Briefly explain whether you agree with the following argument: "Unfortunately, Bolivia does not have a comparative advantage with respect to the United States in the production of any good or service." (*Hint:* You do not need any specific information about the economies of Bolivia or the United States to be able to answer this question.)

2.6 The following table shows the hourly output per worker for Greece and Italy measured as quarts of olive oil and pounds of pasta:

	Output per Hour of Work	
	Olive Oil	Pasta
Greece	4	2
Italy	4	8

Calculate the opportunity cost of producing olive oil and pasta in both Greece and Italy.

2.7 Patrick J. Buchanan, a former presidential candidate, argued in his book on the global economy that there is a flaw in David Ricardo's theory of comparative advantage:

> Classical free trade theory fails the test of common sense. According to Ricardo's law of comparative advantage … if America makes better computers and textiles than China does, but our advantage in computers is greater than our advantage in textiles, we should (1) focus on computers, (2) let China make textiles, and (3) trade U.S. computers for Chinese textiles.… The doctrine begs a question. If Americans are more efficient than Chinese in making clothes … why surrender the more efficient American industry? Why shift to a reliance on a Chinese textile industry that will take years to catch up to where American factories are today?

Do you agree with Buchanan's argument? Briefly explain.

Source: Patrick J. Buchanan, *The Great Betrayal: How American Sovereignty and Social Justice Are Being Sacrificed to the Gods of the Global Economy*, Boston: Little, Brown & Company, 1998, p. 66.

2.8 While running for president, Barack Obama made the following statement: "Well, look, people don't want a cheaper T-shirt if they're losing a job in the process." What did Obama mean by the phrase "losing a job in the process"? Using the economic concept of comparative advantage, explain under what circumstances it would make sense for the United States to produce all of the T-shirts purchased in the United States. Do you agree with President Obama's statement? Briefly explain.

Source: James Pethokoukis, "Democratic Debate Spawns Weird Economics," *U.S. News & World Report*, August 8, 2007.

How Countries Gain from International Trade

LEARNING OBJECTIVE: Explain how countries gain from international trade.

Summary

Autarky is a situation in which a country does not trade with other countries. The **terms of trade** is the ratio at which a country can trade its exports for imports from other countries. When a country specializes in producing goods for which it has a comparative advantage and trades for the other goods it needs, the country will have a higher level of income and consumption. We do not see complete specialization in production for three reasons: (1) Not all goods and services are traded internationally, (2) production of most goods involves increasing opportunity costs, and (3) tastes for products differ across countries. Although the population of a country as a whole benefits from trade, firms—and their workers—that are unable to compete with lower-cost foreign producers lose. Among the main sources of comparative advantage are climate and natural resources, relative abundance of labor and capital, technology, and external economies. **External economies** are reductions in a firm's costs that result from an increase in the size of an industry. A country may develop a comparative advantage in the production of a good, and then as time passes and circumstances change, the country may lose its comparative advantage in producing that good and develop a comparative advantage in producing other goods.

Visit **www.myeconlab.com** to complete these exercises online and get instant feedback.

Review Questions

3.1 Briefly explain how international trade increases a country's consumption.

3.2 What is meant by a country specializing in the production of a good? Is it typical for countries to be completely specialized? Briefly explain.

3.3 What are the main sources of comparative advantage?

3.4 Does everyone gain from international trade? If not, explain which groups lose.

Problems and Applications

3.5 [Related to Solved Problem 3**]** The following table shows the hourly output per worker in two industries in Chile and Argentina:

	Output per Hour of Work	
	Hats	Beer
Chile	8	6
Argentina	1	2

a. Explain which country has an absolute advantage in the production of hats and which country has an absolute advantage in the production of beer.

b. Explain which country has a comparative advantage in the production of hats and which country has a comparative advantage in the production of beer.

c. Suppose that Chile and Argentina currently do not trade with each other. Each has 1,000 hours of labor to use producing hats and beer, and the countries are currently producing the amounts of each good shown in the following table:

	Hats	Beer
Chile	7,200	600
Argentina	600	800

Using this information, give a numerical example of how Chile and Argentina can both gain from trade. Assume that after trading begins, one hat can be exchanged for one barrel of beer.

3.6 [Related to Solved Problem 3**]** A political commentator makes the following statement:

The idea that international trade should be based on the comparative advantage of each country is fine for rich countries like the United States and Japan. Rich countries have educated workers and large quantities of machinery and equipment. These advantages allow them to produce every product more efficiently than poor countries can. Poor countries like Kenya and Bolivia have nothing to gain from international trade based on comparative advantage.

Do you agree with this argument? Briefly explain.

3.7 Briefly explain whether you agree with the following statement: "Most countries exhaust their comparative advantage in producing a good or service before they reach complete specialization."

3.8 Is free trade likely to benefit a large, populous country more than a small country with fewer people? Briefly explain.

3.9 An article in the *New Yorker* magazine states, "the main burden of trade-related job losses and wage declines has fallen on middle- and lower-income Americans. But ... the very people who suffer most from free trade are often, paradoxically, among its biggest beneficiaries." Explain how it is possible that middle- and lower-income Americans are both the biggest losers and at the same time the biggest winners from free trade.

Source: James Surowiecki, "The Free-Trade Paradox," *New Yorker*, May 26, 2008.

3.10 Hal Varian, an economist at the University of California, Berkeley, has made two observations about international trade:

a. Trade allows a country "to produce more with less."

b. There is little doubt who wins [from trade] in the long run: consumers.

Briefly explain whether you agree with either or both of these observations.

Source: Hal R. Varian, "The Mixed Bag of Productivity," *New York Times*, October 23, 2003.

3.11 Imagine that the following graph shows Tanzania's production possibilities frontier for cashew nuts and mangoes. Assume that the output per hour of work is 8 bushels of cashew nuts or 2 bushels of mangoes and that Tanzania has 1,000 hours of labor. Without trade, Tanzania evenly splits its labor hours between cashews and mangoes and produces and consumes at point *A*.

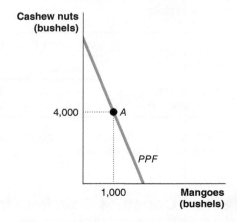

a. Suppose Tanzania opens trade with Kenya, and Kenya's output per hour of work is 1 bushel of cashew nuts or 1 bushel of mangoes. Having the comparative advantage, Tanzania completely specializes in cashew nuts. How many bushels of cashew nuts can Tanzania produce? Denote this point on the graph as point *B*.

b. Suppose Tanzania keeps 5,000 bushels of cashew nuts and exports the remaining 3,000 bushels. If the terms of trade are 1 bushel of mangoes for 2 bushels of cashew nuts, how many bushels of mangoes will Tanzania get in exchange? Denote on the graph the quantity of cashew nuts and mangoes that Tanzania consumes with trade and label this point as point *C*. How does point *C* with trade compare to point *A* without trade?

c. With trade, is Tanzania producing on its production possibilities frontier? With trade, is Tanzania consuming on its production possibilities frontier?

3.12 [Related to the Don't Let This Happen to You**]** In 2011, President Barack Obama described a trade agreement reached with the government of Colombia as a "'win-win' for both our countries." Is everyone in both countries likely to win from the agreement? Briefly explain.

Source: Kent Klein, "Obama: Free Trade Agreement a 'Win-Win' for US, Colombia," Voice of America (voanews.com), accessed April 7, 2011.

3.13 **[Related to the** Making the Connection: **Leave New York City? Risky for Financial Firms]** Instagram is a smartphone app now owned by Facebook. According to an article that discusses the climate for software firms in the San Francisco Bay Area, the success of Instagram "is a tale about the culture of the Bay Area tech scene, driven by a tightly woven web of entrepreneurs and investors who nurture one another's projects with money, advice and introductions to the right people." What advantages does being located in the Bay Area give to startup software firms? In what circumstances can software firms located elsewhere overcome these advantages? Are the advantages the Bay Area has likely to persist over time?

Source: Somini Sengupta, Nicole Perlroth, and Jenna Wortham, "Behind Instagram's Success, Networking the Old Way," *New York Times*, April 13, 2012.

---

4 Government Policies That Restrict International Trade

LEARNING OBJECTIVE: Analyze the economic effects of government policies that restrict international trade.

Summary

Free trade is trade between countries without government restrictions. Government policies that interfere with trade usually take the form of *tariffs, quotas,* or *voluntary export restraints.* A tariff is a tax imposed by a government on imports. A **quota** is a numerical limit imposed by a government on the quantity of a good that can be imported into the country. A **voluntary export restraint (VER)** is an agreement negotiated between two countries that places a numerical limit on the quantity of a good that can be imported by one country from the other country. The federal government's sugar quota costs U.S. consumers $3.9 billion per year, or about $1.3 million per year for each job saved in the sugar industry. Saving jobs by using tariffs and quotas is often very expensive.

Visit **www.myeconlab.com** to complete these exercises online and get instant feedback.

Review Questions

4.1 What is a tariff? What is a quota? Give an example, other than a quota, of a nontariff barrier to trade.

4.2 Who gains and who loses when a country imposes a tariff or a quota on imports of a good?

Problems and Applications

4.3 Political commentator B. Bruce-Briggs once wrote the following in the *Wall Street Journal*: "This is not to say that the case for international free trade is invalid; it is just irrelevant. It is an 'if only everybody …' argument…. In the real world almost everybody sees benefits in economic nationalism." What do you think he means by "economic nationalism"? Do you agree that a country benefits from free trade only if every other country also practices free trade? Briefly explain.

Source: B. Bruce-Biggs, "The Coming Overthrow of Free Trade," *Wall Street Journal*, February 24, 1983.

4.4 Two U.S. senators made the following argument against allowing free trade: "Fewer and fewer Americans support our government's trade policy. They see a shrinking middle class, lost jobs and exploding trade deficits. Yet supporters of free trade continue to push for more of the same—more job-killing trade agreements." Do you agree with these senators that reducing barriers to trade reduces the number of jobs available to workers in the United States? Briefly explain.

Source: Byron Dorgan and Sherrod Brown, "How Free Trade Hurts," *Washington Post*, December 23, 2006.

4.5 The United States produces beef and also imports beef from other countries.
   a. Draw a graph showing the demand and supply of beef in the United States. Assume that the United States can import as much as it wants at the world price of beef without causing the world price of beef to increase. Be sure to indicate on your graph the quantity of beef imported.
   b. Now show on your graph the effect of the United States imposing a tariff on beef. Be sure to indicate on your graph the quantity of beef sold by U.S. producers before and after the tariff is imposed, the quantity of beef imported before and after the tariff, and the price of beef in the United States before and after the tariff.
   c. Discuss who benefits and who loses when the United States imposes a tariff on beef.

4.6 When Congress was considering a bill to impose quotas on imports of textiles, shoes, and other products, the late Milton Friedman, a Nobel Prize–winning economist, made the following comment: "The consumer will be forced to spend several extra dollars to subsidize the producers [of these goods] by one dollar. A straight handout would be far cheaper." Why would a quota result in consumers paying much more than domestic producers receive? Where do the other dollars go? What does Friedman mean by a "straight handout"? Why would a straight handout be cheaper than a quota?

Source: Milton Friedman, "Free Trade," *Newsweek Magazine*, August 27, 1970.

4.7 A student makes the following argument:

> Tariffs on imports of foreign goods into the United States will cause the foreign companies to add the amount of the tariff to the prices they charge in the United States for those goods. Instead of putting a tariff on imported goods, we should ban importing them. Banning imported goods is better than putting tariffs on them because U.S. producers benefit from the reduced competition, and U.S. consumers don't have to pay the higher prices caused by tariffs.

Briefly explain whether you agree with the student's reasoning.

4.8 Suppose China decides to pay large subsidies to any Chinese company that exports goods or services to the United States. As a result, these companies are able to sell products in the United States at far below their cost of production. In addition, China decides to bar all imports from the United States. The dollars that the United States pays to import Chinese goods are left in banks in China. Will this strategy raise or lower the standard of living in China? Will it raise or lower the standard of living in the United States? Briefly explain. Be sure to provide a definition of "standard of living" in your answer.

4.9 The following graph shows the effect on consumer surplus, producer surplus, government tariff revenue, and economic surplus of a tariff of $1 per unit on imports of plastic combs into the United States. Use the areas denoted in the graph to answer the following questions.

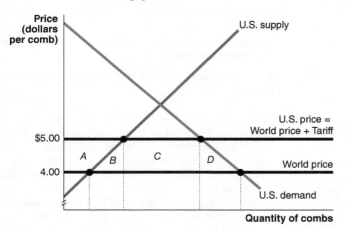

a. Which area shows the losses to U.S. consumers of buying a smaller quantity of combs than they would have if they could have purchased them at the world price?
b. Which area shows the losses to U.S. consumers of having to buy combs from U.S. producers who are less efficient than foreign producers?
c. Which areas show the deadweight loss to the U.S. economy as a result of the tariff on combs?

4.10 The following graph shows the situation after the U.S. government removes a tariff on imports of canned tuna.

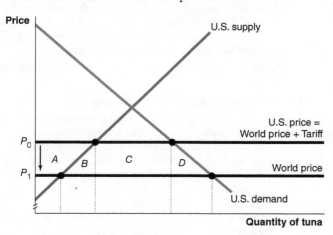

a. Which areas show the gain in consumer surplus?
b. Which area shows the loss in producer surplus?

c. Which area shows the loss in government tariff revenue?
d. Which areas show the gain in economic surplus?

4.11 According to an editorial in the *Washington Post*: "Sugar protectionism is a burden on consumers and a job-killer."
a. In what sense does the United States practice "sugar protectionism"?
b. In what way is sugar protectionism a burden on consumers? In what way is it a job-killer?
c. If sugar protectionism has the bad effects stated in the editorial, why don't Congress and the president eliminate it?

Source: "Sourball," *Washington Post*, March 22, 2010.

4.12 **[Related to** Solved Problem 4**]** Suppose that the United States currently both produces kumquats and imports them. The U.S. government then decides to restrict international trade in kumquats by imposing a quota that allows imports of only 6 million pounds of kumquats into the United States each year. The figure shows the results of imposing the quota.

Fill in the table in the next column using the letters in the figure:

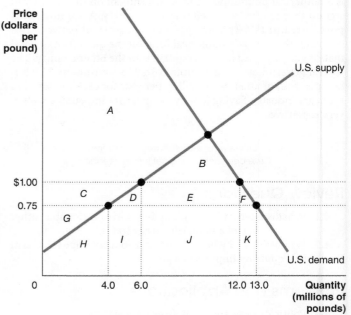

	Without Quota	With Quota
World price of kumquats		
U.S. price of kumquats		
Quantity supplied by U.S. firms		
Quantity demanded		
Quantity imported		
Area of consumer surplus		
Area of domestic producer surplus		
Area of deadweight loss		

4.13 Suppose the government is considering imposing either a tariff or a quota on canned peaches. Assume that the proposed quota has the same effect on the U.S. price of canned peaches as the proposed tariff. Use the graph to answer the following questions.

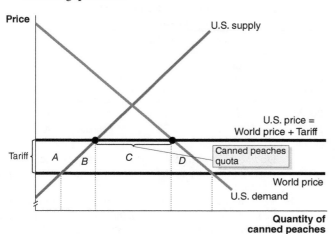

a. If the government imposes a tariff, which area shows the government tariff revenue?

b. If the government imposes a quota, which area shows the gain to foreign producers of canned peaches?

c. As a consumer of peaches, would you prefer the government impose the tariff or the quota? Briefly explain.

4.14 **[Related to the** Making the Connection**: The Effect on the Economy of the Tariff on Chinese Tires]** An economic analysis of a proposal to impose a quota on steel imports into the United States indicated that the quota would save 3,700 jobs in the steel industry but cost about 35,000 jobs in other U.S. industries. Why would a quota on steel imports cause employment to decline in other industries? Which other industries is a steel quota likely to affect?

Source: Douglas A. Irwin, *Free Trade Under Fire*, Princeton, NJ: Princeton University Press, 2002, p. 82.

4.15 **[Related to the** Making the Connection**: The Effect on the Economy of the Tariff on Chinese Tires]** According to the analysis by Hufbauer and Lowry, of the additional $1.1 billion consumers spent on tires as a result of the tariff on Chinese tires, the workers whose jobs were saved in the U.S. tire industry received only about $48 million in wages. Wouldn't it have been cheaper for the federal government to have raised taxes on U.S. consumers and given the money to tire workers rather than to have imposed a tariff? If so, why didn't the federal government adopt this alternative policy?

Source: Gary Clyde Hufbauer and Sean Lowry, "US Tire Tariffs: Saving Few Jobs at High Cost," Peterson Institute for International Economics, Policy Brief Number PB12-9, April 2012.

5	**The Arguments over Trade Policies and Globalization**

LEARNING OBJECTIVE: Evaluate the arguments over trade policies and globalization.

Summary

The **World Trade Organization (WTO)** is an international organization that enforces trade agreements among members. The WTO has promoted **globalization**, the process of countries becoming more open to foreign trade and investment. Some critics of the WTO argue that globalization has damaged local cultures around the world. Other critics oppose the WTO because they believe in **protectionism**, which is the use of trade barriers to shield domestic firms from foreign competition. The WTO allows countries to use tariffs in cases of **dumping**, when an imported product is sold for a price below its cost of production. Economists can point out the burden imposed on the economy by tariffs, quotas, and other government interferences with free trade. But whether these policies should be used is a normative decision.

> Visit www.myeconlab.com to complete these exercises online and get instant feedback.

Review Questions

5.1 What events led to the General Agreement on Tariffs and Trade (GATT)? Why did the WTO eventually replace the GATT?

5.2 What is globalization? Why are some people opposed to globalization?

5.3 What is protectionism? Who benefits and who loses from protectionist policies? What are the main arguments people use to justify protectionism?

5.4 What is dumping? Who benefits and who loses from dumping? What problems arise when anti-dumping laws are implemented?

Problems and Applications

5.5 **[Related to the** Making the Connection**: The Unintended Consequences of Banning Goods Made with Child Labor]** The following excerpt is from a newspaper story on President Bill Clinton's proposal to create a group within the World Trade Organization (WTO) responsible for developing labor standards. The story was published just before a 1999 WTO meeting in Seattle that ended in rioting:

> [President Clinton proposed that] core labor standards ... become "part of every trade agreement. And ultimately I would favor a system in which sanctions would come for violating any provision of a trade agreement...." But the new U.S. stand is sure to meet massive resistance from developing countries, which make up more than 100 of the 135 countries in the WTO. They are not interested in adopting tougher U.S. labor standards.

What did Clinton mean by "core labor standards"? Why would developing countries resist adopting these standards?

Source: Terence Hunt, "Salute to Trade's Benefits Turns into 'Kind of Circus,'" *Associated Press*, December 2, 1999.

5.6 Steven Landsburg, an economist at the University of Rochester, wrote the following in an article in the *New York Times*:

> Free trade is not only about the right of American consumers to buy at the cheapest possible price; it's also about the right of foreign producers to earn a living. Steelworkers in West Virginia struggle hard to make ends meet. So do steelworkers in South Korea. To protect one at the expense of the other, solely because of where they happened to be born, is a moral outrage.

How does the U.S. government protect steelworkers in West Virginia at the expense of steelworkers in South Korea? Is Landsburg making a positive or a normative statement? A few days later, Tom Redburn published an article disagreeing with Landsburg:

> It is not some evil character flaw to care more about the welfare of people nearby than about that of those far away—it's human nature. And it is morally—and economically—defensible.... A society that ignores the consequences of economic disruption on those among its citizens who come out at the short end of the stick is not only heartless, it also undermines its own cohesion and adaptability.

Which of the two arguments do you find most convincing?

Source: Steven E. Landsburg, "Who Cares if the Playing Field Is Level?" *New York Times*, June 13, 2001; and Tom Redburn, "Economic View: Of Politics, Free Markets, and Tending to Society," *New York Times*, June 17, 2001.

5.7 Suppose you are explaining the benefits of free trade and someone states, "I don't understand all the principles of comparative advantage and gains from trade. I just know that if I buy something produced in America, I create a job for an American, and if I buy something produced in Brazil, I create a job for a Brazilian." Do you agree with this statement? When the United States imports products for which it does not have a comparative advantage, does that mean that there are fewer jobs in the United States? In the example with Japan and the United States producing and trading cellphones and tablets, when the United States imports cellphones from Japan, does the number of jobs in the United States decline?

5.8 Every year, the Gallup poll asks a sample of people in the United States whether they believe foreign trade provides "an opportunity for economic growth through increased U.S. exports," or whether they believe foreign trade represents "a threat to the economy from foreign imports." The table shows the responses for two years:

	View of Foreign Trade		
Year	Favorable to Foreign Trade	Unfavorable	State of the U.S. Economy
2008	41%	52%	Deep economic recession
2013	57%	35%	Economic expansion

a. Do you believe that foreign trade helps the economy or hurts it? (Be sure to define what you mean by "helps" or "hurts.")

b. Why might the general public's opinion of foreign trade be substantially different during an economic recession as opposed to during an economic expansion?

c. The poll also showed that while 55 percent of people aged 18 to 29 had a favorable opinion of foreign trade, only 41 percent of people age 65 and over did. Why might younger people have a more favorable view of foreign trade than older people?

Source: Gallup Poll, February 28, 2013, http://www.gallup.com/poll/160748/americans-shift-positive-view-foreign-trade.aspx.

5.9 An article in the *Economist* magazine notes: "One analysis suggests that just getting rid of tariffs could raise Europe's GDP by around 0.4% and America's by a percentage point."

a. Why would getting rid of tariffs be likely to increase the total production of goods and services in Europe and the United States?

b. Why might someone who accepts this analysis still be opposed to eliminating tariffs?

Source: "The Gift That Goes on Giving," *Economist*, December 22, 2012.

5.10 The following appeared in a magazine article that argued against free trade: "The U.S. is currently in a precarious position. In addition to geopolitical threats, we face a severe economic shock. We have already lost trillions of dollars and millions of jobs to foreigners." If a country engages in free trade, is the total number of jobs in the country likely to decline? Briefly explain.

Source: Vladimir Masch, "A Radical Plan to Manage Globalization," *BusinessWeek*, February 14, 2007.

Glossary

Absolute advantage The ability of an individual, a firm, or a country to produce more of a good or service than competitors, using the same amount of resources.

Autarky A situation in which a country does not trade with other countries.

Comparative advantage The ability of an individual, a firm, or a country to produce a good or service at a lower opportunity cost than competitors.

Dumping Selling a product for a price below its cost of production.

Exports Goods and services produced domestically but sold in other countries.

External economies Reductions in a firm's costs that result from an increase in the size of an industry.

Free trade Trade between countries that is without government restrictions.

Globalization The process of countries becoming more open to foreign trade and investment.

Imports Goods and services bought domestically but produced in other countries.

Opportunity cost The highest-valued alternative that must be given up to engage in an activity.

Protectionism The use of trade barriers to shield domestic firms from foreign competition.

Quota A numerical limit a government imposes on the quantity of a good that can be imported into the country.

Tariff A tax imposed by a government on imports.

Terms of trade The ratio at which a country can trade its exports for imports from other countries.

Voluntary export restraint (VER) An agreement negotiated between two countries that places a numerical limit on the quantity of a good that can be imported by one country from the other country.

World Trade Organization (WTO) An international organization that oversees international trade agreements.

Credits

Credits are listed in the order of appearance.

Photo

Rainier Ehrhardt /AP Images; David Ball/Alamy; Joerg Boethling/Alamy; Daniel Acker/Bloomberg/Getty Images

Technology, Production, and Costs

Technology, Production, and Costs

Fracking, Marginal Costs, and Energy Prices

Technological change helps firms create new products and lower the costs of making existing products. As a firm's costs change, how does the firm adjust the price it charges consumers? In recent years, important technological changes have affected the oil industry. For example, oil companies had avoided drilling for oil in shale rock formations such as the Bakken field in North Dakota and Montana because of the high cost. Recent changes in techniques and equipment have lowered the cost of drilling, making producing oil from shale rock formations profitable.

In 2012, the United States experienced the largest increase in oil production in its history. Similar increases occurred in 2013 and were expected for many years to follow. Production of natural gas has also been rapidly increasing. The U.S. Energy Information Administration predicts that by 2025, the United States will be a net exporter of oil for the first time since the 1960s. The increases in oil and gas production are due in large part to a new technology, hydraulic fracturing ("fracking"). Fracking involves injecting a mixture of water, sand, and chemicals into rock formations at high pressure to release oil and natural gas. Fracking remains controversial with some environmentalists who argue that it has the potential to pollute ground water supplies if carried out improperly. But will new production from U.S. shale oil fields reduce the price of oil in the world oil market?

As we will see, the price of a good sold in a competitive market is determined by the marginal cost of producing the good. Marginal cost is the additional cost of producing one more unit of a good or service. In the world oil market, oil is supplied up to the point where the marginal cost of the last barrel just equals the price buyers are willing to pay for that last barrel. Oil produced in North Dakota, Montana, Saudi Arabia, and other relatively low-cost areas is not sufficient to meet all of world demand. In this sense, the last barrel of oil sold is produced in the North Sea, the Arctic, and other areas where production costs are much higher. As Pierre Sigonney, an oil economist for the French oil company Total SA put it: "Costs are still at a very high level because of the complexity of marginal fields...."

In this chapter, we will analyze the basic cost concepts involved in production and see how they affect the operations of firms.

Sources: James Herron, "Oil Price Likely to Stay Buoyed by Marginal Costs," *Wall Street Journal*, May 22, 2012; Richard Mably, "Shale Oil Can't Stop Crude Topping $150 by 2020-Bernstein," *Reuters*, September 11, 2012; and James Herron, "Energy Journal: Big Oil, Big Data," *Wall Street Journal*, June 13, 2013.

Economics in Your Life

Using Cost Concepts in Your Own Business

Suppose that you have the opportunity to open a store that sells recliners. You learn that you can purchase recliners from the manufacturer for $300 each. Bob's Big Chairs is an existing store that is the same size your new store will be. Bob's sells the same recliners you plan to sell and also buys them from the manufacturer for $300 each. Your plan is to sell the recliners for a price of $500. After studying how Bob's is operated, you find that Bob's is selling more recliners per month than you expect to be able to sell and that it is selling them for $450. You wonder how Bob's makes a profit at the lower price. Are there any reasons to expect that because Bob's sells more recliners per month, its costs will be lower than your store's costs? As you read this chapter, see if you can answer this question. You can check your answer against the one we provide at the end of this chapter.

I n this chapter, we look Supply curves are upward sloping because marginal cost increases as firms increase the quantity of a good that they supply. In this chapter, we look more closely at why this is true. In the appendix to this chapter, we extend the analysis by using isoquants and isocost lines to understand the relationship between production and costs.

Technology: An Economic Definition

1 LEARNING OBJECTIVE

Define technology and give examples of technological change.

Technology The processes a firm uses to turn inputs into outputs of goods and services.

Technological change A change in the ability of a firm to produce a given level of output with a given quantity of inputs.

The basic activity of a firm is to use *inputs*, such as workers, machines, and natural resources, to produce *outputs* of goods and services. A pizza parlor, for example, uses inputs such as pizza dough, pizza sauce, cooks, and ovens to produce pizza. A firm's **technology** is the processes it uses to turn inputs into outputs of goods and services. Notice that this economic definition of technology is broader than the everyday definition. When we use the word *technology* in everyday language, we usually refer only to the development of new products. In the economic sense, a firm's technology depends on many factors, such as the skills of its managers, the training of its workers, and the speed and efficiency of its machinery and equipment. The technology of pizza production, for example, includes not only the capacity of the pizza ovens and how quickly they bake the pizza but also how quickly the cooks can prepare the pizza for baking, how well the firm's manager motivates the workers, and how well the manager has arranged the facilities to allow the cooks to quickly prepare the pizzas and get them in the ovens.

Whenever a firm experiences positive **technological change**, it is able to produce more output using the same inputs or the same output using fewer inputs. Positive technological change can come from many sources. A firm's managers may rearrange the factory floor or the layout of a retail store in order to increase production and sales. The firm's workers may go through a training program. The firm may install faster or more reliable machinery or equipment. It is also possible for a firm to experience negative technological change. If a firm, for example, hires less-skilled workers or if a hurricane damages its facilities, the quantity of output it can produce from a given quantity of inputs may decline.

Making the Connection	**Improving Inventory Control at Wal-Mart**

Inventories are goods that have been produced but not yet sold. For a retailer such as Wal-Mart, inventories at any point in time include the goods on the store shelves as well as goods in warehouses. Inventories are an input into Wal-Mart's output of goods sold to consumers. Having money tied up in holding inventories is costly, so firms have an incentive to hold as few inventories as possible and to *turn over* their inventories as rapidly as possible by ensuring that goods do not remain on the shelves long. Holding too few inventories, however, results in *stockouts*—that is, sales being lost because the goods consumers want to buy are not on the shelves.

Improvements in inventory control meet the economic definition of positive technological change because they allow firms to produce the same output with fewer inputs. In recent years, many firms have adopted *just-in-time* inventory systems in which firms accept shipments from suppliers as close as possible to the time the goods will be needed. The just-in-time system was pioneered by Toyota, which used it to reduce the inventories of parts in its automobile assembly plants. Wal-Mart has been a pioneer in using similar inventory control systems in its stores.

Wal-Mart actively manages its *supply chain*, which stretches from the manufacturers of the goods it sells to its retail stores. Entrepreneur Sam Walton, the company founder, built a series of distribution centers spread across the country to supply goods to the retail stores. As goods are sold in the stores, the *point-of-sale* information is sent electronically to the firm's distribution centers to help managers determine what products will be shipped to each store. Depending on a store's location relative to a distribution center, managers can use Wal-Mart's trucks to ship goods overnight. This distribution system allows Wal-Mart to minimize its inventory holdings without running the risk of many stockouts occurring. Because Wal-Mart sells 15 percent to 25 percent of all the toothpaste, disposable diapers, dog food, and many other products sold in the United States, it has been able to involve many manufacturers closely in its supply chain. For example, a company such as Procter & Gamble, which is one of the world's largest manufacturers of toothpaste, laundry detergent, toilet paper, and other products, receives Wal-Mart's point-of-sale and inventory information electronically. Procter & Gamble uses that information to help determine its production schedules and the quantities it should ship to Wal-Mart's distribution centers.

Technological change has been a key to Wal-Mart's becoming one of the largest firms in the world, with 2.2 million employees and revenue of nearly $470 billion in 2013, but to maintain its position Wal-Mart needs to improve its performance in online retailing. Amazon has taken a substantial lead over Wal-Mart in online retailing in part because of Amazon's network of warehouses, some of which use robots to retrieve goods from shelves and box them for shipment. Wal-Mart is attempting to catch up by shipping some goods to online buyers from its retail stores rather than from dedicated warehouses. Because two-thirds of the U.S. population lives within five miles of a Wal-Mart store, the company believes that it can reduce shipping costs by filling online orders from store inventories.

It remains to be seen whether Wal-Mart can reproduce its great success in brick-and-mortar retailing as it tries to catch up with Amazon in online retailing.

Source: Shelly Banjo, "Wal-Mart's E-Stumble with Amazon," *Wall Street Journal*, June 19, 2013.

Your Turn: Test your understanding by doing related problem 1.5 at the end of this chapter.

Better inventory controls have helped Wal-Mart and other firms to reduce their costs.

The Short Run and the Long Run in Economics

2 LEARNING OBJECTIVE

Distinguish between the economic short run and the economic long run.

When firms analyze the relationship between their level of production and their costs, they separate the time period involved into the short run and the long run. In the **short run**, at least one of the firm's inputs is fixed. In particular, in the short run, the firm's technology and the size of its physical plant—its factory, store, or office—are both fixed, while the number of workers the firm hires is variable. In the **long run**, the firm is able to vary all its inputs and can adopt new technology and increase or decrease the size of its physical plant. Of course, the actual length of calendar time in the short run will be different from firm to firm. A pizza parlor may be able to increase its physical plant by adding another pizza oven and some tables and chairs in just a few weeks. General Motors, in contrast, may take more than a year to increase the capacity of one of its automobile assembly plants by installing new equipment.

The Difference between Fixed Costs and Variable Costs

Total cost is the cost of all the inputs a firm uses in production. We have just seen that in the short run, some inputs are fixed and others are variable. The costs of the fixed inputs are called *fixed costs*, and the costs of the variable inputs are called *variable costs*. We can also think of **variable costs** as the costs that change as output changes. Similarly, **fixed costs** are costs that remain constant as output changes. A typical firm's variable costs include its labor costs, raw material costs, and costs of electricity and other utilities. Typical fixed costs include lease payments for factory or retail space, payments for

Short run The period of time during which at least one of a firm's inputs is fixed.

Long run The period of time in which a firm can vary all its inputs, adopt new technology, and increase or decrease the size of its physical plant.

Total cost The cost of all the inputs a firm uses in production.

Variable costs Costs that change as output changes.

Fixed costs Costs that remain constant as output changes.

fire insurance, and payments for online and television advertising. All of a firm's costs are either fixed or variable, so we can state the following:

$$Total\ cost = Fixed\ cost + Variable\ cost$$

or, using symbols:

$$TC = FC + VC.$$

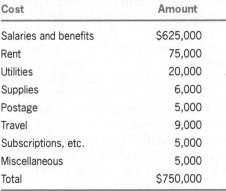

The wages of this worker are a variable cost to the publisher who employs him.

Making the Connection

Fixed Costs in the Publishing Industry

An editor at Cambridge University Press gives the following estimates of the annual fixed cost for a medium-size academic book publisher:

Cost	Amount
Salaries and benefits	$625,000
Rent	75,000
Utilities	20,000
Supplies	6,000
Postage	5,000
Travel	9,000
Subscriptions, etc.	5,000
Miscellaneous	5,000
Total	$750,000

Academic book publishers hire editors, designers, and production and marketing managers who help prepare books for publication. Because these employees work on several books simultaneously, the number of people the company hires does not go up and down with the quantity of books the company publishes during any particular year. Publishing companies therefore consider the salaries and benefits of people in these job categories to be fixed costs.

In contrast, for a company that *prints* books, the quantity of workers varies with the quantity of books printed. The wages and benefits of the workers operating the printing presses, for example, would be a variable cost.

The other costs listed in the table are typical of fixed costs at many firms.

Source: *Handbook for Academic Authors*, 5th edition by Beth Lucy. Copyright © 2010 by Cambridge University Press. Reprinted by permission.

Your Turn: Test your understanding by doing related problems 2.6, 2.7, and 2.8 at the end of this chapter.

Implicit Costs Versus Explicit Costs

Opportunity cost The highest-valued alternative that must be given up to engage in an activity.

Explicit cost A cost that involves spending money.

Implicit cost A nonmonetary opportunity cost.

Economists always measure cost as **opportunity cost**, which is the highest-valued alternative that must be given up to engage in an activity. Costs are either *explicit* or *implicit*. When a firm spends money, it incurs an **explicit cost**. When a firm experiences a nonmonetary opportunity cost, it incurs an **implicit cost**.

For example, suppose that Jill Johnson owns a pizza restaurant. In operating her restaurant, Jill has explicit costs, such as the wages she pays her workers and the payments she makes for rent and electricity. But some of Jill's most important costs are implicit. Before opening her own restaurant, Jill earned a salary of $30,000 per year managing a restaurant for someone else. To start her restaurant, Jill quit her job, withdrew $50,000 from her bank account—where it earned her interest of $3,000 per year—and used the funds to equip her restaurant with tables, chairs, a cash register, and other equipment. To open

Pizza dough, tomato sauce, and other ingredients	$20,000
Wages	48,000
Interest payments on loan to buy pizza ovens	10,000
Electricity	6,000
Lease payment for store	24,000
Forgone salary	30,000
Forgone interest	3,000
Economic depreciation	10,000
Total	$151,000

Table 1

Jill Johnson's Costs per Year

her own business, Jill had to give up the $30,000 salary and the $3,000 in interest. This $33,000 is an implicit cost because it does not represent payments that Jill has to make. Nevertheless, giving up this $33,000 per year is a real cost to Jill. In addition, during the course of the year, the $50,000 worth of tables, chairs, and other physical capital in Jill's store will lose some of its value due partly to wear and tear and partly to better furniture, cash registers, and so forth, becoming available. *Economic depreciation* is the difference between what Jill paid for her capital at the beginning of the year and what she would receive if she sold the capital at the end of the year. If Jill could sell the capital for $40,000 at the end of the year, the $10,000 in economic depreciation represents another implicit cost. (Note that the whole $50,000 she spent on the capital is not a cost because she still has the equipment at the end of the year, although it is now worth only $40,000.)

Table 1 lists Jill's costs. The entries in red are explicit costs, and the entries in blue are implicit costs. The rules of accounting generally require that only explicit costs be used for purposes of keeping the company's financial records and for paying taxes. Therefore, explicit costs are sometimes called *accounting costs*. *Economic costs* include both accounting costs and implicit costs.

The Production Function

Let's look at the relationship in the short run between Jill Johnson's level of production and her costs. We can simplify the situation in Table 1 by assuming that Jill uses only labor—workers—and one type of capital—pizza ovens—to produce a single good: pizzas. Many firms use more than two inputs and produce more than one good, but it is easier to understand the relationship between output and cost by focusing on the case of a firm using only two inputs and producing only one good. In the short run, Jill doesn't have time to build a larger restaurant, install additional pizza ovens, or redesign the layout of her restaurant. So, in the short run, she can increase or decrease the quantity of pizzas she produces only by increasing or decreasing the number of workers she employs.

The first three columns of Table 2 show the relationship between the quantity of workers and ovens Jill uses per week and the quantity of pizzas she can produce. The

Table 2 Short-Run Production and Cost at Jill Johnson's Restaurant

Quantity of Workers	Quantity of Pizza Ovens	Quantity of Pizzas per Week	Cost of Pizza Ovens (Fixed Cost)	Cost of Workers (Variable Cost)	Total Cost of Pizzas per Week	Cost per Pizza (Average Total Cost)
0	2	0	$800	$0	$800	—
1	2	200	800	650	1,450	$7.25
2	2	450	800	1,300	2,100	4.67
3	2	550	800	1,950	2,750	5.00
4	2	600	800	2,600	3,400	5.67
5	2	625	800	3,250	4,050	6.48
6	2	640	800	3,900	4,700	7.34

Production function The relationship between the inputs employed by a firm and the maximum output it can produce with those inputs.

relationship between the inputs employed by a firm and the maximum output it can produce with those inputs is called the firm's **production function**. Because a firm's technology is the processes it uses to turn inputs into output, the production function represents the firm's technology. The first three columns of Table 2 show Jill's *short-run* production function because we are assuming that the time period is too short for Jill to increase or decrease the quantity of ovens she is using.

A First Look at the Relationship between Production and Cost

Table 2 shows Jill Johnson's costs. We can determine the total cost of producing a given quantity of pizzas if we know how many workers and ovens are required to produce that quantity of pizzas and how much Jill has to pay for those workers and ovens. Suppose Jill has taken out a bank loan to buy two pizza ovens. The cost of the loan is $800 per week. Therefore, her fixed costs are $800 per week. If Jill pays $650 per week to each worker, her variable costs depend on how many workers she hires. In the short run, Jill can increase the quantity of pizzas she produces only by hiring more workers. Table 2 shows that if she hires 1 worker, she produces 200 pizzas during the week; if she hires 2 workers, she produces 450 pizzas; and so on. For a particular week, Jill's total cost of producing pizzas is equal to the $800 she pays on the loan for the ovens plus the amount she pays to hire workers. If Jill decides to hire 4 workers and produce 600 pizzas, her total cost is $3,400: $800 to lease the ovens and $2,600 to hire the workers. Her cost per pizza is equal to her total cost of producing pizzas divided by the quantity of pizzas produced. If she produces 600 pizzas at a total cost of $3,400, her cost per pizza, or *average total cost*, is $3,400/600 = $5.67. A firm's **average total cost** is always equal to its total cost divided by the quantity of output produced.

Average total cost Total cost divided by the quantity of output produced.

Panel (a) of Figure 1 uses the numbers in the next-to-last column of Table 2 to graph Jill's total cost. Panel (b) uses the numbers in the last column to graph her average

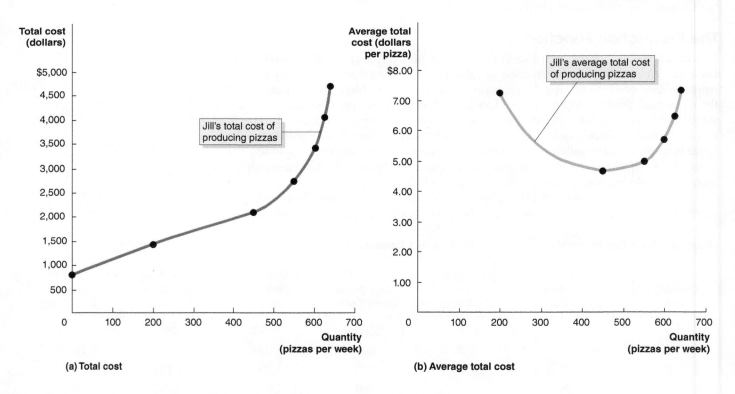

(a) Total cost

(b) Average total cost

Figure 1 Graphing Total Cost and Average Total Cost at Jill Johnson's Restaurant

We can use the information from Table 2 to graph the relationship between the quantity of pizzas Jill produces and her total cost and average total cost. Panel (a) shows that total cost increases as the level of production increases.

Panel (b) shows that her average total cost is roughly U shaped: As production increases from low levels, average total cost falls, before rising at higher levels of production.

total cost. Notice in panel (b) that Jill's average cost curve has a roughly U shape. As production increases from low levels, average total cost falls. Average total cost then becomes fairly flat, before rising at higher levels of production. To understand why average total cost curve has this U shape, we first need to look more closely at the technology of producing pizzas, as shown by the production function for Jill's restaurant. Then we need to look at how this technology determines the relationship between production and cost.

The Marginal Product of Labor and the Average Product of Labor

3 LEARNING OBJECTIVE

Understand the relationship between the marginal product of labor and the average product of labor.

To better understand the choices Jill faces, given the technology available to her, think first about what happens if she hires only one worker. That one worker will have to perform several different activities, including taking orders from customers, baking the pizzas, bringing the pizzas to the customers' tables, and ringing up sales on the cash register. If Jill hires two workers, some of these activities can be divided up: One worker could take the orders and ring up the sales, and one worker could bake the pizzas. With such a division of tasks, Jill will find that hiring two workers actually allows her to produce more than twice as many pizzas as she could produce with just one worker.

The additional output a firm produces as a result of hiring one more worker is called the **marginal product of labor**. We can calculate the marginal product of labor by determining how much total output increases as each additional worker is hired, which we do for Jill's restaurant in Table 3.

Marginal product of labor The additional output a firm produces as a result of hiring one more worker.

When Jill hires only 1 worker, she increases output from 0 pizzas to 200 pizzas per week. So, the marginal product of labor for the first worker is 200 pizzas. When she hires 2 workers, she produces 450 pizzas per week. Hiring the second worker increases her output by 250 pizzas per week. For the second worker, the marginal product of labor rises to 250 pizzas. This increase in marginal product results from the *division of labor* and from *specialization*. By dividing the tasks to be performed—the division of labor—Jill reduces the time workers lose moving from one activity to the next. She also allows them to become more specialized at their tasks. For example, a worker who concentrates on baking pizzas will become skilled at doing so quickly and efficiently.

The Law of Diminishing Returns

In the short run, the quantity of pizza ovens Jill leases is fixed, so as she hires more workers, the marginal product of labor eventually begins to decline. At some point, Jill uses up all the gains from the division of labor and from specialization and starts to experience the effects of the **law of diminishing returns**. This law states that adding more of a variable input, such as labor, to the same amount of a fixed input, such as capital, will eventually cause the marginal product of the variable input to decline. For Jill, the marginal product of labor begins to decline when she hires the third worker. Hiring three workers raises the quantity of pizzas she produces from 450 per week to 550. But the increase in the quantity of pizzas—100—is less than the increase when she hired the second worker—250—so the marginal product of labor has declined.

Law of diminishing returns The principle that, at some point, adding more of a variable input, such as labor, to the same amount of a fixed input, such as capital, will cause the marginal product of the variable input to decline.

Quantity of Workers	Quantity of Pizza Ovens	Quantity of Pizzas	Marginal Product of Labor
0	2	0	—
1	2	200	200
2	2	450	250
3	2	550	100
4	2	600	50
5	2	625	25
6	2	640	15

Table 3

The Marginal Product of Labor at Jill Johnson's Restaurant

If Jill kept adding more and more workers to the same quantity of pizza ovens, workers would eventually begin to get in each other's way, and the marginal product of labor would actually become negative. When the marginal product is negative, the level of total output declines. No firm would actually hire so many workers as to experience a negative marginal product of labor and falling total output.

Graphing Production

Panel (a) in Figure 2 shows the relationship between the quantity of workers Jill hires and her total output of pizzas, using the numbers from Table 3. Panel (b) shows the marginal product of labor. In panel (a), output increases as more workers are hired, but the increase in output does not occur at a constant rate. Because of specialization and the division of labor, output at first increases at an increasing rate, with each additional worker hired causing production to increase by a *larger* amount than did the hiring of the previous worker. But after the second worker has been hired, hiring more workers while

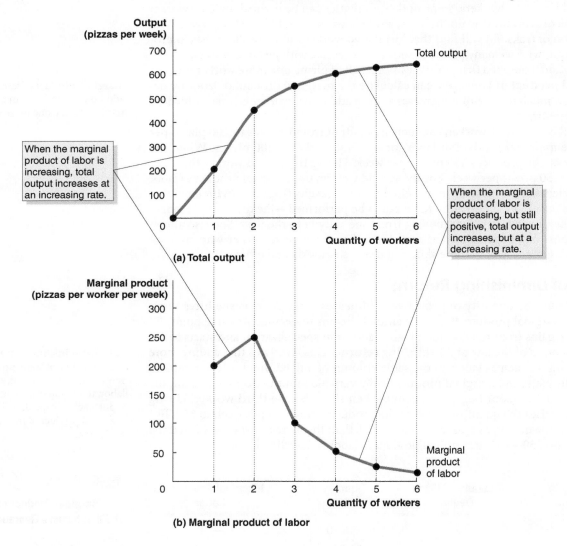

(a) Total output

When the marginal product of labor is increasing, total output increases at an increasing rate.

When the marginal product of labor is decreasing, but still positive, total output increases, but at a decreasing rate.

(b) Marginal product of labor

Figure 2 **Total Output and the Marginal Product of Labor**

In panel (a), output increases as more workers are hired, but the increase in output does not occur at a constant rate. Because of specialization and the division of labor, output at first increases at an increasing rate, with each additional worker hired causing production to increase by a *greater* amount than did the hiring of the previous worker. When the point of diminishing returns is reached, production increases at a decreasing rate. Each additional worker Jill hires after the second worker causes production to increase by a *smaller* amount than did the hiring of the previous worker. In panel (b), the *marginal product of labor* is the additional output produced as a result of hiring one more worker. The marginal product of labor rises initially because of the effects of specialization and division of labor, and then falls because of the effects of diminishing returns.

keeping the quantity of ovens constant results in diminishing returns. When the point of diminishing returns is reached, production increases at a decreasing rate. Each additional worker Jill hires after the second worker causes production to increase by a *smaller* amount than did the hiring of the previous worker. In panel (b), the marginal product of labor curve rises initially because of the effects of specialization and the division of labor, and then falls because of the effects of diminishing returns.

Making the Connection | Adam Smith's Famous Account of the Division of Labor in a Pin Factory

The Wealth of Nations, written in Scotland by Adam Smith in 1776, is the first book to have discussed some of the key ideas of economics. Smith considered the concept of the division of labor important enough to discuss in the first chapter of the book. He illustrated the concept using an example of a pin factory. The following is an excerpt from his account of how pin making was divided into a series of tasks:

> One man draws out the wire, another straightens it, a third cuts it, a fourth points it, a fifth grinds it at the top for receiving the head; to make the head requires two or three distinct operations; to put it on is a … [distinct operation], to whiten the pins is another; it is even a trade by itself to put them into the paper; and the important business of making a pin is, in this manner, divided into eighteen distinct operations.

Because the labor of pin making was divided up in this way, an average worker was able to produce about 4,800 pins per day. Smith estimated that a single worker using the pin-making machinery by himself would make only about 20 pins per day. This lesson from more than 235 years ago, showing the tremendous gains from the division of labor and specialization, remains relevant to most business situations today.

The gains from division of labor and specialization are as important to firms today as they were in the eighteenth century, when Adam Smith first discussed them.

Source: Adam Smith, *An Inquiry into the Nature and Causes of the Wealth of Nations*, Vol. I, Oxford, UK: Oxford University Press, 1976. original edition, 1776, pp. 14–15.

Your Turn: Test your understanding by doing related problem 3.7 on at the end of this chapter.

The Relationship between Marginal Product and Average Product

The marginal product of labor tells us how much total output changes as the quantity of workers hired changes. We can also calculate the average quantity of pizzas workers produce. The **average product of labor** is the total output produced by a firm divided by the quantity of workers. For example, using the numbers in Table 3, if Jill hires 4 workers to produce 600 pizzas, the average product of labor is 600/4 = 150.

We can state the relationship between the marginal and average products of labor this way: *The average product of labor is the average of the marginal products of labor.* For example, the numbers from Table 3 show that the marginal product of the first worker Jill hires is 200, the marginal product of the second worker is 250, and the marginal product of the third worker is 100. Therefore, the average product of labor for three workers is 183.3:

Average product of labor The total output produced by a firm divided by the quantity of workers.

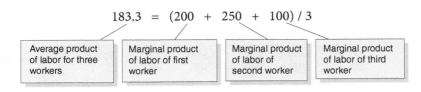

183.3 = (200 + 250 + 100) / 3

| Average product of labor for three workers | Marginal product of labor of first worker | Marginal product of labor of second worker | Marginal product of labor of third worker |

By taking the average of the marginal products of the first three workers, we have the average product of the three workers.

Whenever the marginal product of labor is greater than the average product of labor, the average product of labor must be increasing. This statement is true for the same reason that a person 6 feet, 2 inches tall entering a room where the average height is 5 feet, 9 inches raises the average height of people in the room. Whenever the marginal product of labor is less than the average product of labor, the average product of labor must be decreasing. The marginal product of labor equals the average product of labor at the quantity of workers for which the average product of labor is at its maximum.

An Example of Marginal and Average Values: College Grades

The relationship between the marginal product of labor and the average product of labor is the same as the relationship between the marginal and average values of any variable. To see this point more clearly, think about the familiar relationship between a student's grade point average (GPA) in one semester and his overall, or cumulative, GPA. The table in Figure 3 shows Paul's college grades for each semester, beginning

Figure 3

Marginal and Average GPAs

The relationship between marginal and average values for a variable can be illustrated using GPAs. We can calculate the GPA Paul earns in a particular semester (his "marginal GPA"), and we can calculate his cumulative GPA for all the semesters he has completed so far (his "average GPA"). Paul's GPA is only 1.50 in the fall semester of his first year. In each following semester through the fall of his junior year, his GPA for the semester increases—raising his cumulative GPA. In Paul's junior year, even though his semester GPA declines from fall to spring, his cumulative GPA rises. Only in the fall of his senior year, when his semester GPA drops below his cumulative GPA, does his cumulative GPA decline.

	Semester GPA (marginal GPA)	Cumulative GPA (average GPA)
Freshman year		
Fall	1.50	1.50
Spring	2.00	1.75
Sophomore year		
Fall	2.20	1.90
Spring	3.00	2.18
Junior year		
Fall	3.20	2.38
Spring	3.00	2.48
Senior year		
Fall	2.40	2.47
Spring	2.00	2.41

Average GPA continues to rise, although marginal GPA falls.

With the marginal GPA below the average, the average GPA falls.

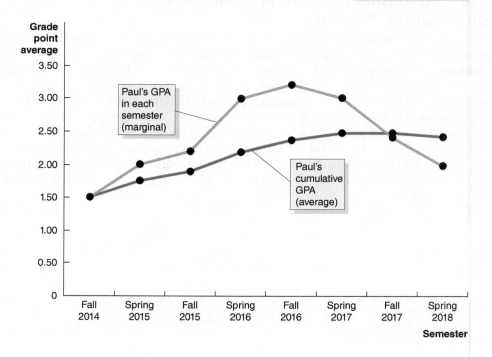

with fall 2014. The graph in Figure 3 plots the grades from the table. Just as each additional worker hired adds to a firm's total production, each additional semester adds to Paul's total grade points. We can calculate what hiring each individual worker adds to total production (marginal product), and we can calculate the average production of the workers hired so far (average product).

Similarly, we can calculate the GPA Paul earns in a particular semester (his "marginal GPA") and we can calculate his cumulative GPA for all the semesters he has completed so far (his "average GPA"). As the table shows, Paul gets off to a weak start in the fall semester of his first year, earning only a 1.50 GPA. In each subsequent semester through the fall of his junior year, his GPA for the semester increases from the previous semester—raising his cumulative GPA. As the graph shows, however, his cumulative GPA does not increase as rapidly as his semester-by-semester GPA because his cumulative GPA is held back by the low GPAs of his first few semesters. Notice that in Paul's junior year, even though his semester GPA declines from fall to spring, his cumulative GPA rises. Only in the fall of his senior year, when his semester GPA drops below his cumulative GPA, does his cumulative GPA decline.

The Relationship between Short-Run Production and Short-Run Cost

4 LEARNING OBJECTIVE

Explain and illustrate the relationship between marginal cost and average total cost.

We have seen that technology determines the values of the marginal product of labor and the average product of labor. In turn, the marginal and average products of labor affect the firm's costs. Keep in mind that the relationships we are discussing are *short-run* relationships: We are assuming that the time period is too short for the firm to change its technology or the size of its physical plant.

The average total cost curve in panel (b) of Figure 1 for Jill Johnson's restaurant has a U shape. As we will soon see, the U shape of the average total cost curve is determined by the shape of the curve that shows the relationship between *marginal cost* and the level of production.

Marginal Cost

One of the key ideas in economics is that optimal decisions are made at the margin. Consumers, firms, and government officials usually make decisions about doing a little more or a little less. As Jill Johnson considers whether to hire additional workers to produce additional pizzas, she needs to consider how much she will add to her total cost by producing the additional pizzas. **Marginal cost** is the change in a firm's total cost from producing one more unit of a good or service. We can calculate marginal cost for a particular increase in output by dividing the change in total cost by the change in output. We can express this idea mathematically (remember that the Greek letter delta, Δ, means, "change in"):

Marginal cost The change in a firm's total cost from producing one more unit of a good or service.

$$MC = \frac{\Delta TC}{\Delta Q}.$$

In the table in Figure 4, we use this equation to calculate Jill's marginal cost of producing pizzas. The other values in the table are from Table 2 and Table 3.

Why Are the Marginal and Average Cost Curves U Shaped?

Notice in the graph in Figure 4 that Jill's marginal cost of producing pizzas declines at first and then increases, giving the marginal cost curve a U shape. The table in Figure 4 also shows the marginal product of labor. This table helps us understand the important relationship between the marginal product of labor and the marginal cost of production: The marginal product of labor is *rising* for the first two workers, but the marginal cost of the pizzas produced by these workers is *falling*. The marginal product of labor is *falling* for the last four workers, but the marginal cost of pizzas produced by

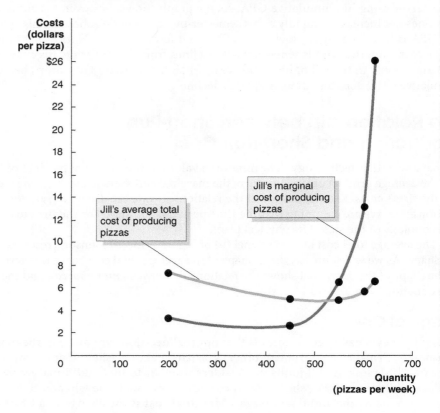

Quantity of Workers	Quantity of Pizzas	Marginal Product of Labor	Total Cost of Pizzas	Marginal Cost of Pizzas	Average Total Cost of Pizzas
0	0	—	$800	—	—
1	200	200	1,450	$3.25	$7.25
2	450	250	2,100	2.60	4.67
3	550	100	2,750	6.50	5.00
4	600	50	3,400	13.00	5.67
5	625	25	4,050	26.00	6.48
6	640	15	4,700	43.33	7.34

Figure 4

Jill Johnson's Marginal Cost and Average Total Cost of Producing Pizzas

We can use the information in the table to calculate Jill's marginal cost and average total cost of producing pizzas. For the first two workers hired, the marginal product of labor is increasing, which causes the marginal cost of production to fall. For the last four workers hired, the marginal product of labor is falling, which causes the marginal cost of production to increase. Therefore, the marginal cost curve falls and then rises—that is, has a U shape—because the marginal product of labor rises and then falls. As long as marginal cost is below average total cost, average total cost will be falling. When marginal cost is above average total cost, average total cost will be rising. The relationship between marginal cost and average total cost explains why the average total cost curve also has a U shape.

these workers is *rising*. We can generalize this point: *When the marginal product of labor is rising, the marginal cost of output is falling. When the marginal product of labor is falling, the marginal cost of output is rising.*

One way to understand the relationship between the marginal product of labor and the marginal cost of output is to notice that the only additional cost to Jill from producing more pizzas is the additional wages she pays to hire more workers. She pays each new worker the same $650 per week. So the marginal cost of the additional pizzas each worker makes depends on that worker's additional output, or marginal product. As long as the additional output from each new worker is rising, the marginal cost of that output is falling. When the additional output from each new worker is falling, the marginal cost of that output is rising. *We can conclude that the marginal cost of output falls and then rises—forming a U shape—because the marginal product of labor rises and then falls.*

The relationship between marginal cost and average total cost follows the usual relationship between marginal and average values. As long as marginal cost is below average total cost, average total cost falls. When marginal cost is above average total cost, average total cost rises. Marginal cost equals average total cost when average total cost is at its lowest point. Therefore, the average total cost curve has a U shape because the marginal cost curve has a U shape.

Solved Problem 4

Calculating Marginal Cost and Average Cost

Santiago Delgado owns a copier store. He leases two copy machines for which he pays $12.50 each per day. He cannot increase the number of machines he leases without giving the office machine company six weeks' notice. He can hire as many workers as he wants, at a cost of $50 per day per worker. These are the only two inputs he uses to produce copies.

a. Fill in the remaining columns in the table by using the definitions of costs.

b. Draw the average total cost curve and marginal cost curve for Santiago's store. Do these curves have the expected shape? Briefly explain.

Quantity of Workers	Quantity of Copies per Day	Fixed Cost	Variable Cost	Total Cost	Average Total Cost	Marginal Cost
0	0					
1	625					
2	1,325					
3	2,200					
4	2,600					
5	2,900					
6	3,100					

Solving the Problem

Step 1: **Review the chapter material.** This problem requires you to understand definitions of costs, so you may want to review the section "The Difference between Fixed Costs and Variable Costs," and the section "Why Are the Marginal and Average Cost Curves U Shaped?"

Step 2: **Answer part (a) by using the definitions of costs.** Santiago's fixed cost is the amount he pays to lease the copy machines. He uses two copy machines and pays $12.50 each to lease them, so his fixed cost is $25. Santiago's variable cost is the amount he pays to hire workers. He pays $50 per worker per day. His total cost is the sum of his fixed cost and his variable cost. His average total cost is his total cost divided by the quantity of copies he produces that day. His marginal cost is the change in total cost divided by the change in output. So, for example, his marginal cost of producing 1,325 copies per day, rather than 625 copies, is:

$$MC = (\$125 - \$75)/(1{,}325 - 625) = \$0.07.$$

Quantity of Workers	Quantity of Copies per Day	Fixed Cost	Variable Cost	Total Cost	Average Total Cost	Marginal Cost
0	0	$25	$0	$25	—	—
1	625	25	50	75	$0.12	$0.08
2	1,325	25	100	125	0.09	0.07
3	2,200	25	150	175	0.08	0.06
4	2,600	25	200	225	0.09	0.13
5	2,900	25	250	275	0.09	0.17
6	3,100	25	300	325	0.10	0.25

Step 3: **Answer part (b) by drawing the average total cost and marginal cost curves for Santiago's store and by explaining whether they have the usual shape.** You can use the numbers from the table to draw your graph:

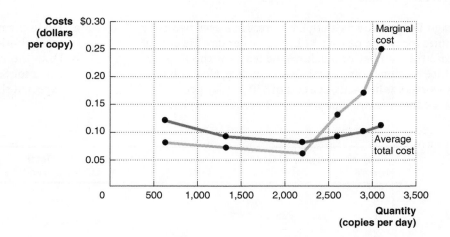

We expect average total cost and marginal cost curves to have a U shape, which Santiago's cost curves do. Both cost curves fall and then rise in the same way as the cost curves in Figure 4.

Your Turn: For more practice, do related problem 4.7 at the end of this chapter.

5 LEARNING OBJECTIVE

Graph average total cost, average variable cost, average fixed cost, and marginal cost.

Average fixed cost Fixed cost divided by the quantity of output produced.

Average variable cost Variable cost divided by the quantity of output produced.

Graphing Cost Curves

We have seen that we calculate average total cost by dividing total cost by the quantity of output produced. Similarly, we can calculate **average fixed cost** by dividing fixed cost by the quantity of output produced. And we can calculate **average variable cost** by dividing variable cost by the quantity of output produced. Or, mathematically, with Q being the level of output, we have:

$$\text{Average total cost} = ATC = \frac{TC}{Q}$$

$$\text{Average fixed cost} = AFC = \frac{FC}{Q}$$

$$\text{Average variable cost} = AVC = \frac{VC}{Q}$$

Finally, notice that average total cost is the sum of average fixed cost plus average variable cost:

$$ATC = AFC + AVC.$$

The only fixed cost Jill incurs in operating her restaurant is the $800 per week she pays on the bank loan for her pizza ovens. Her variable costs are the wages she pays her workers. The table and graph in Figure 5 show Jill's costs.

Before going further, be sure you understand the following three key facts about Figure 5:

1. The marginal cost (MC), average total cost (ATC), and average variable cost (AVC) curves are all U shaped, and the marginal cost curve intersects both the

Quantity of Workers	Quantity of Ovens	Quantity of Pizzas	Cost of Ovens (fixed cost)	Cost of Workers (variable cost)	Total Cost of Pizzas	ATC	AFC	AVC	MC
0	2	0	$800	$0	$800	—	—	—	—
1	2	200	800	650	1,450	$7.25	$4.00	$3.25	$3.25
2	2	450	800	1,300	2,100	4.67	1.78	2.89	2.60
3	2	550	800	1,950	2,750	5.00	1.45	3.54	6.50
4	2	600	800	2,600	3,400	5.67	1.33	4.33	13.00
5	2	625	800	3,250	4,050	6.48	1.28	5.20	26.00
6	2	640	800	3,900	4,700	7.34	1.25	6.09	43.33

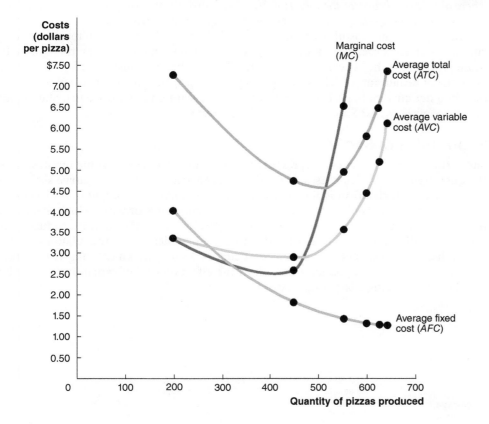

Figure 5

Costs at Jill Johnson's Restaurant

Jill's costs of making pizzas are shown in the table and plotted in the graph. Notice three important facts about the graph: (1) The marginal cost (*MC*), average total cost (*ATC*), and average variable cost (*AVC*) curves are all U shaped, and the marginal cost curve intersects both the average variable cost curve and the average total cost curve at their minimum points. (2) As output increases, average fixed cost (*AFC*) gets smaller and smaller. (3) As output increases, the difference between average total cost and average variable cost decreases. Make sure you can explain why each of these three facts is true. You should spend time becoming familiar with this graph because it is one of the most important graphs in microeconomics.

average variable cost curve and the average total cost curve at their minimum points. When marginal cost is less than either average variable cost or average total cost, it causes them to decrease. When marginal cost is above average variable cost or average total cost, it causes them to increase. Therefore, when marginal cost equals average variable cost or average total cost, they must be at their minimum points.

2. As output increases, average fixed cost gets smaller and smaller. This result occurs because in calculating average fixed cost, we are dividing something that gets larger and larger—output—into something that remains constant—fixed cost. Firms often refer this process of lowering average fixed cost by selling more output as "spreading the overhead" (where "overhead" refers to fixed costs).

3. As output increases, the difference between average total cost and average variable cost decreases. This result occurs because the difference between average total cost and average variable cost is average fixed cost, which gets smaller as output increases.

6 LEARNING OBJECTIVE

Understand how firms use the long-run average cost curve in their planning.

Costs in the Long Run

The distinction between fixed cost and variable cost that we just discussed applies to the short run but *not* to the long run. For example, in the short run, Jill Johnson has fixed costs of $800 per week because she signed a loan agreement with a bank when she bought her pizza ovens. In the long run, the cost of purchasing more pizza ovens becomes variable because Jill can choose whether to expand her business by buying more ovens. The same would be true of any other fixed costs a company like Jill's might have. Once a company has purchased a fire insurance policy, the cost of the policy is fixed. But when the policy expires, the company must decide whether to renew it, and the cost becomes variable. The important point here is this: *In the long run, all costs are variable. There are no fixed costs in the long run.* In other words, in the long run, total cost equals variable cost, and average total cost equals average variable cost.

Managers of successful firms simultaneously consider how they can most profitably run their current store, factory, or office and also whether in the long run they would be more profitable if they became larger or, possibly, smaller. Jill must consider how to run her current restaurant, which has only two pizza ovens, and she must also plan what to do when her current bank loan is paid off and the lease on her store ends. Should she buy more pizza ovens? Should she lease a larger restaurant?

Economies of Scale

Long-run average cost curve A curve that shows the lowest cost at which a firm is able to produce a given quantity of output in the long run, when no inputs are fixed.

Economies of scale The situation when a firm's long-run average costs fall as it increases the quantity of output it produces.

Short-run average cost curves represent the costs a firm faces when some input, such as the quantity of machines it uses, is fixed. The **long-run average cost curve** shows the lowest cost at which a firm is able to produce a given quantity of output in the long run, when no inputs are fixed. A firm may experience **economies of scale**, which means the firm's long-run average costs fall as it increases the quantity of output it produces. We can see the effects of economies of scale in Figure 6, which shows the relationship between short-run and long-run average cost curves. Managers can use long-run average cost curves for planning because they show the effect on cost of expanding output by, for example, building a larger factory or restaurant.

Figure 6

The Relationship between Short-Run Average Cost and Long-Run Average Cost

If a small car company expects to sell only 20,000 cars per year, it will be able to produce cars at the lowest average cost of $52,000 per car if it builds the small factory represented by the *ATC* curve on the left of the figure. A larger factory will be able to produce 200,000 cars per year at a lower cost of $27,000 per car. An automobile factory producing 200,000 cars per year and a factory producing 400,000 cars per year will experience constant returns to scale and have the same average cost. An automobile factory assembling 200,000 cars per year will have reached minimum efficient scale. Very large automobile factories will experience diseconomies of scale, and their average costs will rise as production increases beyond 400,000 cars per year.

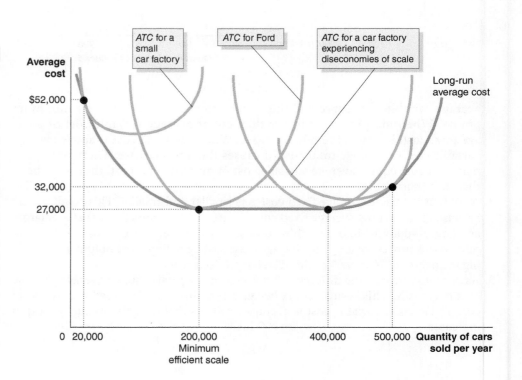

Long-Run Average Cost Curves for Automobile Factories

Figure 6 shows long-run average cost in the automobile industry. If a small company, such as Tesla Motors, expects to sell only 20,000 cars per year, then it will be able to assemble cars at the lowest average cost of $52,000 per car if it builds a small factory, as represented by the *ATC* curve on the left of the figure. A much larger factory, such as those operated by Ford, General Motors, or Toyota, will be able to produce 200,000 cars per year at a lower average cost of $27,000 per car. This decline in average cost from $52,000 to $27,000 represents the economies of scale that exist in manufacturing automobiles. Why would the larger automobile factory have lower average costs? One important reason is that a company like Ford is producing 10 times as many cars per year in one of its factories as Tesla produces in its factory but might need only 6 times as many workers. This saving in labor cost would reduce Ford's average cost of selling cars.

In general, firms may experience economies of scale for several reasons. First, as in the case of automobile production, the firm's technology may make it possible to increase production with a smaller proportional increase in at least one input. Second, both workers and managers can become more specialized, enabling them to become more productive, as output expands. Third, large firms, like Ford, Wal-Mart, or Apple, may be able to purchase inputs at lower costs than smaller competitors. In fact, as Apple and Wal-Mart expanded, their bargaining power with their suppliers increased, and their average costs fell. Finally, as a firm expands, it may be able to borrow money at a lower interest rate, thereby lowering its costs.

Economies of scale do not continue forever. The long-run average cost curve in most industries has a flat segment that often stretches over a substantial range of output. As Figure 6 shows, an automobile factory producing 200,000 cars per year and a factory producing 400,000 cars per year have the same average cost. Over this range of output, firms in the industry experience **constant returns to scale**. As these firms increase their output, they increase their inputs, such as the size of the factory and the quantity of workers, proportionally. The level of output at which all economies of scale are exhausted is known as **minimum efficient scale**. An automobile factory producing 200,000 cars per year has reached minimum efficient scale.

Very large automobile factories experience increasing average costs as managers begin to have difficulty coordinating the operation of the factory. Figure 6 shows that for production above 400,000 cars per year, firms in the industry experience **diseconomies of scale**. For instance, Toyota found that as it expanded production at its Georgetown, Kentucky, plant and its plants in China, its managers had difficulty keeping average cost from rising. According to the president of Toyota's Georgetown plant: "Demand for … high volumes saps your energy. Over a period of time, it eroded our focus … [and] thinned out the expertise and knowledge we painstakingly built up over the years." One analysis of the problems Toyota faced in expanding production concluded: "It is the kind of paradox many highly successful companies face: Getting bigger doesn't always mean getting better."

Constant returns to scale The situation in which a firm's long-run average costs remain unchanged as it increases output.

Minimum efficient scale The level of output at which all economies of scale are exhausted.

Diseconomies of scale The situation in which a firm's long-run average costs rise as the firm increases output.

Solved Problem 6

Using Long-Run Average Cost Curves to Understand Business Strategy

The officials in charge of the port of Rotterdam in the Netherlands decided to expand its capacity from 9.7 million containers processed per year to 18.2 million containers processed per year. An article in the *Wall Street Journal* described the port as attempting to "provide economies of scale to shippers." Shippers using the port expected that the fees charged to process their containers would decline following the expansion.

a. What does it mean to say that expanding the size of the port will "provide economies of scale to shippers"?

b. Use a long-run average cost curve to explain why the expansion of the port might result in lower fees to shippers.

Solving the Problem

Step 1: **Review the chapter material.** This problem is about the long-run average cost curve, so you may want to review the material in the section "Costs in the Long Run."

Step 2: **Answer part (a) by explaining what it means for the port to "provide economies of scale to shippers."** If by expanding, the port of Rotterdam will lower its average cost of processing a shipping container, then the port was operating at less than minimum efficient scale. In that case, the expansion of the port would provide economies of scale to shippers by lowering the average cost of processing a container.

Step 3: **Draw a long-run average cost graph for the port.** The problem provides us with enough information to draw the following graph:

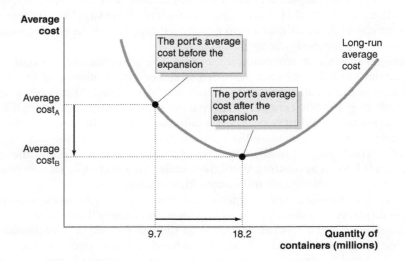

Step 4: **Use your graph to explain why the expansion of the port might result in lower fees to shippers.** Before the expansion, the port was below minimum efficient scale and was processing 9.7 million containers per year, at an average cost of Average cost$_A$. By expanding, the port can move to the minimum efficient scale of 18.2 million containers per year, and average cost falls to Average cost$_B$. (We can't be sure whether the expansion will actually take the port to minimum efficient scale, but it seems likely that the engineers and economists advising the port's managers would suggest an expansion that would raise capacity to that level.) With lower costs, the port may reduce the fees that it charges shippers, which is what shippers were expecting.

Source: John W. Miller, "For Port Expansion, It's Full Speed Ahead," *Wall Street Journal*, October 26, 2010.

Your Turn: For more practice, do related problems 6.7, 6.8, 6.9, and 6.10 at the end of this chapter.

Over time, most firms in an industry will build factories or stores that are at least as large as the minimum efficient scale but not so large that diseconomies of scale occur. For example, in the automobile industry, most factories will produce between 200,000 and 400,000 cars per year. However, firms often do not know the exact shape of their long-run average cost curves. As a result, they may mistakenly build factories or stores that are either too large or too small.

| Making the Connection | **The Colossal River Rouge: Diseconomies of Scale at Ford Motor Company** |

Was Ford's River Rouge plant too big?

When Henry Ford started the Ford Motor Company in 1903, automobile companies produced cars in small workshops, using highly skilled workers. Ford introduced two new ideas to the automobile industry that allowed him to take advantage of economies of scale. First, Ford used identical—or, interchangeable—parts so that unskilled workers could assemble the cars. Second, instead of having groups of workers moving from one stationary automobile to the next, he had the workers remain stationary, while the automobiles moved along an assembly line. Ford built a large factory at Highland Park, outside Detroit, where he used these ideas to produce the famous Model T at an average cost well below what his competitors could match using older production methods in smaller factories.

Ford believed that he could produce automobiles at an even lower average cost by building a still larger plant along the River Rouge in Dearborn, Michigan. Unfortunately, Ford's River Rouge plant was too large and suffered from diseconomies of scale. Ford's managers had great difficulty coordinating the production of automobiles in such a large plant. The following description of the River Rouge plant comes from a biography of Ford by Allan Nevins and Frank Ernest Hill:

> A total of 93 separate structures stood on the [River Rouge] site …. Railroad trackage covered 93 miles, conveyors 27 [miles]. About 75,000 men worked in the great plant. A force of 5000 did nothing but keep it clean, wearing out 5000 mops and 3000 brooms a month, and using 86 tons of soap on the floors, walls, and 330 acres of windows. The Rouge was an industrial city, immense, concentrated, packed with power …. By its very massiveness and complexity, it denied men at the top contact with and understanding of those beneath, and gave those beneath a sense of being lost in inexorable immensity and power.

Beginning in 1927, Ford produced the Model A—its only car model at that time—at the River Rouge plant. Ford failed to achieve economies of scale and actually *lost money* on each of the four Model A body styles.

Ford could not raise the price of the Model A to make it profitable because at a higher price, the car could not compete with similar models produced by competitors such as General Motors and Chrysler. He eventually reduced the cost of making the Model A by constructing smaller factories spread out across the country. These smaller factories produced the Model A at a lower average cost than was possible at the River Rouge plant.

Source: Allan Nevins and Frank Ernest Hill, *Ford: Expansion and Challenge, 1915–1933*, New York: Scribner, 1957, pp. 293, 295.

Your Turn: Test your understanding by doing related problem 6.11 at the end of this chapter.

Don't Let This Happen to You

Don't Confuse Diminishing Returns with Diseconomies of Scale

The concepts of diminishing returns and diseconomies of scale may seem similar, but they are actually unrelated. Diminishing returns applies only to the short run, when at least one of the firm's inputs, such as the quantity of machinery it uses, is fixed. The law of diminishing returns tells us that in the short run, hiring more workers will, at some point, result in less additional output. Diminishing returns explains why marginal cost curves eventually slope upward. Diseconomies of scale apply only in the long run, when the firm is free to vary all its inputs, can adopt new technology, and can vary the amount of machinery it uses and the size of its facility. Diseconomies of scale explain why long-run average cost curves eventually slope upward.

Your Turn: Test your understanding by doing related problem 6.13 at the end of this chapter.

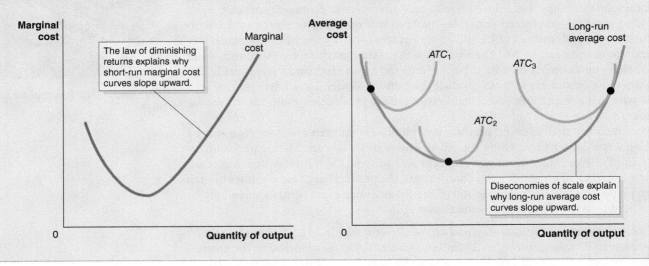

Continued

Economics in Your Life

Using Cost Concepts in Your Own Business

At the beginning of the chapter, we asked you to suppose that you are about to open a store to sell recliners. Both you and a competing store, Bob's Big Chairs, can buy recliners from the manufacturer for $300 each. But because Bob's sells more recliners per month than you expect to be able to sell, his costs per recliner are lower than yours. We asked you to think about why this might be true. In this chapter, we have seen that firms often experience declining average costs as the quantity they sell increases. A key reason Bob's average costs might be lower than yours has to do with fixed costs. Because your store is the same size as Bob's store, you may be paying about the same amount to lease the store space. You may also be paying about the same amounts for utilities, insurance, and advertising. All these are fixed costs because they do not change as the quantity of recliners you sell changes. Because Bob's fixed costs are the same as yours, but he is selling more recliners, his average fixed costs are lower than yours, and, therefore, so are his average total costs. With lower average total costs, he can sell his recliners for a lower price than you do and still make a profit.

Conclusion

In this chapter, we discussed the relationship between a firm's technology, production, and costs. In the discussion, we encountered a number of definitions of costs. It is useful to bring them together in Table 4 for you to review.

We have seen the important relationship between a firm's level of production and its costs. This information is vital to all firms as they attempt to decide the optimal level of production and the optimal prices to charge for their products.

Visit MyEconLab for a news article and analysis related to the concepts in this chapter.

Table 4

A Summary of Definitions of Cost

Term	Definition	Symbols and Equations
Total cost	The cost of all the inputs used by a firm, or fixed cost plus variable cost	TC
Fixed costs	Costs that remain constant as a firm's level of output changes	FC
Variable costs	Costs that change as a firm's level of output changes	VC
Marginal cost	An increase in total cost resulting from producing another unit of output	$MC = \dfrac{\Delta TC}{\Delta Q}$
Average total cost	Total cost divided by the quantity of output produced	$ATC = \dfrac{TC}{Q}$
Average fixed cost	Fixed cost divided by the quantity of output produced	$AFC = \dfrac{FC}{Q}$
Average variable cost	Variable cost divided by the quantity of output produced	$AVC = \dfrac{VC}{Q}$
Implicit cost	A nonmonetary opportunity cost	—
Explicit cost	A cost that involves spending money	—

Chapter Summary and Problems

Key Terms

Average fixed cost	Economies of scale	Long-run average cost curve	Short run
Average product of labor	Explicit cost	Marginal cost	Technological change
Average total cost	Fixed costs	Marginal product of labor	Technology
Average variable cost	Implicit cost	Minimum efficient scale	Total cost
Constant returns to scale	Law of diminishing returns	Opportunity cost	Variable costs
Diseconomies of scale	Long run	Production function	

---

1 Technology: An Economic Definition

LEARNING OBJECTIVE: Define technology and give examples of technological change.

Summary

The basic activity of a firm is to use inputs, such as workers, machines, and natural resources, to produce goods and services. The firm's **technology** is the processes it uses to turn inputs into goods and services. **Technological change** refers to a change in the ability of a firm to produce a given level of output with a given quantity of inputs.

Visit **www.myeconlab.com** to complete these exercises online and get instant feedback.

Review Questions

1.1 What is the difference between technology and technological change?

1.2 Is it possible for technological change to be negative? If so, give an example.

Problems and Applications

1.3 Briefly explain whether you agree with the following observation: "Technological change refers only to the introduction of new products, so it is not relevant to the operations of most firms."

1.4 Which of the following are examples of a firm experiencing positive technological change?
   a. A fall in oil prices leads United Airlines to lower its ticket prices.
   b. A training program makes a firm's workers more productive.
   c. An exercise program makes a firm's workers more healthy and productive.
   d. A firm cuts its workforce and is able to maintain its initial level of output.
   e. A firm rearranges the layout of its factory and finds that by using its initial set of inputs, it can produce exactly as much as before.

1.5 **[Related to the** Making the Connection**: Improving Inventory Control at Wal-Mart]** The 7-Eleven chain of convenience stores in Japan reorganized the timing of truck deliveries of food to their stores, as well as the routes the trucks traveled. This reorganization led to a sharp reduction in the number of trucks the company had to use, while increasing the amount of fresh food on store shelves. Someone discussing 7-Eleven's new system argues: "This is not an example of technological change because it did not require the use of new machinery or equipment." Briefly explain whether you agree with this argument.

---

2 The Short Run and the Long Run in Economics

LEARNING OBJECTIVE: Distinguish between the economic short run and the economic long run.

Summary

In the **short run**, a firm's technology and the size of its factory, store, or office are fixed. In the **long run**, a firm is able to adopt new technology and to increase or decrease the size of its physical plant. **Total cost** is the cost of all the inputs a firm uses in production. **Variable costs** are costs that change as output changes. **Fixed costs** are costs that remain constant as output changes. **Opportunity cost** is the highest-valued alternative that must be given up to engage in an activity. An **explicit cost** is a cost that involves spending money. An **implicit cost** is a nonmonetary opportunity cost. The relationship between the inputs employed by a firm and the maximum output it can produce with those inputs is called the firm's **production function**.

Visit **www.myeconlab.com** to complete these exercises online and get instant feedback.

Review Questions

2.1 What is the difference between the short run and the long run? Is the amount of time that separates the short run from the long run the same for every firm?

2.2 Distinguish between a firm's fixed costs and variable costs and give an example of each.

2.3 What are implicit costs? How are they different from explicit costs?

2.4 What is the production function? What does the short-run production function hold constant?

Problems and Applications

2.5 An article in *Forbes* discussed an estimate that the cost of materials in Apple's iPhone 5 with 64 gigabytes of memory was $230. Apple was selling the iPhone 5 for $849 (most phone carriers made payments to Apple that reduced the price to consumers to $399). Can we conclude from this information that Apple is making a profit of about $619 per iPhone? Briefly explain.

Source: John Gaudiosi, "Research Teardown Details Why the New iPhone 5 Only Costs Apple $207 to Make," *Forbes*, September 19, 2012.

2.6 [Related to the Making the Connection: **Fixed Costs in the Publishing Industry**] Many firms consider their wage costs to be variable costs. Why, then, do publishers usually consider their wage and salary costs to be fixed costs? Are the costs of utilities always fixed, are they always variable, or can they be both? Briefly explain.

2.7 [Related to the Making the Connection: **Fixed Costs in the Publishing Industry**] For Jill Johnson's pizza restaurant, explain whether each of the following is a fixed cost or a variable cost:
a. The payment she makes on her fire insurance policy
b. The payment she makes to buy pizza dough
c. The wages she pays her workers
d. The lease payment she makes to the landlord who owns the building where her store is located
e. The $300-per-month payment she makes to her local newspaper for running her weekly advertisements

2.8 [Related to the Making the Connection: **Fixed Costs in the Publishing Industry**] The *Statistical Abstract of the United States* was published for many years by the U.S. Census Bureau. The *Abstract* provided a summary of business, economic, social, and political statistics. It was available for free online, and a printed copy could also be purchased from the U.S. Government Printing Office for $39. Because government documents are not copyrighted, anyone could print and sell copies of the *Statistical Abstract*. Each year, typically one or two companies would print and sell copies for a significantly lower price than the Government Printing Office did. The copies of the *Statistical Abstract* that these companies sold were usually identical to those sold by the government, except for having different covers. How could these companies have sold the same book for a lower price than the government did and still have covered their costs?

2.9 Suppose that Bill owns an automobile collision repair shop. The following table shows how the quantity of cars Bill can repair per month depends on the number of workers he hires. Assume that he pays each worker $4,000 per month and his fixed cost is $6,000 per month. Using the information provided, complete the table.

Quantity of Workers	Quantity of Cars per Month	Fixed Cost	Variable Cost	Total Cost	Average Total Cost
0	0	$6,000			—
1	20				
2	30				
3	40				
4	50				
5	55				

2.10 In 2008, Clay Bennett, the owner of the then Seattle Supersonics NBA basketball team (now the Oklahoma City Thunder), estimated that if the team remained in Seattle, he would suffer a loss of about $63 million over the following two seasons. If the team were allowed to move to Oklahoma City, he estimated that he would earn a profit of $19 million. What was the opportunity cost to Bennett of his team playing in Seattle rather than in Oklahoma City? Briefly explain.

Source: Jim Brunner, "New Details Emerge from Sonics Owner's Combative Deposition," *Seattle Times*, June 7, 2008.

2.11 Suppose Jill Johnson operates her pizza restaurant in a building she owns in the center of the city. Similar buildings in the neighborhood rent for $4,000 per month. Jill is considering selling her building and renting space in the suburbs for $3,000 per month, but she decides not to make the move. She reasons: "I would like to have a restaurant in the suburbs, but I pay no rent for my restaurant now, and I don't want to see my costs rise by $3,000 per month." Evaluate Jill's reasoning.

2.12 When the DuPont chemical company first attempted to enter the paint business, it was not successful. According to a company report, in one year it "lost nearly $500,000 in actual cash in addition to an expected return on investment of nearly $500,000, which made a total loss of income to the company of nearly a million." Why did this report include as part of the company's loss the amount it had expected to earn—but didn't—on its investment in manufacturing paint?

Source: Alfred D. Chandler, Jr., Thomas K. McCraw, and Richard Tedlow, *Management Past and Present*, Cincinnati, OH: South-Western, 2000.

The Marginal Product of Labor and the Average Product of Labor

LEARNING OBJECTIVE: Understand the relationship between the marginal product of labor and the average product of labor.

Summary

The **marginal product of labor** is the additional output produced by a firm as a result of hiring one more worker. Specialization and division of labor cause the marginal product of labor to rise for the first few workers hired. Eventually, the **law of diminishing returns** causes the marginal product of labor to decline. The **average product of labor** is the total amount of output produced by a firm divided by the quantity of workers hired. When the marginal product of labor is greater than the average product of labor, the average product of labor increases. When the marginal product of labor is less than the average product of labor, the average product of labor decreases.

Visit www.myeconlab.com to complete these exercises online and get instant feedback.

Review Questions

3.1 Draw a graph that shows the usual relationship between the marginal product of labor and the average product of labor. Why do the marginal product of labor and the average product of labor curves have the shapes you drew?

3.2 How do specialization and division of labor typically affect the marginal product of labor?

3.3 What is the law of diminishing returns? Does it apply in the long run?

Problems and Applications

3.4 Fill in the missing values in the following table:

Quantity of Workers	Total Output	Marginal Product of Labor	Average Product of Labor
0	0		
1	400		
2	900		
3	1,500		
4	1,900		
5	2,200		
6	2,400		
7	2,300		

3.5 Use the numbers from problem 3.4 to draw one graph that shows how total output increases with the quantity of workers hired and a second graph that shows the marginal product of labor and the average product of labor.

3.6 A student looks at the numbers in Table 3 and draws this conclusion:

> The marginal product of labor is increasing for the first two workers hired, and then it declines for the next four workers. I guess each of the first two workers must have been hard workers. Then Jill must have had to settle for increasingly bad workers.

Do you agree with the student's analysis? Briefly explain.

3.7 **[Related to the** Making the Connection: **Adam Smith's Famous Account of the Division of Labor in a Pin Factory]** Briefly explain whether you agree with the following argument:

> Adam Smith's idea of the gains to firms from the division of labor makes a lot of sense when the good being manufactured is something complex like automobiles or computers, but it doesn't apply in the manufacturing of less complex goods or in other sectors of the economy, such as retail sales.

3.8 Sally looks at her college transcript and says to you, "How is this possible? My grade point average for this semester's courses is higher than my grade point average for last semester's courses, but my cumulative grade point average still went down from last semester to this semester." Explain to Sally how this is possible.

3.9 Is it possible for a firm to experience a technological change that would increase the marginal product of labor while leaving the average product of labor unchanged? Explain.

3.10 The following table shows the quantity of workers and total output for a local pizza parlor. Answer the following questions based on this table:

Quantity of Workers	Total Output
0	0
1	5
2	—
3	19
4	24
5	28
6	26

a. When the owner hires 4 workers, what is average product of labor?

b. What is the marginal product of the fifth worker?

c. If the marginal product of the second worker is 6, what is the total number of pizzas produced when 2 workers are hired?

d. Assuming the marginal product of the second worker is 6, with which worker hired does the law of diminishing returns set in?

 4

The Relationship between Short-Run Production and Short-Run Cost

LEARNING OBJECTIVE: Explain and illustrate the relationship between marginal cost and average total cost.

Summary

The **marginal cost** of production is the increase in total cost resulting from producing another unit of output. The marginal cost curve has a U shape because when the marginal product of labor is rising, the marginal cost of output is falling, and when the marginal product of labor is falling, the marginal cost of output is rising. When marginal cost is less than average total cost, average total cost falls. When marginal cost is greater than average total cost, average total cost rises. Therefore, the average total cost curve also has a U shape.

Visit www.myeconlab.com to complete these exercises online and get instant feedback.

Review Questions

4.1 What is the difference between the average cost of production and marginal cost of production?

4.2 If the marginal product of labor is rising, is the marginal cost of production rising or falling? Briefly explain.

4.3 Explain why the marginal cost curve intersects the average total cost curve at the level of output where average total cost is at a minimum.

Problems and Applications

4.4 **[Related to the** Chapter Opener**]** Older oil wells that produce fewer than 10 barrels of oil a day are called "stripper" wells. Suppose that you and a partner own a stripper well that can produce eight barrels of oil per day and you estimate that the marginal cost of producing another barrel of oil is $80. In making your calculation, you take into account the cost of labor, materials, and other inputs that increase when you produce more oil. Your partner looks over your calculation of marginal cost and says: "You forgot about that bank loan we received two years ago. If we take into account the amount we pay on that loan, it adds $10 per barrel to our marginal cost of production." Briefly explain whether you should agree with your partner's analysis.

4.5 Is it possible for average total cost to be decreasing over a range of output where marginal cost is increasing? Briefly explain.

4.6 Suppose a firm has no fixed costs, so all its costs are variable, even in the short run.
   a. If the firm's marginal costs are continually increasing (that is, marginal cost is increasing from the first unit of output produced), will the firm's average total cost curve have a U shape?
   b. If the firm's marginal costs are $5 at every level of output, what shape will the firm's average total cost have?

4.7 **[Related to** Solved Problem 4**]** Santiago Delgado owns a copier store. He leases two copy machines for which he pays $20 each per day. He cannot increase the number of machines he leases without giving the office machine company six weeks' notice. He can hire as many workers as he wants, at a cost of $40 per day per worker. These are the only two inputs he uses to produce copies.
   a. Fill in the remaining columns in the following table.
   b. Draw the average total cost curve and marginal cost curve for Santiago's store. Do these curves have the expected shape? Briefly explain.

Quantity of Workers	Quantity of Copies per Day	Fixed Cost	Variable Cost	Total Cost	Average Total Cost	Marginal Cost
0	0					
1	600					
2	1,100					
3	1,500					
4	1,800					
5	2,000					
6	2,100					

4.8 Is Jill Johnson correct when she says the following: "I am currently producing 10,000 pizzas per month at a total cost of $50,000.00. If I produce 10,001 pizzas, my total cost will rise to $50,011.00. Therefore, my marginal cost of producing pizzas must be increasing." Draw a graph to illustrate your answer.

4.9 Is Jill Johnson correct when she says the following: "I am currently producing 20,000 pizzas per month at a total cost of $75,000. If I produce 20,001 pizzas, my total cost will rise to $75,002. Therefore, my marginal cost of producing pizzas must be increasing." Illustrate your answer with a graph.

4.10 (This problem is somewhat advanced.) Using symbols, we can write that the marginal product of labor is equal to $\Delta Q/\Delta L$. Marginal cost is equal to $\Delta TC/\Delta Q$. Because fixed costs by definition don't change, marginal cost is also equal to $\Delta VC/\Delta Q$. If Jill Johnson's only variable cost (VC) is labor cost, then her variable cost equals the wage multiplied by the quantity of workers hired, or wL.
   a. If the wage Jill pays is constant, then what is ΔVC in terms of w and L?
   b. Use your answer to part (a) and the expressions given for the marginal product of labor and the marginal cost of output to find an expression for marginal cost, $\Delta TC/\Delta Q$, in terms of the wage, w, and the marginal product of labor, $\Delta Q/\Delta L$.
   c. Use your answer to part (b) to determine Jill's marginal cost of producing pizzas if the wage is $750 per week and the marginal product of labor is 150 pizzas. If the wage falls to $600 per week and the marginal product of labor is unchanged, what happens to Jill's marginal cost? If the wage is unchanged at $750 per week and the marginal product of labor rises to 250 pizzas, what happens to Jill's marginal cost?

<table>
<tr><td>5</td><td>

Graphing Cost Curves

LEARNING OBJECTIVE: Graph average total cost, average variable cost, average fixed cost, and marginal cost.
</td></tr>
</table>

Summary

Average fixed cost is equal to fixed cost divided by the level of output. **Average variable cost** is equal to variable cost divided by the level of output. Figure 5 shows the relationship among marginal cost, average total cost, average variable cost, and average fixed cost. It is one of the most important graphs in microeconomics.

Review Questions

5.1 Where does the marginal cost curve intersect the average variable cost curve and the average total cost curve?

5.2 As the level of output increases, what happens to the difference between the value of average total cost and average variable cost?

Problems and Applications

5.3 Suppose the total cost of producing 10,000 tennis balls is $30,000 and the fixed cost is $10,000.
  a. What is the variable cost?
  b. When output is 10,000, what are the average variable cost and the average fixed cost?
  c. Assume that the cost curves have the usual shape. Is the dollar difference between the average total cost and the average variable cost greater when the output is 10,000 tennis balls or when the output is 30,000 tennis balls? Explain.

5.4 One description of the costs of operating a railroad makes the following observation: "The fixed … expenses which attach to the operation of railroads … are in the nature of a tax upon the business of the road; the smaller the [amount of] business, the larger the tax." Briefly explain why fixed costs are like a tax. In what sense is this tax smaller when the amount of business is larger?
  Source: Alfred D. Chandler, Jr., Thomas K. McCraw, and Richard Tedlow, *Management Past and Present*, Cincinnati, OH: South-Western, 2000, p. 2–27.

5.5 In the ancient world, a book could be produced either on a scroll or as a codex, which was made of folded sheets glued together, something like a modern book. One scholar has estimated the following variable costs (in Greek drachmas) of the two methods:

	Scroll	Codex
Cost of writing (wage of a scribe)	11.33 drachmas	11.33 drachmas
Cost of paper	16.50 drachmas	9.25 drachmas

Another scholar points out that a significant fixed cost was involved in producing a codex:

> In order to copy a codex … the amount of text and the layout of each page had to be carefully calculated in advance to determine the exact number of sheets … needed. No doubt, this is more time-consuming and calls for more experimentation than the production of a scroll would. But for the next copy, these calculations would be used again.

  a. Suppose that the fixed cost of preparing a codex was 58 drachmas and that there was no similar fixed cost for a scroll. Would an ancient book publisher who intended to sell 5 copies of a book be likely to publish it as a scroll or as a codex? What if he intended to sell 10 copies? Briefly explain.
  b. Although most books were published as scrolls in the first century A.D., by the third century, most were published as codices. Considering only the factors mentioned in this problem, explain why this change may have taken place.
  Sources: T. C. Skeat, "The Length of the Standard Papyrus Roll and the Cost-Advantage of the Codex," *Zeitschrift fur Pspyrologie and Epigraphik*, Germany: Rudolph Habelt, 1982, p. 175; and David Trobisch, *The First Edition of the New Testament*, New York: Oxford University Press, 2000, p. 73.

5.6 Recently some colleges and private companies have launched free online courses that can be taken by anyone with an Internet connection. The most successful of these "massive open online courses" (MOOCs) have attracted tens of thousands of students. An article in the *Economist* magazine discussing MOOCs observed: "Though marginal costs are low, designing enticing online material is costly." Why would the marginal costs of offering a MOOC be low? What is the relationship between the marginal costs, average fixed costs, and average total costs of offering a MOOC? Draw a graph to illustrate your answer.
  Source: "Learning New Lessons," *Economist*, December 22, 2012.

5.7 Use the information in the graph to find the values for the following at an output level of 1,000.

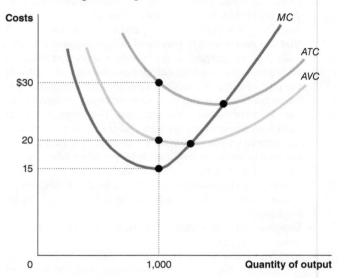

  a. Marginal cost
  b. Total cost
  c. Variable cost
  d. Fixed cost

5.8 List the errors in the following graph. Carefully explain why the curves drawn this way are wrong. In other words, why can't these curves be as they are shown in the graph?

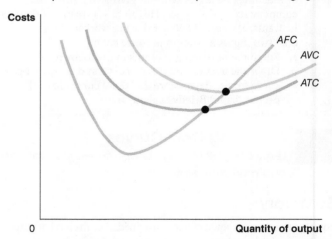

5.9 Explain how the events listed in a. through d. would affect the following costs at Southwest Airlines:
  1. Marginal cost
  2. Average variable cost
  3. Average fixed cost

4. Average total cost
   a. Southwest signs a new contract with the Transport Workers Union that requires the airline to increase wages for its flight attendants.
   b. The federal government starts to levy a $20-per-passenger carbon emissions tax on all commercial air travel.
   c. Southwest decides on an across-the-board 10 percent cut in executive salaries.
   d. Southwest decides to double its television advertising budget.

6 | Costs in the Long Run

LEARNING OBJECTIVE: Understand how firms use the long-run average cost curve in their planning.

Summary

The **long-run average cost curve** shows the lowest cost at which a firm is able to produce a given level of output in the long run. For many firms, the long-run average cost curve falls as output expands because of **economies of scale. Minimum efficient scale** is the level of output at which all economies of scale have been exhausted. After economies of scale have been exhausted, firms experience **constant returns to scale**, where their long-run average cost curve is flat. At high levels of output, the long-run average cost curve turns up as the firm experiences **diseconomies of scale**.

Visit **www.myeconlab.com** to complete these exercises online and get instant feedback.

Review Questions

6.1 What is the difference between total cost and variable cost in the long run?

6.2 What is minimum efficient scale? What is likely to happen in the long run to firms that do not reach minimum efficient scale?

6.3 What are economies of scale? What are four reasons that firms may experience economies of scale?

6.4 What are diseconomies of scale? What is the main reason that a firm eventually encounters diseconomies of scale as it keeps increasing the size of its store or factory?

6.5 Why can short-run average cost never be less than long-run average cost for a given level of output?

Problems and Applications

6.6 Factories for producing computer chips are called "fabs." As the semiconductors used in computer chips have become smaller and smaller, the machines necessary to make them have become more and more expensive. According to an article in the *Economist* magazine:

> To reach the economies of scale needed to make such investments pay, chipmakers must build bigger fabs .... In 1966 a new fab cost $14 million. By 1995 the price had risen to $1.5 billion. Today, says Intel, the cost of a leading-edge fab exceeds $6 billion.

Why would the rising costs of chipmaking machines lead chipmaking companies, such as Intel, to build larger factories?

Source: "The Semiconductor Industry," *Economist*, April 2, 2009.

6.7 **[Related to** Solved Problem 6**]** Suppose that Jill Johnson has to choose between building a smaller restaurant and a larger restaurant. In the following graph, the relationship between costs and output for the smaller restaurant is represented by the curve ATC_1, and the relationship between costs and output for the larger restaurant is represented by the curve ATC_2.

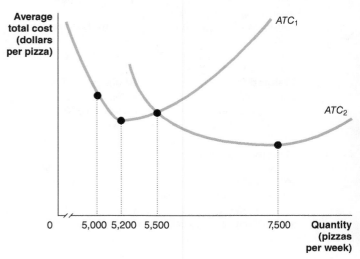

a. If Jill expects to produce 5,100 pizzas per week, should she build a smaller restaurant or a larger restaurant? Briefly explain.

b. If Jill expects to produce 6,000 pizzas per week, should she build a smaller restaurant or a larger restaurant? Briefly explain.

c. A student asks, "If the average cost of producing pizzas is lower in the larger restaurant when Jill produces 7,500 pizzas per week, why isn't it also lower when Jill produces 5,200 pizzas per week?" Give a brief answer to the student's question.

6.8 **[Related to** Solved Problem 6**]** An article in the *Wall Street Journal* discussed the purchase of the small Zipcar rental car firm by the much larger Avis. The article predicted that the purchase would be successful because of the "efficiencies gained by putting the two companies together." The article also observed: "On its own, Zipcar is too small to achieve economies of scale."

a. What economies of scale may exist in the rental car industry? Why would a rental car firm that is too small be unable to achieve these economies of scale?

b. What does the article mean by "efficiencies" that might be gained by putting the two companies together?

c. If Avis had already achieved minimum efficient scale before buying Zipcar, would the combined companies still be more efficient than if they operated separately? Briefly explain.

Source: Rolfe Winkler, "Avis Puts Some Zip in Its Weekend," *Wall Street Journal*, January 2, 2013.

6.9 **[Related to** Solved Problem 6**]** An account of the difficulties of Japanese mobile phone manufacturers argues that these firms made a mistake by concentrating on selling in high-income countries while making little effort to sell in low-income countries:

> The main growth in the wireless industry overall is in emerging markets, which need cheap phones. The world's top three makers—Nokia, Samsung and Motorola—focus on this segment …. Japanese firms are caught in a vicious circle: because they are not selling to poor countries, their volume stays low, which keeps prices high, which makes selling to poor countries infeasible.

Why would the price of Japanese mobile phones be high because Japanese firms are producing these phones in low volumes? Use a graph like Figure 6 to illustrate your answer.

Source: "Dropped Call: Why Japan Lost the Mobile-Phone Wars," *Economist*, March 7, 2008.

6.10 **[Related to** Solved Problem 6**]** At one point, Time Warner and the Walt Disney Company discussed merging their news operations. Time Warner owns Cable News Network (CNN) and Disney owns ABC News. After analyzing the situation, the companies decided that a combined news operation would have higher average costs than either CNN or ABC News had separately. Use a long-run average cost curve graph to illustrate why the companies did not merge their news operations.

Source: Martin Peers and Joe Flint, "AOL Calls Off CNN–ABC Deal, Seeing Operating Difficulties," *Wall Street Journal*, February 14, 2003.

6.11 **[Related to the** Making the Connection: **The Colossal River Rouge: Diseconomies of Scale at Ford Motor Company]** Suppose that Henry Ford had continued to experience economies of scale, no matter how large an automobile factory he built. Discuss what the implications of this would have been for the automobile industry.

6.12 **[Related to the** Chapter Opener**]** Suppose that the economies of scale in using fracking methods in drilling for oil are greater than when using conventional drilling methods. What would the likely consequences be for the number of firms drilling for oil in the United States?

6.13 **[Related to the** Don't Let This Happen to You**]** Explain whether you agree with the following statement: "Henry Ford expected to be able to produce cars at a lower average cost at his River Rouge plant. Unfortunately, because of diminishing returns, his costs were actually higher."

6.14 In 2012, then Barnes & Noble CEO William Lynch predicted that although the firm was suffering losses in selling its Nook tablet, "the Nook business will scale in fiscal 2013, reducing losses from last year."

    a. What did Lynch mean that "the Nook business will scale"?

    b. Why would the Nook business scaling reduce the firm's losses?

    c. In 2013, Barnes & Noble's losses from selling the Nook increased and Lynch resigned as CEO. Can we conclude that the Nook business didn't scale? Briefly explain.

Source: Jeffrey A. Trachtenberg "Nook Loses Ground in Tablet War," *Wall Street Journal*, January 3, 2013.

Appendix

Using Isoquants and Isocost Lines to Understand Production and Cost

Isoquants

In this chapter, we studied the important relationship between a firm's level of production and its costs. In this appendix, we will look more closely at how firms choose the combination of inputs to produce a given level of output. Firms usually have a choice about how they will produce their output. For example, Jill Johnson is able to produce 5,000 pizzas per week by using 10 workers and 2 ovens or by using 6 workers and 3 ovens. We will see that firms search for the *cost-minimizing* combination of inputs that will allow them to produce a given level of output. The cost-minimizing combination of inputs depends on two factors: technology—which determines how much output a firm receives from employing a given quantity of inputs—and input prices—which determine the total cost of each combination of inputs.

An Isoquant Graph

We begin by graphing the levels of output that Jill can produce using different combinations of two inputs: labor—the quantity of workers she hires per week—and capital—the quantity of ovens she uses per week. In reality, of course, Jill uses more than just these two inputs to produce pizzas, but nothing important would change if we expanded the discussion to include many inputs instead of just two. Figure A.1 measures the quantity of capital along the vertical axis and the quantity of labor along the horizontal axis. The curves in the graph are **isoquants**, which show all the combinations of two inputs, in this case capital and labor, that will produce the same level of output.

The isoquant labeled $Q = 5,000$ shows all the combinations of workers and ovens that enable Jill to produce that quantity of pizzas per week. For example, at point A, she produces 5,000 pizzas using 6 workers and 3 ovens, and at point B, she produces the same output using 10 workers and 2 ovens. With more workers and ovens, she can move to a higher isoquant. For example, with 12 workers and 4 ovens, she can produce at point C on the isoquant $Q = 10,000$. With even more workers and ovens, she could move to the isoquant $Q = 13,000$. The higher the isoquant—that is, the further to the upper right on the graph—the more output the firm produces. Although we have shown only three isoquants in this graph, there is, in fact, an isoquant for every level of output.

Isoquant A curve that shows all the combinations of two inputs, such as capital and labor, that will produce the same level of output.

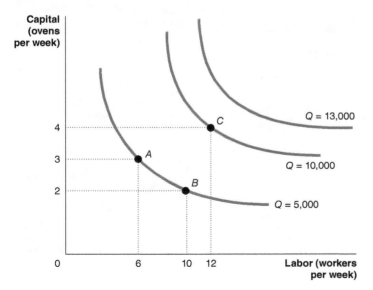

The Slope of an Isoquant

Remember that the slope of a curve is the ratio of the change in the variable on the vertical axis to the change in the variable on the horizontal axis. Along an isoquant, the slope tells us the rate at which a firm is able to substitute one input for another while keeping the level of output constant. This rate is called the **marginal rate of technical substitution (MRTS)**.

We expect that the MRTS will change as we move down an isoquant. In Figure A.1, at a point like A on isoquant Q = 5,000, the isoquant is relatively steep. As we move down the curve, it becomes less steep at a point like B. This shape is the usual one for isoquants: They are bowed in, or convex. The reason isoquants have this shape is that as we move down the curve, we continue to substitute labor for capital. As the firm produces the same quantity of output using less capital, the additional labor it needs increases because of diminishing returns. Remember from the chapter that, as a consequence of diminishing returns, for a given decline in capital, increasing amounts of labor are necessary to produce the same level of output. Because the MRTS is equal to the change in capital divided by the change in labor, it will become smaller (in absolute value) as we move down an isoquant.

Isocost Lines

A firm wants to produce a given quantity of output at the lowest possible cost. We can show the relationship between the quantity of inputs used and the firm's total cost by using an *isocost* line. An **isocost line** shows all the combinations of two inputs, such as capital and labor, that have the same total cost.

Graphing the Isocost Line

Suppose that Jill has $6,000 per week to spend on capital and labor. Suppose, to simplify the analysis, that Jill can rent pizza ovens by the week. The table in Figure A.2 shows the combinations of capital and labor available to her if the rental price of ovens is $1,000 per

Marginal rate of technical substitution (MRTS) The rate at which a firm is able to substitute one input for another while keeping the level of output constant.

Isocost line All the combinations of two inputs, such as capital and labor, that have the same total cost.

Figure A.2

An Isocost Line

The isocost line shows the combinations of inputs with a total cost of $6,000. The rental price of ovens is $1,000 per week, so if Jill spends the whole $6,000 on ovens, she can rent 6 ovens (point A). The wage rate is $500 per week, so if Jill spends the whole $6,000 on workers, she can hire 12 workers (point G). As she moves down the isocost line, she gives up renting 1 oven for every 2 workers she hires. Any combination of inputs along the line or inside the line can be purchased with $6,000. Any combination that lies outside the line cannot be purchased with $6,000.

Combinations of Workers and Ovens with a Total Cost of $6,000			
Point	Ovens	Workers	Total Cost
A	6	0	(6 x $1,000) + (0 x $500) = $6,000
B	5	2	(5 x $1,000) + (2 x $500) = $6,000
C	4	4	(4 x $1,000) + (4 x $500) = $6,000
D	3	6	(3 x $1,000) + (6 x $500) = $6,000
E	2	8	(2 x $1,000) + (8 x $500) = $6,000
F	1	10	(1 x $1,000) + (10 x $500) = $6,000
G	0	12	(0 x $1,000) + (12 x $500) = $6,000

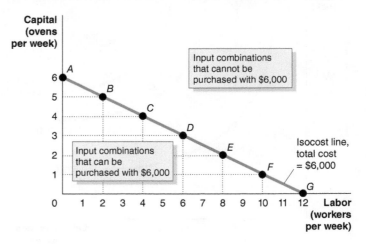

week and the wage rate is $500 per week. The graph uses the data in the table to construct an isocost line. The isocost line intersects the vertical axis at the maximum number of ovens Jill can rent per week, which is shown by point A. The line intersects the horizontal axis at the maximum number of workers Jill can hire per week, which is point G. As Jill moves down the isocost line from point A, she gives up renting 1 oven for every 2 workers she hires. Any combination of inputs along the line or inside the line can be purchased with $6,000. Any combination that lies outside the line cannot be purchased because it would have a total cost to Jill of more than $6,000.

The Slope and Position of the Isocost Line

The slope of the isocost line is constant and equals the change in the quantity of ovens divided by the change in the quantity of workers. In this case, in moving from any point on the isocost line to any other point, the change in the quantity of ovens equals −1, and the change in the quantity of workers equals 2, so the slope equals −1/2. Notice that with a rental price of ovens of $1,000 per week and a wage rate for labor of $500 per week, the slope of the isocost line is equal to the ratio of the wage rate divided by the rental price of capital, multiplied by −1, or −$500/$1,000 = −1/2. In fact, this result will always hold, whatever inputs are involved and whatever their prices may be: *The slope of the isocost line is equal to the ratio of the price of the input on the horizontal axis divided by the price of the input on the vertical axis multiplied by −1.*

The position of the isocost line depends on the level of total cost. Higher levels of total cost shift the isocost line outward, and lower levels of total cost shift the isocost line inward. This can be seen in Figure A.3, which shows isocost lines for total costs of $3,000, $6,000, and $9,000. We have shown only three isocost lines in the graph, but there is, in fact, a different isocost line for each level of total cost.

Choosing the Cost-Minimizing Combination of Capital and Labor

Suppose Jill wants to produce 5,000 pizzas per week. FigureA.1 shows that there are many combinations of ovens and workers that will allow Jill to produce this level of output. There is only one combination of ovens and workers, however, that will allow her to produce 5,000 pizzas *at the lowest total cost*. Figure A.4 shows the isoquant Q = 5,000 along with three isocost lines. Point B is the lowest-cost combination of inputs shown in the graph, but this combination of 1 oven and 4 workers will produce fewer than the 5,000 pizzas needed. Points C and D are combinations of ovens and workers that will produce 5,000 pizzas, but their total cost is $9,000. The combination of 3 ovens and 6 workers at point A produces 5,000 pizzas at the lowest total cost of $6,000.

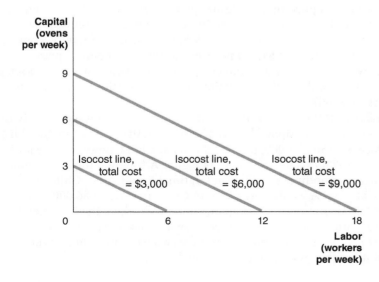

Figure A.3

The Position of the Isocost Line

The position of the isocost line depends on the level of total cost. As total cost increases from $3,000 to $6,000 to $9,000 per week, the isocost line shifts outward. For each isocost line shown, the rental price of ovens is $1,000 per week, and the wage rate is $500 per week.

Figure A.4

Choosing Capital and Labor to Minimize Total Cost

Jill wants to produce 5,000 pizzas per week at the lowest total cost. Point B is the lowest-cost combination of inputs shown in the graph, but this combination of 1 oven and 4 workers will produce fewer than the 5,000 pizzas needed. Points C and D are combinations of ovens and workers that will produce 5,000 pizzas, but their total cost is $9,000. The combination of 3 ovens and 6 workers at point A produces 5,000 pizzas at the lowest total cost of $6,000.

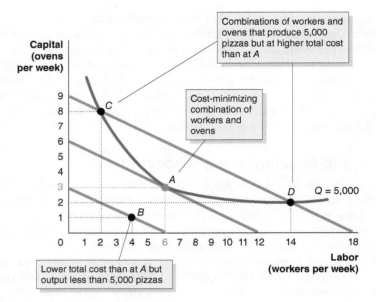

Figure A.4 shows that moving to an isocost line with a total cost of less than $6,000 would mean producing fewer than 5,000 pizzas. Being at any point along the isoquant $Q = 5,000$ other than point A would increase total cost above $6,000. In fact, the combination of inputs at point A is the only one on isoquant $Q = 5,000$ that has a total cost of $6,000. All other input combinations on this isoquant have higher total costs. Notice also that at point A, the isoquant and the isocost lines are tangent, so the slope of the isoquant is equal to the slope of the isocost line at that point.

Different Input Price Ratios Lead to Different Input Choices

Jill's cost-minimizing choice of 3 ovens and 6 workers is determined jointly by the technology available to her—as represented by her firm's isoquants—and by input prices—as represented by her firm's isocost lines. If the technology of making pizzas changes, perhaps because new ovens are developed, her isoquants will be affected, and her choice of inputs may change. If her isoquants remain unchanged but input prices change, then her choice of inputs may also change. This fact can explain why firms in different countries that face different input prices may produce the same good using different combinations of capital and labor, even though they have the same technology available.

For example, suppose that in China, pizza ovens are higher priced and labor is lower priced than in the United States. In our example, Jill Johnson pays $1,000 per week to rent pizza ovens and $500 per week to hire workers. Suppose a businessperson in China must pay a price of $1,500 per week to rent the identical pizza ovens but can hire Chinese workers who are as productive as U.S. workers at a wage of $300 per week. Figure A.5 shows how the cost-minimizing input combination for the businessperson in China differs from Jill's.

Remember that the slope of the isocost line equals the wage rate divided by the rental price of capital multiplied by −1. The slope of the isocost line that Jill and other U.S. firms face is −$500/$1,000, or −1/2. Firms in China, however, face an isocost line with a slope of −$300/$1,500, or −1/5. As Figure A.5 shows, the input combination at point A, which was optimal for Jill, is not optimal for a firm in China. Using the input combination at point A would cost a firm in China more than $6,000. Instead, the Chinese isocost line is tangent to the isoquant at point B, where the input combination is 2 ovens and 10 workers. This result makes sense: Because ovens cost more in China, but workers cost less, a Chinese firm will use fewer ovens and more workers than a U.S. firm, even if it has the same technology as the U.S. firm.

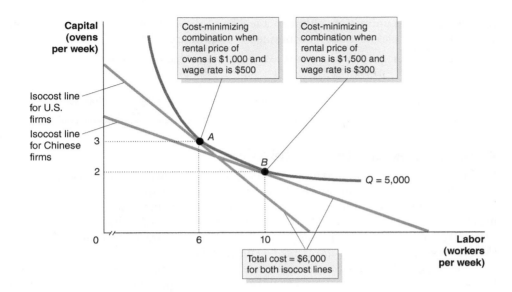

Figure A.5

Changing Input Prices Affects the Cost-Minimizing Input Choice

As the graph shows, the input combination at point *A*, which was optimal for Jill, is not optimal for a businessperson in China. Using the input combination at point *A* would cost businesspeople in China more than $6,000. Instead, the Chinese isocost line is tangent to the isoquant at point *B*, where the input combination is 2 ovens and 10 workers. Because ovens cost more in China but workers cost less, a Chinese firm will use fewer ovens and more workers than a U.S. firm, even if it has the same technology as the U.S. firm.

Making the Connection

The Changing Input Mix in Walt Disney Film Animation

The inputs used to make feature-length animated films have changed dramatically in the past 15 years. Prior to the early 1990s, the Walt Disney Company dominated the market for animated films. Disney's films were produced using hundreds of animators drawing most of the film by hand. Each film would contain as many as 170,000 individual drawings. Then, two developments dramatically affected how animated films are produced. First, in 1994, Disney had a huge hit with *The Lion King*, which cost only $50 million to produce but earned the company more than $1 billion in profit. As a result of this success, Disney and other film studios began to produce more animated films, increasing the demand for animators and more than doubling their salaries. The second development came in 1995, when Pixar Animation Studios released the film *Toy Story*. This was the first successful feature-length film produced using computers, with no hand-drawn animation. In the following years, technological advance continued to reduce the cost of the computers and software necessary to produce an animated film.

As a result of these two developments, the price of capital—computers and software—fell relative to the price of labor—animators. As the figure shows, the change in the price of computers relative to animators changed the slope of the isocost line and resulted in film studios now producing animated films using many more computers and many fewer animators than in the early 1990s. In 2006, Disney bought Pixar, and within a few years, all the major film studios had converted to computer animation, now

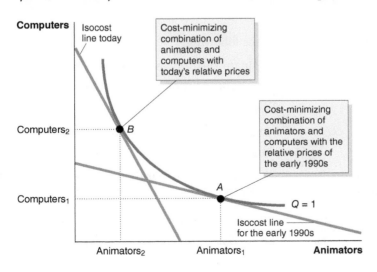

referred to as CGI animation, although a few hand-drawn films, such as Disney's film *Winnie the Pooh* released in 2011, continued to be produced.

Sources: "Magic Restored," *Economist*, April 17, 2008; and Laura M. Holson, "Disney Moves Away from Hand-Drawn Animation," *New York Times*, September 18, 2005.

Your Turn: Test your understanding by doing related problem A.6 at the end of this appendix.

Another Look at Cost Minimization

We know that consumers maximize utility when they consume each good up to the point where the marginal utility per dollar spent is the same for every good. We can derive a very similar cost-minimization rule for firms. Remember that at the point of cost minimization, the isoquant and the isocost line are tangent, so they have the same slope. Therefore, *at the point of cost minimization, the marginal rate of technical substitution* (MRTS) *is equal to the wage rate divided by the rental price of capital.*

The slope of the isoquant tells us the rate at which a firm is able to substitute labor for capital, *keeping the level of output constant.* The slope of the isocost line tells us the rate at which a firm is able to substitute labor for capital, *given current input prices.* Only at the point of cost minimization are these two rates the same.

When we move from one point on an isoquant to another, we end up using more of one input and less of the other input, but the level of output remains the same. For example, as Jill moves down an isoquant, she uses fewer ovens and more workers but produces the same quantity of pizzas. In this chapter, we defined the *marginal product of labor* (MP_L) as the additional output produced by a firm as a result of hiring one more worker. Similarly, we can define the *marginal product of capital* (MP_K) as the additional output produced by a firm as a result of using one more machine. So, when Jill uses fewer ovens by moving down an isoquant, she loses output equal to:

$$-\text{Change in the quantity of ovens} \times MP_K.$$

But she uses more workers, so she gains output equal to:

$$\text{Change in the quantity of workers} \times MP_L.$$

We know that the gain in output from the additional workers is equal to the loss from the smaller quantity of ovens because total output remains the same along an isoquant. Therefore, we can write:

$$-\text{Change in the quantity of ovens} \times MP_K = \text{Change in the quantity of workers} \times MP_L.$$

Loss in output from using fewer ovens

Gain in output from using more workers

If we rearrange terms, we have the following:

$$\frac{-\text{Change in the quantity of ovens}}{\text{Change in the quantity of workers}} = \frac{MP_L}{MP_K}.$$

Because

$$\frac{-\text{Change in the quantity of ovens}}{\text{Change in the quantity of workers}}$$

is the slope of the isoquant, it is equal to the marginal rate of technical substitution (multiplied by negative 1). So, we can write:

$$\frac{-\text{Change in the quantity of ovens}}{\text{Change in the quantity of workers}} = MRTS = \frac{MP_L}{MP_K}.$$

The slope of the isocost line equals the wage rate (w) divided by the rental price of capital (r). We saw earlier in this appendix that at the point of cost minimization, the *MRTS* equals the ratio of the prices of the two inputs. Therefore:

$$\frac{MP_L}{MP_K} = \frac{w}{r}.$$

We can rewrite this to show that at the point of cost minimization:

$$\frac{MP_L}{w} = \frac{MP_K}{r}.$$

This last expression tells us that to minimize cost for a given level of output, a firm should hire inputs up to the point where the last dollar spent on each input results in the same increase in output. If this equality did not hold, a firm could lower its costs by using more of one input and less of the other. For example, if the left side of the equation were greater than the right side, a firm could rent fewer ovens, hire more workers, and produce the same output at lower cost.

Solved Problem A.1

Determining the Optimal Combination of Inputs

Consider the information in the following table for Jill Johnson's restaurant.

Marginal product of capital	3,000 pizzas per oven
Marginal product of labor	1,200 pizzas per worker
Wage rate	$300 per week
Rental price of ovens	$600 per week

Briefly explain whether Jill is minimizing costs. If she is not minimizing costs, explain whether she should rent more ovens and hire fewer workers or rent fewer ovens and hire more workers.

Solving the Problem

Step 1: **Review the chapter material.** This problem is about determining the optimal choice of inputs by comparing the ratios of the marginal products of inputs to their prices, so you may want to review the section "Another Look at Cost Minimization."

Step 2: **Compute the ratios of marginal product to input price to determine whether Jill is minimizing costs.** If Jill is minimizing costs, the following relationship should hold:

$$\frac{MP_L}{w} = \frac{MP_K}{r}.$$

In this case, we have

$$MP_L = 1,200$$
$$MP_K = 3,000$$
$$w = \$300$$
$$r = \$600.$$

So

$$\frac{MP_L}{w} = \frac{1,200}{\$300} = 4 \text{ pizzas per dollar, and } \frac{MP_K}{r} = \frac{3,000}{\$600} = 5 \text{ pizzas per dollar.}$$

Because the two ratios are not equal, Jill is not minimizing cost.

Step 3: **Determine how Jill should change the mix of inputs she uses.** Jill produces more pizzas per dollar from the last oven than from the last worker. This indicates that she has too many workers and too few ovens. Therefore, to minimize cost, Jill should use more ovens and hire fewer workers.

Your Turn: For more practice, do related problems A.7 and A.8 at the end of this appendix.

<table>
<tr><td>

Making
the
Connection

</td><td>

Do National Football League Teams Behave Efficiently?

In the National Football League (NFL), the "salary cap" is the maximum amount each team can spend in a year on salaries for football players. Each year's salary cap results from negotiations

</td></tr>
</table>

between the league and the union representing the players. To achieve efficiency, an NFL team should distribute salaries among players so as to maximize the level of output—in this case, winning football games—given the constant level of cost represented by the salary cap. (Notice that maximizing the level of output for a given level of cost is equivalent to minimizing cost for a given level of output. To see why, think about the situation in which an isocost line is tangent to an isoquant. At the point of tangency, the firm has simultaneously minimized the cost of producing the level of output represented by the isoquant and maximized the output produced at the level of cost represented by the isocost line.)

In distributing the fixed amount of salary payments available, teams should equalize the ratios of the marginal productivity of players, as represented by their contribution to winning games, to the salaries players receive. Just as a firm may not use a machine that has a very high marginal product if its rental price is very high, a football team may not want to hire a superstar player if the salary the team would need to pay is too high.

Economists Cade Massey, of the University of Pennsylvania, and Richard Thaler, of the University of Chicago, have analyzed whether NFL teams distribute their salaries efficiently. NFL teams obtain their players either by signing free agents—who are players whose contracts with other teams have expired—or by signing players chosen in the annual draft of eligible college players. The college draft consists of seven rounds, with the teams with the worst records the previous year choosing first. Massey and Thaler find that, in fact, NFL teams do not allocate salaries efficiently. In particular, the players chosen with the first few picks of the first round of the draft tend to be paid salaries that are much higher relative to their marginal products than are players taken later in the first round. A typical team with a high draft pick would increase its ability to win football games at the constant cost represented by the salary cap if it traded for lower draft picks, providing it could find another team willing to make the trade. Why do NFL teams apparently make the error of not efficiently distributing salaries? Massey and Thaler argue that general managers of NFL teams tend to be overconfident in their ability to forecast how well a college player is likely to perform in the NFL.

General managers of NFL teams are not alone in suffering from overconfidence. Studies have shown that, in general, people tend to overestimate their ability to forecast an uncertain outcome. Because NFL teams tend to overestimate the future marginal productivity of high draft picks, they pay them salaries that are inefficiently high compared to salaries other draft picks receive. NFL teams were aware that they were probably overpaying high draft picks. In 2011, they negotiated a new contract with the NFL Players Union that limited the salaries that drafted players could receive.

This example shows that the concepts developed in this chapter provide powerful tools for analyzing whether firms are operating efficiently.

Source: Cade Massey and Richard Thaler, "The Loser's Curse: Overconfidence vs. Market Efficiency in the National Football League draft," National Bureau of Economic Research Working Paper 11270, April 8, 2010.

Your Turn: Test your understanding by doing related problem A.14 at the end of this appendix.

Did new rules keep the Kansas City Chiefs from paying Eric Fisher too much?

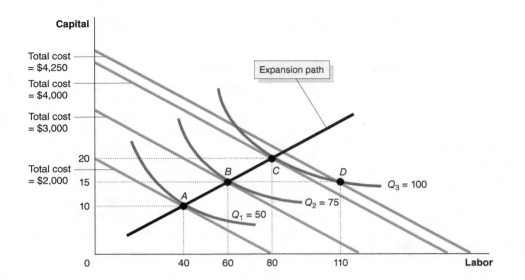

Figure A.6

The Expansion Path

The tangency points *A*, *B*, and *C* lie along the firm's expansion path, which is a curve that shows the cost-minimizing combination of inputs for every level of output. In the short run, when the quantity of machines is fixed, the firm can expand output from 75 bookcases per day to 100 bookcases per day at the lowest cost only by moving from point *B* to point *D* and increasing the number of workers from 60 to 110. In the long run, when it can increase the quantity of machines it uses, the firm can move from point *D* to point *C*, thereby reducing its total costs of producing 100 bookcases per day from $4,250 to $4,000.

The Expansion Path

We can use isoquants and isocost lines to examine what happens as a firm expands its level of output. Figure A.6 shows three isoquants for a firm that produces bookcases. The isocost lines are drawn under the assumption that the machines used in producing bookcases can be rented for $100 per day and the wage rate is $25 per day. The point where each isoquant is tangent to an isocost line determines the cost-minimizing combination of capital and labor for producing that level of output. For example, 10 machines and 40 workers is the cost-minimizing combination of inputs for producing 50 bookcases per day. The cost-minimizing points *A*, *B*, and *C* lie along the firm's **expansion path**, which is a curve that shows the cost-minimizing combination of inputs for every level of output.

An important point to note is that the expansion path represents the least-cost combination of inputs to produce a given level of output *in the long run*, when the firm is able to vary the levels of all of its inputs. We know, though, that in the short run, at least one input is fixed. We can use Figure A.6 to show that as the firm expands in the short run, its costs will be higher than in the long run. Suppose that the firm is currently at point *B*, using 15 machines and 60 workers to produce 75 bookcases per day. The firm wants to expand its output to 100 bookcases per day, but in the short run, it is unable to increase the quantity of machines it uses. Therefore, to expand output, it must hire more workers. The figure shows that in the short run, to produce 100 bookcases per day using 15 machines, the lowest costs it can attain are at point *D*, where it employs 110 workers. With a rental price of machines of $100 per day and a wage rate of $25 per day, in the short run, the firm will have total costs of $4,250 to produce 100 bookcases per day. In the long run, though, the firm can increase the number of machines it uses from 15 to 20 and reduce the number of workers from 110 to 80. This change allows it to move from point *D* to point *C* on its expansion path and to lower its total costs of producing 100 bookcases per day from $4,250 to $4,000. The firm's minimum total costs of production are lower in the long run than in the short run.

Expansion path A curve that shows a firm's cost-minimizing combination of inputs for every level of output.

Key Terms

Expansion path

Isocost line

Isoquant

Marginal rate of technical substitution (*MRTS*)

A Using Isoquants and Isocost Lines to Understand Production and Cost

LEARNING OBJECTIVE: Use isoquants and isocost lines to understand production and cost.

Visit www.myeconlab.com to complete these exercises online and get instant feedback.

Review Questions

A.1 What is an isoquant? What is the slope of an isoquant?

A.2 What is an isocost line? What is the slope of an isocost line?

A.3 How do firms choose the optimal combination of inputs?

Problems and Applications

A.4 Draw an isoquant–isocost line graph to illustrate the following situation: Jill Johnson can rent pizza ovens for $400 per week and hire workers for $200 per week. She is currently using 5 ovens and 10 workers to produce 20,000 pizzas per week and has total costs of $4,000. Make sure to label your graph to show the cost-minimizing input combination and the maximum quantity of labor and capital she can use with total costs of $4,000.

A.5 Use the following graph to answer the questions.

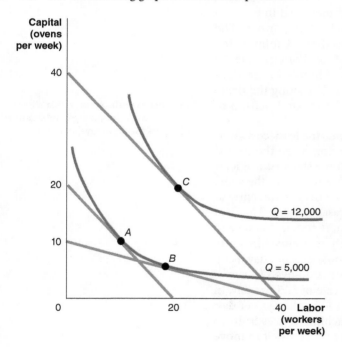

a. If the wage rate and the rental price of ovens are both $100 and total cost is $2,000, is the cost-minimizing point *A*, *B*, or *C*? Briefly explain.

b. If the wage rate is $25, the rental price of ovens is $100, and total cost is $1,000, is the cost-minimizing point *A*, *B*, or *C*? Briefly explain.

c. If the wage rate and the rental price of ovens are both $100 and total cost is $4,000, is the cost-minimizing point *A*, *B*, or *C*? Briefly explain.

A.6 **[Related to the** Making the Connection: **The Changing Input Mix in Walt Disney Film Animation]** During the eighteenth century, the American colonies had much

more land per farmer than did Europe. As a result, the price of labor in the colonies was much higher relative to the price of land than it was in Europe. Assume that Europe and the colonies had access to the same technology for producing food. Use an isoquant–isocost line graph to illustrate why the combination of land and labor used in producing food in the colonies would have been different from the combination used to produce food in Europe.

A.7 **[Related to** Solved Problem A.1**]** Consider the information in the following table for Jill Johnson's restaurant:

Marginal product of capital	4,000
Marginal product of labor	100
Wage rate	$10
Rental price of pizza ovens	$500

Briefly explain whether Jill is minimizing costs. If she is not minimizing costs, explain whether she should rent more ovens and hire fewer workers or rent fewer ovens and hire more workers.

A.8 **[Related to** Solved Problem A.1**]** Draw an isoquant–isocost line graph to illustrate the following situation: Jill Johnson can rent pizza ovens for $200 per week and hire workers for $100 per week. Currently, she is using 5 ovens and 10 workers to produce 20,000 pizzas per week and has total costs of $2,000. Jill's marginal rate of technical substitution (*MRTS*) equals −1. Explain why this means that she's not minimizing costs and what she could do to minimize costs.

A.9 Draw an isoquant–isocost line graph to illustrate the following situation and the change that occurs: Jill Johnson can rent pizza ovens for $2,000 per week and hire workers for $1,000 per week. Currently, she is using 5 ovens and 10 workers to produce 20,000 pizzas per week and has total costs of $20,000. Then Jill reorganizes the way things are done in her business and achieves positive technological change.

A.10 Use the following graph to answer the following questions about Jill Johnson's isoquant curve.

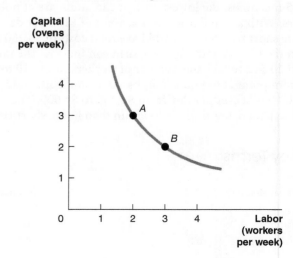

a. Which combination of inputs yields more output: combination A (3 ovens and 2 workers) or combination B (2 ovens and 3 workers)?

b. What will determine whether Jill selects A, B, or some other point along this isoquant curve?

c. Is the marginal rate of technical substitution ($MRTS$) greater at point A or point B?

A.11 Draw an isoquant–isocost line graph to illustrate the following situation: Jill Johnson can rent pizza ovens for $2,000 per week and hire workers for $1,000 per week. She can minimize the cost of producing 20,000 pizzas per week by using 5 ovens and 10 workers, at a total cost of $20,000. She can minimize the cost of producing 45,000 pizzas per week by using 10 ovens and 20 workers, at a total cost of $40,000. She can minimize the cost of producing 60,000 pizzas per week by using 15 ovens and 30 workers, at a total cost of $60,000. Draw Jill's long-run average cost curve and discuss its economies of scale and diseconomies of scale.

A.12 In Brazil, a grove of oranges is picked using 20 workers, ladders, and baskets. In Florida, a grove of oranges is picked using 1 worker and a machine that shakes the oranges off the trees and scoops up the fallen oranges. Using an isoquant–isocost line graph, illustrate why these two different methods are used to pick the same number of oranges per day in these two locations.

A.13 Jill Johnson is minimizing the costs of producing pizzas. The rental price of one of her ovens is $2,000 per week, and the wage rate is $600 per week. The marginal product of capital in her business is 12,000 pizzas. What must be the marginal product of her workers?

A.14 **[Related to the** Making the Connection**: Do National Football League Teams Behave Efficiently?]** If Cade Massey and Richard Thaler are correct, should the team that has the first pick in the draft keep the pick or trade it to another team for a lower pick? Briefly explain. Does the 2011 agreement that limits the salaries of drafted players affect your answer?

A.15 Swift Ellis, Inc. manufactures running shoes. The following graph illustrates the combination of capital and labor (point A) that minimizes the firm's cost of producing 5,000 pairs of shoes. Suppose both the wage rate and the rental price of machinery doubles.

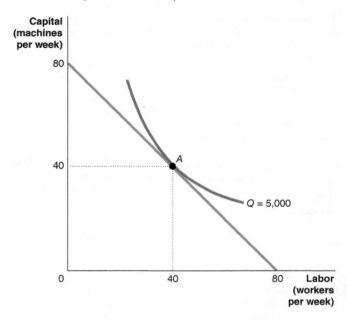

a. Draw a new isocost line to reflect this change in the wage rate and rental price of machinery.

b. Draw a new isoquant to show the combination of capital and labor that minimizes total cost given the increase in input prices. Label this combination point B.

c. Comparing point A to point B, can we be sure that at point B the firm will be using more or less labor? More or less capital? Briefly explain.

Glossary

Average fixed cost Fixed cost divided by the quantity of output produced.

Average product of labor The total output produced by a firm divided by the quantity of workers.

Average total cost Total cost divided by the quantity of output produced.

Average variable cost Variable cost divided by the quantity of output produced.

Constant returns to scale The situation in which a firm's long-run average costs remain unchanged as it increases output.

Diseconomies of scale The situation in which a firm's long-run average costs rise as the firm increases output.

Economies of scale The situation when a firm's long-run average costs fall as it increases the quantity of output it produces.

Explicit cost A cost that involves spending money.

Expansion path A curve that shows a firm's cost-minimizing combination of inputs for every level of output.

Fixed costs Costs that remain constant as output changes.

Isocost line All the combinations of two inputs, such as capital and labor, that have the same total cost.

Isoquant A curve that shows all the combinations of two inputs, such as capital and labor, that will produce the same level of output.

Law of diminishing returns The principle that, at some point, adding more of a variable input, such as labor, to the same amount of a fixed input, such as capital, will cause the marginal product of the variable input to decline.

Long run The period of time in which a firm can vary all its inputs, adopt new technology, and increase or decrease the size of its physical plant.

Long-run average cost curve A curve that shows the lowest cost at which a firm is able to produce a given quantity of output in the long run, when no inputs are fixed.

Marginal cost The additional cost to a firm of producing one more unit of a good or service.

Marginal product of labor The additional output a firm produces as a result of hiring one more worker.

Marginal rate of technical substitution (*MRTS*) The rate at which a firm is able to substitute one input for another while keeping the level of output constant.

Minimum efficient scale The level of output at which all economies of scale are exhausted.

Opportunity cost The highest-valued alternative that must be given up to engage in an activity.

Production function The relationship between the inputs employed by a firm and the maximum output it can produce with those inputs.

Short run The period of time during which at least one of a firm's inputs is fixed.

Technological change A change in the ability of a firm to produce a given level of output with a given quantity of inputs.

Technology The processes a firm uses to turn inputs into outputs of goods and services.

Total cost The cost of all the inputs a firm uses in production.

Variable costs Costs that change as output changes.

Credits

Firms in Perfectly Competitive Markets

Firms in Perfectly Competitive Markets

Chapter Outline and Learning Objectives

1 **Perfectly Competitive Markets**
Explain what a perfectly competitive market is and why a perfect competitor faces a horizontal demand curve.

2 **How a Firm Maximizes Profit in a Perfectly Competitive Market**
Explain how a firm maximizes profit in a perfectly competitive market.

3 **Illustrating Profit or Loss on the Cost Curve Graph**
Use graphs to show a firm's profit or loss.

4 **Deciding Whether to Produce or to Shut Down in the Short Run**
Explain why firms may shut down temporarily.

5 **"If Everyone Can Do It, You Can't Make Money at It": The Entry and Exit of Firms in the Long Run**
Explain how entry and exit ensure that perfectly competitive firms earn zero economic profit in the long run.

6 **Perfect Competition and Efficiency**
Explain how perfect competition leads to economic efficiency.

Perfect Competition in Farmers' Markets

In recent years, the demand for healthier foods has increased. For example, sales of organically grown food have increased at a rate of 20 percent per year. Because farmers' markets typically offer a wide selection of organically grown food, many people have begun buying their fruits and vegetables there. At these markets, local farmers come together at a fairground, a city plaza, or some other open space to sell their products directly to consumers. Many customers are like Tracy Stuntz, who shops at a farmers' market in Fresno, California: "My husband and I prefer to eat ... organically .... The farmer's market has ... produce you don't see [in] other places." Farmers hope that by selling in farmers' markets they can receive higher prices from consumers than they would receive from selling their produce to supermarkets.

In the United States, higher prices and higher profits led to a dramatic increase in the number of farmers' markets, from 1,774 in 1994 to 7,864 in 2012. More markets, though, means more competition for farmers selling their produce. The competition has forced down prices and reduced farmers' profits. As one farmer explained: "You have a certain amount of demand, and the more you spread out the demand, you're making less." Many farmers have found that the profits they earn from selling their produce in farmers' markets are no longer higher than what they earn selling to supermarkets.

The process of new firms entering a profitable market and driving down prices and profits is not unique to agriculture. Throughout the economy, entrepreneurs are continually introducing new products or new ways of selling products, which—when successful—enable them to earn economic profits in the short run. But in the long run, competition among firms forces prices to the level where they just cover the costs of production. This process of competition is at the heart of the market system and is the focus of this chapter.

Sources: Tracie Cone, "USDA: Number of Farmers Markets Up Due to Demand," *Associated Press*, August 3, 2012; Katie Zezima, "As Farmers' Markets Go Mainstream, Some Fear a Glut," *New York Times*, August 20, 2011; and United States Department of Agriculture, *Farmers Market Growth: 1994–2012*, August 3, 2012.

Economics in Your Life

Are You an Entrepreneur?

Were you an entrepreneur during your high school years? Perhaps you didn't have your own store, but you may have worked as a babysitter, or perhaps you mowed lawns for families in your neighborhood. While you may not think of these jobs as being small businesses, that is exactly what they are. How did you decide what price to charge for your services? You may have wanted to charge $25 per hour to babysit or mow lawns, but you probably charged much less. As you read the chapter, think about the competitive situation you faced as a teenage entrepreneur and try to determine why the prices received by most people who babysit and mow lawns are so low. You can check your answers against those we provide at the end of this chapter.

F armers' markets are an example of a *perfectly competitive* industry. Firms in perfectly competitive industries are unable to control the prices of the products they sell and are unable to earn an economic profit in the long run for two main reasons: Firms in these industries sell identical products, and it is easy for new firms to enter these industries. Studying how perfectly competitive industries operate is the best way to understand how markets answer the following fundamental economic questions:

- What goods and services will be produced?
- How will the goods and services be produced?
- Who will receive the goods and services produced?

In fact, though, most industries are not perfectly competitive. In most industries, firms do *not* produce identical products, and in some industries, it may be difficult for new firms to enter. There are thousands of industries in the United States. Although in some ways each industry is unique, industries share enough similarities that economists group them into four market structures. In particular, any industry has three key characteristics:

1. The number of firms in the industry
2. The similarity of the good or service produced by the firms in the industry
3. The ease with which new firms can enter the industry

Economists use these characteristics to classify industries into the four market structures listed in Table 1.

Many industries, including restaurants, clothing stores, and other retailers, have a large number of firms selling products that are differentiated, rather than identical, and fall into the category of *monopolistic competition*. Some industries, such as computers and automobiles, have only a few firms and are *oligopolies*. Finally, a few industries, such as the delivery of first-class mail by the U.S. Postal Service, have only one firm and are *monopolies*.

Table 1

The Four Market Structures

	Market Structure			
Characteristic	Perfect Competition	Monopolistic Competition	Oligopoly	Monopoly
Number of firms	Many	Many	Few	One
Type of product	Identical	Differentiated	Identical or differentiated	Unique
Ease of entry	High	High	Low	Entry blocked
Examples of industries	• Growing wheat • Growing apples	• Clothing stores • Restaurants	• Manufacturing computers • Manufacturing automobiles	• First-class mail delivery • Tap water

Perfectly Competitive Markets

1 LEARNING OBJECTIVE

Explain what a perfectly competitive market is and why a perfect competitor faces a horizontal demand curve.

Why are firms in a **perfectly competitive market** unable to control the prices of the goods they sell, and why are the owners of these firms unable to earn economic profits in the long run? We can begin our analysis by listing the three conditions that make a market perfectly competitive:

1. There must be many buyers and many firms, all of which are small relative to the market.
2. All firms in the market must sell identical products.
3. There must be no barriers to new firms entering the market.

Perfectly competitive market A market that meets the conditions of (1) many buyers and sellers, (2) all firms selling identical products, and (3) no barriers to new firms entering the market.

All three of these conditions hold in markets for agricultural products. For example, no single consumer or producer of apples buys or sells more than a tiny fraction of the total apple crop. The apples sold by each apple grower are identical, and there are no barriers to a new firm entering the apple market by purchasing land and planting apple trees. As we will see, it is the existence of many firms, all selling the same good, that keeps any single apple farmer from affecting the price of apples.

Although the market for apples meets the conditions for perfect competition, the markets for most goods and services do not. In particular, the second and third conditions are very restrictive. In most markets that have many buyers and sellers, firms do not sell identical products. For example, not all restaurant meals are the same, nor is all women's clothing the same. In this chapter, we concentrate on perfectly competitive markets so we can use them as a benchmark to analyze how firms behave when they face the maximum possible competition.

A Perfectly Competitive Firm Cannot Affect the Market Price

Prices in perfectly competitive markets are determined by the interaction of demand and supply for the good or service. The actions of any single consumer or any single firm have no effect on the market price. Consumers and firms have to accept the market price if they want to buy and sell in a perfectly competitive market.

Because a firm in a perfectly competitive market is very small relative to the market and because it is selling exactly the same product as every other firm, it can sell as much as it wants without having to lower its price. If a perfectly competitive firm tries to raise its price, it won't sell anything at all because consumers will switch to buying the product from the firm's competitors. Therefore, the firm will be a **price taker** and will have to charge the same price as every other firm in the market. Although we don't usually think of firms as being too small to affect the market price, consumers are often in the position of being price takers. For instance, suppose your local supermarket is selling bread for $2.50 per loaf. You can load up your shopping cart with 10 loaves of bread, and the supermarket will gladly sell them all to you for $2.50 per loaf. But if you go to the cashier and offer to buy the bread for $2.49 per loaf, he or she will not sell it to you at that price. As a buyer, you are too small relative to the bread market to have any effect on the equilibrium price. Whether you leave the supermarket and buy no bread or you buy 10 loaves, you are unable to change the market price of bread by even 1 cent.

Price taker A buyer or seller that is unable to affect the market price.

The situation you face as a bread buyer is the same one a wheat farmer faces as a wheat seller. In 2013, about 150,000 farmers grew wheat in the United States. The market price of wheat is determined not by any individual wheat farmer but by the interaction of all the buyers and all the sellers in the wheat market. If any one wheat farmer has the best crop the farmer has ever had, or if any one wheat farmer stops growing wheat altogether, the market price of wheat will not be affected *because the market supply curve for wheat will not shift enough to change the equilibrium price by even 1 cent.*

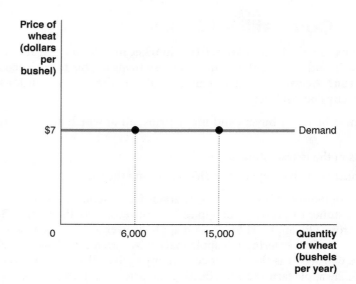

Figure 1

A Perfectly Competitive Firm Faces a Horizontal Demand Curve

A firm in a perfectly competitive market is selling exactly the same product as many other firms. Therefore, it can sell as much as it wants at the current market price, but it cannot sell anything at all if it raises the price by even 1 cent. As a result, the demand curve for a perfectly competitive firm's output is a horizontal line. In the figure, whether the wheat farmer sells 6,000 bushels per year or 15,000 bushels has no effect on the market price of $7.

The Demand Curve for the Output of a Perfectly Competitive Firm

Suppose Bill Parker grows wheat on a 250-acre farm in Washington State. Farmer Parker is selling wheat in a perfectly competitive market, so he is a price taker. Because he can sell as much wheat as he chooses at the market price—but can't sell any wheat at all at a higher price—the demand curve for his wheat has an unusual shape: It is horizontal, as shown in Figure 1. With a horizontal demand curve, Farmer Parker must accept the market price, which in this case is $7 per bushel. Whether Farmer Parker sells 6,000 bushels per year or 15,000 has no effect on the market price.

The demand curve for Farmer Parker's wheat is very different from the market demand curve for wheat. Panel (a) of Figure 2 shows the market for wheat. The demand curve in panel (a) is the *market demand curve for wheat* and has the normal downward slope. Panel (b) of Figure 2 shows the demand curve for Farmer Parker's wheat, which is a horizontal line. By viewing these graphs side by side, you can see that the price Farmer Parker receives for his wheat in panel (b) is determined by the interaction of

Don't Let This Happen to You

Don't Confuse the Demand Curve for Farmer Parker's Wheat with the Market Demand Curve for Wheat

The demand curve for wheat has the normal downward-sloping shape. If the price of wheat goes up, the quantity of wheat demanded goes down, and if the price of wheat goes down, the quantity of wheat demanded goes up. But the demand curve for the output of a single wheat farmer is *not* downward sloping: It is a horizontal line. If an individual wheat farmer tries to increase the price he charges for his wheat, the quantity demanded falls to zero because buyers will purchase from one of the other 150,000 wheat farmers. But any one farmer can sell as much wheat as the farmer can produce without needing to cut the price. Both of these features of this market hold because each

wheat farmer is very small relative to the overall market for wheat.

When we draw graphs of the wheat market, we usually show the market equilibrium quantity in millions or billions of bushels. When we draw graphs of the demand for wheat produced by one farmer, we usually show the quantity produced in smaller units, such as thousands of bushels. It is important to remember this difference in scale when interpreting these graphs.

Finally, it is not just wheat farmers who have horizontal demand curves for their products; any firm in a perfectly competitive market faces a horizontal demand curve.

Your Turn: Test your understanding by doing related problem 1.6 at the end of this chapter.

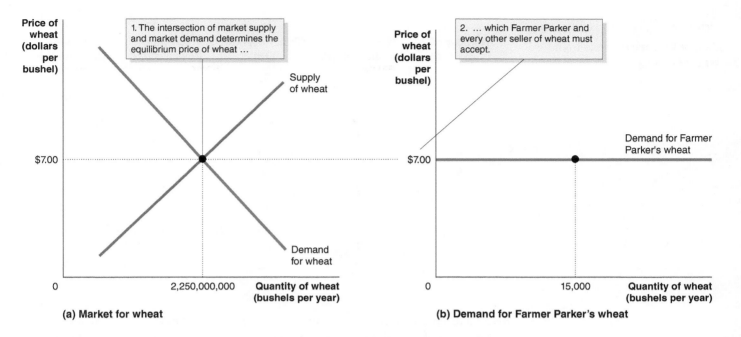

Figure 2 The Market Demand for Wheat versus the Demand for One Farmer's Wheat

In a perfectly competitive market, price is determined by the intersection of market demand and market supply. In panel (a), the demand and supply curves for wheat intersect at a price of $7 per bushel. An individual wheat farmer like Farmer Parker cannot affect the market price for wheat. Therefore, as panel (b) shows, the demand curve for Farmer Parker's wheat is a horizontal line. To understand this figure, it is important to notice that the scales on the horizontal axes in the two panels are very different. In panel (a), the equilibrium quantity of wheat is 2.25 *billion* bushels, and in panel (b), Farmer Parker is producing only 15,000 bushels of wheat.

all sellers and all buyers of wheat in the wheat market in panel (a). Notice, however, that the scales on the horizontal axes in the two panels are very different. In panel (a), the equilibrium quantity of wheat is 2.25 *billion* bushels. In panel (b), Farmer Parker is producing only 15,000 bushels, or less than 0.001 percent of market output. We need to use different scales in the two panels so we can display both of them on one page. Keep in mind this key point: Farmer Parker's output of wheat is very small relative to the total market output.

How a Firm Maximizes Profit in a Perfectly Competitive Market

We have seen that Farmer Parker cannot control the price of his wheat. In this situation, how does he decide how much wheat to produce? We assume that Farmer Parker's objective is to maximize profit. This assumption is reasonable for most firms, most of the time. **Profit** is the difference between total revenue (*TR*) and total cost (*TC*):

$$\text{Profit} = TR - TC.$$

To maximize his profit, Farmer Parker should produce the quantity of wheat where the difference between the total revenue he receives and his total cost is as large as possible.

Revenue for a Firm in a Perfectly Competitive Market

To understand how Farmer Parker maximizes profit, let's first consider his revenue. To keep the numbers simple, we will assume that he owns a very small farm and produces at most 10 bushels of wheat per year. Table 2 shows the revenue Farmer Parker will earn from selling various quantities of wheat if the market price for wheat is $7.

The third column in Table 2 shows that Farmer Parker's *total revenue* rises by $7 for every additional bushel he sells because he can sell as many bushels as he wants at the market price of $7 per bushel. The fourth and fifth columns in the table show Farmer Parker's *average revenue* and *marginal revenue* from selling wheat. His **average revenue (AR)** equals

2 LEARNING OBJECTIVE

Explain how a firm maximizes profit in a perfectly competitive market.

Profit Total revenue minus total cost.

Average revenue (AR) Total revenue divided by the quantity of the product sold.

Table 2

Farmer Parker's Revenue from Wheat Farming

(1) Number of Bushels (Q)	(2) Market Price (per bushel) (P)	(3) Total Revenue (TR)	(4) Average Revenue (AR)	(5) Marginal Revenue (MR)
0	$7	$0	—	—
1	7	7	$7	$7
2	7	14	7	7
3	7	21	7	7
4	7	28	7	7
5	7	35	7	7
6	7	42	7	7
7	7	49	7	7
8	7	56	7	7
9	7	63	7	7
10	7	70	7	7

his total revenue divided by the quantity of bushels he sells. For example, if he sells 5 bushels for a total of $35, his average revenue is $35/5 = $7. Notice that his average revenue is also equal to the market price of $7. In fact, for any level of output, a firm's average revenue is always equal to the market price. This equality holds because total revenue equals price times quantity ($TR = P \times Q$), and average revenue equals total revenue divided by quantity ($AR = TR/Q$). So, $AR = TR/Q = (P \times Q)/Q = P$.

Marginal revenue (MR) The change in total revenue from selling one more unit of a product.

Farmer Parker's **marginal revenue (MR)** is the change in his total revenue from selling one more bushel:

$$\text{Marginal revenue} = \frac{\text{Change in total revenue}}{\text{Change in quantity}}, \text{ or } MR = \frac{\Delta TR}{\Delta Q}.$$

Each additional bushel Farmer Parker sells always adds $7 to his total revenue, so his marginal revenue is $7. Farmer Parker's marginal revenue is $7 per bushel because he is selling wheat in a perfectly competitive market and can sell as much as he wants at the market price. In fact, Farmer Parker's marginal revenue and average revenue are both equal to the market price. This is an important point: *For a firm in a perfectly competitive market, price is equal to both average revenue and marginal revenue.*

Determining the Profit-Maximizing Level of Output

To determine how Farmer Parker can maximize profit, we have to consider his costs as well as his revenue. A wheat farmer has many costs, including the cost of seed and fertilizer, as well as the wages of farm workers. In Table 3, we bring together the revenue data from Table 2 with cost data for Farmer Parker's farm. A firm's *marginal cost* is the increase in total cost resulting from producing another unit of output.

We calculate profit in the fourth column by subtracting total cost in the third column from total revenue in the second column. The fourth column shows that as long as Farmer Parker produces between 3 and 9 bushels of wheat, he will earn a profit. His maximum profit is $13.50, which he will earn by producing 7 bushels of wheat. Because Farmer Parker wants to maximize his profit, we would expect him to produce 7 bushels of wheat. Producing more than 7 bushels reduces his profit. For example, if he produces 8 bushels of wheat, his profit will decline from $13.50 to $11.50. The values for marginal cost given in the last column of the table help us understand why Farmer Parker's profits will decline if he produces more than 7 bushels of wheat: After the seventh bushel of wheat, rising marginal cost causes Farmer Parker's profits to decline.

In fact, comparing the marginal cost and marginal revenue at each level of output is an alternative method of calculating Farmer Parker's profit. We illustrate the two

(1) Quantity (bushels) (Q)	(2) Total Revenue (TR)	(3) Total Cost (TC)	(4) Profit (TR – TC)	(5) Marginal Revenue (MR)	(6) Marginal Cost (MC)
0	$0.00	$10.00	–$10.00	—	—
1	7.00	14.00	–7.00	$7.00	$4.00
2	14.00	16.50	–2.50	7.00	2.50
3	21.00	18.50	2.50	7.00	2.00
4	28.00	21.00	7.00	7.00	2.50
5	35.00	24.50	10.50	7.00	3.50
6	42.00	29.00	13.00	7.00	4.50
7	49.00	35.50	13.50	7.00	6.50
8	56.00	44.50	11.50	7.00	9.00
9	63.00	56.50	6.50	7.00	12.00
10	70.00	72.00	–2.00	7.00	15.50

Table 3

Farmer Parker's Profit from Wheat Farming

methods of calculating profit in Figure 3. We show the total revenue and total cost approach in panel (a) and the marginal revenue and marginal cost approach in panel (b). Total revenue is a straight line on the graph in panel (a) because total revenue increases at a constant rate of $7 for each additional bushel sold. Farmer Parker's profit is maximized when the vertical distance between the line representing total revenue and the total cost curve is as large as possible. Just as we saw in Table 3, his maximum profit occurs at an output of 7 bushels.

The last two columns of Table 3 show the marginal revenue (MR) Farmer Parker receives from selling another bushel of wheat and his marginal cost (MC) of producing another bushel of wheat. Panel (b) of Figure 3 is a graph of Farmer Parker's marginal revenue and marginal cost. Because marginal revenue is always equal to $7, it is

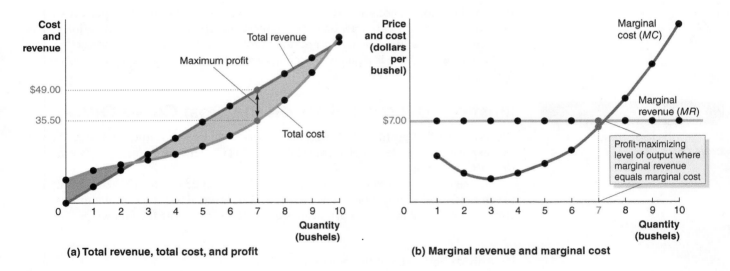

(a) Total revenue, total cost, and profit

(b) Marginal revenue and marginal cost

Figure 3 **The Profit-Maximizing Level of Output**

In panel (a), Farmer Parker maximizes his profit where the vertical distance between total revenue and total cost is the largest, which occurs at an output of 7 bushels. Panel (b) shows that Farmer Parker's marginal revenue (MR) is equal to a constant $7 per bushel. Farmer Parker maximizes profit by producing wheat up to the point where the marginal revenue of the last bushel produced is equal to its marginal cost, or MR = MC. In this case, at no level of output

does marginal revenue exactly equal marginal cost. The closest Farmer Parker can come is to produce 7 bushels of wheat. He will not want to continue to produce once marginal cost is greater than marginal revenue because that would reduce his profits. Panels (a) and (b) show alternative ways of thinking about how Farmer Parker can determine the profit-maximizing quantity of wheat to produce.

a horizontal line at the market price. We have already seen that the demand curve for a perfectly competitive firm is also a horizontal line at the market price. *Therefore, the marginal revenue curve for a perfectly competitive firm is the same as its demand curve.* Farmer Parker's marginal cost of producing wheat first falls and then rises.

We know from panel (a) that profit is at a maximum at 7 bushels of wheat. In panel (b), profit is also at a maximum at 7 bushels of wheat. To understand why profit is maximized at the level of output where marginal revenue equals marginal cost, remember a key economic principle: *Optimal decisions are made at the margin.* Firms use this principle to decide the quantity of a good to produce. For example, in deciding how much wheat to produce, Farmer Parker needs to compare the marginal revenue he earns from selling another bushel of wheat to the marginal cost of producing that bushel. The difference between the marginal revenue and the marginal cost is the additional profit (or loss) from producing one more bushel. As long as marginal revenue is greater than marginal cost, Farmer Parker's profits are increasing, and he will want to expand production. For example, he will not stop producing at 6 bushels of wheat because producing and selling the seventh bushel adds $7.00 to his revenue but only $6.50 to his cost, so his profit increases by $0.50. He wants to continue producing until the marginal revenue he receives from selling another bushel is equal to the marginal cost of producing it. At that level of output, he will make no *additional* profit by selling another bushel, so he will have maximized his profit.

By inspecting Table 3, we can see that there is no level of output at which marginal revenue exactly equals marginal cost. The closest Farmer Parker can come is to produce 7 bushels of wheat. He will not want to produce additional wheat once marginal cost is greater than marginal revenue because that would reduce his profits. For example, the eighth bushel of wheat adds $9.00 to his cost but only $7.00 to his revenue, so producing the eighth bushel *reduces* his profit by $2.00.

From the information in Table 3 and Figure 3, we can draw the following conclusions:

1. The profit-maximizing level of output is where the difference between total revenue and total cost is the greatest.

2. The profit-maximizing level of output is also where marginal revenue equals marginal cost, or $MR = MC$.

Both of these conclusions are true for any firm, whether or not it is in a perfectly competitive industry. We can draw one other conclusion about profit maximization that is true only of firms in perfectly competitive industries: For a firm in a perfectly competitive industry, price is equal to marginal revenue, or $P = MR$. So we can restate the $MR = MC$ condition as $P = MC$.

3 LEARNING OBJECTIVE

Use graphs to show a firm's profit or loss.

Illustrating Profit or Loss on the Cost Curve Graph

We have seen that profit is the difference between total revenue and total cost. We can also express profit in terms of *average total cost* (*ATC*). This allows us to show profit on the cost curve graph.

To begin, we need to work through several steps to determine the relationship between profit and average total cost. Because profit is equal to total revenue minus total cost (*TC*) and total revenue is price times quantity, we can write the following:

$$\text{Profit} = (P \times Q) - TC.$$

If we divide both sides of this equation by Q, we have

$$\frac{\text{Profit}}{Q} = \frac{(P \times Q)}{Q} - \frac{TC}{Q}$$

or

$$\frac{\text{Profit}}{Q} = P - ATC,$$

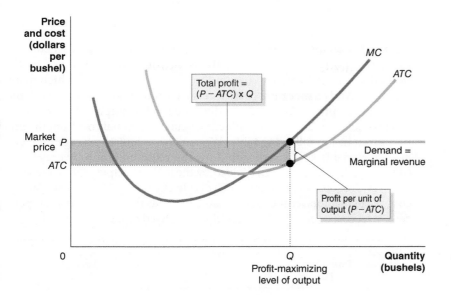

Figure 4

The Area of Maximum Profit

A firm maximizes profit at the level of output at which marginal revenue equals marginal cost. The difference between price and average total cost equals profit per unit of output. Total profit equals profit per unit multiplied by the number of units produced. Total profit is represented by the area of the green-shaded rectangle, which has a height equal to $(P - ATC)$ and a width equal to Q.

because TC/Q equals ATC. This equation tells us that profit per unit (or average profit) equals price minus average total cost. Finally, we obtain the equation for the relationship between total profit and average total cost by multiplying by Q:

$$\text{Profit} = (P - ATC) \times Q.$$

This equation tells us that a firm's total profit is equal to the difference between price and average total cost multiplied by the quantity produced.

Showing a Profit on the Graph

Figure 4 shows the relationship between a firm's average total cost and its marginal cost. In this figure, we also show the firm's marginal revenue curve (which is the same as its demand curve) and the area representing total profit. Using the relationship between profit and average total cost that we just determined, we can say that the area representing total profit has a height equal to $(P - ATC)$ and a base equal to Q. This area is shown by the green-shaded rectangle.

Solved Problem 3

Determining Profit-Maximizing Price and Quantity

Suppose that Andy sells basketballs in the perfectly competitive basketball market. His output per day and his costs are as follows:

Output per Day	Total Cost
0	$10.00
1	20.50
2	24.50
3	28.50
4	34.00
5	43.00
6	55.50
7	72.00
8	93.00
9	119.00

a. Suppose the current equilibrium price in the basketball market is $12.50. To maximize profit, how many basketballs will Andy produce, what price will he charge, and how much profit (or loss) will he make? Draw a graph to illustrate your answer. Your graph should be labeled clearly and should include Andy's demand, ATC, AVC, MC, and MR curves; the price he is charging; the quantity he is producing; and the area representing his profit (or loss).

b. Suppose the equilibrium price of basketballs falls to $6.00. Now how many basketballs will Andy produce, what price will he charge, and how much profit (or loss) will he make? Draw a graph to illustrate this situation, using the instructions in part (a).

Solving the Problem

Step 1: **Review the chapter material.** This problem is about using cost curve graphs to analyze perfectly competitive firms, so you may want to review the section "Illustrating Profit or Loss on the Cost Curve Graph," which begins on.

Step 2: **Calculate Andy's marginal cost, average total cost, and average variable cost.** To maximize profit, Andy will produce the level of output where marginal revenue is equal to marginal cost. We can calculate marginal cost from the information given in the following table. We can also calculate average total cost and average variable cost in order to draw the required graph. Average total cost (ATC) equals total cost (TC) divided by the level of output (Q). Average variable cost (AVC) equals variable cost (VC) divided by output (Q). To calculate variable cost, recall that total cost equals variable cost plus fixed cost. When output equals zero, total cost equals fixed cost. In this case, fixed cost equals $10.00.

Output per Day (Q)	Total Cost (TC)	Fixed Cost (FC)	Variable Cost (VC)	Average Total Cost (ATC)	Average Variable Cost (AVC)	Marginal Cost (MC)
0	$10.00	$10.00	$0.00	—	—	—
1	20.50	10.00	10.50	$20.50	$10.50	$10.50
2	24.50	10.00	14.50	12.25	7.25	4.00
3	28.00	10.00	18.00	9.33	6.00	3.50
4	34.00	10.00	24.00	8.50	6.00	6.00
5	43.00	10.00	33.00	8.60	6.60	9.00
6	55.50	10.00	45.50	9.25	7.58	12.50
7	72.00	10.00	62.00	10.29	8.86	16.50
8	93.00	10.00	83.00	11.63	10.38	21.00
9	119.00	10.00	109.00	13.22	12.11	26.00

Step 3: **Use the information from the table in Step 2 to calculate how many basketballs Andy will produce, what price he will charge, and how much profit he will earn if the market price of basketballs is $12.50.** Andy's marginal revenue is equal to the market price of $12.50. Marginal revenue equals marginal cost when Andy produces 6 basketballs per day. So, Andy will produce 6 basketballs per day and charge a price of $12.50 per basketball. Andy's profit is equal to his total revenue minus his total costs. His total revenue equals the 6 basketballs he sells multiplied by the $12.50 price, or $75.00. So, his profit equals: $75.00 − $55.50 = $19.50.

Step 4: **Use the information from the table in Step 2 to illustrate your answer to part (a) with a graph.**

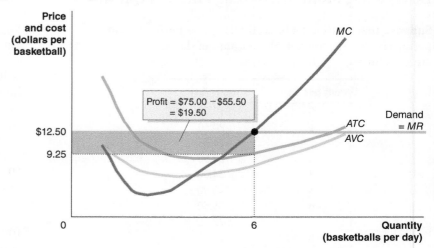

Step 5: **Calculate how many basketballs Andy will produce, what price he will charge, and how much profit he will earn when the market price of basketballs is $6.00.** Referring to the table in Step 2, we can see that marginal revenue equals marginal cost when Andy produces 4 basketballs per day. He charges the market price of $6.00 per basketball. His total revenue is only $24.00, while his total costs are $34.00, so he will have a loss of $10.00. (Can we be sure that Andy will continue to produce even though he is operating at a loss? We answer this question in the next section.)

Step 6: **Illustrate your answer to part (b) with a graph.**

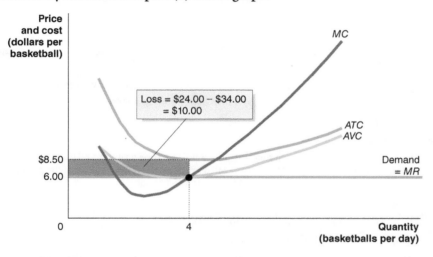

Your Turn: For more practice, do related problems 3.3 and 3.4 at the end of this chapter.

Don't Let This Happen to You

Remember That Firms Maximize Their Total Profit, Not Their Profit per Unit

A student examines the following graph and argues: "I believe that a firm will want to produce at Q_1, not Q_2. At Q_1, the distance between price and average total cost is the greatest. So at Q_1, the firm will be maximizing its profit per unit." Briefly explain whether you agree with the student's argument.

The student's argument is incorrect because firms are interested in maximizing their *total* profit, not their profit per unit. We know that profit is not maximized at Q_1 because at that level of output, marginal revenue is greater than marginal cost. A firm can always increase its profit by producing any unit that adds more to its revenue than it does to its costs. Only when the firm has expanded production to Q_2 will it have produced every unit for which marginal revenue is greater than marginal cost. At that level of output, it will have maximized profit.

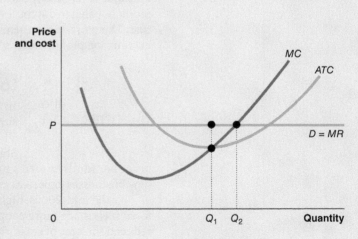

Your Turn: Test your understanding by doing related problem 3.5 at the end of this chapter.

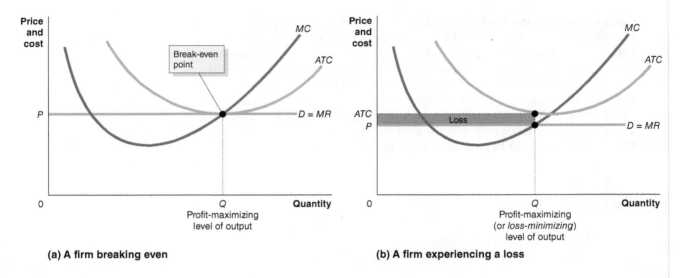

(a) A firm breaking even

(b) A firm experiencing a loss

Figure 5 A Firm Breaking Even and a Firm Experiencing a Loss

In panel (a), price equals average total cost, and the firm breaks even because its total revenue will be equal to its total cost. In this situation, the firm makes zero economic profit.

In panel (b), price is below average total cost, and the firm experiences a loss. The loss is represented by the area of the red-shaded rectangle, which has a height equal to $(ATC - P)$ and a width equal to Q.

Illustrating When a Firm Is Breaking Even or Operating at a Loss

We have already seen that to maximize profit, a firm produces the level of output where marginal revenue equals marginal cost. But will the firm actually make a profit at that level of output? It depends on the relationship of price to average total cost. There are three possibilities:

1. $P > ATC$, which means the firm makes a profit.
2. $P = ATC$, which means the firm *breaks even* (its total cost equals its total revenue).
3. $P < ATC$, which means the firm experiences a loss.

Figure 4 shows the first possibility, where the firm makes a profit. Panels (a) and (b) of Figure 5 show the situations where a firm breaks even or suffers a loss. In panel (a) of Figure 5, at the level of output at which $MR = MC$, price is equal to average total cost. Therefore, total revenue is equal to total cost, and the firm will break even, making zero economic profit. In panel (b), at the level of output at which $MR = MC$, price is less than average total cost. Therefore, total revenue is less than total cost, and the firm suffers a loss. In this case, maximizing profit amounts to *minimizing* loss.

Making the Connection

Losing Money in the Solar Panel Industry

In a market system, a good or service becomes available to consumers only if an entrepreneur brings the product to market. Thousands of new businesses open every week in the United States. Each new business represents an entrepreneur risking his or her funds to earn a profit. Of course, there are no guarantees of success, and many new businesses experience losses rather than earn the profits their owners hoped for.

By the mid-2000s, high oil prices and concern over the pollution caused by burning fossil fuels made more people become interested in solar energy. Technological advances reduced the cost of solar photovoltaic cells used in solar panels. In addition, households installing a solar energy system could receive a federal tax credit equal to 30 percent of the cost of the system. For several years, falling costs and increased demand led entrepreneurs in the United States to start new firms manufacturing solar panels. By 2009, though, large imports of solar panels produced by Chinese firms were driving down the market price. As panel (a) in the following figure shows, the price of solar panels, measured as dollars per watt of power produced, declined by three quarters, from $2.00 per watt in 2009 to $0.50 per watt in 2013.

Panel (b) shows the situation a typical U.S. firm producing solar panels faced. The price of $0.50 was below these firms' average total cost of producing solar panels, so the firms began to suffer losses. U.S. firms argued that Chinese firms were able to sell at low prices because they were receiving subsidies from the Chinese government, which are not allowed under international trade agreements. The U.S. government imposed a tariff of 30 percent on imports of solar panels from China. Most environmentalists opposed the tariff, arguing that if it resulted in higher prices for solar panels, fewer people would convert their homes to use solar power to generate electricity. Some U.S. firms also opposed the tariff because they use solar panels in products they export, which meant the tariff would raise their production costs. In 2013, however, the tariff did not seem to be having much effect on the U.S. market because Chinese imports were largely replaced by imports from Taiwan and South Korea. One energy analyst argued: "The economics of today, and supply and demand of today, aren't going to change because of [the tariff]."

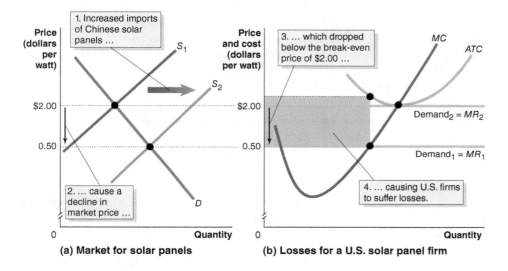

(a) Market for solar panels   **(b) Losses for a U.S. solar panel firm**

Why didn't the U.S. firms producing solar panels just raise the price they charged to the level they needed to break even? We have already seen that any firm that tries to raise the price of its product above the market price loses customers to competing firms. What will happen to the U.S. solar panel industry in the long run is unclear, but by 2013 a number of U.S. solar panel firms had gone out of business. The entrepreneurs who had started those businesses lost most of their investments.

Sources: Keith Bradsher, "U.S. and Europe Prepare to Settle Chinese Solar Panel Cases," *New York Times*, May 20, 2013; "Chinese Solar Imports Drop but Prices Continue to Fall," cleantechnica.com, January 22, 2013; and Diane Cardwell, "Solar Tariffs Upheld, but May Not Help in U.S.," *New York Times*, November 7, 2012.

Your Turn: Test your understanding by doing related problem 3.7 at the end of this chapter.

Deciding Whether to Produce or to Shut Down in the Short Run

4 LEARNING OBJECTIVE

Explain why firms may shut down temporarily.

In panel (b) of Figure 5, we assumed that the firm would continue to produce even though it was operating at a loss. In the short run, a firm experiencing a loss has two choices:

1. Continue to produce
2. Stop production by shutting down temporarily

In many cases, a firm experiencing a loss will consider stopping production temporarily. Even during a temporary shutdown, however, a firm must still pay its fixed costs. For example, if the firm has signed a lease for its building, the landlord will expect to receive a monthly rent payment, even if the firm is not producing anything that month. Therefore, if a firm does not produce, it will suffer a loss equal to its fixed costs. This loss is the maximum the firm will accept. The firm will shut down if producing would cause it to lose an amount greater than its fixed costs.

A firm can reduce its loss below the amount of its total fixed cost by continuing to produce, provided that the total revenue it receives is greater than its variable cost. A firm can use the revenue over and above variable cost to cover part of its fixed cost. In this case, a firm will have a smaller loss by continuing to produce than if it shuts down.

Sunk cost A cost that has already been paid and cannot be recovered.

In analyzing the firm's decision to shut down, we are assuming that its fixed costs are *sunk costs*. Remember that a **sunk cost** is a cost that has already been paid and cannot be recovered. We assume, as is usually the case, that the firm cannot recover its fixed costs by shutting down. For example, if a farmer has taken out a loan to buy land, the farmer is legally required to make the monthly loan payment whether he grows any wheat that season or not. The farmer has to spend those funds and cannot get them back, *so the farmer should treat his sunk costs as irrelevant to his short-run decision making*. For any firm, whether total revenue is greater or less than *variable costs* is the key to deciding whether to shut down or to continue producing in the short run. As long as a firm's total revenue is greater than its variable costs, it should continue to produce no matter how large or small its fixed costs are.

Solved Problem 4

When to Pull the Plug on a Movie

In the summer of 2013, Walt Disney released *The Lone Ranger*, starring Johnny Depp and produced by Jerry Bruckheimer. The film bombed at the box office: Worldwide, it earned about $245 million in revenue, well below the $375 million it cost to produce and market. Before Disney completed the film, executives became concerned that it might not be successful. They were disappointed in the early work on the film and temporarily stopped production. According to media reports, Disney executives took several factors into account as they considered whether to continue with production: Depp and Bruckheimer had made the very successful *Pirates of the Caribbean* for the studio; Depp and Bruckheimer agreed to accept smaller salaries if Disney agreed to finish the film; and Disney had already spent tens of millions of dollars on the film. How should Disney have decided whether to finish *The Lone Ranger* and release it to theaters? What role should the money Disney executives had already spent on the film have played in their decision?

Solving the Problem

Step 1: **Review the chapter material.** This problem is about the role of sunk costs in business decision making, so you may want to review the section "Deciding Whether to Produce or to Shut Down in the Short Run."

Step 2: **Use the concept of sunk costs to analyze Disney's decision about whether to finish the film.** In this case, Disney was not considering whether to shut down the company but whether to shut down production of this particular film. Disney had already invested millions of dollars in *The Lone Ranger* at the time they were considering whether to finish the film. It is tempting to argue that unless Disney completed the film, these millions of dollars would be lost. It is important to see, however, that the millions were a sunk cost: Whether Disney shut down the film or finished it and released it to theaters, the company would not be able to get back what it had already invested. Therefore, the millions were irrelevant to Disney's decision. Instead, Disney should have made the decision based on comparing the additional cost of completing and releasing the film to the revenue the film was expected to earn. In other words, Disney should have completed the film if marginal revenue was expected to be greater than marginal cost, and it should have shut down the film if marginal cost was expected to be greater than marginal revenue.

Although Disney knew the marginal cost of completing and releasing the film, it had to estimate the marginal revenue based on its forecasts of ticket sales and later sales of DVDs and streaming video. Disney decided to finish the film. The additional cost to complete the film was more than $300 million, but it earned only about $245 million at the box office. With hindsight, Disney made the wrong decision, but on the basis of the past success of the *Pirates of the Caribbean* films Depp and Bruckheimer made together, Disney overestimated ticket sales.

Sources: Lucas Shaw, "'Lone Ranger' Fallout: Jerry Bruckheimer May Lose Final Cut on 'Pirates 5,'" Reuters, August 7, 2013; Brooks Barnes, "Masked Lawman Stumbles at the Gate," *New York Times*, July 7, 2013; and Mike Fleming, Jr., "Shocker! Disney Halts 'Lone Ranger' with Johnny Depp and Gore Verbinski," www.dealince.com, August 12, 2011.

Your Turn: Test your understanding by doing related problems 4.8 and 4.9 at the end of this chapter.

One option not available to a firm with losses in a perfectly competitive market is to raise its price. If the firm did raise its price, it would lose all its customers, and its sales would drop to zero. For example, during the past 15 years, the price of wheat has typically been high enough for a typical wheat farmer in the United States to at least break even. But in 2004, the price of wheat was $3.16 per bushel. At that price, the typical U.S. wheat farmer lost $9,500. At a price of about $4.25 per bushel, the typical wheat farmer would have broken even. But any wheat farmer who tried to raise his price to $4.25 per bushel would have seen his sales quickly disappear because buyers could purchase all the wheat they wanted at $3.16 per bushel from the thousands of other wheat farmers.

The Supply Curve of a Firm in the Short Run

The supply curve for a firm tells us how many units of a product the firm is willing to sell at any given price. Notice that the marginal cost curve for a firm in a perfectly competitive market tells us the same thing. The firm will produce at the level of output where $MR = MC$. Because price equals marginal revenue for a firm in a perfectly competitive market, the firm will produce where $P = MC$. For any given price, we can determine from the marginal cost curve the quantity of output the firm will supply. *Therefore, a perfectly competitive firm's marginal cost curve is also its supply curve.* There is, however, an important qualification to this fact. We have seen that if a firm is experiencing a loss, it will shut down if its total revenue is less than its variable cost:

$$\text{Total revenue} < \text{Variable cost},$$

or, in symbols:

$$(P \times Q) < VC.$$

If we divide both sides by Q, we have the result that the firm will shut down if

$$P < AVC.$$

If the price drops below average variable cost, the firm will have a smaller loss if it shuts down and produces no output. *So, the firm's marginal cost curve is its supply curve only for prices at or above average variable cost.*

The marginal cost curve intersects the average variable cost where the average variable cost curve is at its minimum point. Therefore, as shown in Figure 6, the firm's supply curve is its marginal cost curve above the minimum point of the average variable cost curve. For prices below minimum average variable cost (P_{MIN}), the firm will shut down, and its output will drop to zero. The minimum point on the average variable cost curve is called

Figure 6

The Firm's Short-Run Supply Curve

Because price equals marginal revenue for a firm in a perfectly competitive market, the firm will produce where $P = MC$. For any given price, we can determine the quantity of output the firm will supply from the marginal cost curve, so the marginal cost curve is the firm's supply curve. But the firm will shut down if the price falls below average variable cost. The marginal cost curve crosses the average variable cost at the firm's shutdown point at the output level Q_{SD}. For prices below P_{MIN}, the supply curve is a vertical line along the price axis, which shows that the firm will supply zero output at those prices. The red line is the firm's short-run supply curve.

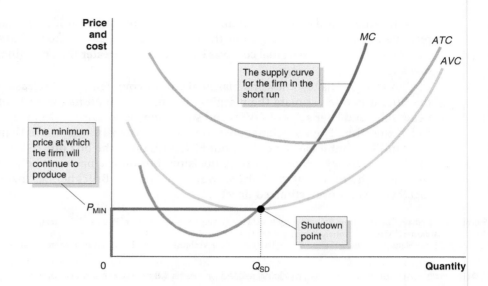

Shutdown point The minimum point on a firm's average variable cost curve; if the price falls below this point, the firm shuts down production in the short run.

the **shutdown point**, and it occurs at the output level Q_{SD}. The dark red line in Figure 6 shows the supply curve for the firm in the short run.

The Market Supply Curve in a Perfectly Competitive Industry

The market demand curve is determined by adding up the quantity demanded by each consumer in the market at each price. Similarly, the market supply curve is determined by adding up the quantity supplied by each firm in the market at each price. Each firm's marginal cost curve tells us how much that firm will supply at each price. So, the market supply curve can be derived directly from the marginal cost curves of the firms in the market. Panel (a) of Figure 7 shows the marginal cost

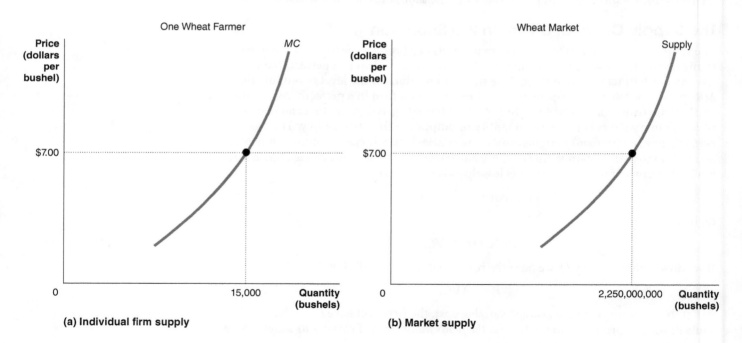

(a) Individual firm supply

(b) Market supply

Figure 7 Firm Supply and Market Supply

We can derive the market supply curve by adding up the quantity that each firm in the market is willing to supply at each price. In panel (a), one wheat farmer is willing to supply 15,000 bushels of wheat at a price of $7 per bushel. If every wheat farmer supplies the same amount of wheat at this price and if there are 150,000 wheat farmers, the total amount of wheat supplied at a price of $7 will equal

15,000 bushels per farmer × 150,000 farmers = 2.25 billion bushels of wheat. This amount is one point on the market supply curve for wheat shown in panel (b). We can find the other points on the market supply curve by determining how much wheat each farmer is willing to supply at each price.

curve for one wheat farmer. At a price of $7, this wheat farmer supplies 15,000 bushels of wheat. If every wheat farmer supplies the same amount of wheat at this price and if there are 150,000 wheat farmers, the total amount of wheat supplied at a price of $7 will be

15,000 bushels per farmer × 150,000 farms = 2.25 billion bushels of wheat.

Panel (b) shows a price of $7 and a quantity of 2.25 billion bushels as a point on the market supply curve for wheat. In reality, of course, not all wheat farms are alike. Some wheat farms supply more at the market price than the typical farm; other wheat farms supply less. The key point is that we can derive the market supply curve by adding up the quantity that each firm in the market is willing and able to supply at each price.

"If Everyone Can Do It, You Can't Make Money at It": The Entry and Exit of Firms in the Long Run

5 LEARNING OBJECTIVE

Explain how entry and exit ensure that perfectly competitive firms earn zero economic profit in the long run.

In the long run, unless a firm can cover all its costs, it will shut down and exit the industry. In a market system, firms continually enter and exit industries. In this section, we will see how profits and losses provide signals to firms that lead to entry and exit.

Economic Profit and the Entry or Exit Decision

To begin, let's look more closely at how economists characterize the profits earned by the owners of a firm. Suppose Sacha Gillette decides to start her own business. After considering her skills and interests and preparing a business plan, she decides to start an organic vegetable farm rather than a restaurant or clothing boutique. After 10 years of effort, Sacha has saved $100,000, and she is able to borrow another $900,000 from a bank. With these funds, she has bought the land and farm equipment necessary to start her farm. She intends to sell the carrots she grows in a local farmer's market. When someone invests her own funds in her firm, the opportunity cost to the firm is the return the funds would have earned in their best alternative use. If Farmer Gillette could have earned a 10 percent return on her $100,000 in savings in their best alternative use—which might have been, for example, to buy a small restaurant—then her carrot business incurs a $10,000 opportunity cost. We can also think of this $10,000 as being the minimum amount that Farmer Gillette needs to earn on her $100,000 investment in her farm to remain in the industry in the long run.

Table 4 lists Farmer Gillette's costs. In addition to her explicit costs, we assume that she has two implicit costs: the $10,000 that represents the opportunity cost of the funds she invested in her farm and the $30,000 salary she could have earned managing someone else's farm instead of her own. Her total costs are $125,000. If the market price of carrots is $15 per box and Farmer Gillette sells 10,000 boxes, her total revenue will be $150,000, and her economic profit will be $25,000 (total revenue of $150,000 minus total costs of $125,000). **Economic profit** equals a firm's revenues minus all its costs, implicit and explicit. So, Farmer Gillette is covering the $10,000 opportunity cost of the funds invested in her firm, and she is also earning an additional $25,000 in economic profit.

Economic profit A firm's revenues minus all its costs, implicit and explicit.

Table 4

Farmer Gillette's Costs per Year

Explicit Costs	
Water	$10,000
Wages	$15,000
Fertilizer	$10,000
Electricity	$5,000
Payment on bank loan	$45,000
Implicit Costs	
Forgone salary	$30,000
Opportunity cost of the $100,000 she has invested in her farm	$10,000
Total cost	**$125,000**

Economic Profit Leads to Entry of New Firms Unfortunately, Farmer Gillette is unlikely to earn an economic profit for very long. Suppose other farmers are just breaking even by selling their carrots to supermarkets. In that case, they will have an incentive to switch to selling at farmers' markets so they can begin earning an economic profit. As we saw in the chapter opener, in recent years many small farmers have begun to sell their produce in farmers' markets in the hope of earning higher profits. The more firms there are in an industry, the farther to the right the market supply curve is. Panel (a) of Figure 8 shows that as more farmers begin selling carrots in farmers' markets, the market supply curve shifts to the right. Farmers will continue entering the market until the market supply curve has shifted from S_1 to S_2.

With the supply curve at S_2, the market price will fall to $10 per box. Panel (b) shows the effect on Farmer Gillette, whom we assume has the same costs as other carrot farmers. As the market price falls from $15 to $10 per box, Farmer Gillette's demand curve shifts down, from D_1 to D_2. In the new equilibrium, Farmer Gillette is selling 8,000 boxes, at a price of $10 per box. She and the other carrot farmers are no longer earning any economic profit. They are just breaking even, and the return on their investment is just covering the opportunity cost of these funds. New farmers will stop entering the market because the rate of return from selling carrots in farmers' markets is now no better than they can earn by selling them elsewhere.

Will Farmer Gillette continue to sell carrots at farmers' markets even though she is just breaking even? She will because selling carrots at farmers' markets earns her as high a return on her investment as she could earn elsewhere. It may seem strange that new firms will continue to enter a market until all economic profits are eliminated and that established firms remain in a market despite not earning any economic profit. But it seems strange only because we are used to thinking in terms of accounting profit rather than *economic* profit. accounting rules generally require that only explicit costs be included on a firm's financial statements. The opportunity cost of the funds Farmer Gillette invested in her farm—$10,000—and her forgone salary—$30,000—are

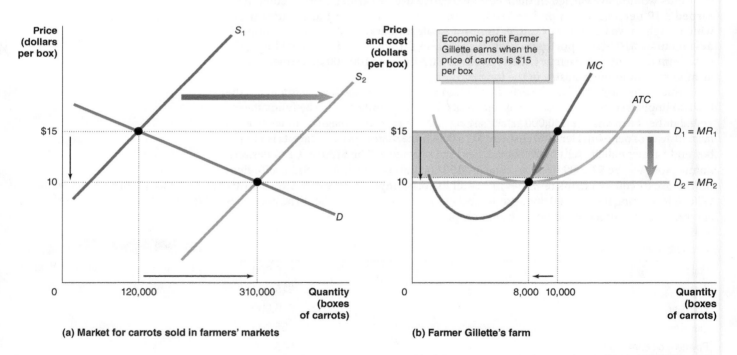

(a) Market for carrots sold in farmers' markets

(b) Farmer Gillette's farm

Figure 8 The Effect of Entry on Economic Profit

Initially, Farmer Gillette and other farmers selling carrots in farmers' markets are able to charge $15 per box and earn an economic profit. Farmer Gillette's economic profit is represented by the area of the green box in panel (b). Panel (a) shows that as other farmers begin to sell carrots in farmers' markets, the market supply curve shifts to the right, from S_1 to S_2, and the market price drops to $10 per box.

Panel (b) shows that the falling price causes Farmer Gillette's demand curve to shift down from D_1 to D_2, and she reduces her output from 10,000 boxes to 8,000. At the new market price of $10 per box, carrot growers are just breaking even: Their total revenue is equal to their total cost, and their economic profit is zero. Notice the difference in scale between the graphs in panels (a) and (b).

economic costs, but neither of them is an accounting cost. So, although an accountant would see Farmer Gillette as earning a profit of $40,000, an economist would see her as just breaking even. Farmer Gillette must pay attention to her accounting profit when preparing her financial statements and when paying her income tax. But because economic profit takes into account all her costs, it gives a more accurate indication of the financial health of her farm.

Economic Losses Lead to Exit of Firms Suppose some consumers decide that there are no important benefits from locally grown produce sold at farmers' markets, and they switch back to buying their produce in supermarkets. Panel (a) of Figure 9 shows that the demand curve for carrots sold in farmers' markets will shift to the left, from D_1 to D_2, and the market price will fall from $10 per box to $7. Panel (b) shows that as the price falls, a farmer, like Sacha Gillette, will move down her marginal cost curve to a lower level of output. At the lower level of output and lower price, she will be suffering an **economic loss** because she will not cover all her costs. As long as price is above average variable cost, she will continue to produce in the short run, even when suffering losses. But in the long run, firms will exit an industry if they are unable to cover all their costs. In this case, some farmers will switch back to selling carrots to supermarkets rather than selling them in farmers' markets.

Economic loss The situation in which a firm's total revenue is less than its total cost, including all implicit costs.

Panel (c) of Figure 9 shows that as firms exit from selling at farmers' markets, the market supply curve shifts to the left. Firms will continue to exit, and the supply curve will continue to shift to the left until the price has risen back to $10 and the market supply curve is at S_2. Panel (d) shows that when the price is back to $10, the remaining firms in the industry will be breaking even.

Long-Run Equilibrium in a Perfectly Competitive Market

We have seen that economic profits attract firms to enter an industry. The entry of firms forces down the market price until a typical firm is breaking even. Economic losses cause firms to exit an industry. The exit of firms forces up the equilibrium market price until the typical firm is breaking even. In **long-run competitive equilibrium**, entry and exit have resulted in the typical firm breaking even. In the long run, firms can also vary their scale by becoming larger or smaller. The *long-run average cost curve* shows the lowest cost at which a firm is able to produce a given quantity of output in the long run. So, we would expect that in the long run, competition drives the market price to the minimum point on the typical firm's long-run average cost curve.

Long-run competitive equilibrium The situation in which the entry and exit of firms has resulted in the typical firm breaking even.

The long run in selling produce in farmers' markets appears to be several years, which is the amount of time it takes for new farmers' markets to be organized and for farmers to make the investment necessary to sell directly to consumers. As we discussed in the chapter opener, the number of farmers' markets operating in the United States had increased from 1,774 in 2005 to 7,864 in 2012. But some farmers have begun to exit the market because the prices they were receiving were lower than they could get by selling their produce elsewhere. In Oregon, 32 of 62 farmers' markets that had opened in recent years have since closed.

Firms in perfectly competitive markets are in a constant struggle to stay one step ahead of their competitors. They are always looking for new ways to provide a product, such as selling carrots in farmers' markets. It is possible for firms to find ways to earn an economic profit for a while, but competition typically eliminates those profits in just a few years. This observation is not restricted to agriculture. In any perfectly competitive market, an opportunity to make economic profits never lasts long. As Sharon Oster, an economist at Yale University, has put it: "If everyone can do it, you can't make money at it."

The Long-Run Supply Curve in a Perfectly Competitive Market

If a typical farmer selling carrots in a farmers' market breaks even at a price of $10 per box, in the long run the market price will always return to this level. If an increase in demand causes the market price to rise above $10, farmers will be earning economic profits. These profits will attract additional farmers into the market, and the market supply curve will shift to the right until the price is back to $10.

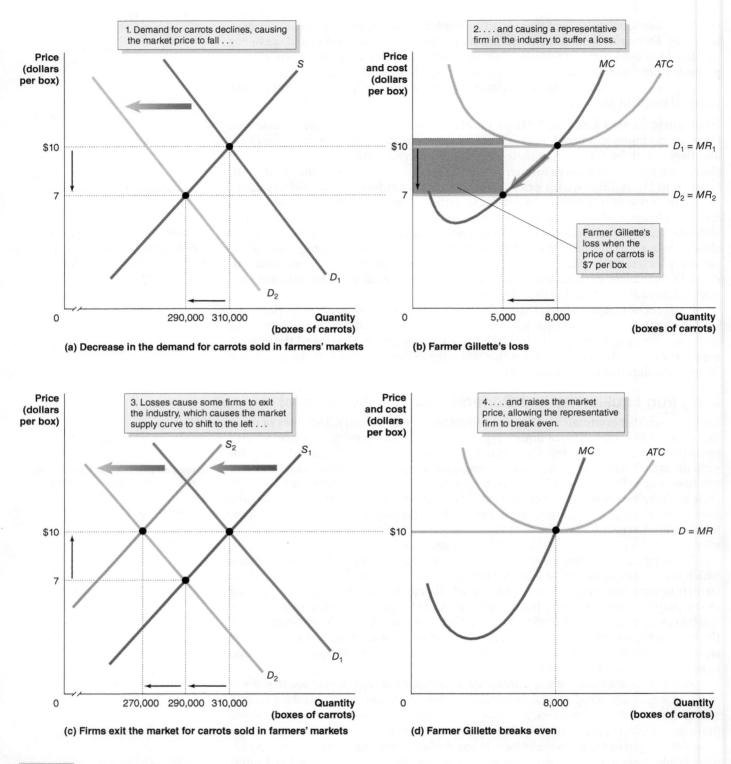

Figure 9 **The Effect of Exit on Economic Losses**

When the price of carrots is $10 per box, Farmer Gillette and other farmers are break-ing even. A total quantity of 310,000 boxes is sold in the market. Farmer Gillette sells 8,000 boxes. Panel (a) shows a decline in the demand for carrots sold in farmers' markets from D_1 to D_2 that reduces the market price to $7 per box. Panel (b) shows that the falling price causes Farmer Gillette's demand curve to shift down from D_1 to D_2 and her output to fall from 8,000 to 5,000 boxes. At a market price of $7 per box,

farmers have economic losses, represented by the area of the red box. As a result, some farmers will exit the market, which shifts the market supply curve to the left. Panel (c) shows that exit continues until the supply curve has shifted from S_1 to S_2 and the mar-ket price has risen from $7 back to $10. Panel (d) shows that with the price back at $10, Farmer Gillette will break even. In the new market equilibrium in panel (c), total sales of carrots in farmers' markets have fallen from 310,000 to 270,000 boxes.

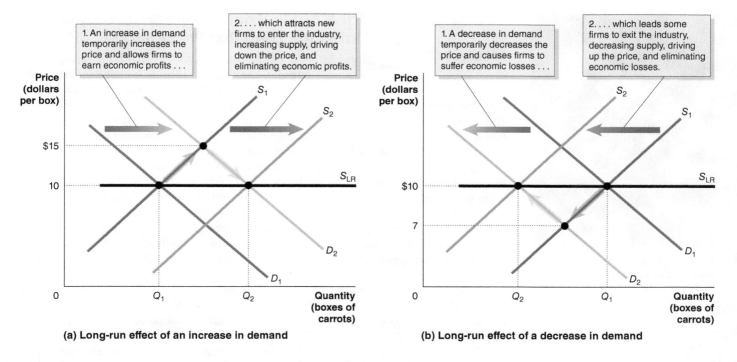

(a) Long-run effect of an increase in demand

(b) Long-run effect of a decrease in demand

Figure 10 **The Long-Run Supply Curve in a Perfectly Competitive Industry**

Panel (a) shows that an increase in demand for carrots sold in farmers' markets will lead to a temporary increase in price from $10 to $15 per box, as the market demand curve shifts to the right, from D_1 to D_2. The entry of new firms shifts the market supply curve to the right, from S_1 to S_2, which will cause the price to fall back to its long-run level of $10. Panel (b) shows that a decrease in demand will lead to a temporary decrease in price from $10 to $7 per box, as the market

demand curve shifts to the left, from D_1 to D_2. The exit of firms shifts the market supply curve to the left, from S_1 to S_2, which causes the price to rise back to its long-run level of $10. The long-run supply curve (S_{LR}) shows the relationship between market price and the quantity supplied in the long run. In this case, the long-run supply curve is a horizontal line.

Panel (a) in Figure 10 illustrates the long-run effect of an increase in demand. An increase in demand from D_1 to D_2 causes the market price to temporarily rise from $10 per box to $15. At this price, farmers are making economic profits selling carrots at farmers' markets, but these profits attract the entry of new farmers. The result is an increase in supply from S_1 to S_2, which forces the price back down to $10 per box and eliminates the economic profits.

Similarly, if a decrease in demand causes the market price to fall below $10, farmers will experience economic losses. These losses will cause some farmers to exit the market, the supply curve will shift to the left, and the price will return to $10. Panel (b) in Figure 10 illustrates the long-run effect of a decrease in demand. A decrease in demand from D_1 to D_2 causes the market price to fall temporarily from $10 per box to $7. At this price, farmers are suffering economic losses, but these losses cause some farmers to exit the market for selling carrots in farmers' markets. The result is a decrease in supply from S_1 to S_2, which forces the price back up to $10 per box and eliminates the losses.

The **long-run supply curve** shows the relationship in the long run between market price and the quantity supplied. In the long run, the price will be $10 per box, no matter how many boxes of carrots are produced. So, as Figure 10 shows, the long-run supply curve (S_{LR}) is a horizontal line at a price of $10. Remember that the price returns to $10 in the long run because at this price a typical firm in the industry just breaks even. The typical firm breaks even because $10 is at the minimum point on the firm's average total cost curve. We can draw the important conclusion that *in the long run, a perfectly competitive market will supply whatever amount of a good consumers demand at a price determined by the minimum point on the typical firm's average total cost curve.*

Because the position of the long-run supply curve is determined by the minimum point on the typical firm's average total cost curve, anything that raises or lowers the costs of the typical firm in the long run will cause the long-run supply curve to shift. For example, if a new disease infects carrots and the costs of treating the disease adds $2 per box to every farmer's cost of producing carrots, the long-run supply curve will shift up by $2.

Long-run supply curve A curve that shows the relationship in the long run between market price and the quantity supplied.

Economic profits are rapidly competed away in the iTunes apps store.

In the Apple iPhone Apps Store, Easy Entry Makes the Long Run Pretty Short

Apple introduced the first version of the iPhone in June 2007. Although popular, the original iPhone had some drawbacks, including a slow connection to the Internet and an inability to run any applications except those written by Apple. The iPhone 3G, released in July 2008, could connect to the Internet more quickly and easily, had a faster processor, and had a larger capacity. Perhaps more importantly, Apple announced that a section of its immensely popular iTunes music and video store would be devoted to applications (or "apps") for the iPhone 3G. Independent software programmers would write these iPhone apps. Apple would approve the apps and make them available in the iTunes app store in exchange for receiving 30 percent of the purchase price. Major software companies, as well as individuals writing their first software programs, have posted games, calendars, dictionaries, and many other types of apps to the iTunes store.

Apple sold more than 3 million iPhones within a month of launching the iPhone 3G. Demand for apps from the iTunes store soared along with sales of the iPhone. Ethan Nicholas, who was a programmer at Sun Microsystems but had never written a game before, decided to teach himself the coding language used in iPhone apps. His game, iShoot, with an initial price of $4.99, was a great success. Within one week of posting to iTunes, enough people had downloaded iShoot to earn Nicholas $200,000. At the end of five months, he had earned $800,000.

But could Nicholas's success last? As we have seen, when firms earn economic profits in a market, other firms have a strong economic incentive to enter that market. This is exactly what happened with iPhone apps, and by April 2009, more than 25,000 apps were available in the iTunes store. The cost of entering this market was very small. Anyone with the programming skills and the available time could write an app and have it posted in the store. As a result of this enhanced competition, the ability to get rich quick with a killer app was quickly fading. As an article in the *New York Times* put it: "The chances of hitting the iPhone jackpot keep getting slimmer: the Apple store is already crowded with look-alike games ... and fresh inventory keeps arriving daily. Many of the simple but clever concepts that sell briskly ... are already taken."

To try to maintain sales, Ethan Nicholas was forced to drop the price of iShoot from $4.99 in October 2008 to $2.99 in April 2009 to $1.99 in May 2009, and finally to $0.99 in September 2010. His profits from the game continued to decline. In a competitive market, earning an economic profit in the long run is extremely difficult. And the ease of entering the market for iPhone apps has made the long run pretty short.

Sources: Jenna Wortham, "The iPhone Gold Rush," *New York Times*, April 5, 2009; and Bruce X. Chen, "Coder's Half-Million-Dollar Baby Proves iPhone Gold Rush Is Still On," wired.com, February 12, 2009.

Your Turn: Test your understanding by doing related problem 5.9 at the end of this chapter.

Increasing-Cost and Decreasing-Cost Industries

Any industry in which the typical firm's average costs do not change as the industry expands production will have a horizontal long-run supply curve, like the one in Figure 10. These industries, the carrot industry, for example, are called *constant-cost industries*. It's possible, however, for the typical firm's average costs to change as an industry expands.

For example, if an input used in producing a good is available in only limited quantities, the cost of the input will rise as the industry expands. If only a limited amount of land is available on which to grow the grapes to make a certain variety of wine, an increase in demand for wine made from these grapes will result in competition for the land and will drive up its price. As a result, more of the wine will be produced in the long run only if the price rises to cover the typical firm's higher average costs. In this case, the long-run supply curve will slope upward. Industries with upward-sloping long-run supply curves are called *increasing-cost industries*.

Finally, in some cases, the typical firm's costs may fall as the industry expands. Suppose that someone invents a new microwave oven that uses as an input a specialized memory chip that is currently produced only in small quantities. If demand for the microwave increases, firms that produce microwaves will increase their orders for the memory chip. If there are *economies of scale* in producing a good, its average cost will decline as output increases. If there are economies of scale in producing this memory chip, the average cost of producing it will fall, and competition will result in its price falling as well. This price decline, in turn, will lower the average cost of producing the new microwave. In the long run, competition will force the price of the microwave to fall to the level of the typical firm's new lower average cost. In this case, the long-run supply curve will slope downward. Industries with downward-sloping long-run supply curves are called *decreasing-cost industries*.

Perfect Competition and Efficiency

6 LEARNING OBJECTIVE

Explain how perfect competition leads to economic efficiency.

Notice how powerful consumers are in a market system. If consumers want more locally grown carrots, the market will supply them. More carrots are supplied not because a government bureaucrat in Washington, DC, or an official in a carrot growers' association gives orders. The additional carrots are produced because an increase in demand results in higher prices and a higher profit from selling at farmers' markets. Carrot growers, trying to get the highest possible return on their investments, begin to switch from selling to supermarkets to selling at farmers' markets. If consumers lose their taste for locally grown carrots and demand falls, the process works in reverse.

Productive Efficiency

In a market system, consumers get as many carrots as they want, produced at the lowest average cost possible. The forces of competition will drive the market price to the typical firm's minimum average cost. **Productive efficiency** refers to the situation in which a good or service is produced at the lowest possible cost. As we have seen, perfect competition results in productive efficiency.

Productive efficiency The situation in which a good or service is produced at the lowest possible cost.

    The managers of every firm strive to earn an economic profit by reducing costs. But in a perfectly competitive market, other firms quickly copy ways of reducing costs. Therefore, in the long run, only the consumer benefits from cost reductions.

Solved Problem 6

How Productive Efficiency Benefits Consumers

Financial writer Michael Lewis once remarked: "The sad truth, for investors, seems to be that most of the benefits of new technologies are passed right through to consumers free of charge."

a. What do you think Lewis means by the benefits of new technology being "passed right through to consumers free of charge"? Use a graph like Figure 8 to illustrate your answer.
b. Explain why this result is a "sad truth" for investors.

Solving the Problem

Step 1: **Review the chapter material.** This problem is about perfect competition and efficiency, so you may want to review the section "Perfect Competition and Efficiency," which begins above.

Step 2: **Use the concepts from this chapter to explain what Lewis means.** By "new technologies," Lewis means new products—such as smartphones or LED television sets—or lower-cost ways of producing existing products. In either case, new technologies will allow firms to earn economic profits for a while, but these profits will lead new firms to enter the market in the long run.

Step 3: **Use a graph like Figure 8 to illustrate why the benefits of new technologies are "passed right through to consumers free of charge."** Figure 8 shows the situation in which a firm is making economic profits in the short run but has these profits eliminated by entry in the long run. We can draw a similar graph to analyze what happens in the long run in the market for LED televisions.

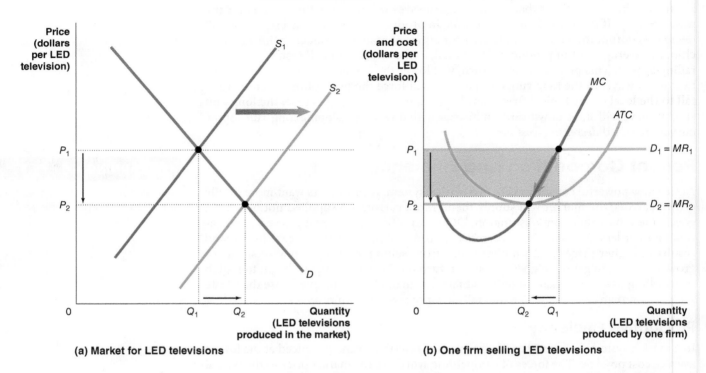

(a) Market for LED televisions

(b) One firm selling LED televisions

When LED televisions were first introduced, prices were high, and only a few firms were in the market. Panel (a) shows that the initial equilibrium price in the market for LED televisions is P_1. Panel (b) shows that at this price, the typical firm in the industry is earning an economic profit, which is shown by the green-shaded box. The economic profit attracts new firms into the industry. This entry shifts the market supply curve from S_1 to S_2 in panel (a) and lowers the equilibrium price from P_1 to P_2. Panel (b) shows that at the new market price, P_2, the typical firm is breaking even. Therefore, LED televisions are being produced at the lowest possible cost, and productive efficiency is achieved. Consumers receive the new technology "free of charge" in the sense that they only have to pay a price equal to the lowest possible cost of production.

Step 4: **Answer part (b) by explaining why the result in part (a) is a "sad truth" for investors.** We have seen in answering part (a) that in the long run, firms only break even on their investment in producing high-technology goods. That result implies that investors in these firms are also unlikely to earn an economic profit in the long run.

Extra Credit: Lewis is using a key result from this chapter: In the long run, the entry of new firms competes away economic profits. We should notice that, strictly speaking, the high-technology industries Lewis is discussing are not perfectly competitive. Smartphones or LED televisions, for instance, are not identical, and each smartphone company produces a quantity large enough to affect the market price. However these deviations from perfect competition do not change the important conclusion that the entry of new firms benefits consumers by forcing prices down to the level of average cost. In fact, the price of LED televisions dropped by more than 35 percent within three years of their first becoming widely available.

Source: Michael Lewis, "In Defense of the Boom," *New York Times*, October 27, 2002.

Your Turn: For more practice, do related problems 6.6, 6.7, and 6.8 at the end of this chapter.

Allocative Efficiency

Not only do perfectly competitive firms produce goods and services at the lowest possible cost, they also produce the goods and services that consumers value most. Firms will produce a good up to the point where the marginal cost of producing another unit is equal to the marginal benefit consumers receive from consuming that unit. In other words, firms will supply all those goods that provide consumers with a marginal benefit at least as great as the marginal cost of producing them. This result holds because:

1. The price of a good represents the marginal benefit consumers receive from consuming the last unit of the good sold.

2. Perfectly competitive firms produce up to the point where the price of the good equals the marginal cost of producing the last unit.

3. Therefore, firms produce up to the point where the last unit provides a marginal benefit to consumers equal to the marginal cost of producing it.

These statements are another way of saying that entrepreneurs in a market system efficiently *allocate* labor, machinery, and other inputs to produce the goods and services that best satisfy consumer wants. In this way, perfect competition achieves **allocative efficiency**. Many goods and services sold in the U.S. economy are not produced in perfectly competitive markets. Nevertheless, productive efficiency and allocative efficiency are useful benchmarks against which to compare the actual performance of the economy.

Allocative efficiency A state of the economy in which production represents consumer preferences; in particular, every good or service is produced up to the point where the last unit provides a marginal benefit to consumers equal to the marginal cost of producing it.

Continued

Economics in Your Life

Are You an Entrepreneur?

At the beginning of the chapter, we asked you to think about why you can charge only a relatively low price for performing services such as babysitting or lawn mowing. In the chapter, we saw that firms selling products in competitive markets can't charge prices higher than those being charged by competing firms. The market for babysitting and lawn mowing is very competitive because in most neighborhoods there are many teenagers willing to supply these services. The price you can charge for babysitting may not be worth your time when you are 20 but is enough to cover the opportunity cost of a 14-year-old eager to enter the market. In other words, the ease of entry into babysitting and lawn mowing is high. So, in your career as a teenage entrepreneur, you may have become familiar with one of the lessons of this chapter: A firm in a competitive market has no control over price.

Conclusion

The competitive forces of the market impose relentless pressure on firms to produce new and better goods and services at the lowest possible cost. Firms that fail to adequately anticipate changes in consumer tastes or that fail to adopt the latest and most efficient technology do not survive in the long run. In the nineteenth century, the biologist Charles Darwin developed a theory of evolution based on the idea of the "survival of the fittest." Only those plants and animals that are best able to adapt to the demands of their environment are able to survive. Darwin first realized the important role that the struggle for existence plays in the natural world after reading early nineteenth-century economists' descriptions of the role it plays in the economic world. Just as "survival of the fittest" is the rule in nature, so it is in the economic world.

At the start of this chapter, we saw that there are four market structures: perfect competition, monopolistic competition, oligopoly, and monopoly. Now we have studied perfect competition.

Visit MyEconLab for a news article and analysis related to the concepts in this chapter.

Chapter Summary and Problems

Key Terms

Allocative efficiency

Average revenue (*AR*)

Economic loss

Economic profit

Long-run competitive equilibrium

Long-run supply curve

Marginal revenue (*MR*)

Perfectly competitive market

Price taker

Productive efficiency

Profit

Shutdown point

Sunk cost

1 Perfectly Competitive Markets

LEARNING OBJECTIVE: Explain what a perfectly competitive market is and why a perfect competitor faces a horizontal demand curve.

Summary

A **perfectly competitive market** must have many buyers and sellers, firms must be producing identical products, and there must be no barriers to new firms entering the market. The demand curve for a good or service produced in a perfectly competitive market is downward sloping, but the demand curve for the output of one firm in a perfectly competitive market is a horizontal line at the market price. Firms in perfectly competitive markets are **price takers**, and their sales drop to zero if they attempt to charge more than the market price.

Visit www.myeconlab.com to complete these exercises online and get instant feedback.

Review Questions

1.1 What are the three conditions for a market to be perfectly competitive?

1.2 What is a price taker? When are firms likely to be price takers?

1.3 Draw a graph showing the market demand and supply curves for corn and the demand curve for the corn produced by one corn farmer. Be sure to indicate the market price and the price the corn farmer receives.

Problems and Applications

1.4 Explain whether each of the following is a perfectly competitive market. For each market that is not perfectly competitive, explain why it is not.
   a. Corn farming
   b. Coffee shops
   c. Automobile manufacturing
   d. New home construction

1.5 Why are consumers usually price takers when they buy most goods and services, while relatively few firms are price takers?

1.6 **[Related to the** Don't Let This Happen to You**]** Explain whether you agree with the following remark:

> According to the model of perfectly competitive markets, the demand curve for wheat should be a horizontal line. But this can't be true: When the price of wheat rises, the quantity of wheat demanded falls, and when the price of wheat falls, the quantity of wheat demanded rises. Therefore, the demand curve for wheat is not a horizontal line.

1.7 The financial writer Andrew Tobias described an incident that occurred when he was a student at the Harvard Business School: Each student in the class was given large amounts of information about a particular firm and asked to determine a pricing strategy for the firm. Most of the students spent hours preparing their answers and came to class carrying many sheets of paper with their calculations. Tobias came up with the correct answer after just a few minutes and without having made any calculations. When his professor called on him in class for an answer, Tobias stated: "The case said the XYZ Company was in a very competitive industry ... and the case said that the company had all the business it could handle." Given this information, what price do you think Tobias argued the company should charge? Briefly explain. (Tobias says the class greeted his answer with "thunderous applause.")

Source: Andrew Tobias, *The Only Investment Guide You'll Ever Need*, Houghton Mifflin Harcourt, 2010, pp. 7–8.

2 How a Firm Maximizes Profit in a Perfectly Competitive Market

LEARNING OBJECTIVE: Explain how a firm maximizes profit in a perfectly competitive market.

Summary

Profit is the difference between total revenue (*TR*) and total cost (*TC*). **Average revenue** (*AR*) is total revenue divided by the quantity of the product sold. A firm maximizes profit by producing the level of output where the difference between revenue and cost is the greatest. This is the same level of output where marginal revenue is equal to marginal cost. **Marginal revenue (*MR*)** is the change in total revenue from selling one more unit.

Visit www.myeconlab.com to complete these exercises online and get instant feedback.

Review Questions

2.1 Explain why it is true that for a firm in a perfectly competitive market, $P = MR = AR$.

2.2 Explain why at the level of output where the difference between TR and TC is at its maximum positive value, MR must equal MC.

2.3 Explain why it is true that for a firm in a perfectly competitive market, the profit-maximizing condition $MR = MC$ is equivalent to the condition $P = MC$.

Problems and Applications

2.4 A student argues: "To maximize profit, a firm should produce the quantity where the difference between marginal revenue and marginal cost is the greatest. If a firm produces more than this quantity, then the profit made on each additional unit will be falling." Briefly explain whether you agree with this reasoning.

2.5 Why don't firms maximize revenue rather than profit? Briefly explain whether a firm that maximized revenue would be likely to produce a smaller or larger quantity than if it were maximizing profit.

2.6 Refer to Table 3. Suppose the price of wheat falls to $5.50 per bushel. How many bushels of wheat will Farmer Parker produce, and how much profit will he make? Briefly explain.

2.7 Refer to Table 3. Suppose that the marginal cost of wheat is $0.50 higher for every bushel of wheat produced. For example, the marginal cost of producing the eighth bushel of wheat is now $9.50. Assume that the price of wheat remains $7 per bushel. Will this increase in marginal cost change the profit-maximizing level of production for Farmer Parker? Briefly explain. How much profit will Farmer Parker make now?

2.8 In Table 3, what are Farmer Parker's fixed costs? Suppose that his fixed costs increase by $10. Will this increase in fixed costs change the profit-maximizing level of production for Farmer Parker? Briefly explain. How much profit will Farmer Parker make now?

---

 3 | ## Illustrating Profit or Loss on the Cost Curve Graph
LEARNING OBJECTIVE: Use graphs to show a firm's profit or loss.

Summary

From the definitions of profit and average total cost, we can develop the following expression for the relationship between total profit and average total cost: Profit $= (P - ATC) \times Q$. Using this expression, we can determine the area showing profit or loss on a cost curve graph: The area of profit or loss is a rectangle with a height equal to price minus average total cost (for profit) or average total cost minus price (for loss) and a base equal to the quantity of output.

Visit **www.myeconlab.com** to complete these exercises online and get instant feedback.

Output per Day	Total Cost
0	$1.00
1	2.50
2	3.50
3	4.20
4	4.50
5	5.20
6	6.80
7	8.70
8	10.70
9	13.00

Review Questions

3.1 Draw a graph showing a firm that is making a profit in a perfectly competitive market. Be sure your graph includes the firm's demand curve, marginal revenue curve, marginal cost curve, average total cost curve, and average variable cost curve, and make sure to indicate the area representing the firm's profit.

3.2 Draw a graph showing a firm that is operating at a loss in a perfectly competitive market. Be sure your graph includes the firm's demand curve, marginal revenue curve, marginal cost curve, average total cost curve, and average variable cost curve, and make sure to indicate the area representing the firm's loss.

Problems and Applications

3.3 **[Related to** Solved Problem 3**]** Frances sells earrings in the perfectly competitive earrings market. Her output per day and her costs are as follows:

a. If the current equilibrium price in the earring market is $1.80, how many earrings will Frances produce, what price will she charge, and how much profit (or loss) will she make? Draw a graph to illustrate your answer. Your graph should be clearly labeled and should include Frances's demand, ATC, AVC, MC, and MR curves; the price she is charging; the quantity she is producing; and the area representing her profit (or loss).

b. Suppose the equilibrium price of earrings falls to $1.00. Now how many earrings will Frances produce, what price will she charge, and how much profit (or loss) will she make? Show your work. Draw a graph to illustrate this situation, using the instructions in part (a).

c. Suppose the equilibrium price of earrings falls to $0.25. Now how many earrings will Frances produce, what price will she charge, and how much profit (or loss) will she make?

3.4 **[Related to** Solved Problem 3**]** Review Solved Problem 3 and then answer the following: Suppose the equilibrium price of basketballs falls to $2.50. Now how many basketballs will Andy produce? What price will he charge? How much profit (or loss) will he make?

3.5 [Related to the Don't Let This Happen to You**]** A student examines the following graph and argues: "I believe that a firm will want to produce at Q_1, not at Q_2. At Q_1, the distance between price and marginal cost is the greatest. Therefore, at Q_1, the firm will be maximizing its profit." Briefly explain whether you agree with the student's argument.

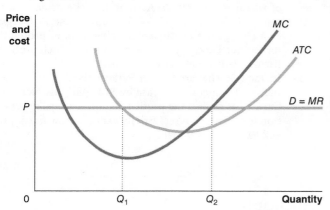

3.6 A newspaper article discussed the financial results for Texas Instruments Inc., a semiconductor manufacturer, during the first quarter of 2013. "First quarter profit jumped 37 percent to $362 million, or 32 cents per share, but revenue declined 6.8 percent to $2.89 billion from a year earlier." How is it possible for Texas Instruments' revenue to decrease but its profit to increase? Doesn't Texas Instruments have to maximize its revenue to maximize its profit?

Source: Sheryl Jean, "TI Narrows its 2nd-Quarter Projections," *The Dallas Morning News*, June 11, 2013.

3.7 [Related to the Making the Connection: **Losing Money in the Solar Panel Industry]** Suppose that the price of oil

doubles, raising the cost of home-heating oil and electricity. What effect would this development have on U.S. firms manufacturing solar panels? Illustrate your answer with two graphs: one showing the situation in the market for solar panels and another graph showing the situation for a representative firm in the industry. Be sure your graph for the industry shows any shifts in the market demand and supply curve and any changes in the equilibrium market price. Be sure that your graph for the representative firm includes the firm's demand curve, marginal revenue curve, marginal cost curve, and average total cost curve.

3.8 The following graph represents the situation of Marguerite's Caps, a firm selling caps in the perfectly competitive cap industry:

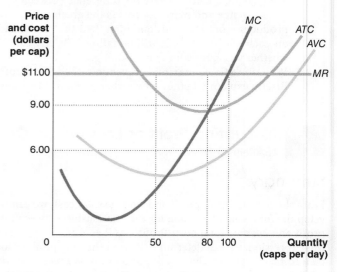

a. How much output should Marguerite produce to maximize her profits?

b. How much profit will she earn?

c. Suppose Marguerite decides to shut down. What would her loss be?

 Deciding Whether to Produce or to Shut Down in the Short Run

LEARNING OBJECTIVE: Explain why firms may shut down temporarily.

Summary

In deciding whether to shut down or produce in the short run, a firm should ignore its *sunk costs*. A **sunk cost** is a cost that has already been paid and that cannot be recovered. In the short run, a firm continues to produce as long as its price is at least equal to its average variable cost. A perfectly competitive firm's **shutdown point** is the minimum point on the firm's average variable cost curve. If price falls below average variable cost, the firm shuts down in the short run. For prices above the shutdown point, a perfectly competitive firm's marginal cost curve is also its supply curve.

Visit **www.myeconlab.com** to complete these exercises online and get instant feedback.

Review Questions

4.1 What is the difference between a firm's shutdown points in the short run and in the long run? Why are firms willing to accept losses in the short run but not in the long run?

4.2 What is the relationship between a perfectly competitive firm's marginal cost curve and its supply curve?

4.3 How is the market supply curve derived from the supply curves of individual firms?

Problems and Applications

4.4 Edward Scahill produces table lamps in the perfectly competitive desk lamp market.
  a. Fill in the missing values in the following table:

Output per Week	Total Cost	AFC	AVC	ATC	MC
0	$100				
1	150				
2	175				
3	190				
4	210				
5	240				
6	280				
7	330				
8	390				
9	460				
10	540				

b. Suppose the equilibrium price in the desk lamp market is $50. How many table lamps should Scahill produce, and how much profit will he make?

c. If next week the equilibrium price of desk lamps drops to $30, should Scahill shut down? Explain.

4.5 Matthew Rafferty produces hiking boots in the perfectly competitive hiking boot market.

a. Fill in the missing values in the following table:

Output per Week	Total Cost	AFC	AVC	ATC	MC
0	$100.00				
1	155.70				
2	205.60				
3	253.90				
4	304.80				
5	362.50				
6	431.20				
7	515.10				
8	618.40				
9	745.30				
10	900.00				

b. Suppose the equilibrium price in the hiking boot market is $100. How many boots should Rafferty produce, what price should he charge, and how much profit will he make?

c. If next week the equilibrium price of boots drops to $65, how many boots should Rafferty produce, what price should he charge, and how much profit (or loss) will he make?

d. If the equilibrium price of boots falls to $50, how many boots should Rafferty produce, what price should he charge, and how much profit (or loss) will he make?

4.6 The following graph represents the situation of a perfectly competitive firm. Indicate on the graph the areas that represent the following:

a. Total cost

b. Total revenue

c. Variable cost

d. Profit or loss

Briefly explain whether the firm will continue to produce in the short run.

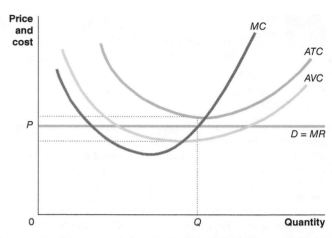

4.7 Look again at the *Making the Connection*: Losing Money in the Solar Panel Industry that discusses the U.S. solar panel industry. According to an article in the *New York Times*, interest payments on bank loans make up more than half the costs of a typical solar panel manufacturer. The owner of a firm that imports solar panels made this observation about solar panel manufacturers: "So as long as companies can cover their variable costs and earn at least some revenue to put toward interest payments, they will continue to operate even at a loss."

a. Are the interest payments these firms make a variable cost or a fixed cost? Briefly explain.

b. Does the quotation accurately describe the behavior of solar panel manufacturers in the short run? Does it accurately describe their behavior in the long run? Briefly explain.

Source: Diane Cardwell, "Solar Tariffs Upheld, but May Not Help in U.S.," *New York Times*, November 7, 2012.

4.8 **[Related to** Solved Problem 4**]** Suppose you decide to open a copy store. You rent store space (signing a one-year lease to do so), and you take out a loan at a local bank and use the money to purchase 10 copiers. Six months later, a large chain opens a copy store two blocks away from yours. As a result, the revenue you receive from your copy store, while sufficient to cover the wages of your employees and the costs of paper and utilities, doesn't cover all your rent and the interest and repayment costs on the loan you took out to purchase the copiers. Should you continue operating your business?

4.9 **[Related to** Solved Problem 4**]** According to an article in the *Wall Street Journal*, in 2007 the insurance company AXA Equitable signed a long-term lease on 2 million square feet of office space in a skyscraper on Sixth Avenue in Manhattan in New York City. In 2013, AXA decided that it only needed 1.7 million square feet of office space, so it subleased 300,000 square feet of space to several other firms. Although AXA is paying a rent of $88 per square foot on all 2 million square feet it is leasing, it is only receiving $40 per square foot from the firms it is subleasing the 300,000 square feet to. Briefly explain why AXA's actions might make economic sense in the short run. Would these actions make sense in the long run? Briefly explain.

Source: Molly Hensley-Clancy, "A Slump on Sixth Avenue," *Wall Street Journal*, June 16, 2013.

5 "If Everyone Can Do It, You Can't Make Money at It": The Entry and Exit of Firms in the Long Run

LEARNING OBJECTIVE: Explain how entry and exit ensure that perfectly competitive firms earn zero economic profit in the long run.

Summary

Economic profit is a firm's revenue minus all its costs, implicit and explicit. **Economic loss** is the situation in which a firm's total revenue is less than its total cost, including all implicit costs. If firms make economic profits in the short run, new firms enter the industry until the market price has fallen enough to wipe out the profits. If firms make economic losses, firms exit the industry until the market price has risen enough to wipe out the losses. **Long-run competitive equilibrium** is the situation in which the entry and exit of firms has resulted in the typical firm breaking even. The **long-run supply curve** shows the relationship between market price and the quantity supplied.

Visit **www.myeconlab.com** to complete these exercises online and get instant feedback.

Review Questions

5.1 When are firms likely to enter an industry? When are they likely to exit an industry?

5.2 Would a firm earning zero economic profit continue to produce, even in the long run?

5.3 Discuss the shape of the long-run supply curve in a perfectly competitive market. Suppose that a perfectly competitive market is initially at long-run equilibrium and then there is a permanent decrease in the demand for the product. Draw a graph showing how the market adjusts in the long run.

Problems and Applications

5.4 Suppose an assistant professor of economics is earning a salary of $75,000 per year. One day she quits her job, sells $100,000 worth of bonds that had been earning 3 percent per year, and uses the funds to open a bookstore. At the end of the year, she shows an accounting profit of $80,000 on her income tax return. What is her economic profit?

5.5 Why does the entry of firms into an industry decrease the economic profits of the existing firms? Why does the exit of firms from an industry increase the economic profits of the existing firms?

5.6 Briefly explain whether you agree with the following statement: "The products for which demand is the greatest will also be the products that are most profitable to produce."

5.7 In panel (b) of Figure 9, Sacha Gillette reduces her output from 8,000 to 5,000 boxes of carrots when the price falls to $7. At this price and this output level, she is operating at a loss. Why doesn't she just continue charging the original $10 and continue producing 8,000 boxes of carrots?

5.8 For a given decrease in demand, will more firms exit a constant-cost industry or an increasing-cost industry? Briefly explain.

5.9 [Related to the Making the Connection: **In the Apple iPhone Apps Store, Easy Entry Makes the Long Run**

Pretty Short] Ethan Nicholas developed his first game while still working as a programmer for Sun Microsystems. After his first game was a success, he quit Sun to form his own company—with himself as the only employee. How did Nicholas's quitting Sun to work full time for himself affect the cost to him of developing games?

Source: Jenna Wortham, "The iPhone Gold Rush," *New York Times*, April 5, 2009.

5.10 A student in a principles of economics course makes the following remark:

The economic model of perfectly competitive markets is fine in theory but not very realistic. It predicts that in the long run, a firm in a perfectly competitive market will earn no profits. No firm in the real world would stay in business if it earned zero profits.

Do you agree with this remark?

5.11 In 2011, National Public Radio ran a story about the market for gold. It reported:

The price of gold in the international market is steadily rising: more than fivefold in the past decade alone. It's currently selling for about $1,500 an ounce, paving the way for a new gold rush. Ten old mines have reopened in remote mountain and desert areas of the American West over the past decade.

a. The new gold rush is not just in the United States. It is also in Australia, Africa, Asia, and elsewhere. If old gold mines still have gold in them, why weren't they being operated before the increase in the price of gold?

b. Assuming the increased demand for gold continues, in the long run, what will the entry of new firms into gold mining do to the price of gold and the economic profits from gold mining?

Sources: Ruxandra Guidi, "Mining Companies on Quest to Cash In on Gold," National Public Radio, July 7, 2011; Jeanne Baron, "Gold Fever Draws African Farmers from Fields," National Public Radio, July 2, 2011; "China Mining Company, Zijin Mining Group to Expand Gold Mines Exploration in Australia," *Mining Exploration News*, August 2, 2011; "Sixteen New Firms to Prospect for Gold in Turkey's Kaz Mountains," *Hurriyet Daily News*, August 22, 2011.

5.12 Suppose that the laptop computer industry is perfectly competitive and that the firms that assemble laptops do not also make the displays, or screens. Suppose that the laptop display industry is also perfectly competitive. Finally, suppose that because the demand for laptop displays is currently relatively small, firms in the laptop display industry have not been able to take advantage of all the economies of scale in laptop display production. Use a graph of the laptop computer market to illustrate the long-run effects on equilibrium price and quantity in the laptop computer market of a substantial and sustained increase in the demand for laptop computers. Use another graph to show the effect on the cost curves of a typical firm in the laptop computer industry. Briefly explain your graphs. Do your graphs indicate that the laptop computer industry is a constant-cost industry, an increasing-cost industry, or a decreasing-cost industry?

5.13 [Related to the Chapter Opener**]** If in the long run vegetable growers who sell in farmers' markets make no greater rate of return on their investment than vegetable growers who sell to supermarkets, why did a significant number of vegetable growers switch from selling to supermarkets to selling in farmers' markets in the first place?

5.14 Suppose that some soybean farmers experience losses over a long period and therefore decide to exit the market. What effect will this exit have on the market supply of soybeans? How will the change in supply affect the market price of soybeans and the ability of farmers remaining in the soybean market to earn a profit?

Perfect Competition and Efficiency

LEARNING OBJECTIVE: Explain how perfect competition leads to economic efficiency.

Summary

Perfect competition results in **productive efficiency**, which means that goods and services are produced at the lowest possible cost. Perfect competition also results in **allocative efficiency**, which means the goods and services are produced up to the point where the last unit provides a marginal benefit to consumers equal to the marginal cost of producing it.

Visit **www.myeconlab.com** to complete these exercises online and get instant feedback.

Review Questions

6.1 Why are consumers so powerful in a market system?

6.2 What is meant by allocative efficiency? What is meant by productive efficiency? Briefly discuss the difference between these two concepts.

6.3 How does perfect competition lead to allocative and productive efficiency?

Problems and Applications

6.4 The chapter states, "Firms will supply all those goods that provide consumers with a marginal benefit at least as great as the marginal cost of producing them." A student objects to this statement, arguing, "I doubt that firms will really do this. After all, firms are in business to make a profit; they don't care about what is best for consumers." Evaluate the student's argument.

6.5 The following graph represents the situation of Karl's Kumquats, a kumquat grower.
  a. How much profit is Karl earning?
  b. Does the current situation of Karl's firm illustrate productive efficiency or allocative efficiency? If so, briefly explain how.

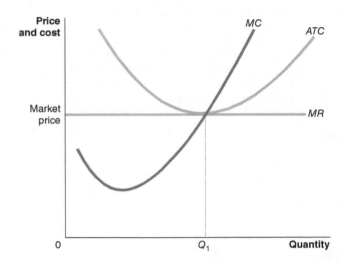

6.6 [Related to Solved Problem 6**]** Discuss the following statement: "In a perfectly competitive market, in the long run consumers benefit from reductions in costs, but firms don't." Don't firms also benefit from cost reductions because they are able to earn larger profits?

6.7 [Related to Solved Problem 6**]** Suppose you read the following item in a newspaper article, under the headline "Price Gouging Alleged in Pencil Market":

Consumer advocacy groups charged at a press conference yesterday that there is widespread price gouging in the sale of pencils. They released a study showing that whereas the average retail price of pencils was $1.00, the average cost of producing pencils was only $0.50. "Pencils can be produced without complicated machinery or highly skilled workers, so there is no justification for companies charging a price that is twice what it costs them to produce the product. Pencils are too important in the life of every American for us to tolerate this sort of price gouging any longer," said George Grommet, chief spokesperson for the consumer groups. The consumer groups advocate passage of a law that would allow companies selling pencils to charge a price no more than 20 percent greater than their average cost of production.

Do you believe such a law would be advisable in a situation like this? Explain.

6.8 **[Related to** Solved Problem 6**]** In 2013, Sony announced that it had suffered losses selling televisions for the ninth straight year. Given the strong consumer demand for plasma, LCD, and LED television sets, shouldn't Sony have been able to raise prices to earn a profit? Briefly explain.

Source: Daisuke Wakabayashi, "Investor Pushes Sony to Take Entertainment Unit Public," *Wall Street Journal*, May 14, 2013.

6.9 An article in the *Wall Street Journal* discusses the visual effects industry, which is made up of firms that provide visual effects for films and television programs. The article notes: "Blockbusters … often have thousands of visual effects shots. Even dramas and comedies today can include hundreds of them." But the article notes that the firms producing the effects have not been very profitable. Some

firms have declared bankruptcy, and the former general manager of one firm was quoted as saying: "A good year for us was a 5% return." If demand for visual effects is so strong, why is it difficult for the firms that supply them to make an economic profit?

Source: Ben Fritz, "Visual Effects Industry Does a Disappearing Act," *Wall Street Journal*, February 22, 2013.

6.10 Although New York State is second only to Washington State in production of apples, its production has been declining during the past 20 years. The decline has been particularly steep in counties close to New York City. In 1985, there were more than 11,000 acres of apple orchards in Ulster County, which is 75 miles north of New York City. Today, only about 6,000 acres remain. As it became difficult for apple growers in the county to compete with lower-cost producers elsewhere, the resources these entrepreneurs were using to produce apples—particularly land—became more valuable in other uses. Many farmers sold their land to housing developers. Suppose a nutritionist develops a revolutionary new diet that involves eating 10 apples per day. The new diet becomes wildly popular. What effect is the new diet likely to have on the number of apple orchards within 100 miles of New York City? What effect is the diet likely to have on housing prices in New York City?

Glossary

Allocative efficiency A state of the economy in which production is in accordance with consumer preferences; in particular, every good or service is produced up to the point where the last unit provides a marginal benefit to society equal to the marginal cost of producing it.

Average revenue (*AR*) Total revenue divided by the quantity of the product sold.

Economic loss The situation in which a firm's total revenue is less than its total cost, including all implicit costs.

Economic profit A firm's revenues minus all its costs, implicit and explicit.

Long-run competitive equilibrium The situation in which the entry and exit of firms has resulted in the typical firm breaking even.

Long-run supply curve A curve that shows the relationship in the long run between market price and the quantity supplied.

Marginal revenue (*MR*) The change in total revenue from selling one more unit of a product.

Perfectly competitive market A market that meets the conditions of (1) many buyers and sellers, (2) all firms selling identical products, and (3) no barriers to new firms entering the market.

Price taker A buyer or seller that is unable to affect the market price.

Productive efficiency A situation in which a good or service is produced at the lowest possible cost.

Profit Total revenue minus total cost.

Shutdown point The minimum point on a firm's average variable cost curve; if the price falls below this point, the firm shuts down production in the short run.

Sunk cost A cost that has already been paid and cannot be recovered.

Credits

Credits are listed in the order of appearance.

Photo

Michael Nolan/Robert Harding; Alex Segre/Alamy

Text

Sharon M. Oster, *Modern Competitive Analysis*, Third Edition, New York: Oxford University Press, 1999.

Monopoly and Antitrust Policy

From Chapter 15 of *Economics*, Fifth Edition. R. Glenn Hubbard and Anthony Patrick O'Brien. Copyright © 2015 by Pearson Education, Inc.

Monopoly and Antitrust Policy

Chapter Outline and Learning Objectives

A Monopoly on Lobster Dinners in Maine?

A *New York Times* article written from Stonington, Maine, explained that: "Lobsters are flooding the market here." The reporter observed that the huge lobster harvest was not good news for fishermen because "the law of supply and demand has forced the price down to a 40-year low" of $1.35 per pound. Yet shortly after this article appeared, a columnist for *Slate*, an online magazine, had dinner with his father at the only lobster restaurant in Stonington, The Fisherman's Friend. He was surprised that the restaurant charged $20.99 for each dinner.

How could The Fisherman's Friend charge so much for a lobster dinner when the price of lobsters was so low? The answer is that The Fisherman's Friend is the *only* seafood restaurant in Stonington. The reporter and his father couldn't eat at "the competitor next door" because there wasn't one. To eat lobster while staying in Stonington, they had to eat at that restaurant or buy lobsters in a store and cook the lobsters themselves. In other words,

The Fisherman's Friend has a *monopoly* on selling seafood dinners in that town.

Few firms in the United States are monopolies because in a market system whenever a firm earns an economic profit, typically other firms will enter that market. Therefore, it is very difficult for a firm to remain the only provider of a good or service. Only if the gap between the price of lobsters and the price of lobster dinners in Stonington fails to attract a competitor would The Fisherman's Friend be able to maintain its monopoly. Although not common, monopolies are worth studying because they provide a benchmark for how firms behave when they face the minimum possible competition. In this chapter, we will build a model to analyze monopolies.

Sources: Katharine Q. Seelye, "In Maine, More Lobsters Than They Know What to Do With," *New York Times*, July 28, 2012; and Matthew Yglesias, "The Mystery of the Market Price" www.slate.com, August 21, 2012.

Economics in Your Life

Is There a Monopoly in Your Dorm?

You and your roommate Fatma come up with an idea for a business: You will buy rolls, lunch meat, lettuce, and tomatoes and become the sole seller of submarine sandwiches in your school's dormitories on Saturday and Sunday evenings when there are no other food vendors open on campus. You believe that there will be many hungry customers when students return to campus from the library and off-campus events. But you and Fatma must decide on the prices to charge for the subs. Fatma argues that because your business is a monopoly, you can charge prices much higher than what local shops charge for subs during the day—hungry students will have to buy your subs or stay hungry until the following day. You want to make a profit from your business but are not sure if Fatma is right. Is your business a monopoly? Should you charge high prices for your sandwiches? As you read this chapter, try to answer these questions. You can check your answers against those we provide at the end of this chapter.

Although few firms are monopolies, the economic model of monopoly can be quite useful. As we have seen, even though perfectly competitive markets are rare, the competitive market model provides a benchmark for how a firm acts in the most competitive situation possible: when it is in an industry with many firms that all supply the same product. Monopoly provides a benchmark for the other extreme, where a firm is the only one in its market and, therefore, faces no competition from other firms supplying its product. The monopoly model is also useful in analyzing situations in which firms agree to *collude*, or not compete, and act together as if they were a monopoly. As we will discuss in this chapter, collusion is illegal in the United States, but it occasionally happens.

Monopolies pose a dilemma for the government. Should the government allow monopolies to exist? Are there circumstances in which the government should actually promote the existence of monopolies? Should the government regulate the prices monopolies charge? If so, will such price regulation increase economic efficiency? In this chapter, we will explore these public policy issues.

1 LEARNING OBJECTIVE

Define monopoly.

Monopoly A firm that is the only seller of a good or service that does not have a close substitute.

Is Any Firm Ever Really a Monopoly?

A **monopoly** is a firm that is the only seller of a good or service that does not have a close substitute. Because substitutes of some kind exist for just about every product, are there actually any monopolies? The answer is "yes," provided that the substitutes are not "close" substitutes. But how do we decide whether a substitute is a close substitute? A narrow definition of monopoly that some economists use is that a firm has a monopoly if it can ignore the actions of all other firms. In other words, if a firm can ignore the prices other firms charge, the firm has a monopoly because other firms must not be producing close substitutes. For example, candles are a substitute for electric lights, but your local electric company can ignore candle prices because however low the price of candles becomes, almost no customers will give up using electric lights and switch to candles. Therefore, your local electric company is clearly a monopoly.

Many economists, however, use a broader definition of *monopoly*. For example, consider again The Fisherman's Friend seafood restaurant in Stonington, Maine, that we discussed in the chapter opener. Does this restaurant have a monopoly? Substitutes for lobster dinners certainly exist. If the price of lobster dinners is too high, people will switch to steak dinners or spaghetti dinners or some other food. People do not have to eat at The Fisherman's Friend or starve. The restaurant is in competition with several other local restaurants. So, The Fisherman's Friend does not meet the narrow definition of a monopoly. Many economists, however, would still argue that it is useful to think of the restaurant as having a monopoly.

Although steak and spaghetti are substitutes for lobster, competition from firms selling them is not enough to keep The Fisherman's Friend from earning an economic profit. We have seen that when firms earn economic profits, we can expect new firms to enter the industry, and in the long run, the economic profits are competed away. The Fisherman's Friend's profits will not be competed away as long as it is the *only* seller of lobster dinners. The *Slate* reporter mentioned in the chapter opener noted that: "Stonington is a great place to visit. But it's also a very small town." So it's possible that no other seafood restaurants will choose to open in the town. In that case, using the broader definition of monopoly, The Fisherman's Friend has a monopoly because there are no other firms selling a substitute close enough that its economic profits are competed away in the long run.

Making the Connection | **Is Google a Monopoly?**

As we will discuss later in this chapter, the federal government can take legal action against a firm under *antitrust laws* if the government believes that the firm has created a monopoly. The U.S. Federal Trade Commission (FTC) spent two years beginning in 2011 investigating whether Google had violated antitrust laws before concluding that it hadn't. The European Union, which is an organization of 28 European countries, has similar rules against firms forming monopolies. The European Commission enforces these rules. In early

2011, Microsoft filed a complaint with the European Commission that Google was using its dominant position as an Internet search engine to exclude competitors. In 2013, Google reached a settlement with the European Commission in which the firm agreed to clearly label any search results that directed users to sites that Google owns. Still, many critics argued that both the FTC and the European Commission should take further actions against some of Google's practices.

Google has a dominant market share in the United States and in Europe. Can other search engines effectively compete?

But is Google a monopoly? Clearly, Google is not the only Internet search option available. Yahoo! has for a number of years operated a search engine, Microsoft operates the Bing search engine, and there are a number of smaller search engines. Critics point out, though, that Google has a dominant market share of 70 percent in the United States and 90 percent in Europe. Can the other search engines effectively compete with Google? Microsoft argues that Google has taken steps to create an effective monopoly:

> [Google] understands as well as anyone that search engines depend upon the openness of the Web in order to function properly…. Unfortunately, Google has engaged in a broadening pattern of walling off access to content and data that competitors need to provide search results to consumers and to attract advertisers.

Microsoft was particularly concerned that Google was limiting the access of other search engines to YouTube, which Google owns: "Without proper access to YouTube, Bing and other search engines cannot stand with Google on an equal footing in returning search results with links to YouTube videos and that, of course, drives more users away from competitors and to Google." Microsoft also complained that Google was limiting the access of other search engines to many of the books that Google had scanned and made available on the Web.

Google, naturally, takes a different view of its position. The company argues that its dominant market share is due to the higher quality of its search engine, not any attempts the company has made to reduce the access of other search engines to online content. In a response to the FTC investigation, Google noted: "We want [users of search engines] to stay with us because we're innovating and making our products better—not because [they are] locked in."

As we have seen, many economists consider a firm to have a monopoly if other firms are unable to compete away its profit in the long run. Some economists argue that rapid technological advances affecting search engines and other aspects of the Internet make it unlikely that Google would be able to maintain its current level of profitability indefinitely. The debate over whether other search engines can compete with Google or whether it is effectively a monopoly is likely to continue.

Sources: Vanessa Mock, "Google's Grand Bargain," *Wall Street Journal*, April 18, 2013; Miguel Helft, "Google Confirms F.T.C. Antitrust Inquiry," *New York Times*, June 24, 2011; Amit Singhal, "Supporting Choice, Ensuring Economic Opportunity," www.googleblog.blogspot.com, June 24, 2011; David Goldman, "Microsoft Accuses Google of Antitrust Violations," www.money.cnn.com, March 31, 2011; and Brad Smith, "Adding Our Voice to Concerns about Search in Europe," www.blogs.technet.com, March 31, 2011.

Your Turn: Test your understanding by doing related problems 1.6 and 1.7 at the end of this chapter.

Where Do Monopolies Come From?

2 LEARNING OBJECTIVE

Explain the four main reasons monopolies arise.

Because monopolies do not face competition, every firm would like to have a monopoly. But to have a monopoly, barriers to entering the market must be so high that no other firms can enter. *Barriers to entry* may be high enough to keep out competing firms for four main reasons:

1. Government action blocks the entry of more than one firm into a market.
2. One firm has control of a key resource necessary to produce a good.
3. There are important *network externalities* in supplying the good or service.
4. Economies of scale are so large that one firm has a *natural monopoly*.

Government Action Blocks Entry

As we will discuss later in this chapter, governments ordinarily try to promote competition in markets, but sometimes governments take action to block entry into a market. In the United States, governments block entry in two main ways:

1. By granting a *patent*, *copyright*, or *trademark* to an individual or a firm, giving it the exclusive right to produce a product

2. By granting a firm a *public franchise*, making it the exclusive legal provider of a good or service

Patents, Copyrights, and Trademarks The U.S. government grants patents to firms that develop new products or new ways of making existing products. A **patent** gives a firm the exclusive right to a new product for a period of 20 years from the date the patent is filed with the government. Because Microsoft has a patent on the Windows operating system, other firms cannot sell their versions of Windows. The government grants patents to encourage firms to spend money on the research and development necessary to create new products. If other firms could have freely copied Windows, Microsoft would have been unlikely to spend the money necessary to develop it. Sometimes a firm is able to maintain a monopoly in the production of a good without patent protection, provided that it can keep secret how the product is made.

Patent protection is of vital importance to pharmaceutical firms as they develop new prescription drugs. Pharmaceutical firms start research and development work on a new prescription drug an average of 12 years before the drug is available for sale. A firm applies for a patent about 10 years before it begins to sell the product. The average 10-year delay between the government granting a patent and the firm actually selling the drug is due to the federal Food and Drug Administration's requirements that the firm demonstrate that the drug is both safe and effective. Therefore, during the period before the drug can be sold, the firm will have significant costs to develop and test the drug. If the drug does not successfully make it to market, the firm will have a substantial loss.

Once a drug is available for sale, the profits the firm earns from the drug will increase throughout the period of patent protection—which is usually about 10 years—as the drug becomes more widely known to doctors and patients. After the patent has expired, other firms are free to legally produce chemically identical drugs called *generic drugs*. Gradually, competition from generic drugs will eliminate the profits the original firm had been earning. For example, when patent protection expired for Glucophage, a diabetes drug manufactured by Bristol-Myers Squibb, sales of the drug declined by more than $1.5 billion in the first year due to competition from 12 generic versions of the drug produced by other firms. When the patent expired on Prozac, an antidepressant drug manufactured by Eli Lilly, sales dropped by more than 80 percent. Most economic profits from selling a prescription drug are eliminated 20 years after the drug is first offered for sale.

A *trademark* grants a firm legal protection against other firms using its product's name. Trademarks are also referred to as *brand names*. The U.S. Patent and Trademark Office defines a trademark as "any word, name, symbol, device, or any combination, used or intended to be used to identify and distinguish the goods/services of one seller or provider from those of others, and to indicate the source of the goods/services." Firms often vigorously defend their trademarks, including by filing lawsuits against other firms for selling goods that infringe on their trademarks. For example, Christian Louboutin filed a lawsuit against Yves Saint Laurent claiming that Yves Saint Laurent had infringed on Louboutin's trademark on women's shoes with red soles.

Patent The exclusive right to a product for a period of 20 years from the date the patent is filed with the government.

Making
the
Connection

Does Hasbro Have a Monopoly on Monopoly?

To receive a copyright, patent, or trademark, a work has to be substantially new. Once a work no longer has legal protection, it is in the *public domain* and available to be freely used. It wouldn't be possible, for example, to make small changes to Mark Twain's novel *Huckleberry Finn* and then claim copyright on the book because it has been in the public domain for decades. (If you drew new illustrations for the book, however, it would be possible to copyright those illustrations independently of the text of the book.)

Hasbro is the multinational American company that owns Monopoly, one of the world's most popular board games. The company estimates that more than 275 million copies of the game have been sold, and it is available in 43 languages. According to Hasbro, Charles Darrow invented the game in the 1930s. After selling many homemade copies, Darrow sold the game to Parker Brothers. In 1935, the U.S. Patent and Trademark Office issued Parker Brothers a trademark on the use of the name Monopoly for a board game. Hasbro bought Parker Brothers in 1991. Trademarks, unlike patents and copyrights, never expire, so Hasbro continues to have a trademark on the name Monopoly.

Hasbro's trademark on its Monopoly game prevents other companies from creating and selling similar games using the same title. In 2013, Hasbro displayed its new cat token at a toy fair.

Economics professor Ralph Anspach of California State University, San Francisco, received an unexpected lesson in the law of trademarks when he decided in the 1970s to sell a game about competition that he titled Anti-Monopoly. The game was a hit, selling 200,000 copies the first year. Parker Brothers sued Anspach, though, on the grounds that his game infringed on their Monopoly trademark. In the course of defending the lawsuit, Anspach believed he had uncovered evidence that in 1904 a woman named Elizabeth Magie had developed The Landlord's Game, which was very similar to Monopoly. The game was never trademarked and was played for years on the east coast. According to Anspach, Darrow became aware of The Landlord's Game in the mid-1930s, made a few changes to it, and sold it to Parker Brothers in 1935. A federal appeals court largely agreed with Anspach that given the history of the game, the name Monopoly was in the public domain and so couldn't be trademarked. Congress later amended the law, though, in a way that reinstated Parker Brothers' trademark. Eventually, Anspach and Hasbro worked out a settlement under which Anspach was allowed to sell his Anti-Monopoly game under a license from Hasbro.

Losing the trademark on its Monopoly game would have cost Hasbro millions of dollars per year because other companies could have begun to market similar games using the same title. The long legal fight the company had with Professor Anspach illustrates that companies consider it critical to retain exclusive control over their products.

Sources: Mary Pilon, "How a Fight Over a Board Game Monopolized an Economist's Life," *Wall Street Journal*, October 20, 2009; Ralph Anspach, *The Billion Dollar Monopoly® Swindle*, 2nd ed., Bloomington, IN: Xlibris, 2007; and Rachel Doepker, "Monopoly Patented," Business Reference Services, Library of Congress, www.loc.gov/rr/business /businesshistory/December/monopoly.html.

Your Turn: Test your understanding by doing related problem 2.10 at the end of this chapter.

Just as the government grants a new product patent or trademark protection, it grants books, films, and pieces of music **copyright** protection. U.S. law grants the creator of a book, film, or piece of music the exclusive right to use the creation during the creator's lifetime. The creator's heirs retain this exclusive right for 70 years after the creator's death. In effect, copyrights create monopolies for the copyrighted items. Without copyrights, individuals and firms would be less likely to invest in creating new books, films, and software.

Copyright A government-granted exclusive right to produce and sell a creation.

Public Franchises In some cases, the government grants a firm a **public franchise** that allows it to be the only legal provider of a good or service. For example, state and local governments often designate one company as the sole provider of electricity, natural gas, or water.

Public franchise A government designation that a firm is the only legal provider of a good or service.

Occasionally, a government may decide to provide certain services directly to consumers through a *public enterprise*. This is much more common in Europe than in the United States. For example, the governments in most European countries own the railroad systems. In the United States, many city governments provide water and sewage service rather than rely on private firms.

Control of a Key Resource

Another way for a firm to become a monopoly is by controlling a key resource. This happens infrequently because most resources, including raw materials such as oil or iron ore, are widely available from a variety of suppliers. There are, however, a few prominent examples of monopolies based on control of a key resource, such as the Aluminum Company of America (Alcoa) and the International Nickel Company of Canada.

For many years until the 1940s, Alcoa either owned or had long-term contracts to buy nearly all of the available bauxite, the mineral needed to produce aluminum. Without access to bauxite, competing firms had to use recycled aluminum, which limited the amount of aluminum they could produce. Similarly, the International Nickel Company of Canada controlled more than 90 percent of available nickel supplies. Competition in the nickel market increased when the Petsamo nickel fields in northern Russia were developed after World War II.

In the United States, a key resource for a professional sports team is a large stadium. The teams that make up the major professional sports leagues—Major League Baseball, the National Football League, and the National Basketball Association—usually either own or have long-term leases with the stadiums in major cities. Control of these stadiums is a major barrier to new professional baseball, football, or basketball leagues forming.

Making the Connection	**Are Diamond Profits Forever?** **The De Beers Diamond Monopoly**

The most famous monopoly based on control of a raw material is the De Beers diamond mining and marketing company of South Africa. Before the 1860s, diamonds were extremely rare. Only a few pounds of diamonds were produced each year, primarily from Brazil and India. Then in 1870, enormous deposits of diamonds were discovered along the Orange River in South Africa. It became possible to produce thousands of pounds of diamonds per year, and the owners of the new mines feared that the price of diamonds would plummet. To avoid financial disaster, the mine owners decided in 1888 to merge and form De Beers Consolidated Mines, Ltd.

De Beers became one of the most profitable and longest-lived monopolies in history. The company carefully controlled the supply of diamonds to keep prices high. As new diamond deposits were discovered in Russia and Zaire, De Beers was able to maintain prices by buying most of the new supplies.

Because diamonds are rarely destroyed, De Beers has always worried about competition from the resale of stones. Heavily promoting diamond engagement and wedding rings with the slogan "A Diamond Is Forever" was a way around this problem. Because engagement and wedding rings have great sentimental value, they are seldom resold, even by the heirs of the original recipients. De Beers advertising has been successful even in some countries, such as Japan, that have had no custom of giving diamond engagement rings. As the populations in De Beers's key markets age, its advertising in recent years has focused on middle-aged men presenting diamond rings to their wives as symbols of financial success and continuing love and on professional women buying "right-hand rings" for themselves.

Over the years, competition has gradually increased in the diamond business. By 2000, De Beers directly controlled only about 40 percent of world diamond production. The company became concerned about how much it was spending to buy diamonds from other sources to keep them off the market. It decided to abandon its strategy of attempting to control the worldwide supply of diamonds and to concentrate instead on differentiating its diamonds by relying on its name recognition. Each De Beers diamond is now marked with a microscopic brand—a "Forevermark"—to reassure consumers of its high quality. Other firms, such as BHP Billiton, which owns mines in northern Canada, have followed

De Beers promoted the sentimental value of diamonds as a way to maintain its position in the diamond market.

suit by branding their diamonds. Whether consumers will pay attention to brands on diamonds remains to be seen, although through 2013, the branding strategy had helped De Beers to maintain about a 35 to 40 percent share of the diamond market.

Sources: Alex MacDonald, "De Beers Brings Oppenheimer Era to End," *Wall Street Journal*, October 3, 2012; William J. Holstein, "De Beers Reworks Its Image as Rivals Multiply," *New York Times*, December 12, 2008; Edward Jay Epstein, "Have You Ever Tried to Sell a Diamond?" *Atlantic Monthly*, February 1982; and Donna J. Bergenstock, Mary E. Deily, and Larry W. Taylor, "A Cartel's Response to Cheating: An Empirical Investigation of the De Beers Diamond Empire," *Southern Economic Journal*, Vol. 73, No. 1, July 2006, pp. 173–189.

Your Turn: Test your understanding by doing related problem 2.11 at the end of this chapter.

Network Externalities

There are **network externalities** in the consumption of a product if its usefulness increases with the number of people who use it. If you owned the only HD television in the world, for example, it would not be very valuable because firms would not have an incentive to develop HD programming. The more HD televisions there are in use, the more valuable they become to consumers.

Some economists argue that network externalities can serve as barriers to entry. For example, in the early 1980s, Microsoft gained an advantage over other software companies by developing MS-DOS, the operating system for the first IBM personal computers. Because IBM sold more computers than any other company, software developers wrote many application programs for MS-DOS. The more people who used MS-DOS–based programs, the greater the value to a consumer of using an MS-DOS–based program. By the 1990s, Microsoft had replaced MS-DOS with Windows. Today, Windows has an 85 percent share in the market for personal computer operating systems, with Apple's operating system having a 10 percent share, and other operating systems, including the open-source Linux system, having shares of about 1 percent or less. If another firm introduced a new operating system, some economists argue that relatively few people would use it initially, and few applications would run on it, which would limit the operating system's value to other consumers.

eBay was the first Internet site to attract a significant number of people to its online auctions. Once a large number of people began to use eBay to buy and sell collectibles, antiques, and many other products, it became a more valuable place to buy and sell. Yahoo .com, Amazon.com, and other Internet sites eventually started online auctions, but they had difficulty attracting buyers and sellers. On eBay, a buyer expects to find more sellers, and a seller expects to find more potential buyers than on Amazon or other auction sites.

As these examples show, from a firm's point of view, network externalities can set off a *virtuous cycle*: If a firm can attract enough customers initially, it can attract additional customers because the value of its product has been increased by more people using it, which attracts even more customers, and so on. With products such as computer operating systems and online auctions, it might be difficult for new firms to enter the market and compete away the profit being earned by the first firm in the market.

Economists engage in considerable debate, however, about the extent to which network externalities are important barriers to entry in the business world. Some economists argue that Microsoft and eBay have dominant positions primarily because they are efficient in offering products that satisfy consumer preferences rather than because of the effects of network externalities. In this view, the advantages existing firms gain from network externalities would not be enough to protect them from competing firms offering better products. For example, many people have switched from computers to tablets and smartphones that run on Apple's iOS or Google's Android operating system, making Microsoft's domination of computer operating systems less important.

Natural Monopoly

Economies of scale exist when a firm's long-run average costs fall as it increases the quantity of output it produces. A **natural monopoly** occurs when economies of scale are so large that one firm can supply the entire market at a lower

Network externalities A situation in which the usefulness of a product increases with the number of consumers who use it.

Natural monopoly A situation in which economies of scale are so large that one firm can supply the entire market at a lower average total cost than can two or more firms.

Figure 1

Average Total Cost Curve for a Natural Monopoly

With a natural monopoly, the average total cost curve is still falling when it crosses the demand curve (point *A*). If only one firm is producing electric power in the market, and it produces where the average cost curve intersects the demand curve, average total cost will equal $0.04 per kilowatt-hour of electricity produced. If the market is divided between two firms, each producing 15 billion kilowatt-hours, the average cost of producing electricity rises to $0.06 per kilowatt-hour (point *B*). In this case, if one firm expands production, it can move down the average total cost curve, lower its price, and drive the other firm out of business.

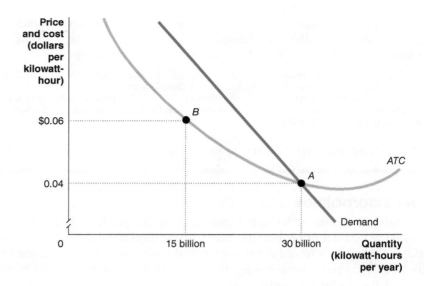

average total cost than can two or more firms. In that case, there is "room" in the market for only one firm.

Figure 1 shows the average total cost curve for a firm producing electricity and the total demand for electricity in the firm's market. Notice that the average total cost curve is still falling when it crosses the demand curve at point *A*. If the firm is a monopoly and produces 30 billion kilowatt-hours of electricity per year, its average total cost of production will be $0.04 per kilowatt-hour. Suppose instead that two firms are in the market, each producing half of the market output, or 15 billion kilowatt-hours per year. Assume that each firm has the same average total cost curve. The figure shows that producing 15 billion kilowatt-hours would move each firm back up its average cost curve so that the average cost of producing electricity would rise to $0.06 per kilowatt-hour (point *B*). In this case, if one of the firms expands production, it will move down the average total cost curve. With lower average costs, it will be able to offer electricity at a lower price than the other firm can offer. Eventually, the other firm will be driven out of business, and the remaining firm will have a monopoly. Because a monopoly would develop automatically—or *naturally*—in this market, it is a natural monopoly.

Natural monopolies are most likely to occur in markets where fixed costs are very large relative to variable costs. For example, a firm that produces electricity must make a substantial investment in machinery and equipment necessary to generate the electricity and in the wires and cables necessary to distribute it. Once the initial investment has been made, however, the marginal cost of producing another kilowatt-hour of electricity is relatively small.

Solved Problem 2

Can a Seafood Restaurant Be a Natural Monopoly?

We saw in the chapter opener that there is only one seafood restaurant in the town of Stonington, Maine. While eating at the restaurant, a principles of economics student visiting Stonington makes the following observation: "This restaurant must be a natural monopoly. We can reach this conclusion because it is making a large profit by selling lobster dinners for high prices even though the price of live lobsters has fallen to very low levels. If the restaurant wasn't a natural monopoly, other restaurants would open in Stonington and compete away this restaurant's profit." Briefly explain whether you agree with the student's observation. Does the amount of time the restaurant has been earning a large profit on lobster dinners matter for your answer? Include a graph in your answer showing the demand for this restaurant's meals and its cost curves.

Solving the Problem

Step 1: **Review the chapter material.** This problem is about natural monopoly, so you may want to review the section "Natural Monopoly."

Step 2: **Begin your answer by explaining what must be true for the restaurant to be a natural monopoly.** We know for a firm to be a natural monopoly, its average total cost curve should still be declining when it crosses the firm's demand curve. If the market for lobster dinners in Stonington were a natural monopoly, then if there were two seafood restaurants in Stonington, the average cost of supplying lobster dinners would be higher than if only one restaurant were in the market. So, we would expect one restaurant to expand, thereby moving down its average total cost curve, lowering its price of lobster dinners, and driving the other restaurant out of business.

Step 3: **Explain whether it is likely that the seafood restaurant in Stonington is a natural monopoly and draw a graph to illustrate your answer.** Restaurants are not usually natural monopolies. Most towns have at least several restaurants in each category—seafood, Italian, Chinese, and so on—which would not be true if the restaurants were natural monopolies. It is possible, though, that in a very small town, demand for seafood dinners might be limited enough that the demand curve intersects the average total cost at a quantity where the average total cost curve is still falling. The following graph illustrates this situation.

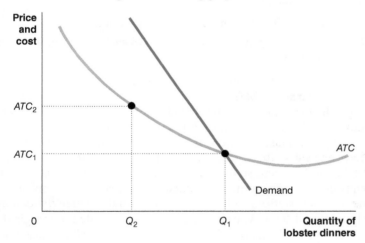

As shown in the graph, the market for seafood dinners in Stonington is a natural monopoly because if one restaurant can supply Q_1 dinners at an average total cost of ATC_1, then dividing the business equally between two restaurants each supplying Q_2 dinners would raise average total cost to ATC_2.

Step 4: **Complete your answer by explaining whether the amount of time the restaurant has been earning a large profit on lobster dinners matters to your answer.** The chapter opener indicates that the large profit earned by The Fisherman's Friend was largely due to low prices for lobsters following a record harvest. It can take time for potential competitors to decide whether it would be profitable to enter an industry. The longer the restaurant continues to operate without significant competition, the more likely it is that the firm actually is a natural monopoly in the small Stonington market.

Extra Credit: Keep in mind that competition is not good for its own sake. It is good because it can lead to lower costs, lower prices, and better products. In certain markets, however, cost conditions are such that competition is likely to lead to higher costs and higher prices. These markets are natural monopolies that are best served by one firm. The market for restaurant meals is rarely a natural monopoly, but the market for seafood in tiny Stonington, Maine, might be an example.

Your Turn: For more practice, do related problem 2.13 at the end of this chapter.

How Does a Monopoly Choose Price and Output?

Like every other firm, a monopoly maximizes profit by producing where marginal revenue equals marginal cost. A monopoly differs from other firms in that *a monopoly's demand curve is the same as the market demand curve for the product*. When discussing perfect competition, we emphasized that the market demand curve for wheat was very different from the demand curve for the wheat produced by any one farmer. If, however, one farmer had a monopoly on wheat production, the two demand curves would be exactly the same.

Marginal Revenue Once Again

Firms in perfectly competitive markets—such as a farmer in the wheat market—face horizontal demand curves. These firms are *price takers*. All other firms, including monopolies, are *price makers*. If price makers raise their prices, they will lose some, but not all, of their customers. Therefore, they face both a downward-sloping demand curve and a downward-sloping marginal revenue curve. Let's review why a firm's marginal revenue curve slopes downward if its demand curve slopes downward.

Remember that when a firm cuts the price of a product, one good thing happens, and one bad thing happens:

- *The good thing.* It sells more units of the product.
- *The bad thing.* It receives less revenue from each unit than it would have received at the higher price.

For example, consider the table in Figure 2, which shows information on the market for Time Warner Cable's basic cable package. To operate a cable system in a city, firms typically need a license from the city government. Time Warner is the only cable television available in some cities. For simplicity, we assume that a particular market has only 10 potential subscribers. If Time Warner charges a price of $60 per month, it won't have any subscribers. If it charges a price of $57, it sells 1 subscription. At $54, it sells 2 subscriptions, and so on. Time Warner's total revenue is equal to the number of subscriptions sold per month multiplied by the price. The firm's average revenue—or revenue per subscription sold—is equal to its total revenue divided by the quantity of subscriptions sold. Time Warner is particularly interested in marginal revenue because marginal revenue tells the firm how much its revenue will increase if it cuts the price to sell one more subscription.

Notice that Time Warner's marginal revenue is less than the price for every subscription sold after the first subscription. To see why, think about what happens if Time Warner cuts the price of its basic cable package from $42 to $39, which increases its subscriptions sold from 6 to 7. Time Warner increases its revenue by the $39 it receives for the seventh subscription. But it also loses revenue of $3 per subscription on the first 6 subscriptions because it could have sold them at the old price of $42. So, its marginal revenue on the seventh subscription is $39 − $18 = $21, which is the value shown in the table. The graph in Figure 2 plots Time Warner's demand and marginal revenue curves, based on the information in the table.

Profit Maximization for a Monopolist

Figure 3 shows how Time Warner combines the information on demand and marginal revenue with information on average and marginal costs to decide how many subscriptions to sell and what price to charge. We assume that the firm's marginal cost and average total cost curves have the usual U shapes. In panel (a), we see how Time Warner can calculate its profit-maximizing quantity and price. As long as the marginal cost of selling one more subscription is less than the marginal revenue, the firm should sell additional subscriptions because it is adding to its profits. As Time Warner sells more cable subscriptions, rising marginal cost will eventually equal marginal revenue, and the firm will be selling

Subscribers per Month (Q)	Price (P)	Total Revenue (TR = P x Q)	Average Revenue (AR = TR/Q)	Marginal Revenue (MR = ΔTR/ΔQ)
0	$60	$0	–	–
1	57	57	$57	$57
2	54	108	54	51
3	51	153	51	45
4	48	192	48	39
5	45	225	45	33
6	42	252	42	27
7	39	273	39	21
8	36	288	36	15
9	33	297	33	9
10	30	300	30	3

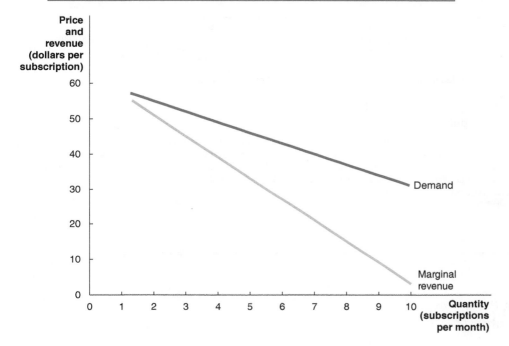

Figure 2

Calculating a Monopoly's Revenue

Time Warner Cable faces a downward-sloping demand curve for subscriptions to basic cable. To sell more subscriptions, it must cut the price. When this happens, it gains revenue from selling more subscriptions but loses revenue from selling at a lower price the subscriptions that it could have sold at a higher price. The firm's marginal revenue is the change in revenue from selling another subscription. We can calculate marginal revenue by subtracting the revenue lost as a result of a price cut from the revenue gained. The table shows that Time Warner's marginal revenue is less than the price for every subscription sold after the first subscription. Therefore, Time Warner's marginal revenue curve will be below its demand curve.

the profit-maximizing quantity of subscriptions. Time Warner maximizes profit with the sixth subscription, which adds $27 to the firm's costs and $27 to its revenues—point A in panel (a) of Figure 3. The demand curve tells us that Time Warner can sell 6 subscriptions for a price of $42 per month. We can conclude that Time Warner's profit-maximizing quantity of subscriptions is 6, and its profit-maximizing price is $42.

Panel (b) shows that the average total cost of 6 subscriptions is $30 and that Time Warner can sell 6 subscriptions at a price of $42 per month (point B on the demand curve). Time Warner is making a profit of $12 per subscription—the price of $42 minus the average cost of $30. Its total profit is $72 (= 6 subscriptions × $12 profit per subscription), which is shown by the area of the green-shaded rectangle in the figure. We could also have calculated Time Warner's total profit as the difference between its total revenue and its total cost. Its total revenue from selling 6 subscriptions is $252. Its total cost equals its average total cost multiplied by the number of subscriptions sold, or $30 × 6 = $180. So, its profit is $252 − $180 = $72.

It's important to note that even though Time Warner is earning an economic profit, new firms will *not* enter the market unless they can obtain licenses from the city. If it holds the only license, Time Warner has a monopoly and will not face competition from other cable operators. Therefore, if other factors remain unchanged, Time Warner will be able to continue to earn an economic profit, even in the long run.

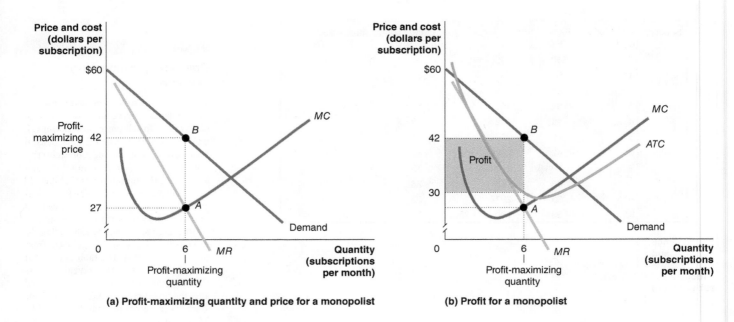

Figure 3 **Profit-Maximizing Price and Output for a Monopoly**

Panel (a) shows that to maximize profit, Time Warner should sell subscriptions up to the point where the marginal revenue from selling the last subscription equals its marginal cost (point A). In this case, both the marginal revenue from selling the sixth subscription and the marginal cost are $27. Time Warner maximizes profit by selling 6 subscriptions per month and charging a price of $42 (point B).

In panel (b), the green rectangle represents Time Warner's profit. The rectangle has a height equal to $12, which is the price of $42 minus the average total cost of $30, and a base equal to the quantity of 6 cable subscriptions. Time Warner's profit therefore equals $12 × 6 = $72.

Solved Problem 3

Finding the Profit-Maximizing Price and Output for a Cable Monopoly

Suppose that Comcast has a cable monopoly in Philadelphia. The following table gives Comcast's demand and costs per month for subscriptions to basic cable (for simplicity, we once again keep the number of subscribers artificially small):

Price	Quantity	Total Revenue	$\left(MR = \dfrac{\Delta TR}{\Delta Q} \right)$	Total Cost	$\left(MC = \dfrac{\Delta TC}{\Delta Q} \right)$
$27	3			$56	
26	4			73	
25	5			91	
24	6			110	
23	7			130	
22	8			151	

a. Fill in the missing values in the table.

b. If Comcast wants to maximize profit, what price should it charge, and how many cable subscriptions per month should it sell? How much profit will Comcast make? Briefly explain.

c. Suppose the local government imposes a $25-per-month tax on cable companies. Now what price should Comcast charge, how many subscriptions should it sell, and what will its profit be?

Solving the Problem

Step 1: **Review the chapter material.** This problem is about finding the profit-maximizing quantity and price for a monopolist, so you may want to review the section "Profit Maximization for a Monopolist."

Step 2: **Answer part (a) by filling in the missing values in the table.** Remember that to calculate marginal revenue and marginal cost, you must divide the change in total revenue or total cost by the change in quantity.

We don't have enough information from the table to fill in the values for marginal revenue and marginal cost in the first row.

Price	Quantity	Total Revenue	Marginal Revenue $\left(MR = \dfrac{\Delta TR}{\Delta Q} \right)$	Total Cost	Marginal Cost $\left(MC = \dfrac{\Delta TC}{\Delta Q} \right)$
$27	3	$81	—	$56	—
26	4	104	$23	73	$17
25	5	125	21	91	18
24	6	144	19	110	19
23	7	161	17	130	20
22	8	176	15	151	21

Step 3: **Answer part (b) by determining the profit-maximizing quantity and price.** We know that Comcast will maximize profit by selling subscriptions up to the point where marginal cost equals marginal revenue. In this case, that means selling 6 subscriptions per month. From the information in the first two columns, we know Comcast can sell 6 subscriptions at a price of $24 each. Comcast's profit is equal to the difference between its total revenue and its total cost: Profit = $144 − $110 = $34 per month.

Step 4: **Answer part (c) by analyzing the effect of the tax.** This tax is a fixed cost to Comcast because it is a flat $25 no matter how many subscriptions it sells. Because the tax doesn't affect Comcast's marginal revenue or marginal cost, the profit-maximizing level of output has not changed. So, Comcast will still sell 6 subscriptions per month at a price of $24, but its profit will fall by the amount of the tax, from $34 per month to $9 per month.

Your Turn: For more practice, do related problems 3.4 and 3.5 at the end of this chapter.

Don't Let This Happen to You

Don't Assume That Charging a Higher Price Is Always More Profitable for a Monopolist

In answering part (c) of Solved Problem 3, it's tempting to argue that Comcast should increase its price to make up for the tax. After all, Comcast is a monopolist, so why can't it just pass along the tax to its customers? The reason it can't is that Comcast, like any other monopolist, must pay attention to demand. Comcast is not interested in charging high prices for the sake of charging high prices; it is interested in maximizing profit. Charging a price of $1,000 for a basic cable subscription sounds nice, but if no one will buy at that price, Comcast would hardly be maximizing profit.

To look at it another way, before the tax is imposed, Comcast has already determined that $24 is the price that will maximize its profit. After the tax is imposed, it must determine whether $24 is still the profit-maximizing price. Because the tax has not affected Comcast's marginal revenue or marginal cost (or had any effect on consumer demand), $24 is still the profit-maximizing price, and Comcast should continue to charge it. The tax reduces Comcast's profit but doesn't cause it to increase the price of cable subscriptions.

Your Turn: Test your understanding by doing related problem 3.8 at the end of this chapter.

Does Monopoly Reduce Economic Efficiency?

We have seen that a perfectly competitive market is economically efficient. How would economic efficiency be affected if instead of being perfectly competitive, a market were a monopoly? *Economic surplus* provides a way of characterizing the economic efficiency in a market. *Equilibrium in a perfectly competitive market results in the greatest amount of economic surplus, or total benefit to society, from the production of a good or service.* What happens to economic surplus under a monopoly? We can begin the analysis by considering the hypothetical case of what would happen if the market for smartphones begins as perfectly competitive and then becomes a monopoly.

Comparing Monopoly and Perfect Competition

Panel (a) in Figure 4 illustrates the situation if the market for smartphones is perfectly competitive. Price and quantity are determined by the intersection of the demand and supply curves. Remember that none of the individual firms in a perfectly competitive industry has any control over price. Each firm must accept the price determined by the market. Panel (b) shows what happens if the smartphone market becomes a monopoly. We know that the monopoly will maximize profit by producing where marginal revenue equals marginal cost. To do this, the monopoly reduces the quantity of smartphones that would have been produced if the industry were perfectly competitive and increases the price. Panel (b) illustrates an important conclusion: *A monopoly will produce less and charge a higher price than would a perfectly competitive industry producing the same good.*

Measuring the Efficiency Losses from Monopoly

Figure 5 uses panel (b) from Figure 4 to illustrate how monopoly affects consumers, producers, and the efficiency of the economy. Recall that *consumer surplus* measures the net benefit received by consumers from purchasing a good or service.

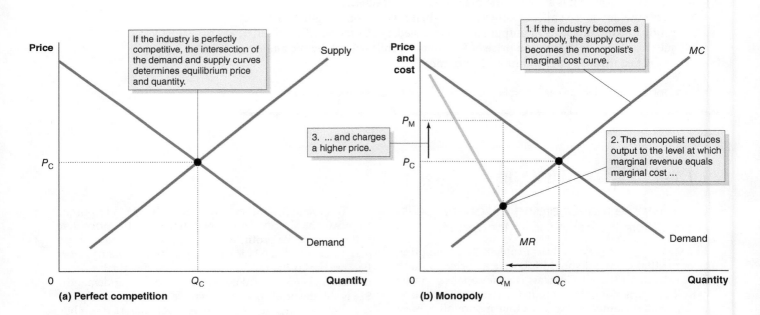

Figure 4 **What Happens If a Perfectly Competitive Industry Becomes a Monopoly?**

In panel (a), the market for smartphones is perfectly competitive, and price and quantity are determined by the intersection of the demand and supply curves. In panel (b), the perfectly competitive smartphone market becomes a monopoly. As a result:

1. The industry supply curve becomes the monopolist's marginal cost curve.

2. The monopolist reduces output to where marginal revenue equals marginal cost, Q_M.

3. The monopolist raises the price from P_C to P_M.

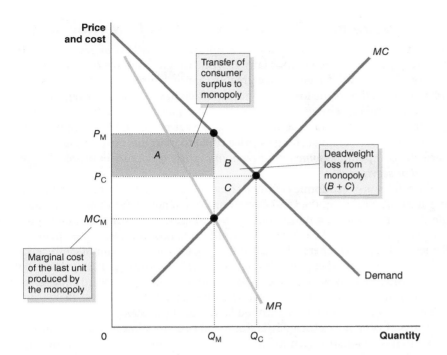

Figure 5

The Inefficiency of Monopoly

A monopoly charges a higher price, P_M, and produces a smaller quantity, Q_M, than a perfectly competitive industry, which charges price P_C and produces Q_C. The higher price reduces consumer surplus by the area equal to the rectangle A and the triangle B. Some of the reduction in consumer surplus is captured by the monopoly as producer surplus, and some becomes deadweight loss, which is the area equal to triangles B and C.

We measure consumer surplus as the area below the demand curve and above the market price. The higher the price, the smaller the consumer surplus. Because a monopoly raises the market price, it reduces consumer surplus. In Figure 5, the loss of consumer surplus is equal to rectangle A plus triangle B. Remember that *producer surplus* measures the net benefit to producers from selling a good or service. We measure producer surplus as the area above the supply curve and below the market price. The increase in price due to monopoly increases producer surplus by an amount equal to rectangle A and reduces it by an amount equal to triangle C. Because rectangle A is larger than triangle C, we know that a monopoly increases producer surplus compared with perfect competition.

Economic surplus is equal to the sum of consumer surplus plus producer surplus. By increasing price and reducing the quantity produced, the monopolist has reduced economic surplus by an amount equal to the areas of triangles B and C. This reduction in economic surplus is called *deadweight loss* and represents the loss of economic efficiency due to monopoly.

The best way to understand how a monopoly causes a loss of economic efficiency is to recall that price is equal to marginal cost in a perfectly competitive market. As a result, a consumer in a perfectly competitive market is always able to buy a good if she is willing to pay a price equal to the marginal cost of producing it. As Figure 5 shows, the monopolist stops producing smartphones at a point where the price is well above marginal cost. Consumers are unable to buy some smartphones for which they would be willing to pay a price greater than the marginal cost of producing them. Why doesn't the monopolist produce these additional smartphones? Because the monopolist's profit is greater if it restricts output and forces up the price. A monopoly produces the profit-maximizing level of output but fails to produce the efficient level of output from the point of view of society.

We can summarize the effects of monopoly as follows:

1. Monopoly causes a reduction in consumer surplus.

2. Monopoly causes an increase in producer surplus.

3. Monopoly causes a deadweight loss, which represents a reduction in economic efficiency.

How Large Are the Efficiency Losses Due to Monopoly?

Market power The ability of a firm to charge a price greater than marginal cost.

We know that there are relatively few monopolies, so the loss of economic efficiency due to monopoly must be small. Many firms, though, have **market power**, which is the ability of a firm to charge a price greater than marginal cost. The analysis we just completed shows that some loss of economic efficiency will occur whenever a firm has market power and can charge a price greater than marginal cost, even if the firm is not a monopoly. The only firms that do *not* have market power are firms in perfectly competitive markets, which must charge a price equal to marginal cost. Because few markets are perfectly competitive, *some loss of economic efficiency occurs in the market for nearly every good or service.*

Is the total loss of economic efficiency due to market power large or small? It is possible to put a dollar value on the loss of economic efficiency by estimating for every industry the size of the deadweight loss triangle, as in Figure 5. The first economist to do this was Arnold Harberger of the University of California, Los Angeles. His estimates—largely confirmed by later researchers—indicated that the total loss of economic efficiency in the U.S. economy due to market power is relatively small. According to his estimates, if every industry in the economy were perfectly competitive, so that price were equal to marginal cost in every market, the gain in economic efficiency would equal less than 1 percent of the value of total production in the United States, or about $500 per person.

The loss of economic efficiency is this small primarily because true monopolies are very rare. In most industries, competition keeps price much closer to marginal cost than would be the case in a monopoly. The closer price is to marginal cost, the smaller the size of the deadweight loss.

Market Power and Technological Change

Some economists have raised the possibility that the economy may actually benefit from firms having market power. This argument is most closely identified with Joseph Schumpeter, an Austrian economist who spent many years as a professor of economics at Harvard. Schumpeter argued that economic progress depends on technological change in the form of new products. For example, the replacement of horse-drawn carriages by automobiles, the replacement of ice boxes by refrigerators, and the replacement of mechanical calculators by electronic computers all represent technological changes that significantly raised living standards. In Schumpeter's view, new products unleash a "gale of creative destruction" that drives older products—and, often, the firms that produced them—out of the market. Schumpeter was not concerned that firms with market power would charge higher prices than perfectly competitive firms:

> It is not that kind of [price] competition which counts but the competition from the new commodity, the new technology, the new source of supply, the new type of organization ... competition which commands a decisive cost or quality advantage and which strikes not at the margins of the profits and outputs of the existing firms but at their foundations and their very lives.

Economists who support Schumpeter's view argue that the introduction of new products requires firms to spend funds on research and development. It is possible for firms to raise this money by borrowing from investors or banks. But investors and banks are usually skeptical of ideas for new products that have not yet passed the test of consumer acceptance in the market. As a result, firms are often forced to rely on their profits to finance the research and development needed for new products. Because firms with market power are more likely to earn economic profits than are perfectly competitive firms, they are also more likely to carry out research and development and introduce new products. In this view, the higher prices firms with market power charge are unimportant compared with the benefits from the new products these firms introduce to the market.

Some economists disagree with Schumpeter's views. These economists point to the number of new products developed by smaller firms, including, for example, Steve Jobs and Steve Wozniak inventing the first Apple computer in Jobs's garage, and Larry Page and Sergey Brin inventing the Google search engine as graduate students at Stanford. As we will see in the next section, government policymakers continue to struggle with the issue of whether, on balance, large firms with market power are good or bad for the economy.

Government Policy toward Monopoly

Because monopolies reduce consumer surplus and economic efficiency, most governments have policies that regulate their behavior. **Collusion** refers to an agreement among firms to charge the same price or otherwise not to compete. In the United States, *antitrust laws* are designed to prevent monopolies and collusion. Governments also regulate firms that are natural monopolies, often by controlling the prices they charge.

Collusion An agreement among firms to charge the same price or otherwise not to compete.

Antitrust Laws and Antitrust Enforcement

The first important law regulating monopolies in the United States was the Sherman Act, which Congress passed in 1890 to promote competition and prevent the formation of monopolies. Section 1 of the Sherman Act outlaws "every contract, combination in the form of trust or otherwise, or conspiracy in restraint of trade." Section 2 states that "every person who shall monopolize, or attempt to monopolize, or combine or conspire with any other person or persons, to monopolize any part of the trade or commerce … shall be deemed guilty of a felony."

The Sherman Act targeted firms in several industries that had combined together during the 1870s and 1880s to form "trusts." In a trust, the firms were operated independently but gave voting control to a board of trustees. The board enforced collusive agreements for the firms to charge the same price and not to compete for each other's customers. The most notorious of the trusts was the Standard Oil Trust, organized by John D. Rockefeller. In the years following passage of the Sherman Act, business trusts disappeared, but the term **antitrust laws** has lived on to refer to the laws aimed at eliminating collusion and promoting competition among firms.

Antitrust laws Laws aimed at eliminating collusion and promoting competition among firms.

The Sherman Act prohibited trusts and collusive agreements, but it left several loopholes. For example, it was not clear whether it would be legal for two or more firms to merge to form a new, larger firm that would have substantial market power. A series of Supreme Court decisions interpreted the Sherman Act narrowly, and the result was a wave of mergers at the turn of the twentieth century. Included in these mergers was U.S. Steel Corporation, which was formed from dozens of smaller companies. U.S. Steel, organized by J. P. Morgan, was the first billion-dollar corporation, and it controlled two-thirds of steel production in the United States. The Sherman Act also left unclear whether any business practices short of outright collusion were illegal.

To address the loopholes in the Sherman Act, in 1914 Congress passed the Clayton Act and the Federal Trade Commission Act. Under the Clayton Act, a merger was illegal if its effect was "substantially to lessen competition, or to tend to create a monopoly." The Federal Trade Commission Act set up the Federal Trade Commission (FTC), which was given the power to police unfair business practices. The FTC has brought lawsuits against firms employing a variety of business practices, including deceptive advertising. In setting up the FTC, Congress divided the authority to police mergers. Currently, both the Antitrust Division of the U.S. Department of Justice and the FTC are responsible for merger policy. Table 1 lists the most important U.S. antitrust laws and the purpose of each.

Table 1	Law	Date Enacted	Purpose
Important U.S. Antitrust Laws	Sherman Act	1890	Prohibited "restraint of trade," including price fixing and collusion. Also outlawed monopolization.
	Clayton Act	1914	Prohibited firms from buying stock in competitors and from having directors serve on the boards of competing firms.
	Federal Trade Commission Act	1914	Established the Federal Trade Commission (FTC) to help administer antitrust laws.
	Robinson–Patman Act	1936	Prohibited firms from charging buyers different prices if the result would reduce competition.
	Cellar–Kefauver Act	1950	Toughened restrictions on mergers by prohibiting any mergers that would reduce competition.

Making the Connection | Did Apple Violate the Law in Pricing e-Books?

Did Apple try to artificially restrict competition to raise prices of e-books?

People who buy e-books got some bad news in 2010 when Apple introduced the iPad: The prices of new books and best sellers increased from $9.99 to $12.99 or $14.99. The price increases were not just for books sold in Apple's iBookstore but also for books Amazon was selling for its Kindle. Why did this big jump in prices happen? The U.S. Justice Department had a straightforward answer: Apple had organized an agreement with five large book publishers to raise the prices of e-books. As one Justice Department lawyer put it, Apple had directed "an old-fashioned, straight-forward price-fixing agreement." Accordingly, the Justice Department sued Apple for violating antitrust laws. The lawsuit was a civil action, meaning that the Justice Department was not pursuing criminal charges against Apple executives.

When Amazon introduced its Kindle e-reader in 2007, it priced most new books and best sellers at $9.99, even though this price was less than the price the publishers were charging Amazon for the books. Amazon believed that by selling e-books at a loss, it would increase sales of the Kindle. Most publishers were unhappy with Amazon's low e-book prices, however, because they believed the prices reduced sales of hardcover copies of best sellers on which the publishers made a larger profit. According to the Justice Department, Apple took advantage of the publishers' unhappiness to propose an "agency pricing model." Under this model, the publishers would set the retail price of e-books, and Apple would keep 30 percent of the price of every e-book it sold.

In addition, Apple negotiated a clause in its contracts with the publishers that allowed Apple to match the retail prices of other e-book sellers. By invoking this clause, Apple would be able to sell e-books for $9.99 if Amazon continued to do so. The publishers then insisted that Amazon switch to an agency pricing model. If Amazon failed to switch, the publishers said they would not allow Amazon to sell e-versions of their books until months after the hardcover editions were first published, which would give Apple a huge advantage in the e-book market. Faced with this situation, Amazon also adopted the agency pricing model, and the publishers were able to raise the prices of most new books to $12.99 or $14.99.

At the trial, Apple argued that it had not attempted to organize a price-fixing agreement with the publishers. Instead, Apple had simply proposed a pricing model similar to the one they were already using for songs in their iTunes store. As Apple's executive in charge of negotiating with the publishers put it: "I didn't raise prices. The publishers set the prices." Representatives of the publishers also testified during the trial that they had not conspired with Apple or with each other to fix the prices of e-books.

Monopoly and Antitrust Policy

In the end, the judge in charge of the case decided that Apple had conspired with the publishers to raise e-book prices. Following the decision, the Justice Department proposed that the judge bar Apple from entering agency pricing contracts with publishers for a period of five years. The Justice Department also proposed that it be given oversight of pricing of music, television shows, and movies in Apple's iTunes online store. Apple appealed the judge's decision and continued to maintain that it had not violated the law.

The lawsuit the Justice Department brought against Apple is an example of attempts by the government to keep firms from artificially restricting competition to raise prices. As we have seen, higher prices reduce consumer surplus and economic efficiency.

Sources: Chad Bray, "Apple's E-Book Damages Trial Set to Begin in May," *Wall Street Journal*, August 15, 2013; Bob Van Voris, "Apple Awaits e-Book Decision with State, Private Suits in Wings," *Bloomberg BusinessWeek*, June 22, 2013; Joe Palazolo and Chad Bray, "Apple's Civil Antitrust Trial: The Highlights," *Wall Street Journal*, June 20, 2013; and Julie Bosman, "Publishers Tell of Disputes with Apple on e-Book Prices," *New York Times*, June 5, 2013.

Your Turn: Test your understanding by doing related problem 5.12 at the end of this chapter.

Mergers: The Trade-off between Market Power and Efficiency

The federal government regulates business mergers because if firms gain market power by merging, they may use that market power to raise prices and reduce output. As a result, the government is most concerned with **horizontal mergers**, or mergers between firms in the same industry. Two airlines or two candy manufacturers merging are examples of a horizontal merger. Horizontal mergers are more likely to increase market power than **vertical mergers**, which are mergers between firms at different stages of the production of a good. An example of a vertical merger would be a merger between a company making soft drinks and a company making aluminum cans.

Horizontal merger A merger between firms in the same industry.

Vertical merger A merger between firms at different stages of production of a good.

Two factors can complicate regulating horizontal mergers. First, the "market" that firms are in is not always clear. For example, if Hershey Foods wants to merge with Mars, Inc., maker of M&Ms, Snickers, and other candies, what is the relevant market? If the government looks just at the candy market, the newly merged company would have more than 70 percent of the market, a level at which the government would likely oppose the merger. What if the government looks at the broader market for snacks? In this market, Hershey and Mars compete with makers of potato chips, pretzels, and peanuts—and perhaps even producers of fresh fruit. Of course, if the government looked at the very broad market for food, then both Hershey and Mars have very small market shares, and there would be no reason to oppose their merger. In practice, the government defines the relevant market on the basis of whether there are close substitutes for the products being made by the merging firms. In this case, potato chips and the other snack foods mentioned are not close substitutes for candy. So, the government would consider the candy market to be the relevant market and would oppose the merger, on the grounds that the new firm would have too much market power.

The second factor that complicates merger policy is the possibility that the newly merged firm might be more efficient than the merging firms were individually. For example, one firm might have an excellent product but a poor distribution system for getting the product into the hands of consumers. A competing firm might have built a great distribution system but have an inferior product. Allowing these firms to merge might be good for both the firms and consumers. Or, two competing firms might each have an extensive system of warehouses that are only half full, but if the firms merged, they could consolidate their warehouses and significantly reduce their average costs.

Most of the mergers that come under scrutiny by the Department of Justice and the FTC are between large firms. For simplicity, though, let's consider a case in which all

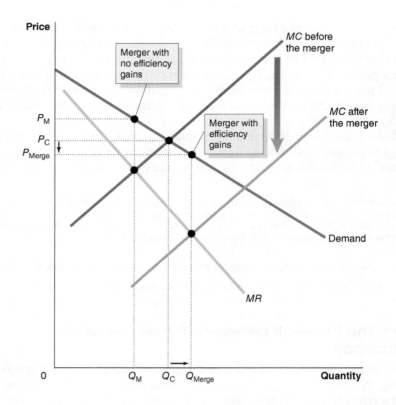

Figure 6

A Merger That Makes Consumers Better Off

This figure shows the result of all the firms in a perfectly competitive industry merging to form a monopoly. If the merger does not affect costs, the result is the same as in Figure 5: Price rises from P_C to P_M, quantity falls from Q_C to Q_M, consumer surplus declines, and a loss of economic efficiency results. If, however, the monopoly has lower costs than the perfectly competitive firms, as shown by the marginal cost curve shifting to MC after the merger, it is possible that the price of the good will actually decline from P_C to P_{Merge} and that output will increase from Q_C to Q_{Merge} following the merger.

the firms in a perfectly competitive industry want to merge to form a monopoly. As we saw in Figure 5, as a result of this merger, prices will rise and output will fall, leading to a decline in consumer surplus and economic efficiency. But what if the larger, newly merged firm actually is more efficient than the smaller firms were? Figure 6 shows a possible result.

If the merger doesn't affect costs, we get the same result as in Figure 5: Price rises from P_C to P_M, quantity falls from Q_C to Q_M, consumer surplus declines, and a loss of economic efficiency results. If the monopoly has lower costs than the competitive firms, it is possible for price to decline and quantity to increase. In Figure 6, note that after the merger MR crosses MC at the new profit-maximizing quantity, Q_{Merge}. The demand curve shows that the monopolist can sell this quantity of the good at a price of P_{Merge}. Therefore, the price declines after the merger from P_C to P_{Merge}, and the quantity increases from Q_C to Q_{Merge}. We have the following seemingly paradoxical result: *The newly merged firm has a great deal of market power, but consumers are better off and economic efficiency is increased because the firm is more efficient.* Of course, sometimes a merged firm will be more efficient and have lower costs, and other times it won't. Even if a merged firm is more efficient and has lower costs, the lower costs may not offset the increased market power of the firm enough to increase consumer surplus and economic efficiency.

As you might expect, whenever large firms propose a merger, they claim that the newly merged firm will be more efficient and have lower costs. They realize that without these claims, the Department of Justice and the FTC, along with the court system, are unlikely to approve the merger.

The Department of Justice and FTC Merger Guidelines

For many years after the passage of the Sherman Act in 1890, lawyers from the Department of Justice enforced the antitrust laws. The lawyers rarely considered economic arguments, such as the possibility that consumers might be made better off by a merger if economic efficiency were significantly improved. This situation began to change in 1965, when Donald Turner became the first Ph.D. economist to head the Antitrust Division of the Department of Justice. Under Turner and his successors, economic analysis shaped antitrust policy. In 1973, the Economics Section of the Antitrust Division was established and staffed with economists who evaluate the economic consequences of proposed mergers.

Economists played a major role in the development of merger guidelines by the Department of Justice and the FTC in 1982. The guidelines made it easier for firms considering a merger to understand whether the government was likely to allow the merger or to oppose it. The guidelines were modified in 2010 and have three main parts:

1. Market definition
2. Measure of concentration
3. Merger standards

Market Definition A market consists of all firms making products that consumers view as close substitutes. Economists can identify close substitutes by looking at the effect of a price increase. If the definition of a market is too narrow, a price increase will cause firms to experience a significant decline in sales—and profits—as consumers switch to buying close substitutes.

Identifying the relevant market involved in a proposed merger begins with a narrow definition of the industry. For a hypothetical merger of Hershey Foods and Mars, Inc., economists might start with the candy industry. If all firms in the candy industry increased price by 5 percent, would their profits increase or decrease? If profits would increase, the market is defined as being just these firms. If profits would decrease, economists would try a broader definition—say, by adding in potato chips and other snacks. Would a price increase of 5 percent by all firms in the broader market raise profits? If profits increase, the relevant market has been identified. If profits decrease, economists consider a broader definition. Economists continue the process until a market has been identified.

Measure of Concentration A market is *concentrated* if a relatively small number of firms have a large share of total sales in the market. A merger between firms in a market that is already highly concentrated is very likely to increase market power. A merger between firms in an industry that has a very low concentration is unlikely to increase market power and can be ignored. The guidelines use the *Herfindahl-Hirschman Index (HHI)* of concentration, which squares the market shares of each firm in the industry and adds up the values of the squares. The following are some examples of calculating HHI:

- 1 firm, with 100 percent market share (a monopoly):

$$HHI = 100^2 = 10,000.$$

- 2 firms, each with a 50 percent market share:

$$HHI = 50^2 + 50^2 = 5,000.$$

- 4 firms, with market shares of 30 percent, 30 percent, 20 percent, and 20 percent:

$$HHI = 30^2 + 30^2 + 20^2 + 20^2 = 2,600.$$

- 10 firms, each with a 10 percent market share:

$$HHI = 10 \times (10)^2 = 1,000.$$

Merger Standards The Department of Justice and the FTC use the HHI calculation for a market to evaluate proposed horizontal mergers according to these standards:

- *Postmerger HHI below 1,500.* These markets are not concentrated, so mergers in them are not challenged.
- *Postmerger HHI between 1,500 and 2,500.* These markets are moderately concentrated. Mergers that raise the HHI by fewer than 100 points probably will not be challenged. Mergers that raise the HHI by more than 100 points may be challenged.

- *Postmerger HHI above 2,500.* These markets are highly concentrated. Mergers that increase the HHI by fewer than 100 points will not be challenged. Mergers that increase the HHI by 100 to 200 points may be challenged. Mergers that increase the HHI by more than 200 points will likely be challenged.

Increases in economic efficiency will be taken into account and can lead to approval of a merger that otherwise would be opposed, but the burden of showing that the efficiencies exist lies with the merging firms:

> The merging firms must substantiate efficiency claims so that the [Department of Justice and the FTC] can verify by reasonable means the likelihood and magnitude of each asserted efficiency.... Efficiency claims will not be considered if they are vague or speculative or otherwise cannot be verified by reasonable means.

Regulating Natural Monopolies

If a firm is a natural monopoly, competition from other firms will not play its usual role of forcing price down to the level where the company earns zero economic profit. As a result, local or state *regulatory commissions* usually set the prices for natural monopolies, such as firms selling natural gas or electricity. What price should these commissions set? Economic efficiency requires the last unit of a good or service produced to provide an additional benefit to consumers equal to the additional cost of producing it. We can measure the additional benefit consumers receive from the last unit by the price of the product, and we can measure the additional cost to the monopoly of producing the last unit by marginal cost. Therefore, to achieve economic efficiency, regulators should require that the monopoly charge a price equal to its marginal cost. There is, however, an important drawback to doing so, as illustrated in Figure 7, which shows the situation of a typical regulated natural monopoly.

Remember that with a natural monopoly, the average total cost curve is still falling when it crosses the demand curve. If unregulated, the monopoly will charge a price equal to P_M and produce Q_M. To achieve economic efficiency, regulators should require the monopoly to charge a price equal to P_E. The monopoly will then produce Q_E. But here is the drawback: P_E is less than average total cost, so the monopoly will be suffering a loss, shown by the area of the red-shaded rectangle. In the long run, the owners of the monopoly will not continue in business if they are experiencing losses. Realizing this, most regulators will set the regulated price, P_R, equal to the level of average total cost at which the demand curve intersects the *ATC* curve. At that price, the owners of the monopoly are able to break even on their

Figure 7

Regulating a Natural Monopoly

A natural monopoly that is not subject to government regulation will charge a price equal to P_M and produce Q_M. If government regulators want to achieve economic efficiency, they will set the regulated price equal to P_E, and the monopoly will produce Q_E. Unfortunately, P_E is below average total cost, and the monopoly will suffer a loss, shown by the red rectangle. Because the monopoly will not continue to produce in the long run if it suffers a loss, government regulators set a price equal to average total cost, which is P_R in the figure. The resulting production, Q_R, will be below the efficient level.

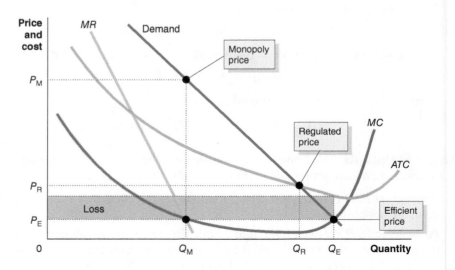

investment by producing the quantity Q_R, although this quantity is below the efficient quantity, Q_E.

Continued

Economics in Your Life

Is There a Monopoly in Your Dorm?

At the beginning of the chapter, we asked if the submarine sandwich business you and your roommate, Fatma, start in your dorm was a monopoly, and if you should charge high prices for the subs to increase your profit. In this chapter, we have seen that a monopoly is a firm that is the only seller of a good or service that does not have a close substitute. Even though you and Fatma would be the only sellers of submarine sandwiches on campus during the evening hours of Saturdays and Sundays, there could be other options for hungry students. For example, students could buy food from nearby off-campus stores, have it delivered to campus from those stores, or buy from vendors open earlier in the day. Most goods have substitutes, and you and Fatma should realize that for many students pizza and hamburgers are good substitutes for subs. High prices are likely to lead many of your customers to search for these substitutes.

Conclusion

The more intense the level of competition among firms, the better a market works. In this chapter, we have seen that, compared with perfect competition, in a monopoly, the price of a good or service is higher, output is lower, and consumer surplus and economic efficiency are reduced. Fortunately, true monopolies are rare. Even though most firms resemble monopolies in being able to charge a price above marginal cost, most markets have enough competition to keep the efficiency losses from market power low.

Visit MyEconLab for a news article and analysis related to the concepts in this chapter.

Chapter Summary and Problems

Key Terms

Antitrust laws	Horizontal merger	Natural monopoly	Public franchise
Collusion	Market power	Network externalities	Vertical merger
Copyright	Monopoly	Patent	

1 Is Any Firm Ever Really a Monopoly?
LEARNING OBJECTIVE: Define monopoly.

Summary

A **monopoly** exists only in the rare situation in which a firm is producing a good or service for which there are no close substitutes. A narrow definition of monopoly that some economists use is that a firm has a monopoly if it can ignore the actions of all other firms. Many economists favor a broader definition of monopoly. Under the broader definition, a firm has a monopoly if no other firms are selling a substitute close enough that the firm's economic profit is competed away in the long run.

Visit **www.myeconlab.com** to complete these exercises online and get instant feedback.

Review Questions

1.1 What is a monopoly? Can a firm be a monopoly if close substitutes for its product exist?

1.2 If you own the only hardware store in a small town, do you have a monopoly?

Problems and Applications

1.3 The great baseball player Ty Cobb was known for being very thrifty. Near the end of his life, he was interviewed by a reporter who was surprised to find that Cobb used candles, rather than electricity, to light his home. From Ty Cobb's point of view, was the local electric company a monopoly?

1.4 Some observers say that changes in the past few years have eroded the monopoly power of local cable television companies, even if no other cable firms have entered their markets. What are these changes? Do these "monopoly" firms still have monopoly power?

1.5 Are there any products for which there are no substitutes? Are these the only products for which it would be possible to have a monopoly? Briefly explain.

1.6 **[Related to** Making the Connection: **Is Google a Monopoly?]** A newspaper article has the headline "Google Says It's Actually Quite Small." According to the article:

> Google rejects the idea that it's in the search advertising business, an industry in which it holds more than a 70 percent share of revenue. Instead, the company says its competition is all advertising, a category broad enough to include newspaper, radio and highway billboards.

Why does Google care whether people think it is large or small? Do highway billboards actually provide competition for Google? Briefly explain.

Source: Jeff Horwitz, "Google Says It's Actually Quite Small," *Washington Post*, June 7, 2009.

1.7 **[Related to** Making the Connection: **Is Google a Monopoly?]** Why is access to YouTube by other search engines such as Yahoo and Bing relevant to the question of whether Google has a monopoly in the Internet search engine market?

2 Where Do Monopolies Come From?
LEARNING OBJECTIVE: Explain the four main reasons monopolies arise.

Summary

To have a monopoly, barriers to entering the market must be so high that no other firms can enter. Barriers to entry may be high enough to keep out competing firms for four main reasons: (1) A government blocks the entry of more than one firm into a market by issuing a **patent**, which is the exclusive right to make a product for 20 years, a **copyright**, which is the exclusive right to produce and sell a creation, or a *trademark*, which grants a firm legal protection against other firms using its product's name, or by giving a firm a **public franchise**, which is the right to be the only legal provider of a good or service; (2) one firm has control of a key raw material necessary to produce a good; (3) there are important *network externalities* in supplying the good or service; or (4) economies of scale are so large

that one firm has a *natural monopoly*. **Network externalities** refer to the situation where the usefulness of a product increases with the number of consumers who use it. A **natural monopoly** is a situation in which economies of scale are so large that one firm can supply the entire market at a lower average cost than can two or more firms.

Visit **www.myeconlab.com** to complete these exercises online and get instant feedback.

Review Questions

2.1 What are the four most important ways a firm becomes a monopoly?

2.2 If patents, copyrights, and trademarks reduce competition, why does the federal government grant them?

2.3 What is a public franchise? Are all public franchises natural monopolies?

2.4 What is "natural" about a natural monopoly?

Problems and Applications

2.5 The U.S. Postal Service (USPS) is a monopoly because the federal government has blocked entry into the market for delivering first-class mail. Is the USPS also a natural monopoly? How can we tell? What would happen if the law preventing competition in this market were removed?

2.6 Patents are granted for 20 years, but pharmaceutical companies can't use their patent-guaranteed monopoly powers for anywhere near this long because it takes several years to acquire approval of drugs from the Food and Drug Administration (FDA). Should the life of drug patents be extended to 20 years *after* FDA approval? What would be the costs and benefits of such an extension?

2.7 Under U.S. copyright law, authors have the exclusive right to their writings during their lifetimes—unless they sell this right, as most authors do to their publishers—and their heirs retain this exclusive right for 70 years after their death. The historian Thomas Macaulay once described the copyright law as "a tax on readers to give a bounty to authors." In what sense does the existence of the copyright law impose a tax on readers? What "bounty" do copyright laws give authors? Discuss whether the government would be doing readers a favor by abolishing the copyright law.

Source: Thomas Mallon, *Stolen Words: The Classic Book on Plagiarism*, Boston: Houghton Mifflin Harcourt, 2001 (original ed. 1989), p. 59.

2.8 If firms incurred no cost in developing new technologies and new products, would there be any need for patents? Briefly explain.

2.9 The German company Koenig & Bauer has 90 percent of the world market for presses that print currency. Discuss the factors that would make it difficult for new companies to enter this market.

2.10 **[Related to** Making the Connection: **Does Hasbro Have a Monopoly on Monopoly Game?]** Why should it matter legally whether Professor Anspach is correct that Hasbro's Monopoly game closely resembles a game that had been

played for decades before Charles Darrow claimed to have invented it? Does it matter economically? Briefly explain.

2.11 **[Related to** Making the Connection: **Are Diamond Profits Forever? The De Beers Diamond Monopoly]** Why was De Beers worried that people might resell their old diamonds? How did De Beers attempt to convince consumers that previously owned diamonds were not good substitutes for new diamonds? How did De Beers's strategy affect the demand curve for new diamonds? How did De Beers's strategy affect its profit?

2.12 In China, the government owns many more firms than in the United States. A former Chinese government official argued that a number of government-run industries such as oil refining were natural monopolies. Is it likely that oil refining is a natural monopoly? How would you be able to tell?

Source: Shen Hong, "Former State Assets Regulator: SOE Monopolies 'Natural'," *Wall Street Journal*, January 4, 2012.

2.13 **[Related to** Solved Problem 2] Suppose that the quantity demanded per day for a product is 90 when the price is $35. The following table shows costs for a firm with a monopoly in this market:

Quantity (per day)	Total Cost
30	$1,200
40	1,400
50	2,250
60	3,000

Briefly explain whether this firm has a natural monopoly.

2.14 As noted in this chapter, many generic versions of the diabetes drug Glucophage were introduced within the first year of Glucophage's patent expiration. Recently, the U.S. Supreme Court ruled that patients who become ill taking generic drugs cannot sue the manufacturer of those drugs, even though: "People who are hurt by a brand-name drug can sue the drug maker for damages." How might the Supreme Court's decision affect the willingness of pharmaceutical firms to invest in research and development on new drugs?

Source: David G. Savage, "Supreme Court Rules Drug Makers Can't Be Sued over Defects," *Los Angeles Times*, June 25, 2013.

---

3 ## How Does a Monopoly Choose Price and Output?

LEARNING OBJECTIVE: Explain how a monopoly chooses price and output.

Summary

Monopolists face downward-sloping demand and marginal revenue curves and, like all other firms, maximize profit by producing where marginal revenue equals marginal cost. Unlike a perfect competitor, a monopolist that earns an economic profit does not face the entry of new firms into the market. Therefore, a monopolist can earn an economic profit even in the long run.

Visit **www.myeconlab.com** to complete these exercises online and get instant feedback.

Review Questions

3.1 What is the relationship between a monopolist's demand curve and the market demand curve? What is the

relationship between a monopolist's demand curve and its marginal revenue curve?

3.2 In what sense is a monopolist a *price maker*? Will charging the highest possible price always maximize a monopolist's profit? Briefly explain.

3.3 Draw a graph that shows a monopolist earning a profit. Be sure your graph includes the monopolist's demand, marginal revenue, average total cost, and marginal cost curves. Be sure to indicate the profit-maximizing level of output and price.

Problems and Applications

3.4 **[Related to** Solved Problem 3] Ed Scahill has acquired a monopoly on the production of baseballs (don't ask how) and faces the demand and cost situation shown in the following table:

Price	Quantity (per week)	Total Revenue	Marginal Revenue	Total Cost	Marginal Cost
$20	15,000			$330,000	
19	20,000			365,000	
18	25,000			405,000	
17	30,000			450,000	
16	35,000			500,000	
15	40,000			555,000	

a. Fill in the remaining values in the table.

b. If Scahill wants to maximize profit, what price should he charge, and how many baseballs should he sell? How much profit (or loss) will he make? Draw a graph to illustrate your answer. Your graph should be clearly labeled and should include Scahill's demand, *ATC*, *AVC*, *AFC*, *MC*, and *MR* curves, the price he is charging, the quantity he is producing, and the area representing his profit (or loss).

c. Suppose the government imposes a tax of $50,000 per week on baseball production. Now what price should Scahill charge, how many baseballs should he sell, and what will his profit (or loss) be?

d. Suppose that the government raises the tax in part (c) to $70,000. Now what price should Scahill charge, how many baseballs should he sell, and what will his profit (or loss) be? Will his decision on what price to charge and how much to produce be different in the short run than in the long run? Briefly explain.

3.5 **[Related to** Solved Problem 3**]** Use the information in Solved Problem 3 to answer the following questions.

a. What will Comcast do if the tax is $36.00 per month instead of $25.00? (*Hint:* Will its decision be different in the long run than in the short run?)

b. Suppose that the flat per-month tax is replaced with a tax on the firm of $25.00 per cable subscriber. Now how many subscriptions should Comcast sell if it wants to maximize profit? What price should it charge? What is its profit? (Assume that Comcast will sell only the quantities listed in the table.)

3.6 Before inexpensive pocket calculators were developed, many science and engineering students used slide rules to make numerical calculations. Slide rules are no longer produced, which means nothing prevents you from establishing a monopoly in the slide rule market. Draw a graph showing the situation your slide rule firm would be in. Be sure to include on your graph your demand, marginal revenue, average total cost, and marginal cost curves. Indicate the price you would charge and the quantity you would produce. Are you likely to make a profit or a loss? Show this area on your graph.

3.7 Does a monopolist have a supply curve? Briefly explain. (*Hint:* Look at the definition of a supply curve and consider whether this definition applies to a monopolist.)

3.8 **[Related to the** Don't Let This Happen to You**]** A student argues: "If a monopolist finds a way of producing a good at lower cost, he will not lower his price. Because he is a monopolist, he will keep the price and the quantity the same and just increase his profit." Do you agree? Use a graph to illustrate your answer.

3.9 When homebuilders construct a new housing development, they usually sell to a single cable television company the rights to lay cable. As a result, anyone buying a home in that development is not able to choose between competing cable companies. Some cities have begun to ban such exclusive agreements. Williams Township, Pennsylvania, decided to allow any cable company to lay cable in the utility trenches of new housing developments. The head of the township board of supervisors argued: "What I would like to see and do is give the consumers a choice. If there's no choice, then the price [of cable] is at the whim of the provider." In a situation in which the consumers in a housing development have only one cable company available, is the price really at the whim of the company? Would a company in this situation be likely to charge, say, $500 per month for basic cable services? Briefly explain why or why not.

Source: Sam Kennedy, "Williams Township May Ban Exclusive Cable Provider Pacts," (Allentown, PA), *Morning Call* November 5, 2004.

3.10 Will a monopoly that maximizes profit also be maximizing revenue? Will it be maximizing production? Briefly explain.

---

4 ## Does Monopoly Reduce Economic Efficiency?

LEARNING OBJECTIVE: Use a graph to illustrate how a monopoly affects economic efficiency.

Summary

Compared with a perfectly competitive industry, a monopoly charges a higher price and produces less, which reduces consumer surplus and economic efficiency. Some loss of economic efficiency will occur whenever firms have **market power** and can charge a price greater than marginal cost. The total loss of economic efficiency in the U.S. economy due to market power is small, however, because true monopolies are very rare. In most industries, competition will keep price much closer to marginal cost than would be the case in a monopoly.

Visit www.myeconlab.com to complete these exercises online and get instant feedback.

Review Questions

4.1 Suppose that a perfectly competitive industry becomes a monopoly. Describe the effects of this change on consumer surplus, producer surplus, and deadweight loss.

4.2 Explain why market power leads to a deadweight loss. Is the total deadweight loss from market power for the economy large or small?

Problems and Applications

4.3 Review Figure 5 on the inefficiency of monopoly. Will the deadweight loss due to monopoly be larger if the demand is elastic or if it is inelastic? Briefly explain.

4.4 Economist Harvey Leibenstein argued that the loss of economic efficiency in industries that are not perfectly competitive has been understated. He argued that when competition is weak, firms are under less pressure to adopt the best techniques or to hold down their costs. He referred to this effect as "x-inefficiency." If x-inefficiency causes a firm's marginal costs to rise, use a graph to show that the deadweight loss in Figure 5 understates the true deadweight loss caused by a monopoly.

4.5 Most cities own the water system that provides water to homes and businesses. Some cities charge a flat monthly fee, while other cities charge by the gallon. Which method of pricing is more likely to result in economic efficiency in the water market? Be sure to refer to the definition of *economic efficiency* in your answer. Why do you think the same method of pricing isn't used by all cities?

4.6 Review the concept of externalities. If a market is a monopoly, will a negative externality in production always lead to production beyond the level of economic efficiency? Use a graph to illustrate your answer.

4.7 [**Related to the** Chapter Opener] Suppose a second seafood restaurant opens in Stonington, Maine. Will consumer surplus and economic efficiency necessarily increase? Briefly explain.

4.8 Suppose that the city has given Jorge a monopoly selling baseball caps at the local minor league stadium. Use the following graph to answer the questions:

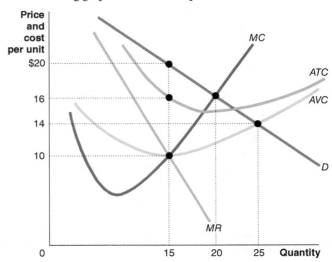

a. What quantity will Jorge produce, and what price will he charge?

b. How much profit will he earn?

c. Review the definition of allocatively efficiency. If Jorge produced at the allocatively efficient level of output, what quantity would he produce?

d. How much deadweight loss did Jorge create by acting like a monopolist rather than a perfect competitor? (Assume that the marginal cost curve is linear (a straight line) between the two relevant points.)

<table>
<tr><td>**5**</td><td></td></tr>
</table>

Government Policy toward Monopoly

LEARNING OBJECTIVE: Discuss government policies toward monopoly.

Summary

Because monopolies reduce consumer surplus and economic efficiency, governments often regulate monopolies. Firms that are not monopolies have an incentive to avoid competition by **colluding**, or agreeing to charge the same price or otherwise not to compete. In the United States, **antitrust laws** are aimed at deterring monopoly, eliminating collusion, and promoting competition among firms. The Antitrust Division of the U.S. Department of Justice and the Federal Trade Commission share responsibility for enforcing the antitrust laws, including regulating mergers between firms. A **horizontal merger** is a merger between firms in the same industry. A **vertical merger** is a merger between firms at different stages of production of a good. Local governments often regulate the prices charged by natural monopolies.

Visit **www.myeconlab.com** to complete these exercises online and get instant feedback.

Review Questions

5.1 What is the purpose of the antitrust laws? Who is in charge of enforcing these laws?

5.2 What is the difference between a horizontal merger and a vertical merger? Which type of merger is more likely to increase the market power of a newly merged firm?

5.3 Why would it be economically efficient to require a natural monopoly to charge a price equal to marginal cost? Why do most regulatory agencies require natural monopolies to charge a price equal to average cost instead?

Problems and Applications

5.4 Use the following graph for a monopoly to answer the questions:

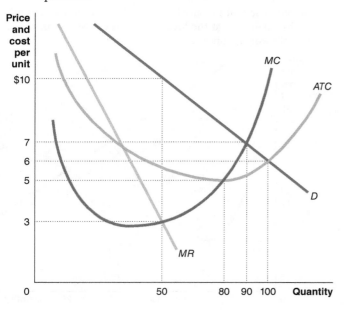

a. What quantity will the monopoly produce and what price will the monopoly charge?

b. Suppose the monopoly is regulated. If the regulatory agency wants to achieve economic efficiency, what price should it require the monopoly to charge? How much output will the monopoly produce at this price? Will the monopoly make a profit if it charges this price? Briefly explain.

5.5 Use the following graph of a monopoly to answer the questions:

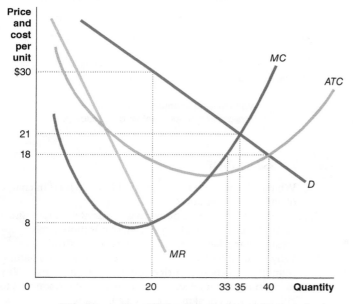

a. What quantity will the monopoly produce, and what price will the monopoly charge?

b. Suppose the government decides to regulate this monopoly and imposes a price ceiling of $18 (in other

words, the monopoly can charge less than $18 but can't charge more). Now what quantity will the monopoly produce, and what price will the monopoly charge? Will every consumer who is willing to pay this price be able to buy the product? Briefly explain.

5.6 In Pennsylvania, wine and liquor can only be purchased from "state stores," which are stores that are owned and operated by the state government. According to an analysis by Katja Seim of the University of Pennsylvania and Joel Waldfogel of the University of Minnesota, if the state of Pennsylvania were to allow unlimited entry of private liquor stores, the number of stores would increase by 2.5 times and consumer surplus would increase by 9 percent. Are these results sufficient to decide whether the state of Pennsylvania should abolish the system of state stores and allow free entry of private stores? In your answer, discuss the distinction between positive and normative analysis.

Source: Katja Seim and Joel Waldfogel, "Public Monopoly and Economic Efficiency: Evidence from the Pennsylvania Liquor Control Board's Entry Decisions," *American Economic Review*, Vol. 103, No. 2, April 2013, pp. 811–862.

5.7 Consider the natural monopoly shown in Figure 7. Assume that the government regulatory agency sets the regulated price, P_R, at the level of average total cost at which the demand curve intersects the *ATC* curve. If the firm knows that it will always be able to charge a price equal to its average total cost, does it have an incentive to reduce its average cost? Briefly explain.

5.8 Draw a graph like Figure 6 that shows a merger lowering costs. On your graph, show producer surplus and consumer surplus before a merger and consumer surplus and producer surplus after a merger.

5.9 Look again at the section "The Department of Justice and FTC Merger Guidelines." Evaluate the following situations.

a. A market initially has 20 firms, each with a 5 percent market share. Of the firms, 4 propose to merge, leaving a total of 17 firms in the industry. Are the Department of Justice and the Federal Trade Commission likely to oppose the merger? Briefly explain.

b. A market initially has 5 firms, each with a 20 percent market share. Of the firms, 2 propose to merge, leaving a total of 4 firms in the industry. Are the Department of Justice and the Federal Trade Commission likely to oppose the merger? Briefly explain.

5.10 In October 2008, Delta Air Lines completed its acquisition of Northwest Airlines. The newly merged company is the largest airline in the world. The following statement regarding the merger is from a Justice Department press release:

> After a thorough, six-month investigation, during which the [Antitrust] Division obtained extensive information from a wide range of market participants—including the companies, other airlines, corporate customers and travel agents—the Division has determined that the proposed merger between Delta and Northwest is likely to produce substantial and credible efficiencies that will benefit U.S. consumers and is not likely to substantially lessen competition.

What does the Justice Department mean by "substantial and credible efficiencies," and how might they benefit U.S. consumers? Why would a merger between two large airlines not be "likely to substantially lessen competition"?

Sources: Andrew Ross Sorkin, "Regulators Approve Delta–Northwest Merger," *New York Times*, October 30, 2008; and Department of Justice, "Statement of the Department of Justice's Antitrust Division on Its Decision to Close Its Investigation of the Merger of Delta Air Lines Inc. and Northwest Airlines Corporation," October 29, 2008.

5.11 The following table shows the market shares during the first three months of 2013 for companies in the U.S. personal computer (PC) market, which includes desk-based PCs and mobile PCs, such as mini-notebooks, but not tablet computers, such as the iPad:

Company	Market Share
Hewlett-Packard	25%
Dell	22
Apple	10
Toshiba	9
Lenovo	9
Other	25

Use the information in the section "The Department of Justice and FTC Merger Guidelines," to predict whether the Department of Justice and the Federal Trade Commission would be likely to oppose a merger between any of the five firms listed in the table. Assume that "Other" in the table consists of five firms, each of which has a 5 percent share of the market.

Source: Eric Slivka, "Apple's U.S. Mac Shipments Fall 7.5% as Overall PC Market Plunges 14% Year-Over-Year," www.macrumors.com, April 10, 2013.

5.12 **[Related to** Making the Connection: **Did Apple Violate the Law in Pricing e-Books?]** After a federal court judge had found Apple guilty of conspiring with book publishers to raise e-book prices, the Department of Justice recommended that the judge order Apple not to sign agency pricing model contracts with publishers for five years. The publishers objected to the recommendation, arguing that the recommendation would "effectively punish the [publishers] by prohibiting agreements with Apple using an agency model."
a. What is an agency pricing model?
b. Why would the Department of Justice want to keep Apple from signing agency pricing model contracts with publishers? Why would the publishers want to continue signing such contracts?

Source: Chad Bray, "Publishers Object to E-Book Plan for Apple," *Wall Street Journal*, August 7, 2013.

Glossary

Antitrust laws Laws aimed at eliminating collusion and promoting competition among firms.

Collusion An agreement among firms to charge the same price or otherwise not to compete.

Copyright A government-granted exclusive right to produce and sell a creation.

Horizontal merger A merger between firms in the same industry.

Market power The ability of a firm to charge a price greater than marginal cost.

Monopoly A firm that is the only seller of a good or service that does not have a close substitute.

Natural monopoly A situation in which economies of scale are so large that one firm can supply the entire market at a lower average total cost than can two or more firms.

Network externalities A situation in which the usefulness of a product increases with the number of consumers who use it.

Patent The exclusive right to a product for a period of 20 years from the date the patent is filed with the government.

Public franchise A government designation that a firm is the only legal provider of a good or service.

Vertical merger A merger between firms at different stages of production of a good.

Credits

Credits are listed in the order of appearance.

Photo

Katja Heinemann/Aurora Photos/Robert Harding; Paul Sakuma/AP Images; Jason DeCrow/Invision/AP Images; Roussel Bernard/Alamy;Migstock/Alamy

Monopolistic Competition:
The Competitive Model in a More Realistic Setting

From Chapter 13 of *Economics*, Fifth Edition. R. Glenn Hubbard and Anthony Patrick O'Brien. Copyright © 2015 by Pearson Education, Inc.
All rights reserved.

Monopolistic Competition: The Competitive Model in a More Realistic Setting

Chapter Outline and Learning Objectives

Starbucks: The Limits to Growth through Product Differentiation

Like many other large firms, Starbucks started small. In 1971, entrepreneurs Gordon Bowker, Gerald Baldwin, and Zev Siegl opened the first Starbucks in Seattle, Washington. Current CEO Howard Schultz joined the company 10 years later. Schultz realized that many consumers wanted a coffeehouse where they could relax, read, chat, and drink higher-quality coffee than was typically served in diners or donut shops. Designing Starbucks coffeehouses to provide this experience was the key to Schultz's success. But it was easy for other coffeehouses to copy the Starbucks approach.

By 2009, fierce competition and a weak economy led Starbucks to close hundreds of stores in the United States and cut prices as it tried to overcome the impression that it was the "home of the $4 coffee." Starbucks became profitable once more in 2010, partly due to expansion of its overseas markets, with sales in Asia exceeding $1 billion in 2013. Starbucks also made its coffeehouses friendlier to customers using smartphones and other mobile devices. The following quote from Schultz shows that he realizes that his company faces a constant challenge to stay ahead of its competitors and satisfy its customers: "I feel it's so important to remind us all of how fleeting success ... can be."

Perfectly competitive markets, share three key characteristics:

1. There are many firms.
2. All firms sell identical products.
3. There are no barriers to new firms entering the industry.

The market Starbucks competes in shares two of these characteristics: There are many coffeehouses, and the barriers to entering the market are very low. But the coffee at Starbucks is not identical to what competing coffeehouses offer. Selling coffee in coffeehouses is not like selling wheat: The products that Starbucks and its competitors sell are *differentiated* rather than identical. So, the coffeehouse market is *monopolistically competitive* rather than perfectly competitive. As we will see, most monopolistically competitive firms are unable to earn economic profits in the long run.

Sources: Annie Gasparro, "Starbucks Shuffles Global Management Team," *Wall Street Journal*, May 2, 2013; Annie Gasparo, "U.S., China Boost Starbucks," *Wall Street Journal*, April 25, 2013; and Claire Cain Miller, "A Changed Starbucks. A Changed C.E.O.," *New York Times*, March 12, 2011.

Economics in Your Life

Opening Your Own Restaurant

After you graduate, you plan to realize your dream of opening your own Italian restaurant. You are confident that many people will enjoy the pasta prepared with your grandmother's secret sauce. Although your hometown already has three Italian restaurants, you are convinced that you can enter this market and make a profit.

You have many choices to make in operating your restaurant. Will it be "family style," with sturdy but inexpensive furniture, where families with small—and noisy!—children will feel welcome, or will it be more elegant, with nice furniture, tablecloths, and candles? Will you offer a full menu or concentrate on pasta dishes that use your grandmother's secret sauce? These and other choices you make will distinguish your restaurant from competitors. What's likely to happen in the restaurant market in your hometown after you open your restaurant? How successful are you likely to be? Try to answer these questions as you read this chapter. You can check your answers against those we provide at the end of this chapter.

Many markets in the U.S. economy are similar to the coffeehouse market: They have many buyers and sellers, and the barriers to entry are low, but the goods and services offered for sale are differentiated rather than identical. Examples of these markets include restaurants, movie theaters, supermarkets, and clothing manufacturing. In fact, the majority of the firms you buy from are competing in **monopolistically competitive** markets.

We have seen how perfect competition benefits consumers and results in economic efficiency. Will these same desirable outcomes also hold for monopolistically competitive markets? This question is important because monopolistically competitive markets are common.

Monopolistic competition A market structure in which barriers to entry are low and many firms compete by selling similar, but not identical, products.

1 LEARNING OBJECTIVE

Explain why a monopolistically competitive firm has downward-sloping demand and marginal revenue curves.

Demand and Marginal Revenue for a Firm in a Monopolistically Competitive Market

If the Starbucks coffeehouse located a mile from where you live raises the price of a caffè latte from $3.00 to $3.25, it will lose some, but not all, of its customers. Some customers will switch to buying their coffee at another store, but other customers will be willing to pay the higher price for a variety of reasons: This store may be closer to them, or they may prefer Starbucks caffè lattes to similar coffees at competing stores. Because changing the price affects the quantity of caffè lattes sold, a Starbucks store will face a downward-sloping demand curve rather than the horizontal demand curve that a wheat farmer faces.

The Demand Curve for a Monopolistically Competitive Firm

Figure 1 shows how a change in price affects the quantity of caffè lattes Starbucks sells. The increase in the price from $3.00 to $3.25 decreases the quantity of caffè lattes sold from 3,000 per week to 2,400 per week.

Marginal Revenue for a Firm with a Downward-Sloping Demand Curve

For a firm in a perfectly competitive market, the demand curve and the marginal revenue curve are the same. A perfectly competitive firm faces a horizontal demand curve and does not have to cut the price to sell a larger quantity. A monopolistically competitive firm, on the other hand, must cut the price to sell more, so its marginal revenue curve will slope downward and will be below its demand curve.

The data in Table 1 illustrate this point. To keep the numbers simple, let's assume that your local Starbucks coffeehouse is very small and sells at most 10 caffè lattes per week.

Figure 1

The Downward-Sloping Demand for Caffè Lattes at a Starbucks

If a Starbucks increases the price of caffè lattes, it will lose some, but not all, of its customers. In this case, raising the price from $3.00 to $3.25 reduces the quantity of caffè lattes sold from 3,000 to 2,400. Therefore, unlike a perfect competitor, a Starbucks coffeehouse faces a downward-sloping demand curve.

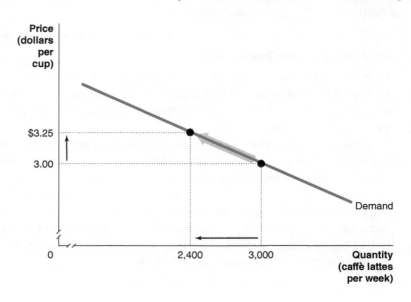

Caffè Lattes Sold per Week (Q)	Price (P)	Total Revenue (TR = P × Q)	Average Revenue $\left(AR = \dfrac{TR}{Q} \right)$	Marginal Revenue $\left(MR = \dfrac{\Delta TR}{\Delta Q} \right)$
0	$6.00	$0.00	—	—
1	5.50	5.50	$5.50	$5.50
2	5.00	10.00	5.00	4.50
3	4.50	13.50	4.50	3.50
4	4.00	16.00	4.00	2.50
5	3.50	17.50	3.50	1.50
6	3.00	18.00	3.00	0.50
7	2.50	17.50	2.50	−0.50
8	2.00	16.00	2.00	−1.50
9	1.50	13.50	1.50	−2.50
10	1.00	10.00	1.00	−3.50

Table 1

Demand and Marginal Revenue at a Starbucks

If the local Starbucks charges a price of $6.00 or more, all of its potential customers will buy their coffee somewhere else. If it charges $5.50, it will sell 1 caffè latte per week. For each additional $0.50 this Starbucks reduces the price, it increases the number of caffè lattes it sells by 1. The third column in the table shows how the firm's *total revenue* changes as it sells more caffè lattes. The fourth column shows the firm's revenue per unit, or its *average revenue*. Average revenue is equal to total revenue divided by quantity. Because total revenue equals price multiplied by quantity, dividing by quantity leaves just price. Therefore, *average revenue is always equal to price*. This result will be true for firms selling in any of the four market structures: perfect competition, monopolistic competition, oligopoly, and monopoly.

The last column in Table 1 shows the firm's marginal revenue, or the change in total revenue as the firm sells 1 more caffè latte. For a perfectly competitive firm, the additional revenue received from selling 1 more unit is just equal to the price. That will not be true for this Starbucks because to sell another caffè latte, it has to reduce the price. When the firm cuts the price by $0.50, one good thing and one bad thing happen:

- **The good thing.** It sells 1 more caffè latte; we can call this the *output effect*.
- **The bad thing.** It receives $0.50 less for each caffè latte that it could have sold at the higher price; we can call this the *price effect*.

Figure 2 illustrates what happens when the firm cuts the price from $3.50 to $3.00. Selling the sixth caffè latte adds the $3.00 price to the firm's revenue; this is the

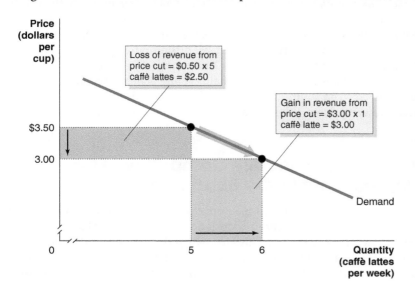

Figure 2

How a Price Cut Affects a Firm's Revenue

If a local Starbucks reduces the price of a caffè latte from $3.50 to $3.00, the number of caffè lattes it sells per week will increase from 5 to 6. Its marginal revenue from selling the sixth caffè latte will be $0.50, which is equal to the $3.00 additional revenue from selling 1 more caffè latte (the area of the green box) minus the $2.50 loss in revenue from selling the first 5 caffè lattes for $0.50 less each (the area of the red box).

Figure 3

The Demand and Marginal Revenue Curves for a Monopolistically Competitive Firm

Any firm that has the ability to affect the price of the product it sells will have a marginal revenue curve that is below its demand curve. We plot the data from Table 1 to create the demand and marginal revenue curves. After the sixth caffè latte, marginal revenue becomes negative because the additional revenue received from selling 1 more caffè latte is smaller than the revenue lost from receiving a lower price on the caffè lattes that could have been sold at the original price.

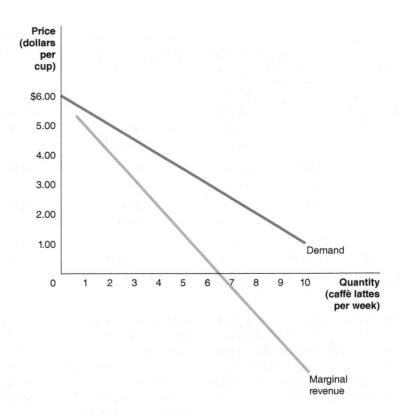

output effect. But this Starbucks now receives a price of $3.00, rather than $3.50, on the first 5 caffè lattes sold; this is the price effect. As a result of the price effect, the firm's revenue on these 5 caffè lattes is $2.50 less than it would have been if the price had remained at $3.50. So, the firm has gained $3.00 in revenue on the sixth caffè latte and lost $2.50 in revenue on the first 5 caffè lattes, for a net change in revenue of $0.50. Marginal revenue is the change in total revenue from selling 1 more unit. Therefore, the marginal revenue of the sixth caffè latte is $0.50. Notice that the marginal revenue of the sixth unit is far below its price of $3.00. In fact, for each additional caffè latte this Starbucks sells, marginal revenue will be less than price. There is an important general point: *Every firm that has the ability to affect the price of the good or service it sells will have a marginal revenue curve that is below its demand curve.* Only firms in perfectly competitive markets, which can sell as many units as they want at the market price, have marginal revenue curves that are the same as their demand curves.

Figure 3 shows the relationship between the demand curve and the marginal revenue curve for the local Starbucks. Notice that after the sixth caffè latte, marginal revenue becomes negative. Marginal revenue is negative because the additional revenue received from selling 1 more caffè latte is smaller than the revenue lost from receiving a lower price on the caffè lattes that could have been sold at the original price.

2 LEARNING OBJECTIVE

Explain how a monopolistically competitive firm maximizes profit in the short run.

How a Monopolistically Competitive Firm Maximizes Profit in the Short Run

All firms use the same approach to maximize profits: They produce the quantity where marginal revenue is equal to marginal cost. So the local Starbucks will maximize profits by selling the quantity of caffè lattes for which the last caffè latte sold adds the same amount to the firm's revenue as to its costs. Let's look more carefully at how monopolistically competitive firms maximize profits by considering the situation the local Starbucks faces in the short run. In the short run, at least one factor of production is fixed, and there is not enough time for new firms to enter the market. A Starbucks has many costs, including the cost of purchasing the ingredients for its caffè lattes and other coffees, the electricity it uses, and the wages of its employees. A firm's *marginal cost* is the increase in total cost resulting from producing another unit of output. For many firms, the marginal cost curve has a U shape. We will assume that the marginal cost curve for this Starbucks has the usual shape.

We combine the revenue data for this Starbucks from Table 1 with cost data to create the table in Figure 4. The graphs in Figure 4 plot the data from the table. In panel (a), we see how this Starbucks can determine its profit-maximizing quantity and price. As long as the marginal cost of selling 1 more caffè latte is less than the marginal revenue, the firm should sell additional caffè lattes. For example, increasing the quantity of caffè lattes sold from 3 per week to 4 per week increases cost by $1.00 but increases

Caffè Lattes Sold per Week (Q)	Price (P)	Total Revenue (TR)	Marginal Revenue (MR)	Total Cost (TC)	Marginal Cost (MC)	Average Total Cost (ATC)	Profit
0	$6.00	$0.00	—	$5.00	—	—	−$5.00
1	5.50	5.50	$5.50	8.00	$3.00	$8.00	−2.50
2	5.00	10.00	4.50	9.50	1.50	4.75	0.50
3	4.50	13.50	3.50	10.00	0.50	3.33	3.50
4	4.00	16.00	2.50	11.00	1.00	2.75	5.00
5	3.50	17.50	1.50	12.50	1.50	2.50	5.00
6	3.00	18.00	0.50	14.50	2.00	2.42	3.50
7	2.50	17.50	−0.50	17.00	2.50	2.43	0.50
8	2.00	16.00	−1.50	20.00	3.00	2.50	−4.00
9	1.50	13.50	−2.50	23.50	3.50	2.61	−10.00
10	1.00	10.00	−3.50	27.50	4.00	2.75	−17.50

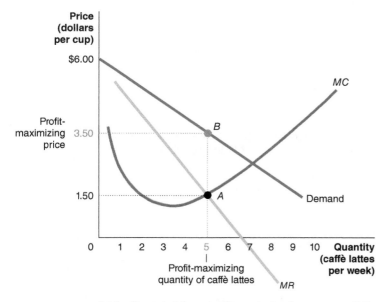

(a) Profit-maximizing quantity and price for a monopolistic competitor

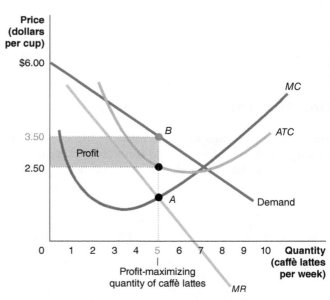

(b) Short-run profits for a monopolistic competitor

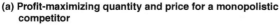

Figure 4 Maximizing Profit in a Monopolistically Competitive Market

To maximize profit, a Starbucks coffeehouse wants to sell caffè lattes up to the point where the marginal revenue from selling the last caffè latte is just equal to the marginal cost. As the table shows, selling the fifth caffè latte—point A in panel (a)—adds $1.50 to the firm's costs and $1.50 to its revenues. The firm then uses the demand curve to find the price that will lead consumers to buy this quantity of caffè lattes (point B). In panel (b), the green box represents the firm's profits. The box has a height equal to $1.00, which is the $3.50 price minus the average total cost of $2.50, and it has a base equal to the quantity of 5 caffè lattes. So, for this Starbucks profit equals $1 × 5 = $5.00.

revenue by $2.50. So, the firm's profits are increased by $1.50 as a result of selling the fourth caffè latte.

As this Starbucks sells more caffè lattes, rising marginal cost eventually equals marginal revenue, and the firm sells the profit-maximizing quantity of caffè lattes. Marginal cost equals marginal revenue with the fifth caffè latte, which adds $1.50 to the firm's costs and $1.50 to its revenues—point *A* in panel (a) of Figure 4. The demand curve tells us the price at which the firm is able to sell 5 caffè lattes per week. In Figure 4, if we draw a vertical line from 5 caffè lattes up to the demand curve, we can see that the price at which the firm can sell 5 caffè lattes per week is $3.50 (point *B*). We can conclude that for this Starbucks, the profit-maximizing quantity is 5 caffè lattes, and the profit-maximizing price is $3.50. If the firm sells more than 5 caffè lattes per week, its profit will fall. For example, selling a sixth caffè latte adds $2.00 to its costs and only $0.50 to its revenues. So, its profit will fall from $5.00 to $3.50.

Panel (b) adds the average total cost curve for Starbucks. The panel shows that the average total cost of selling 5 caffè lattes is $2.50.

$$\text{Profit} = (P - ATC) \times Q.$$

In this case, profit = ($3.50 − $2.50) × 5 = $5.00. The green rectangle in panel (b) shows the amount of profit. The rectangle has a base equal to Q and a height equal to $(P - ATC)$, so its area equals profit.

Notice that, unlike a perfectly competitive firm, which produces where $P = MC$, a monopolistically competitive firm produces where $P > MC$. In this case, this Starbucks is charging a price of $3.50, although marginal cost is $1.50. For a perfectly competitive firm, price equals marginal revenue, $P = MR$. Therefore, to fulfill the $MR = MC$ condition for profit maximization, a perfectly competitive firm will produce where $P = MC$. $P > MR$ for a monopolistically competitive firm because the firm's marginal revenue curve is below its demand curve. Therefore, a monopolistically competitive firm will maximize profits by producing where $P > MC$.

Solved Problem 2

Does Minimizing Cost Maximize Profit at Apple?

Suppose Apple finds that the relationship between the average total cost of producing iPhones and the quantity of iPhones produced is as shown in the following graph.

Will Apple maximize profits if it produces 800,000 iPhones per month? Briefly explain.

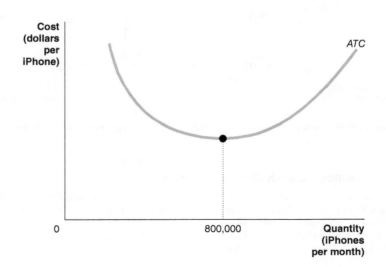

Solving the Problem

Step 1: **Review the chapter material.** This problem is about how monopolistically competitive firms maximize profits, so you may want to review the section "How a Monopolistically Competitive Firm Maximizes Profit in the Short Run."

Step 2: **Discuss the relationship between minimizing costs and maximizing profits.** Firms often talk about the steps they take to reduce costs. The graph shows that by producing 800,000 iPhones per month, Apple will minimize its average cost of production. But remember that minimizing cost is not the firm's ultimate goal; the firm's ultimate goal is to maximize profit. Depending on demand, a firm may maximize profit by producing a quantity that is either larger or smaller than the quantity that would minimize average total cost.

Step 3: **Draw a graph that shows Apple maximizing profit at a quantity where average cost is not minimized.** Note that in the graph, average total cost reaches a minimum at a quantity of 800,000, but profit is maximized at a quantity of 600,000.

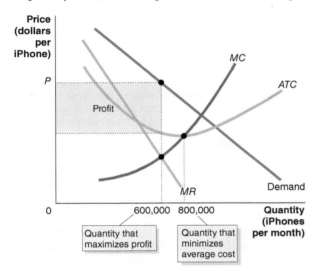

Your Turn: For more practice, do related problem 2.5 at the end of this chapter.

What Happens to Profits in the Long Run?

3 LEARNING OBJECTIVE

Analyze the situation of a monopolistically competitive firm in the long run.

A firm makes an economic profit when its total revenue is greater than all of its costs, including the opportunity cost of the funds invested in the firm by its owners. Because cost curves include the owners' opportunity costs, the Starbucks coffeehouse represented in Figure 4 is making an economic profit. This economic profit gives entrepreneurs an incentive to enter this market and establish new firms. If a Starbucks is earning an economic profit selling caffè lattes, new coffeehouses are likely to open in the same area.

How Does the Entry of New Firms Affect the Profits of Existing Firms?

As new coffeehouses open near a local Starbucks, the firm's demand curve will shift to the left. The demand curve will shift because the Starbucks will sell fewer caffè lattes at each price when there are additional coffeehouses in the area selling similar drinks. The demand curve will also become more elastic because consumers have additional coffeehouses from which to buy coffee, so the Starbucks will lose more sales if it raises its prices. Figure 5 shows how the demand curve for the local Starbucks shifts as new firms enter its market.

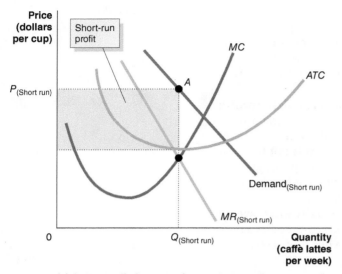

(a) A monopolistic competitor may earn a short-run profit

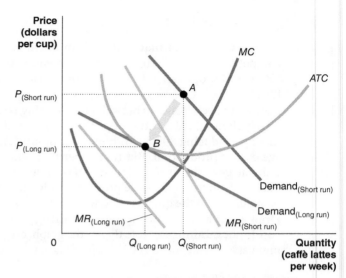

(b) A monopolistic competitor's profits are eliminated in the long run

Figure 5   **How Entry of New Firms Eliminates Profits**

Panel (a) shows that in the short run, the local Starbucks faces the demand and marginal revenue curves labeled "Short run." With this demand curve, Starbucks can charge a price above average total cost (point A) and make a profit, shown by the green rectangle. But this profit attracts new firms to enter the market, which shifts the demand and marginal revenue curves to the curves labeled "Long run" in panel (b). Because price is now equal to average total cost (point B), Starbucks breaks even and no longer earns an economic profit.

In panel (a) of Figure 5, the short-run demand curve shows the relationship between the price of caffè lattes and the quantity of caffè lattes this Starbucks sells per week before the entry of new firms. With this demand curve, this Starbucks can charge a price above average total cost—shown as point A in panel (a)—and make a profit. But this profit attracts additional coffeehouses to the area and shifts the demand curve for this Starbucks' caffè lattes to the left. As long as this Starbucks is making an economic profit, there is an incentive for additional coffeehouses to open in the area, and the demand curve will continue shifting to the left. As panel (b) shows, eventually the demand curve will have shifted to the point where it is just touching—or tangent to—the average total cost curve.

In the long run, at the point where the demand curve is tangent to the average total cost curve, price is equal to average total cost (point B), the firm is breaking even, and it no longer earns an economic profit. In the long run, the demand curve is also more elastic because the more coffeehouses there are in the area, the more sales this Starbucks will lose to other coffeehouses if it raises its price.

Don't Let This Happen to You

Don't Confuse Zero Economic Profit with Zero Accounting Profit

Economistscount the opportunity cost of the owner's investment in a firm as a cost. Suppose you invest $200,000 opening a pizza parlor, and the return you could earn on those funds each year in a similar investment—such as opening a sandwich shop—is 10 percent. Therefore, the annual opportunity cost of investing the funds in your own business is 10 percent of $200,000, or $20,000. This $20,000 is part of your profit in the accounting sense, and

you would have to pay taxes on it. But in an economic sense, the $20,000 is a cost. In long-run equilibrium, we would expect that entry of new firms would keep you from earning more than 10 percent on your investment. So, you would end up breaking even and earning zero economic profit, even though you were earning an accounting profit of $20,000.

Your Turn: Test your understanding by doing related problem 3.6 at the end of this chapter.

Of course, it is possible that a monopolistically competitive firm will suffer an economic loss in the short run. As a consequence, the owners of the firm will not be covering the opportunity cost of their investment. We expect that, in the long run, firms will exit an industry if they are suffering economic losses. If firms exit, the demand curve for the output of a remaining firm will shift to the right. This process will continue until the representative firm in the industry is able to charge a price equal to its average total cost and break even. Therefore, in the long run, monopolistically competitive firms will experience neither economic profits nor economic losses. Table 2 summarizes the short run and the long run for a monopolistically competitive firm.

Table 2 **The Short Run and the Long Run for a Monopolistically Competitive Firm**

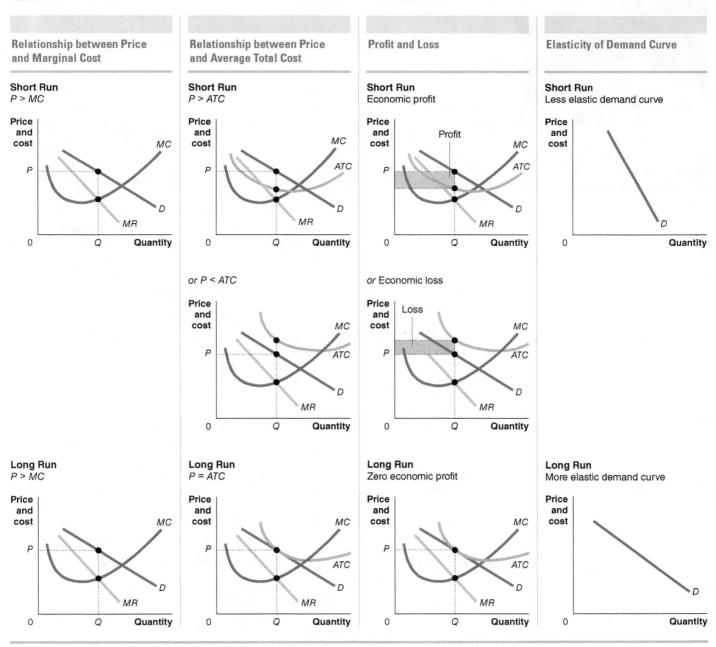

Making the Connection

The Rise and Decline and Rise of Starbucks

In the spring of 2009, an article from Bloomberg News summed up the situation that Starbucks was in: "After more than a decade of sensational buzz, Starbucks is struggling nationwide as it faces slowing sales growth and increased competition." The initial success and later struggles of Starbucks are a familiar pattern for firms in monopolistically competitive markets.

When Starbucks began rapidly expanding, CEO Howard Schultz knew that fresh-brewed coffee was widely available in restaurants, diners, and donut shops. He believed, though, that he had a strategy that would differentiate Starbucks from competitors: Starbucks would offer a European espresso bar atmosphere, with large, comfortable chairs, music playing, and groups of friends dropping in and out during the day. From the mid-1990s through the mid-2000s, this strategy worked very well, and Starbucks opened nearly 17,000 stores worldwide. But the profitability of Starbucks attracted competitors. Other nationwide chains, such as Caribou Coffee, Peet's Coffee, and Diedrich Coffee, and regional chains, such as Dunn Brothers Coffee, provided stores with similar atmospheres, as did many individually owned coffeehouses.

Starbucks used innovations such as Wi-Fi to return to profitability after several years of struggling with intense competition from other firms.

In addition, McDonald's and Dunkin' Donuts began competing more directly with Starbucks. Dunkin' Donuts began building more upscale restaurants, and McDonald's began selling espresso-based coffee drinks for prices considerably below those at Starbucks. Schultz was also worried that in opening thousands of coffeehouses worldwide, Starbucks had made the customers' experience less distinctive and easier for competitors to copy.

Beginning in 2010, Schultz managed a remarkable turnaround, with Starbucks' sales and profits increasing. Some of the success was attributable to an expansion in overseas markets, where competition was not as strong as in the United States. By 2013, the firm had sales of more than $1 billion in Asia and plans to open thousands of additional stores in China. But the firm's focus remained on staying one step ahead of its competition in the United States. The revival of Starbucks in the United States was based on several factors: The firm gave customers more freedom to customize drinks; it started a loyalty program that included free refills and other perks for regular customers; it started a mobile payment system that allowed customers to pay with a smartphone; and it provided stores with machines that brewed higher-quality coffees. Stephen Gillett, the firm's chief information officer, improved in-store Wi-Fi so customers could use it without having to go through a logon screen and could get free access to content from sources such as the *Wall Street Journal* and *USA Today*, as well as see exclusive movie trailers. The objective was to keep customers in the store longer so they would buy more coffee. The customer loyalty program, by reducing the average price for frequent customers, helped fight the impression that Starbucks coffee was too expensive to buy a cup every day.

In mid-2013, Starbucks's strategy appeared to be working as its U.S. stores experienced increasing sales while sales at Dunkin' Donuts and McDonald's were flat or declining. Schulz declared: "Anyone who suggested in '08 or '09 that Starbucks was reaching saturation in the U.S. was just flat out wrong," and he announced that Starbucks would open an additional 300 stores in the United States by the end of the year.

In a monopolistically competitive industry, maintaining profits in the long run is very difficult. Only by constantly innovating has Starbucks been able to return to profitability after several years of struggling with intense competition from other firms.

Sources: Annie Gasparro, "Starbucks Shuffles Global Management Team," *Wall Street Journal*, May 2, 2013; Annie Gasparo, "U.S., China Boost Starbucks," *Wall Street Journal*, April 25, 2013; Andrew Harrer, "Starbucks Corporation," Bloomberg News, April 13, 2009; and Janet Adamy, "Dunkin' Donuts Tries to Go Upscale, But Not Too Far," *Wall Street Journal*, April 8, 2006.

Your Turn: Test your understanding by doing related problem 3.8 at the end of this chapter.

Is Zero Economic Profit Inevitable in the Long Run?

The economic analysis of the long run shows the effects of market forces over time. Owners of monopolistically competitive firms, of course, do not have to passively accept this long-run result. The key to earning an economic profit is either to sell a differentiated product or to find a way of producing an existing product at a lower cost. If a monopolistically competitive firm selling a differentiated product is earning a profit, the profit will attract the entry of additional firms, and the entry of those firms will eventually eliminate the firm's profit. If a firm introduces new technology that allows it to sell a good or service at a lower cost, competing firms will eventually duplicate that technology and eliminate the firm's profit. *But this result holds only if the firm stands still and fails to find new ways of differentiating its product or fails to find new ways of lowering the cost of producing its product.* Starbucks had great initial success, had difficulty maintaining its profitability after the entry of new firms, and then found its way back to profitability by introducing new products and improving its customers' experience through a loyalty program and other innovations. Firms continually struggle to find new ways of differentiating their products as they try to stay one step ahead of other firms that are attempting to copy their success.

The owner of a competitive firm is in a position like that of Ebenezer Scrooge in Charles Dickens's *A Christmas Carol*. When the Ghost of Christmas Yet to Come shows Scrooge visions of his own death, he asks the ghost, "Are these the shadows of the things that Will be, or are they shadows of things that May be, only?" The shadow of the end of their profits haunts owners of every firm. Firms try to continue earning profits by reducing costs, by improving their products, by providing exceptional customer service, or by convincing consumers that their products are indeed different from what competitors offer. To stay one step ahead of its competitors, a firm has to offer consumers goods or services that they perceive to have greater *value* than those competing firms offer. Value can take the form of product differentiation that makes the good or service more suited to consumers' preferences, or it can take the form of a lower price.

Solved Problem 3

Can It Be Profitable to Be the High-Price Seller?

h.h.gregg is an appliance and electronics retailer with stores in 20 states. As a relatively small firm, it has to pay more for its appliances, televisions, and other goods from manufacturers than does a large chain, such as Best Buy. Because h.h.gregg must pay higher prices to manufacturers, it must charge higher prices to consumers. How is h.h.gregg able to succeed in competition with Best Buy, Wal-Mart, Amazon, and other big retailers, despite charging higher prices?

According to an article in the *Wall Street Journal*: "h.h.gregg's commissioned sales staff is an advantage over national chains with young, lower-paid hourly workers that tend to stay for shorter periods." h.h.gregg's CEO noted that: "We have sales people that have been with us 10 to 20 years, and customers who come in and ask for them by name."

Use this information to explain how an h.h.gregg store might be more profitable than a similar Best Buy store, despite the fact that the h.h.gregg store charges higher prices. Use a graph for h.h.gregg and a graph for Best Buy to illustrate your answer.

Solving the Problem

Step 1: Review the chapter material. This problem is about how a monopolistically competitive firm maximizes profits and about how firms attempt to earn economic profits in the long run, so you may want to review the section "How a Monopolistically Competitive Firm Maximizes Profit in the Short Run," and the section "Is Zero Economic Profit Inevitable in the Long Run?"

Step 2: Explain how h.h.gregg can remain profitable despite its high costs. If an h.h.gregg store has higher costs than a comparable Best Buy store, it can have greater profits only if the demand for its goods is higher. According to the *Wall Street Journal* article, h.h.gregg has differentiated itself from the competition, particularly from large chain stores such as Best Buy, by offering better customer service. By having salespeople who are more knowledgeable and more experienced than the salespeople hired by competitors, h.h.gregg has attracted consumers who need help in buying televisions and appliances. The higher demand from these consumers must be enough to offset h.h.gregg's higher costs.

Step 3: Draw graphs to illustrate your argument. For simplicity, the graphs here assume that televisions are the product being sold. Panel (a) shows the situation for h.h.gregg, and panel (b) shows the situation for Best Buy.

The graphs show that the h.h.gregg store has both greater demand and higher costs than the Best Buy store. Because the greater demand more than offsets the higher costs, the h.h.gregg store makes a larger profit.

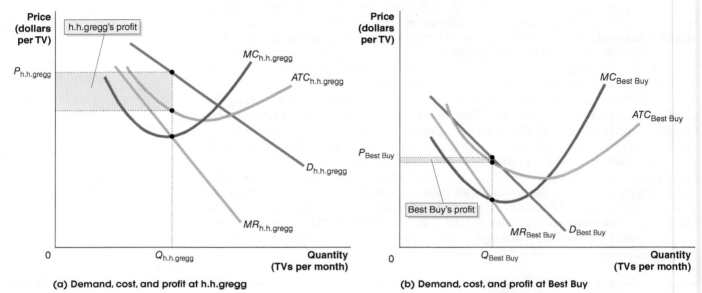

(a) Demand, cost, and profit at h.h.gregg

(b) Demand, cost, and profit at Best Buy

Extra Credit: As we have seen, firms constantly search for means of differentiating themselves from their competitors. Often, differentiation works for a while but then breaks down as competitors copy the strategy. After a number of years of success, by 2013, the competition may have caught up with h.h.gregg, as its sales were declining.

Sources: Debbi Cai, "Hhgregg 4th-Quarter Profit Down 82% on Weaker Same-Store Sales," *Wall Street Journal*, May 20, 2013; Scott Tilghman, "Hhgregg Could Get a Leg Up," Barron's, June 2, 2011; and Miguel Bustillo, "Small Electronics Chains Thrive in Downturn," *Wall Street Journal*, May 27, 2009.

Your Turn: For more practice, do related problem 3.9 at the end of this chapter.

4 LEARNING OBJECTIVE

Compare the efficiency of monopolistic competition and perfect competition.

Comparing Monopolistic Competition and Perfect Competition

We have seen that monopolistic competition and perfect competition share the characteristic that in long-run equilibrium firms earn zero economic profits. As Figure 6 shows, however, there are two important differences between long-run equilibrium in the two markets:

- Monopolistically competitive firms charge a price greater than marginal cost.
- Monopolistically competitive firms do not produce at minimum average total cost.

Excess Capacity under Monopolistic Competition

A firm in a perfectly competitive market faces a perfectly elastic demand curve that is also its marginal revenue curve. Therefore, the firm maximizes profit by producing the quantity where price equals marginal cost. As panel (a) of Figure 6 shows, in long-run equilibrium, a perfectly competitive firm produces at the minimum point of its average total cost curve.

Panel (b) of Figure 6 shows that the profit-maximizing level of output for a monopolistically competitive firm comes at a level of output where price is greater than marginal cost, and the firm is not at the minimum point of its average total cost curve. A monopolistically competitive firm has *excess capacity*: If it increased its output, it could produce at a lower average total cost.

Is Monopolistic Competition Inefficient?

. *Productive efficiency* refers to the situation where a good is produced at the lowest possible cost. *Allocative efficiency* refers to the situation where every good or service is

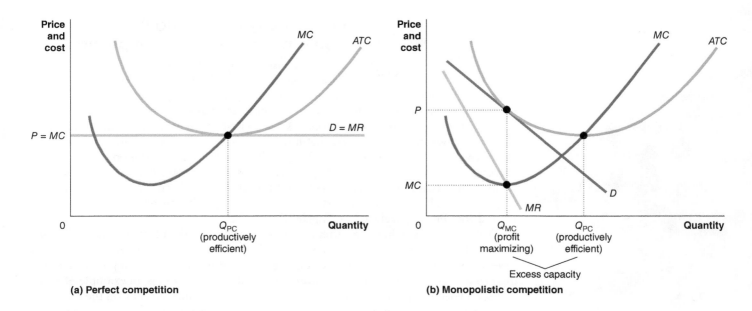

(a) Perfect competition

(b) Monopolistic competition

Figure 6 Comparing Long-Run Equilibrium under Perfect Competition and Monopolistic Competition

In panel (a), a perfectly competitive firm in long-run equilibrium produces at Q_{PC}, where price equals marginal cost, and average total cost is at a minimum. The perfectly competitive firm is both allocatively efficient and productively efficient. In panel (b), a monopolistically competitive firm produces at Q_{MC}, where price is greater than marginal cost, and average total cost is not at a minimum. As a result, the monopolistically competitive firm is neither allocatively efficient nor productively efficient. The monopolistically competitive firm has excess capacity equal to the difference between its profit-maximizing level of output and the productively efficient level of output.

produced up to the point where the last unit provides a marginal benefit to consumers equal to the marginal cost of producing it. For productive efficiency to hold, firms must produce at the minimum point of average total cost. For allocative efficiency to hold, firms must charge a price equal to marginal cost. In a perfectly competitive market, both productive efficiency and allocative efficiency are achieved, but in a monopolistically competitive market, neither is achieved. Does it matter? Economists have debated whether monopolistically competitive markets being neither productively nor allocatively efficient results in a significant loss of well-being to society in these markets compared with perfectly competitive markets.

How Consumers Benefit from Monopolistic Competition

Looking again at Figure 6, you can see that the key difference between the monopolistically competitive firm and the perfectly competitive firm is that the demand curve for the monopolistically competitive firm slopes downward, whereas the demand curve for the perfectly competitive firm is a horizontal line. The demand curve for the monopolistically competitive firm slopes downward because the good or service the firm is selling is differentiated from the goods or services being sold by competing firms. The perfectly competitive firm is selling a good or service identical to those being sold by its competitors. A key point to remember is that *firms differentiate their products to appeal to consumers.* For example, when Starbucks coffeehouses begin offering slower-brewed, higher-quality coffees, when Wal-Mart begins carrying more Blu-ray discs and fewer regular DVDs, when General Mills introduces Apple-Cinnamon Cheerios, or when PepsiCo introduces Diet Wild Cherry Pepsi, they are all attempting to attract and retain consumers through product differentiation. The success of these product differentiation strategies indicates that some consumers find these products preferable to the alternatives. Consumers, therefore, are better off than they would have been had these companies not differentiated their products.

We can conclude that consumers face a trade-off when buying the product of a monopolistically competitive firm: They are paying a price that is greater than marginal cost, and the product is not being produced at minimum average cost, but they benefit from being able to purchase a product that is differentiated and more closely suited to their tastes.

Making the Connection

Peter Thiel, e-Cigarettes, and the Monopoly in Monopolistic Competition

The term *monopolistic competition* is a combination of two words with opposite economic meanings: monopoly—meaning an industry with one firm—and competition—meaning an industry with many firms. A true monopoly—like a town's water department delivering tap water to homes—has no competition and is very rare, but the economists who first began using the term monopolistic competition wanted to emphasize that most firms have, in a sense, a *limited* monopoly. If you open a pizza parlor on the corner, yours will be the only pizza parlor on that corner and probably the only pizza parlor on that block and possibly—if you are lucky!—the only pizza parlor in that part of town. The "competition" in monopolistic competition was meant to emphasize that if your firm is a success and you make a profit, new firms will enter the market and your profit is likely to be competed away.

Peter Thiel is a billionaire entrepreneur. He was co-founder of PayPal, the online payment system, and was an early investor in firms such as LinkedIn, Zynga, and Facebook. Thiel has emphasized that the key to starting a successful firm is rarely to provide an existing product at a higher quality or lower price—although Toyota is an example of a firm that succeeded using that approach. Instead, Thiel recommends focusing on the monopoly part of monopolistic competition by coming up with a new product or service or a product or service that meets an existing consumer demand in an entirely new way. Before PayPal, people could pay for Internet services using a credit card or by sending a check. But these ways of paying had drawbacks: In the early days of the Internet, many sellers on eBay and elsewhere didn't have the ability to accept credit cards or wanted to avoid the fees that credit card companies charge sellers. Checks take time to clear through banks, making sellers wait for payment and buyers wait for goods to be shipped. PayPal gave consumers using eBay and other Web sites a new way to pay for purchases.

One columnist summarized Thiel's approach: "He's talking about doing something so creative that you establish a distinct market, niche and identity. You've established a creative monopoly and everybody has to come to you if they want that service, at least for a time." In a course Thiel gave at Stanford University, he argued that an entrepreneur should aim for "owning a market"—at least for a period: "For a company to own its market, it must have some combination of brand, scale cost advantages, network effects, or proprietary technology."

Thiel's latest project is investing in NJOY, a firm that makes e-cigarettes. E-cigarettes look like regular tobacco cigarettes but use a battery to turn a liquid containing nicotine into a vapor. E-cigarettes have a potential advantage over conventional cigarettes in providing nicotine to smokers without the risks of cancer, heart disease, and other health problems. U.S. consumers spend about $100 billion per year on conventional cigarettes, so converting even a small percentage of smokers to e-cigarettes could prove very profitable. But a firm selling e-cigarettes faces a number of problems. The U.S. Food and Drug Administration has stated that further research is necessary to determine whether e-cigarettes may pose health risks to smokers. Some states have banned their sale to minors, and some businesses—including Starbucks—have banned their use.

Time will tell whether NJOY will succeed in owning an important market—at least for a time.

Sources: Mike Esterl, "E-Cigarettes Fire Up Investors, Regulators," *Wall Street Journal*, June 9, 2013; Teresa Novellino, "With Cash, Sean Parker and Peter Thiel Follow NJOY's Vapor Trail," http://upstart.bizjournals.com, June 10, 2013; David Brooks, "The Creative Monopoly," *New York Times*, April 23, 2012; and Blake Masters, "Ten Lessons from Peter Thiel's Class on Startups," *Forbes*, June 7, 2012.

Your Turn: Test your understanding by doing related problem 4.8 at the end of this chapter.

Will NJOY own the e-cigarette market?

---

5 LEARNING OBJECTIVE

Define marketing and explain how firms use marketing to differentiate their products.

How Marketing Differentiates Products

Firms can differentiate their products through **marketing**, which refers to all the activities necessary for a firm to sell a product to a consumer. Marketing includes activities such as determining which product to sell, designing the product, advertising the product, deciding how to distribute the product—for example, in retail stores or through a Web site—and monitoring how changes in consumer tastes are affecting the market for the product. Peter F. Drucker, a leading business strategist, described marketing as follows: "It is the whole business seen from the point of view of its final result, that is, from the consumer's point of view.... True marketing ... does not ask, 'What do we want to sell?' It asks, 'What does the consumer want to buy?' "

For monopolistically competitive firms to earn economic profits and defend those profits from competitors, they must differentiate their products. Firms use two marketing tools to differentiate their products: brand management and advertising.

Brand Management

Once a firm has succeeded in differentiating its product, it must try to maintain that differentiation over time through **brand management**. As we have seen, whenever a firm successfully introduces a new product or a significantly different version of an old product, it earns an economic profit in the short run. But the success of the firm inspires competitors to copy the new or improved product, and, in the long run, the firm's economic profit will be competed away. Firms use brand management to postpone the time when they will no longer be able to earn economic profits.

Advertising

An innovative advertising campaign can make even long-established and familiar products, such as Coke or McDonald's Big Mac hamburgers, seem more desirable than competing products. When a firm advertises a product, it is trying to shift the demand curve for the product to the right and to make it more inelastic. If the firm is successful, it will sell more of the product at every price, and it will be able to increase the price it charges without losing as many customers. Of course, advertising also increases a firm's costs. If the increase in revenue that results from the advertising is greater than the increase in costs, the firm's profits will rise.

Defending a Brand Name

Once a firm has established a successful brand name, it has a strong incentive to defend it. A firm can apply for a *trademark*, which grants legal protection against other firms using its product's name.

One threat to a trademarked name is the possibility that it will become so widely used for a type of product that it will no longer be associated with the product of a specific company. Courts in the United States have ruled that when this happens, a firm is no longer entitled to legal protection of the brand name. For example, "aspirin," "escalator," and "thermos" were originally all brand names of the products of particular firms, but each became so widely used to refer to a type of product that none remains a legally protected brand name. Firms spend substantial amounts of money trying to make sure that this does not happen to them. Coca-Cola, for example, employs people to travel to restaurants around the country and order a "Coke" with their meal. If the restaurant serves Pepsi or some other cola, rather than Coke, Coca-Cola's legal department sends the restaurant a letter reminding the owner that "Coke" is a trademarked name and not a generic name for any cola. Similarly, Xerox Corporation spends money on advertising to remind the public that "Xerox" is not a generic term for making photocopies.

Legally enforcing trademarks can be difficult. Estimates are that each year, U.S. firms lose hundreds of billions of dollars in sales worldwide as a result of unauthorized use of their trademarked brand names. U.S. firms often find it difficult to enforce their trademarks in the courts of some foreign countries, although recent international agreements have increased the legal protections for trademarks.

Firms that sell their products through franchises rather than through company-owned stores encounter the problem that if a franchisee does not run his or her business well, the firm's brand may be damaged. Automobile firms send "roadmen" to visit their dealers to make sure the dealerships are clean and well maintained and that the service departments employ competent mechanics and are well equipped with spare parts. Similarly, McDonald's sends employees from corporate headquarters to visit McDonald's franchises to make sure the bathrooms are clean and the French fries are hot.

Marketing All the activities necessary for a firm to sell a product to a consumer.

Brand management The actions of a firm intended to maintain the differentiation of a product over time.

Figure 7

What Makes a Firm Successful?

The factors under a firm's control—the ability to differentiate its product and the ability to produce it at lower cost—combine with the factors beyond its control to determine the firm's profitability.

Source: Adapted from Figure 9.2 in David Besanko, David Dranove, Mark Shanley, and Scott Schaefer, *The Economics of Strategy*, 6th edition, New York: John Wiley & Sons, Inc., 2012, p. 295.

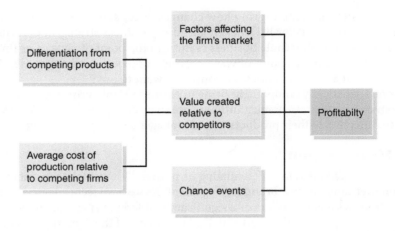

6 LEARNING OBJECTIVE

Identify the key factors that determine a firm's success.

What Makes a Firm Successful?

A firm's owners and managers control some of the factors that make a firm successful and allow it to earn economic profits. The most important of these is the firm's ability to differentiate its product or to produce it at a lower average cost than competing firms. A firm that successfully does one or both of these things creates *value* for its customers. Consumers will buy a product if they believe it meets a need not met by competing products or if its price is below that of competitors.

Some factors that affect a firm's profitability are not directly under the firm's control. Certain factors will affect all the firms in a market. For example, rising prices for jet fuel will reduce the profitability of all airlines. When some consumers decided that rather than buy DVDs, they preferred to download or stream movies from Netflix, iTunes, or Amazon, the profitability of all stores selling DVDs was reduced.

Sheer chance also plays a role in business, as it does in all other aspects of life. A struggling McDonald's franchise may see profits increase dramatically after the county unexpectedly decides to build a new road nearby. Many businesses in New York City, including restaurants, hotels, and theaters, experienced a marked drop in customers and profits as a result of the effects of Hurricane Sandy in October 2012. Figure 7 illustrates the important point that factors within the firm's control and factors outside the firm's control interact to determine the firm's profitability.

Making the Connection

Is Being the First Firm in the Market a Key to Success?

Some business analysts argue that the first firm to enter a market can have important *first-mover advantages*. By being the first to sell a particular good, a firm may find its name closely associated with the good in the public's mind, as, for instance, Amazon is closely associated with ordering books online or eBay is associated with online auctions. This close association may make it more difficult for new firms to enter the market and compete against the first mover.

Surprisingly, though, recent research has shown that the first firm to enter a market often does *not* have a long-lived advantage over later entrants. Consider, for instance, the market for pens. Until the 1940s, the only pens available were fountain pens that had to be refilled frequently from an ink bottle and used ink that dried slowly and smeared easily. In October 1945, entrepreneur Milton Reynolds introduced the first ballpoint pen, which did not need to be refilled. When it went on sale at Gimbel's department store in New York City, it was an instant success. Although the pen had a price of $12.00—the equivalent of about $155.00 at today's prices—hundreds of thousands were sold, and Milton Reynolds became a millionaire. Unfortunately, it didn't last. Although Reynolds had guaranteed that his pens would write for two years—later raised to five years—in fact, the pens often leaked and frequently stopped writing after only limited use. Sales began to collapse, the flood of pens returned under the company's guarantee wiped out its profits, and within a few years, Reynolds International Pen Company stopped selling pens in the United States. By the late 1960s, firms such as Bic, selling inexpensive—but reliable—ballpoint pens, dominated the market.

Although not first to market, Bic ultimately was more successful than the firm that pioneered ballpoint pens.

What happened to the Reynolds International Pen Company turns out to be more the rule than the exception. For example, Apple's iPod was not the first digital music player to appear on the U.S. market. Both SeaHan's MPMan and Diamond's PMP300 were released in the United States in 1998, three years before the iPod. Similarly, although Hewlett-Packard currently leads the market for laser printers, with a market share of more than 35 percent, it did not invent the laser printer. Xerox invented the laser printer, and IBM sold the first commercial laser printers, although neither firm is important in the market today. Nor was Procter & Gamble the first firm to sell disposable diapers when it introduced Pampers in 1961. Microsoft's Internet Explorer was not the first Web browser: Before Internet Explorer, there was Netscape; before Netscape, there was Mosaic; and before Mosaic, there were several other Web browsers that for a time looked as if they might dominate the market. In all these cases, the firms that were first to introduce a product ultimately lost out to latecomers who did a better job of providing consumers with products that were more reliable, less expensive, more convenient, or otherwise provided greater value.

Sources: Steven P. Schnaars, *Managing Imitation Strategies: How Late Entrants Seize Markets from Pioneers*, New York: The Free Press, 1994; and Gerard J. Tellis and Peter N. Golder, *Will and Vision: How Latecomers Grow to Dominate Markets*, Los Angeles: Figueroa Press, 2002.

Your Turn: Test your understanding by doing related problem 6.5 at the end of this chapter.

Continued

Economics in Your Life

Opening Your Own Restaurant

At the beginning of the chapter, we asked you to think about how successful you are likely to be in opening an Italian restaurant in your hometown. As you learned in this chapter, if your restaurant is successful, other people are likely to open competing restaurants, and all your economic profit will eventually disappear. Your new competitors will sell Italian food, but it won't be exactly like your Italian food—after all, they don't have your grandmother's secret sauce recipe! Each restaurant will have its own ideas on how best to appeal to people who like Italian food. Unless your food is very different from your competitors' food—or your service is much better—in the long run you will be unable to charge prices high enough to allow you to earn an economic profit.

In a monopolistically competitive market, free entry will reduce prices and lead to zero economic profits in the long run. In addition to lowering prices, competition benefits consumers by leading firms to offer somewhat different versions of the same product; for example, two Italian restaurants will rarely be exactly alike.

Conclusion

In this chapter, we have applied many of the ideas about competition we developed in discussing perfect competition to the more common market structure of monopolistic competition. We have seen that these ideas apply to monopolistically competitive markets, just as they do to perfectly competitive markets. At the end of the chapter on perfect competition, we concluded: "The competitive forces of the market impose relentless pressure on firms to produce new and better goods and services at the lowest possible cost. Firms that fail to adequately anticipate changes in consumer tastes or that fail to adopt the latest and most efficient production technology do not survive in the long run." These conclusions are as true for coffeehouses and firms in other monopolistically competitive markets as they are for wheat farmers and carrot growers.

Chapter Summary and Problems

Key Terms

Brand management   Marketing   Monopolistic competition

 Demand and Marginal Revenue for a Firm in a Monopolistically Competitive Market

LEARNING OBJECTIVE: Explain why a monopolistically competitive firm has downward-sloping demand and marginal revenue curves.

Summary

A firm competing in a **monopolistically competitive** market sells a differentiated product. Therefore, unlike a firm in a perfectly competitive market, it faces a downward-sloping demand curve. When a monopolistically competitive firm cuts the price of its product, it sells more units but must accept a lower price on the units it could have sold at the higher price. As a result, its marginal revenue curve is downward sloping. Every firm that has the ability to affect the price of the good or service it sells will have a marginal revenue curve that is below its demand curve.

Visit **www.myeconlab.com** to complete these exercises online and get instant feedback.

Review Questions

1.1 What are the most important differences between perfectly competitive markets and monopolistically competitive markets? Give two examples of products sold in perfectly competitive markets and two examples of products sold in monopolistically competitive markets.

1.2 Why does a local McDonald's face a downward-sloping demand curve for its Quarter Pounders? If McDonald's raises the price of Quarter Pounders above the prices other fast-food restaurants charge for hamburgers, won't it lose all its customers?

1.3 With a downward-sloping demand curve, why is average revenue equal to price? Why is marginal revenue less than price?

Problems and Applications

1.4 In 2013, Purell announced that the new chemical formula for its hand sanitizer was so effective that: "Just 1 squirt of Purell Advanced Hand Sanitizer kills as many germs as two squirts of any other national brand." If Purell succeeds in convincing consumers that its claims are correct, would its demand curve become flatter or steeper? Briefly explain.

Source: http://www.purell.com/purell-advanced.aspx.

1.5 Complete the following table, which shows the demand for snow skiing lessons per day:

Snow Skiing Lessons per Day (Q)	Price (P)	Total Revenue $(TR = P \times Q)$	Average Revenue $\left(AR = \dfrac{TR}{Q} \right)$	Marginal Revenue $\left(MR = \dfrac{\Delta TR}{\Delta Q} \right)$
0	$80.00			
1	75.00			
2	70.00			
3	65.00			
4	60.00			
5	55.00			
6	50.00			
7	45.00			
8	40.00			

1.6 A student makes the following argument:

When a firm sells another unit of a good, the additional revenue the firm receives is equal to the price: If the price is $10, the additional revenue is also $10. Therefore, this chapter is incorrect when it says that marginal revenue is less than price for a monopolistically competitive firm.

Briefly explain whether you agree with this argument.

1.7 There are many wheat farms in the United States, and there are also more than 7,000 Starbucks coffeehouses. Why, then, does a Starbucks coffeehouse face a downward-sloping demand curve, while a wheat farmer faces a horizontal demand curve?

1.8 Is it possible for marginal revenue to be negative for a firm selling in a perfectly competitive market? Is it possible for marginal revenue to be negative for a firm selling in a monopolistically competitive market? Briefly explain.

1.9 In the following figure, consider the marginal revenue of the eleventh unit sold. When the firm cuts the price from $5.00 to $4.75 to sell the eleventh unit, what area in the graph denotes the output effect, and what is the dollar value of the output effect? What area in the graph denotes the price effect, and what is the dollar value of the price effect? What is the marginal revenue of the eleventh unit?

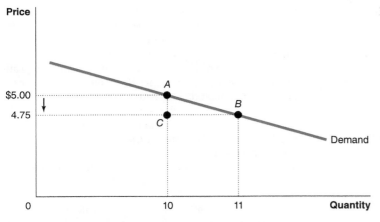

1.10 Sally runs a vegetable stand. She is selling 100 pounds of heirloom tomatoes per week, at a price of $3.75 per pound. If she lowers the price to $3.70, she will sell 101 pounds of heirloom tomatoes. What is the marginal revenue of the 101st pound of heirloom tomatoes?

2 How a Monopolistically Competitive Firm Maximizes Profit in the Short Run

LEARNING OBJECTIVE: Explain how a monopolistically competitive firm maximizes profit in the short run.

Summary

A monopolistically competitive firm maximizes profit at the level of output where marginal revenue equals marginal cost. Price equals marginal revenue for a perfectly competitive firm, but price is greater than marginal revenue for a monopolistically competitive firm. Therefore, unlike a perfectly competitive firm, which produces where $P = MC$, a monopolistically competitive firm produces where $P > MC$.

Visit www.myeconlab.com to complete these exercises online and get instant feedback.

Review Questions

2.1 Why doesn't a monopolistically competitive firm produce where $P = MC$, as a perfectly competitive firm does?

2.2 Stephen runs a pet salon. He is currently grooming 125 dogs per week. If instead of grooming 125 dogs, he grooms 126 dogs, he will add $68.50 to his costs and $60.00 to his revenues. What will be the effect on his profit of grooming 126 dogs instead of 125 dogs?

2.3 If Daniel sells 350 Big Macs at a price of $3.25 each, and his average cost of producing 350 Big Macs is $3.00 each, what is his profit?

Problems and Applications

2.4 Maria manages a bakery that specializes in ciabatta bread, and she has the following information on the bakery's demand and costs:

Ciabatta Bread Sold per Hour (Q)	Price (P)	Total Cost (TC)
0	$6.00	$3.00
1	5.50	7.00
2	5.00	10.00
3	4.50	12.50
4	4.00	14.50
5	3.50	16.00
6	3.00	17.00
7	2.50	18.50
8	2.00	21.00

a. To maximize profit, how many loaves of ciabatta bread should Maria sell per hour, what price should she charge, and how much profit will she make?

b. What is the marginal revenue Maria receives from selling the profit-maximizing quantity of ciabatta bread? What is the marginal cost of producing the profit-maximizing quantity of ciabatta bread?

2.5 [Related to Solved Problem 2] Suppose a firm producing table lamps has the following costs:

Quantity	Average Total Cost
1,000	$15.00
2,000	9.75
3,000	8.25
4,000	7.50
5,000	7.75
6,000	8.50
7,000	9.75
8,000	10.50
9,000	12.00

Ben and Jerry are managers at the company, and they have this discussion:

Ben: We should produce 4,000 lamps per month because that will minimize our average costs.

Jerry: But shouldn't we maximize profits rather than minimize costs? To maximize profits, don't we need to take demand into account?

Ben: Don't worry. By minimizing average costs, we will be maximizing profits. Demand will determine how high the price we can charge will be, but it won't affect our profit-maximizing quantity.

Evaluate the discussion between the two managers.

2.6 During the last three months of 2011, the Abercrombie & Fitch clothing chain cut the prices of many of its products. During that period, its profits per item of clothing declined, and its total profits declined by 79 percent. An article discussing Abercrombie's situation had the headline: "Abercrombie Markdowns Cut Profit." Do we have enough information to decide whether Abercrombie's decision to markdown—or cut the prices—of its clothing caused its profit to fall? Is it possible that Abercrombie's decision to cut prices was a profit-maximizing strategy? Briefly explain.

Source: Karen Talley and Mia Lamar, "Abercrombie Markdowns Cut Profit," *Wall Street Journal*, February 16, 2012.

2.7 William Germano previously served as the vice president and publishing director at the Routledge publishing company. He once gave the following description of how a publisher might deal with an unexpected increase in the cost of publishing a book:

> It's often asked why the publisher can't simply raise the price [if costs increase].... It's likely that the editor [is already] ... charging as much as the market will bear .... In other words, you might be willing to pay $50.00 for a ... book on the Brooklyn Bridge, but if ... production costs [increase] by 25 percent, you might think $62.50 is too much to pay, though that would be what the publisher needs to charge. And indeed the publisher may determine that $50.00 is this book's ceiling—the most you would pay before deciding to rent a movie instead.

a. According to what you have learned in this chapter, how do firms adjust the price of a good when there is an increase in cost? Use a graph to illustrate your answer.

b. Does the model of monopolistic competition seem to fit Germano's description? If a publisher does not raise the price of a book following an increase in its production cost, what will be the result?

c. How would the elasticity of demand for published books affect the ability of the publishing company to raise book prices when costs increase?

Source: William Germano, *Getting It Published: A Guide to Scholars and Anyone Else Serious About Serious Books*, 2nd edition, Chicago: University of Chicago Press, 2008, p. 107.

2.8 In 1916, Ford Motor Company produced 500,000 Model T Fords, at a price of $440 each. The company made a profit of $60 million that year. Henry Ford told a newspaper reporter that he intended to reduce the price of the Model T to $360, and he expected to sell 800,000 cars at that price. Ford said, "Less profit on each car, but more cars, more employment of labor, and in the end we get all the total profit we ought to make."

a. Did Ford expect the total revenue he received from selling Model Ts to rise or fall following the price cut?

b. Use the information given above to calculate the price elasticity of demand for Model Ts. Use the midpoint formula to make your calculation.

c. What would the average total cost of producing 800,000 Model Ts have to be for Ford to make as much profit selling 800,000 Model Ts as it made selling 500,000 Model Ts? Is this smaller or larger than the average total cost of producing 500,000 Model Ts?

d. Assume that Ford would make the same total profit when selling 800,000 cars as when selling 500,000 cars. Was Henry Ford correct in saying he would make less profit per car when selling 800,000 cars than when selling 500,000 cars?

2.9 Use the following graph for Elijah's Burgers to answer the questions:

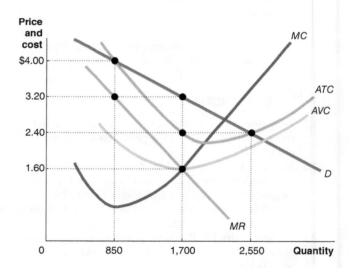

a. If Elijah produces at the profit-maximizing level of output, how much is his total revenue? How much is his total cost? Briefly explain your calculations.

b. How much economic profit is Elijah earning? Briefly explain your calculation.

3 What Happens to Profits in the Long Run?

LEARNING OBJECTIVE: Analyze the situation of a monopolistically competitive firm in the long run.

Summary

If a monopolistically competitive firm earns an economic profit in the short run, entry of new firms will eliminate the profit in the long run. If a monopolistically competitive firm is suffering an economic loss in the short run, exit of existing firms will eliminate the loss in the long run. Monopolistically competitive firms continually struggle to find new ways of differentiating their products as they try to stay one step ahead of other firms that are attempting to copy their success.

Visit **www.myeconlab.com** to complete these exercises online and get instant feedback.

Review Questions

3.1 What effect does the entry of new firms have on the economic profits of existing firms?

3.2 Why does the entry of new firms cause the demand curve of an existing firm in a monopolistically competitive market to shift to the left and to become more elastic?

3.3 What is the difference between zero accounting profit and zero economic profit?

3.4 Is it possible for a monopolistically competitive firm to continue to earn an economic profit as new firms enter the market?

Problems and Applications

3.5 Suppose Angelica opens a small store near campus, selling beef brisket sandwiches. Use the graph below, which shows the demand and cost for Angelica's beef brisket sandwiches, to answer the following questions.

   a. If Angelica wants to maximize profit, how many beef brisket sandwiches should she sell per day, and what price should she charge? Briefly explain your answer.

   b. How much economic profit (or loss) is Angelica making? Briefly explain.

   c. Is Angelica likely to continue selling this number of beef brisket sandwiches in the long run? Briefly explain.

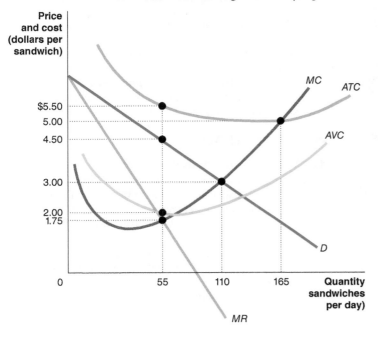

3.6 [Related to the Don't Let This Happen to You**]** A student remarks:

> If firms in a monopolistically competitive industry are earning economic profits, new firms will enter the industry. Eventually, a representative firm will find that its demand curve has shifted to the left, until it is just tangent to its average total cost curve and it is earning zero profit. Because firms are earning zero profit at that point, some firms will leave the industry, and the representative firm will find that its demand curve will shift to the right. In long-run equilibrium, price will be above average total cost by just enough so that each firm is just breaking even.

Briefly explain whether you agree with this analysis.

3.7 A columnist for the *Wall Street Journal* made the following observation: "The [oil] refining business is just too competitive, which is great for consumers, but not shareholders." Briefly explain why the high level of competition in the oil refining industry is good for consumers but bad for the shareholders who own these firms.

Source: James B. Stewart, "Coping with the Inevitable: The Losers in Your Portfolio," *Wall Street Journal*, December 3, 2008.

3.8 [Related to the Making the Connection: **The Rise and Decline and Rise of Starbucks]** An article in *Forbes* magazine in 2013 discussed the reasons for the ability of Starbucks to remain profitable despite competition. The author argued the most important reason for the firm's success was "Right market segmentation. The company has stayed with the upper-scale of the coffee market, competing on comfort rather than convenience...."

   a. What does the author mean by "market segmentation"?

   b. What does the author mean by the "upper-scale" of the coffee market? Why might it be more difficult for other firms to compete with Starbucks in that segment of the coffeehouse market?

Source: Panos Mourdoukoutas, "Starbucks and McDonald's Winning Strategy," *Forbes*, April 25, 2013.

3.9 [Related to Solved Problem 3**]** h.h.gregg has been successful in retailing appliances and electronics by combining high prices with excellent customer service. In late 2008, Saks Fifth Avenue tried a new strategy in retailing luxury clothing. Saks decided to slash prices on designer clothing by 70 percent just before the beginning of the holiday sales season. According to an article in the *Wall Street Journal*, "Saks's risky price-cut strategy was to be one of the first to discount deeply, rather than one of the last." The article continued:

> Saks's maneuver marked an open abandonment of the longstanding unwritten pact between retailers and designers.... Those old rules boiled down to this: Leave the goods at full price at least two months, and don't do markdowns until the very end of the season.

Is Saks's strategy of becoming the low-priced luxury clothing retailer likely to succeed? Contrast Saks's strategy with the strategy of h.h.gregg in terms of how likely the two strategies are to be successful over the long run.

Source: Vanessa O'Connell and Rachel Dodes, "Saks Upends Luxury Market with Strategy to Slash Prices," *Wall Street Journal*, February 9, 2009.

3.10 Michael Korda was, for many years, editor-in-chief at the Simon & Schuster book publishing company. He has written about the many books that have become bestsellers by promising to give readers financial advice that will make them wealthy, by, for example, buying and selling real estate. Korda is skeptical about the usefulness of the advice in these books because "I have yet to meet anybody who got rich by buying a book, though quite a few people got rich by writing one." On the basis of the analysis in this chapter, discuss why it may be very difficult to become rich by following the advice found in a book.

Source: Michael Korda, *Making the List: A Cultural History of the American Bestseller, 1900–1999*, New York: Barnes & Noble Books, 2001, p. 168.

3.11 **[Related to the** Chapter Opener**]** John Quelch, a marketing professor at the Harvard Business School, commented on the situation facing Starbucks: "Starbucks is fundamentally selling an experience, but by no means is coffee the only part of the experience." Why might Starbucks have problems if selling coffee were the only part of the Starbucks "experience"?

Source: Sarah Skidmore, "Starbucks Gives Logo a New Look," *Associated Press*, January 5, 2011.

3.12 In 2011, some Starbucks stores in New York City began putting metal plates over electric outlets to limit the

time people using laptop computers could sit at tables. A spokesman for Starbucks stated that individual stores could make the decision whether to cover up power outlets. Why might some Starbucks stores cover up the outlets while others leave them uncovered?

Source: Emily Maltby, "Should Coffee Shop Owners Limit Laptop Usage?" *Wall Street Journal*, August 4, 2011.

3.13 The *Wall Street Journal* reported that Western European brewers such as Heineken, Carlsberg, and Anheuser-Busch InBev are increasing their production and marketing of nonalcoholic beer. The article quotes a Carlsberg executive for new-product development as saying:

> Nonalcoholic beer is a largely unexploited opportunity for big brewers. It is quite a natural move when you see that the overall beer market [in Western Europe is] going down. So, of course, we're battling for market share.

The article further states that "brewers are hoping to capitalize on health consciousness" and that "recent brewing advances are helping improve the taste of nonalcoholic beers."

a. In what sense is nonalcoholic beer an "unexploited opportunity" for big brewers?

b. Are the brewers responding to consumer desires, or are brewers exploiting consumers? Briefly explain.

c. How will the "recent brewing advances" that improve taste affect the market for nonalcoholic beer?

Source: Ilan Brat, "Taking the Buzz out of Beer," *Wall Street Journal*, August 30, 2011.

4	**Comparing Monopolistic Competition and Perfect Competition**

LEARNING OBJECTIVE: Compare the efficiency of monopolistic competition and perfect competition.

Summary

Perfectly competitive firms produce at a quantity where price equals marginal cost and at minimum average total cost. Perfectly competitive firms achieve both allocative and productive efficiency. Monopolistically competitive firms produce at a quantity where price is greater than marginal cost and above minimum average total cost. Monopolistically competitive firms do not achieve either allocative or productive efficiency. Consumers face a trade-off when buying the product of a monopolistically competitive firm: They are paying a price that is greater than marginal cost, and the product is not being produced at minimum average total cost, but they benefit from being able to purchase a product that is differentiated and more closely suited to their tastes.

Visit **www.myeconlab.com** to complete these exercises online and get instant feedback.

Review Questions

4.1 What are the differences between the long-run equilibrium of a perfectly competitive firm and the long-run equilibrium of a monopolistically competitive firm?

4.2 Why is a monopolistically competitive firm not productively efficient? In what sense does a monopolistically competitive firm have excess capacity?

4.3 Why is a monopolistically competitive firm not allocatively efficient?

4.4 Does the fact that monopolistically competitive markets are not allocatively or productively efficient mean that there is a significant loss in economic well-being to society in these markets? In your answer, be sure to define what you mean by "economic well-being."

Problems and Applications

4.5 A student makes the following comment:

> I can understand why a perfectly competitive firm will not earn a profit in the long run because a perfectly competitive firm charges a price equal to marginal cost. But a monopolistically competitive firm can charge a price greater than marginal cost, so why can't it continue to earn a profit in the long run?

How would you answer this question?

4.6 Consider the following graph:

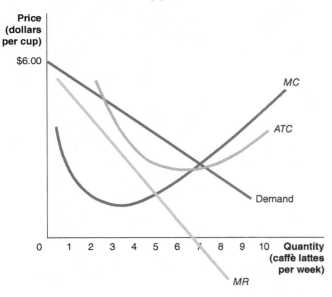

a. Is it possible to say whether this firm is a perfectly competitive firm or a monopolistically competitive firm? If so, explain how you are able to make this determination.

b. Does the graph show a short-run equilibrium or a long-run equilibrium? Briefly explain.

c. What quantity on the graph represents long-run equilibrium if the firm is perfectly competitive?

4.7 Before the fall of Communism, most basic consumer products in Eastern Europe and the Soviet Union were standardized. For example, government-run stores would offer for sale only one type of bar soap or one type of toothpaste. Soviet economists often argued that this system of standardizing basic consumer products avoided the waste associated with the differentiated goods and services produced in Western Europe and the United States. Do you agree with this argument?

4.8 [**Related to the** Making the Connection] According to Peter Thiel: "For a company to own its market, it must have some combination of brand, scale cost advantages, network effects, or proprietary technology." Thiel has invested in the NJOY e-cigarette firm.

a. What does Thiel mean by a company "owning" its market?

b. What information would you need to know to determine whether NJOY owns—or is likely to own in the future—the e-cigarette market?

Source: Blake Masters, "Ten Lessons from Peter Thiel's Class on Startups," *Forbes*, June 7, 2012.

4.9 Consider the following graph:

a. At the profit-maximizing level of output, how much economic profit is this firm earning? Briefly explain.

b. Is this firm allocatively efficient? Is it productively efficient? Briefly explain.

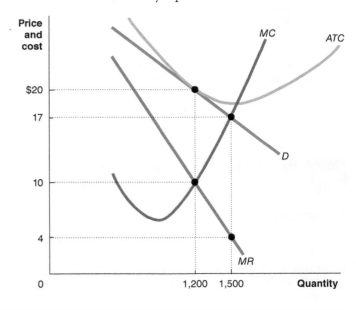

---

5 | How Marketing Differentiates Products

LEARNING OBJECTIVE: Define marketing and explain how firms use marketing to differentiate their products.

Summary

Marketing refers to all the activities necessary for a firm to sell a product to a consumer. Firms use two marketing tools to differentiate their products: brand management and advertising. **Brand management** refers to the actions of a firm intended to maintain the differentiation of a product over time. When a firm has established a successful brand name, it has a strong incentive to defend it. A firm can apply for a *trademark*, which grants legal protection against other firms using its product's name.

Visit **www.myeconlab.com** to complete these exercises online and get instant feedback.

Review Questions

5.1 Define *marketing*. Is marketing just another name for advertising?

5.2 Why are many companies so concerned about brand management?

Problems and Applications

5.3 Draw a graph that shows the effect on a firm's profits when it increases spending on advertising but the increased advertising has *no* effect on the demand for the firm's product.

5.4 A skeptic says: "Marketing research and brand management are unnecessary. If a company wants to find out what customers want, it should simply look at what they're already buying." Do you agree with this comment? Explain.

5.5 The National Football League (NFL) has a trademark on the name "Super Bowl" for its championship game. Advertisers can use the words Super Bowl in their advertising only if they pay the NFL a fee. Many companies attempt to get around this trademark by using the phrase "the big game" in their advertising. For example, a few days before the Super Bowl, a consumer electronics store might have an advertisement with the phrase "Watch the big game on a new LED TV." In 2006, the National Football League filed for a trademark on the phrase "Big Game," although it eventually withdrew the filing after firms such as Domino's Pizza, Dell, Time Warner Cable, and some universities filed an objection with the U.S. Patent and Trademark Office.

a. Why does the government allow firms to trademark their products?

b. Would consumers gain or lose if the NFL were allowed to trademark the phrase "Big Game"? Briefly explain.

Source: Richard Sandomir, "Not Quite Saying 'Super Bowl,' but Cashing In on It," *New York Times*, February 6, 2010.

5.6 Some companies have done a poor job protecting the images of their products. For example, Hormel's Spam brand name is widely ridiculed and is associated with annoying commercial messages received via e-mail. Think of other cases of companies failing to protect their brand names. What can companies do about the situation now? Should the companies re-brand their products?

5.7 Walgreens, one of the largest drugstore chains in the United States, recently built new flagship stores and expanded and upgraded existing stores. As a newspaper article described it: "More than a drugstore, Walgreens wants customers to be able to grab a smoothie, pick up a prescription, find a bottle of wine for dinner and get a mini makeover—all on their lunch hour." In addition, to take advantage of changes in the pharmacy business as a result of the continued implementation of the Affordable Care Act, Walgreens is expanding its immunization program and increasing the time pharmacists have to assist customers with their health care needs. Briefly discuss Walgreens' strategy in the context of marketing and brand management.

Source: Hadley Malcolm, "A Chi-Chi Pharmacy? Walgreens Goes All Out," *USA Today*, June 14, 2013.

---

 6 | ## What Makes a Firm Successful?

LEARNING OBJECTIVE: Identify the key factors that determine a firm's success.

Summary

A firm's owners and managers control some of the factors that determine the profitability of the firm. Other factors affect all the firms in the market or are the result of chance, so they are not under the control of the firm's owners. The interactions between factors the firm controls and factors it does not control determine its profitability.

Visit **www.myeconlab.com** to complete these exercises online and get instant feedback.

Review Questions

6.1 What are the key factors that determine the profitability of a firm in a monopolistically competitive market?

6.2 How might a monopolistically competitive firm continually earn an economic profit?

Problems and Applications

6.3 According to an article in the *Wall Street Journal*:

In early January last year, after a disappointing Christmas season and amid worries about competition from discount retailers, Zale Corp. decided to shake things up: The self-proclaimed jeweler to Middle America was going to chase upscale customers.... The move was a disaster. The Irving, Texas, retailer lost many of its traditional customers without winning the new ones it coveted.

Why would a firm like Zale abandon one market niche for another market niche? We know that in this case the move was not successful. Can you think of other cases where such a move has been successful?

Source: Ann Zimmerman and Kris Hudson, "Chasing Upscale Customers Tarnishes Mass-Market Jeweler," *Wall Street Journal*, June 26, 2006.

6.4 7-Eleven, Inc., operates more than 20,000 convenience stores worldwide. Edward Moneypenny, 7-Eleven's chief financial officer, was asked to name the biggest risk the company faced. He replied, "I would say that the biggest risk that 7-Eleven faces, like all retailers, is competition ... because that is something that you've got to be aware of in this business." In what sense is competition a "risk" to a business? Why would a company in the retail business need to be particularly aware of competition?

Source: Company Report, "CEO Interview: Edward Moneypenny—7-Eleven, Inc.," The Wall Street Transcript Corporation, February 24, 2003.

6.5 **[Related to the** Making the Connection**: Is Being the First Firm in the Market a Key to Success?]** A firm that is first to market with a new product frequently discovers that there are design flaws or problems with the product that were not anticipated. For example, the ballpoint pens made by the Reynolds International

Pen Company often leaked. What effect do these problems have on the innovating firm, and how do these unexpected problems open up possibilities for other firms to enter the market?

6.6 Wealthy investors often invest in hedge funds. Hedge fund managers use investors' money to buy stocks, bonds, and other investments with the intention of earning high returns. But an article in the *New York Times* notes that: "Even professionals have a problem in evaluating hedge fund performance, because distinguishing skill from luck ... is extremely difficult." Is it ever easy to determine whether a firm making an economic profit is doing so because of the skills of the firm's managers or because of luck? Briefly explain.

Source: Jesse Eisinger, "Pruning Hedge Fund Regulation Without Cultivating Better Rules," *New York Times*, September 5, 2012.

Glossary

Brand management The actions of a firm intended to maintain the differentiation of a product over time.

Marketing All the activities necessary for a firm to sell a product to a consumer.

Monopolistic competition A market structure in which barriers to entry are low and many firms compete by selling similar, but not identical, products.

Credits

Credits are listed in the order of appearance.

Photo

Lou Linwei/Alamy; Robert Alexander/Archive Photos/Getty Images; Steve Helber/AP Images; Studiomode/Alamy

Text

Peter F. Drucker, *Management: Tasks, Responsibilities, Practices*, New York: Harper & Row, 1974

The Markets for Labor and Other Factors of Production

From Chapter 17 of *Economics*, Fifth Edition. R. Glenn Hubbard and Anthony Patrick O'Brien. Copyright © 2015 by Pearson Education, Inc.
All rights reserved.

The Markets for Labor and Other Factors of Production

Chapter Outline and Learning Objectives

Who Is Zach Greinke and Why Is He Being Paid $147 Million?

Few businesses generate as much passion as sports teams. Sports fans admire the skills of star athletes, but many people question why they are paid high salaries "just for playing a game." Some fans also get frustrated when their teams lose star players to wealthier teams that can afford to sign players to long-term contracts for large salaries. Zack Greinke is a star baseball pitcher who won the Cy Young Award in 2009 as the best pitcher in the American League. Yet in 2013, Greinke was playing for the fourth team since he started his major league career in 2004 with the Kansas City Royals. The Royals couldn't afford to sign Greinke to a long-term contract and traded him to the Milwaukee Brewers in 2010, who in turn traded him to the Los Angeles Angels in 2012. Following the 2012 season, Greinke became a free agent and was eligible to sign with any team. The Los Angeles Dodgers signed Greinke to a contract that will pay him $147 million over six years—making him one of the highest paid players in history.

In 2013, the Dodgers sold the rights to televise their games to Time Warner Cable for more than $6 *billion* over a 25-year period. Because of the high revenues the Dodgers generate from ticket sales, cable television, and broadcast television and radio, they can afford to pay more for players than teams such as the Milwaukee Brewers and Kansas City Royals that play in smaller cities.

We will use some of the demand and supply models in this chapter to analyze the markets for labor and other factors of production. But there are important differences between the markets for factors of production and the markets for goods and services. The most obvious difference is that in factor markets, firms are demanders and households are suppliers.

Another difference between the labor market and the markets for goods and services is that concepts of fairness arise more frequently in labor markets. When an athlete signs a contract for millions of dollars, people often wonder: "Why should someone playing a game get paid so much more than teachers, nurses, and other people doing more important jobs?" Because people typically earn most of their income from wages and salaries, they often view the labor market as the most important market in which they participate.

Sources: Jonah Keri, "Pondering Zack Greinke's $147 Million Deal," www.grantland.com, December 10, 2012; and Bill Shaikin, "Dodgers to Keep More than $6 Billion from TV Contract in Tentative Pact," *Los Angeles Times*, June 13, 2013.

Economics in Your Life

How Can You Convince Your Boss to Give You a Raise?

Imagine that you have worked for a local sandwich shop for over a year and are preparing to ask for a raise. You might tell the manager that you are a good employee, with a good attitude and work ethic. You might also explain that you have learned more about your job and are now able to make sandwiches more quickly, track inventory more accurately, and work the cash register more effectively than when you were first hired. Will this be enough to convince your manager to give you a raise? How can you convince your manager that you are worth a higher wage than you are currently being paid? As you read this chapter, try to answer these questions. You can check your answers against those we provide at the end of this chapter.

Factors of production Labor, capital, natural resources, and other inputs used to produce goods and services.

Firms use **factors of production**—such as labor, capital, and natural resources—to produce goods and services. For example, the Los Angeles Dodgers use labor (baseball players), capital (Dodger Stadium), and natural resources (the land on which Dodger Stadium sits) to produce baseball games. In this chapter, we will explore how firms choose the profit-maximizing quantity of labor and other factors of production. The interaction between firms' demand for labor and households' supply of labor determines the equilibrium wage rate.

Because there are many different types of labor, there are many different labor markets. The equilibrium wage in the market for baseball players is much higher than the equilibrium wage in the market for college professors. We will analyze why. We will also analyze how factors such as discrimination, unions, and compensation for dangerous or unpleasant jobs help explain differences in wages. We will then look at *personnel economics*, which is concerned with how firms can use economic analysis to design their employee compensation plans. Finally, we will analyze the markets for other factors of production.

1 LEARNING OBJECTIVE

Explain how firms choose the profit-maximizing quantity of labor to employ.

Derived demand The demand for a factor of production; it depends on the demand for the good the factor produces.

The Demand for Labor

Until now, we have concentrated on consumer demand for final goods and services. The demand for labor is different from the demand for final goods and services because it is a *derived demand*. A **derived demand** for a factor of production depends on the demand for the good the factor produces. You demand an Apple iPhone because of the utility you receive from making phone calls, texting, posting to Facebook, playing games, and listening to music. Apple's demand for the labor to make iPhones is derived from the underlying consumer demand for iPhones. As a result, we can say that Apple's demand for labor depends primarily on two factors:

1. The additional iPhones Apple can produce if it hires one more worker
2. The additional revenue Apple receives from selling the additional iPhones

(In fact, Apple's suppliers, rather than Apple itself, manufacture the iPhone. For simplicity, we are assuming here that Apple does the manufacturing.)

The Marginal Revenue Product of Labor

Let's consider an example. To keep the main point clear, we'll assume that in the short run, Apple can increase production of iPhones only by increasing the quantity of labor it employs. The table in Figure 1 shows the relationship between the quantity of workers Apple hires, the quantity of iPhones it produces, the additional revenue from selling the additional iPhones, and the additional profit from hiring each additional worker.

For simplicity, we are keeping the scale of Apple's factory very small. We will also assume that Apple is a perfect competitor both in the market for selling cellphones and in the market for hiring labor. As a result, Apple is a *price taker* in both markets. Although this assumption is not realistic, the basic analysis would not change if we assumed that Apple can affect the price of cellphones and the wage paid to workers. Suppose that Apple can sell as many iPhones as it wants at a price of $200 and can hire as many workers as it wants at a wage of $600 per week. Remember that the additional output a firm produces as a result of hiring one more worker is called the **marginal product of labor**. In the table in Figure 1, we calculate the marginal product of labor as the change in total output as each additional worker is hired. Because of *the law of diminishing returns*, the marginal product of labor declines as a firm hires more workers.

When deciding how many workers to hire, a firm is not interested in how much *output* will increase as it hires another worker but in how much *revenue* will increase as it hires another worker. In other words, what matters is how much the firm's revenue will rise when it sells the additional output it can produce by hiring one more worker.

Marginal product of labor The additional output a firm produces as a result of hiring one more worker.

Number of Workers	Output of iPhones per Week	Marginal Product of Labor (iPhones per week)	Product Price	Marginal Revenue Product of Labor (dollars per week)	Wage (dollars per week)	Additional Profit from Hiring One More Worker (dollars per week)
L	Q	MP	P	MRP = P x MP	W	MRP – W
0	0	—	$200	—	$600	—
1	6	6	200	$1,200	600	$600
2	11	5	200	1,000	600	400
3	15	4	200	800	600	200
4	18	3	200	600	600	0
5	20	2	200	400	600	–200
6	21	1	200	200	600	–400

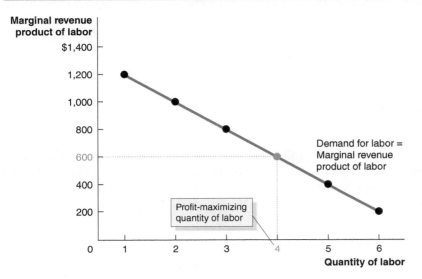

Figure 1

The Marginal Revenue Product of Labor and the Demand for Labor

The marginal revenue product of labor equals the marginal product of labor multiplied by the price of the good. The marginal revenue product curve slopes downward because diminishing returns cause the marginal product of labor to decline as more workers are hired. A firm maximizes profits by hiring workers up to the point where the wage equals the marginal revenue product of labor. The marginal revenue product of labor curve is the firm's demand curve for labor because it tells the firm the profit-maximizing quantity of workers to hire at each wage. For example, using the demand curve shown in this figure, if the wage is $600, the firm will hire 4 workers.

We can calculate this amount, which is called the **marginal revenue product of labor (MRP)**, by multiplying the additional output produced by the product price. For example, consider what happens if Apple increases the number of workers hired from 2 to 3. The table in Figure 1 shows that hiring the third worker allows Apple to increase its weekly output of iPhones from 11 to 15, so the marginal product of labor is 4 iPhones. The price of the iPhones is $200, so the marginal revenue product of the third worker is 4 × $200 or $800. In other words, Apple adds $800 to its revenue as a result of hiring the third worker. In the graph, we plot the values of the marginal revenue product of labor at each quantity of labor.

To decide how many workers to hire, Apple must compare the additional revenue it earns from hiring another worker to the increase in its costs from paying that worker. The difference between the additional revenue and the additional cost is the additional profit (or loss) from hiring one more worker. This additional profit is shown in the last column of the table in Figure 1 and is calculated by subtracting the wage from the marginal revenue product of labor. As long as the marginal revenue product of labor is greater than the wage, Apple's profits are increasing, and it should continue to hire more workers. When the marginal revenue product of labor is less than the wage, Apple's profits are falling, and it should hire fewer workers. When the marginal revenue product of labor is equal to the wage, Apple has maximized its profits by hiring the optimal number of workers. The values in the table show that Apple should hire 4 workers. If Apple hires a fifth worker, the marginal revenue product of $400 will be less than the wage of $600, and its profits will fall by $200. Table 1 summarizes the relationship between the marginal revenue product of labor and the wage.

Marginal revenue product of labor (MRP) The change in a firm's revenue as a result of hiring one more worker.

Table 1

The Relationship between the Marginal Revenue Product of Labor and the Wage

When ...	the firm ...
MRP > W,	should hire more workers to increase profits.
MRP < W,	should hire fewer workers to increase profits.
MRP = W,	is hiring the optimal number of workers and is maximizing profits.

We can see from Figure 1 that if Apple has to pay a wage of $600 per week, it should hire 4 workers. If the wage rises to $1,000, then applying the rule that profits are maximized where the marginal revenue product of labor equals the wage, Apple should hire only 2 workers. Similarly, if the wage falls to $400 per week, Apple should hire 5 workers. In fact, the marginal revenue product curve tells a firm how many workers it should hire at any wage rate. In other words, *the marginal revenue product of labor curve is the demand curve for labor.*

Solved Problem 1

Hiring Decisions by a Firm That Is a Price Maker

We have assumed that Apple can sell as many iPhones as it wants without having to cut the price. A firm in a perfectly competitive market is in this situation. These firms are *price takers*. Suppose instead that a firm has market power and is a *price maker*, so that to increase sales, it must reduce the price.

Assume that Apple faces the situation shown in the following table. Fill in the blanks and then determine the profit-maximizing quantity of workers for Apple to hire. Briefly explain why hiring this quantity of workers is profit maximizing.

(1) Quantity of Labor	(2) Output of iPhones per Week	(3) Marginal Product of Labor	(4) Product Price	(5) Total Revenue	(6) Marginal Revenue Product of Labor	(7) Wage	(8) Additional Profit from Hiring One Additional Worker
0	0	—	$200		—	$500	—
1	6	6	180			500	
2	11	5	160			500	
3	15	4	140			500	
4	18	3	120			500	
5	20	2	100			500	
6	21	1	80			500	

Solving the Problem

Step 1: Review the chapter material. This problem is about determining the profit-maximizing quantity of labor for a firm to hire, so you may want to review the section "The Demand for Labor."

Step 2: Fill in the blanks in the table. As Apple hires more workers, it sells more iPhones and earns more revenue. You can calculate how revenue increases by multiplying the quantity of iPhones produced—shown in column (2)—by the price—shown in column (4). Then you can calculate the marginal revenue product of labor as the change in revenue as each additional worker is hired. (Notice that in this case, marginal revenue product is *not* calculated by multiplying the marginal product by the product price. Because Apple is a price maker, its marginal revenue from selling additional iPhones is less than the price of iPhones.) Finally, you can calculate the additional profit from hiring one more worker by subtracting the wage—shown in column (7)—from each worker's marginal revenue product.

(1) Quantity of Labor	(2) Output of iPhones per Week	(3) Marginal Product of Labor	(4) Product Price	(5) Total Revenue	(6) Marginal Revenue Product of Labor	(7) Wage	(8) Additional Profit from Hiring One Additional Worker
0	0	—	$200	$0	—	$500	—
1	6	6	180	1,080	$1,080	500	$580
2	11	5	160	1,760	680	500	180
3	15	4	140	2,100	340	500	−160
4	18	3	120	2,160	60	500	−440
5	20	2	100	2,000	−160	500	−660
6	21	1	80	1,680	−320	500	−820

Step 3: **Use the information in the table to determine the profit-maximizing quantity of workers to hire.** To determine the profit-maximizing quantity of workers to hire, you need to compare the marginal revenue product of labor with the wage. Column (8) makes this comparison by subtracting the wage from the marginal revenue product. As long as the values in column (8) are positive, the firm should continue to hire workers. The marginal revenue product of the second worker is $680, and the wage is $500, so column (8) shows that hiring the second worker will add $180 to Apple's profits. The marginal revenue product of the third worker is $340, and the wage is $500, so hiring the third worker would reduce Apple's profits by $160. Therefore, Apple will maximize profits by hiring 2 workers.

Your Turn: For more practice, do related problem 1.6 at the end of this chapter.

The Market Demand Curve for Labor

We can determine the market demand curve for labor in the same way we determine the market demand curve for a good—by adding up the quantity of the good demanded by each consumer at each price. Similarly, we find the market demand curve for labor by adding up the quantity of labor demanded by each firm at each wage, holding constant all other variables that might affect the willingness of firms to hire workers.

Factors That Shift the Market Demand Curve for Labor

In constructing the demand curve for labor, we held constant all variables—except for the wage—that would affect the willingness of firms to demand labor. An increase or a decrease in the wage causes *an increase or a decrease in the quantity of labor demanded*, which we show by a movement along the demand curve. If any variable other than the wage changes, the result is *an increase or a decrease in the demand for labor*, which we show by a shift of the demand curve. The following are the five most important variables that cause the labor demand curve to shift:

Human capital The accumulated training and skills that workers possess.

1. *Increases in human capital.* **Human capital** represents the accumulated training and skills that workers possess. For example, a worker with a college education generally has more skills and is more productive than a worker who has only a high school diploma. If workers become more educated and are therefore able to produce more output per day, the demand for their services will increase, shifting the labor demand curve to the right.

2. *Changes in technology.* As new and better machinery and equipment are developed, workers become more productive. This effect causes the labor demand curve to shift to the right over time.

3. *Changes in the price of the product.* The marginal revenue product of labor depends on the price a firm receives for its output. A higher price increases the marginal revenue product and shifts the labor demand curve to the right. A lower price shifts the labor demand curve to the left.

4. *Changes in the quantity of other inputs.* Workers are able to produce more if they have more machinery and other inputs available to them. The marginal product of labor in the United States is higher than the marginal product of labor in most other countries in large part because U.S. firms provide workers with more machinery and equipment. Over time, workers in the United States have had increasing amounts of other inputs available to them, which has increased their productivity and caused the labor demand curve to shift to the right.

5. *Changes in the number of firms in the market.* If new firms enter the market, the labor demand curve will shift to the right. If firms exit the market, the demand for labor will shift to the left. The result is similar to the effect that increasing or decreasing the number of consumers in a market has on the demand for a good.

2 LEARNING OBJECTIVE

Explain how people choose the quantity of labor to supply.

The Supply of Labor

Having discussed the demand for labor, we can now consider the supply of labor. Of the many trade-offs each of us faces in life, one of the most important is how to divide up the 24 hours in a day between labor and leisure. Every hour spent posting to Facebook, walking on the beach, or in other forms of leisure is one hour less spent working. Because in devoting an hour to leisure we give up an hour's earnings from working, the *opportunity cost* of leisure is the wage. The higher the wage we could earn working, the higher the opportunity cost of leisure. Therefore, as the wage increases, we tend to take less leisure and work more. As Figure 2 shows, the result is that the labor supply curve for most people is upward sloping.

Figure 2

The Labor Supply Curve

As the wage increases, the opportunity cost of leisure increases, causing individuals to supply a greater quantity of labor. Therefore, the labor supply curve is upward sloping.

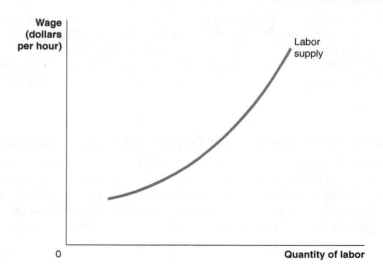

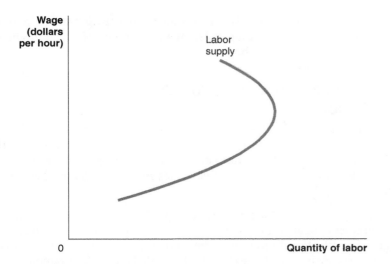

Figure 3

A Backward-Bending Labor Supply Curve

As the wage rises, a greater quantity of labor is usually supplied. As the wage rises above a certain level, the individual is able to afford more leisure even though the opportunity cost of leisure is higher. The result may be that an increase in the wage leads to a smaller quantity of labor supplied.

Although we normally expect the labor supply curve for an individual to be upward sloping, it is possible that at very high wage levels, the labor supply curve of an individual might be *backward bending*, so that higher wages actually result in a *smaller* quantity of labor supplied, as shown in Figure 3. To understand why, recall the definitions of the *substitution effect* and the *income effect*. The substitution effect of a price change refers to the fact that an increase in price makes a good more expensive *relative* to other goods. In the case of a wage change, the substitution effect refers to the fact that an increase in the wage raises the opportunity cost of leisure and causes a worker to devote *more* time to working and less time to leisure.

The income effect of a price change refers to the change in the quantity demanded of a good that results from changes in consumer purchasing power as the price changes. An increase in the wage will clearly increase a consumer's purchasing power for any given number of hours worked. For a normal good, the income effect leads to a larger quantity demanded. Because leisure is a normal good, the income effect of a wage increase will cause a worker to devote *less* time to working and more time to leisure. So, the substitution effect of a wage increase causes a worker to supply a larger quantity of labor, but the income effect causes a worker to supply a smaller quantity of labor. Whether a worker supplies more or less labor following a wage increase depends on whether the substitution effect is larger than the income effect. Figure 3 shows the typical case of the substitution effect being larger than the income effect at low levels of wages—so the worker supplies a larger quantity of labor as the wage rises—and the income effect being larger than the substitution effect at high levels of wages—so the worker supplies a smaller quantity of labor as the wage rises. For example, suppose an attorney has become quite successful and can charge clients very high fees. Or suppose a rock band has become very popular and receives a large payment for every performance. In these cases, there is a high opportunity cost for the lawyer to turn down another client to take a longer vacation or for the band to turn down another concert. But because their incomes are already very high, they may decide to give up additional income for more leisure. In this case, for the lawyer or the rock band, the income effect is larger than the substitution effect, and a higher wage causes them to supply *less* labor.

The Market Supply Curve of Labor

We can determine the market supply curve of labor in the same way we determine a market supply curve of a good. We find the market supply curve of a good by adding up the quantity of the good supplied by each firm at each price. Similarly, we find the market supply curve of labor by adding up the quantity of labor supplied by each worker at each wage, holding constant all other variables that might affect the willingness of workers to supply labor.

Factors That Shift the Market Supply Curve of Labor

In constructing the market supply curve of labor, we hold constant all other variables that would affect the willingness of workers to supply labor, except the wage. If any of these other variables change, the market supply curve will shift. The following are the three most important variables that cause the market supply curve of labor to shift:

1. *Increasing population.* As the population grows due to the number of births exceeding the number of deaths and due to immigration, the supply curve of labor shifts to the right. The effects of immigration on labor supply are largest in the markets for unskilled workers. In some large cities in the United States, for example, the majority of taxi drivers and workers in hotels and restaurants are immigrants. Some supporters of reducing immigration argue that wages in these jobs have been depressed by the increased supply of labor from immigrants.

2. *Changing demographics. Demographics* refers to the composition of the population. The more people who are between the ages of 16 and 65, the greater the quantity of labor supplied. During the 1970s and 1980s, the U.S. labor force grew particularly rapidly as members of the Baby Boom generation—born between 1946 and 1964—first began working. In contrast, a low birthrate in Japan has resulted in an aging population. The number of working-age people in Japan actually began to decline during the 1990s, causing the labor supply curve to shift to the left.

   A related demographic issue is the changing role of women in the labor force. In 1900, only 21 percent of women in the United States were in the labor force. By 1950, this figure had risen to 30 percent, and today it is 60 percent. This increase in the *labor force participation* of women has significantly increased the supply of labor in the United States.

3. *Changing alternatives.* The labor supply in any particular labor market depends, in part, on the opportunities available in other labor markets. For example, the problems in the financial services industry that began in 2007 reduced the opportunities for investment bankers, stockbrokers, and other financial workers. Many workers left this industry—causing the labor supply curve to shift to the left—and entered other markets, causing the labor supply curves to shift to the right in those markets. People who have lost jobs or who have low incomes are eligible for unemployment insurance and other payments from the government. The more generous these payments are, the less pressure unemployed workers have to quickly find another job. In many European countries, it is much easier than in the United States for unemployed workers to replace a larger fraction of their wage income with government payments. Many economists believe generous unemployment benefits help explain the higher unemployment rates experienced in some European countries.

3 LEARNING OBJECTIVE

Explain how equilibrium wages are determined in labor markets.

Equilibrium in the Labor Market

In Figure 4, we bring together labor demand and labor supply to determine equilibrium in the labor market. We can use demand and supply to analyze changes in the equilibrium wage and the level of employment for the entire labor market, and we can also use it to analyze markets for different types of labor, such as baseball players or college professors.

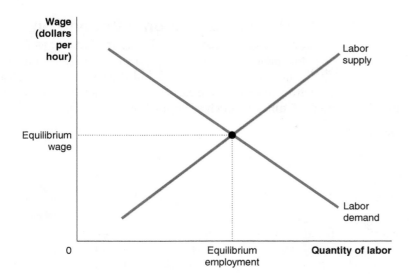

Figure 4

Equilibrium in the Labor Market

As in other markets, equilibrium in the labor market occurs where the demand curve for labor and the supply curve of labor intersect.

The Effect on Equilibrium Wages of a Shift in Labor Demand

In many labor markets, increases over time in labor productivity will cause the demand for labor to increase. As Figure 5 shows, if labor supply is unchanged, an increase in labor demand will increase both the equilibrium wage and the number of workers employed.

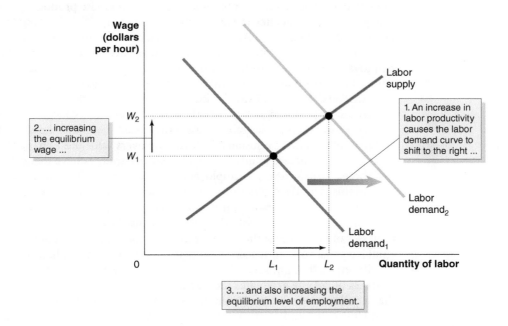

Figure 5 **The Effect of an Increase in Labor Demand**

Increases in labor demand will cause the equilibrium wage and the equilibrium level of employment to rise:

1. If the productivity of workers rises, the marginal revenue product increases, causing the labor demand curve to shift to the right.

2. The equilibrium wage rises from W_1 to W_2.
3. The equilibrium level of employment rises from L_1 to L_2.

Making the Connection

Will Your Future Income Depend on Which Courses You Take in College?

Most people realize the value of a college education. As the following chart shows, in 2013, full-time workers aged 25 and over with a college degree earned more per week than other workers; for example, they earned 2.5 times as much as high school dropouts.

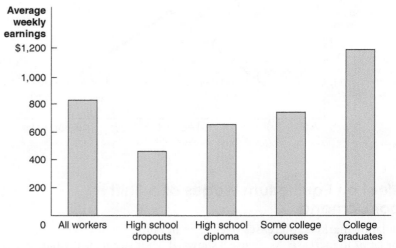

Source: U.S. Bureau of Labor Statistics, "Usual Weekly Earnings of Wage and Salary Workers," April 18, 2013.

Why do college graduates earn more than others? The obvious answer would seem to be that a college education provides skills that increase productivity. Some economists, though, advocate an alternative explanation, known as the *signaling hypothesis*, first proposed by Nobel Laureate A. Michael Spence of New York University. This hypothesis is based on the idea that job applicants will always have more information than will potential employers about how productive the applicants are likely to be. Although employers attempt through job interviews and background checks to distinguish "good workers" from "bad workers," they are always looking for more information.

According to the signaling hypothesis, employers see a college education as a signal that workers possess certain desirable characteristics: self-discipline, the ability to meet deadlines, and the ability to make a sustained effort. Employers value these characteristics because they usually lead to success in any activity. People generally believe that college graduates possess these characteristics, so employers often require a college degree for their best-paying jobs. In this view, the signal that a college education sends about a person's inherent characteristics—which the person presumably already possessed *before* entering college—is much more important than any skills the person may have learned in college. Or, as a college math professor of one of the authors put it (only half-jokingly): "The purpose of college is to show employers that you can succeed at something that's boring and hard."

Recently, though, several economic studies have provided evidence that the higher incomes of college graduates are due to their greater productivity rather than the signal that a college degree sends to employers. Orley Ashenfelter and Cecilia Rouse of Princeton University studied the relationship between schooling and income among 700 pairs of identical twins. Identical twins have identical genes, so differences in their inherent abilities should be relatively small. Therefore, if they have different numbers of years in school, differences in their earnings should be mainly due to the effect of schooling on their productivity. Ashenfelter and Rouse found that identical twins had returns of about 9 percent per additional year of schooling, enough to account for most of the gap in income between high school graduates and college graduates.

Daniel Hamermesh and Stephen G. Donald of the University of Texas studied the determinants of the earnings of college graduates 5 to 25 years after graduation. They collected extensive information on each person in their study, including the person's SAT scores, rank in high school graduating class, grades in every college course taken, and college major. Hamermesh and Donald discovered that, holding constant all other factors, business and engineering majors earned more than graduates with other majors. They also discovered that taking science and math courses has a large effect on future earnings: "A student who takes 15 credits of upper-division science and math courses and obtains a B average in them will earn about 10% more than an otherwise identical student in the same major … who takes no upper-division classes in these areas." This result held even after adjusting for a student's SAT score. The study by Hamermesh and Donald contradicts the signaling hypothesis because if that hypothesis is correct, the choice of courses taken in college should be of minor importance compared with the signal workers send to employers just by having completed college.

Sources: Orley Ashenfelter and Cecilia Rouse, "Income, Schooling, and Ability: Evidence from a New Sample of Identical Twins," *Quarterly Journal of Economics*, Vol. 113, No. 1, February 1998, pp. 253–284; and Daniel S. Hamermesh and Stephen G. Donald, "The Effect of College Curriculum on Earnings: An Affinity Identifier for Non-Ignorable Non-Response Bias," *Journal of Econometrics*, Vol. 144, No. 2, June 2008, pp. 479–491.

Your Turn: Test your understanding by doing related problem 3.3 at the end of this chapter.

The Effect on Equilibrium Wages of a Shift in Labor Supply

What is the effect on the equilibrium wage of an increase in labor supply due to population growth? As Figure 6 shows, if labor demand is unchanged, an increase in labor supply will decrease the equilibrium wage but increase the number of workers employed.

Whether the wage rises in a market depends on whether demand increases faster than supply. For example, as Facebook, Twitter, Pinterest, and other social networking sites became increasingly popular, the demand for software engineers in California's Silicon Valley began to increase faster than the supply of new engineers graduating from college. Starting salaries for new graduates had increased from about $80,000 in 2009 to as much as $150,000 in 2013. To keep their engineers from jumping to other employers, Google, Tagged, and other firms had to give their existing employees across-the-board raises. Start-up firms found that the salaries they needed to pay were raising their costs to levels that made it difficult to compete. If these escalating salaries lead more students to graduate with degrees in software engineering, the increased labor supply could eventually bring down salaries.

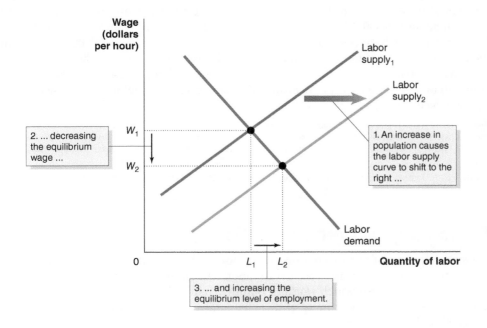

Figure 6

The Effect of an Increase in Labor Supply

Increases in labor supply will cause the equilibrium wage to fall but the equilibrium level of employment to rise:

1. As population increases, the labor supply curve shifts to the right.
2. The equilibrium wage falls from W_1 to W_2.
3. The equilibrium level of employment increases from L_1 to L_2.

Making the Connection

Veterinarians Fall Victim to Demand and Supply

A rapid increase in demand and a slow increase in supply has driven up the salaries of software engineers. Veterinarians have been hurt, rather than helped, by changes in demand and supply in recent years. Schools of veterinary medicine in the United States have continued to turn out about 2,500 new veterinarians each year, while demand for the most important veterinary specialty—small animal medicine—has been declining. Over the long run, as more women have entered the workforce, some families have had greater difficulty caring for pets that may have to be left home alone during the day. The decline in incomes and employment during the 2007–2009 recession and the slow recovery that followed have also left many families looking for ways to cut back spending. As a result, the number of dogs and cats in the United States has declined, thereby reducing the demand for small animal vets.

The following figure shows that increases in the supply of small animal vets combined with a decrease in the demand for their services caused the equilibrium annual income of these vets to decline from $139,000 in 2003 to $121,000 in 2013 (both values are measured in dollars of 2013 purchasing power) at the same time that the number of small animal vets increased from 42,000 to 47,000.

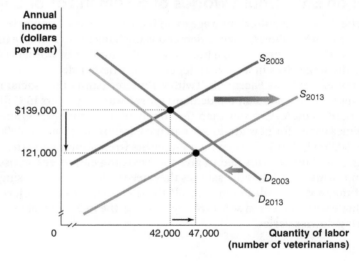

The situation for new vets is worse than the graph indicates. Although an annual income of $121,000 may sound comfortable, the average annual income of *new* vets in 2013 was only about $46,000. Many new vets graduate from schools of veterinary medicine with large student loan balances as average out-of-state tuition has risen to $63,000 per year. In fact, the ratio of debt to income for new vets is double the ratio for new medical doctors.

Basic demand and supply analysis indicates that as long as the supply of vets continues to increase while the population of dogs and cats continues to fall, the incomes of vets will be declining.

Sources: David Segal, "High Debt and Falling Demand Trap New Vets," *New York Times*, February 23, 2013; American Veterinary Medical Association, *Veterinary Market Statistics*, various issues; and Committee to Assess the Current and Future Workforce Needs in Veterinary Medicine, *Workforce Needs in Veterinary Medicine*, Washington, D.C.: The National Academies Press, 2013.

Your Turn: Test your understanding by doing related problem 3.8 at the end of this chapter.

---

4 LEARNING OBJECTIVE

Use demand and supply analysis to explain how compensating differentials, discrimination, and labor unions cause wages to differ.

Explaining Differences in Wages

A key conclusion of our discussion of the labor market is that the equilibrium wage equals the marginal revenue product of labor. The more productive workers are and the higher the price for which workers' output can be sold, the higher the wages workers will receive. At the beginning of this chapter, we raised the question of why Major League Baseball players are paid so much more than most other workers. We are now

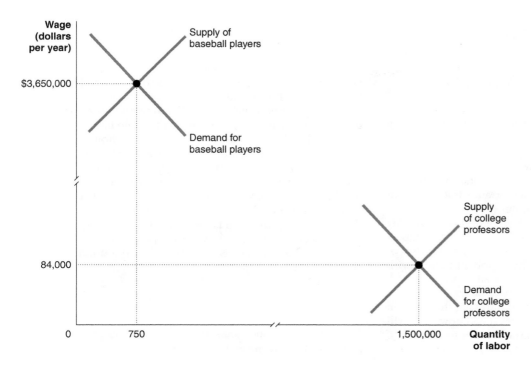

Figure 7

Baseball Players Are Paid More Than College Professors

The marginal revenue product of baseball players is very high, and the supply of people with the ability to play Major League Baseball is low. The result is that the 750 Major League Baseball players receive an average wage of $3,650,000. The marginal revenue product of college professors is much lower, and the supply of people with the ability to be college professors is much higher. The result is that the 1.5 million college professors in the United States receive an average wage of $84,000, far below the average wage of baseball players.

ready to use demand and supply analysis to answer this question. Figure 7 shows the demand and supply curves for Major League Baseball players and the demand and supply curves for college professors.

Consider the marginal revenue product of baseball players, which is the additional revenue a team owner will receive from hiring one more player. Baseball players are hired to produce baseball games that are then sold to fans, who pay admission to baseball stadiums, and to radio and television stations and to cable systems that broadcast the games. Because a Major League Baseball team can sell each baseball game for a large amount, the marginal revenue product of baseball players is high. The supply of people with the ability to play Major League Baseball is also very limited. As a result, the average annual salary of the 750 Major League Baseball players was $3,650,000 in 2013.

The marginal revenue product of college professors is much lower than for baseball players. College professors are hired to produce college educations that are sold to students and their parents. Although one year's college tuition is quite high at many colleges, hiring one more professor allows a college to admit at most a few more students. So, the marginal revenue product of a college professor is much lower than the marginal revenue product of a baseball player. There are also many more people who possess the skills to be a college professor than possess the skills to be a Major League Baseball player. As a result, the average annual salary of the country's 1.5 million college professors was about $84,000 in 2013.

This discussion still leaves unanswered the question raised at the beginning of this chapter: Why are the Los Angeles Dodgers willing to pay Zack Greinke more than the Kansas City Royals or Milwaukee Brewers, two of his previous teams, were? Greinke's marginal product—which we can think of as the extra games a team will win by employing him—should be about the same in Los Angeles as in Kansas City or Milwaukee. But his *marginal revenue product* will be higher in Los Angeles. Because the Dodgers play in the second largest metropolitan area in the United States, the number of Dodgers fans is much greater than the number of Kansas City or Milwaukee fans, so winning additional games will result in a greater increase in attendance at Dodgers games than it would at Royals or Brewers games. It will also result in a greater increase in viewers for Dodgers games on television. Therefore, the Dodgers are able to sell the extra wins that Greinke produces for much more than the Royals or Brewers can. This difference explains why the Dodgers were willing to pay Greinke much more than the Royals or Brewers were.

Don't Let This Happen to You

Remember That Prices and Wages Are Determined at the Margin

You have probably heard some variation of the following remark: "We could live without baseball, but we can't live without the trash being hauled away. In a more rational world, trash collectors would be paid more than baseball players." This remark seems logical: The total value to society of having the trash hauled away certainly is greater than the total value of baseball games. But wages—like prices—do not depend on total value but on *marginal* value. The *additional* baseball games the Los Angeles Dodgers expect to win by signing Zack Greinke will result in millions of dollars in increased revenue. The supply of people with the ability to play Major League Baseball is very limited. The supply of people with the ability to be trash haulers is much greater. If a trash-hauling firm hires another worker, the *additional* trash-hauling services it can now offer will bring in a relatively small amount of revenue. The *total* value of baseball games and the *total* value of trash hauling

are not relevant in determining the relative salaries of baseball players and trash collectors.

This point is related to the diamond and water paradox first noted by Adam Smith. On the one hand, water is very valuable—we literally couldn't live without it—but its price is very low. On the other hand, apart from a few industrial purposes, diamonds are used only for jewelry, yet their price is quite high. We resolve the paradox by noting that the price of water is low because the supply is very large and the additional benefit consumers receive from the last gallon purchased is low. The price of diamonds is high because the supply is very small, and the additional benefit consumers receive from the last diamond purchased is high.

Your Turn: Test your understanding by doing related problem 4.7 at the end of this chapter.

Why does Brad Pitt earn more today relative to the typical actor than stars did in the 1940s?

Making the Connection

Technology and the Earnings of "Superstars"

The gap between Zack Greinke's salary and the salary of the lowest-paid baseball players is much greater than the gap between the salaries paid during the 1950s and 1960s to top players such as Mickey Mantle and Willie Mays and the salaries of the lowest-paid players. Similarly, the gap between the $30 million Brad Pitt is paid to star in a movie and the salary paid to an actor in a minor role is much greater than the gap between the salaries paid during the 1930s and 1940s to stars such as Clark Gable and Cary Grant and the salaries paid to bit players. In fact, in most areas of sports and entertainment, the highest-paid performers—the "superstars"—now have much higher incomes relative to other members of their professions than was true a few decades ago.

The increase in the relative incomes of superstars is mainly due to technological advances. The spread of cable television has increased the number of potential viewers of Dodgers games, but many of those viewers will watch only if the Dodgers are winning. This increases the value to the Dodgers of winning games and, therefore, increases Greinke's marginal revenue product and the salary he can earn.

With Blu-ray discs, DVDs, Internet streaming video, and pay-per-view cable, the value to movie studios of producing a hit movie has greatly risen. Not surprisingly, movie studios have also increased their willingness to pay large salaries to stars such as Brad Pitt and Leonardo DiCaprio because they think these superstars will significantly increase the chances that a film will be successful.

This process has been going on for a long time. For instance, before the invention of the motion picture, anyone who wanted to see a play had to attend the theater and see a live performance. Limits on the number of people who could see the best actors and actresses perform created an opportunity for many more people to succeed in the acting profession, and the gap between the salaries earned by the best actors and the salaries earned by average actors was relatively small. Today, when a hit movie starring Brad Pitt is available on DVD or for downloading, millions of people will buy or rent it, and they will not be forced to spend money to see a less popular actor, as their great-great-grandparents might have been.

Your Turn: Test your understanding by doing related problems 4.10 and 4.11 at the end of this chapter.

Differences in marginal revenue products are the most important factor in explaining differences in wages, but they are not the whole story. To provide a more complete explanation for differences in wages, we must take into account three important aspects of labor markets: compensating differentials, discrimination, and labor unions.

Compensating Differentials

Suppose Paul runs a pizza parlor and acquires a reputation for being a bad boss who yells at his workers and is generally unpleasant. Two blocks away, Brendan also runs a pizza parlor, but he is always very polite to his workers. We would expect in these circumstances that Paul will have to pay a higher wage than Brendan to attract and retain workers. Higher wages that compensate workers for unpleasant aspects of a job are called **compensating differentials**.

If working in a dynamite factory requires the same degree of training and education as working in a semiconductor factory but is much more dangerous, a larger number of workers will want to work making semiconductors than will want to work making dynamite. As a consequence, the wages of dynamite workers will be higher than the wages of semiconductor workers. We can think of the difference in wages as being the price of risk. As each worker decides on his or her willingness to assume risk and decides how much higher the wage must be to compensate for assuming more risk, wages will adjust so that dynamite factories will pay wages that are just high enough to compensate workers who choose to work there for the extra risk they assume. Only when workers in dynamite factories have been fully compensated with higher wages for the additional risk they assume will dynamite companies be able to attract enough workers.

One surprising implication of compensating differentials is that *laws protecting the health and safety of workers may not make workers better off*. To see this point, suppose that dynamite factories pay wages of $25 per hour and semiconductor factories pay wages of $20 per hour, with the $5 difference in wages being a compensating differential for the greater risk of working in a dynamite factory. Suppose that the government passes a law regulating the manufacture of dynamite in order to improve safety in dynamite factories. As a result of this law, dynamite factories are no longer any more dangerous than semiconductor factories. Once this change occurs, the wages in dynamite factories will decline to $20 per hour, the same as in semiconductor factories. Are workers in dynamite factories any better or worse off? Before the law was passed, their wages were $25 per hour, but $5 per hour was a compensating differential for the extra risk they were exposed to. Now their wages are only $20 per hour, but the extra risk has been eliminated. The conclusion seems to be that dynamite workers are no better off as a result of the safety legislation.

This conclusion is true, though, only if the compensating differential actually does compensate workers fully for the additional risk. Nobel Laureate George Akerlof of the University of California, Berkeley, and William Dickens of the Brookings Institution have argued that the psychological principle known as *cognitive dissonance* might cause workers to underestimate the true risk of their jobs. According to this principle, people prefer to think of themselves as intelligent and rational and tend to reject evidence that seems to contradict this image. Because working in a very hazardous job may seem irrational, workers in such jobs may refuse to believe that the jobs really are hazardous. Akerlof and Dickens present evidence that workers in chemical plants producing benzene and workers in nuclear power plants underestimate the hazards of their jobs. If Akerlof and Dickens are correct, the wages of these workers will not be high enough to

Compensating differentials Higher wages that compensate workers for unpleasant aspects of a job.

compensate them fully for the risk they have assumed. So, in this situation, safety legislation may make workers better off.

Discrimination

Table 2 shows that in the United States, white males on average earn more than other groups. One possible explanation for this fact is **economic discrimination**, which involves paying a person a lower wage or excluding a person from an occupation on the basis of an irrelevant characteristic such as race or gender.

If employers discriminated by hiring only white males for high-paying jobs or by paying white males higher wages than other groups working the same jobs, white males would have higher earnings, as Table 2 shows. However, excluding groups from certain jobs or paying one group more than another has been illegal in the United States since the passage of the Equal Pay Act of 1963 and the Civil Rights Act of 1964. Nevertheless, it is possible that employers are ignoring the law and practicing economic discrimination.

Most economists believe that only part of the gap between the wages of white males and the wages of other groups is due to discrimination. Instead, some of the gap is explained by three main factors:

1. Differences in education
2. Differences in experience
3. Differing preferences for jobs

Differences in Education Some of the difference between the incomes of white workers and the incomes of black workers can be explained by differences in education. Historically, African Americans have had less schooling than have whites. Although the gap has closed significantly over the years, 88 percent of adult white males in 2012 had graduated from high school as opposed to 84 percent of adult African-American males. Thirty-two percent of white males had graduated from college as opposed to 19 percent of African-American males. These statistics understate the true gap in education between blacks and whites because many blacks receive a substandard education in inner-city schools. Not surprisingly, studies have shown that differing levels of education can account for a significant part of the gap between the earnings of white and black males. Some of the difference in educational levels between blacks and whites may itself reflect past and current discrimination by governments in failing to provide equal educational opportunities.

Differences in Experience Women are much more likely than men to leave their jobs for a period of time after having a child. Women with several children will sometimes have several interruptions in their careers. Some women leave the workforce for several years until their children are of school age. As a result, on average, women

Economic discrimination Paying a person a lower wage or excluding a person from an occupation on the basis of an irrelevant characteristic such as race or gender.

Table 2

Why Do White Males Earn More Than Other Groups?

Group	Annual Earnings
White males	$56,247
White females	42,171
Black males	39,816
Black females	35,090
Hispanic males	32,516
Hispanic females	29,508

Note: The values are median annual earnings for persons who worked full time, year-round in 2012. Persons of Hispanic origin can be of any race.
Source: U.S. Bureau of the Census, Table PINC-01, "Current Population Survey," *2013 Annual Social and Economic Supplement.*

with children have less workforce experience than do men of the same age. Because workers with greater experience are, on average, more productive, the difference in levels of experience helps to explain some of the difference in earnings between men and women. Providing some support for this explanation is the fact that, on average, married women earn about 25 percent less than married men, but women who have never been married—and whose careers are less likely to have been interrupted—earn only about 9 percent less than men who have never been married.

Differing Preferences for Jobs Significant differences exist between the types of jobs held by women and men. Women represent 90 percent or more of the people employed in some relatively low-paying jobs, such as preschool teachers, dental assistants, and childcare workers, while men represent more than 90 percent of the people employed in some relatively high-paying jobs, such as airline pilots, engineering managers, and electricians. Although the overrepresentation of women in low-paying jobs and men in high-paying jobs may be due, in part, to discrimination, it is also likely to reflect differences in job preferences between men and women. For example, because many women interrupt their careers—at least briefly—when their children are born, they are more likely to take jobs where work experience is less important. More women may also be likely to take jobs, such as teaching, that allow them to be home in the afternoons when their children return from school.

Solved Problem 4

Is Passing "Comparable Worth" Legislation a Good Way to Close the Gap between Men's and Women's Pay?

As we have seen, because of either discrimination or differing preferences, certain jobs are filled primarily by men, and other jobs are filled primarily by women. On average, the "men's jobs" have higher wages than the "women's jobs." Some commentators have argued that many "men's jobs" are more highly paid than "women's jobs," despite the jobs being comparable in terms of the education and skills required and the working conditions involved. These commentators have argued that the earnings gap between men and women could be closed at least partially if the government required employers to pay the same wages for jobs that have *comparable worth*. Many economists are skeptical of these proposals because they believe allowing markets to determine wages results in a more efficient outcome.

Suppose that electricians are currently being paid a market equilibrium wage of $800 per week, and dental assistants are being paid a market equilibrium wage of $500 per week. Comparable-worth legislation is passed, and a study finds that an electrician and a dental assistant have comparable jobs, so employers will now be required to pay workers in both jobs $650 per week. Analyze the effects of this requirement on the market for electricians and on the market for dental assistants. Be sure to use demand and supply graphs.

Solving the Problem

Step 1: **Review the chapter material.** This problem is about economic discrimination, so you may want to review the section "Discrimination."

Step 2: **Draw the graphs.** When the government sets the price in a market, the result is a surplus or a shortage, depending on whether the government-mandated price is above or below the competitive market equilibrium. A wage of $650 per week is below the market wage for electricians and above the market wage for dental assistants. Therefore, we expect the requirement to result in a shortage of electricians and a surplus of dental assistants.

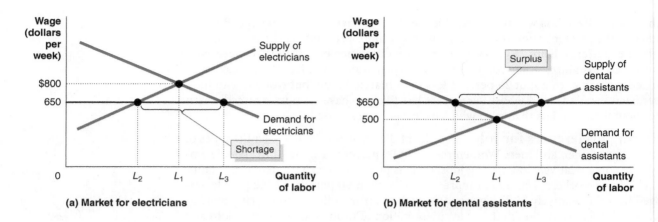

(a) Market for electricians

(b) Market for dental assistants

In panel (a), without comparable-worth legislation, the equilibrium wage for electricians is $800, and the equilibrium quantity of electricians hired is L_1. Setting the wage for electricians below equilibrium at $650 reduces the quantity of labor supplied in this occupation from L_1 to L_2 but increases the quantity of labor demanded by employers from L_1 to L_3. The result is a shortage of electricians equal to $L_3 - L_2$, as shown by the bracket in the graph.

In panel (b), without comparable-worth legislation, the equilibrium wage for dental assistants is $500, and the equilibrium quantity of dental assistants hired is L_1. Setting the wage for dental assistants above equilibrium at $650 increases the quantity of labor supplied in this occupation from L_1 to L_3 but reduces the quantity of labor demanded by employers from L_1 to L_2. The result is a surplus of dental assistants equal to $L_3 - L_2$, as shown by the bracket in the graph.

Extra Credit: Most economists are skeptical of government attempts to set wages and prices, as comparable-worth legislation would require. Supporters of comparable-worth legislation, by contrast, see differences between men's and women's wages as being mainly due to discrimination and see government legislation as a solution.

Your Turn: For more practice, do related problems 4.17 and 4.18 at the end of this chapter.

The Difficulty of Measuring Discrimination When two people are paid different wages, discrimination may be the explanation. But differences in productivity or preferences may also be an explanation. Labor economists have attempted to measure what part of differences in wages between black workers and white workers and between men and women is due to discrimination and what part is due to other factors. Unfortunately, it is difficult to precisely measure differences in productivity or in worker preferences. As a result, we can't know exactly the extent of economic discrimination in the United States today.

Making the Connection	**Does Greg Have an Easier Time Finding a Job Than Jamal?**

One difficulty in accurately measuring economic discrimination is that two workers may not only differ in race and gender but also in characteristics that employers expect will affect the workers' productivity. If Worker A is hired instead of Worker B, is it because A is a white male, while B is a black female, or is it because of A's and B's other characteristics?

Marianne Bertrand of the University of Chicago and Sendhil Mullainathan of Harvard found an ingenious way of gaining insight into the extent of economic discrimination. They responded to help wanted ads in newspapers by sending identical résumés, with the exception that half of the résumés were assigned an African-American–sounding name and half were assigned a white-sounding name. In other words, the characteristics of these fictitious people were the same, except for their names. In the absence of discrimination, résumés with African-American–sounding names, such as Jamal Jones, should have been as likely to get job interviews as the identical résumés with white-sounding names, such as Greg Baker. Bertrand and Mullainathan sent out more than 5,000 résumés to many different employers who were advertising for jobs in sales, administrative support, clerical services, and customer services. They found that employers were 50 percent more likely to interview workers with white-sounding names than workers with African-American–sounding names.

Some economists have questioned whether the study by Bertrand and Mullainathan, as well as other similar studies, actually do show that employers discriminate. They argue that employers may believe that the typical white job applicant and the typical black job applicant have different characteristics, apart from those included in the résumés, that may affect their productivity. If so, the employers may be responding to these differences in productivity rather than solely to the job applicant's race. Because Bertrand and Mullainathan based their artificial résumés on actual résumés, however, the artificial résumés probably include all the characteristics that actual job applicants think are relevant. Bertrand and Mullainathan believe that the results of their experiment show that "differential treatment by race ... appears to still be prominent in the U.S. labor market."

Does having an African-American–sounding name make it more difficult to find a job?

Sources: Marianne Bertrand and Sendhil Mullainathan, "Are Emily and Greg More Employable Than Lakisha and Jamal? A Field Experiment on Labor Market Discrimination," *American Economic Review*, Vol. 94, No. 4, September 2004, pp. 991–1013; and David Neumark, "Detecting Discrimination in Audit and Correspondence Studies," *Journal of Human Resources*, Vol. 47, No. 4, Fall 2012, pp. 1128–1157.

Your Turn: Test your understanding by doing related problem 4.19 at the end of this chapter.

Does It Pay to Discriminate? Many economists believe that in the long run, markets can undermine economic discrimination. One reason is that *employers who discriminate pay an economic penalty*. To see why, let's consider a simplified example. Suppose that men and women are equally qualified to be airline pilots and that, initially, airlines do not discriminate. In Figure 8, we divide the airlines into two groups: "A" airlines and "B" airlines. If neither group of airlines discriminates, we would expect them to pay an equal wage of $1,100 per week to both men and women pilots. Now suppose that "A" airlines decide to discriminate and to fire all their women pilots. This action will reduce the supply of pilots to these airlines and, as shown in panel (a), will force up the wage from $1,100 to $1,300 per week. At the same time, as women fired from the jobs with "A" airlines apply for jobs with "B" airlines, the supply of pilots to "B" airlines will increase, and the equilibrium wage will fall from $1,100 to $900 per week. All the women pilots will end up being employed at the nondiscriminating airlines and will be paid a lower wage than the men who are employed by the discriminating airlines.

But this situation cannot persist for two reasons. First, male pilots employed by "B" airlines will also receive the lower wage. This lower wage gives them an incentive to quit their jobs at "B" airlines and apply at "A" airlines, which will shift the labor supply curve for "B" airlines to the left and the labor supply curve for "A" airlines to the right. Second, "A" airlines are paying $1,300 per week to hire pilots who are no more productive than the pilots being paid $900 per week by "B" airlines. As a result, "B" airlines will have lower costs and will be able to charge lower prices. Eventually, high-price "A" airlines will lose their customers to low-price "B" airlines and will be driven out of business. The

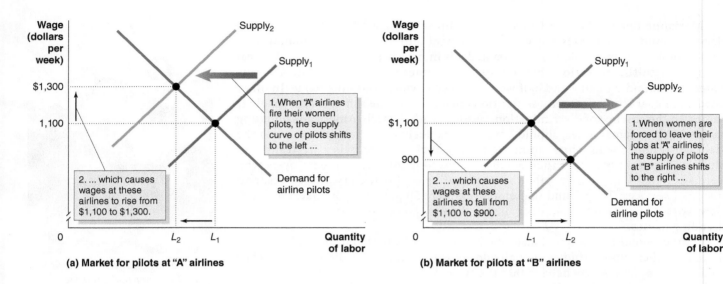

Figure 8 Discrimination and Wages

In this hypothetical example, we assume that initially neither "A" airlines nor "B" airlines discriminate. As a result, men and women pilots receive the same wage of $1,100 per week at both groups of airlines. We then assume that "A" airlines discriminate by firing all their women pilots. Panel (a) shows that discrimination reduces the supply of pilots to "A" airlines and raises the wage paid by these airlines from $1,100 to $1,300. Panel (b) shows that discrimination increases the supply of pilots to "B" airlines and lowers the wage paid by these airlines from $1,100 to $900. All the women pilots will end up being employed at the nondiscriminating airlines and will be paid a lower wage than the men who are employed by the discriminating airlines.

market will have imposed an economic penalty on the discriminating airlines. So, discrimination will not persist, and the wages of men and women pilots will become equal.

Can we conclude from this analysis that competition in markets will eliminate all economic discrimination? Unfortunately, this optimistic conclusion is not completely accurate. We know that until the Civil Rights Act of 1964 was passed, many firms in the United States refused to hire black workers. Even though this practice had persisted for decades, nondiscriminating competitors did not drive these firms out of business. Why not? There were three important factors:

1. *Worker discrimination.* In some cases, white workers refused to work alongside black workers. As a result, some industries—such as the important cotton textile industry in the South—were all white. Because of discrimination by white workers, an entrepreneur who wanted to use low-cost black labor might need to hire an all-black workforce. Some entrepreneurs tried this approach, but because black workers had been excluded from these industries, they often lacked the skills and experience to form an effective workforce.

2. *Customer discrimination.* Some white consumers were unwilling to buy from companies in certain industries if they employed black workers. This discrimination was not a significant barrier in manufacturing industries, where customers would not know the race of the workers producing the good. It was, however, a problem for firms in industries in which workers came into direct contact with the public.

3. *Negative feedback loops.* Our analysis in Figure 8 assumed that men and women pilots were equally qualified. However, if discrimination makes it difficult for a member of a group to find employment in a particular occupation, his or her incentive to be trained to enter that occupation is reduced. Consider the legal profession as an example. In 1952, future Supreme Court Justice Sandra Day O'Connor graduated third in her class at Stanford University Law School and was an editor of the *Stanford Law Review*, but for some time she was unable to get a job as a lawyer because in those years, many law firms would not hire women. Given such bleak job prospects, it's not surprising that relatively few women entered law school. As a

result, a law firm that did not discriminate would have been unable to hire women lawyers at a lower salary and use this cost advantage to drive discriminating law firms out of business. Notice the difference between this situation and the airline example discussed earlier. In this situation, an unfortunate feedback loop was in place: Few women prepared to become lawyers because many law firms discriminated against women, and nondiscriminating law firms were unable to drive discriminating law firms out of business because there were too few women lawyers available.

Most economists agree that the market imposes an economic penalty on firms that discriminate, but because of the factors just discussed, it may take the market a very long time to eliminate discrimination entirely. The passage of the Civil Rights Act of 1964, which outlawed hiring discrimination on the basis of race and sex, greatly sped up the process of reducing economic discrimination in the United States.

Labor Unions

Workers' wages can differ depending on whether the workers are members of **labor unions**, which are organizations of employees that have the legal right to bargain with employers about wages and working conditions. If a union is unable to reach an agreement with a company, it has the legal right to call a *strike*, which means its members refuse to work until a satisfactory agreement has been reached. As Figure 9 shows, a smaller fraction of the U.S. labor force is unionized than in most other high-income countries.

As Table 3 shows, in the United States, workers who are in unions receive higher wages than workers who are not in unions. Do union members earn more than non-union members because they are in unions? The answer might seem to be "yes," but many union workers are in industries, such as automobile manufacturing, in which their marginal revenue products are high, so their wages would be high even if they were not unionized. Economists who have attempted to estimate statistically the effect of unionization on wages have concluded that being in a union increases a worker's wages about 10 percent, holding constant other factors, such as the industry the worker is in. A related question is whether unions raise the total amount of wages received by all workers, whether unionized or not. Because the share of national income received by workers has remained roughly constant over many years, most economists do not believe that unions have raised the total amount of wages received by workers.

Labor union An organization of employees that has a legal right to bargain with employers about wages and working conditions.

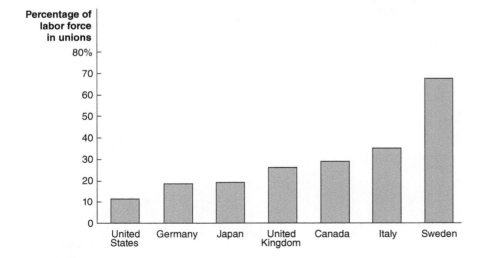

Figure 9

The United States Is Less Unionized Than Most Other High-Income Countries

The percentage of the labor force belonging to unions is lower in the United States than in most other high-income countries.
Source: Organization for Economic Cooperation and Development.

	Average Weekly Earnings
Union workers	$943
Nonunion workers	742

Note: "Union workers" includes union members as well as workers who are represented by unions but who are not members of them.
Source: U.S. Bureau of Labor Statistics, *Union Members Summary*, January 23, 2013.

5 LEARNING OBJECTIVE

Discuss the role personnel economics can play in helping firms deal with human resources issues.

Personnel economics The application of economic analysis to human resources issues.

Personnel Economics

Traditionally, labor economists have focused on issues such as the effects of labor unions on wages or the determinants of changes in average wages over time. They have spent less time analyzing *human resources issues*, which address how firms hire, train, and promote workers and set their wages and benefits. In recent years, some labor economists, including Edward Lazear of Stanford University and William Neilson of the University of Tennessee, have begun exploring the application of economic analysis to human resources issues. This new focus has become known as *personnel economics*.

Personnel economics analyzes the link between differences among jobs and differences in the way workers are paid. Jobs have different skill requirements, require more or less interaction with other workers, have to be performed in more or less unpleasant environments, and so on. Firms need to design compensation policies that take into account these differences. Personnel economics also analyzes policies related to other human resources issues, such as promotions, training, and pensions. In this brief overview, we look only at compensation policies.

Should Workers' Pay Depend on How Much They Work or on How Much They Produce?

One issue personnel economics addresses is when workers should receive *straight-time pay*—a certain wage per hour or salary per week or month—and when they should receive *commission* or *piece-rate pay*—a wage based on how much output they produce.

Suppose that Anne owns a car dealership and is trying to decide whether to pay her salespeople a salary of $800 per week or a commission of $200 on each car they sell. Figure 10 compares the compensation a salesperson would receive under the two systems, according to the number of cars the salesperson sells.

Figure 10

Paying Car Salespeople by Salary or by Commission

This figure compares the compensation a car salesperson receives if she is on a straight salary of $800 per week and if she receives a commission of $200 for each car she sells. With a straight salary, she receives $800 per week, no matter how many cars she sells. This outcome is shown by the horizontal line in the figure. If she receives a commission of $200 per car, her compensation will increase with every car she sells. This outcome is shown by the upward-sloping line. If she sells fewer than 4 cars per week, she would be better off with the $800 salary. If she sells more than 4 cars per week, she would be better off with the $200-per-car commission.

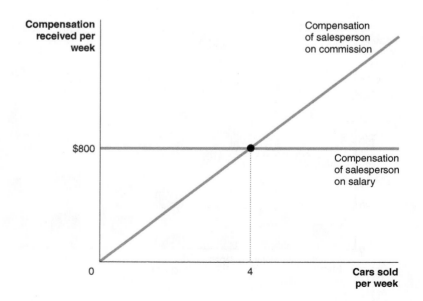

With a straight salary, the salesperson receives $800 per week, no matter how many cars she sells. This outcome is shown by the horizontal line in Figure 10. If she receives a commission of $200 per car, her compensation will increase with every car she sells. This outcome is shown by the upward-sloping line. A salesperson who sells fewer than 4 cars per week would earn more by receiving a straight salary of $800 per week. A salesperson who sells more than 4 cars per week would be better off receiving the $200-per-car commission. We can identify two advantages Anne would receive from paying her salespeople commissions rather than salaries: She would attract and retain the most productive employees, and she would provide an incentive to her employees to sell more cars.

Suppose that other car dealerships are all paying salaries of $800 per week. If Anne pays her employees on commission, any of her employees who are unable to sell at least 4 cars per week can improve their pay by going to work for one of her competitors. And any salespeople at Anne's competitors who can sell more than 4 cars per week can raise their pay by quitting and coming to work for Anne. Over time, Anne will find her least productive employees leaving, while she is able to hire new employees who are more productive.

Paying a commission also increases the incentive Anne's salespeople have to sell more cars. If Anne paid a salary, her employees would receive the same amount no matter how few cars they sold. An employee on salary might decide on a particularly hot or cold day that it was less trouble to stay inside the building than to go out on the car lot to greet potential customers. An employee on commission would know that the additional effort expended on selling more cars would be rewarded with additional compensation.

| Making the Connection | **Raising Pay, Productivity, and Profits at Safelite AutoGlass** |

Safelite Group, headquartered in Columbus, Ohio, is the parent company of Safelite AutoGlass, the nation's largest installer of auto glass, with 600 repair shops. In the mid-1990s, Safelite shifted from paying its glass installers hourly wages to paying them on the basis of how many windows they installed. Safelite already had in place a computer system that allowed it to easily track how many windows each worker installed per day. To make sure quality did not suffer, Safelite added a rule that if a workmanship-related defect occurred with an installed windshield, the worker would have to install a new windshield and would not be paid for the additional work.

Edward Lazear analyzed data provided by the firm and discovered that under the new piece-rate system, the number of windows installed per worker jumped 44 percent. Lazear estimated that half of this increase was due to increased productivity from workers who continued with the company and half was due to new hires being more productive than the workers they replaced who had left the company. Worker pay rose on average by about 9.9 percent. Ninety-two percent of workers experienced a pay increase, and one-quarter received an increase of at least 28 percent. Safelite's profit also increased as the cost to the company per window installed fell from $44.43 under the hourly wage system to $35.24 under the piece-rate system.

A piece-rate system at Safelite AutoGlass led to increased worker wages and firm profits.

Sociologists sometimes question whether worker productivity can be increased through the use of monetary incentives. The experience of Safelite AutoGlass provides a clear example of workers reacting favorably to the opportunity to increase output in exchange for higher compensation.

Source: Edward P. Lazear, "Performance Pay and Productivity," *American Economic Review*, Vol. 90, No. 5, December 2000, pp. 1346–1361.

Your Turn: Test your understanding by doing related problem 5.8 at the end of this chapter.

Other Considerations in Setting Compensation Systems

The discussion so far indicates that companies will find it more profitable to use a commission or piece-rate system of compensation rather than a salary system. In fact, many firms continue to pay their workers salaries, which means they are paying their workers on the basis of how long they work rather than on the basis of how much they produce. Firms may choose a salary system for several good reasons:

- *Difficulty measuring output.* Often firms have difficulty attributing output to any particular worker. For example, an engineering firm may carry out a project using teams of workers whose individual contributions are difficult to distinguish. On assembly lines, such as those used in the automobile industry, the amount produced by each worker is determined by the speed of the line, which is set by managers rather than by workers. Managers at many firms perform such a wide variety of tasks that measuring their output would be costly, if it could be done at all.

- *Concerns about quality.* If workers are paid on the basis of the number of units produced, they may become less concerned about quality. An office assistant who is paid on the basis of the quantity of letters typed may become careless about how many typos the letters contain. In some cases, there are ways around this problem; for example, the assistant may be required to correct the mistakes on his or her own time, without pay.

- *Worker dislike of risk.* Piece-rate or commission systems of compensation increase the risk to workers because sometimes output declines for reasons not connected to the worker's effort. For example, if there is a very snowy winter, few customers may show up at Anne's auto dealership. Through no fault of their own, her salespeople may have great difficulty selling any cars. If they are paid a salary, their income will not be affected, but if they are on commission, their incomes may drop to low levels. The flip side of this is that by paying salaries, Anne assumes a greater risk. During a snowy winter, her payroll expenses will remain high even though her sales are low. With a commission system of compensation, her payroll expenses will decline along with her sales. But owners of firms are typically better able to bear risk than are workers. As a result, some firms may find that workers who would earn more under a commission system will prefer to receive a salary to reduce their risk. In these situations, paying a lower salary may reduce the firm's payroll expenses compared with what they would have been under a commission or piece-rate system.

Personnel economics is a relatively new field, but it holds great potential for helping firms deal more efficiently with human resources issues.

6 LEARNING OBJECTIVE

Show how equilibrium prices are determined in the markets for capital and natural resources.

The Markets for Capital and Natural Resources

The approach we have used to analyze the market for labor can also be used to analyze the markets for other factors of production. We have seen that the demand for labor is determined by the marginal revenue product of labor because the value to a firm of hiring another worker equals the increase in the firm's revenue from selling the additional output it can produce by hiring the worker. The demand for capital and natural resources is determined in a similar way.

The Market for Capital

Physical capital includes machines, equipment, and buildings. Firms sometimes buy capital, but we will focus on situations in which firms rent capital. A chocolate manufacturer renting a warehouse and an airline leasing a plane are examples of firms renting capital. Like the demand for labor, the demand for capital is a derived demand. When a firm is considering increasing its capital by, for example, employing another machine, the value it receives equals the increase in the firm's revenue from selling the additional

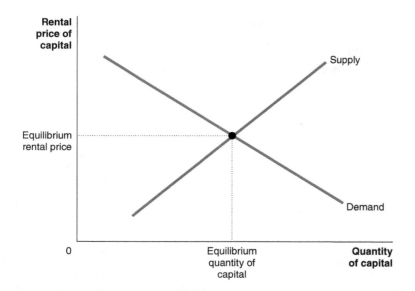

Figure 11

Equilibrium in the Market for Capital

The rental price of capital is determined by demand and supply in the market for capital. In equilibrium, the rental price of capital is equal to the marginal revenue product of capital.

output it can produce by employing the machine. The *marginal revenue product of capital* is the change in the firm's revenue as a result of employing one more unit of capital, such as a machine. We have seen that the marginal revenue product of labor curve is the demand curve for labor. Similarly, the marginal revenue product of capital curve is the demand curve for capital.

Firms producing capital goods face increasing marginal costs, so the supply curve of capital goods is upward sloping. Figure 11 shows equilibrium in the market for capital. In equilibrium, suppliers of capital receive a rental price equal to the marginal revenue product of capital, just as suppliers of labor receive a wage equal to the marginal revenue product of labor.

The Market for Natural Resources

The market for natural resources can be analyzed in the same way as the markets for labor and capital. When a firm is considering employing more natural resources, the value it receives equals the increase in the firm's revenue from selling the additional output it can produce by buying the natural resources. So, the demand for natural resources is also a derived demand. The *marginal revenue product of natural resources* is the change in a firm's revenue as a result of employing one more unit of natural resources, such as a barrel of oil. The marginal revenue product of natural resources curve is also the demand curve for natural resources.

Although the total quantity of most natural resources is ultimately fixed—as the humorist Will Rogers once remarked: "Buy land. They ain't making any more of it"—in many cases, the quantity supplied still responds to the price. For example, although the total quantity of oil deposits in the world is fixed, an increase in the price of oil will result in an increase in the quantity of oil supplied during a particular period. The result, as shown in panel (a) of Figure 12, is an upward-sloping supply curve. In some cases, however, the quantity of a natural resource that will be supplied is fixed and will not change as the price changes. The land available at a busy intersection is fixed, for example. In panel (b) of Figure 12, we illustrate this situation with a supply curve that is a vertical line, or perfectly inelastic. The owner of a factor of production that is in fixed supply receives an **economic rent** (or a **pure rent**). In this case, the price of the factor is determined only by demand. For example, if a new highway diverts much of the traffic from a previously busy intersection, the demand for the land will decline, and the price of the land will fall, but the quantity of the land will not change.

Economic rent (or **pure rent**) The price of a factor of production that is in fixed supply.

379

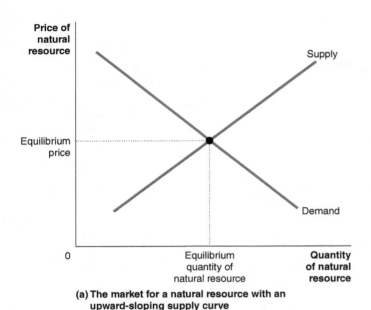

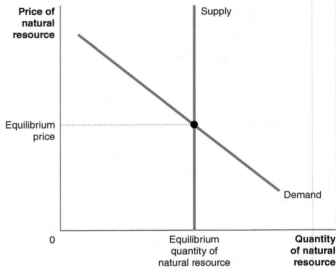

Figure 12 **Equilibrium in the Market for Natural Resources**

In panel (a), the supply curve of a natural resource is upward sloping. The price of the natural resource is determined by the interaction of demand and supply. In panel (b), the supply curve of the natural resource is a vertical line, indicating that the quantity supplied does not respond to changes in price. In this case, the price of the natural resource is determined only by demand. The price of a factor of production with a vertical supply curve is called an *economic rent*, or a *pure rent*.

Monopsony

Monopsony The situation in which a firm is sole buyer of a factor of production.

We have analyzed the case of *monopoly*, where a firm is the sole *seller* of a good or service. What happens if a firm is the sole *buyer* of a factor of production? This case, which is called **monopsony**, is comparatively rare. An example is a firm in an isolated town—perhaps a lumber mill in a small town in Washington or Oregon—that is the sole employer of labor in that location. In the nineteenth and early twentieth centuries, some coal mining firms were the sole employers in certain small towns in West Virginia, and some pineapple plantations were the sole employers on certain small islands in Hawaii. In these cases, not only would the firm own the mill, mine, or plantation, but it would also own the stores and other businesses in the town. Workers would have the choice of working for the sole employer in the town or moving to another town.

We know that a firm with a monopoly in an output market takes advantage of its market power to reduce the quantity supplied to force up the market price and increase its profits. A firm that has a monopsony in a factor market would employ a similar strategy: It would restrict the quantity of the factor demanded to force down the price of the factor and increase profits. A firm with a monopsony in a labor market will hire fewer workers and pay lower wages than would be the case in a competitive market. Because fewer workers are hired than would be hired in a competitive market, monopsony results in a deadweight loss. Monopoly and monopsony have similar effects on the economy: In both cases, a firm's market power results in a lower equilibrium quantity, a deadweight loss, and a reduction in economic efficiency compared with a competitive market.

In some cases, monopsony in labor markets is offset by worker membership in a labor union. A notable example of this is professional sports. For instance, Major League Baseball effectively has a monopsony on employing professional baseball players. (Although independent baseball leagues exist, none of the best players play for these teams, and the teams pay salaries that are a small fraction of those paid by Major League Baseball teams.) The monopsony power of the owners of Major League Baseball teams is offset by the power of the Major League Baseball Players Association, the union that represents baseball players. Bargaining between the representatives of Major League Baseball and the players' union has resulted in baseball players being paid something close to what they would be receiving in a competitive market.

The Marginal Productivity Theory of Income Distribution

We have seen that in equilibrium each factor of production receives a price equal to its marginal revenue product. We can use this fact to explain the distribution of income. Marginal revenue product represents the value of a factor's marginal contribution to producing goods and services. Therefore, individuals will receive income equal to the marginal contributions to production from the factors of production they own, including their labor. The more factors of production an individual owns and the more productive those factors are, the higher the individual's income will be. This approach to explaining the distribution of income is called the **marginal productivity theory of income distribution**. The theory was developed by John Bates Clark, who taught at Columbia University in the late nineteenth and early twentieth centuries.

Marginal productivity theory of income distribution The theory that the distribution of income is determined by the marginal productivity of the factors of production that individuals own.

Continued

Economics in Your Life

How Can You Convince Your Boss to Give You a Raise?

At the beginning of this chapter, we asked you to imagine that you work at a local sandwich shop and that you plan to ask your manager for a raise. One way to show the manager your worth is to demonstrate how many dollars your work earns for the sandwich shop: your marginal revenue product. You could certainly suggest that as you have become better at your job and have gained new skills, you have become a more productive employee. But more importantly, you could say that your productivity results in increased revenue for the sandwich shop. By showing how your employment contributes to higher revenue and profit, you may be able to convince your manager to give you a raise.

Conclusion

In this chapter, we used the demand and supply model to explain why wages differ among workers. The demand for workers depends on their productivity and on the prices firms receive for the output the workers produce. The supply of workers to an occupation depends on the wages and working conditions offered by employers and on the skills required. The demand and supply for labor can also help us analyze issues such as economic discrimination and the effect of labor unions.

Visit MyEconLab for a news article and analysis related to the concepts in this chapter.

Chapter Summary and Problems

Key Terms

Compensating differentials	Economic rent (or pure rent)	Labor union	Marginal revenue product of labor (*MRP*)
Derived demand	Factors of production	Marginal product of labor	Monopsony
Economic discrimination	Human capital	Marginal productivity theory of income distribution	Personnel economics

The Demand for Labor

LEARNING OBJECTIVE: Explain how firms choose the profit-maximizing quantity of labor to employ.

Summary

The demand for labor is a **derived demand** because it depends on the demand consumers have for goods and services. The additional output produced by a firm as a result of hiring another worker is called the **marginal product of labor**. The amount by which a firm's revenue will increase as a result of hiring one more worker is called the **marginal revenue product of labor (*MRP*)**. A firm's marginal revenue product of labor curve is its demand curve for labor. Firms maximize profit by hiring workers up to the point where the wage is equal to the marginal revenue product of labor. We find the market demand curve for labor by adding up the quantity of labor demanded by each firm at each wage, holding constant all other variables that might affect the willingness of firms to hire workers. The most important variables that shift the labor demand curve are changes in human capital, technology, the price of the product, the quantity of other inputs, and the number of firms in the market. **Human capital** is the accumulated training and skills that workers possess.

Visit **www.myeconlab.com** to complete these exercises online and get instant feedback.

Review Questions

1.1 In what sense is the demand for labor a derived demand?

1.2 What is the difference between the marginal product of labor and the marginal revenue product of labor?

1.3 Why is the demand curve for labor downward sloping?

1.4 What are the five most important variables that cause the market demand curve for labor to shift?

Problems and Applications

1.5 Frank Gunter owns an apple orchard. He employs 87 apple pickers and pays them each $8 per hour to pick apples, which he sells for $1.60 per box. If Frank is maximizing profit, what is the marginal revenue product of the last worker he hired? What is that worker's marginal product?

1.6 **[Related to** Solved Problem 1**]** Complete the following table for Terrell's Televisions:

Number of Workers (L)	Output of Televisions per Week (Q)	Marginal Product of Labor (television sets per week) (MP)	Product Price (P)	Marginal Revenue Product of Labor (dollars per week)	Wage (dollars per week) (W)	Additional Profit from Hiring One More Worker (dollars per week)
0	0	_____	$300	_____	$1,800	_____
1	8	_____	300	_____	1,800	_____
2	15	_____	300	_____	1,800	_____
3	21	_____	300	_____	1,800	_____
4	26	_____	300	_____	1,800	_____
5	30	_____	300	_____	1,800	_____
6	33	_____	300	_____	1,800	_____

a. From the information in the table, can you determine whether this firm is a price taker or a price maker? Briefly explain.

b. Use the information in the table to draw a graph like Figure 1 that shows the demand for labor by this firm. Be sure to indicate the profit-maximizing quantity of labor on your graph.

1.7 State whether each of the following events will result in a movement along the market demand curve for labor in electronics factories in China or whether it will cause the market demand curve for labor to shift. If the demand curve shifts, indicate whether it will shift to the left or to the right and draw a graph to illustrate the shift.

a. The wage rate declines.

b. The price of televisions declines.

c. Several firms exit the television market in China.

d. Chinese high schools introduce new vocational courses in assembling electronic products.

1.8 Baseball writer Rany Jazayerli assessed the Kansas City Royals outfielder Jose Guillen as follows: "Guillen has negative value the way his contract stands." How could a baseball player's contract cause him to have negative value to a baseball team?

Source: Rany Jazayerli, "Radical Situations Call for Radical Solutions," www.ranyontheroyals.com, June 6, 2009.

2 | The Supply of Labor

LEARNING OBJECTIVE: Explain how people choose the quantity of labor to supply.

Summary

As the wage increases, the opportunity cost of leisure increases, causing individuals to supply a greater quantity of labor. Normally, the labor supply curve is upward sloping, but it is possible that at very high wage levels, the supply curve might be backward bending. This outcome occurs when someone with a high income is willing to accept a somewhat lower income in exchange for more leisure. We find the market labor supply curve by adding up the quantity of labor supplied by each worker at each wage, holding constant all other variables that might affect the willingness of workers to supply labor. The most important variables that shift the labor supply curve are increases in population, changing demographics, and changing alternatives.

Visit **www.myeconlab.com** to complete these exercises online and get instant feedback.

Review Questions

2.1 How can we measure the opportunity cost of leisure? What are the substitution effect and the income effect resulting from a wage change? Why is the supply curve of labor usually upward sloping?

2.2 What are the three most important variables that cause the market supply curve of labor to shift?

Problems and Applications

2.3 Daniel was earning $65 per hour and working 45 hours per week. Then Daniel's wage rose to $75 per hour, and as a result, he now works 40 hours per week. What can we conclude from this information about the income effect and the substitution effect of a wage change for Daniel?

2.4 A columnist writing in the *Wall Street Journal* argues that because "hourly wages in real terms" rose, the "price of time" also rose. What is the "price of time"? Is the columnist correct that when real hourly wages rise, the price of time increases? Briefly explain.
Source: Brett Arends, "Spend Some Time, Save Some Money," *Wall Street Journal*, May 19, 2009.

2.5 Most labor economists believe that many adult males are on a vertical section of their labor supply curves. Use the concepts of income and substitution effects to explain under what circumstances an individual's labor supply curve would be vertical.
Source: Robert Whaples, "Is There Consensus among American Labor Economists? Survey Results on Forty Propositions," *Journal of Labor Research*, Vol. 17, No. 4, Fall 1996.

2.6 Suppose that a large oil field is discovered in Michigan. By imposing a tax on the oil, the state government is able to eliminate the state income tax on wages. What is likely to be the effect on the labor supply curve in Michigan?

2.7 A columnist in the *New York Times* notes that the U.S. labor supply "in the next decade is expected to expand at less than half the pace of the 1960s, 1970s and 1980s." What explains these changing growth rates in the U.S. labor supply?
Source: Eduardo Porter, "The Payoff in Delaying Retirement," *New York Times*, March 5, 2013.

2.8 State whether each of the following events will result in a movement along the market supply curve of agricultural labor in the United States or whether it will cause the market supply curve of agricultural labor to shift. If the supply curve shifts, indicate whether it will shift to the left or to the right and draw a graph to illustrate the shift.
   a. The agricultural wage rate declines.
   b. Wages outside agriculture increase.
   c. The law is changed to allow for unlimited immigration into the United States.

3 | Equilibrium in the Labor Market

LEARNING OBJECTIVE: Explain how equilibrium wages are determined in labor markets.

Summary

The intersection between labor supply and labor demand determines the equilibrium wage and the equilibrium level of employment. If labor supply is unchanged, an increase in labor demand will increase both the equilibrium wage and the number of workers employed. If labor demand is unchanged, an increase in labor supply will lower the equilibrium wage and increase the number of workers employed.

Visit **www.myeconlab.com** to complete these exercises online and get instant feedback.

Review Questions

3.1 If the labor demand curve shifts to the left and the labor supply curve remains unchanged, what will happen to the equilibrium wage and the equilibrium level of employment? Illustrate your answer with a graph.

3.2 If the labor supply curve shifts to the left and the labor demand curve remains unchanged, what will happen to the equilibrium wage and the equilibrium level of employment? Illustrate your answer with a graph.

Problems and Applications

3.3 **[Related to** Making the Connection: **Will Your Future Income Depend on Which Courses You Take in College?]** Over time, the gap between the wages of workers with college degrees and the wages of workers without college degrees has been increasing. Shouldn't this gap have increased the incentive for workers to earn college degrees, thereby increasing the supply of college-educated workers and reducing the size of the gap?

3.4 Reread the discussion of changes in the salaries of software engineers. Use a graph to illustrate this situation. Make sure your graph has labor demand and supply curves for 2009 and 2013 and that the equilibrium point for each year is clearly indicated.

3.5 Sean Astin, who played Sam in *The Lord of the Rings* movies, wrote the following about an earlier film he had appeared in: "Now I was in a movie I didn't respect, making obscene amounts of money (five times what a teacher makes, and teachers do infinitely more important work)." Are salaries determined by the importance of the work being done? If not, what are salaries determined by?

Source: Sean Astin, with Joe Layden, *There and Back Again: An Actor's Tale*, New York: St. Martin's Press, 2004, p. 35.

3.6 A newspaper article summarizes a study showing that "a standout kindergarten teacher is worth about $320,000 a year. That's the present value of the additional money that a full class of students can expect to earn over their careers. This estimate doesn't take into account social gains, like better health and less crime." Why are even standout kindergarten teachers paid salaries much lower than $320,000?

Source: David Leonhardt, "The Case for $320,000 Kindergarten Teachers," *New York Times*, July 27, 2010.

3.7 In 541 A.D., an outbreak of bubonic plague hit the Byzantine Empire. Because the plague was spread by flea-infested rats that often lived on ships, ports were hit particularly hard. In some ports, more than 40 percent of the population died. The emperor, Justinian, was concerned that the wages of sailors were rising very rapidly as a result of the plague. In 544 A.D., he placed a ceiling on the wages of sailors. Use a demand and supply graph of the market for sailors to show the effect of the plague on the wages of sailors. Use the same graph to show the effect of Justinian's wage ceiling. Briefly explain what is happening in your graph.

Source: Michael McCormick, *The Origins of the European Economy: Communications and Commerce, A.D., 300–900*, New York: Cambridge University Press, 2001, p. 109.

3.8 **[Related to** Making the Connection**: Veterinarians Fall Victim to Demand and Supply]** If the incomes of veterinarians are falling, why has the number of students enrolling in schools of veterinary medicine in the United States not declined?

---

4 | Explaining Differences in Wages

LEARNING OBJECTIVE: Use demand and supply analysis to explain how compensating differentials, discrimination, and labor unions cause wages to differ.

Summary

The equilibrium wage is determined by the intersection of the labor demand curve and the labor supply curve. Some differences in wages are explained by **compensating differentials**, which are higher wages that compensate workers for unpleasant aspects of a job. Wages can also differ because of **economic discrimination**, which involves paying a person a lower wage or excluding a person from an occupation on the basis of irrelevant characteristics, such as race or gender. **Labor unions** are organizations of employees that have the legal right to bargain with employers about wages and working conditions. Being in a union increases a worker's wages about 10 percent, holding constant other factors, such as the industry the workers are in.

Visit **www.myeconlab.com** to complete these exercises online and get instant feedback.

Review Questions

4.1 What is a compensating differential? Give an example.

4.2 Define *economic discrimination*. Is the fact that one group in the population has higher earnings than other groups evidence of economic discrimination? Briefly explain.

4.3 In what sense do employers who discriminate pay an economic penalty? Is this penalty enough to eliminate discrimination? Briefly explain.

4.4 Is the fraction of U.S. workers in labor unions larger or smaller than in other countries?

Problems and Applications

4.5 Writing on the Baseball Prospectus Web site, Dan Fox argued: "What a player is really worth depends a great deal on the teams that are interested in signing him." Do you agree? Shouldn't a baseball player with a particular level of ability be worth the same to every team? Briefly explain.

Source: Dan Fox, "Schrodinger's Bat," www.baseballprospectus.com, May 17, 2007.

4.6 **[Related to the** Chapter Opener**]** A student remarks: "I don't think the idea of marginal revenue product really helps explain differences in wages. After all, a ticket to a baseball game costs much less than college tuition, yet baseball players are paid much more than college professors." Do you agree with the student's reasoning?

4.7 **[Related to the** Don't Let This Happen to You**]** Joe Morgan is a sportscaster and former baseball player. After he stated that he thought the salaries of Major League Baseball players were justified, a baseball fan wrote the following to Rob Neyer, a sports columnist:

> Mr. Neyer,
> What are your feelings about Joe Morgan's comment that players are justified in being paid what they're being paid? How is it ok for A-Rod [New York Yankees infielder Alex Rodriguez] to earn $115,000 per GAME while my boss works 80 hour weeks and earns $30,000 per year?

How would you answer this fan's questions?

Source: ESPN.com, August 30, 2002.

4.8 Buster Olney, a columnist for ESPN.com, wondered why baseball teams pay the teams' managers and general managers less than they pay most baseball players:

> About two-thirds of the players on the [New York] Mets' roster will make more money than [manager Willie] Randolph; Willie will get somewhere in the neighborhood of half of an average major league salary for 2007. But Randolph's deal is right in line with what other managers are making, and right in the range of what the highest-paid general managers are

making…. I have a hard time believing that Randolph or general manager Omar Minaya will have less impact on the Mets than left-handed reliever Scott Schoeneweis, who will get paid more than either the manager or GM.

Provide an economic explanation of why baseball managers and general managers are generally paid less than baseball players.

Source: Buster Olney, "Managers Low on Pay Scale," ESPN.com, January 25, 2007.

4.9 When Nick Saban agreed to leave his job as head coach of the Miami Dolphins National Football League team to take a job as head football coach at the University of Alabama, he received a salary of $4 million per year for eight years. Ivan Maisel, a columnist for ESPN.com, wondered whether Saban was worth such a large salary: "Is Saban eight times better than the coach who outmaneuvered Bob Stoops of Oklahoma on Monday night? Boise State paid Chris Petersen $500,000 this season—and he still hasn't lost a game." Might Saban still be worth a salary of $4 million per year to Alabama even if he is not "eight times better" than a coach being paid $500,000 at another school? In your answer, be sure to refer to the difference between the marginal product of labor and the marginal revenue product of labor.

Source: Ivan Maisel, "Saban Will Find Crowded Pond in Tuscaloosa," ESPN.com, January 3, 2007.

4.10 **[Related to** Making the Connection: **Technology and the Earnings of "Superstars"]** According to Alan Krueger, an economist at Princeton University, the share of concert ticket revenue received by the top 1 percent of all acts rose from 26 percent in 1982 to 56 percent in 2003. Does this information indicate that the top acts in 2003 must have been much better performers relative to other acts than was the case in 1982? If not, can you think of another explanation?

Source: Eduardo Porter, "More Than Ever, It Pays to Be the Top Executive," *New York Times*, May 25, 2007.

4.11 **[Related to** Making the Connection: **Technology and the Earnings of "Superstars"]** Why are there superstar basketball players but no superstar plumbers?

4.12 **[Related to the** Chapter Opener**]** Sam Goldwyn, a movie producer during Hollywood's Golden Age, once remarked about one of his stars: "We're overpaying him, but he's worth it."

a. In what sense did Goldwyn mean that he was overpaying this star?

b. If he was overpaying the star, why would the star have still been worth it?

4.13 Prior to the early twentieth century, a worker who was injured on the job could collect damages only by suing his employer. To sue successfully, the worker—or his family, if the worker had been killed—had to show that the injury was due to the employer's negligence, that the worker did not know the job was hazardous, and that the worker's own negligence had not contributed to the accident. These lawsuits were difficult for workers to win, and even workers who had been seriously injured on the job often were unable to collect any damages from their employers. Beginning in 1910, most states passed workers' compensation laws that required employers to purchase insurance that

would compensate workers for injuries suffered on the job. A study by Price Fishback, of the University of Arizona, and Shawn Kantor, of the University of California, Merced, shows that after the passage of workers' compensation laws, wages received by workers in the coal and lumber industries fell. Briefly explain why passage of workers' compensation laws would lead to a fall in wages in some industries.

Source: Price V. Fishback and Shawn Everett Kantor, "Did Workers Pay for the Passage of Workers' Compensation Laws?" *Quarterly Journal of Economics*, Vol. 110, No. 3, August 1995, pp. 713–742.

4.14 The following table is similar to Table 2, except that it includes the earnings of Asian males and females. Does the fact that Asian males are the highest-earning group in the table affect the likelihood that economic discrimination is the best explanation for why earnings differ among the groups listed in the table? Briefly explain your argument.

Group	Annual Earnings
Asian males	$60,253
White males	56,247
Asian females	46,371
White females	42,171
Black males	39,816
Black females	35,090
Hispanic males	32,516
Hispanic females	29,508

Source: U.S. Bureau of the Census, Table PINC-01, "Current Population Survey," *2013 Annual Social and Economic Supplement*.

4.15 During the 1970s, many women changed their minds about whether they would leave the labor force after marrying and having children or whether they would be in the labor force most of their adult lives. In 1968, the National Longitudinal Survey asked a representative sample of women aged 14 to 24 whether they expected to be in the labor force at age 35. Twenty-nine percent of white women and 59 percent of black women responded that they expected to be in the labor force at that age. In fact, when these women were 35 years old, 60 percent of those who were married and 80 percent of those who were unmarried were in the labor force. In other words, many more women ended up being in the labor force than expected to be when they were of high school and college age. What effect did this fact have on the earnings of these women? Briefly explain.

Source: Claudia Goldin, *Understanding the Gender Gap: An Economic History of American Women*, New York: Oxford University Press, 1990, p. 155.

4.16 Lawrence Katz, an economist at Harvard, was quoted in a newspaper article as arguing that differences between the incomes of male physicians and female physicians "are largely explained by individual choices." He also noted that discrimination could account for part of the gap "though it isn't clear how much."

a. What did Katz mean by "individual choices"? How can individual choices result in differences between how much men and women are paid?

b. Why is it difficult to estimate how much of the gap between what men and women are paid is due to discrimination?

Source: Josh Mitchell, "Women Notch Progress," *Wall Street Journal*, December 4, 2012.

4.17 **[Related to** Solved Problem 4**]** Use the following graphs to answer the questions:

Market for trash collectors

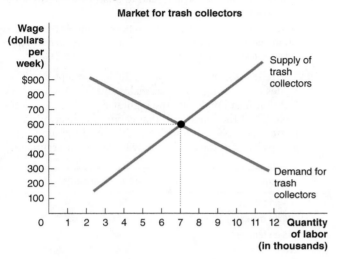

Market for receptionists

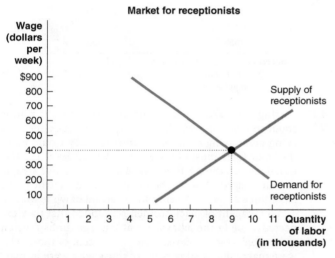

a. What is the equilibrium quantity of trash collectors hired, and what is the equilibrium wage?

b. What is the equilibrium quantity of receptionists hired, and what is the equilibrium wage?

c. Briefly discuss why trash collectors might earn a higher weekly wage than receptionists.

d. Suppose that comparable-worth legislation is passed, and the government requires that trash collectors and receptionists be paid the same wage, $500 per week. Now how many trash collectors will be hired and how many receptionists will be hired?

4.18 **[Related to** Solved Problem 4**]** In most universities, economics professors receive larger salaries than English professors. Suppose that the government requires that from now on, all universities must pay economics professors the same salaries as English professors. Use demand and supply graphs to analyze the effect of this requirement.

4.19 **[Related to** Making the Connection: **Does Greg Have an Easier Time Finding a Job Than Jamal?]** Why might employers be more likely to interview a job applicant with a white-sounding name than an applicant with an African-American–sounding name? Leaving aside legal penalties, will employers who follow this practice incur an economic penalty? Briefly explain.

4.20 According to data from the Bureau of Labor Statistics, the unemployment rate among whites in June 2013 was 6.6 percent, while the unemployment rate among African Americans was 13.7 percent. If a news commentator concluded that economic discrimination is the best explanation for the difference in unemployment rates, would you agree? Briefly explain.

Source: U.S. Department of Labor, Bureau of Labor Statistics, *The Employment Situation—June 2013*, July 5, 2013.

4.21 Daniel Hamermesh is an economist at the University of Texas who has done a great deal of research on labor markets. According to an article in *Forbes*, Hamermesh writes that "below-average-looking men earn 17% less than those considered good-looking, while below-average-looking females earn 12% less than their attractive counterparts." Is this difference in earnings due to economic discrimination? Briefly explain.

Source: Susan Adams, "Does Beauty Really Pay?" *Forbes*, August 30, 2011.

4.22 Anthony Carnevale, director of the Center on Education and the Workforce at Georgetown University, recently noted that even among college graduates, unemployment rates can vary quite a bit. However, Carnevale also found that unemployment rates during 2010 and 2011 "were 9 to 10 percent for noncollege graduates, compared to 4.6 to 4.7 percent for college graduates 25 years or older." What could explain this difference in unemployment rates between college graduates and noncollege graduates?

Source: Gail MarksJarvis, "Costs vs. Benefits of College," *The Dallas Morning News*, June 30, 2013.

---

 5 **Personnel Economics**

LEARNING OBJECTIVE: Discuss the role personnel economics can play in helping firms deal with human resources issues.

Summary

Personnel economics is the application of economic analysis to human resources issues. One insight of personnel economics is that the productivity of workers can often be increased if firms move from straight-time pay to commission or piece-rate pay.

Visit **www.myeconlab.com** to complete these exercises online and get instant feedback.

Review Questions

5.1 What is personnel economics?

5.2 What are the two ways that the productivity of a firm's employees may increase when a firm moves from straight-time pay to commission or piece-rate pay?

5.3 If piece-rate or commission systems of compensating workers have important advantages for firms, why don't more firms use them?

Problems and Applications

5.4 According to a study, the number of jobs in which firms used bonuses, commissions, or piece rates to tie workers' pay to their performance increased from an estimated 30 percent of all jobs in the 1970s to 40 percent in the 1990s. Why would systems that tie workers' pay to how much they produce have become increasingly popular with firms? The same study found that these pay systems were more common in higher-paid jobs than in lower-paid jobs. Briefly explain this result.

Source: Thomas Lemieux, W. Bentley MacLeod, and Daniel Parent, "Performance Pay and Wage Inequality," *Quarterly Journal of Economics*, Vol. 124, No. 1, February 2009, pp. 1–49.

5.5 Many companies that pay workers an hourly wage require some minimum level of acceptable output. Suppose a company that has been using this system decides to switch to a piece-rate system under which workers are compensated on the basis of how much output they produce. Is it likely that workers under a piece-rate system will end up choosing to produce less than the minimum output required under the hourly wage system? Briefly explain.

5.6 In most jobs, the harder you work, the more you earn. Some workers would rather work harder and earn more; others would rather work less hard, even though as a result they earn less. Suppose, though, that all workers at a company fall into the "work harder and earn more" group. Suppose also that the workers all have the same abilities. In these circumstances, would output per worker be the same under an hourly wage compensation system as under a piece-rate system? Briefly explain.

5.7 For years, the Goodyear Tire & Rubber Company compensated its sales force by paying a salesperson a salary plus a bonus, based on the number of tires he or she sold. Eventually, Goodyear made two changes to this policy: (1) The basis for the bonus was changed from the *quantity* of tires sold to the *revenue* from the tires sold; and (2) salespeople were required to get approval from corporate headquarters in Akron, Ohio, before offering to sell tires to customers at reduced prices. Explain why these changes were likely to increase Goodyear's profits.

Source: Timothy Aeppel, "Amid Weak Inflation, Firms Turn Creative to Boost Prices," *Wall Street Journal*, September 18, 2002.

5.8 **[Related to** Making the Connection: **Raising Pay, Productivity, and Profits at Safelite AutoGlass]** What effect did the incentive pay system have on Safelite's marginal cost of installing replacement car windows? If all firms that replace car windows adopted an incentive pay system, what would happen to the price of replacing automobile glass? Who would ultimately benefit?

---

6 | The Markets for Capital and Natural Resources

LEARNING OBJECTIVE: Show how equilibrium prices are determined in the markets for capital and natural resources.

Summary

The approach used to analyze the market for labor can also be used to analyze the markets for other factors of production. In equilibrium, the price of capital is equal to the marginal revenue product of capital, and the price of natural resources is equal to the marginal revenue product of natural resources. The price received by a factor that is in fixed supply is called an **economic rent** (or a **pure rent**). A **monopsony** is a situation in which a firm is the sole buyer of a factor of production. According to the **marginal productivity theory of income distribution**, the distribution of income is determined by the marginal productivity of the factors of production individuals own.

Visit **www.myeconlab.com** to complete these exercises online and get instant feedback.

Review Questions

6.1 In equilibrium, what determines the price of capital? What determines the price of natural resources? What is an economic rent?

6.2 What is a monopsony?

6.3 What is the marginal productivity theory of income distribution?

Problems and Applications

6.4 Adam operates a pin factory. Suppose Adam faces the situation shown in the following table and the cost of renting a machine is $550 per week.

a. Fill in the blanks in the table and determine the profit-maximizing number of machines for Adam to rent. Briefly explain why renting this number of machines is profit maximizing.

b. Draw Adam's demand curve for capital.

Number of Machines	Output of Pins (boxes per week)	Marginal Product of Capital	Product Price (dollars per box)	Total Revenue	Marginal Revenue Product of Capital	Rental Cost per Machine	Additional Profit from Renting One Additional Machine
0	0	___	$100		___	$550	
1	12		100			550	
2	21		100			550	
3	28		100			550	
4	34		100			550	
5	39		100			550	
6	43		100			550	

6.5 Many people have predicted, using a model like the one in panel (b) of Figure 12, that the price of natural resources should rise consistently over time in comparison with the prices of other goods because the demand curve for natural resources is continually shifting to the right, while the supply curve must be shifting to the left as natural resources are used up. However, the relative prices of most natural resources have not been increasing. Draw a graph showing the demand and supply for natural resources that can explain why prices haven't risen even though demand has.

6.6 In 1879, economist Henry George published *Progress and Poverty*, which became one of the best-selling books of the nineteenth century. In this book, George argued that all existing taxes should be replaced with a single tax on land. Tax incidence refers to the actual division of the burden of a tax between buyers and sellers in a market. If land is taxed, how will the burden of the tax be divided between the sellers of land and the buyers of land? Illustrate your answer with a graph of the market for land.

6.7 The total amount of oil in the earth is not increasing. Does this mean that in the market for oil, the supply curve is perfectly inelastic? Briefly explain.

6.8 In a competitive labor market, imposing a minimum wage should reduce the equilibrium level of employment. Will this result still hold if the labor market is a monopsony? Briefly explain.

Glossary

Compensating differentials Higher wages that compensate workers for unpleasant aspects of a job.

Derived demand The demand for a factor of production; it depends on the demand for the good the factor produces.

Economic discrimination Paying a person a lower wage or excluding a person from an occupation on the basis of an irrelevant characteristic such as race or gender.

Economic rent (or **pure rent**) The price of a factor of production that is in fixed supply.

Factors of production Labor, capital, natural resources, and other inputs used to produce goods and services.

Human capital The accumulated knowledge and skills that workers acquire from formal training and education or from life experiences.

Labor union An organization of employees that has a legal right to bargain with employers about wages and working conditions.

Marginal product of labor The additional output a firm produces as a result of hiring one more worker.

Marginal productivity theory of income distribution The theory that the distribution of income is determined by the marginal productivity of the factors of production that individuals own.

Marginal revenue product of labor (*MRP*) The change in a firm's revenue as a result of hiring one more worker.

Monopsony The situation in which a firm is the sole buyer of a factor of production.

Personnel economics The application of economic analysis to human resources issues.

Credits

Credits are listed in the order of appearance.

Photo

Pricing Strategy

From Chapter 16 of *Economics*, Fifth Edition. R. Glenn Hubbard and Anthony Patrick O'Brien. Copyright © 2015 by Pearson Education, Inc.
All rights reserved.

Pricing Strategy

Chapter Outline and Learning Objectives

1 **Pricing Strategy, the Law of One Price, and Arbitrage**
   Define the law of one price and explain the role of arbitrage.

2 **Price Discrimination: Charging Different Prices for the Same Product**
   Explain how a firm can increase its profits through price discrimination.

3 **Other Pricing Strategies**
   Explain how some firms increase their profits by using odd pricing, cost-plus pricing, and two-part tariffs.

Getting into Walt Disney World: One Price Does Not Fit All

When you visit Walt Disney World's Magic Kingdom in Florida, your age, home address, and occupation can determine how much you pay for admission. In 2013, the price for a one-day ticket for an adult was $101.18. The same ticket for a child, aged three to nine, was $94.79. Children under three were free. Students at the University of Central Florida paid $65. Active members of the military paid $98, and were charged $82 for their children aged three to nine. Why does Disney charge so many different prices for the same product?

We can assume that firms charge all consumers the same price for a given product. In reality, many firms charge customers different prices, based on differences in their willingness to pay for the product. Firms often face complicated pricing problems. For example, the Walt Disney Company faces the problem of determining the profit-maximizing prices to charge different groups of consumers for admission to its Disneyland and Walt Disney World theme parks.

In the early 1950s, most amusement parks were collections of unrelated rides, such as roller coasters and Ferris wheels. Walt Disney believed that a theme park, with attractions that emphasized storytelling over thrills, would be more appealing to families than were amusement parks. Disney hired an economist to evaluate the feasibility of such a park. Managers of existing parks gave this advice to the economist: "Tell your boss . . . to stick to what he knows and leave the amusement business to people who know it." Eventually, Disney convinced the ABC television network to provide funding in exchange for his providing them with a weekly television program.

When Disneyland opened in 1955, Disney charged a low price—$1 for adults and $0.50 for children—for admission into the park and charged for tickets to the rides. This system of separate charges for admission and for rides continued until the early 1980s. Today, the Walt Disney Company charges a high price for admission to its theme parks, but once a customer is in the park, the rides are free. In this chapter, we will study some common pricing strategies, and we will see how Disney and other firms use these strategies to increase their profits.

Sources: Disney World prices from www.mousesavers.com, June 27, 2013; Harrison Price, *Walt's Revolution! By the Numbers*, Ripley Entertainment, Inc., 2004, p. 31; and Bruce Gordon and David Mumford, *Disneyland: The Nickel Tour*, Santa Clarita, CA: Camphor Tree Publishers, 2000, pp. 174–175.

Economics in Your Life

Why So Many Prices to See a Movie?

How much do you, as a student, pay to get into a movie theater? Would your parents pay the same amount? What about your grandparents? How about your little brother or sister? Is the price the same in the evening as in the afternoon? Why do you suppose movie theaters charge different prices to different groups of consumers?

If you buy popcorn at the movie theater, you pay the same price as everyone else. Why do you suppose people in certain age groups get a discount on movie admission but not on popcorn? As you read this chapter, try to answer these questions. You can check your answers against those we provide at the end of this chapter.

R ecall that entrepreneurs continually seek out economic profit. Using pricing strategies is one way firms can attempt to increase their economic profit. One of these strategies, called *price discrimination*, involves firms setting different prices for the same good or service, as Disney does when setting admission prices at Walt Disney World. In this chapter, we will see how a firm can increase its profit by charging a higher price to consumers who value the good more and a lower price to consumers who value the good less.

We will also analyze the widely used strategies of *odd pricing* and *cost-plus pricing*. Finally, we will analyze situations in which firms are able to charge consumers one price for the right to buy a good and a second price for each unit of the good purchased. Disney's old pricing scheme of charging for admission to Disney World and also charging for each ride is an example of a strategy economists call a *two-part tariff*.

1 LEARNING OBJECTIVE

Define the law of one price and explain the role of arbitrage.

Pricing Strategy, the Law of One Price, and Arbitrage

We saw in the chapter opener that sometimes firms can charge different prices for the same good. In fact, many firms rely on economic analysis to practice *price discrimination* by charging higher prices to some customers and lower prices to others. Some firms practice a sophisticated form of price discrimination in which they use technology to gather information on the preferences of consumers and their responsiveness to changes in prices. Managers use the information to rapidly adjust the prices of their goods and services. This practice of rapidly adjusting prices, called *yield management*, has been particularly important to airlines and hotels. There are limits, though, to the ability of firms to charge different prices for the same product. The key limit is the possibility in some circumstances that consumers who can buy a good at a low price will resell it to consumers who would otherwise have to buy at a high price.

Arbitrage

According to the *law of one price*, identical products should sell for the same price everywhere. Let's explore why the law of one price usually holds true. Suppose that an Apple iPad sells for $499 in stores in Atlanta and for $429 in stores in San Francisco. Anyone who lives in San Francisco could buy iPads for $429 and resell them for $499 in Atlanta. They could sell them on eBay or Craigslist or ship them to someone they know in Atlanta who could sell them in local flea markets. Buying a product in one market at a low price and reselling it in another market at a high price is called *arbitrage*. The profits received from engaging in arbitrage are called *arbitrage profits*.

As people take advantage of the price difference to earn arbitrage profits, the supply of iPads in Atlanta will increase and the price of iPads in Atlanta will decline. At the same time, the supply of iPads in San Francisco will decrease and the price of iPads in San Francisco will rise. Eventually, the arbitrage process will eliminate most, but not all, of the price difference. Some price difference will remain because sellers must pay to list iPads on eBay or to ship them to Atlanta. The costs of carrying out a transaction—by, for example, listing items on eBay and shipping them across the country—are called **transactions costs**. The law of one price holds exactly *only if transactions costs are zero*. As we will soon see, in cases in which it is impossible to resell a product, the law of one price will not hold, and firms will be able to practice price discrimination. Apart from this important qualification, we expect that arbitrage will result in a product selling for the same price everywhere.

Transactions costs The costs in time and other resources that parties incur in the process of agreeing to and carrying out an exchange of goods or services.

Solved Problem 1

Is Arbitrage Just a Rip-Off?

People are often suspicious of arbitrage. Buying something at a low price and reselling it at a high price exploits the person buying at the high price. Or does it? Is this view correct? If so, do the auctions on eBay serve any useful economic purpose?

Solving the Problem

Step 1: **Review the chapter material.** This problem is about arbitrage, so you may want to review the section "Arbitrage."

Step 2: **Use the discussion of arbitrage to answer the questions.** Many of the goods on eBay have been bought at low prices and are being resold at higher prices. In fact, some people supplement their incomes by buying collectibles and other goods at garage sales and reselling them on eBay. Does eBay serve a useful economic purpose? Economists would say that it does. Consider the case of Lou, who buys collectible movie posters and resells them on eBay. Suppose Lou buys a *Guardians of the Galaxy* poster at a garage sale for $30 and resells it on eBay for $60. Both the person who sold to Lou at the garage sale and the person who bought from him on eBay must have been made better off by the deals *or they would not have made them*. Lou has performed the useful service of locating the poster and making it available for sale on eBay. In carrying out this service, Lou has incurred costs, including the opportunity cost of his time spent searching garage sales, the opportunity cost of the funds he has tied up in posters he has purchased but not yet sold, and the cost of the fees eBay charges him. It is easy to sell goods on eBay, so over time, competition among Lou and other movie poster dealers should cause the difference between the prices of posters sold at garage sales and the prices on eBay to shrink until they are equal to the dealers' costs of reselling the posters, including the opportunity cost of their time.

Your Turn: For more practice, do related problems 1.5 and 1.6 at the end of this chapter.

Why Don't All Firms Charge the Same Price?

The law of one price may appear to be violated even where transactions costs are zero and a product can be resold. For example, different Web sites may sell what seem to be identical products for different prices. We can resolve this apparent contradiction if we look more closely at what "product" an Internet Web site—or another business— actually offers for sale.

Suppose you want to buy a copy of the Blu-ray disc for *The Amazing Spider-Man 2*. You use Google, Pricegrabber.com, or some other search engine to compare prices at various Web sites. You get the results shown in Table 1.

Because they have the lowest prices, would you automatically buy from one of the last two sites listed rather than from Amazon.com or Wal-Mart.com? We can think about why you might not. Consider what these sites offer for sale. Amazon.com is not just offering *The Amazing Spider-Man 2*; it is offering *The Amazing Spider-Man 2*

Product: *The Amazing Spider-Man 2* Blu-ray Disc

Company	Price
Amazon.com	$24.99
Wal-Mart.com	24.98
WaitForeverForYourOrder.com	22.50
JustStartedinBusinessLastWednesday.com	21.25

delivered quickly to your home, well packaged so it's not damaged in the mail, and charged to your credit card using a secure method that keeps your credit card number safe from computer hackers. As we have discussed, firms differentiate the products they sell in many ways. One way is by providing faster and more reliable delivery than competitors.

Amazon.com and Wal-Mart.com have built reputations for fast and reliable service. New Internet sellers who lack that reputation will have to differentiate their products on the basis of price, as the two fictitious firms listed in the table have done. So, the difference in the prices of products offered on Web sites does *not* violate the law of one price. A Blu-ray disc Amazon.com offers for sale is not the same product as a Blu-ray disc JustStartedinBusinessLastWednesday.com offers for sale.

Explain how a firm can increase its profits through price discrimination.

Price discrimination Charging different prices to different customers for the same product when the price differences are not due to differences in cost.

Price Discrimination: Charging Different Prices for the Same Product

We saw at the beginning of this chapter that the Walt Disney Company charges different prices for the same product: admission to Disney World. Charging different prices to different customers for the same good or service when the price differences are not due to differences in cost is called **price discrimination**. But doesn't price discrimination contradict the law of one price? Why doesn't the possibility of arbitrage profits lead people to buy at the low price and resell at the high price?

Don't Let This Happen to You

Don't Confuse Price Discrimination with Other Types of Discrimination

Don't confuse price discrimination with discrimination based on race or gender. Discriminating on the basis of arbitrary characteristics, such as race or gender, is illegal under the civil rights laws. Price discrimination is legal because it involves charging people different prices on the basis of their willingness to pay rather than on the basis of arbitrary characteristics. There is a gray area, however, when companies charge different prices on the basis of gender. For example, insurance companies usually charge women lower prices than men for automobile insurance. The courts have ruled that this is not illegal discrimination under the civil rights laws because women, on average, have better driving records than men. Because the costs of insuring men are higher than the costs of insuring women, insurance companies are allowed to charge men higher prices. Notice that this is not actually price discrimination as we have defined it here. Price discrimination involves charging different prices for the same product *where the price differences are not due to differences in cost.*

Your Turn: Test your understanding by doing related problem 2.10 at the end of this chapter.

The Requirements for Successful Price Discrimination

A successful strategy of price discrimination has three requirements:

1. A firm must possess market power.

2. Some consumers must have a greater willingness to pay for the product than other consumers, and the firm must be able to know which consumers have a greater willingness to pay.

3. The firm must be able to divide up—or *segment*—the market for the product so that consumers who buy the product at a low price are not able to resell it at a high price. In other words, price discrimination will not work if arbitrage is possible.

A firm selling in a perfectly competitive market cannot practice price discrimination because it can only charge the market price. Because most firms do not sell in perfectly competitive markets, they have market power and can set the price of the good they sell. Many firms may also be able to determine that some consumers have a greater willingness to pay for a product than others. However, the third requirement—that markets be segmented so that consumers buying at a low price will not be able to resell the product—can be difficult to fulfill. For example, some people really love Big Macs and would be willing to pay $10 rather than do without one. Other people would not be willing to pay a penny more than $1 for a Big Mac. Even if McDonald's could identify differences in the willingness of consumers to pay for Big Macs, it would not be able to charge them different prices. Suppose McDonald's knows that Joe is willing to pay $10, whereas Jill will pay only $1. If McDonald's tries to charge Joe $10, he will just have Jill buy a Big Mac for him.

Only firms that can keep consumers from reselling a product are able to practice price discrimination. Because buyers cannot resell the product, the law of one price does not hold. For example, movie theaters know that many people are willing to pay more to see a movie in the evening than during the afternoon. As a result, theaters usually charge higher prices for tickets to evening showings than for tickets to afternoon showings. They keep these markets separate by making the tickets to afternoon showings a different color or by having the time printed on them and by having a ticket taker examine the tickets. That practice makes it difficult for someone to buy a lower-priced ticket in the afternoon and use the ticket to gain admission to an evening showing.

Figure 1 illustrates how the owners of movie theaters use price discrimination to increase their profits. The marginal cost to the movie theater owner from another person attending a showing is very small: a little more wear on a theater seat and a few more kernels of popcorn to be swept from the floor. We can assume that the marginal cost curve has a U shape. In Figure 1, we assume for simplicity that marginal cost is a constant $0.50, shown as a horizontal line. Panel (a) shows the demand for afternoon showings. In this segment of its market, the theater should maximize profit by selling the quantity of tickets for which marginal revenue equals marginal cost, or 450 tickets. We know from the demand curve that the theater can sell 450 tickets at a price of $7.25 per ticket. Panel (b) shows the demand for evening showings. Notice that charging $7.25 per ticket would *not* be profit maximizing in this market. At a price of $7.25, the theater sells 850 tickets, which is 225 more tickets than the profit-maximizing quantity of 625. By charging $7.25 for tickets to afternoon showings and $9.75 for tickets to evening showings, the theater has maximized profit.

Figure 1 also illustrates another important point about price discrimination: When firms can practice price discrimination, they will charge customers who are less sensitive to price—those whose demand for the product is *less elastic*—a higher price and charge customers who are more sensitive to price—those whose demand is *more elastic*—a lower price. In this case, the demand for tickets to evening showings is less elastic, so the price charged is higher, and the demand for tickets to afternoon showings is more elastic, so the price charged is lower.

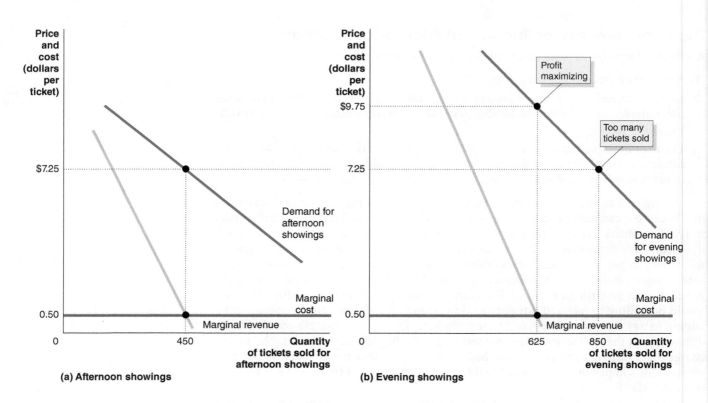

Figure 1 Price Discrimination by a Movie Theater

Fewer people want to go to the movies in the afternoon than in the evening. In panel (a), the profit-maximizing price for a ticket to an afternoon showing is $7.25. Charging this same price for evening showings would not be profit maximizing, as

panel (b) shows. At a price of $7.25, the theater would sell 850 tickets to evening showings, which is more than the profit-maximizing number of 625 tickets. To maximize profit, the theater should charge $9.75 for tickets to evening showings.

Solved Problem 2

How Apple Uses Price Discrimination to Increase Profits

During the summer of 2013, Apple was selling MacBook Pro laptop computers with 13-inch retina displays on its Web site and in its retail stores for $1,499. But college students and faculty members could buy the same laptop from Apple

for $1,399. Why would Apple charge different prices for the same laptop, depending on whether the buyer is an education customer? Draw two graphs to illustrate your answers: one for the general public and one for education customers.

Solving the Problem

Step 1: **Review the chapter material.** This problem is about using price discrimination to increase profits, so you may want to review the section "Price Discrimination: Charging Different Prices for the Same Product."

Step 2: **Explain why charging different prices to education customers and other customers will increase Apple's profit.** It makes sense for Apple to charge different prices if education customers have a different price elasticity of demand than do other customers. In that case, Apple will charge the market segment with the less elastic demand a higher price and the market segment with the more elastic demand a lower price. Because Apple is charging education customers the lower price, they must have a more elastic demand than do other customers.

Step 3: **Draw a graph to illustrate your answer.** Your graphs should look like the following ones, where we have chosen hypothetical quantities to illustrate the ideas. As in the case of movie theaters, you can assume for simplicity that marginal cost is constant; in the graph we assume that marginal cost is $400.

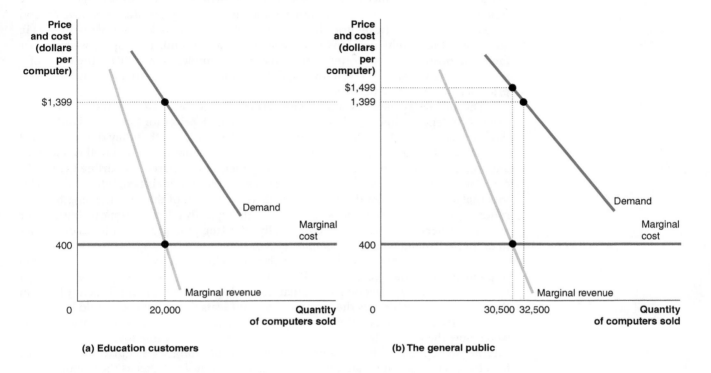

(a) Education customers

(b) The general public

Panel (a) shows that in the education customers segment of the market, marginal revenue equals marginal cost at 20,000 laptops sold. Therefore, Apple should charge a price of $1,399 to maximize profits. But if Apple also charges $1,399 in the general public segment of the market, shown in panel (b), it will sell 32,500 laptops, which is more than the profit-maximizing quantity. By charging $1,499 to the general public, Apple will sell 30,500 laptops, the profit-maximizing quantity. We have shown that Apple maximizes its profits by charging education customers a lower price than it charges the general public. Notice that although the demand curve in panel (a) is more elastic, it is also steeper. This reminds us of the important point that elasticity is different from slope.

Your Turn: For more practice, do problems 2.11, 2.12, and 2.13 at the end of this chapter.

Airlines: The Kings of Price Discrimination

Airline seats are a perishable product. Once a plane has taken off from Chicago for Los Angeles, any seat that has not been sold on that particular flight will never be sold. In addition, the marginal cost of flying one additional passenger is low. As a result, airlines have a strong incentive to manage prices to fill as many seats as possible on each flight.

Airlines divide their customers into two main categories: business travelers and leisure travelers. Business travelers often have inflexible schedules, can't commit until the last minute to travel on a particular day, and, most importantly, are not very sensitive to changes in price. The opposite is true for leisure travelers: They are flexible about when they travel, willing to buy their tickets well in advance, and sensitive to changes in price. Based on what we discussed earlier in this chapter, you can see that airlines will maximize profits by charging business travelers higher ticket prices than leisure travelers, but they need to determine who is a business traveler and who is a leisure traveler. Some airlines do this by requiring people who want to buy a ticket at the leisure price to buy 14 days in advance and to stay at their destination over a Saturday night. Anyone unable to meet these requirements must pay a much higher price. Business travelers end up paying the higher ticket price because they often cannot make their plans 14 days in advance of their flight and don't want to stay over a weekend. The gap between leisure fares and business fares is often substantial. For example, in mid-2013, the price of a leisure-fare ticket between New York and San Francisco on U.S. Airways was $460. The price of a business-fare ticket was $1,016.

The airlines go well beyond a single leisure fare and a single business fare in their pricing strategies. Although they ordinarily charge high prices for tickets sold only a few days in advance, airlines are willing to reduce prices for seats that they doubt they will be able to sell at current prices. Since the late 1980s, airlines have employed economists and mathematicians to construct computer models of the market for airline tickets. To calculate a suggested price each day for each seat, these models take into account factors that affect the demand for tickets, such as the season of the year, the length of the route, the day of the week, and whether the flight typically attracts primarily business or leisure travelers. This practice of continually adjusting prices to take into account fluctuations in demand is called *yield management*.

Since the late 1990s, Internet sites such as Priceline.com have helped the airlines to implement yield management. On Priceline.com, buyers commit to paying a price of their choosing for a ticket on a particular day and agree that they will fly at any time on that day. This gives airlines the opportunity to fill seats that otherwise would have gone empty, particularly on late-night or early-morning flights, even though the price may be well below the normal leisure fare. In 2001, several airlines came together to form the Internet site Orbitz, which became another means of filling seats at discount prices. In fact, the chance that you paid the same price for your airline ticket as the person sitting next to you has become quite small. Figure 2 shows an actual United Air Lines flight from Chicago to Los Angeles. The 33 passengers on the flight paid 27 different prices for their tickets, including one passenger who used frequent flyer miles to obtain a free ticket.

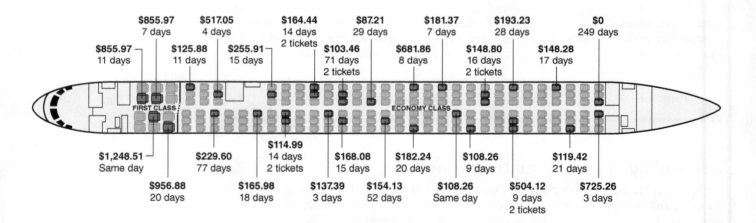

Figure 2   **33 Customers and 27 Different Prices**

To fill as many seats on a flight as possible, airlines charge many different ticket prices. The 33 passengers on this United Air Lines flight from Chicago to Los Angeles paid 27 different prices for their tickets, including one passenger who used frequent flyer miles to obtain a free ticket. The first number in the figure is the price paid for the ticket; the second number is the number of days in advance that the customer purchased the ticket.

How Colleges Use Yield Management

Traditionally, colleges have based financial aid decisions only on the incomes of prospective students. In recent years, however, many colleges have started using yield management techniques, first developed for the airlines, to determine the amount of financial aid they offer different students. Colleges typically use a name such as *financial aid engineering* or *student enrollment management* rather than yield management to describe what they are doing. There is an important difference between the airlines and colleges: Colleges are interested not just in maximizing the revenue they receive from student tuition but also in increasing the academic quality of the students who enroll. As one newspaper article puts it, many colleges will "offer merit scholarships to attract smart students whose grades and test scores will increase their academic profile."

The "price" a college charges equals the full tuition minus any financial aid it provides students. When colleges use yield management techniques, they increase financial aid offers to students who are likely to be more price sensitive, and they reduce financial aid offers to students who are likely to be less price sensitive. As Stanford economist Caroline Hoxby puts it: "Universities are trying to find the people whose decisions will be changed by these [financial aid] grants." Some of the factors colleges use to judge how sensitive students are likely to be to price include whether they applied for early admission, whether they came for an on-campus interview, their intended major, their home state, and the level of their family's income. William F. Elliott, vice president for enrollment management at Carnegie Mellon University, advises: "If finances are a concern, you shouldn't be applying any place [for] early decision" because you are less likely to receive a large financial aid offer.

Many students (and their parents) are critical of colleges that use yield management techniques in allocating financial aid. Some colleges, such as those in the Ivy League, have large enough endowments to meet all of their students' financial aid needs, so they don't practice yield management. Less well-endowed colleges defend the practice on the grounds that it allows them to recruit the best students at a lower cost in financial aid.

Some colleges use yield management techniques to determine financial aid.

Sources: Paul Sullivan, "College Admission Roulette: Ask for Financial Aid, or Not?" *New York Times*, March 1, 2013; Jacques Steinberg, "Early Signs That College Yields Did Not Change Dramatically," *New York Times*, May 8, 2009; and Jane J. Kim and Anjali Athavaley, "Colleges Seek to Address Affordability," *Wall Street Journal*, May 3, 2007; Albert B. Crenshaw, "Price Wars on Campus: Colleges Use Discounts to Draw Best Mix of Top Students, Paying Customers," *Washington Post*, October 15, 2002 .

Your Turn: Test your understanding by doing related problem 2.14 at the end of this chapter.

Perfect Price Discrimination

If a firm knew every consumer's willingness to pay—and could keep consumers who bought a product at a low price from reselling it—the firm could charge every consumer a different price. In this case of *perfect price discrimination*—also known as *first-degree price discrimination*—each consumer would have to pay a price equal to the consumer's willingness to pay and, therefore, would receive no consumer surplus. To see why, remember that consumer surplus is the difference between the highest price a consumer is willing to pay for a product and the price the consumer actually pays. But if the price the consumer pays is the maximum the consumer would be willing to pay, there is no consumer surplus.

Figure 3 shows the effects of perfect price discrimination. To simplify the discussion, we assume that the firm is a monopoly and that it has constant marginal and average total costs. Panel (a) shows the case of a monopolist who cannot practice

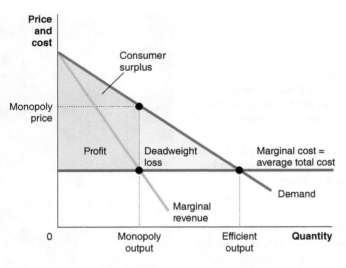

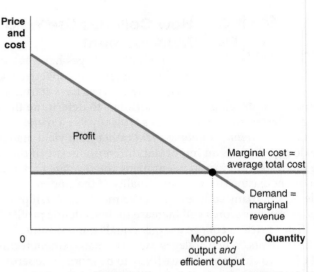

(a) A monopolist who cannot practice price discrimination

(b) A monopolist practicing perfect price discrimination

Figure 3 **Perfect Price Discrimination**

Panel (a) shows the case of a monopolist who cannot practice price discrimination and, therefore, can charge only a single price for its product. The graph shows that to maximize profit, the monopolist will produce the level of output where marginal revenue equals marginal cost. The resulting profit is shown by the area of the green rectangle. Given the monopoly price, the amount of consumer surplus in this market is shown by the area of the blue triangle. The economically efficient level of output occurs where price equals marginal cost. Because the monopolist stops production at a level of output where price is above marginal cost, there is a deadweight loss equal to the area of the yellow triangle. In panel (b), the monopolist is able to practice perfect price discrimination by charging a different price to each consumer. The result is to convert both the consumer surplus *and* the deadweight loss from panel (a) into profit.

price discrimination and, therefore, can charge only a single price for its product. The monopolist maximizes profit by producing the level of output where marginal revenue equals marginal cost. Recall that the economically efficient level of output occurs where price is equal to marginal cost, which is the level of output in a perfectly competitive market. Because the monopolist produces where price is greater than marginal cost, it causes a loss of economic efficiency equal to the area of the deadweight loss triangle in the figure.

Panel (b) shows the situation of a monopolist practicing perfect price discrimination. Because the firm can charge each consumer the maximum each consumer is willing to pay, its marginal revenue from selling one more unit is equal to the price of that unit. Therefore, the monopolist's marginal revenue curve becomes equal to its demand curve, and the firm will continue to produce up to the point where price is equal to marginal cost. It may seem like a paradox, but the ability to practice perfect price discrimination causes the monopolist to produce the efficient level of output. By doing so, the monopolist converts the consumer surplus *and* the deadweight loss in panel (a) into profits. In both panel (a) and panel (b), the profit shown is also producer surplus.

Even though the result in panel (b) is more economically efficient than the result in panel (a), consumers clearly are worse off because the amount of consumer surplus has been reduced to zero. We probably will never see a case of perfect price discrimination in the real world because firms typically do not know how much each consumer is willing to pay and, therefore, cannot charge each consumer a different price. Still, this extreme case helps us to see the two key results of price discrimination:

1. Profits increase.

2. Consumer surplus decreases.

Perfect price discrimination improves economic efficiency. Can we also say that this will be the case if price discrimination is less than perfect? Often, less-than-perfect price discrimination will improve economic efficiency. But under certain circumstances, it may actually reduce economic efficiency, so we can't draw a general conclusion.

Price Discrimination across Time

Firms are sometimes able to engage in price discrimination over time. With this strategy, firms charge a higher price for a product when it is first introduced and a lower price later. Some consumers are *early adopters* who will pay a high price to be among the first to own certain new products. This pattern helps explain why DVD players, Blu-ray players, digital cameras, and flat-screen plasma televisions all sold for very high prices when they were first introduced. After the demand of the early adopters was satisfied, the companies reduced prices to attract more price-sensitive customers. For example, the price of DVD players dropped by 95 percent within five years of their introduction. Some of the price reductions over time for these products were also due to falling costs, as companies took advantage of economies of scale, but some represented price discrimination across time.

Book publishers routinely use price discrimination across time to increase profits. Hardcover editions of novels have much higher prices and are published months before paperback editions. For example, the hardcover edition of John Grisham's novel *The Racketeer* was published in October 2012 at a price of $28.95. The paperback edition was published in August 2013 for $9.99. Although this difference in price might seem to reflect the higher costs of producing hardcover books, in fact, it does not. The marginal cost of printing another copy of the hardcover edition is about $1.50. The marginal cost of printing another copy of the paperback edition is only slightly less, about $1.25. So, the difference in price between the hardcover and paperback editions is explained primarily by differences in demand. John Grisham's most devoted fans want to read his next book at the earliest possible moment and are not very sensitive to price. Many casual readers are also interested in Grisham's books but will read something else if the price of Grisham's latest book is too high.

As Figure 4 shows, a publisher will maximize profit by segmenting the market—in this case, across time—and by charging a higher price to the less elastic market segment and a lower price to the more elastic segment. (This example is similar to our earlier analysis of movie tickets in Figure 1.) If the publisher had skipped the hardcover and issued only the paperback version at a price of $9.99 when the book was first published in October, its revenue would have dropped by the number of readers who bought the hardcover edition multiplied by the difference in price between the hardcover and paperback editions, or 500,000 × ($28.95 − $9.99) = $9,480,000.

Can Price Discrimination Be Illegal?

Price discrimination may be illegal if its effect is to reduce competition in an industry. In 1936, Congress passed the Robinson–Patman Act, which outlawed price discrimination that reduced competition. The act also contained language that could be interpreted as making illegal *all* price discrimination not based on differences in cost. In the 1960s, the Federal Trade Commission sued Borden, Inc., under this act because Borden was selling the same evaporated milk for two different prices. Cans with the Borden label were sold for a high price, and cans the company sold to supermarkets to be repackaged as the supermarkets' private brands were sold for a much lower price. The courts ultimately ruled that Borden had not violated the law because the price differences increased, rather than reduced, competition in the market for evaporated milk. In recent years, the courts have interpreted the Robinson–Patman Act narrowly, allowing firms to use the types of price discrimination described in this chapter.

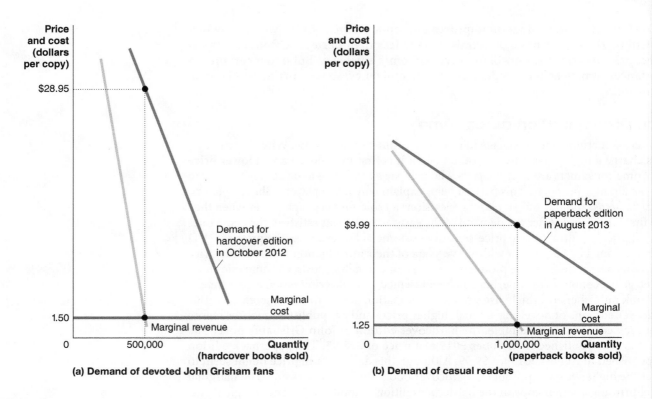

(a) Demand of devoted John Grisham fans

(b) Demand of casual readers

Figure 4 | **Price Discrimination across Time**

Publishers issue most novels in hardcover editions at high prices to satisfy the demand of the novelists' most devoted fans. Later, publishers issue paperback editions at much lower prices to capture sales from casual readers. In panel (a), with a marginal cost of $1.50 per copy for a hardcover edition, the profit-maximizing level of output is 500,000 copies, which can be sold at a price of $28.95. In panel (b), the more elastic demand of casual readers and the slightly lower marginal cost result in a profit-maximizing output of 1,000,000 for the paperback edition, which can be sold at a price of $9.99.

Making
the
Connection

The Internet Leaves You Open to Price Discrimination

Have you ever used Google or Pricegrabber.com to search for the best price for a book, a computer, or an airline ticket? Although the Internet can help you compare prices among different Web sites, it can also be a way for some sellers to price discriminate. When you log on to a Web site, its servers can gather important information about you, including your location—which can be determined from the address of your Internet Service Provider (ISP)—and your browsing history. If the site already has your e-mail address, it may be able to use an Internet data firm to learn facts about you, including your age, race, gender, and income.

Reporters for the *Wall Street Journal* performed an experiment by logging on to the Web site of Staples, the office supply store, from computers in many different zip codes. They found that the Staples Web site displayed different prices for several items based on the zip code of the person who logged on to the site. For example, some people saw a price of $15.79 for a Swingline stapler, while other people saw a price of $14.29 for the same stapler. Similarly, some people saw a price of $28.49 for a 12-pack of Bic roller ball pens, while other people saw a price of $25.99. From the analysis in this chapter, we know that Staples was attempting to use the information it had gathered to estimate the price elasticities of demand of people shopping on its site. Those people Staples believed to have a low price elasticity of demand would see the high price for goods, and those Staples believed to have a high price elasticity of demand would see the low price. Staples managers declined to explain their pricing strategy, so the reporters did a statistical analysis of the characteristics of the zip codes. The most important characteristic turned out to be whether a zip code was within 20 miles of an OfficeMax or Office Depot store, which are Staples's main competitors. People living in zip codes close to a rival store were likely to see the low price, and people in zip codes far away from a rival store were likely to see the high price.

A number of firms in addition to Staples use this pricing strategy. Is the strategy an effective way of increasing profits? In the case of Staples, the firm was able to gather only limited information on potential buyers, so it was unable to effectively price discriminate. For example, the *Wall Street Journal* reporters found that the zip codes seeing the higher-priced stapler had lower average income than the

The price of this stapler may change depending on the consumer's zip code.

zip codes seeing the lower-priced stapler, even though people with lower incomes might be expected to be more sensitive to price. More generally, Web sites using personal information to price discriminate run the risk of upsetting consumers. For instance, when told of Staples's price strategy, one person who had used the firm's Web site asked: "How can they get away with that?" For a brief time, Amazon varied prices on its site depending on a shopper's buying history. One customer saw a DVD price of $26.24 when he first logged on to the site. After deleting the "cookies" in his browser, so that he appeared to Amazon's servers to be a new customer, the price of the DVD dropped to $22.74. Widespread complaints about this pricing strategy caused Amazon to quickly drop it.

As Web sites become more sophisticated in gathering information about shoppers, they will have a greater ability to price discriminate. Whether negative reactions from consumers will cause sites to avoid this pricing strategy remains to be seen.

Sources: Jennifer Valentino-Devries, Jeremy Singer-Vine, and Ashkan Soltani, "Websites Vary Prices, Deals Based on Users' Information," *Wall Street Journal*, December 24, 2012; Jennifer Valentino-Devries and Jeremy Singer-Vine, "They Know What You're Shopping For," *Wall Street Journal*, December 7, 2012; and Anita Ramasastry, "Web Sites Change Prices Based on Customers' Habits," www.cnn.com, June 24, 2005.

Your Turn: Test your understanding by doing related problem 2.16 at the end of this chapter.

Other Pricing Strategies

3 LEARNING OBJECTIVE

Explain how some firms increase their profits by using odd pricing, cost-plus pricing, and two-part tariffs.

In addition to price discrimination, firms use many other pricing strategies, depending on the nature of their products, the level of competition in their markets, and the characteristics of their customers. In this section, we consider three important strategies: odd pricing, cost-plus pricing, and two-part tariffs.

Odd Pricing: Why Is the Price $2.99 Instead of $3.00?

Many firms use *odd pricing*—for example, charging $4.95 instead of $5.00, or $199 instead of $200. Surveys show that 80 percent to 90 percent of the products sold in supermarkets have prices ending in "9" or "5" rather than "0." Odd pricing has a long history. In the early nineteenth century, most goods in the United States were sold in general stores and did not have fixed prices. Instead, prices were often determined by haggling, much as prices of new cars are often determined today by haggling on dealers' lots. Later in the nineteenth century, when most products began to sell for a fixed price, odd pricing became popular.

There are different explanations for the origin of odd pricing. One explanation is that it began because goods imported from Great Britain had a reputation for high quality. When the prices of British goods in British currency—the pound—were translated into U.S. dollars, the result was an odd price. Because customers connected odd prices with high-quality goods, even sellers of domestic goods charged odd prices. Another explanation is that odd pricing began as an attempt to guard against employee theft. An odd price forced an employee to give the customer change, which reduced the likelihood that the employee would simply pocket the customer's money without recording the sale.

Whatever the origins of odd pricing, why do firms still use it today? The most obvious answer is that an odd price, say $9.99, seems somehow significantly—more than a penny—cheaper than $10.00. But do consumers really have this illusion? To find out, three market researchers conducted a study. We have seen that demand curves can be estimated statistically. If consumers have the illusion that $9.99 is significantly cheaper than $10.00, they will demand a greater quantity of goods at $9.99—and other odd prices—than the estimated demand curve predicts. The researchers surveyed consumers about their willingness to purchase six different products—ranging from a block of cheese to an electric blender—at a series of prices. Ten of the prices were either odd cent prices—99 cents or 95 cents—or odd dollar prices—$95 or $99. Nine of these 10 odd prices resulted in an odd-price effect, with the quantity demanded being greater than predicted using the estimated demand curve. The study was not conclusive because it relied on surveys rather than on observing actual purchasing behavior and because it used only a small group of products, but the study does provide some evidence that using odd prices makes economic sense.

Another study carried out in the 1990s used mail-order catalogs for women's clothing. With the cooperation of the clothing firm, some women were mailed catalogs with even dollar prices and other women received catalogs with prices ending in 99 cents. The women receiving the catalogs with prices ending in 99 cents bought 8 percent more clothes than the women receiving catalogs with even dollar prices.

Many firms have begun to use sales strategies that rely on insights from *behavioral economics*, which is the study of situations in which people make choices that do not appear to be economically rational. Odd pricing is an old strategy that is consistent with the modern analysis of behavioral economics.

Why Do McDonald's and Other Firms Use Cost-Plus Pricing?

Many firms use *cost-plus pricing*, which involves adding a percentage *markup* to average total cost. With this pricing strategy, the firm first calculates average total cost at a particular level of production, usually equal to the firm's expected sales. The firm then applies a percentage markup, say 30 percent, to the estimated average total cost to arrive at the price. For example, if average total cost is $100 and the percentage markup is 30 percent, the price will be $130. For a firm selling multiple products, the markup is intended to cover all costs, including those that the firm cannot assign to any particular product. Most firms have costs that are difficult to assign to one particular product. For example, the work performed by the employees in the accounting and finance departments at McDonald's applies to all of McDonald's products and can't be assigned directly to Big Macs or Happy Meals.

Making the Connection

Cost-Plus Pricing in the Publishing Industry

Book publishing companies incur substantial costs for editing, designing, marketing, and warehousing books. These costs are difficult to assign directly to any particular book. Most publishers arrive at a price for a book by applying a markup to their production costs, which are usually divided into plant costs and manufacturing costs. Plant costs include typesetting the manuscript and preparing graphics or artwork for printing. Manufacturing costs include the costs of printing, paper, and binding the book.

Consider the following example for the hypothetical new book by Adam Smith, *How to Succeed at Economics without Really Trying*. We will assume that the book is 250 pages long, the publisher expects to sell 5,000 copies, and plant and manufacturing costs are as given in the following table:

Plant Costs		
	Typesetting	$3,500
	Other plant costs	2,000
Manufacturing Costs		
	Printing	$5,750
	Paper	6,250
	Binding	5,000
Total Production Cost		
		$22,500

With total production cost of $22,500 and production of 5,000 books, the per-unit production cost is $22,500/5,000 = $4.50. Many publishers multiply the unit production cost number by 7 or 8 to arrive at the retail price they will charge customers in bookstores. In this case, multiplying by 7 results in a price of $31.50 for the book. The markup seems quite high, but publishers typically sell books to bookstores at a 40 percent discount. Although a customer in a bookstore will pay $31.50 for the book—or less, of course, if it is purchased from a bookseller that discounts the retail price—the publisher receives only $18.90. The difference between the $18.90 received from the bookstore and the $4.50 production cost equals the cost of editing, marketing, warehousing, paying a royalty to the author of the book, and all other costs, including the opportunity cost of the investment in the firm by its owners, plus any economic profit the owners receive.

Source: Beth Luey, *Handbook for Academic Authors*, 5th ed., New York: Cambridge University Press, 2010.

Your Turn: Test your understanding by doing related problem 3.8 at the end of this chapter.

We have seen that firms maximize profit by producing the quantity where marginal revenue equals marginal cost and charging a price that will cause consumers to buy that quantity. The cost-plus approach doesn't appear to maximize profit unless the cost-plus price turns out to be the same as the price that will cause the marginal revenue earned on the last unit to equal the unit's marginal cost. Economists have two views of cost-plus pricing. One is that cost-plus pricing is simply a mistake that firms should avoid. The other view is that cost-plus pricing is a good way to come close to the profit-maximizing price when either marginal revenue or marginal cost is difficult to calculate.

Small firms often like cost-plus pricing because it is easy to use. Unfortunately, these firms can fall into the trap of mechanically applying a cost-plus pricing rule, which may result in charging prices that do not maximize profit. The most obvious problems with cost-plus pricing are that it ignores demand and focuses on average total cost rather than marginal cost. If a firm's marginal cost is significantly different from its average total cost at its current level of production, cost-plus pricing is unlikely to maximize profit.

Despite these problems, cost-plus pricing is used by some large firms that have the knowledge and resources to devise a better method of pricing if cost-plus pricing fails to maximize profit. Economists conclude that using cost-plus pricing may be the best way to determine the optimal price in two situations:

1. When marginal cost and average total cost are roughly equal

2. When a firm has difficulty estimating its demand curve

In fact, most large firms that use cost-plus pricing do not just mechanically apply a markup to their estimate of average total cost. Instead, they adjust the markup to reflect their best estimate of current demand. A large firm is likely to have a pricing policy committee that adjusts prices based on the current state of competition in the industry and the current state of the economy. If competition is strong in a weak economy, the pricing committee may decide to set price significantly below the cost-plus price.

In general, firms that take demand into account will charge lower markups on products that are more price elastic and higher markups on products that are less elastic. Supermarkets, where cost-plus pricing is widely used, have markups in the 5 to 10 percent range for products with more elastic demand, such as soft drinks and breakfast cereals, and markups in the 50 percent range for products with less elastic demand, such as fresh fruits and vegetables.

Why Do Some Firms Use Two-Part Tariffs?

Some firms require consumers to pay an initial fee for the right to buy their product and an additional fee for each unit of the product purchased. For example, many golf and tennis clubs require members to buy an annual membership in addition to paying a fee each time they use the golf course or tennis court. Sam's Club requires consumers to pay a membership fee before shopping at its stores. Cellphone companies sometimes charge a monthly fee and then have a per-minute charge after a certain number of minutes have been used. Economists call this pricing strategy a **two-part tariff**.

Two-part tariff A situation in which consumers pay one price (or tariff) for the right to buy as much of a related good as they want at a second price.

The Walt Disney Company is in a position to use a two-part tariff by charging consumers for admission to Walt Disney World or Disneyland and also charging them to use the rides in the parks. As mentioned at the beginning of this chapter, at one time, the admission price to Disneyland was low, but people had to purchase tickets to go on the rides. Today, you must pay a high price for admission to Disneyland or Disney World, but the rides are free once you're in the park. Figure 5 helps us understand which of these pricing strategies is more profitable for Disney. The numbers in the figure are simplified to make the calculations easier.

Once visitors are inside the park, Disney is in the position of a monopolist: No other firm is operating rides in Disney World. So, we can draw panel (a) in Figure 5 to represent the market for rides at Disney World. This graph looks like the standard monopoly graph. (Note that the marginal cost of another rider is quite low. We assume that it is a constant $2 and equal to the average total cost.) It seems obvious—but it will turn out to be wrong!—that Disney should determine the profit-maximizing quantity of ride tickets by setting marginal revenue equal to marginal cost. In this case, the result would be 20,000 ride tickets sold per day at a price of $26 per ride. Disney's profit from selling *ride tickets* is shown by the area of rectangle B. The area equals the difference between the $26 price and the average total cost of $2, multiplied by the 20,000 tickets sold, or ($26 − $2) × 20,000 = $480,000. Disney also has a second source of profit from selling *admission tickets* to the park. Given the $26 price for ride tickets, what price would Disney be able to charge for admission tickets?

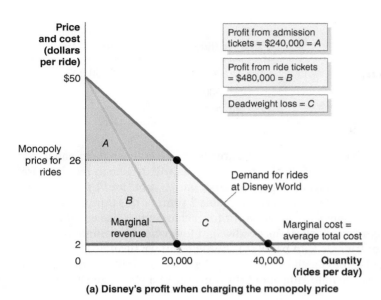

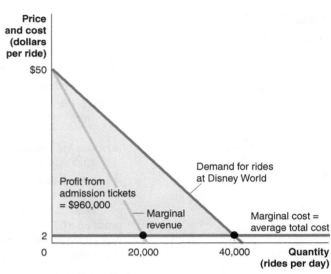

Figure 5 **A Two-Part Tariff at Disney World**

In panel (a), Disney charges the monopoly price of $26 per ride ticket and sells 20,000 ride tickets. Its profit from *ride tickets* is shown by the area of rectangle *B*, or $480,000. If Disney is in the position of knowing every consumer's willingness to pay, it can also charge a price for *admission tickets* that would result in the total amount paid for admission tickets being equal to total consumer surplus from the rides. Total consumer surplus from the rides equals the area of the triangle, *A*, or $240,000. So, when charging the monopoly price, Disney's total profit equals $480,000 + $240,000 or $720,000. In panel (b), Disney charges the perfectly competitive price of $2, which results in a quantity of 40,000 ride tickets sold. At the lower ride ticket price, Disney can charge a higher price for admission tickets, which will increase its total profits from operating the park to the area of the green triangle, or $960,000.

Let's assume the following for simplicity: The only reason people want admission to Disney World is to go on the rides, all consumers have the same individual demand curve for rides, and Disney knows what this demand curve is. This last assumption allows Disney to practice perfect price discrimination. More realistic assumptions would make the outcome of the analysis somewhat different but would not affect the main point of how Disney uses a two-part tariff to increase its profits. With these assumptions, we can use the concept of consumer surplus to calculate the maximum total amount consumers would be willing to pay for admission. Remember that consumer surplus is equal to the area below the demand curve and above the price line, shown by the the area of triangle *A* in panel (a). Consumers would not be willing to pay more for admission to the park than the consumer surplus they receive from the rides. In panel (a) of Figure 5, the total consumer surplus when Disney charges a price of $26 per ride is $240,000. (This number is easy to calculate if you remember that the formula for the area of a triangle is ½ × base × height, or ½ × 20,000 × $24.) Disney can set the price of admission tickets so that the *total* amount spent by buyers would be $240,000. In other words, Disney can set the price of admission to capture the entire consumer surplus from the rides. So, Disney's total profit from Disney World would be the $240,000 it receives from admission tickets plus the $480,000 in profit from the rides, or $720,000 per day.

Is this the most profit Disney can earn from selling admission tickets and ride tickets? The answer is "no." The key to understanding why is to notice that *the lower the price Disney charges for ride tickets, the higher the price it can charge for admission tickets.* Lower-priced ride tickets increase consumer surplus from the rides and, therefore, increase the willingness of buyers to pay a higher price for admission tickets. In panel (b) of Figure 5, we assume that Disney acts as it would in a perfectly competitive market and charges a price for ride tickets that is equal to marginal cost, or $2. Charging this price increases consumer surplus—*and* the maximum total amount that Disney can charge for admission tickets—from $240,000 to $960,000. (Once again, we use the

	Monopoly Price for Rides	Competitive Price for Rides
Profits from admission tickets	$240,000	$960,000
Profits from ride tickets	480,000	0
Total profit	720,000	960,000

Table 2

Disney's Profits per Day from Different Pricing Strategies

formula for the area of a triangle to calculate the area of the green triangle in panel (b): ½ × 40,000 × 48 = $960,000.) Disney's profits from the rides will decline to zero because it is now charging a price equal to average total cost, *but its total profit from Disney World will rise from $720,000 to $960,000 per day.* Table 2 summarizes this result.

What is the source of Disney's increased profit from charging a price equal to marginal cost? Disney has converted what was deadweight loss when the monopoly price was charged—the area of triangle *C* in panel (a)—into consumer surplus. Disney then turns this consumer surplus into profit by increasing the price of admission tickets.

It is important to note the following about the outcome of a firm using an optimal two-part tariff:

1. Because price equals marginal cost at the level of output supplied, the outcome is economically efficient.
2. All consumer surplus is transformed into profit.

Notice that, in effect, Disney is practicing perfect price discrimination. As we noted in our discussion of perfect price discrimination, Disney's use of a two-part tariff has increased the amount of the product—in this case, rides at Disney World—consumers are able to purchase but has eliminated consumer surplus. Although it may seem paradoxical, consumer surplus was actually higher when consumers were being charged the monopoly price for the rides. The solution to the paradox is that although consumers pay a lower price for the rides when Disney employs a two-part tariff, the overall amount they pay to be at Disney World increases.

Disney actually does follow the profit-maximizing strategy of charging a high price for admission to the park and a very low price—zero—for the rides. It seems that Disney could increase its profits by raising the price for the rides from zero to the marginal cost of the rides. But the marginal cost is so low that it would not be worth the expense of printing ride tickets and hiring additional workers to sell the tickets and collect them at each ride. Finally, note that in practice Disney can't convert all consumer surplus into profit because (1) the demand curves of customers are not all the same, and (2) Disney does not know precisely what these demand curves are.

Continued

Economics in Your Life

Why So Many Prices to See a Movie?

At the beginning of the chapter, we asked you to think about what you pay for a movie ticket and what people in other age groups pay. A movie theater will try to charge different prices to different consumers, based on their willingness to pay. If you have two otherwise identical people, one a student and one not, you might assume that the student has less income, and therefore a lower willingness to pay, than the nonstudent, and the movie theater would like to charge the student a lower price. The movie theater employee can ask to see a student ID to ensure that the theater is giving the discount to a student.

But why don't theaters practice price discrimination at the concession stand? It is likely that a student will also have a lower willingness to pay for popcorn, and the theater can check for a student ID at the time of purchase, but unlike with the entry ticket, the theater would have a hard time preventing the student from giving the popcorn to a nonstudent once inside the theater. Because it is easier to limit resale in movie admissions, we often see different prices for different groups. Because it is difficult to limit resale of popcorn and other movie concessions, everyone will typically pay the same price.

Conclusion

Firms in perfectly competitive industries must sell their products at the market price. For firms in other industries—which means, of course, the vast majority of firms—pricing is an important part of the strategy used to maximize profits. We have seen in this chapter, for example, that if firms can successfully segment their customers into different groups on the basis of the customers' willingness to pay, the firms can increase their profits by charging different segments different prices.

Visit MyEconLab for a news article and analysis related to the concepts in this chapter.

Chapter Summary and Problems

Key Terms

Price discrimination   Transactions costs   Two-part tariff

Pricing Strategy, the Law of One Price, and Arbitrage

LEARNING OBJECTIVE: Define the law of one price and explain the role of arbitrage.

Summary

According to the *law of one price*, identical products should sell for the same price everywhere. If a product sells for different prices, it will be possible to make a profit through *arbitrage*: buying a product at a low price and reselling it at a high price. The law of one price will hold as long as arbitrage is possible. Arbitrage is sometimes blocked by high **transactions costs**, which are the costs in time and other resources incurred to carry out an exchange or because the product cannot be resold. Another apparent exception to the law of one price occurs when companies offset the higher price they charge for a product by providing superior or more reliable service to customers.

Visit **www.myeconlab.com** to complete these exercises online and get instant feedback.

Review Questions

1.1 What is the law of one price? What is arbitrage?
1.2 Does a product always have to sell for the same price everywhere? Briefly explain.

Problems and Applications

1.3 A newspaper article contains the following description of New York consumers avoiding the state's 8.375 percent sales tax by shopping in New Jersey:

> For years, shoppers from New York City have played a game of retail arbitrage, traveling to the many malls in northern New Jersey, a state where there is no tax on clothing and shoes.

Does this article use the word arbitrage as it is used in this chapter? Briefly explain.

Source: Ken Belson and Nate Schweber, "Sales Tax Cut in City May Dim Allure of Stores Across Hudson," *New York Times*, January 18, 2007.

1.4 The following table contains the actual prices four Web sites charged for a Blu-ray disc of the movie *X-Men: First Class*:

Amazon	$24.99
Wal-Mart	24.96
OrlandsBricks	21.58
ranch_records	17.75

On Google's price comparison Web site, which allows customers to rate the seller, Amazon had been rated by 6,233 people, Wal-Mart had been rated by 835 people, ranch_records had been rated by 153 people, and OrlandsBricks had not been rated by anyone. Briefly explain whether the information in this table contradicts the law of one price.

1.5 **[Related to** Solved Problem 1**]** Suppose California has many apple trees, and the price of apples there is low. Nevada has few apple trees, and the price of apples there is high. Abner buys low-priced California apples and ships them to Nevada, where he resells them at a high price. Is Abner exploiting Nevada consumers by doing this? Is Abner likely to earn an economic profit in the long run? Briefly explain.

1.6 **[Related to** Solved Problem 1**]** Suspicions about arbitrage have a long history. For example, Valerian of Cimiez, a Catholic bishop who lived during the fifth century, wrote: "When something is bought cheaply only so it can be retailed dearly, doing business always means cheating." What might Valerian think of eBay? Do you agree with his conclusion? Briefly explain.

Source: Michael McCormick, *The Origins of the European Economy: Communications and Commerce,* A.D. *300–900,* New York: Cambridge University Press, 2001, p. 85.

Price Discrimination: Charging Different Prices for the Same Product

LEARNING OBJECTIVE: Explain how a firm can increase its profits through price discrimination.

Summary

Price discrimination occurs if a firm charges different prices for the same product when the price differences are not due to differences in cost. Three requirements must be met for a firm to successfully practice price discrimination: (1) A firm must possess market power; (2) some consumers must have a greater willingness to pay for the product than other consumers, and firms must be able to know what consumers are willing to pay; and (3) firms must be able to divide up—or segment—the market for the product so that consumers who buy the product at a low price cannot resell it at a high price. In the case of *perfect price discrimination*, each consumer pays a price equal to the consumer's willingness to pay.

Visit **www.myeconlab.com** to complete these exercises online and get instant feedback.

Review Questions

2.1 What is price discrimination? Under what circumstances can a firm successfully practice price discrimination?

2.2 In 2013, the Rock and Roll Hall of Fame and Museum charged adults $22 for admission. Seniors (65 years and older) and military personnel were charged $17, and children between 9 and 12 years old were charged $13. Use the admission fees to rank these groups based on their elasticities of demand from highest to lowest.

Source: www.rockhall.com.

2.3 What is yield management? Give an example of a firm using yield management to increase profits.

2.4 What is perfect price discrimination? Is it likely to ever occur? Explain. Is perfect price discrimination economically efficient? Explain.

2.5 Is it possible to practice price discrimination across time? Briefly explain.

Problems and Applications

2.6 According to an article in the *Wall Street Journal*:

> Airlines have increased restrictions on cheap fares by raising overnight requirements, upping what had commonly been only a one-night stay requirement to two and three nights. The overnights can be weeknights, so those tickets aren't as onerous as Saturday-night stay tickets. But the three-night requirement does limit the utility of discounted fares for road warriors.

What is a "road warrior"? Why would a company put restrictions on a service that make the service less desirable to some of its customers?

Source: Scott McCartney, "Airlines Revive Minimum Stays on Cheap Fares," *Wall Street Journal*, August 19, 2008.

2.7 A newspaper article provides advice to airline travelers: "The ideal time to book domestic travel last year was 21 to 35 days before departure and within three months before departure for international travel." Why would airlines offer their lowest prices so far in advance of the day of the flight? Wouldn't the airlines be better off discounting only

just before the day of the flight when they know how many empty seats they have left to fill?

Source: Scott McCartney, "The Best Places to Fly This Summer," *Wall Street Journal*, May 1, 2013.

2.8 Political columnist Michael Kinsley wrote: "The infuriating [airline] rules about Saturday night stayovers and so on are a crude alternative to administering truth serum and asking, 'So how much are you really willing to pay?'" Would a truth serum—or some other way of knowing how much people would be willing to pay for an airline ticket—really be all the airlines need in order to practice price discrimination? Briefly explain.

Source: Michael Kinsley, "Consuming Gets More Complicated," *Slate*, November 21, 2001.

2.9 Journalist Timothy Noah discovered that when he called up the *New York Times* and threatened to end his subscription, he was offered a 50 percent discount on the regular subscription price. He became convinced that anyone who called up and threatened to end his or her subscription would be offered the same discount. Briefly explain whether the *New York Times* is practicing price discrimination.

Source: Timothy Noah, "Wise Up, Print Addicts!" www.slate.com, November 17, 2010.

2.10 **[Related to the** Don't Let This Happen to You**]** A state law in California makes it illegal for businesses to charge men and women different prices for dry cleaning, laundry, tailoring, or hair grooming. The state legislator who introduced the law did so after a dry cleaner charged her more to have her shirts dry cleaned than to have her husband's shirts dry cleaned. According to a newspaper article, the owner of the dry cleaner told the legislator that his costs for cleaning women's shirts were higher because he had to iron them by hand rather than use an automatic press. The law proved difficult to enforce, with many dry cleaners continuing to ignore it years after it was passed.

a. Was the dry cleaner practicing price discrimination, as defined in this chapter? Briefly explain.

b. Do you support laws like this one? Briefly explain.

Source: Veronique de Turenne, "Santa Monica Sues Nine Dry Cleaners under Gender Discrimination Law," *Los Angeles Times*, May 13, 2008; and Harry Brooks, "Law Mandates Equality in Dry Cleaning, Hair Styling," *North County (California) Times*, October 7, 2001.

2.11 **[Related to** Solved Problem 2**]** Use the graphs on the next page to answer the questions.

a. If this firm wants to maximize profits, what price will it charge in Market 1, and what quantity will it sell?

b. If this firm wants to maximize profits, what price will it charge in Market 2, and what quantity will it sell?

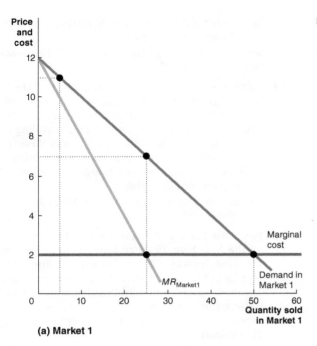

(a) Market 1

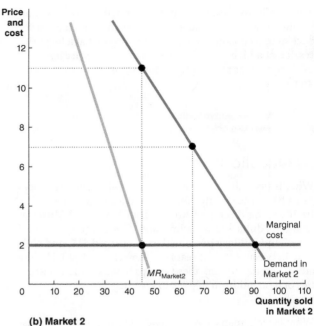

(b) Market 2

2.12 **[Related to** Solved Problem 2**]** In mid-2013, Apple was offering a $100 discount to students on MacBook Pro laptops but only $50 on MacBook Air laptops. The MacBook Air is a very thin, light laptop that is particularly aimed at businesspeople who travel frequently. Why would Apple cut the price more for MacBook Pros than for MacBook Airs?

2.13 **[Related to** Solved Problem 2**]** In addition to discounting the price of computers purchased by students and faculty, Apple sells certain computer models only to schools and universities. According to a discussion on the MacRumors blog:

> Apple has quietly launched a lower cost $999 iMac for educational institutions this morning. The new low-end model is labeled "Education only" and is not available for individuals.... Apple, in the past, has also offered special education only models for institutions ... [and] has adjusted the hardware down in order to fit the sub-$1000 price point.

Is Apple engaging in price discrimination in following this policy? If so, why does it prepare special models for educational institutions rather than cutting the prices of existing models purchased by educational buyers? If this is not an example of price discrimination, why doesn't Apple offer these computers to the general public?

Source: "Apple Launches $999 iMac for Educational Institutions," by Arnold Kim. From www.macrumors.com, August 8, 2011. Reprinted with permission.

2.14 **[Related to** Making the Connection: **How Colleges Use Yield Management]** Assume that the marginal cost of admitting one more student is constant for every university. Also assume that at every university, the demand for places in the freshman class is downward sloping. Now, suppose that the public becomes upset that universities charge different prices to different students. Responding to these concerns, the

federal government requires universities to charge the same price to each student. In this situation, who will gain, and who will lose?

2.15 **[Related to the** Chapter Opener**]** Walt Disney World charges residents of Florida lower prices for various theme park ticket packages than it charges non-Florida residents. For example, in 2013 an adult Florida resident was charged $190.64 for a three-day "Magic Your Way" package that included lodging at a Disney Resort hotel and a ticket to one theme park per day. The price of the same package for a non-Florida resident was $326.96.

a. What is Disney assuming about the willingness to pay of Florida residents? Why might it make this assumption?

b. How might Disney keep Florida residents from buying Walt Disney World tickets at discounted prices and reselling them to non-Florida residents at higher prices?

c. Disney offers discount tickets to students at universities located in Florida, but does not offer discount tickets to students at most universities in other states. Briefly explain Disney's strategy. Would you expect the discount Disney offers to students at Florida universities to be higher or lower than the discount it offers to other residents of Florida? Briefly explain.

Source: Disney prices from allears.net, June 23, 2013.

2.16 **[Related to** Making the Connection: **The Internet Leaves You Open to Price Discrimination]** Many supermarkets provide regular shoppers with "loyalty cards" that the shoppers swipe each time they checkout. By swiping the card, the shopper receives reduced prices on a few goods and the supermarket compiles information on all the shoppers' purchases. Recently, some supermarkets have switched from giving the same price reductions to all shoppers to giving shoppers differing price reductions depending on their shopping history. A manager at one company that uses this approach said: "It comes down to understanding elasticity at a household level."

a. Is the use of loyalty cards that provide the same price discounts for every shopper who uses them a form of price discrimination? Briefly explain.

b. Why would making price discounts depend on a shopper's buying history involve "elasticity at a household level"? What information from a shopper's buying history would be relevant in predicting the shopper's response to a price discount?

Source: Stephanie Clifford, "Shopper Alert: Price May Drop for You Alone," *New York Times*, August 9, 2012.

2.17 One company sells underpads that can be used on the beds of people who are ill or the sleeping area for dogs that are being house trained. The packages for dogs are different and have a different brand name than the packages for people, but the pads in the packages are identical. Recently on Amazon, the company was selling the pads for dogs at a price that was 11 percent higher than the price they charged for the pads for people.

a. How is the company able to price discriminate in this situation?

b. Why would the company sell the pads for dogs at a higher price than the pads for people?

2.18 General Mills periodically puts $1 coupons in Sunday newspapers and online for large boxes of its Cheerios breakfast cereal. Why doesn't General Mills just charge $1 less for Cheerios instead of using coupons? Is issuing coupons a form of price discrimination? Briefly explain.

2.19 Yasiel has a monopoly on sales of pizzas in the small town of North Key Largo, Florida. Use the following information on the demand for Yasiel's pizzas to answer the questions:

Price	Quantity Demanded
$30	0
25	1
20	2
15	3
10	4
5	5
0	6

a. If Yasiel can produce pizzas at a constant cost of $5 per pizza, how many pizzas does he produce, what price does he charge, and how much profit does he make?

b. If Yasiel is able to engage in perfect price discrimination, what is his total revenue for 3 units? What is the marginal revenue of the third unit?

c. If Yasiel is able to engage in perfect price discrimination, how many pizzas does he produce and how much profit does he make?

d. Draw a graph showing producer surplus, consumer surplus, and deadweight loss if Yasiel does not price discriminate. Draw a second graph showing producer surplus, consumer surplus, and deadweight loss if he practices perfect price discrimination.

---

3   Other Pricing Strategies

LEARNING OBJECTIVE: Explain how some firms increase their profits by using odd pricing, cost-plus pricing, and two-part tariffs.

Summary

In addition to price discrimination, firms use odd pricing, cost-plus pricing, and two-part tariffs as pricing strategies. Firms use *odd pricing*—for example, charging $1.99 rather than $2.00—because consumers tend to buy more at odd prices than would be predicted from estimated demand curves. With *cost-plus pricing*, firms set the price for a product by adding a percentage markup to average total cost. Using cost-plus pricing may be a good way to come close to the profit-maximizing price when marginal revenue or marginal cost is difficult to measure. Some firms can require consumers to pay an initial fee for the right to buy their product and an additional fee for each unit of the product purchased. Economists refer to this situation as a **two-part tariff**. Sam's Club, cellphone companies, and many golf and tennis clubs use two-part tariffs in pricing their products.

Visit www.myeconlab.com to complete these exercises online and get instant feedback.

Review Questions

3.1 What is odd pricing?

3.2 What is cost-plus pricing? Is using cost-plus pricing consistent with a firm maximizing profit? How does the elasticity of demand affect the percentage price markup that firms use?

3.3 Give an example of a firm using a two-part tariff as part of its pricing strategy.

Problems and Applications

3.4 One leading explanation for odd pricing is that it allows firms to trick buyers into thinking they are paying less than they really are. If this explanation is correct, in what types of markets and among what groups of consumers would you be most likely to find odd pricing? Should the government ban this practice and force companies to round up their prices to the nearest dollar?

3.5 According to an article in the *Wall Street Journal*, McDonald's and Burger King have much larger markups on French fries and sodas than on hamburgers. Is it likely that the companies believe that the demand for French fries and sodas is more elastic or less elastic than the demand for hamburgers? Briefly explain.

Source: Diana Ransom, "Can They Really Make Money Off the Dollar Menu?" *Wall Street Journal*, May 21, 2009.

3.6 According to an article in the *Wall Street Journal*, most restaurants in New York City price wine at a 300 percent markup over the price the restaurants pay for the wine. The restaurants use a much smaller markup on the food they serve. What might explain the difference in the markups?

Source: Lettie Teague, "Highs and (Rare) Lows in Restaurant Wine Prices," *Wall Street Journal*, June 21, 2013.

3.7 An article in the *Wall Street Journal* gave the following explanation of how products were traditionally priced at Parker-Hannifin Corporation:

> For as long as anyone at the 89-year-old company could recall, Parker used the same simple formula to determine prices of its 800,000 parts—from heat-resistant seals for jet engines to steel valves that hoist buckets on cherry pickers. Company managers would calculate how much it cost to make and deliver each product and add a flat percentage on top, usually aiming for about 35%. Many managers liked the method because it was straightforward.

Is it likely that this system of pricing maximized the firm's profit? Briefly explain.

Source: Timothy Aeppel, "Seeking Perfect Prices, CEO Tears Up the Rules," *Wall Street Journal*, March 27, 2007.

3.8 **[Related to** Making the Connection: **Cost-Plus Pricing in the Publishing Industry]** Would you expect a publishing company to use a strict cost-plus pricing system for all its books? How might you find some indication about whether a publishing company actually was using cost-plus pricing for all its books?

3.9 Some professional sports teams charge fans a one-time lump sum for a personal seat license. The personal seat license allows a fan the right to buy season tickets each year. No one without a personal seat license can buy season tickets. After the original purchase from the team, the personal seat licenses usually can be bought and sold by fans—whoever owns the seat license in a given year can buy season tickets—but the team does not earn any additional revenue from this buying and selling. Suppose a new sports stadium has been built, and the team is trying to decide on the price to charge for season tickets.

   a. Will the team make more profit from the combination of selling personal seat licenses and season tickets if it keeps the prices of the season tickets low or if it charges the monopoly price? Briefly explain.

   b. After the first year, is the team's strategy for pricing season tickets likely to change?

   c. Will it make a difference in the team's pricing strategy for season tickets if all the personal seat licenses are sold in the first year?

3.10 During the nineteenth century, the U.S. Congress encouraged railroad companies to build transcontinental railways across the Great Plains by giving them land grants. At that time, the federal government owned most of the land on the Great Plains. The land grants consisted of the land on which the railway was built and alternating sections of 1 square mile each on either side of the railway to a distance of 6 to 40 miles, depending on the location. The railroad companies were free to sell this land to farmers or anyone else who wanted to buy it. The process of selling the land took decades. Some economic historians have argued that the railroad companies charged lower prices to ship freight because they owned so much land along the tracks. Briefly explain the reasoning of these economic historians.

3.11 **[Related to the** Chapter Opener**]** If you visited Disneyland between 1955 and 1982, you could not go on most rides without buying a ticket for the ride—in addition to the ticket necessary to enter the park. Explain why this pricing strategy earned Disney a lower profit than the current strategy of requiring visitors to purchase a ticket to enter the park but not requiring an additional ticket to be purchased for each ride.

3.12 Thomas Kinnaman, an economist at Bucknell University, has analyzed the pricing of garbage collection:

> Setting the appropriate fee for garbage collection can be tricky when there are both fixed and marginal costs of garbage collection.... A curbside price set equal to the average total cost of collection would have high garbage generators partially subsidizing the fixed costs of low garbage generators. For example, if the time that a truck idles outside a one-can household and a two-can household is the same, and the fees are set to cover the total cost of garbage collection, then the two-can household paying twice that of the one-can household has subsidized a portion of the collection costs of the one-can household.

Briefly explain how a city might solve this pricing problem by using a two-part tariff in setting the garbage collection fees it charges households.

Source: Thomas C. Kinnaman, "Examining the Justification for Residential Recycling," *Journal of Economic Perspectives*, Vol. 20, No. 4, Fall 2006.

Glossary

Price discrimination Charging different prices to different customers for the same product when the price differences are not due to differences in cost.

Transactions costs The costs in time and other resources that parties incur in the process of agreeing to and carrying out an exchange of goods or services.

Two-part tariff A situation in which consumers pay one price (or tariff) for the right to buy as much of a related good as they want at a second price.

Credits

Credits are listed in the order of appearance.

Photo

Katja Kreder/imagebroker/Alamy; Bruce Newman/AP Images

Index

network, 297, 301, 318, 324